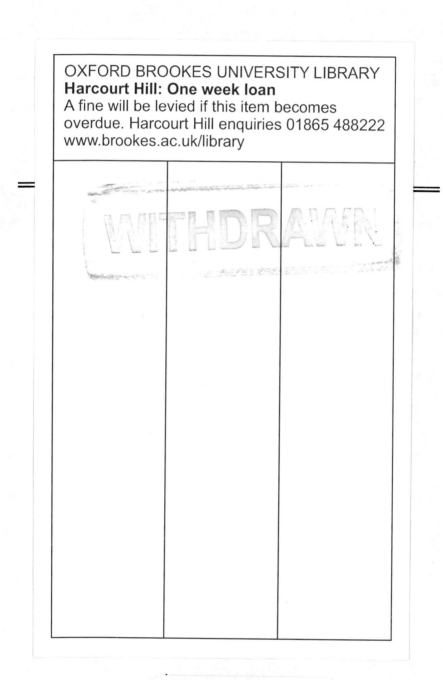

LEA's COMMUNICATION SERIES
Jennings Bryant/Dolf Zillmann, General Editors

For a complete list of titles in LEA's Communication Series, please contact Lawrence Erlbaum Associates, Publishers.

Human Communication Theory and Research

Concepts, Contexts, and Challenges

Second Edition

Robert L. Heath
University of Houston
Jennings Bryant
University of Alabama

Routledge
Taylor & Francis Group
New York London

Transferred to Digital Printing 2008

First published by Lawrence Erlbaum Associates, Inc., Publishers
10 Industrial Avenue
Mahwah, New Jersey 07430

Reprinted 2008 by Routledge
Routledge
Taylor & Francis Group
270 Madison Avenue
New York, NY 10016

Routledge
Taylor & Francis Group
2 Park Square
Milton Park, Abingdon
Oxon OX14 4RN

Cover design by Kathryn Houghtaling Lacey

Library of Congress Cataloging-in-Publication Data

Heath, Robert L. (Robert Lawrence), 1941–
      Human communication theory and research : concepts, contexts, and challenges /
Robert Heath,—2nd ed.
        p.   cm. — (LEA's communication series)
      Includes bibliographical references and index.
      ISBN 0-8058-3007-3 (alk. Paper) — 0-8058-3008-1 (pbk. :
alk. paper)
      1. Communication. I. Bryant, Jennings. II. Title. III. Series.

P90 .H39 2000
302.2'01—dc21   00-033166

Publisher's Note
The publisher has gone to great lengths to ensure the quality of this reprint but points
out that some imperfections in the original may be apparent

Contents

Preface

T he study of communication theory asks that for a moment we step back and look at the field. It forces us to consider what communication is, where it occurs in relatively unique contexts, and how it affects people. We also realize that people affect it. Communication is a process that changes because of how people use it. Communication is often very much taken for granted. Why study communication when everyone can communicate? Does one need special insight to understand communication? Is a scholar's insight better than a person's who is not specially trained in research and the study of theory?

In 1993, Robert Craig asked, why are there so many communication theories? He hoped that the discipline would have fewer theories and would find integration instead of differences. He offered a challenge:

> Dialogue in the discipline will be advanced as we reflect on the various modes of theory and their characteristic biases and limitations. Situated within such a dialogue, work in our field cannot fail to engage with issues of broad concern through the human sciences. (p. 32)

This book does not make particular efforts to reconcile differences, but it does suggest where theories work together and at odds. It also looks for some molar concerns: the human desire to reduce uncertainty; the desire to influence and the willingness to yield to influence; the desire for quality, satisfying relationships; and the desire to entertain and be entertained.

This volume introduces students to the growing body of theory and research regarding communication. In the past half century, communication has come to be a particularly important and fruitful topic of research. It has drawn the attention of hundreds of scholars who have devoted thousands of hours to unlocking its mysteries.

The design of this book is simple. We have sought to draw together the best ideas on theory and research. We want to chart developments and linkages within and between ways of looking at communication. Topics selected for discussion in this book reflect the desire that students will understand and appreciate the difficulties of making discoveries that can help them to increase their insights into communication, one of the most unique qualities of the human species. What is discussed here has implications for how individuals relate to one another as well as for the development of public policy regarding the effects media have on society.

This book acknowledges the contributions of researchers from psychology, political science, and sociology departments. Although their contributions are important, one of the most significant developments in recent decades is the emergence of communication as a research discipline, largely advanced through the development of major departments, schools, and colleges named communication and devoted to that discipline. Most of the work presented here has been drawn from scholars who find their academic affiliation with such programs. The chapters that comprise this book were selected and arranged to give insight into the breadth of studies unique to communication.

Chapter 1 sets an orientation for the social scientific study of communication. It discusses principles of research and outlines the requirements for the development and evaluation of theories. One of the important points made in that chapter is the need for system and rigor in the development of hypotheses, generation of data, and creation of theory. Development of theory entails more than merely thinking abstractly. Only by testing and arguing about theories can they be improved. To know how to do this requires careful examination of the methods and assumptions of social science research as well as re-examination of key assumptions about the communication process, especially those that are sensitive to the similarities and differences involved in how communication occurs in the individual, interpersonal, group, organizational, and mass-mediated contexts.

Chapter 2 examines the dynamic shifts that have occurred in scholars' efforts to define communication and isolate its key variables. Taking the tone of a scholar serving as detective who is intent on determining "who done it," the chapter examines the anatomy of the communication process and discusses the difficulty in knowing which aspects of the process deserve the most attention. By examining key aspects of communication, such as message, source, and channel, the chapter lays a foundation of terminology that is useful to discussing the elements of the process.

Chapter 3 concentrates on language, meaning, and messages. Of particular interest in this chapter is the description and comparison of the three overarching approaches to how words are meaningful. This examination features representationalism or referentialism, linguistic relativity, and the interactional or purposive approach to language. Each theory helps explain how words are meaningful, but none of the theories completely explains this process. Words are a unique part of the human communication process. Their meaning and impact deserve careful attention.

Chapter 4 focuses attention on the importance of uncertainty as a universal motive that leads people to seek and think about information. This chapter examines information as the foundation of communication that leads to a comparison of theories of what information is and how it has meaning for humans who need to learn about and make decisions regarding events that are important to their lives. Once the chapter has established this foundation, it examines how information is important to communication in interpersonal, organizational, and mass-mediated contexts. From this analysis, a case is made that people communicate about something; the essence of that something is information.

Chapter 5 provides an important complement to the discussion on information by addressing the dynamics of social influence, persuasion. Rather than seeing information and persuasion at odds, the chapter demonstrates how leading theories treat them as interdependent parts of social influence and decision making. Starting from findings produced by the seminal Yale research project, this chapter progresses to explain how leading researchers have refined the work of each other to establish several leading theories by conducting experiments. As was the case of chapter 4, attention is given to persuasion in the typical communication contexts.

Chapter 6 is the first of two chapters that discuss interpersonal communication. Whereas chapter 6 focuses on factors that improve or harm relationships, chapter 7 studies the processes people use to reduce uncertainty about themselves and their relational partners. Of particular importance to relationship development is the need for disclosure. This examination requires that consideration be given to which variables differentiate between good and bad relationships. As well as looking at the impact of nonverbal communication, this chapter discusses expectations people have of one another and of the conditions that lead to social conflict.

Chapter 7 extends the attention given in previous chapters to how people reduce uncertainty in their interpersonal relationships. Essential to this process is the ways people attribute causes to explain why they and others act as they do. Also important are the communication tactics people use to seek information about relationships, trying to know, for instance, whether other people like them. Research is reported about the processes of second guessing and debiasing. In subtle ways people accommodate to one another and employ communication plans to negotiate relationships.

Chapter 8 captures the dynamics of communication that are typical of organizations. Focal points in organizational communication involve what people think about the companies in which they work, the interpersonal relationships that occur as they work together, and the groups that are used for collective decision making. The chapter compares various approaches to explain how communication allows people to create and act in organizations. This analysis seeks to explain how communication interacts with the climate and culture of each organization. As well as looking at the communication that transpires inside organizations, insights are provided into the communication that organizations use to affect people outside of them.

Chapter 9 concentrates on the dynamics of mass-mediated communication. This discussion is warranted because of the important roles media play in each person's daily activities. Starting with analysis of early approaches to media studies, the chapter introduces and discusses up-to-date theories that are being used to guide regulatory policies as well as programming and editorial policy. Several key theories enjoy a great deal of scholarly debate and research in the effort to determine how media affect people, as well as to understand how people affect media. A theme central to this analysis is the importance of maintaining attention on the cognitive processes involved in media attentiveness, as well as the interaction between interpersonal communication and media utilization.

Chapter 10 is brand new to the second edition. In this chapter we attempt to come to grips with communication theories that are being developed to chart and explain the advanced communication technologies that are so dramatically affecting all of our lives. Quite frankly, communication theory for the new media is in its infancy, but as it cuts its teeth, we wanted to include an early discussion of its development.

We want to publicly praise and profusely thank three people who were inordinately helpful in preparing this second edition: Susan Thompson for her superb research skills and for her invaluable writing assistance; Mary Maxwell, who served as copyeditor par excellence; and Mike Little, who added his monumental creative skills in production and design. We are also grateful to the wonderful staff at Lawrence Erlbaum Associates, with whom it is always a pleasure to collaborate.

Each day leading researchers and theorists shed new insights onto the processes of communication. In the late 1950s, some scholars had come to believe that nothing new would be discovered about the nature of communication. Since then, we have had a revolutionary growth in the study of this topic. Since the first edition of this book appeared, we have become more alert to the influence of critical studies and cultural theory. We are challenged to think not of communication merely as a process, but as a very human (humanizing and dehumanizing) process. Since this first edition, we have seen the emergence of cyberspace, about which we are only beginning to learn.

From relatively primitive starting points, a steady march continues. This trek is beginning to demonstrate how much integration exists between the communication efforts that are typical of interpersonal, organizational, and mass-mediated settings. Welcome to this journey.

—Robert L. Heath
—Jennings Bryant

1

Why Study Theories and Conduct Research?

For a moment, consider one of your typical days. Let's imagine the following events. You get up in the morning, awakened by your favorite early morning radio program. Perhaps the movement of someone else getting up in the morning awakens you. You engage in conversation. You get ready for school, work, a day of chores, or merely hang around your apartment or house. During the morning you call someone about some service you need performed, perhaps a car repair. You read part, then want to read more, of a newspaper before leaving. While waiting for your car to be repaired, you read a magazine or novel. You have explained the needed repair to the service person, but as you go over the bill you note that something seems incorrect. You get into an argument. As you drive across town, you listen to the radio, tape, or CD player in your car. You meet a friend for lunch and have a pleasant conversation. After lunch you wave, "Good bye, see you later." In the evening you listen to television news and write a birthday card to a cousin. You spend some time after the news visiting with a neighbor. The landlord comes to see whether you have the rent. You say, "My parents have not sent the money they promised me," or "The check is in the mail; it should be here tomorrow." Are those statements deception on your part? You start watching evening television and decide to go to a friend's house. There you watch a couple of sitcoms and part of a cable movie that turns out to be boring. You discuss going to a movie over the weekend. But now you need to study. Does the person have some notes for one class? "What kinds of tests does the faculty member give?" "What classes are you taking in the spring?" you ask. You go home, and call someone in a student organization. You make plans for the meeting on Thursday when you will begin to get organized for the fall social event. You listen to the CD player. Then you turn on your favorite late night shows. You set the remote control to shut the television off in 30 minutes. You think that tomorrow you need to e-mail a friend who is studying abroad this semester. And you need to do some research using the Internet. You drift into sleep. Then the radio alarm turns on. Another day has begun.

For a moment, think about the features that most distinguish human beings from other animals? People build tools. Other animals do as well, but human tools are more complex and sophisticated. Chimpanzees, for instance, use wet branches to extract termites from their mounds so they can be eaten. Many other fascinating instances of tools can be found throughout many animal species, including playing with snowballs. Humans have much more sophisticated tools, such as automobiles, computers, space travel vehicles, and remote controls for televiewing or for operating radio receivers. Human toys can be as simple as snowballs or as complex as interactive computer games. Each day we more fully develop and understand what is called the information age. If we were impressed before by the ability of humans to communicate, we now have even more opportunities and tools with the advent of cyberspace. It is an ingenious linking of mass communication with interpersonal communication.

Another trait that distinguishes humans is their ability to communicate in quite complex ways. Humans communicate, but so do other animals. Bands of animals could not cooperate for the survival of their species without communication. Animals express emotions, such as grieving over the loss of loved ones. They play and exhibit joy. They let one another know where they are and if they need help. Elephants can communicate over long distances, as can various species of whales. Although we are impressed by the communication capability of other beings, even casual observation leads us to be impressed by how much more vast human communication skills are.

Communication is one of the perspectives that gives us the most insight into human nature. Human beings are "symbol users," as well as "symbol makers" and "symbol misusers." With this observation, Burke (1966) underscored how people communicate to manage interpersonal relationships, express feelings, share views of reality, and disseminate informative and persuasive messages through media. Through words, great and magnificent cities are created, problems of health and famine are solved, and great dramas and comedies are written. Words and other symbols allow people to plumb the depths of their souls as well as those of their friends and enemies. People share ideas in order to work together. They can plan and operate complex business, nonprofit, and governmental organizations that span the globe. Other animals, such as humpback whales and elephants, communicate for social purposes by calling to others of their species. Whether other animals use symbols to communicate is a moot issue here; people are more elaborate and complex communicators.

As Burke said, people are symbol misusers. Through symbols, people define and categorize one another in ways that lead them to discriminate against some and think favorably of others. If people hold one religious orientation too firmly, they can become intolerant of people who do not hold similar views. Symbols can lead nations to wage war in order to impose their values on enemies. Symbols allow people to scream racial or ethnic slurs at persons they do not like. Words support the development of the science needed to go to the moon and to solve health problems; words provide means to attempt genocide. Words can be used to cast people away as well as to welcome them. Advertisers can use misleading advertisements to entice people to buy defective products unworthy of their cost. They also provide customers with details so they can make intelligent purchases.

We begin this chapter by asking, why should we study communication? One answer is that people study communication because it is vital to their lives. From infancy, you have watched other people communicate. You have imitated some communication behavior to see if you could successfully use those strategies to improve relationships, motivate others, or persuade people to go along with your ideas and plans. As a child, you enacted conversations that you observed between your parents and teachers. By this time in your life, you have engaged in thousands of communication interactions. You know that friendship and business success require effective communication. You learned early in life that communication can help you satisfy your needs, perhaps by making requests of your parents or by creating friendships with other children in your neighborhood.

Whether you actually stopped to think about it or not, you were quick to realize that communication is strategic. Some words are appropriate in certain social contexts but not in others. You noticed that the method in which messages are framed and delivered nonverbally increased their chances of success or failure. Even though you may not have formal theories about how people communicate, you have informal ones. Now it is time to study communication instructively, perhaps to make it serve your interests even more.

Communication research is not interested in knowing about the world independent of people. It focuses on how people interact in all contexts: interpersonal, group, organizational, and mediated.

This chapter lays a foundation for the remainder of the book by setting the study of communication into perspective. It (a) explains the conditions and processes of inquiry, (b) presents the criteria that can be used to compare and evaluate theories, (c) supplies key terms that are vital to understanding how scholars think, (d) examines several broad research perspectives, (e) discusses assumptions that we make about human nature that have implications for our thoughts on communication, and (f) shows how communication is best understood by taking a broad perspective based on research into key subdisciplines. These subdisciplines are featured as chapters in this book.

SYSTEMATIC STUDY OF COMMUNICATION

Understanding of the phenomena of our lives begins with a hypothesis that can be tested and a theory that can be examined. In explaining the usefulness of theories, McGuire (1981) called them *maps.* "Knowledge is not a perfect map of the thing known but without it one has to move through the environment with no map at all" (p. 42). Each of us has maps, theories about communication.

The trick is in making proper use of the theory, which involves recognizing the brilliant partial insight into reality that is provided by any theory's special perspective, seeing its applicability to a specific problem whose puzzling aspects it can illuminate, while at the same time recognizing its limitations and being open to alternative theoretical insights from which guidance can be obtained as one's initial theory begins to prove unsatisfactory. (p. 42)

Theory is needed because no matter how long and hard people examine any object of inquiry—communication in this case—it will not reveal itself. Only by developing and testing hypotheses and weighing the lines of arguments advanced by different theories can the secrets of human communication be unlocked.

This book offers many maps. Each should increase your understanding of communication even if you do not agree with the points it makes. The theories may give you insights into how to communicate more effectively. Many theories in the chapters that follow probably will confirm your own observations about the dynamics of how people communicate in relationships, in organizations, and as they encounter mass media. The discussions may give you new and important insights into how communication works. Without maps, people wander helplessly and aimlessly. A good theory should help you to avoid being helpless and aimless. In fact, you have spent a lifetime developing theories of communication, probably without realizing what you were doing.

When you ask why you should study communication theories and research, realize that you already are a communication theorist. Each day you may watch television programs to be entertained, view commercial advertisements to learn about new products, or watch news broadcasts to find out information. You might say, "Tonight I deserve to reward myself with a couple of laughs on TV." Or you might decide to tune into the news to find out what is happening or to see how the weather report might affect your weekend plans. Researchers, as well as you, want to know why and how people select, think about, and respond to such programs.

When you begin to converse with someone, you follow a theory that you have worked out regarding interpersonal interaction. If you want to borrow something from someone, you are likely to use a theory about what to say and do if the person is reluctant to grant your wish. You might be less mindful of what you say on the way into an office to work than if you are going to visit a friend who is suffering from cancer. When you participate in a meeting you do so according to some theory you have formed about group dynamics, leadership, and turn taking. You may not consciously think of these theories all the time, or even much of the time, but, if you were pressed to do so, you would be able to explain why you are communicating as you are. To understand and explain why people do what they do are key roles of theories.

Scholars have discovered that people employ theories they have created to guide the way they engage in communication. Exploring this line of analysis, B. J.

O'Keefe and McCornack (1987) reasoned that during conversations, each participant operates out of a theory of conversation. The success of each set of conversational participants may depend on the extent to which their conversational goals are similar and whether they use their theories competently as they communicate to achieve their outcomes.

Theory can give orderly, as opposed to whimsical, explanations of events, interactions, and processes in which you engage each day. When you study theories and research that supports them, you should be able to clarify and improve your theories. Reading the theories and research in this book should increase your insight and help you communicate better, but we make no guarantees.

Theory, research, and practice of communication are interrelated. Broadcasters and editors want to understand how and why viewers use television, listeners use radio, or readers use print journalism. This knowledge can help them develop programming. It can shape editorial policies. By understanding communication, government regulators and media managers can create laws and policies, such as designating movies by codes (G, PG, R, or NC-17). Research is used by advertisers of products and services, public relations practitioners, public speakers, and other professional communicators. Many large advertising and public relations companies support extensive applied research programs. Insight into communication can improve employee performance in many occupational contexts: business, health and medical service, legal practice, and others. For instance, researchers study doctor–patient communication to increase the likelihood that patients will tell their doctors the truth about symptoms and to improve the likelihood that doctors can persuade patients to take the prescribed medication. Understanding interpersonal communication may help people communicate more effectively with family members, thereby increasing the pleasure of family life.

For these reasons, we are convinced that studying communication is a benefit. People are naturally curious about communication and generate explanations for the vital aspect of their lives. Professional researchers (e.g., faculty members) study theory and research to be able to assist students' understanding of the phenomena of their life experiences. Applied researchers use theory and research to increase the effectiveness of applied communication, such as advertising. For these reasons, the study of communication is not merely an intellectual challenge. It has value because it can make our personal and professional lives better.

This chapter lays a foundation for studying communication. It explains how systematic inquiry entails observation, analysis, generalization, and prediction. As people engage in daily communication activities, they naively construct and apply theories of communication. In contrast, social scientists go beyond mere intuition and personal observation to understand human communication by constructing theories and then conducting research to test them. Behind systematic inquiry and research is the desire to discover order in our social universe. Systematic study requires researchers to go beyond mere observation of behavior, such as noting that some people watch more television or are more persuasive than others. Researchers are interested in observable behavior patterns, such as noting that people meet and greet one another ritualistically. Research probes the human mind and looks for patterns of communication behavior to discover why people communicate as they do and to learn what effects communication has on opinions and relationships.

Your study of human communication will be easier and more rewarding, even fascinating, if you catch the spirit of observing and thinking about communication behavior with a sense of wonder. You may, for instance, wonder why sometimes a person will understand you quite clearly and at other times you can't seem to get that person to understand you no matter what strategies you try. Are you causing the problem or is the other person? Or are both of you at fault?

Many other questions may prompt research. Why are some television shows entertaining and others not? Why do some people prefer one kind of television show over other programs? Why do some television programs make you laugh and others make you cry? Do all people greet one another in the same ways, for instance, saying "Good morning," even when the weather is miserable and they are ill? If not, why are there differences? And what are the different greeting patterns? Why do people ask the questions they do when they meet for the first time? How do they communicate to reduce the uncertainty they feel toward the world around them, their relationships with other people, and their own sense of competence? Why do some companies run smoothly with each employee seeming to understand what is going on, whereas in other companies nothing goes properly? Why do some employees feel miserable about their jobs and believe that no one in the department involves them in the flow of information and decision making?

Questions such as these show how inquisitive people can be about the ways they communicate. Seeking answers to these and other questions indicates the desire to understand communication to make it serve us better. To do so requires systematic investigation of the major factors that influence how and why people communicate as they do.

THEORIES AS COMPETING PERSPECTIVES

Warning! You will encounter many theories and research findings in this book. Some theories and research findings challenge and contradict one another. Some findings support one theory but not another.

This book does not present one theory but demonstrates the robust debate that results when many researchers strive to unlock the mysteries of communication.

The goal of this book is not to convince you that any one or even several theories can best explain the phenomena of communication. Rather the purpose of the book is to help you expand your capacity to investigate and understand communication from different perspectives by weighing one theory against another. For this reason, the book features a philosophy of social scientific inquiry, touches on factors related to that way of approaching intellectual problems, and uses a variety of theories and research findings to demonstrate problems and progress of such inquiry.

Life would be ideal if we had only one theory that explained all communication behavior and processes. It would be nice if all hypotheses led to helpful and noncontradictory results. But life is imperfect. Communication research and theory building are dynamic activities. Any theory may compete against one or several alternative explanations. The activities of research and theory construction are a debate between alternative views. One researcher thinks she or he has a sound explanation of some phenomenon. That explanation is set out as a theory. Persons agree or disagree with that explanation. Other theories, explanations, are proposed. So the process of academic inquiry progresses.

Posing theories and producing research findings are informative and persuasive activities. Researchers work to explain their ideas and their research findings. They build what they believe is a persuasive argument to support the conclusions they draw. No theory is without flaws; each has its critics and detractors. In the study of communication, as in other social and physical sciences, you will benefit from thinking of researchers and theorists as advocates who assert a thesis on a topic. They are expected to provide research to support their assertions. Without research findings, a theory is mere speculation.

Nature, Processes, and Limits of Human Inquiry

What makes one theory better than another? How do we know which theory is worth our attention? Questions such as these direct our attention to an examination of the processes and criteria of inquiry.

Each theory is tested by the extent to which it is insightful, accurate, encompassing, and predictive. A theory must accurately describe and account for the important observable events in the communication behavior being scrutinized. Any theory is only as good as its ability to explain what happens and make predictions. It should be useful. Keep in mind that scholars do not dream up theories just to frustrate students—not usually anyway! To more fully understand the process of inquiry, let's focus on some key topics.

Inquiry Begins With a Sense of Curiosity. You probably can remember some of the fascinations and wonderments you have had. When you were a child, you might have watched fish in an aquarium and wondered about their behavior. You might have wondered how they breathe and why they chased each other and hid from one another. This observation could have led you to understand how dominance, caution, and hierarchy are vital to the ecology of an aquarium. And you probably examined the hardness or softness of some object by seeing whether you could scratch it or break it. You tested the durability of things by throwing rocks at them until they broke, or you learned that they didn't, or that you shouldn't throw rocks at some things in some places. Inquiry begins with wondering about some phenomenon.

These valuable lessons taught you something about your world and yourself. That activity also taught you the attitudes and methods of "scientific" inquiry. Without knowing it, you engaged in the scientific method. You wondered about some observable phenomenon, formed a theory, acquired facts about your world, and tested hypotheses to learn more about the nature and relationships of objects. You wondered "what is?" "why?" "if then, what?" and "what if?" If your curiosity continues today, you are poised to learn in a sophisticated way.

Inquiry Requires Accurate and Insightful Observation. Inquiry consists of observation and analysis of what you observe. You note patterns. You realize that events don't just happen. They happen in the same way. For that reason, some factor must cause these patterns. Let's think for a moment about your communication behavior. If you have choices, do you just watch any television program? Is all music equally appealing to you? Do you like some people—even love some—more than others? Do you like talking to some people, but avoid others? Do you communicate in the same way when you are telling the truth as you do when you are telling a lie—OK, a fib? How do you act in class when the teacher is in the room and when she or he is out of the room? Do you communicate the same way during a job interview as you do when visiting with friends in the student union? Do you use words in conversations with your friends that you would not use when visiting with your grandmother?

Inquiry Must Have System. To be successful in these activities, you need to know how to discriminate between the important elements of communication activity. Learning the names other people have assigned (or assigning names yourself) to the key elements of communication is vital. Inquiry is systematic when it is used to look for patterns, that is, when communication events are observed to occur in repeatable and predictable ways. A goal of inquiry is to recognize similarities and dissimilarities. Having the same name other persons do to refer to categories of observable phenomena is important. We need a systematic way to communicate our thoughts and findings. We also need to know how to test theories and hypotheses.

As you look for consistency between communication events, patterns, and relationships, you may discover anomalies, which are events, patterns, or facts that do not seem to fit your theory. Kuhn (1970) concluded that inquiry is driven by recognition of anomaly (awareness that some fact, event, behavior, or relationship occurs in violation of what a theory says). He believed that inquiry continues until anomalies have been explained. Just when you think you understand an aspect of communication, you may recognize that your conclusions do not completely square with some facts that you see. You may ask yourself whether the "facts" are incorrect or trivial and whether your theory is inadequate.

How you progress from curiosity and systematic observation to draw conclusions about communication is important. You cannot understand communication without a game plan. Systematic inquiry begins by forming theories and testing hypotheses inductively to create, expand, refine, or challenge each theory. Through deductive reasoning, analysis focuses on how well each hypothesis supports the theory and whether competing theories are relevant to the analysis you are conducting.

Inquiry Requires Imagination. Persons can observe with different degrees of insightfulness. They also have more or less ability to imagine different explanations. The scientific process requires that we discard explanations that are unsupportable.

Inquiry Requires That Key Variables be Systematically Isolated and Their Interaction be Understood and Explained. Theories help organize hypotheses basic to research and findings that result from it. Some research is conducted merely to observe interaction between two or more variables. This *variable analytic* approach to the study of communication may lead to interesting conclusions, but each conclusion stands alone because it does not relate to any others or an encompassing theory. For instance, consider this research finding: Television viewing does not hamper children's academic achievement until it exceeds about 10 hours a week; if young viewers are exposed to programs that are high in information content, television viewing actually enhances their academic achievement (Potter, 1987). This finding is interesting and important. It demonstrates important relationships between variables. It may help parents to know what limits they may set on the televiewing habits of their children. But the research finding does not support or deny a theory. Although a widely used, tried and tested approach, researchers must be cautious to not overlook important dimensions of communication by focusing only on variables that are testable.

A Definition of Theory

To this point, the word *theory* has been used but not defined. Our intention is to have you think about the process of inquiry and to see what it does for people before we define it. We want to convince you that you are a theorist before we proceed into more detail about the nature and requirements of theory building.

We intend for the study of theory to enrich your imagination, not limit it. Toward that end, we suggest that you consider the observation by McQuail (1987) that you can have four kinds of theories: social scientific, normative, working, and common sense. Social scientific theories are proposed, supported, challenged, and refined by well-trained researchers, often in universities. Normative theories are advanced to propose ways to improve human communication. Working theories are under examination, often at an exploratory level of development. Common sense is a wonderful gift. Even the best social scientists are expected to advance theories that exhibit common sense. At times throughout this book, you may say, "That is nothing but common sense." That is a compliment, not a criticism of good theory.

The word *theory* refers to the processes of observing and speculating. It is similar to making an educated guess about some phenomenon. You might think, "I guess people communicate in such and such a way because. . . ." To make such observations combines a bit of what a theory is and a bit of what a hypothesis is.

A theory is a systematic and plausible set of generalizations that explain some observable phenomena by linking concepts (constructs and variables) in terms of an organizing principle that is internally consistent. For example,

- Cultivation theory states that people who view large amounts of television tend to adopt the view of reality, no matter how incorrect it is, that is portrayed in programs they watch.
- Involvement theory proposes that people who believe their self-interests are affected by a choice, action, or opinion are prone to invest more cognitive effort (think more) into becoming informed and forming a point of view on the topic.
- Uncertainty reduction theory says that people communicate in all contexts—interpersonal, organizational, and mediated—to obtain information because uncertainty is uncomfortable.

These are a few of the theories this book discusses in more detail in subsequent chapters. You could use the index to read more about them at the moment so they will not seem so mysterious.

What does a communication theory do? It defines key concepts and explains systematically and rationally the relationships among variables basic to communication behaviors, outcomes, and cognitive processes. A good theory can guide additional speculation, observation, explanation, and prediction. For example, uncertainty reduction theory argues that people strategically communicate to obtain information they need to be comfortable when faced with conditions of social relations and the world around them. Based on this theory, you might predict (hypothesize) that people who are scheduled to meet one another again will ask different or more questions during initial interaction than if they know they are unlikely to meet again. Or social learning theory argues that people learn acceptable and unacceptable opinions and behavior by observing what actions or opinions produce rewards or punishments for other people. Using this theory, you might predict that when persons see behavior rewarded (such as other people becoming more attractive by using an advertised product), they will buy the product.

A Theory Differs From a Hypothesis. Often when you think that you have a theory of how communication works, you may only have a hypothesis, or it may be a conclusion based on observed facts: a tested hypothesis. A hypothesis is a single conjectural statement regarding relationships between two or more variables that can be tested by empirical observation. For example, someone might hypothesize that, in a business organization, personnel will have higher morale if bosses allow them to participate in departmental decision making rather than merely telling the employees what the policy is.

Organizational communication researchers might ask, for instance, "What if bosses praise their employees' performance frequently, seldom, or never?" These researchers may wonder whether the praise needs to be specific and accurate, such as, "You are doing a good job by entering a lot of data and doing your job accurately," or whether general praise, "You are a good worker," will affect employees' performance of tedious jobs. A researcher interested in organizational communication might wonder what kinds and amounts of questions successful and unsuccessful applicants ask during employment interviews.

Or as researchers discovered, when bargainers are held accountable for the outcome of their bargaining efforts, their initial offers are more extreme, and they are perceived as being less cooperative. Under such circumstances, according to Roloff and Campion (1987), employees who are assigned the task of being negotiators take more time to negotiate, are more likely to deadlock, and are less satisfied with the outcome. These kinds of questions are empirically testable, as were those when as children we learned what happens to a worn-out TV picture tube laying in the junk if we hit it with a rock, or a bigger rock.

Hypotheses are the "work horses" of inquiry. They are single, testable statements, the answer to which may help support or deny a theory. Testing a hypothesis may supply evidence to support a conclusion on which a theory may be based, but the results from testing one hypothesis do not constitute a theory. Testing a hypothesis gives researchers the opportunity to frame a proposition, generate data to test the validity of that hypothesis, and determine whether those results support or do not support the hypothesis.

As work horses, results derived from testing several hypotheses may be used to postulate and support a theory or challenge one. After a theory has been postulated, several relevant hypotheses may be tested to support or challenge that theory.

Observing patterns, events, and facts does not result in a theory. Knowing that most people answer a telephone or greet one another by saying "hello" does not make a theory. But it does say something about communication behavior that should, and can, be explained by a theory. A theory is a more encompassing statement of many facts, events, relationships, and conclusions. It has a larger scope than can be captured in one hypothesis. Rather than being a proposition, as is the case for a hypothesis, a theory is often reducible to a summarizing metaphor or overarching concept. For instance, uncertainty reduction theory postulates that much communication behavior is motivated by people's desire to predict which actions and judgments produce positive or negative outcomes.

Theories and Hypotheses Interact. Conclusions drawn from several tested hypotheses may be grouped in support of an encompassing statement or generalization that we would call a theory. That is, someone might have a theory in mind that seems intuitively to be an accurate explanation of the relationships between some facts and conclusions. By systematically testing relevant hypotheses, the explanatory power of the theory can be examined. Inquiry is guided by asking whether facts and conclusions support a theory.

Stressing how theories impose structure on and give names to observable phenomena, Kaplan (1964) reasoned, "A theory must somehow fit God's world, but in an important sense it creates a world of its own" (p. 309). Kaplan made the vital point that theory imposes a view on reality that may not be accurate, but may be believed and used nonetheless. A good example is the belief that persuasive messages always change attitudes and thereby alter behavior. Following that questionable line of reasoning, some communication students reason that if ads did not alter attitudes and influence behavior they would not be used widely to sell products and services. Advocates of that position draw that conclusion without realizing that they buy and use very few of the products or services they see advertised. Or as the magic bullet theory proposes, media, particularly television, virtually control people's thoughts and lives. These conclusions have been severely criticized over the years, but they neverthess continue to be believed by persons who have not carefully examined the evidence against them.

For these reasons, we see theory as making broader generalizations than is possible with any hypothesis. Hypotheses are tested as part of the formulation of a theory. They are examined empirically to determine whether the theory is sound. In this way, researchers seek to determine whether theories express accurate views of the phenomena they are designed to explain. Drawing this conclusion suggests that theories can be evaluated by the extent to which they meet specific criteria. That topic is discussed in the next section.

Criteria of Theory Construction

How can you know whether one theory is better than another? A good theory explains and predicts, and thereby assists efforts to control communication activities and outcomes. In addition, it is useful (heuristic), parsimonious, internally consistent, capable of being falsified or disproved, and addresses the ethical challenges of being morally responsible for using theory and research to advance humanity. Let's examine each of these criteria in more detail.

A Good Theory Must Explain. Building a theory begins with observation and leads to explanation. As you observe communication events and patterns, you might speculate on what is going on and hypothesize how these events will work out to some end. The tendency is to ask "what?" "how?" "why?" or "if then, what?" Observation breaks the communication process into discrete, definable elements, events, processes, and relationships. Different kinds of communication events and activities can be observed. For instance, an argument is different from a joke. Salutations are different from saying good-bye. Watching television is different from reading a newspaper or sending and receiving memos in a company. Holding a meeting or participating in an interview is not the same as preparing and delivering a speech.

Even though these communication events may be different, we can also discover themes that are similar in several. For instance reading a newspaper, listening to radio news, and televiewing the evening news are similar processes; at least they are processes conducted for similar ends. In all three cases, the person wants to reduce uncertainty by being informed on current events.

Sophisticated Theories Predict Sequences of Actions, Events, and Outcomes. Prediction entails being able to say what is likely to occur given a set of communication strategies and events in a given situation. Prediction entails if–then reasoning. Although prediction is unnecessary for a theory to be good, it is nevertheless a valuable goal. For instance, academic and applied researchers may work to understand the principles of attracting attention to increase their ability to design advertisements that are more likely than others to attract readers', listeners', or televiewers' interest. Or the applied or academic researchers may want to better understand the characteristics of an entertaining and popular sitcom. If they know what makes sitcoms more entertaining, they can use that theory to create successful programming. Theories must describe, but they can also predict how people will behave or respond under certain circumstances. To appreciate the usefulness of predicting outcomes, imagine a communicator who wants to be persuasive (raise a listener's willingness to receive a message and yield to it). The communicator could use fear appeals; in this effort, the person designing the message would have to know what fear appeals are (as a concept) and understand how they interact with cognitive processes of reception and yielding (McGuire, 1968a, 1968b).

Theories Are Best When They Allow People to Understand and Predict Processes So They Can Better Control What Occurs in Communication. A theory can be used to explain and predict, thereby helping people to be more able to control the communication events, processes, strategies, and outcomes that affect their lives. Control can be seen as manipulative, but it also means that communication can be strategically used to achieve good ends. Control works out of an equation such as this: If this situation, then these communication processes can lead to positive or negative outcomes. Or, we can think of a variation: If I use these strategies in this circumstance, I am likely to achieve my desired outcomes. People learn to drive so that they can control the motion of their car, including avoiding collisions with other drivers. In a similar fashion, people want to understand the key communication processes so that they can achieve positive outcomes and avoid negative ones. If people understand theories of social conflict, for instance, they may be more likely to avoid conflict, at least conflict that is harmful and unproductive. With insights supplied by good theories, they may be able to resolve social conflict if it occurs. In this way, insights into the processes of communication can help people more successfully navigate the events of their lives in productive and satisfying ways.

A good theory is heuristic. That means it can be used to do something valuable. It may guide the design and execution of a communication campaign. A person designing a political campaign, for instance, might be interested in knowing what types of messages (a) will attract voters' attention to candidates, (b) reinforce committed voters' preferences to vote, (c) sway uncommitted voters, (d) convert opponents, and (e) motivate supporters to vote for one candidate or against an opponent. A theory is heuristic if it helps researchers to generate testable hypotheses.

A theory is heuristic if it leads to productive hypothesis testing. Until hypotheses are tested, they and the theory of which they are a part are nothing but speculation based on intuition or general observation. A good way to think about a hypothesis is that it is the "what if?" "what is?" "why is?" or "if then, what?" statements that are used to focus the research effort so that the answer supports or contradicts the theory that is being explored.

One heuristic aspect of a theory is the extent to which it can be reduced to a paradigm. What is a paradigm? It is the archetypal example or principle that a researcher keeps in mind when thinking about an ideal concept, relationship, or set of relationships. As Kaplan (1964) wrote, a paradigm is "the clearest instance of the general category. In this respect the paradigm functions like an ideal type, but is an actuality rather than an abstract construction, an individual to be generalized rather than a concept already generic in form" (p. 118). A paradigm differs from a theory that requires full explanation of relationships between variables. In contrast, a paradigm reduces a theory to its essence, a single summary model or example.

A Good Theory is Parsimonious. It can be briefly and succinctly stated—what some call the "back of the envelope" test. Can the theory be explained in the space available on an envelope? Even though one or more books could be devoted to the explanation and justification of a theory, it should be capable of being summarized in few words. It often is framed around a term or two, such as uncertainty reduction theory or information integration theory. The first suggests that people seek communication in order to reduce uncertainty because uncertainty is uncomfortable. The second, information integration theory, suggests that people form attitudes that result from a blending of positives and negatives. For instance, your car probably has positive and negative features; you like some things about it and dislike others. Cultivation theory postulates that as individuals are exposed to more of certain kinds of television programs, each exposure plants seeds that grow into a perspective that is largely influenced by the themes presented in the programs. For instance, people who watch more television—and television portrays a lot of violence—believe that society is more violent than do people who watch less television. The impact of this kind of programming may result in people being more able to imagine such events occurring, especially to themselves. If we watch a lot of programming about crime, we come to have lots of episodic information that forms more vivid thoughts about specific crimes. Such thoughts are updated or kept current by repeated heavy viewing (Shrum, 1996).

A Good Theory is Internally Consistent. This means that it is logical and reasonable. It must not make statements in one part or on one aspect of communication that are contradicted by other explanations. This criterion is one of those universal standards of a well-argued point of view. It is weakened to the extent that it is not internally consistent.

A Good Theory is Capable of Being Falsified. If a theory cannot be disproven, it probably cannot be proven. In such a circumstance, the "theory" is interesting, but it is not useful for empirical research. A theory is tested by its ability to be subjected to examination of the hypotheses that give it support. If the hypotheses can not be supported, then the theory is false.

As well as satisfying the criteria specified above, good theories do not ignore value issues. Good theory addresses "good communication" (Penman, 1992). Rather than merely reducing phenomena to empircally provable conclusions, theory is challenged to address issues that are central to the concern of helping people to improve their condition through communication. *Thus, a good theory addresses the ethical challenges of being morally responsible.*

This list of criteria can help you determine which theories do a good job of explaining the phenomena that you are trying to understand. Not all theories are equal. Some are better than others. Throughout this book you have ample opportunities to be persuaded by the soundness of the arguments presented in support of some theories and you may doubt the quality of the reasoning and evidence provided by advocates of other theories. Such analysis suggests that each theory is only as strong as its ability to withstand the challenge of critics.

Concepts: Building Blocks of Theory

A term, *concept,* was used frequently in the discussion earlier. Thanks for patiently waiting for us to define the term. What is a concept? It is a building block of a theory and each hypothesis.

Sometimes people use the terms *concept* and *construct* interchangeably. At other times, scholars will suggest that a concept is more general than its more precisely expressed counterpart, a construct, which typically is thought to be created by scientists to help understand a phenomon under investigation. Here we use concept in preference to construct. If we use construct, we also mean concept but think of it as having been more precisely defined by researchers than its more embracing, less discriminating counterpart.

Concepts are the names for unique categories of recognizable, distinguishable phenomena. Once different events, relationships, patterns, and processes are observed, they can be named. Each of these categories is a concept or construct.

Researchers try to identify key concepts in communication. For instance, information may be distinguished from persuasion, or conflict from cooperation. What is entertainment? What is pornography, meaning, channel, or attraction? Is propaganda the same as persuasion? What is trust in interpersonal relationships? What is attitude or belief? You may notice how difficult these concepts are to define. Often, just as some concept seems to be stabilizing in meaning, someone comes along and frustrates the effort by demonstrating flaws in conceptualization, definition, or measurement. For instance, in order to study the effects of watching pornography, a researcher must have a viable concept of what pornography is and what distinguishes it from art. Just as researchers think they have achieved a standard definition, culture changes and so does the definition of pornography. Yesterday's pornography may be today's made-for-television movie. Another example: The concept of channels and how they differ from messages seemed reasonably clear until Marshall McLuhan (1964) called the "medium the message" (p. 23). His observation was designed to show how a medium, such as television, is also a message because each medium gives unique shape to the information it conveys.

Let's think about some of the obvious concepts that are likely to be central to research and theory to explain communication processes. Entertainment is a concept, typically associated with the outcomes people feel or desire to feel if they read, listen, see a movie, or watch a television program. Meaning is a concept. We often seek to understand what meaning is and to explain how what one person says becomes meaningful to another. Attitude is a concept frequently associated with the study of persuasion. Deception is a concept used to understand interpersonal communication; deception refers to the goals and communication styles that are associated with one person lying (not telling the truth, or the whole truth) to another. We can imagine that an organization has a climate (the feelings employees have about where they work). We can conceptualize media impact as the social, psychological, and cultural effects consuming media messages has on readers, listeners, or televiewers.

Naming events, processes, and relationships in communication is difficult. For instance, if researchers are going to base their research on the assumption that uncertainty reduction is a powerful motive of how and when people communicate, we need to be certain that those researchers know for sure what the concept of uncertainty means? What is uncertainty? Or, what is a question? For instance, researchers who study how people conduct themselves during interviews are interested in strategic questioning activities. A question—a concept vital to interviewing strategies—can be defined as an interrogative statement, "What did you study in college?" But we may also ask, is an imperative ("Tell me what you studied in college") also a question?

A concept is useful to the extent that other researchers see and define the same phenomenon. Some phenomena are directly observable. We can calculate the total amount of time persons spend watching television. We can count the references to men or women in a series of news stories over several years of reporting. We can observe the beginning of a conversation and realize that it is different from the ending of a conversation. The glare of a person angered during a conversation is observable; we can even capture it on video as part of an experiment.

All of those phenomena are directly observable; they can be seen as we watch people communicate. Other phenomena are not directly observable. Communication research is often interested in what happens inside of people's minds. We want to know how they think and how watching a program, for instance, affects them. In that way, we might be interested in studying entertainment. How do you measure entertainment? As you think about your own experiences, how do you know when you are being entertained? How does that feeling compare with being bored? Attitudes, beliefs, or values cannot be directly observed. Nor can researchers know whether a person is being entertained or enlightened by a television program.

All that researchers can use to build theory is what they believe constitutes evidence of these phenomena. When a research participant fills out a questionnaire, the researcher hopes the response corresponds to an attitude, organizational climate, or entertainment, for instance.

Observation and naming are crucial aspects of theory building because understanding can be advanced only if phenomena are named with sufficient accuracy that people can agree with the terms and find them useful to understand and explain what is going on.

Two terms, *reliability* and *validity*, set standards of precision that help researchers determine whether they can accurately define key concepts and properly measure the phenomenon being examined. Two research and conceptual flaws are likely to mar research and theory construction. One flaw is that terms used to express a concept actually do not accurately capture the essence of the phenomonon under scrutiny. For instance, if researchers want to study the impact of watching pornography, they have to agree which content of what people read, view, or hear actually constitutes pornography. What is pornography for some persons may be art for others. A researcher who says that there is not such communication phenomena as pornography cannot study it, because for that person it does not exist. A second flaw is that researchers use different terms to refer to the same phenomenon or the same terms to refer to different phenomena. Oh my, that can be a tangle. But knowing the process helps researchers and students.

Reliability is a test of whether repeated studies can produce the same results. A concept is well understood, and measures are reliable, if they consistently give the same results. If we were to give the same response items to the same persons over several weeks or months, giving them time to forget how they have previously responded to the items, we could determine whether the measures are unreliable. If those persons answered differently each time, all else being equal, the measures were unreliable. If we attempt to measure a specific phenomenon by using certain items on a questionnaire, we should get highly similar results every time we conduct the study. If we get different results from different groups of research participants, then we either have bad measures or we have a flawed sense of the concept that we are attempting to measure. If we do not get reliable results, they are a function only of the study and are not an accurate definition and understanding of the phenomena that are being examined. Researchers have developed many research methodologies and statistical procedures to increase the quality of measures and their ability to know whether they have quality measures that accurately capture the true essence of the concepts being studied.

Validity refers to the accuracy of the definitions of concepts and the tools used to measure them. Again we can think of validity in terms of researchers' ability to accurately measure the concept being investigated. Validity exists if researchers actually measure what they are seeking to measure. For example, what is an attitude? Is it an opinion obtained by having participants think about an object, situation, or behavior and complete a scale, such as

Strongly like ____, ____, ____, ____, ____ Strongly dislike

Is the best measure of an attitude respondents' answers to questions that ask them to think about statements and then complete questionnaire items that ask them to express whether they agree ____, disagree ____, or don't know____, with the statement?

A theory based on concepts that lack validity or reliability is not useful. It is not an accurate statement of the phenomenon that people want to understand. We have several types of validity to consider.

- Face validity exists if other researchers agree that, on the "face of things," the measures and definitions of the concept seem to capture the essence of the concept under consideration.
- Construct validity entails lots of thought, measurement, and scholarly discussion. The essence of construct validity centers on the ability of researchers to reliably measure a concept and to persuade other researchers that the definition and measurement are accurate.
- Predictive validity can be assessed by seeing whether some expected measure actually measures what it is designed to measure. Prediction is the crux of this kind of validity. If we predict that attitudes toward specific products lead customers to purchase those products, we can measure the persons' attitudes as preferences and then see whether they act based on those preferences.
- Concurrent validity exists when we can use a measure to differentiate between two (or more) groups of individuals based on control of a key factor. We might examine media impact by comparing two groups of people, those who watch more than 30 hours of television a week against those who watch less than 1 hour a day. Those people who view more television should be more likely to state that they learned their opinions from watching television than those people who watch less television.

By understanding and having means for examining the accuracy of the terms they use (the attributes of the phenomena under consideration), researchers can be more comfortable in thinking that their conclusions are accurate. If they understand the essence of the phenomonon they are examining and can measure it reliably, they can with substantial confidence assert that the conclusions are accurate.

Models and Other Means for Expressing Relationships Between Concepts

Once concepts are identified, the next step is to define or explain the relationships between them. Merely being interested in concepts leaves researchers far from their mark of knowing and explaining the phenomena they are studying. Identifying the key concepts (the basic phenomena) is vital, but the real intellectual breakthrough occurs when the relationships between the variables can be explained. If researchers are to formulate useful and valuable theories, they need not only to know which concepts are vital to the processes under discussion, but they also need to be able to indicate how the presence of one concept can affect other related concepts. If they find changes in one concept, will they discover other changes as well? If the processes of communication being studied transpire over time, what is the sequence? These sorts of questions demonstrate the need to know concepts and the relationships between them.

One way to deal with concepts is to put them into a model. Since the 1950s, many articles and communication texts have contained primitive pictorial models. Some of these are shown in chapter 2, where we discuss the history of many of the early researchers and the models they proposed. Whereas a theory explains key concepts and their relationships, most models are mere pictorial representations that may not be isomorphic analogues of the phenomenon being described (Hawes, 1975). To be isomorphic, a model must accurately represent the phenomenon under consideration. Few models meet this requirement.

As you study communication, you will encounter at least three kinds of models:

- A taxonomy, the most primitive model, merely lists the key concepts relevant to understanding some phenomenon, but does nothing more than suggest that the featured concepts are related in some way. A good example of a taxonomy is a list of components typically used to describe the communication process: source, message, channel, receiver, feedback, and context. In this taxonomy, no effort is made to account for how any concept relates to, affects, or is affected by any other. As you proceed through this book, you will encounter lists of variables that scholars have identified as being relevant but that they do not fully understand and have not formed into more sophisticated explanations.
- A pictorial or graphic model is a more sophisticated presentation that conceptually describes the phenomenon. These "spaghetti" models frequently consist of lines going in all directions as they suggest in the most general manner how concepts relate to one another. A typical example of a pictorial representation model results when someone takes the taxonomy of source, message, channel, receiver, feedback, and context and draws elaborate complexes of lines and arrows attempting to describe the relationships between them. Although such models are always incomplete and imprecise, they can help researchers to capture the key variables, indicate to others what the variables are, and suggest the relationships. The postulated relationships can be discussed so that hypotheses can be posed. This type of model is used to help students understand key concepts and relationships, as long as it is understood that they are not accurate replicas of the phenomenon being considered.

- The mathematical formula models feature sufficient sophistication that relationships between concepts can be calculated with mathematical precision. Few mathematical models have been developed to explain communication events and processes. This book presents two algebraic formulas, one to define attitude (p. 203) and related concepts, the other to explain the potential gratifications media users seek to satisfy (p. 361). Close inspection will reveal that the first of these two models supplies the intellectual foundation for the second.

Quantitative and Qualitative Assessment

The scientific scrutiny of concepts usually results in their treatment as variables. A variable is a concept to which a set of values can be assigned. These values can be numerical (quantitative) or nonnumerical (qualitative). Quantitative methods are those by which an instrument generates data. A questionnaire, for instance, generates quantitative information, as does a meter that records which television stations (channels) a family selects to watch each day. If you ask a person to rate a movie according to several criteria (e.g., quality of the story line, using responses such as very satisfactory, satisfactory, neither satisfactory nor unsatisfactory, unsatisfactory, or very unsatisfactory), you have generated quantitative information. If you ask people to rank 10 popular music groups favorate to least favorite, you have obtained quantitative information.

Qualitative research requires a lot of involvement on the part of the researcher. If a researcher has to interpret answers to open-ended questions (those that allow respondents the option of saying what is on their minds), the researcher has qualitative information. Many qualitative methods are available to the researcher, and these are explained in many research methdology texts. Here, we only want to demonstrate briefly that research requires the generation of information and the interpretation of it by qualitative and quantitative methods.

Variables: Concepts Come to Life

In the previous two sections, we defined and explained concepts and showed how researchers can imagine the relationships between them. In that discussion, a term kept coming up. The term is *variable*. Each kind of model mentioned in the previous section attempted to express the relationship between concepts and variables.

Social scientists typically use the term *variable* to describe what happens when concepts interact or when a concept is measured. As Kerlinger (1973) observed, "A variable is a property that takes on different values." This change in value is not a moral issue but a mathematical one. That means that researchers can measure changes in a concept by seeing it change, for instance, from high to low.

Viewing the matter that way, Kerlinger continued, "A variable is something that varies" (p. 29). A variable is a concept that can be measured numerically. A concept becomes a variable when it can be seen to take on different numerical weights. For instance, we could imagine the amount of televiewing as a variable. In fact, in chapter 9, we indicate that some researchers have studied the different media impact that occurs when people watch lots of television versus when they watch very little television. We can quantify the variable (amount of televiewing) as ranging from heavy (25–40 hours per week) to light (less than 8 hours per week). In this way, we can compare heavy to light viewers, for instance.

We can think of many other variables. Understanding is a concept; one person can "understand" another. But we know that people misunderstand as well as understand. So we can conceptualize the variable as ranging from misunderstanding to totally understanding. Attitudes can be strong or weak. As a concept, uncertainty can become a variable ranging from no uncertainty to extreme uncertainty. In terms of media impact of viewers, listeners, or readers, we can imagine (and measure) no effect, minimal effect, modest effect, and dominant effect.

In terms of the methodologies used in social science research, researchers often measure variables by asking research participants to "respond to" different survey questions by circling a number or providing a quantifiable response. For instance, you might ask research participants to indicate on a scale of 1 to 5 how much they like their job: 1 could mean *don't like job very much,* and 5 could mean *like job very much.* The other numbers would measure points between 1 and 5. You might also ask participants how much they believe they are allowed to participate in organizational decision making (1 to 5, with 1 meaning *very little,* and 5 meaning *a great deal*). In these ways, concepts come alive as variables that can be measured. The key to measuring the variables is to determine whether changes in the value of one variable corresponds to the changes in value of another variable.

For instance, the amount of televiewing could be studied to see whether it affects school performance. Amount of televiewing could be measured and compared to students' academic grade point averages. Or, following the organizational communication study in the previous paragraph, we could be interested in finding out whether job satisfaction (like/dislike my job) is influenced by the amount of participation people believe they have in organizational decision making.

To enlarge your vocabulary of social science, you may want to learn the names of various kinds of varibles. Variables may be dichotomous, (for instance, demographic characteristics such as male or female), or continuous, such as degree of opinion change or amount of enjoyment produced by watching a particular television program. A dichotomous variable is one where you have only either/or opinions. A person is either biologically male or female. A continuous variable is one where you can have a range of measures that is infinite. Usually social science research is limited to a few increments in any range of measures. For instance, to measure the amount of enjoyment a viewer experiences from television, a researcher might use a 3-, 5-, 7-, or even 9-point scale from 1 (*not enjoyable*) to 9 (*very enjoyable*). The researcher could use any number of interval measures, even an extreme such as hundreds (1–100) or thousands (1–1,000). Science has many measures in those extremes and more. For instance, temperature can be measured in hundreds of degrees. Such extremes in social science are not usual, at least not at this point of research development. The trick to measurement is not to use more than the reasonable number of intervals. To be reasonable, you need some rationale for believing that more than 3, 5, 7, or 9 points yields useful data. Most of the measures mentioned or implied in the studies in this book were no more than 9, and probably most were fewer.

Variables are the heart of the social scientific process of observing and predicting. By assigning numbers to variables and calculating the relationship or differences between them, researchers seek to make accurate observations and predictions. For instance, a speaker might want to know whether fear appeals of a particular magnitude (high, moderate, low) increase a listener's willingness to receive and yield to a message. That example contains two other kinds of variables: independent and dependent. An independent variable is one that is presumed to produce changes in the dependent variable. Here fear appeals is the independent variable, whereas reception and yielding are dependent variables. As an independent variable changes in value (such as heat under a pan of water), the dependent variable is predicted to change (such as the molecular action in the water in the pan). One of the keys to using theory and research to make predictions is to know which variables (independent) produce changes in other variables (dependent).

We can find many examples of analysis that examine the relationship between independent and dependent variables. One study examined the impact of television watching (independent variable) on children's book reading. Televiewing led to lowered amounts of reading. Moreover, it also resulted in deteriorated attitudes toward book reading and children's ability to concentrate on reading (Koolstra & Van Der Voort, 1996).

A mediating variable influences how an independent variable, such as message, will affect the dependent variable, such as attitude; the degree to which a receiver is personally affected by (self-interested in) the topic of a message mediates its impact on recall or attitude change. In the example of water boiling as heat increases under the pan, altitude (atmospheric pressure) is a mediating variable. As atmosphere decreases, less heat is required to bring water to a boil.

A confounding variable interferes with the routine or ordinary relationship between the independent and the dependent variable. In doing research on the amount of time children watch television, for example, results could be confounded by a variable such as attention (attentiveness); even though television sets may be on, and children are in front of them, the children may not be paying attention.

Researchers and theorists use variables as their basic way of thinking. Variables are the essence of hypothesis testing. Hypotheses are based on testable relationships between two or more other variables. The logic behind testing a hypothesis is that as one variable changes, one or more variables will also change. Being able to make such observations allows researchers to understand phenomena and to observe patterns. Variables over time become the essence of theory construction because researchers want to know how a few dominant concepts and variables can explain some phenomenon that is being investigated.

This line of analysis can also be applied to communication. Let's look at communication as a variable. It can be treated as a dependent variable by looking for factors that influence it as an outcome. For instance, if persons experience high enough levels of uncertainty, they are likely to engage in specific communication behavior: question asking. If people want to know something, to reduce uncertainty, they ask questions. On the other hand, communication can be treated as an independent variable by examining the variables it influences. For instance, in interpersonal communication, researchers find that the more relational partners communicate openly, the more they like and trust one another. Studies of mediated communication treat communication as an independent variable that has impact on how people form opinions on matters of current events and public policies.

Relationships Between Variables

Throughout your study of communication, your inquiry should be guided by the goal of achieving a precise understanding of the relationship between key variables. It is not enough to learn that certain communication variables correspond to one another. The higher level of analysis is to know how and why they affect one another. The following discussion features some major types of relationships that occur between variables.

Linear Versus Nonlinear. Some relationships are linear. That means as one variable changes, so do one or more other variables. Linear relationships may imply the presence of independent and dependent variables. This means that the events that occur early in any communication event (concepts and variables) influence those that follow in a predictable manner. For instance, as persons become more cognitively involved (interested) in a topic, they are more likely to receive and think about information on that topic. As we explain later, causal relationships, as well as correlations, are linear relationships. For instance, as one variable increases (as in the case of heat on the bottom of a pan of water), another also increases (the activity of the water in the pan).

The earliest popular communication model portrayed the process as starting from a sender who creates a message that is sent through a channel to have an effect on a receiver. Another linear relationship between variables would occur when a persuasive message is a stimulus (independent variable) that creates a response, such as attitude change, which subsequently leads to a change in behavior. Or, the message in an advertisement may stimulate a salient attitude in the mind of the potential buyer and thereby prompt the person to buy (or at least prefer) the product or use the service. A linear model of communication behavior assumes that a logical, causal, sequential relationship exists between key concepts so that each preceding element affects those that follow.

Many relationships between the elements of the communication process are nonlinear. (The discussion in chap. 2 should help you understand this point more clearly.) Each element in a process interacts dynamically with others. In the aforementioned example of the advertisement, a linear view would assume that the advertisement's message content led to an attitude that could in turn motivate a person to prefer to buy one product instead of another. But a person's reaction to advertising is typically nonlinear, depending on (a) the time of day when the ad is encountered, (b) the buyer's awareness of competing purchasing choices, (c) peer approval, (d) source credibility, (e) willingness to refute the persuasive message, (f) the buyer's mood, (g) the ease or difficulty of making the purchase, (h) the buyer's cash flow, and (i) the size of last month's credit card statement. These factors will impinge on (mediate) the likelihood that the message will lead to the desired purchasing behavior. Also, because buyers are dynamic, at least to some extent, they seek information and ask questions about products and services. In this way, they select information strategically rather than merely yielding to ad content. Each of us has experienced this nonlinear relationship as we weigh factors involved in making a purchasing decision.

Here is another example of the problems of looking for linear relationships and assuming that the source directly affects the receiver of a message. What if you give advice to a friend or receive advice from a friend? Do you or your friend necessarily follow that advice? Researchers discovered that the answer was no. Goldsmith and Fitch (1997) found that the advice people give to one another can be viewed either as being helpful or an instance of butting in. It is thought to be helpful if it is interpreted as being honest and supportive. If people follow each other's advice, it confirms the person who offers the advice, but the person who receives the advice reserves the right to accept or reject it. So, the influence is not linear. The sender does not put an idea into the mind of the receiver, who merely accepts it.

Colinear. A relationship is colinear when two variables act together to produce a predicted outcome in another variable. For instance, persuasion research has observed a colinear relationship between attitude toward a behavior (what we want to do) and the belief that we should adhere to norms others would expect us to follow as we decide whether to behave as we prefer. For this reason, one predictor of a person's behavior is the attitude toward the behavior, whether the person thinks it will lead to positive or negative outcomes. The second factor (colinear) in predicting what the person will do is his or her sense of what significant others want him or her to do (Ajzen & Fishbein, 1980; Shepherd, 1987). This means that, even though you might have a favorable attitude toward an action, such as going out to a movie instead of studying for a final, you consider the norm expressed by your best friend who says, "Going to a movie can clear your mind so you can study more effectively later." Or you may not have a positive attitude toward the directive, "Give blood," but you decide to donate because your friends agree to give and think you should as well. In this case, neither variable (attitude toward action or norm) necessarily precedes or follows the other. They may occur simultaneously in the process of persuasive influence.

Curvilinear. A curvilinear relationship between variables means that the relationship between two variables is U-shaped. In a linear relationship, in contrast, high levels of a variable, such as noise, might require that the listener strain to hear and understand a message. Thus, the higher the noise, the harder a person has to strain to listen.

In contrast, a curvilinear relationship occurs when the greatest and least amount of one variable corresponds to increases in a corresponding variable. For instance, a curvilinear relationship exists between the impact of source credibility on attitudes and the degree to which receivers are interested in finding out information on the topic. As interest increases, source credibility increases attitude up to a point, after which further interest in the topic lessens attitude change (Stiff, 1986). Researchers found that moderate fear appeals have more impact than minimal or extreme fear appeals. Minimal fear appeals are not significant enough to motivate thought or action. Extreme fear appeals may not be persuasive because the person can be in denial if he or she is sufficiently frightened by the prospect of negative outcomes.

Positive Versus Negative. The relationship between variables can be positive or negative. For instance, high credibility sources have a positive effect on attitude change, whereas low credibility sources may have a negative effect. That positive relationship means that as people have more respect for a speaker they are more likely to believe that person. A positive relationship occurs when as one variable increases its companion variable also increases. Another example of a positive relationship is when, in interpersonal communication, individuals are attracted to those persons who share the same attitudes. In contrast, a negative relationship exists between persons who have dissimilar attitudes. Thus, a negative relationship exists when as one variable rises the other falls, or becomes lower. As trust increases, reluctance to disclose becomes lower. As the amount of television viewing increases, the sense that the world is a safe place (free from crime) diminishes.

Causation Versus Correlation. As they engage in research and develop theories, academics consider whether a relationship between two or more variables is due to causation or correlation. Causation assumes that the relationship between two variables, events, or behaviors is such that as one changes it causes changes in the other. As Perry (1996) reasoned, three conditions must be met for a relationship to be causal: (1) The two variables must go together—be associated with one another; (2) the variable thought to be the cause must precede the one it is thought to affect; and (3) the effect cannot exist in the absence of the cause, and no other variable can be the cause of the effect.

Let's apply the criteria of causality to a common relationship, one we mentioned earlier in this chapter. You know that increased amounts of heat (cause) applied to the bottom of a tea kettle will increase the speed (effect) with which the water will boil. Are heat and boiling associated with one another? Does the rise in temperature precede the boiling? Can water boil without sufficient heat?

A correlation exists when two variables change (increase or decrease) in proportion to one another, but not in a way where one produces the change in the other. Two variables may change as a consequence of being the effects of a common independent variable. One can imagine that more ice cream is eaten during the summer when people also wear less clothing. Thus, increased amounts of ice cream consumption occur as less clothing is worn. But the one does not cause the other. Both are caused by rising temperatures from summer heat.

One perplexing example of this causation–correlation relationship is what occurs between high amounts of television viewing and low academic achievement. Achievement tends to drop once viewing exceeds 10 hours per week. But studies on this topic are inconclusive as to whether low achievers watch more television or whether watching high amounts of television causes lower achievement. Perhaps high amounts of watching and low achievement are products of some mutual cause (Potter, 1987).

Correlation states that two events occur or variables change (covary) in either a positive or negative relationship to one another. Even if a causal link cannot be established, the researcher knows that a relationship exists between events. Do we have cause or correlation? This is a vital question. Let's examine an everyday event. Two coworkers frequently go to lunch together. Near lunch time, one or the other shows up at the other's office and says, "Lunch?" A causal model would argue that the invitation produces the response, "I'm ready; let's go." But sometimes the invitation is declined: "I have a different lunch arrangement today." Is the fact that they often go to lunch together due to correlation or causality? The probability is high that one person's arrival will prompt the other person to make a choice, but the arrival does not cause the choice. If the two people go to lunch together routinely, that is likely to be a correlation, but not a causal relationship.

A researcher might wonder whether high amounts of television viewing cause viewers to believe the world is more violent than it is (because TV portrays more violence than actually occurs in the real world). Does watching large amounts of television cause people to perceive high levels of violence? Or do fearful people watch more TV than nonfearful people do, taking solace in the fact that in television drama, most violence is punished, and justice is usually restored in each episode. Some researchers are intent on finding out the causality, if any exists, in this tangle. Others may settle for some unexplained relationship (in causal terms) between high amounts of televiewing and a sense of apprehension about the amount of violence that occurs in society

Efforts to solve intellectual challenges of these kinds are brain teasers. However, the effort to dig deeply and see what variables produce changes in other variables is vital to achieving lasting academic, social scientific insights. As we argued in this chapter, the objective of social scientists is to observe and explain. If observation and explanation are sufficiently accurate and insightful, researchers are able to make useful predictions. Causation occurs when they conclude that changes in one variable affect changes in another. Correlation is an adequate but not an optimal way of thinking. It notes change occurring in relationships between variables, but researchers do not know what causes these changes.

APPROACHES TO THE STUDY OF COMMUNICATION: META-THEORIES

By now you know that the processes of communication behavior are not merely random. Researchers could never explain communication behavior, strategies, styles, and effects if they could not observe and make sense of the patterns. As we explained earlier, theory must be based on observation and understanding of phenomena in the attempt to make predictions about the processes of communication.

Early in their efforts to solve the mystery of communication, researchers conducted many research projects to test hypotheses. Then they realized that if they only found a huge list of relationships between variables, they would never actually understand communication. They needed theories to group the research discoveries into meaningful generalizations.

As one of the major steps toward theory development, scholars discussed which theoretical assumptions are most likely to guide effective theory development. That led researchers to consider what are called meta-theories—theories about theories. To solve this riddle, researchers have examined four meta-theories: Scientific laws meta-theory, rules meta-theory, systems meta-theory, and covering law meta-theory.

Scientific Laws

Some researchers aspired to discover invariant "scientific" laws. Oh, if life were only that easy! An invariant scientific law meta-theory assumes that a constant, causal relationship always exists when the change of one variable, as antecedent, invariably produces a change in another variable. A scientific laws meta-theory assumes that if a few of these major generalizations could be made, then all relevant research findings would make more sense.

A scientific laws meta-theory argues that research findings always conform to this equation: Variable Y varies as a function of variable X under condition Z. Such logic might explain physical events such as objects falling at the same speed under the same conditions or water boiling at the same temperature at the same altitude. But this standard of law-like causal relations is too demanding for building theory and conducting communication research. People are too complex in what they do and why they do it to yield to absolute scientific explanation.

An invariant scientific laws meta-theory assumes that human communication behavior is motion, not action. This is an unrealistically mechanistic view of human behavior. Motion is the product of cause and effect relationships. A truck rolling down a hill without a driver controlling its direction or speed is in motion; it is not acting. Action assumes willed choices.

As action, communication behavior is subject to a variety of choices that may not always lead to the same behavior. It is complex and subject to influences and choices due to (a) the unique nature of situations, (b) personality and maturity of persons involved, (c) personal preferences regarding communication styles and strategies, and (d) the ability to perform expected communication activity. Communication interaction is a web of multiple causes or correlations so complex that relationships among variables probably are not invariable. Communication phenomena are often multidimensional, rather than unidimensional and straightforward in their relationships.

Once researchers realized that strictly deterministic, law-like models did not accurately predict communication behavior, they asked themselves which theoretical assumptions would help them generate significant conclusions. To solve for this methodological challenge, researchers proposed three meta-theories: rules, systems, and covering law.

Rules

Rules meta-theory assumes that people learn to "play the game" of communication as they learn to play any other game. According to this approach to the study of communication, people make strategic choices in their communication behavior. Because communication is a "game," people learn its rules and strive to behave in ways that conform to those rules. People generate, learn, and use rules to make judgments and interact in specific ways so that each knows what to do and how to respond to the other. For instance, the rules of arguing differ from those of getting to know one another. We follow different rules when we communicate with our friends than when we participate in job interviews. We even have rules about when and how people can watch television. One such rule is that programs occur at predictable times each day, week, or month. They last for predictable, rule-bound, lengths of time. In this way, people can communicate because they learn and use the appropriate set of rules and their corresponding behaviors.

Researchers who favor a rules perspective claim that it treats humans more as masters of their fate and less as robots who merely respond to environmental cues. It reasons that strategic interaction choices are guided by learned rules of action, not causal laws of motion. To explain why communicators know which choices to make and when to make them, theorists search for the cybernetic (feedback) mechanism by which people judge whether their choices bring about the results they desire. This principle can be expressed in this fashion: If X outcome is desired, then Y behavior or opinion will produce the desired result under Z circumstances. People choose rules that increase their chances of being rewarded through interaction. In this way, for instance, conversations occur because participants know and follow rules of turn taking and topic development (McLaughlin, 1984).

Let's look at some examples. People take turns during a conversation to be perceived as pleasant and amenable. They answer questions during an interview to be viewed as competent candidates for a job. They use ingratiation, which follows the rule that if they compliment someone, that person is obliged to reciprocate or comply with some request in exchange. They know that they must "yield the floor" to allow communication partners to have a turn during a conversation. During an argument, they keep the floor to prevent the other person from having their say. They believe that they can obtain a favorable outcome by holding a particular attitude, such as believing a specific product is better than other products under the circumstances. The rule "people should buy cars that are economical and durable" contains attitudes that can guide behavior. By similar reasoning, persons might watch a funny television program to put themselves in a happy mood. The rules perspective assumes that communication transpires as people follow knowable rules to interact as well as to make judgments (Bandura, 1986; Reardon, 1981).

People use rules out of convenience or conviction. Reardon (1981) differentiated between rules that are "owned" and those that are "borrowed." Owned rules are part of an individual's personal repertoire, whereas some rules are borrowed only to "get along." Whether someone uses a rule that is owned or borrowed is important. Does the person believe the rule or use it for mere social convenience? Knowing whether someone owns or borrows a rule can let us determine whether he or she is responding to self-oriented or other-oriented rules. People respond differently under those circumstances.

Rules give researchers insights into why and how people communicate as they do. Social science searches to observe and explain patterns and processes. Rules are "what if" statements that link communication behavior to goals that can be satisfied by interacting with other people. Thus, a person might ask, what strategies should I employ if I want to start a conversation? Or the tactical relationship can be stated as "if–then." If person A says "Hello," then person B should respond appropriately if he or she wants to seem (be seen as being) friendly. Each rule links a goal with the communication strategy likely to achieve it: If goal X, in situation Z, then action Y. If hungry, then eat. If an attitude is unrewarding, then change it. If person A wants to impress the boss (goal X), when the boss needs a favor (situation Z), the employee will volunteer (action Y).

Rules meta-theory can help researchers gain insights because communication behavior exhibits patterns that are knowable and followable, but not invariant. Rules meta-theory reasons that patterns result when people choose to apply specific rules to guide their interactions to achieve specific goals. Based on this logic, researchers seek to discover the rules people systematically and repeatedly employ to coordinate their efforts and achieve goals in the contexts typical of human existence.

Rules meta-theory can shed light on strategic behavior in all communication contexts. Many examples used in this section feature interpersonal processes. Rules meta-theory also aids analysis of how organizations operate— organizational communication. On behalf of an organization, key personnel, such as receptionists and sales personnel, follow rules that are appropriate to their roles. Superiors and subordinates have rules to follow during their interactions. Staff meetings follow rules. Sexual harrassment has been a serious problem in organizations. It occurs when persons use one set of conversational and interaction rules as opposed to a much more appropriate and less offensive set.

Rules also help explain mass-mediated communication. Television formats follow rules. Those formats are segmented into predictable and definable time units. For instance, programs start on the hour or half hour and last for a predictable period of time. Rules—codes of regulation—are prescribed by federal agencies to regulate broadcasts. Characters on sitcoms follow role-dependent rules. For instance, villains act in villainous ways and say villainous things. Episodes follow plots that are based on rules people use to build and dissolve interpersonal relationships. The interaction patterns that occur in Internet communication follow rules.

Critics of the rules perspective argue that it is impossible to develop a complete list of all of the rules that can apply to all situations and to know which ones will govern the strategic plans and actions of persons as they communicate. Rules perspectives assume that people are reasonably thoughtful and strategic. What if communication behavior is mindless and routine. Maybe what is discovered as a rule, which assumes thoughtfulness and strategy, is merely a habit. Despite such reservations, many researchers cling to key assumptions of rules meta-theory. For these researchers, the power of the rules perspective is its ability to capture the structure and logic of interaction without being required to explain all communication behavior.

Systems

Systems meta-theory features communication as transpiring according to the principles unique to systems (Fisher, 1982; Monge, 1977). This meta-theory allows researchers to think holistically to capture the breadth and dynamism of the communication process. For these reasons, systems meta-theory has substantial impact on how researchers build communication theory.

Systems meta-theory originated to explain the dynamic interaction and exchange among biological organisms in an ecosystem. Researchers wanted to analyze the adaptive changes organisms make in their efforts to survive (Bertalanffy, 1968). According to that logic, research can analyze the earth as an ecosystem. It can feature the adaptation of individual species. It can look at each person as a system that consists of subsystems, for instance, respiratory, reproductive, nervous, gastrointestinal, and cardiovascular.

Systems theory assumes that reality (including human interaction) is so complex that its variables and relationships can never be known completely. Despite this complexity, patterns and processes become apparent to researchers and theorists. These patterns are the product of the characteristics of a system. Thus, the logic goes, if people know those characteristics and the dynamics of a system, they can use that knowledge to better understand the principles, processes, strategies, and effects of communication.

Systems meta-theory treats relationships among people as complex, interdependent, dynamic, self-adjusting, and goal oriented. It treats media as systems. Audiences are part of that system. Media obtain information, process it, and output it to viewers, readers, and listeners. In this manner, meta-systems can also explain how organizations are systems that engage in input, processing, and output. For instance, a restaurant buys (input) food goods, which it prepares (processes) into meals (output).

Systems meta-theory helps researchers to get a perspective on various levels of analysis. According to this research perspective, each person is a communication system as well as a part of many other systems, such as families, businesses, social organizations, universities, news or entertainment media, and countries.

Systems meta-theory helps researchers grasp the dynamics of communication. As people interact with one another and their environment, they take in information (input), think about it (processing), and respond to it (output). A newspaper publishing company, for instance, obtains information (input) gathered by reporters, which the editorial staff processes into stories. Eventually the paper is printed and sold to customers (output). In terms of interpersonal communication, one person notices another (input), and thinks about dating the person (processing), and eventually asks the other person to lunch (output).

Systems meta-theory can provide insights into how communication events occur as each system interacts with other systems. Each system's components holistically and dynamically function to achieve the purpose for which it was created. If, for example, researchers want to understand the health of a business, they can use a systems approach to determine how effectively each employee uses communication to survive and excel in the system, and on behalf of it. Researchers may believe that an open system is healthier than one that is closed (does not interact with its environment). Interchange occurs when one system receives information (input) from another system. This input is processed and output for other systems.

Systems theory has been especially influential on organizational communication theory and research. It explains how and why people form groups, each of which is a system as well as part of a larger system. For instance, a student can be part of an academic club or social group on campus. Each of these is a subsystem, a part of the entire college or university (system). Each college or university is a part of a larger system that contains other campuses, such as a conference or league. That is kind of confusing to comprehend at first, but it is simple when you think of each system as a system, even though it is part of a larger system or composed of subsystems (each of which can be thought of as a system).

The systems perspective rests on many assumptions, particularly the cybernetic principle of regulation and adjustment. Communication systems are self-regulating because of the cybernetic principle that actions are selected and designed to achieve goals; if persons' actions do not achieve their goals, they use feedback to change the goals or tactics so that they can be more successful.

Used to analyze communication, systems meta-theory emphasizes the characteristics of the system, the hierarchies of subsystems in the system, and the dynamic balance between the subsystems within each system as well as between it and other systems in its environment. The parts of a system are interdependent.

For example, a university has several kinds of systems: administration, staff, students, and faculty. If a part of a university (system) changes (such as an influx of students), so does the system itself (need for more faculty or increased class size) so that it can accomplish the required processing and output.

This line of analysis could focus on a receptionist as a person who interfaces (input) with the public (a system) to see if he or she uses appropriate greeting behavior (output) to give customers the feeling that the organization is friendly and thereby attracts their business (input). Analysis might focus on customer relations personnel who interact with unhappy and dissatisfied customers. A systems approach might encourage researchers to examine whether cordiality by customer relations personnel enhances a business system's ability to succeed, at least to the extent the business depends on customer satisfaction. Parts of a system are interdependent; what affects one part affects all other parts.

The systems approach demands that theorists acknowledge that communication events and interactions are dynamic and complex. This approach cautions researchers to view communication as a system of interdependent parts. A change in one part affects all other parts. This perspective can apply to interaction between two people or capture the dynamics of a corporation with thousands of employees. It explains how people in one system interact with persons in other systems. Thus, a company uses marketing and public relations (bolstered by opinion research) to function constructively with customers and the general public (components of an environment that affects the company's ability to achieve its goals). This observation makes us aware of one last characteristic of a system: *equifinality*. This term refers to the fact that each system can achieve the same goal by different means.

Systems theory has assisted researchers in their efforts to avoid the limits placed on them by an invariant laws perspective. Fisher (1978) reasoned that the systems meta-theory is more compatible with a rule-conforming meta-theory than it is with the law-governed meta-theory. When studying complex systems, it is often difficult to make inferences on the basis of antecedent conditions—the analysis of causal relationships between independent and dependent variables. Thus, he believed, systems theory provides an encompassing rationale for developing communication theory and generating research hypotheses. In its own right, rules meta-theory can be used to explain the form and processes of individual episodes of communication interaction.

Each of these two meta-theories (rules and systems) was adopted and developed to assist researchers and theorists to know where to look to discover the patterns that make a difference in their understanding of key communication processes. Researchers know that social science cannot advance if it is unable to observe patterns and processes as well as describe relationships among key variables.

Covering Law

The covering law meta-theory was adopted to fill a void in research and theory development. It is less demanding than the scientific laws meta-theory. Rather than expecting research to discover invariant laws, this meta-theory reasons that social science makes acceptable progress when it discovers highly probable, but not absolute connections between events, behaviors, and variables (C. R. Berger, 1977a).

This meta-theory assumes that individuals learn patterns of communication behavior. Then they enact these patterns in a fashion that is probable or predictable. If we stop to think for a moment, we recognize the truth in that observation. As we interact with our friends, for instance, we have a pretty good idea—we know what is probable and predictable—what will happen if we say something to someone in any of several ways. We might refrain from using certain terms that might offend a friend. We realize that people seek information and ask questions in predictable and probable ways. For instance, if a person is romantically interested in someone else, he or she might seek information to see if the target of that interest shares those romantic feelings.

This meta-theory acknowledges that a covering law must be general enough to account for a broad range of individual behaviors that (a) can be captured within one statement, (b) can express the essence of the behavior, and (c) can be tested empirically. A covering law is more abstract and encompassing than a theory; it embraces many individual behaviors under a general statement. Such conclusions need only to address the vital aspects of communication. As C. R. Berger (1977a) contended, many differences that occur during communication exhibit "irrelevant variety." Researchers need to ignore those aspects of communication behavior that are irrelevant.

A covering law allows for predictions by specifying which communication activities go with specific conditions and outcomes. For instance, researchers interested in the dynamics of interpersonal communication might offer an axiom, such as, "Increases in uncertainty level produce decreases in liking; decreases in uncertainty level produce increases in liking" (C. R. Berger & Calabrese, 1975, p. 107). This means that as people have a chance to become acquaintances and friends, they are more likely to achieve that end if they are able to reduce uncertainty about one another. So, researchers can look for probable and predictable patterns (those worth making a bet they will occur) without having to rely on only those patterns they know will certainly occur. As long as people can chose, they will not always act in the exact manner every time, but the covering laws meta-theory assumes that they will more likely act in one way than other ways. This is the essence of the covering law meta-theory.

In summary, your knowledge of these three meta-theories (rules, systems, and covering law) should help you grasp the essence of communication processes, strategies, and styles. These meta-theories complement more often than compete with one another (Cronen & Davis, 1978). Even more important, as is demonstrated in chapter 2, rules and systems meta-theories have helped convince scholars that the linear, "hypodermic needle paradigm" does not adequately explain how communication occurs. The hypodermic needle paradigm (also called the magic bullet approach) assumes that a message is sent by the source (as a lump or bullet) and is received and accepted uncritically by the receiver, as medicine is injected through a hypodermic needle into a patient. This view has become outdated as researchers realize that people interpret messages rather than merely receive and accept them uncritically.

Critical Theory and Cultural Studies

Another option merits consideration before we end our discussion of meta-theoretic assumptions. For at least 2 decades, what has come to be called the critical theory and cultural studies approach to communication has challenged many, if not all, of the assumptions that underpin an empirical approach to communication science. In place of this ostensibly neutral approach, critical scholars advocate the value of normative theory. Advocates of this view reason that communication theory should help people realize their "true nature": "Through critical assessment of the conditions of modern institutional life we may better overcome the multiple forms of alienation that follow as a consequence of humans dominating other humans" (Huspek, 1997, p. 274).

Critical theory and cultural studies approaches propose that knowledge simply is too vast and illusive to be reduced to neat, empirically driven conclusions that are true at some degree of probability. Second, these scholars demand that ethics be central to considerations of all aspects of communication. Ethical choices are central to the communication process. To ignore these choices denies the human spirit, which is the essence of communication. A third challenge made by this research perspective is to improve communication by enhancing rather than denying the human spirit. These scholars argue that reducing the process to barebone empirical conclusions denies the ethical challenges essential to the humanity of the process (Penman, 1992). In this way, the critical theory and cultural studies perspective challenges all research to avoid being reductionist, value free, and indifferent to humanity.

Cultural studies injects ethical judgment into the analysis of the role communication plays in people's lives. Nelson, Treichler, and Grossberg (1992) concluded that, "because cultural studies is concerned with the interrelationships between supposedly separate cultural domains, it necessarily interrogates the mutual determination of popular belief and other discursive formations" (p. 11). This intellectual perspective challenges students of communication to seek not only to understand communication but also to be vigilant in their efforts to achieve insight into how communication is a power resource. The politics of communication come into play as we think about information, language, and persuasion, as well as the contexts: interpersonal communication, organizational communication, and mass-mediated communication.

Competing Assumptions About Human Nature

We end our discussion in chapter 1 by considering assumptions that can lead people to one set of conclusions as opposed to others when they think about communication. If people make one set of assumptions about human nature, they opt for a corresponding set of conclusions about communication. If they preferred different assumptions, they would favor another view of communication. Thus, we must examine our assumptions to be sure that we don't merely discover that communication is what we think it is as opposed to truly discovering what it is.

Some research views people as passive receivers of information who are primarily influenced by outside persons, media, and environmental conditions. Other researchers take the opposite view, that human beings are active participants, dynamically seeking and giving information or persuading and being persuaded. Several questions help illustrate the difference these assumptions make.

Activity Versus Passivity? Do readers or viewers actively seek information from media outlets or do they passively and uncritically accept and believe the information the media provide? Do persons who receive a persuasive message consider its merits and refute some or all of its claims, or do they passively and uncritically accept all of those claims? Your experiences probably help you make up your mind as to whether people are passive or active. You may decide that people are passive or active depending on circumstances, a position taken by many current communication scholars. One study suggests that young children's viewing behavior (time spent watching TV and types of shows viewed), their understanding of the reality of what is presented on TV, and the degree to which they are discriminating viewers depends on their parents. Children view less, understand better, and are more discriminating when they are coached by their parents and when their parents show them more affection (Desmond, Singer, Singer, Calam, & Colimore, 1985).

Persons who are more argumentative generate more counter arguments when they encounter persuasive messages. They are less likely, in comparison to their less argumentative counterparts, to be influenced by persuasive messages (Kazoleas, 1993). Persons who are more cognitively involved with a message (see it related to their self-interests) are more thoughtful about the message, more likely to receive information about it, and more likely to prefer messages that have many supporting points (Petty & Cacioppo, 1981, 1986a).

Mindless Versus Mindful? When people interact, are they mindless, merely voicing scripts that they have learned from other conversations, or do they mindfully (thoughtfully) create each conversational statement anew? Some researchers think that much communication behavior is relatively mindless, requiring little, if any, strategic thought and analysis. Scripted behavior exists as long as it is successful; when it fails, individuals probably have to improvise. In chapter 5, the point is made that, depending on how important a topic is to us, we may be mindful or mindless in our efforts to obtain and think about information and persuasive messages. In chapter 7 we discuss the problems people face when they develop and use plans during their interpersonal communication.

Mindfulness assumes that people think about what they are going to say and do because they are goal directed. If they consider the accuracy and implications of information they obtain, they are being mindful.

Kellermann (1992) reasoned that communication is inherently purposeful, but primarily automatic. What we do is designed to achieve some purpose, but we usually do not think about all of the choices we could make as we enact our communication behavior.

However mindful, communication requires that short-term and long-term memory be applied as we select words, design sentences, and craft conversations (Bavalas & Coates, 1992; Motley, 1992). We recall vocabulary. We retrieve the structural rules we have learned regarding the options our language culture allows for the construction of sentences. We negotiate conversations with others, not only recalling the protocols we have learned but also remembering the relational and conversational history we have with the other person. Related processes can be used to account for what happens when we receive and interpret a message. Interpretation requires recognition of vocabulary, sentence structure, and conversational routines and histories. Researchers apply similar principles to the processes individuals use as they interpret a television program. As is explained in chapter 9, such processes include recalling vocabulary, episode, characters, and program design options as we watch television programs.

Complex Versus Simple? Are people complex or simple? Do they prefer detailed, in-depth discussions? When they encounter what they think to be "too much" information, do they reduce it to manageable amounts? Some researchers believe that people are complex and insightful as they communicate. This view argues that people prefer a lot of information and subject it to careful scrutiny. It assumes that people create complex plans during interpersonal communication; those plans are designed and used to create positive impressions on the interaction partner. This view might also assume that persons view television or read newspapers to obtain lots of information and scrutinize it thoughtfully. The contrasting view approaches the human mind as being relatively uncluttered with detail and disinterested in complex analysis. Sillars (1982), for one, found that people are neither complex nor accurate in their judgments of the reasons why other people behave as they do. In chapter 5, cognitive involvement theory reasons that people are either complex or simple depending on how much they believe a topic relates to their self-interest—how relevant it is to them.

Of related interest is the fact that when receiving and processing news about public policy issues, persons tend to reduce the information they receive to manageable amounts. People obtain, store in memory, recall, think about, and talk about limited amounts of information in proportion to all of the data that could inform their opinions (Graber, 1989).

Complexity can also be viewed from the point of view of the design and interpretation of messages. In martial situations, for instance, wives are significantly more likely than husbands to use openness, networks, and task strategies during their interactions. This means, in part, that relational partners calculate the effort they put into a relationship and compare it against what they think their partners invest in the relationship. Wives use more sharing-task strategies and other relationship-maintenance strategies than do their husbands (Ragsdale, 1996).

Rational Versus Emotional? Are persons rational or emotional? Some theories of communication, especially those related to persuasion, examine the extent to which judgment is guided by careful, rational analysis versus feelings that lead people to overlook arguments and respond emotionally. Some researchers contend that emotions and reasoning are virtually inseparable. The key to understanding their impact requires examination of how emotional and rational processes undergird decision making. As you watch television, do you like to concentrate on some programs because of their content? Do you like to analyze the news or carefully dissect the plays during a football game? Or do you just like to empathize with characters, for instance those in a good novel, without much in-depth analysis?

Single Influence or Multiple Causality? Is a communication event the product of a single influence, multiple causes, or neither? Researchers try to guard against using too few causes or factors to explain communication activities, but they know that an infinite list of multiple causes could be used to explain human communication behavior. Addressing this quandary, C. R. Berger (1977a) emphasized the goal of discounting "irrelevant variety," as he concluded that "it is probably the case that relatively few variables ultimately can account for most of the action. We simply do not know what many of these variables are yet" (p. 15). Evidence suggests that people are not particularly good at sorting through the influence communication has on them. For instance, people confuse sources from which they receive information. They even cannot recall accurately whether their view on some topic was influenced by news or entertainment television. Persons who watch more television are even less able to recall accurately whether something they believe to be true came to them via news or entertainment television (Mares, 1996).

Research by Domain: Subdisciplines

Communication can be studied by examining core concepts (e.g., uncertainty, relationship, information, meaning, or persuasion) and/or by considering how people communicate in different contexts (e.g., interpersonal, organizational, or mediated). Some concepts (e.g., information, persuasion, and meaning) are universal to all research domains. Persuasion can be studied in general or as it occurs in context. Persuasion in face-to-face contact typical of interpersonal communication may introduce different concepts and variables than does a corporate public relations effort. Any of these focal points can be considered subdisciplines; each can be studied by itself or as part of the total communication discipline. Holistic views are more illuminating than particular ones.

Communication behaviors differ, at least to some degree, in each unique context. Context domains include levels of analysis ranging from intraindividual cognitive processes, interpersonal interaction, organizational communication, to mass-mediated communication. Interpersonal communication can be narrowed to the domains of marital communication, doctor–patient communication, platonic/romantic relationships, or relationship dissolution. In narrow domains such as these, research could focus on persuasion or compliance-gaining strategies.

Although each context raises interesting and unique questions, we must never think that any context is completely independent from all others. They interrelate. For years, the academic side of the field departmentalized these contexts so that faculty members would specialize in one to the exclusion of others. Departmentalization led to budget battles that divided the field in ways that were not only deep but also unnatural. As Wiemann, Hawkins, and Pingree (1988) observed, "Perceiving communication as substantially subdivided by channel, level, or audience characteristics is both incorrect and harmful to the development of the discipline" (p. 309). Echoing this theme, Reardon and Rogers (1988) observed that similarity of interests outweighs the differences between the study of interpersonal and mass-mediated communication. People often encounter mass-mediated communication through interpersonal interaction. For instance, we watch television together. We talk about what we heard on the radio or read in the newspaper. We share tapes and CDs as a form of "conversation." Mass media—think of sitcoms—use interpersonal interaction as recurring themes. People talk to one another. They create and dissolve relationships.

What is a domain? Shapere (1974) defined a *domain* as "a body of related information about which there is a problem, well defined usually and raised on the basis of specific considerations" (pp. 521–522). A domain focuses on a related group of problems that are worthy and capable of being solved through analysis and research. A domain may feature a general concept, such as persuasion; a context, for instance mediated communication; or an application, such as advertising. Nonverbal communication and meaning, for example, are domains in their own right but are also relevant to other domains, such as interpersonal, organizational, or mediated communication.

Thinking about research by domain should help you understand the continuity and structure of research so that you are not lost in a tangle of competing theories, hypotheses, and contexts. Intuitively, you should notice how research conclusions might differ if source variables, such as credibility, are studied in general, or in one or a combination of the following contexts: public speaking, interpersonal communication, television news, or public relations. You will also note that, increasingly scholars are viewing communication as being more integrated than segmented. At one point, mass communication scholars and interpersonal communication scholars had little to say to one another. Now, efforts are being made to discover connections between television and the family. Portrayals of families and interpersonal relationships on television may affect the development and dissolution of real-life relationships. Also, power relationships in families determine who watches certain programs, when they watch the programs, and on which specific television set (Bryant, 1990).

The chapters in the remainder of this book present research and theory by concept and context, with some attention to application. Effort has been made to demonstrate how the domains integrate. Each chapter addresses an aspect of communication and features competing interpretations but advocates no single theory of communication.

COMMUNICATION SCIENCE: THE STUDY OF COMMUNICATION

Some researchers study communication for sheer intellectual curiosity. Their efforts are like those of astronomers, for instance, who want to understand the universe but do not intend to travel there. Many communication researchers are goaded by curiosity to understand human communication but have no practical applications in mind as they conduct their studies.

Some researchers not only do applied research, but they also adapt findings of pure researchers to solve real problems in practical settings. For instance, researchers have become increasingly sensitive to the effects that media have on culture. They may be interested in understanding how people use media so that they can help networks decide which programs to run at specific times. Public policy regarding programming in many countries reflects regulators' views of the effects television or newspapers have on society and culture.

Communication researchers are interested in whether news media set the agenda for public policy discussions or merely report the debate as it is conducted by politicians and special interest groups. Some researchers study viewing patterns of persons to determine whether television creates "a reality" whereby persons who view lots of television believe that there is more violence in society than do light viewers. Such studies tell us about communication and how to communicate more effectively. This research can lead to improved media policy and programming decisions—practical outcomes, whether self-imposed or promulgated through regulatory agencies.

Research has helped explain why some people suffer from speech fright or speech reticence. It offers insight into why some people are better than others at interpersonal communication. Some people use interpersonal communication research and theory to help people to create more successful relationships; similar efforts apply organizational communication research to improve businesses and increase employee satisfaction. Results of persuasion studies are applied by advertisers, public relations practitioners, and political consultants. Some persons worry that social science can be applied by corporate communicators to "manipulate" or "brainwash" the public. By the same token research reveals that advertisers are unlikely to do either of these. Each person who studies communication may be more able to guard against the abuse of such research.

During your initial encounter with the many competing theoretical explanations of communication, you may become frustrated. You may find yourself wishing that one explanation could account for the phenomena under consideration. Social science does not operate that way. Scholars advance knowledge by creating arguments, supporting them with data and reasoning, and challenging as well as defending competing explanations of communication processes, strategies, effects, styles, and behavior.

At times research findings tell us what we knew intuitively about communication behaviors or outcomes. So why conduct research and create theories? The answer: to be sure that what we intuit is correct and to understand communication phenomena in a systematic and holistic way.

You can study communication more constructively if you keep in mind five assumptions:

- Each person uses communication to reduce uncertainty. People communicate to learn what they need and want to know to cope with their physical and social reality. They tune into the news to get the weather report. They ask questions and share comments to learn how to be social, to know what to say and when, to learn whether they fit in, and to know the ropes of the business in which they work. Communication helps people adapt to their social and physical realms.

- Through communication people create and manage social knowledge, a view of reality that reflects beliefs unique to each group. By sharing meaning with one another, humans can live together with a degree of organization, coordination, and predictability.
- People communicate to join with others they encounter in ways that increase their sense of self-efficacy—personal competence. They learn strategies of interaction that will help them adapt to one another. Each person is unique to some extent in his or her need to reduce uncertainty and to adjust and adapt to the communication styles used by other people. Some people are extremely competent; others are painfully awkward. But each person is stuck with the problem of needing to be as competent as he or she can be to achieve the desired rewards and avoid the pitfalls of incompetence.
- Because people are symbol users, they communicate to get pleasure from the act of communicating. As you think about why you like to entertain and be entertained through communication, you may realize that entertainment also helps us to reduce uncertainty. Television programs give information about social and physical realities. You can watch people be rewarded and punished for their opinions and efforts. Entertainment viewing or reading reinforces as well as challenges opinions or values. But in addition to this kind of information, you watch, listen, and read simply for pleasure. We also like to talk to friends and relatives.
- Because communication is inherent in the nature of the human being, considerations of ethics must be central to the study of communication. Because empiricism has no ethical soul, it must be rejected or challenged, so as not to overlook or ignore ethical implications inherent in research, theory, and practice.

This chapter should arm you with an understanding of key assumptions and methods necessary to appreciate how communication is studied. Along with this foundation, you should be convinced that you have been studying communication throughout your life. By systematically studying communication, you should become more knowledgeable and a better researcher. And you may become a better communicator.

2

Anatomy of the Communication Process

W hat is communication? How and why does it occur? Which variables help us understand why some people communicate more effectively than others do? Is communication a process or an act? Is it a series of acts that occur as a process? Is communication a function? Can it break down? Can people "uncommunicate"? Is it the use of symbols to transmit ideas and information from one person to another? Is it a means by which we interpret what each other does and says? Are those interpretations the basis for our communication? Is communication interaction that occurs between people a form of sharing or relationship development? Can people form their identities and build interpersonal relationships without communication? Are some interpersonal relationships better than others because of how well the persons involved are able to communicate? If communication can help relationships, is the opposite true? Do relationships help people in those relationships communicate with one another? Does mass-mediated communication (radio, television, or newspapers, for instance) control listeners' and readers' thoughts? Do readers and listeners shape the content of mass-mediated communication by their selections of which shows to watch or listen to or which papers or magazines to buy and read?

This is a long list of questions. It may seem overwhelming. In fact, it reflects only a few of the questions that theorists and researchers attempt to answer. They seek to discover how and why humans communicate. They want to know how and why people plan and execute communication plans. They want to understand how and why communication succeeds—and fails. They work to know how one person or organization affects other people through the process of communication.

To address topics such as these requires that researchers and theorists dissect the anatomy of the communication process much as biologists would dissect an organism to better understand how it functions. The discussion in this chapter should help you appreciate the effort researchers have undertaken to decide which concepts are vital to the process of communication.

This chapter portrays dramatic shifts that have occurred in regard to how communication is conceptualized and researched. This chapter begins by examining several definitions of communication and challenges you to propose your own definition. You should appreciate how researchers' definitions of communication affect they way they analyze key concepts. As you become more aware of these concepts, you should better understand why researchers and theorists work so hard to achieve reliable and valid definitions of these key terms. Along the way in this chapter, your attention will be directed by key shifts in perspectives that affect how researchers and theorists view and study communication. As you encounter these shifts, we ask that you appreciate why competing and conflicting viewpoints affect how people think about communication.

To examine the anatomy of the communication process, this chapter reviews several definitions, thinks of communication as a process, examines early models of the process, and discusses components of the process. We devote the last section in this chapter to a summary of key themes that drive the study of communication in all of its contexts. This discussion is designed to challenge you to refine your definition of communication and to decide which concepts best explain the communication process.

COMMUNICATION—A HARD TERM TO DEFINE

What is communication? Hundreds of definitions have been proposed over the past 50 years, but none is entirely satisfactory. A good definition accurately and completely features the key concepts and it points to the relationship between them. For this reason, one definition can be better than another because it more accurately and completely captures the essence of the phenomenon being considered. Think about that as you dissect the definitions that follow.

The following examples show the variety of definitions that have been offered. Before studying these examples, jot down your definition of communication and compare it against them. What concepts does your definition feature? Can your definition explain what happens in the four dominant contexts: interpersonal, group, organizational, mass-mediated communication?

Featuring what is called a transmission paradigm, Devito (1986) said that communication is "the process or act of transmitting a message from a sender to a receiver, through a channel and with the interference of noise; the actual message or messages sent and received; the study of the processes involved in the sending and receiving of messages" (p. 61). This view of communication has been very popular but offers a limited view. For a moment, consider what is implied by a transmission approach to communication. It assumes that a source or sender creates a message that contains information and transmits that message to the receiver. This view postulates that communication works properly when the message received is the same as the message sent. This linear transmission view of communication assumes that the source "injects" information and other influence into the receiver's mind. Viewed this way, a message is a "lump" of meaning—like a bullet—that transports and inserts an idea into the receiver's brain.

Think again about this definition before we proceed. Note that Devito said that communication is *either* a process *or* an act. Is it both? Is it sometimes an act and a process at other times? Later in this chapter, you encounter reasons to think of communication as process.

Viewing communication as interaction, Gerbner (1967) defined it as "interaction through messages. Messages are formally coded symbolic or representational events of some shared significance in a culture, produced for the purpose of evoking significance" (p. 430). This view of communication differs radically from the transmission of ideas or information. To indicate how communication occurs, Gerbner used the term *evoke*. He, as most others, thought that a message stimulates or evokes a meaning. This view of communication rests on a stimulus–response paradigm. What one person says (stimulus) has meaning based on the interpretations (response) others make of those statements.

Note that Gerbner said that messages are "formally" coded. Does his definition exclude informal, unintentional behavior, such as nonverbal cues such as head nodding in agreement or glaring at someone? Does one person communicate with another even if he or she does not intend to do so? Later in this book, we discuss speech accommodation theory. It reasons that nonverbal response matching behavior occurs; if one person likes the other, he or she is prone to act similar to the other person. Do you think that such nonverbal behavior is communication?

If interaction is the essence of communication, to what end does interaction lead? Featuring convergence theory to answer that question, E. M. Rogers and Kincaid (1981) argued that through communication "participants create and share information with one another in order to reach a mutual understanding" (p. 63). The incentive behind communication is to achieve mutual understanding through conversation. As one corporate communication firm's letterhead optimistically proclaims, "Communication is the beginning of understanding."

Also featuring interaction, Cronen, Pearce, and Harris (1982) viewed communication as "a process through which persons create, maintain, and alter social order, relationships, and identities" (pp. 85–86). They challenged communication researchers to concentrate on how humans "achieve coordination by managing the ways messages take on meaning" (p. 68). W. B. Pearce and Cronen (1980) contended that through communication "persons collectively create and manage social reality" (p. 7). As did E. M. Rogers and Kincaid (1981), W. B. Pearce and Cronen reasoned that people interact because they must coordinate—come to share—meaning sufficiently well to live together with a degree of predictable social order.

An interaction view of communication emphasizes the dynamic efforts persons make while communicating with one another. This paradigm does not feature sources sending or receivers being injected with information. Rather it assumes that people need to achieve social coordination and communicate toward that end. If we are to adopt this view of communication, what sense do we make of the concept of social coordination? What does that term mean to you?

This analysis demonstrates how interaction occurs through patterns and for ends that are crucial to the study of interpersonal communication. Making that point, McLaughlin (1984) reasoned that conversations do not grow randomly; they follow specific, knowable turn-taking patterns that follow rules. (Recall the discussion of rules meta-theory in chap. 1.) How people evaluate each situation in which they interact influences how they communicate. People use rules to achieve their goals in light of their definition of the situation (Cody & McLaughlin, 1985). For instance, one person may want a favor. They promise a favor to have their favor granted: "I will work overtime for you if you will work overtime for me." According to this view, people do not randomly change communication topics; conversations have flow and follow linkages. People take turns sharing the conversational floor with others. Thus, is it safe to define communication as an interaction "game" that is played to achieve outcomes by applying sets of rules that we learn?

Additional reasons can be found to support an interaction view by building a definition of communication on systems meta-theory. In this way, communication can be said to occur when information output from one system becomes input for another (Ashby, 1963). A systems meta-theory features processes of input, processing, and output. For instance, you receive information from a book or television (or from a conversation) as input. You think about the information (process it) and tell someone else (output). You might find out that your favorite music group is putting together a new CD. You think about that and hint that it would be a nice present. Is that the communication process, at least from a systems perspective? Note that your output (hint) can be input to your parents or friend (who thinks, "I will buy that for a present.") The present is the output. Is it also communication? What does the present communicate? Is it information? Does it help build a relationship? Is it the coordination of relationships and the management of meaning?

You might notice that most of these definitions feature the processes of influence—social influence. In a similar way, Hewes and Planalp (1987) argued that communication occurs when one person's behavior affects another. Twenty years earlier, Dance (1967) defined communication "as the eliciting of a response" (p. 289). These definitions make communication synonymous with all stimuli—anything that produces a response or has impact. Do those definitions make communication too basic? Can they account for that range of activities that goes from two people talking, to the sharing of information and influence in a business, to the mass dissemination of information and influence through the media?

So far, we have thought about definitions that have featured linear transmission, interpretation (stimulus–response), and co-created meaning through ongoing discourse and interaction. That seems like a lot to consider.

At this point in the chapter, you are probably wanting to shout, "Stop. No more definitions. Can't somebody come up with one definition that satisfies everyone else?" If you look closely, you can find even more definitions of communication, as did Dance (1970), who found 15 different types. Each stressed a different focal point: symbols and verbal speech; understanding; interaction; uncertainty reduction; process; transmission; linking and binding; common experience; channel; memory; modification; stimuli; purpose/intent; time/situation; and power. After this review, he observed, "We are trying to make the concept of 'communication' do too much work for us. The concept, in its present state, is overburdened and thus exhibits strain within itself and within the field which uses it. What may help is the creation of a family of concepts" (p. 210).

Rather than deciding on one definition, you are wise to look for key concepts and assumptions that make up the anatomy of the communication process. You should learn the role each plays in the communication process. As you become skilled in your study of communication, you should be able to spot the unique assumptions each author is making as he or she proposes a definition. Such insight is the same as that used by a good detective who can solve a "whodunit" by using clues to ferret out the culprit. You can understand the crucial differences reflected in each definition and appreciate the assumptions it bears.

Through your analysis you may conclude that communication is a process or set of actions by which people share symbols as they create meaning through interaction. Do you conclude that that is a good definition? Does it explain what happens in all contexts: interpersonal, group, organizational, and mass-mediated communication? To better answer that question, let's consider the implications of thinking about communication as a process that is universal to such contexts (Reardon & Rogers, 1988; Wiemann et al., 1988).

COMMUNICATION AS PROCESS

Imagine yourself going into a town or country that is unfamiliar to you. You do not know the names of its streets, roads, and places. You do not know where the important places are or where you should be safe, get food, or receive shelter. You do not have a map to help you find your way. This feeling is similar to that experienced by communication theorists of the 1950s and 1960s. They knew that communication played a major role in thought, relationships, and society. They had an idea of where they wanted their research to lead them, but they did not know which concepts were important. They were unsure which questions were worth answering.

Many questions motivated and guided their inquiry:

- What impact do media have on society?
- How do people understand and influence one another?
- How do they know when other people understand them?
- Can communication occur even though there is misunderstanding?
- Do relationships hinge on the extent to which people understand one another, influence each other, or bring about liking or disliking?
- Is communication intentional, fairly random, or virtually mindless, scripted behavior?
- What motivates people to communicate?
- Is one of the major motives the desire to reduce uncertainty?
- Do other motives include seeking to be socially competent or achieving shared meaning?
- How do people use communication to manage relationships?

Questions such as these have been central to communication research and theorizing.

Questions such as these centered on another key question. Is communication an act or a process? That debate raged for more than a decade. Some people wanted to focus their attention on each act of communication, such as a conversation, a public speech, or a television program. Others said that each act or episode is part of a much larger process. Process suggests that lots has occurred prior to the act. Some residue of the act will continue into the future.

Treating it as process, Berlo (1960) featured communication

> events and relationships as dynamic, on-going, ever-changing, continuous. When we label something as a process, we also mean that it does not have a beginning, an end, or even a fixed sequence of events. It is not static, at rest. It is moving. The ingredients within a process interact; each affects all of the others. (p. 24)

Process does not mean that communication is aimless. In Berlo's view, "we communicate to influence—to affect with intent" (p. 12). As process, communication transpires over time and is relatively strategic. Each act or episode has a history, a present, and a future.

Nearly two decades after alerting communication scholars to feature process, Berlo (1977) observed that four versions had developed:

- Process as mystery: Communication has no starting points, no boundaries, only patterns of development and interaction.
- Process as complex organization: Individual behavior is not the unit of study; relationships are. They change over time.

- Process as effect: This view measures change over time in increments such as attitude shifts or relationship improvement and decline.
- Process as activity and change: People develop, change, and use information to guide behavior and create a shared social reality. The process of communication is central to ongoing changes in social agreement. Information is the fundamental unit of analysis in understanding the presence of communication in society.

The study of communication as process has substantial justification. One is the assumption of process that permeates the physical sciences. Think of the changing of the seasons as process. Biologists see it this way. Imagine the deterioration of metals (rust, for instance) or changing chemical properties of water as salt is added to it. This is process.

Another school of thought supported the commitment to process. Advocates of general semantics reasoned that the meanings of words are not static, but constantly changing. General semanticists, such as Korzybski (1948), Johnson (1946), and I. J. Lee (1952), stressed how meanings of words are not static because the world is in flux. They founded their discussion on the word–thing–thought relationship, which assumes that meaning consists of what words mean in relationship to the things they represent. One method they employed to remind people of the process nature of meaning was to "date" key terms. For instance, instead of merely using the word war, they might say war 1863, war 1917, war 1941, war 1952, or war 1967. (Or they would ask that people realize that the war changes each day because on one day one side is winning, whereas on another day that same side is losing.) Each of these is a different war having its own set of enemies, problems, materials, logistical tactics, and heroes. Or they might remind us to avoid thinking of our high school chums as though they do not age or change. Words must be used in ways that are sensitive to the passing of time.

One quick way that you can think about the evolutionary and changing process of meaning is to compare your language today with the terms that were typical of the era in which William Shakespeare wrote his plays and sonnets. Today, those terms sound peculiar, even foreign. They may be a language "foreign" to us. Would Shakespeare be insulting or complimentary if he called you a "twanging Jack"? Those terms were quite familiar to persons who would have read his sonnets and attended his plays. He was a very popular playwright. His language was understood and appreciated by audiences of his time. But, through process, words change in meaning, new words are invented, and words die.

Let's summarize the characteristics of process. A process is something that has no apparent beginning or end. It is irreversible. It is unbounded. It always goes forward. For instance, even when you and a friend try to resolve a difference that occurred a week ago, those efforts will carry forward to subsequent communication. Most of us recall instances, whether in friendly conversation, at work, or on television, that linger in our memory. These parts of our memory are recalled and used later. How you communicated with someone before can help or hinder how you deal with that person again.

Conversations do not start anew; they have a history. A maxim should help you understand this point: People cannot not communicate nor can they uncommunicate. Efforts to not say something communicate any number of messages: dislike, shyness, rejection, unwillingness to communicate, inability to communicate, and so forth. Telling someone you are sorry for what you said does not erase the statement; it merely adds to it. Recall how a heated argument with someone colors subsequent conversation with that person.

Some writers say that a process model commits researchers to view communication merely as a product of causality that eliminates the possibility of choice. "Process" is often viewed as being mechanistic, whereas "act" is thought to be the product of choice. If you fall and roll down a hill, that is process. If you get up, dust yourself off, and climb back up the hill, that is an act.

Let's summarize the issue of process this way. Some actions that occur during communication are intentional, the result of willed behavior, and others are unintentional. The key to understanding communication is not found in trying to determine what is intentional or willed, but in acknowledging that the process continues without end. Each conversation builds on previous ones. Ads people view or read today are filtered through ads previously encountered. Movies or television programs are viewed in the context of previous entertainment fare.

As process, communication has no beginning or end. The process of communication was occurring when you arrived in the world, and it will continue after you are gone. Communication efforts leave a residue of interaction patterns, experiences, ideas, meanings, and feelings that become part of subsequent encounters. How you communicate is a product of your communication in the past as well as the past communication of the persons with whom you interact.

To call something a process means that individual events or episodes occur over time in ways that are reasonably, but not totally, predictable. Carried far enough, process can be viewed as motion instead of action. According to this view, events change, but they do so because of causality rather than random chance or willed choice. Some communication is random or unplanned. You know this because sometimes you say something you did not mean to say, or a comment by a friend provokes a nonverbal reaction that you never intended to make. Communication can be viewed as a process of ongoing events, separate acts such as conversations, or the viewing of individual television episodes, all of which prompt subsequent acts.

The degree to which communication is mindful and willed or automatic and unplanned is a major issue concerning communication in all contexts: interpersonal, organizational, and mass-mediated. Bargh (1988) saw free will as a challenge to researchers who seek to comprehend how people process information and manage perception, affection, and attribution. Some communication is automatic, but some is purposeful, strategic, and willful. Even with a moment's reflection, we realize that we can choose to interact in a particular way at a particular time. We can be pleasant or unpleasant, agreeable or disagreeable. We can decide to ask questions of our boss or co-worker. Or we can elect not to ask those questions. We can choose to watch TV, read a book, or listen to the radio. Or we can decide not to. All of this suggests that we make choices in the process of communication.

Researchers struggle with the dilemma of viewing communication as process while using research methods and theories that do not meet the requirements of process. For instance, D. H. Smith (1972) noted the irony of Berlo's (1960) call to treat communication as process even though he reduced it to a linear Sender-Message-Channel-Receiver (SMCR) model. That model violates assumptions required for a process view of communication, because it views communication primarily from the perspective of the sender, and only sees the receiver as a target of messages.

If communication is to be viewed as process, then appropriate theories and research methods must be formulated. Cappella (1977) argued that to understand communication as process, researchers must treat it as ever changing, unbounded, unsequenced, totally interdependent, and consisting of interaction sequences. It is time dependent because no two communication events are the same. Each event is different, and each moment in each event is different. Thinking about your reactions when watching an entertaining or informational television program can help illustrate time dependency. Each scene builds, as do bricks in a wall, on one another to produce an entire episode. Each episode is a part of a series, a season's run. Some episodes are more entertaining than others. Some parts of each episode are more entertaining. In this way televiewing is time dependent, and it is a process that is a complex series of acts.

One telling question central to this line of inquiry is whether media have a dominant effect on people because they transmit ideas that those people receive and accept uncritically. Taking an interaction approach to message impact, Grimes and Meadowcraft (1995) concluded the following:

> What a viewer learns, as far as television messages are concerned, derives from the interaction between the message and the human information-processing system. Communication researchers long ago put to rest the notion of the magic bullet theory of message reception, in which a reality that exists apart from us directly enters our minds. We now understand that complex media messages are rarely entered and stored unaltered in long-term memory. (p. 154)

Such conclusions challenge researchers and other persons interested in media impact to realize that receivers are not passive vessels into which media pour messages that are received uncritically.

Some researchers chide their colleagues to be sure that their research assumptions and procedures match their commitment to view communication as process. For instance, Meyer, Trandt, and Anderson (1980) noted that mass communication studies often fail to adopt a process approach. Many mass communication studies, they argued, are static, looking at discrete variables such as those at play in a single episode or program. They noted how measures used to study television effects "focus on either one minute act or several measured in a single point in time, rather than identifying the interplay of many elements and their changing levels that compose media usage" (p. 264). To begin to correct this mistake, studies of mass-mediated communication need to acknowledge that listeners, viewers, and readers receive information and entertainment from many sources. Each of these sources is one of many factors that affect how a particular reading, viewing, or listening experience is likely to be accomplished and whether its impact is minimal or substantial. For instance, as you see a new episode of your favorite program, you compare it against previous episodes and even imagine how this one will turn out given the plots that are routinely developed in each episode and throughout the series.

Losing sight of the process nature of communication often results from the set of assumptions that researchers and scholars bring to their efforts. Those assumptions are often the unchallenged baggage of popular research activities. Stressing that point, Reeves, Chaffee, and Tims (1982) claimed that mass communication research has been unduly influenced by Lasswell's (1948) famous linear model. That model asks us to focus our attention on who says what to whom through which channel with what effect. Because Lasswell's model is sender oriented, it leads researchers to stress the role of the source as we consider the control, content, channel, audience, and effects that result from media watching, listening, or reading. Slowly, the influence of Lasswell is giving way to an interest in the receiver. Encouraging this shift, Reeves et al. (1982) advised researchers to concentrate on the "pictures" in people's heads that are created and influenced by what they seek and receive from mass media

Stressing the influence that people seek from their experiences from the media, Reeves et al. advocated using a social cognition approach. This view of the mass-media process assumes that each receiver "is mentally active, organizing and processing stimuli from the environment rather than simply responding directly to them" (p. 289). A social cognition orientation to human communication argues that people construct views of reality. These views of reality are created by the information and opinions they obtain from media and their social contacts. The impact of this contact results in opinions that become a residue of multiple influences. By taking a social cognition view, researchers are more likely to be able to understand how people think about one another and about the programs they watch on television, for instance. As active participants in the communication process, people are capable of recalling and adding information and thoughts to that which they receive from the media. What they do and how they respond is likely to be influenced by their goals for watching each program.

In this section we have demonstrated that communication should be studied as process. The process is a series of acts that people perform; they engage in communication to listen, to ignore, and to interact in one way as opposed to another. In the remainder of this chapter, we examine components of the process and explain how researchers have changed their views on these components. Those changes continue to challenge us to refine our definition and thinking about communication. To begin this investigation, we review this history of communication theory.

ORIGINS OF COMMUNICATION THEORY

Communication theory and research have a long and rich heritage. For more than 2,000 years, many people have contributed to the body of literature that defines the discipline of communication. Most of what is thought of as communication theory has strong social science foundations, but along the way much has been contributed by the humanities. Recently, the cultural school of thought has denounced the value of empirically testing hypotheses and theories. This group of scholars has argued that all too easily the ethical problems associated with communication choices become lost or denied with a narrow, theory-driven investigation of concepts, variables, and processes.

What is called communication science resulted from the merger of at least four lines of inquiry in this century: (a) the rhetorical tradition, (b) propaganda and media effects, (c) transmission and reception of information, as well as (d) group dynamics and interpersonal relationship development. Academic disciplines such as social psychology, sociology, and anthropology have also contributed valuable insights into the process of communication. A glance at key lines of thought can help you appreciate the effort that has been spent to advance the study of communication.

The Rhetoric Tradition

The study of human influence through communication is probably timeless. Interest in influence is likely to extend back to the distant origins of human beings as we know them today. Humans have always been fascinated with the communication processes that lead one person to be effective in communicating with his or her fellow beings.

At least 2,000 years ago, public speaking became a vital part of the formal study and training of the ancient Greeks. After the overthrow of the tyrants in Syracuse, citizens were required to speak in public to exert self-government and to reclaim their lands that had been confiscated. Thus, people with keen insights into the process of effective public speaking began to teach that art. From those humble origins, the tradition of rhetorical theory has been uninterrupted since at least 500 BC. Most of rhetorical theory has focused on the strategies and conditions that make one speaker effective, whereas others might have less impact on their audiences.

Theory in the early part of the 20th century was based on a speaker-speaking-to-audience paradigm that had its roots in ancient Greece. One of the seminal studies influencing this tradition is Aristotle's *Rhetoric,* which was written in the 4th century BC. He studied the tactics speakers used to affect the thoughts, ideas, and behavior of an audience—other members of society. He wanted to know the principles of effective public speaking that distinguished the effective from ineffective speaker.

Aristotle's inquiry reasoned that speakers have more impact if they possess sound moral character. He observed that they are more persuasive if they create sound arguments that are framed in clear, appropriate, and vivid language. His study of audiences led him to note that what appealed to one group of people might be ineffective with others. He was interested in the logical aspects of messages (evidence and reasoning) as well as appeals to emotions. He realized that ethical speakers were likely to have more impact than unethical ones. Aristotle discussed the impact they gain through their vocal and physical delivery.

Following the seminal work by Aristotle, hundreds of refinements have amplified and corrected his original ideas. Burke (1969b), for instance, added to our understanding of rhetoric by noting that people use language to identify with one another. They identify with one another as they come to share perspectives. For instance, environmentalists identify with one another based on their concern for the survival of species and their commitment to improve air and water quality.

Today, the heritage of Aristotle is not only found in studies of persuasion, but also in interpersonal conversation. This heritage provides the rationale for unlocking the dynamics of strategic plans people use during interpersonal communication. By being interested in such plans, scholars are working to disclose the ways people develop and utilize message design logics (B. J. O'Keefe, 1988; B. J. O'Keefe & McCornack, 1987) as they plan what to say during conversations (Hewes & Planalp, 1987). In these ways, the works of the ancients, especially Aristotle, taught researchers and scholars to focus on the factors that explain the processes of social influence and persuasive impact. The assumption was that messages could be designed to more effectively inform, persuade, and entertain if people understood the factors of those processes.

Propaganda and Media Effects

Another major impetus in the development of communication theory was the concern that mass communication was having enormous influence on people's opinions and lives. Mass communication studies prior to the mid-1950s were conducted primarily in departments of psychology, political science, and sociology, or in interdisciplinary institutes. Social psychology studies were heavily oriented to understanding mass persuasion, which was also called propaganda. Prevailing interests in rhetoric and persuasion as well as fondness for stimulus–response psychology offered some of the theoretical underpinning scholars needed as they set out to study mass communication impact.

Early theoretical developments began when Lasswell (1948) asked who says what to whom through what channel with what purpose and effect? This transmission–effects paradigm was compatible with the rhetoric/persuasion tradition and seemed ideal for comprehending the dynamics of mass communication, particularly under the umbrella of propaganda. This view of communication assumed that a savvy and strategic (even devious) sender could design a message that listeners, readers, and viewers could not resist. The assumption was that sources put ideas and motivations into the minds of passive and relatively unthinking, uncritical audiences. The assumption—and dominant fear—was that clever sources could use the media to control the thoughts and actions of the members of society.

That paradigm has been important because many communication researchers are steeped in a search to understand how communication strategies produce effects. Lasswell's interest in propaganda techniques produced *Propaganda Technique in the World War,* published in 1927. This book is often used to mark the beginning of mass communication research. It took the orientation that scholars must know how mass communication affects thought and culture to protect society against unwanted effects.

Concern for the role of propaganda in society grew enormously after thinking people around the world realized the power that a despot such as Hitler could have through the control of mass media and the manipulation of mass audiences. The cold war ideological battle between the Soviet bloc countries and the western bloc countries added fuel to the desire to understand—and control—the processes of mass persuasion. Motivation for this line of study was the apprehension that persons who had primary access to a few dominant and exciting media could shape and control thoughts of millions of people. Critics worried that the media could intrude into the lives of relatively independent people. By watching and reading the same material, these people could be led to have similar rather than unique and heterogeneous ideas. They could be controlled and manipulated. Democracy assumes difference of opinion. Propaganda presumes the control of thought and the elimination of divergent opinion. Thus began the concept of a mass society created by mass media.

Out of this apprehension, decades of sound research have debated the role media play in society, especially their impact. This analysis centers on four dominant concepts: selection, creation, dissemination, and reception. Research has centered on the role played by individuals and organizations who select the information and other content that go into mass-communicated messages. For instance, we might want to know why reporters, editors, and news directors choose to cover or not cover certain stories. Issues of creation address features of messages such as the topics that are discussed, themes that are explored, and styles in which ideas are presented. Processes of dissemination include programming decisions such as the level of adult material that is shown in different primetime slots. Researchers, interested in reception, examine why people choose to watch some television programs and not others. Reception can include the media people select to obtain entertainment. Some people read novels. Others watch television. Some prefer the movies. Purist film buffs would not think of watching a movie on a television. For other viewers, the ability to command the VCR and cable delivery systems fits their viewing style (Greenberg & Salwen, 1996).

Information Theory: Transmission and Reception

Independent of these lines of analysis—rhetoric and mass-mediated influence—arose a series of studies that focused on the principles of information transmission and reception. These studies were conducted in the middle decades of this century, primarily at industrial research facilities such as Bell Labs. Researchers wanted to understand how information in the form of messages could be electronically transmitted and received with the greatest efficiency and fidelity. This thinking featured a linear model, a sender seeking to get a message to a receiver. It often was more concerned with the quality of communication technology than with the nature of the people who were using those technologies.

This line of analysis helped to lay a foundation for systems meta-theory. It featured the role of channels in the communication process. It stressed efficiency in creating, transmitting, and receiving messages. It forced people to realize even more how strategic communication message design could be. Featuring outcomes and processes needed to achieve those outcomes, this line of research gave us cybernetics and laid a portion of the foundation for our adventures into cyberspace, what is being called the information age.

Group Dynamics and Interpersonal Relations

In the 1930s, the work of Mead, especially *Mind, Self, and Society* (1934), was extremely influential. His primary contribution to the study of communication was the proposition that people can know one another and themselves only through communication. The essence of communication, he thought, was symbolic interaction. Individuals communicate by doing something that could be interpreted by and reacted to by others. What each of us does may be responded to by others—the essence of interaction. What we think about them and their response to us defines our identity. We become the product of how others communicate with us.

A major breakthrough in the study of interpersonal communication occurred in 1958 when Heider published *The Psychology of Interpersonal Relations*. He made the point that people can know one another only by experiencing each other's behavior. As we see people behaving in one way as opposed to another, we attribute motives to explain these choices. We believe that we come to know others by the choices they make. For instance, if you visit a person's apartment, do you try to figure out who they are by the kind of books they read and the sort of CDs they like?

Leadership was a topic of primary interest to scholars and political figures who wanted to understand what makes some people leaders. Lewin's (1951) studies of leadership and the influence people exert on one another in small group situations offered an interactional paradigm from which to study communication. Groups are a vital part of our lives, as is the role of leadership. For these reasons, scholars were encouraged to unlock the factors that predict which people will be leaders.

Additional efforts were made to discover the dynamics of groups. As society became more complex people found themselves involved in more small group activities. This topic became vital to understanding how to improve the quality of communication in large, complex organizations, such as businesses and governmental agencies.

This brief review demonstrated that four lines of influence merged in subtle ways to weave a fabric that came to be called communication studies. This fabric consisted of an interest in rhetoric, propaganda and media impact, information technologies and processes, interaction, personal identity, leadership, and group dynamics.

Without full appreciation for the dramatic changes they would bring, this diverse array of scholars initiated lines of inquiry that formed and then altered the study of communication. Slowly, the term *communication* came to be used to label the content of the study, often replacing terms such as *psychology* or *mass persuasion*. Mass communication studies supplanted mass persuasion or mass psychology studies. Communication slowly evolved into a term with its own intellectual territory and research domains, fostered by departments, schools, and colleges of communication that have burgeoned since 1960.

Particularly since 1960, scholars adopted *communication* as the central term because they want to study it as a significant and unique aspect of human behavior, not as a manifestation of the psychological, sociological, or political sides of human experience. Communication became the central term modified by many adjectives to characterize domains of study, such as interpersonal communication, organizational communication, speech communication, mass communication, and telecommunication. Each of these domains has its own scope and importance. This body of analysis grows and prospers.

REEMERGENCE OF COMMUNICATION SCIENCE

During the 1940s and 1950s, scholars from many fields examined those aspects of communication that were particularly relevant to their disciplines. For instance, political scientists were fascinated with political communication. They wanted to understand the forces, largely mass mediated, they thought, that influence voters' decisions. Scholars worried that new media such as film or television might corrupt the morals of society and blunt the democratic process. People could become controlled by a dominant elite that lulled people into complacency. Public opinion could be manipulated by what were feared to be powerful media forces.

A robust period of communication research generated many interesting research findings that were reported at various academic societies. At one such convention, a distinguished panel of speakers considered the future of communication studies. One of the featured speakers, Berelson (1959), proclaimed that communication research lacked promise. He claimed that all of the major research topics had been explored satisfactorily to their conclusions. No new research was on the horizon. The field had reached its end.

Few academic predictions could have been more inaccurate. One year after this dire prediction by one of its leading figures, an explosion of studies began that would prove him wrong. Two outstanding contributions were made by Klapper (1960), who argued that media had limited effects, and Berlo (1960) who popularized his S–M–C–R model as the definitive essence of communication, that linked the classical studies of rhetoric with the contemporary interest in the person who achieves identity through communication.

Limited Media Effects

In 1960, Klapper challenged the prevailing fear that the media dominate the thoughts and actions of people. In a book entitled, *The Effects of Mass Communication,* Klapper argued that television plays an important role in the lives of people but does not dominate them. He questioned the prevailing belief that television audiences are passive and reasoned that TV is one of many influences that account for public opinions and mass behavior. He advised a shift from the hypodermic (linear-transmission) model that assumes that media "inject" influence directly into a passive audience. He demonstrated that people resist media influence by relying on community norms, beliefs, and values. When mass communication does change widely held values and norms, one of two conditions is likely to exist: (a) Factors, such as group norms and values, that counter media effects are inoperative, or (b) these factors actually encourage large numbers of people to change their opinions for views that are better.

Klapper's work gave new direction to communication studies by denying the singularity of media influence, by establishing it as one of many mediating influences on opinion, and by showing how audiences are influenced by selective perception, recall, and attention. He was aware that interpersonal influences contribute to and mediate media influence; people talk about issues and programs. This talk shapes their reactions to program content and sets norms that may be as or more influential than the media on judgment and behavior. This research was among the first to challenge the linear model of communication. It demonstrated how the influence of communication is more likely to result from many causes rather than one.

A Model for the Process

In the evolution of communication studies, few books had more impact than did Berlo's (1960) *Communication: An Introduction to Theory and Practice.* By the time his book arrived on the scene, the ideas he expressed were not new, as will be noted in the next section. Many people had voiced and written the lines of argument he featured in this book, but he popularized the notion that communication is a process and offered an enduring model (S–M–C–R) that contained the now standard concepts: (a) the communication source (the encoder), (b) the message, (c) the channel, and (d) the receiver (the decoder).

Reflecting major themes that defined the study of communication in the first 60 years of this century, Berlo acknowledged the influence of Aristotle and the general semanticists, as well as Shannon and Weaver. Aristotle's approach to communication stressed how the speech process originates with a speaker who seeks to use a message to influence an audience. This sequence of events transpires in a context, such as a court or public legislative assembly.

Another influence on Berlo was George Herbert Mead (1934), who helped him recognize the impact communication has on the development of individual personality—the self. Borrowing from Mead, Berlo (1960) concluded that *"the concept of self does not precede communication. It is developed through communication"* (p. 125). Mead's primary contribution to communication is the claim that minds, self-concepts, and societies mature and take shape only through the dynamics of symbolic interaction.

In Berlo's discussion, the term *process* had enormous implications for how communication is viewed. It flew in the face of traditional studies, which treated each speech as an act separable from what came before it and what followed it. Persons who approached communication as "act" tended to think that an audience listens to a speech, or any other communication message, as a whole unit of thought. What actually happens is that each person hears a speech as a sequence of words and thoughts on a "lump" of meaning taken in at once. In addition, what the person hears is filtered through opinions and beliefs that were created by his or her own personal, previous communication. What is learned and assimilated from one speech becomes part of the memories that affect how subsequent messages are interpreted.

Berlo (1960) used classical learning theory as the rationale for how and why people communicate. The S in source, he believed, is equivalent to the S in stimulus. The R's in receiver and response are roughly parallel. Thus he concluded that *"a stimulus is anything that a person can receive through one of his senses,"* and *"a response is anything that the individual does as a result of perceiving the stimulus"* (pp. 74–75). A key to his approach is the observation, *"The source wants the receiver to change, to learn"* (p. 77). This fondness for learning theory made the S–R paradigm an underpinning for explaining the process of communication.

Learning theory is one of the long-term underpinnings of communication theory. In its most primitive sense, as discovered by Pavlov, people create associations when two things occur simultaneously. Pavlov, you may remember, conditioned some dogs to salivate when they heard a bell ring. He did this by ringing a bell as he gave them meat. After a while, the bell alone could cause the dogs to salivate. The stimulus, bell, produced the response, salivation. As you see in this chapter and in chapter 3, many theories of meaning depend on learning theory.

For some researchers, process means that multiple causal relationships exist between events. Others think of process in terms of an ongoing, uninterrupted flow of events that interact but are not reducible to cause–effect relationships. Communication behavior is viewed by the former group as causal patterns—akin to movement. The latter group views behavior as strategic, willful choices regarding how to act during communication. This action–motion duality forces researchers to consider whether people act willfully or move as a product of causes. Researchers consider how intentional communication behavior is. Do people communicate thoughtfully and intentionally or do they respond to one another without much insight, thought, or strategy?

That theme is explored throughout this book. It addresses the balance between mindful communication, as calculated action, and the flow of communication behavior that lacks thought and premeditation. To better understand this line of reasoning, we can recall the efforts of some of the giant thinkers of the field who worked to feature key concepts and processes so they could be captured and expressed in pictorial models.

EFFORTS TO CREATE A COMMUNICATION MODEL

During the middle decades of this century, leading thinkers began to use pictorial or schematic models to feature the key concepts in communication. Recall that in chapter 1 we discussed three kinds of models: taxonomies, pictorial (schematic), and mathematical. Taxonomies are not very good models because they merely list key variables and do not describe how they interact during communication. In contrast, pictorial models use lines, boxes, arrows, circles, and such to demonstrate which variables precede others and lead to one another.

Many studies in the first half of the 20th century operated on a linear model, which assumed that sources produce messages that influence passive receivers. This paradigm was reinforced by a desire to understand how people get a message across to one another clearly and efficiently. Work by Shannon and Weaver (1949) at Bell Labs culminated in an influential explanation of those concepts that can be controlled and manipulated to increase the clarity and efficiency in the way people communicate. Their model was noticeably mechanistic, in part, because Shannon wanted to help engineers understand electronic transmission and reception. Despite its limitations, their model prompted other researchers to describe the communication process by using a complex of boxes, circles, and lines.

As limited as their approach was, Shannon and Weaver contributed a systematic approach to the study of communication. As Ritchie (1986) observed, Shannon was more interested in explaining how to achieve accurate and efficient signal transmission, particularly to improve telephone communication, than he was in proposing a theory of communication. Weaver extended these ideas and intentions to form a rudimentary theory of communication. Shannon wanted to discuss information as it pertained to signal transmission; in this regard, he wanted to be able to deal with information as though it were a fixed entity contained in a message or a series of messages. Weaver, however, wanted to apply this theory more broadly to issues being addressed by social scientists. Together, they showed how uncertainty reduction motivates people's communication behavior.

Shannon and Weaver (1949) broadly defined *communication* as "all of the procedures by which one mind may affect another" (p. 3). Weaver showed how their theory could address three broad concerns: (a) the technical problem of achieving efficient transmission and reception; (b) the semantic problem of increasing the precision with which one person conveys a message to another by selecting the appropriate words; and (c) the effectiveness problem of understanding whether the meaning of the message affected the receiver's conduct in the manner the sender intended.

Their classic model (see Fig. 2.1) consisted of an information source: the source's message, transmitter, signal, receiver: the receiver's message: and destination. Eventually, the standard communication model featured the source or encoder, who encodes a message by translating an idea into a code. A code is a language or other set of symbols or signs that can be used to transmit a thought through one or more channels to elicit a response in a receiver or decoder. In this

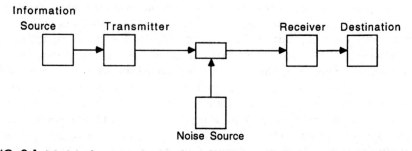

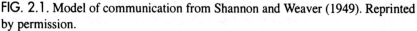

FIG. 2.1. Model of communication from Shannon and Weaver (1949). Reprinted by permission.

process, the decoder receives the transmitted message and decodes, or translates, it. Shannon and Weaver also worked to account for how noise could interfere in the transmission/reception process. They tracked down the places where noise might occur.

As viewed through this model, the communication process started with an information source, such as Person A's mind. The process begins, they postulated, because Person A wants to get information or an idea across to Person B. Person A uses a telephone (transmitter) to ask a friend (receiver—Person B) to dinner (message). The signal is the electrical impulse sent over the telephone line to B's telephone. Person B listens to Person A despite some noise and understands the invitation. In this view, noise is any interference in transmission or reception. To refine this model, researchers such as Krippendorff (1975) concluded that "noise competes with the information that is transmitted from a source to a receiver" (p. 375). Applying information theory as an explanation, he observed that "noise is the random variable that reduces predictability" (p. 375). This means that noise will affect a sender's ability to predict how a receiver will receive and decode a message. Noise is any factor in the process that works against that predictability.

That last notion may seem a bit complex to you, but it becomes simple with a moment's reflection. Think about the communication in which you engage. As people speak or do something in ways that can be meaningful, we expect that you "predict" what those sounds and actions mean. If you are trying to hear the person in the midst of a noisy crowd, you might have difficulty understanding what the person is saying. The physical noise created by the crowd around you creates sounds that interfere with your attempts to make sense of what your friend is saying. This is noise. It comes in many forms, but let's focus on distracting sounds to stress the point, one that seriously concerned Bell Laboratory researchers. In your own time, you might experience the breakup on a cellular phone, which is a kind of noise that your cellular phone company wants to eliminate so that you can hear clearly and accurately what your friend is saying.

Addressing issues of this kind, Shannon and Weaver helped lay the foundation for using information theory as a foundation for communication theory. This line of analysis takes two major orientations. One stresses the engineering principles of transmission and reception. Typical considerations are the engineering design of telephone sending/receiving mechanisms and the fidelity of the transmitted signal as it is passed via telephone lines or through the air. This line of study currently has its greatest influence in the development of new communication technologies, such as fiber optics, satellite communication, or computer messaging.

The other orientation considers how people are able or unable to communicate accurately because they have different experiences and attitudes. They may speak different languages. Differences of opinion, background, and experience provide some of the noise that keeps two people from communicating accurately on a topic. Noise, for example, occurs when people do not share the same meaning of key words or have different attitudes, values, and knowledge.

The study conducted by Shannon and Weaver was motivated by the desire to increase the efficiency and accuracy or fidelity of transmission and reception. Efficiency refers to the bits of information per second that can be sent and received. Accuracy is the extent to which signals of information can be understood. In this sense, accuracy refers more to clear reception than to the meaning of a message. This engineering model asks quite different questions than do other approaches to human communication research. Engineers want to achieve efficiency and fidelity by understanding technical aspects of transmission and reception. But communication entails more than this. An engineering model does not account for human factors that produce problems, such as inattentiveness, difference of experience, or disagreement.

A major step in the evolution of human communication occurred when the focus of study shifted from transmission to an interest in the forces that influence human interaction. Early researchers adhered to the hypodermic, or powerful direct-effects model. Researchers adopted this perspective because they worried that media could virtually control people's thought and judgment. For many years, this view of media effects prevailed even though researchers had little if any hard evidence to support it (Bineham, 1988; Chaffee, 1988).

One of the strongest critics of the direct effects model, Schramm (1954, 1973) advocated a limited effects model. To explain communication effects, he sought to develop a model that would define how communication occurs in many settings, including, as he said, an author seeking to influence a reader, a person reporting a house on fire, two young lovers talking, and a newspaper trying to stress the virtues of Republicanism.

Schramm contributed substantially to the understanding of the communication process by noting that communicators simultaneously send and receive. In this way, he fostered the trend toward an interaction paradigm for communication. His model (see Fig 2.2) could explain that while one person is speaking, the other is listening. How this listening is done constitutes information for the sender. If a receiver frowns, that provides different information than if he or she smiles supportively. Recognizing the dynamics of interaction countered the tendency to view communication as a linear progression of steps leading to or "causing" each following step. He understood that people respond idiosyncratically to messages as a function of their personality, group influences, and the situation under which the communication occurs.

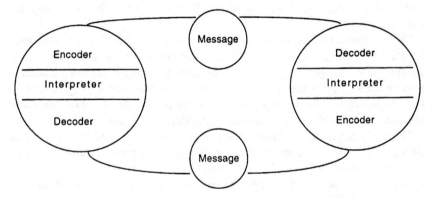

FIG. 2.2. Elements of communication from Schramm (1954). Reprinted by permission.

Wanting to explain the role of mass media in people's lives, Westley and MacLean (1957), alert to the implications of the previous models, noted that Shannon and Weaver did not apply their model to mass communication. So Westley and MacLean developed a basic sender–receiver model to show how communication transpires in many contexts ranging from face-to-face to mass mediated.

They relied on Newcomb (1953) for the intellectual foundation for their model. Newcomb contributed two important dimensions to the basic model of Person A speaking with Person B. He postulated that the relationship between A and B influenced the perceptions B had of A's views on the topic of discussion, X. Thus he examined A speaking to B about X. Newcomb believed that if B likes A, and if A speaks favorably about X, a topic on which B has no opinion, then because B likes A, B will also like X. This scheme has many possibilities. If B likes X and does not like A, what happens if A speaks positively or negatively about X? For instance, you might like your roommate's taste in music. If he or she likes a particular group or album, you will tend to like it as well. If your favorite editorialist takes a particular stand on a tax measure, you may agree. If someone you don't like prefers a particular kind of music you might be motivated to dislike that music. This line of analysis seemed to add dynamism to the basic process model.

On this foundation, Westley and MacLean (1957) built four versions of the S–R model (see Fig. 2.3). In the first figure (a), they characterize how B receives information directly from X, some aspect of the immediate environment. For instance, B might look at a scenic view. In the second figure (b), A intervenes to tell B something about an aspect of X. Now A is communicating to B about X, and the FBA (feedback from B to A) loop makes feedback part of the communication system. In (c), the Person C added is a gatekeeper, who can withhold or transmit information about X to B.

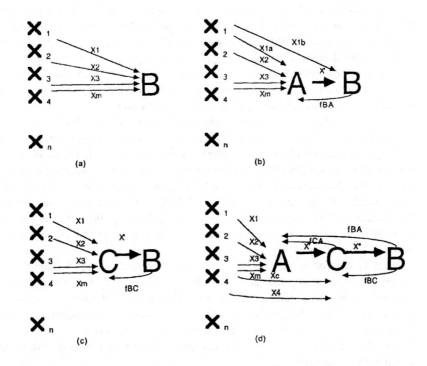

FIG. 2.3. Conceptual model of communication from Westley and MacLean (1957). Reprinted by permission.

In this case, C is the same as a newspaper—a source of information about X. If B is receiving information about X from A and C, we have an even more complex model as portrayed in (d), which combines interpersonal and mass communication. In this instance, C is like a channel—a formal news source that communicates information that B wants to know. Westley and MacLean utilized learning theory to reason that B will turn to C as a channel of information only if B is satisfied by (learns from) the information received. Learning theory postulates that a response to a stimuli is learned and will be repeated if it results in what the person believes are rewards. This is one of many views of communication that have employed learning theory.

Westley and MacLean progressed beyond Shannon and Weaver by showing how various communication settings could be modeled, and they underscored how feedback helps a source estimate whether and how a receiver understands a message. By demonstrating how each setting—given its unique context, relationships, people, channels—could be modeled, they also gave evidence of how limited a pictorial model can be in its ability to capture the dynamics of some phenomenon. Think, for instance, what it would be like to draw a pictorial model to encompass the dynamics of 20 teenagers (10 females and 10 males) at a party chaperoned by one teacher who is well liked and one teacher who is disliked. The dynamics would be impossible to capture. Efforts to model the communication process led to what were called "spaghetti" or "freeway" models. As scholars tried to use pictorial models to capture all of the concepts and their relationships, the lines, boxes, and circles hopelessly tangled.

Early theories featured a stimulus–response (S–R) paradigm, which dominated social science. As Thomas Kuhn (1970) noted, paradigms change when they can no longer explain the phenomena under consideration. The S–R paradigm states that a sender causes or stimulates a "meaning" in the receiver. Researchers soon realized that that paradigm was limited and imprecise. A major shift occurred when an M was inserted to produce an S–M–R version of the model, which emphasizes that messages—their content and design—are the stimulus for the receiver. That means a receiver translates into his or her own thoughts what the message "seems" to mean.

Berlo (1960) drew on this analysis to feature his S–M–C–R model. He assumed that a source has an idea, which is expressed in a message and transmitted through a channel to a receiver. The receiver interprets the message depending on many factors, such as knowledge, culture, and experience. The receiver's reaction to the message could serve as feedback to the source. Feedback could be used to determine whether the message was received and interpreted as intended.

Struggling as they did to capture the essence of the communication process, the scholars reviewed in this section played dominant roles in the development of communication models. They identified concepts and relationships basic to the communication process. They built their models on theoretical foundations and assumptions that led later scholars to adopt their approaches or to have to provide research and theories to refine, correct, or repudiate them. By now you should understand how research relies on key assumptions to explain how and why the process functions as it does. The key assumptions that researchers hold are best exhibited in the definitions they provide for key concepts, which might be called the anatomy of the communication process.

ANATOMY OF THE COMMUNICATION PROCESS

Now that we have reviewed early explanations of the dynamics of the communication process, we have laid the foundation to examine the anatomy of the process. To do so requires that we think about key variables that are commonly featured in discussions of communication. We want to consider definitions—and the problems of creating them—for key terms that often are taken for granted. Through this analysis, you can increase and sharpen the vocabulary you use to discuss communication. You may feel frustration that comes from thinking that you have acquired a definition of a concept or understood a principle only to learn that it has shortcomings. Such is the nature of research and theory construction.

As we explore the following terms, we need to keep in mind that the original meaning of these terms was often used to explain a transmission model of communication. It assumed that a sender (like an archer) created a message (like an arrow), which was transferred (launched) to be received by a receiver (target). This mechanistic sense of communication sees it as something that can "break down." It can treat a message as transferred or transmitted; that view of communication is quite different from one that sees a message as something a receiver interprets. These distinctions are crucial to an accurate and insightful understanding of communication. We explore them in the sections that follow.

Source/Receiver

Early communication models distinguished sources from receivers, as though people were not both. Featuring this distinction in his S–M–C–R model, Berlo (1960) said that a source is "some person or group of persons with a purpose, a reason for engaging in communication" (p. 30). Does the receiver not have a reason for communicating? Such linear models of the communication process emphasize the sender as the dominant figure: A source creates a message that is sent, as a stimulus, through a channel to effect a response in a receiver.

One version of the model features transmission. Taken literally, transmission occurs when a message containing information is transmitted to a receiver, who gets the information exactly as the source intended. In the narrowest sense, this process would be similar to loading furniture (or any cargo) onto a truck and hauling it from point A to point B.

A variation on that model stresses communication as a process of stimulus and response. What the sender does stimulates a response in the receiver. The stimulus created by the sender could be a message that is received and interpreted by the receiver.

Explaining this view of communication, researchers use the term *encoding* to describe the source's efforts to design a message that is used to supply information to the receiver. Encoding refers to the process by which the source translates his or her ideas into words and other symbols—encapsulates those ideas into one or more codes. Ideas are translated into messages, which are sent to the receiver, who decodes them. Decoding occurs when the receiver translates the words and other symbols into a message that might be similar to, exactly the same as, or quite different from the one intended by the sender. Sometimes the encoder is portrayed as being the decoder of his or her own message.

In this way, the process of communication can easily be segmented so that the contribution of each part may be examined. This approach to communication assumes that a message could be transferred from one person to another. It postulates that a message is designed to be received and to have an intended effect. When design does not achieve this effect, some writers concluded, a communication "breakdown" occurs.

Today, if researchers employ this linear view of sender and receiver, they are cautious to note that only at a moment is one person a sender and the other a receiver. Because communication is interaction, participants take turns "sending" and "receiving." This turn-taking is even true for mass-mediated communication, for instance, the process whereby an entertainment program is created, programmed, and aired for an audience's enjoyment. If the audience watches and enjoys the program, it is likely to continue to be aired. If the audience is not amused, the program is canceled. Interaction can mature into fan clubs. People can identify with characters and use their names and lines in conversation. That confirms the popularity of the program. Viewers can respond to the program directors and actors by using e-mail addresses and Web sites. Some viewers may make a telephone call in which they say "Hey, I don't like your program." However, in the vast majority of cases, they just don't watch the program, preferring something else instead. They interact with advertisers. They buy some products and avoid others. Programs that are less appealing attract fewer viewers, lower ratings, and less advertising revenue. All of that is interaction.

Interaction means that both parties—persons or entities—can affect the other. In this way, both parties are senders and receivers. They are also co-persuaders in that they may take turns trying to affect one another by sharing symbols. Once researchers acknowledge this dynamic of communication—interpersonal, organizational, and mass mediated—they begin to use *sender* and *receiver* as terms more as a convenience than to accurately describe the anatomy of the process. Current researchers prefer to use other terms, such as *actors, interactants, communication partners, communicators, audiences, viewers, listeners, readers, televiewers, consumers,* or merely *persons* or *individuals.*

When they discuss new communication technologies, such as the Internet and the World Wide Web, they are prone to think of the persons as *users*.

Terms such as these avoid conceptual problems associated with determining who is sending and who is receiving, and when one person is sending or receiving. Both parties may be doing both simultaneously. As you are speaking with a friend, he or she is communicating with you, even if the reaction is only listening.

A major improvement on early studies occurred when researchers found that people are willing and able to avoid being dominated or influenced by a source. McLeod, Becker, and Byrnes (1974) discovered that persons who are self-motivated to participate in a political campaign actively seek information from newspapers and are less likely to form an issue agenda that only corresponds to that of the newspaper they read. They are more likely to seek alternative information than are people who lack self-motivation. These researchers concluded that "cognitive theories require that we take seriously the mechanisms people use to think about mass communications. We must concentrate on the process of thinking rather than the results of thinking" (p. 318).

This shift in focus, Bryant and Street (1988) reasoned, is moving from an emphasis on receptivity to activity and action. The new paradigm features agents who act and are acted on in interpersonal, organizational, and mediated contexts. People select and evaluate information and influence and, in turn, exert influence and provide information that affects other people.

Theories such as constructivism stress cognitive activities persons use to obtain and process information. As Delia (1977) argued, constructivism assumes that people are able to construct views of their environment. According to this theory, people perceive reality and engage in communication by imposing an image on what they experience. How they communicate can be predicted by the ways they view other persons with whom they communicate. As persons interact, they see one another as dynamic or weak, active or passive, and in myriad other ways. Delia continued, "Since competence at interaction ultimately rests upon individual competencies in social perception and the control of language, variations in communication performance can be understood in terms of differences in the underlying competencies of interactants" (p. 72).

The communication process is more complex than a source sending information expressed in a message to elicit a response in a receiver. Enlightened views of communication reason that how each person communicates is a function of his or her competencies, motivation, and idiosyncrasies, a view that goes beyond mere transmission and reception or stimulus–response patterns. The original sending and receiving model of Shannon and Weaver may be appropriate for an elementary engineering explanation of the communication process that features electrons being sent and received, but it is too simplistic to account for the dynamics of most communication interaction. For these reasons, we can use the language of a sender and a receiver, but we are wise to be extremely cautious in that regard to avoid thinking in limited terms about the dynamics of the communication process.

Intent/Purpose

Several of the definitions used earlier in this chapter focused on intent or purpose as a key element in the anatomy of the communication process. Think for a moment about how purposive (purposeful) your communication is. If you see a friend and wave, what purpose motivated that wave? If you sit down to watch television or listen to a new CD, what is your purpose? If you approach someone whom you find attractive and engage in conversation, what is your purpose? If you think someone is approaching you in ways that cause you to distrust them, how do you respond; what is your purpose? Your thoughts about these questions can help you zero in on the role intention, or purpose, plays in the communication process. You probably begin your analysis by agreeing that communication is not random. Choices are made, whether in terms of what to say and when to say it or which television program or movie to watch.

This line of questioning should lead you to believe that your communication may be quite purposeful as well as quite unintentional. We like to think that human action is purposeful and that communication therefore is purposeful. But a lot of what happens is more automatic than purposeful, and individuals often have trouble thinking about the purposes for which they are communicating.

A second issue to address is the unlimited number of purposes or intentions that we might pose as reasons for why people communicate. Can you list as many as 100? Focusing on that issue, McQuail (1987) reasoned that "it is difficult to discover any systematic functional framework for theory and research that is widely accepted or that spans the several levels of communication analysis" (p. 327), such as interpersonal, organizational, and mass mediated. We could have an unmanageably long list of functions or purposes or so few that they are useless to focus our thinking. We know that some functions operate as strategic options for obtaining other functions. For instance, a person might suggest going to a movie for entertainment. Entertainment is a purpose that actually is embedded in the larger purpose of getting a date for a romantic night out—another purpose. That purpose is related to the creation or maintenance of a romantic relationship. Thinking broadly, and exclusively, McQuail offered four candidates for the universally relevant functions that define communication: Being, adapting, controlling, and affiliating. What do you think of this list, or other candidates?

One of the most problematic aspects of communication theory is determining the extent to which communication events are purposeful. Early models probably stressed purpose too much and did so primarily from the sender's point of view, giving little account of why receivers (seen as passive) acted as they did. In contrast, more recent views of the communication process reason that intentionality is "a jointly constructed product" (Knapp, Miller, & Fudge, 1994, p. 15). As Parks (1994) noted, "Communication is inherently strategic and goal directed. We take it as axiomatic that there would be no reason to communicate if we were not dependent upon others for the fulfillment of our wishes and that these wishes or needs are fulfilled by influencing or controlling others' response to us" (p. 592).

Rhetorical theories that treat the sender as the artistic creator of messages and Lasswell's interest in who says what to whom and with what effect relied heavily on intention or purpose. The linear model relies on the stimulus–response paradigm to determine how the source could achieve its purpose. Applied areas of communication, such as advertising, continue to stress purpose.

In contrast to linear models, uses and gratification theory explains how and why people utilize mass media by predicting that audiences purposefully seek and use television programs and other media to gratify their needs and satisfy their wants. The rules meta-theory assumes that communicators follow a kind of syllogistic logic that is oriented toward purposeful behavior. Purposes are chosen, as are the means to achieve them. Thus, communication is said to follow this pattern:

- A intends to bring about C.
- A considers that to bring about C, he or she must do B.
- Therefore, A sets out to do B, if C seems to be worth the effort of B.

This reasoning suggests that communication is not random, nor is it always precisely purposeful, although it can be.

Each of us communicates messages we never intended. Have you ever said something to a friend or relative that you did not intend to say? Have your intentions ever been misunderstood? Communication occurs accidentally or incidentally, even if it lacks a well-defined purpose. If you go to a club and see someone who interests you, did that person intend for you to be interested in her or him? We suppose that people strive to be appealing or attractive, but are all people equally motivated? Did that specific person intend for you to find him or her appealing?

Many purposes can come together at the same time, and sometimes communication occurs for reasons quite different than what is intended. Most newspapers or television stations have multiple purposes for presenting their wares in an appealing manner, especially to attract audiences in order to sell advertising space or time and earn a profit. Some media managers have a larger purpose, such as persuading readers or listeners to an editorial point of view. Programming and editorial policy are largely a matter of attracting audiences that have the disposable income to purchase the products or services advertised in commercials, rather than having the purpose of converting them to a point of view.

Stressing the problems associated with understanding the role purpose plays in communication, Bowers and Bradac (1982) reported that most researchers are vague or ambivalent regarding the matter of intentionality. People, when asked why they communicate as they do, may or may not be able to articulate their intentions. Ironically, when people interact, they usually do so by attributing intentions to one another. An interesting communication question is how accurately people attribute intention to one another as they interact.

To challenge those who believe that all communication is purposeful, C. R. Berger and Douglas (1982) proposed "that it is a mistake to assume that most utterances in social interactions are the result of highly conscious thought processes" (p. 43). They continued, "Only under rather specific conditions can people be expected to be highly cognizant of concurrent behavior" (p. 46). They contended that much interpersonal communication is a product of scripts (patterns that involve low levels of decision making about what is being said under the circumstances). Thus, "self-consciousness or self-awareness cannot be assumed to be at consistently high levels across persons or situations" (p. 53).

Purpose—what we speculate or actually know about why someone is communicating—helps us interpret the meaning of one's statements or actions. As we discuss in chapter 2, communicators use purpose as a focal point for interpreting what others mean by what they say and do. For instance, if someone says, "I like you," do you consider why the person is saying that as you interpret what that statement means? If your parents say that, does it have a different meaning than if someone with whom you are romantically involved says it? If a stranger says it, what does that mean? If a person follows that statement with a request for a favor, what do you think the expression of liking meant? We deal with this issue in more detail in chapter 3.

Purpose or intention can be found to occur along a continuum from highly strategic and mindful to scripted, mindless, and ritualistic. At times, what people do and say is purposeful, the result of carefully defined message design logic and plans. People tune in radio or television programs intent on learning what is happening or to be entertained. They engage in conversations to be perceived as friendly or to borrow class notes or to get a ride home. In these instances, purpose occurs in well-defined or vague ways. Nevertheless, communication occurs whether intended or not.

Let's conclude by noting how purpose or intention is jointly constructed. Both parties have to share an intention or goal to have an argument. One person cannot sustain an argument if the other party refuses to argue. If a boss wants to evaluate the work of an employee, the employee has to accept that intention (even silently the employee can ignore the instructions). If one of the networks decides to put a comedy at one of its prime times, some number of people—its audience—must agree to use it as entertainment if the show is going to continue to be aired. We conclude with a comment by Kellermann (1992): "No reason to communicate exists apart from a dependence on others for need satisfaction. A communication is, consequently, purposive and goal-directed" (p. 289). This is the case even though much of what people do and say is automatic.

Feedback

Feedback: Perhaps no other term is used more loosely and imprecisely when referring to the communication process. Early approaches to communication were fond of the concept of feedback because it fit nicely with the transmission–reception model. Feedback was based on the principle of cybernetics, which postulated that people set goals and use strategies to accomplish them. Feedback is the interpretation of information they receive that helps them to determine whether their strategies are accomplishing their goals. We use the term incorrectly when we say, "Give me some feedback." Whatever the person says or does at that point can be used as feedback, but it is not feedback.

Let's make that distinction by drawing on a common experience. If you shoot a basketball to the hoop, you may sink or miss. If you shoot it too hard (i.e., "throw up a brick"), you are likely to use that feedback to throw the ball easier on the next try. If the ball falls short of the hoop (i.e., "air ball"), you are likely to use that information as feedback to decide to shoot harder. At no point did the ball give you feedback. Likewise, if you ask a co-worker to give you some "feedback" on a proposal you are writing, you will decide what to do with the person's comments. For instance, if the person says, "I think this draft stinks," will you agree and change it or defend the quality of the draft by ignoring the comment? See, the comment is not actually feedback. Feedback is what you use to decide what to do. You can ignore the person's "feedback." If that is the case, then it was not feedback.

Based on the influence of cybernetics, *feedback* is defined as information a person (or machine) receives and interprets that allows him or her to determine whether his or her action (such as message) had the desired effect to achieve a goal, such as inform a receiver. In this sense, feedback is not what person B says that can lead to a correction in what person A says or does to achieve some outcome. Feedback is the interpretation of what is said or done. For instance, person B might respond to a statement by person A by saying, "I don't understand," or, "That is a good point." Either statement might be used as feedback that person A would use to decide what to do or say next. Or the person might change the goal that was being sought.

N. Weiner (1948) fueled enthusiasm for this concept by using a cybernetic model to demonstrate how elements of a system feed back information to one another, so that the efforts of one part could be corrected by assessing the extent to which it was effective or ineffective. This self-regulating mechanism offered hope for researchers who wanted to understand how responses from the receiver could be used by the sender to determine whether the message was getting across as intended. Systems meta-theory relies on the concept of feedback, as do the rules meta-theory and learning theory. Feedback stresses the strategic and interactive nature of communication.

Feedback is not a simple concept to define. How does feedback differ from any other kind of statement made during communication interaction? If an irate reader sends a letter to the editor of a newspaper, is it feedback or merely an additional phase in a communication episode? If you say, "Good morning," and a friend replies, "What's good about a rainy day?," is that comment feedback that the receiver did not understand your message or disagreed with it? Or is it a comment that has nothing to do with the accuracy of the statement? Are survey results used to determine the success of a public relations or advertising campaign feedback? Are television viewer ratings feedback or an actual part of the communication process?

Used precisely, feedback is quite a useful concept. If extended beyond its original meaning, it loses precision and blurs our understanding of the process.

Message

Message is one of the most taken-for-granted parts of the anatomy of communication. It is a difficult term to define. We use it in a variety of ways and feature it as the essence of communication without noting the imprecision that surrounds its use.

Writers comment on message, message variables, and message impact. They believe that message variables can account for differences in impact that one person has in contrast with another. For this reason, communication researchers and practitioners focus their attention on many characteristics of messages: purpose, style, content, delivery, order of points made, or arguments asserted, for instance. They blur distinctions between message and the source of the message. We may say, "That message is not credible" when we mean that its source is not credible.

At least three views of message can be found. One features the transmission of message as a "bullet" that penetrates receivers' skulls and injects the source's idea into their minds. A second view defines message as a stimulus the meaning of which is interpreted by the receiver. The third view treats message as meaning that may be cocreated or codefined through ongoing interactions by the persons involved. In this sense, meaning is the interpretation each person makes of what is done and said over time. For instance, the message, "I love you," is likely to be defined, redefined, and codefined during the development, maintenance, and perhaps dissolution of a relationship.

What is a message? A transmission view of message treats it as a vehicle by which an idea is transferred from person A to person B. In this way, a message is similar to the arrow an archer launches into a target. Considering this line of analysis, Cherry (1978) scoffed that we do not transmit a message; we share it. Even after we talk with someone about something, Cherry wrote, we "still have it" (p. 306). People do not transmit information, they share it.

Communication occurs, not by transmitting meaning, but because messages elicit meaning stored in receivers' minds. Devito (1986) said that it is "any signal or combination of signals that serves as a stimulus for a receiver" (p. 201). This view is oriented toward a stimulus–response paradigm rather than a transmission paradigm. It treats message as something that a receiver interprets rather than as something a source sends and a receiver receives.

If we argue that communication is what happens when one person's behavior affects another, what then is the difference between communication—the whole process—and message—a means (part of the process) by which the process transpires? What is the message of a television entertainment program? Are visual images a part of television news's message, as well as the words spoken by the reporter? Is the message of a news report conceptually similar to that of entertainment? Does entertainment programming contain a message? If we believe that television news constitutes a message that creates in viewers an impression of reality, what is that message? (Seeing the same news, one person might fear the amount of crime because so much is reported, whereas another person might be reassured that the cops catch the bad guys.) Are interpersonal communication messages the same as those in mediated communication or organizational communication? Is the touch of one romantic partner on the arm of another as much of a message as the words, "You are very special to me"? Is the "touch" the message? Is being "special" the meaning? What happens if the message received differs from that intended? In that case, which is "the message"?

Any solid discussion of message eventually brings in another term: *meaning*. In our discussion of message, the real issue is meaning. Addressing this point, McQuail (1987) observed: "Messages . . . are symbolic constructs that have a meaningful reference to sender, receiver, or environment" (p. 330).

During communication, participants become meaningful to one another through interaction. Meaning is the product that results as a person interprets the behavior—verbal and nonverbal—of another. This definition fits comfortably with the cognitive processes associated with attribution, the means by which one person interprets (makes sense of) the behavior of others. This analysis of message and meaning can be applied to mass communication. For instance, if an audience watches the first episode of a series but decides not to watch the program again, what is the message and its meaning? If the audience does not watch, the persons who create the program may interpret the audience's behavior as a message and attribute any of several meanings. "The program was too sophisticated for them." Another interpretation is possible: "The audience is sovereign. If they say it is no good, then it is no good."

Discussions of messages may imply that they are communicated only through words. This is not the case. Nonverbal communication plays a major role in how people pay attention to and interpret messages. For instance, the intensity of the words used to state a message can increase or decrease its impact—meaning. When nonverbal communication does not conform to what is expected under the circumstances, person B may infer that person A is lying.

Messages—verbal and nonverbal—affect the meaning the communicators create in each other. Visual messages have a grammar as do verbal messages. For instance, if an advertisement features a product in a pleasant setting, the "visual" statement is this: Product X is pleasant. The news may visually present "good" people in "good settings" and "bad" people in "bad settings." In our more enlightened age, people are sensitive as to whether members of minority groups are visually presented as being inferior or subservient.

Many writers have attempted to explain the interaction of message and meaning. Typical of writers of his time, Schramm (1955) adopted a referential model to explain how messages achieve meaning. A referential approach views words as having meaning insofar as they stand for things (i.e., refer to a person's experience with those things). According to this view, if we want to know what a term means we need to see the thing to which it refers. He wrote, "Messages are made up of signs. A sign is a signal that stands for something in experience. The word 'dog' is a sign that stands for our generalized experience with dogs" (p. 6).

This view of messages relies heavily on a stimulus–response explanation and is discussed in more detail in chapter 3. It parallels the view taken by Ogden and Richards (1923). They argued that meaning results because people share experiences of things, feelings, and events, and use words to refer to those experiences. A word causes the mind to think of the thing. Seeing the thing elicits the thought in the mind, which in turn prompts the word to pop into mind. For example, each of us knows what the word *dog* means because of what we have learned; we share a generalized meaning of *dog*.

More than mere tools for eliciting meaning, words affect the views people have (the interpretations they make) of the world around them, including the behavior of others. This point was argued by Sapir and Whorf (Whorf, 1956), who contended that the meanings of the terms and the grammar of the language of each unique group of people contain their peculiar view of the world. This view of language is called linguistic relativity, which also is discussed in more detail in chapter 3. According to this theory, people express their culture and identity in their language, and their language expresses their culture and identity. This line of analysis challenges the referential model. Indeed, it argues that words "define" reality rather than reality "telling" what words mean. As Burke (1966) argued, people should think of things as signs of words rather than words as signs of things. If, for instance, you hear, "John is a bum," you do not look at John to better understand the meaning of the word bum. Rather, you look at him to see how much of a bum he is.

In addition to a referential approach and a linguistic relativity view of meaning and language, some researchers stress the role that purpose and interaction play in the process of creating message and meaning. Messages may be the negotiated product of interaction. Some writers (e.g., Cronen, Pearce, & Harris, 1982; Delia, O'Keefe, & O'Keefe, 1982) believed that people negotiate meaning as they interact. Typical of this line of discussion, B.J. O'Keefe and Delia (1982) showed how, from the speaker's orientation, "messages are those configurations of elements or features in behavior or human manufactures that are designed to communicate" (p. 47). To communicate, senders "make publicly available some mental state (such as wants, beliefs, or ideas) of the message producer" (p. 47). Viewed from an interaction perspective, message and meaning are created through the dynamic process whereby participants in communication affect each other. This view of message and meaning is also discussed in more detail in chapter 3.

If we define *message* from the sender's viewpoint, it is the vehicle by which information is sent or made available and social influence exerted or attempted. Defined from the receiver's point of view, message is the interpretation of one person's verbal and nonverbal behavior by another. In this way, we distinguish the message of the source (message^s) and the message received and interpreted (message^R). This distinction may remind us that messages whether seen from sender or receiver viewpoints may be quite unintentional and mindless. It also suggests that ultimately meaning results from some set of experiences we have personally and share with others. The key, however, is realizing that all messages are interpreted by the communicators. Through actions and reactions that constitute messages, meanings become codefined and negotiated.

Channels

Channels are typically defined as any means by which a message is sent by a source or obtained by a receiver. When we think of channel, we often think of a technology, such as print, radio, television, film, faxes, pagers, or the Internet.

If we define channels as technologies, we are likely to view the communication process as one by which people select channels depending on the kind of message they intend to convey. For instance, people may prefer giving bad news in writing and good news in person. A person ending a romance or a friendship may do so in writing or through a third party (e.g., a mutual friend). If you are going to share good news with someone close, are you likely to want to do so face to face, through writing, or through a third party? People rarely propose marriage by placing the proposal on a billboard. In this less-than-orderly world, receivers often obtain messages they were not intended to receive. They get messages via channels other than the ones intended.

We may also use the key elements of human reception to discuss the concept of channel. For instance, people obtain messages and form meaning through their senses, which include the following: hearing, touch, taste, sight, smell, sense of motion, temperature, and time. Defining channels this way, Berlo (1960) reasoned that every way people experience reality and interact with one another is a communication channel. People communicate by hearing, seeing, smelling, tasting, and touching.

Senses are important for studying interpersonal communication. Researchers have made substantial inroads in determining the influence of various channels, verbal and nonverbal. One channel is what is said. But other channels include myriad nonverbal means including eye contact, vocal quality, touching, proximity, body position, and appearance. During interpersonal communication, many channels operate simultaneously because parties are in proximity.

In organizational and mediated communication contexts, channels are means by which experts learn how people send and receive information and exert influence, even when they are not in proximity. Communication specialists identify and analyze formal and informal channels to understand communication networks and information flow in organizations. Formal channels typically correspond to chains of command, whereas informal channels are synonymous with "grapevines" and "rumor mills." Gatekeepers are persons who are positioned where they control the flow of information. They determine what information gets into channels. For instance, a boss is a gatekeeper of information that subordinates want to send upward. Likewise, a boss can prevent subordinates from receiving information from above. Reporters and editors are gatekeepers.

In mass communication, each medium is a distinct channel. Key members of a media organization, such as newspaper editors and television program producers, are gatekeepers. Channels also include the hardware used in telecommunications; typical examples would be satellites or computer networks. Researchers who study mediated communication analyze the effects channels have on messages and on the people who use the media to obtain those messages. Advertising media planners spend much of their day deciding which channels are ideal vehicles for their clients.

Before we close this section, let's muddy the water. We discussed source and receiver earlier. Here we are discussing channel. We have said that a channel may be defined as a technology, such as print. We have noted that the transmission model of communication sees a source as creating a message that is transmitted through a channel to a receiver. Now, let's apply that logic and see how clearly it defines the process of communication.

If you read a news story, is the newspaper a source (you got the information from it) or is it a channel. People tend to refer to channels as sources: "I read this fact in the newspaper." In this sense, the newspaper is the source, not the reporter. Or the person who gave an account of some event is the source, and the reporter is the channel by which the person's eye witness account came to you. So, source and channel are not clearly distinguished, at least in the way people talk and think about them.

Now, we can confuse this issue more, by thinking that the channel—the medium—might be the message. Taking that view, McLuhan (1964) challenged conventional definitions when he claimed that the medium is the message. With this claim, he stressed how channels differ, not only in terms of their content, but also in regard to how they awaken and alter thoughts and senses. Channels allow experiences to be shared directly (television) or indirectly (print). Radio, he wrote, uses spoken writing. Television combines seeing and hearing. He distinguished media by the cognitive processes each required. Reading is an example of linear thought because readers take in one word at a time. In contrast, television is multisensory and nonlinear because viewers see and hear simultaneously, as they do in conversation. Televiewing, he claimed, demands a kind of thought different from reading. A society heavily dependent on reading becomes rigid and linear in thought. Verbal/visual communication, typical of television or face-to-face conversations, can make society less rigid and more multisensory. He reasoned that people who were reared in a predominantly "print" society exhibit different thought processes than do those reared on heavy doses of television. Following the lead of his mentor, Innis (1951), McLuhan popularized the idea that channels are a dominant force that must be understood to know how the media influence society and culture.

So, we began this section by thinking of channel as a technology or as the means by which people perceive the world around them. Now, we have suggested that the medium is the message. We don't tantalize you with these twists of logic and definition to torment you—really we don't. But we want to challenge your thinking so that you do not easily jump to simplistic conclusions about the communication process.

Stressing the notion that a medium is a message, researchers have discovered that mediated channels convey information differently. For instance, a book of pictures presents discrete and static images, whereas film and television create an illusion of movement through a continuous display of images. Media convey different material with varying degrees of ease; for instance, body and facial gestures are easy to depict visually, but figurative language is not. Messages conveyed in one medium have more impact than if they were presented in another. Preschoolers recall content better if a story is read to them rather than viewed on television, even though the scripts are identical (Meringoff et al., 1983).

If we start with a message, a description of a skunk for instance, we can see that each time we add a channel, we can enrich the message that is formed in the receiver's mind. We can say that a skunk is a black and white animal that stinks. We can show a picture of a skunk, which helps define *black* and *white*. We can bring in some skunk odor to define *stinks*. Each channel added in the presentation of a message enriches it. Viewing scenery through television enhances the message regarding a vacation spot, and sampling different kinds of chocolate (taste is a channel) enhances a discussion of candy. Perfume ads in magazines often include a sample of the fragrance along with text and pictures—to the great displeasure of many readers. A community with only one medium of information is not as information "rich" as is a community with several media.

This brief summary leaves us with three potentially incompatible definitions of channel: technology, perceptual process, or message. These may not be divergent if we note that we perceive differently with each technology. And, we get what we interpret as messages through seeing and hearing others, not a technology. Let's conclude by defining *channel* as the perceptual means by which we obtain stimuli that we interpret as meaning. We see a friend's smile. We hear radio. We taste food. We hear and see television. We see and touch a newspaper. We see text on a computer screen. We feel touch. We smell colognes. We move with or against someone, such as dancing with a romantic partner. These perceptions are channels.

Interaction

Over the years, views on communication shifted from a transmission–reception model to a perspective that emphasized interaction as the essence of the process. The transmission–reception model is linear; each component transpires in a linear time sequence at the initiation of the sender.

In contrast, interaction is dynamic; all parties influence the events, sequence, and outcomes of each communication event or act. One scholar who contributed to this view was Darnell (1971), who argued that "focus on messages or on symbolic transmission is . . . unrealistically narrow" (p. 5). He encouraged researchers to study all of the ways people "affect each other *and* the interactions of those systems of influence" (p. 5).

As early as 1960, Berlo proclaimed that interaction is the "goal of human communication" (p. 129). His claim reflected the undercurrent of symbolic interaction, which, Mead (1934) argued, viewed people as dynamic, not passive. They receive their understanding of themselves, their mind and self, as well as their society, through symbolic interaction.

Berlo (1960) discussed two forms of interaction. One features feedback, a means that the source can use to determine whether the message as designed was received as intended and if it had the desired effect. This view of communication implies that the quality of interaction depends on cybernetic principles of whether messages are sent and received accurately. That view is sender oriented;

it treats the receiver as a passive target of the sender's influence (N. Weiner, 1948, 1950).

A better approach to interaction is based on empathy, a concept associated with the study of interpersonal communication by examining whether a high quality relationship exists. Stressing this orientation, Berlo (1960) concluded, *"If two individuals make inferences about their own roles and take the roles of the other at the same time, if their communication behavior depends on the reciprocal taking of roles, then they are communicating by interacting with each other"* (p. 130). Communication theory is enriched by the argument that rapport between interactants is a major factor in the process of communication.

What is communication interaction? It consists of a series of interrelated communication events that transpire between communication partners over time and space (Hawes, 1973). Communication transpires through a series of comments and actions between people. A conversation can be tracked to see how each statement leads to subsequent ones and eventually to an end, which may be the beginning for a subsequent conversation. What a friend says to you (a component of the interaction) serves as the antecedent to your response, which in turn prompts your friend to reply. And so develops communication interaction.

Hawes (1973) cautioned against believing the process of communication has easily delineated segments and that any segment is free from previous influence and will not shape subsequent segments. If you doubt this notion, think about how you approach someone with whom you have had a heated, angry argument. The new encounter will be shaped in many ways by the memory of what happened before. Interaction not only involves progression, by which a conversation develops, but also interdependent behaviors that occur simultaneously.

To examine how interactions transpire, Hawes (1973) suggested that communication research should concentrate on "two dimensions simultaneously—the content and the relationship" (p. 15). He showed how an emphasis on message transmission and reception can distort the view of the communication process. Theorists who adopt a transmission–reception approach think of words and other symbols as something communicators use as a medium of exchange like money, which can be traded back and forth. He took a different view, that *"communication functions to create and validate symbol systems which define social reality and regulate social action"* (p. 15).

This stance stresses how a symbol system is sustained by interaction. Language is not some static entity that can be codified into dictionaries and used to elicit responses. One person's meaning for a term, at a particular time, cannot actually be imposed on another. Each symbol system is a product of interaction between relatively unique yet similar people. Thus, communication is a means people use to reduce the uncertainty they have about their world, which happens to contain, among other things, many other human beings. Each has similar and different needs and personalities. Communication can decrease or increase uncertainty about others.

Interaction can be understood by appreciating how people conduct conversation. They shift conversational topics based on goals they have for the conversation. They attend to their conversational partner's statements for many reasons, one of which is to show regard through attentiveness. In reciprocation for attentiveness, they can shift topics based on linkages between what is being discussed and what they want to say (Tracy, 1984).

This sense of development highlights the dynamic nature of interaction. Relationships, in this sense, are best thought of as "unfinished business" (Duck, 1990, p. 5). They are ongoing, rather than finished. This perspective is useful for researchers as well as persons who tend to think of their relationships as static rather than dynamic. It underpins communication that transpires in organizations; interaction occurs between co-workers, superiors and subordinates, and even between the organization and its employees.

We interact with the media. We select some programs or movies instead of others. We react to the shows, by being emotionally moved, for instance. We become loyal viewers of soap operas. We identify with characters. We have favorite authors. We call talk shows. We engage in conversations and act interactively with persons and vendors—as well as data bases—on the Internet and World Wide Web. Thus, interaction captures the dynamics of the communication process.

Context

Early process models exhibited little awareness of the impact context has on communication. Then researchers became aware of the role context plays. Where—the situation in which—communication occurs influences how the process is likely to occur and be studied. Bateson (1978) concluded that "without context, words and actions have no meaning at all" (p. 15). Where we say something can have a lot of impact on how it is said and how people interpret the statement. Where we find ourselves—such as a job interview—is likely to influence what we say, how and when we say it.

So important is context that a few major contexts define the domains of communication science: (a) interpersonal communication, (b) group communication, (c) organizational communication, (d) mass or mediated communication, and (e) public communication. In these ways, and others, context can be examined:

- as social settings (such as friends having coffee or attending a party);
- as institutional settings (such as school or employment);
- as a combination of roles and relationships (for instance, father ⊛ family; mother ⊛ family, superior–subordinate);

- as objects in reality (such as location where a conversation occurs or the physical objects of reality);
- as message variables (for instance, grammatical sequence or the order of comments—"At that point she said . . . and then I replied . . .").

One study gave us insights into context as generational differences. Williams and Giles (1996) asked young adults to describe satisfying and dissatisfying conversations with older adults. Dissatisfying conversations were characterized by older persons as being less similar in communication style to the younger persons, as well as expressing negative comments and stereotypic responses. Young adults found intragenerational conversations more comfortable than intergenerational conversations. Generational differences are a context factor influencing the satisfaction people have with interpersonal communication.

Context can be thought of as the place or conditions under which communication transpires; it can also be defined as the relationship between communicants. A doctor's office is a context; in this instance, the nonverbal decoration and arrangement of the office are part of context. Doctor–patient communication is a context. In organizational communication, superior–subordinate relationships are a context. If a subordinate is reprimanded in front of fellow employees, that context is different than if the counseling occurs in the privacy of the boss's office.

Contexts often interlock or overlap. While watching television (mediated context), a family is typically also functioning as a small group or interpersonal unit. In this regard, researchers can be quite interested in how one context shapes another. Some researchers think that organizational communication—that which transpires in large and complex organizations—is actually a matter of many interlocking and overlapping instances of interpersonal communication (two people communicating with one another face to face, over the phone, via memos or letters, and so on). Others conceive of organizational communication as a special domain of small group communication, and this influences the way the organization is examined.

Cognitive Processes

Many theorists assume that communication reflects humans' unique ability to have and communicate abstract thoughts. Following this line of thought, Dance (1978) argued that mentation is a primary element in human communication—especially because it is unique by comparison to other communication, such as that of chimpanzees or dolphins. Although he acknowledged that it is "a vital and essential component of human communication," Dance (1978) doubted that it is the "primary goal." Rather, he argued, the fundamental motivation for "human communication is mentation, or the facilitation of conceptualization" (p. 17). He reasoned that many species of animals use communication, but only humans use it to think and conceptualize—to share information and ideas (Dance, 1985).

Not all theorists believe that much goes on in people's minds as they communicate. Some researchers argue that much communication is the product of relatively mindless applications of scripts. An example of a script is phatic communication, those relatively mindless, but not always meaningless comments people make when greeting one another. "Good morning" may be the most inaccurate statement that most of us ritualistically make.

On the other hand, people are more or less argumentative. People who are argumentative generate more counterarguments—think of reasons not to agree—as they encounter messages that they perceive to be persuasive. Argumentative persons are more resistant to persuasive messages (Kazoleas, 1993).

An original motivation for studying mass communication was to know its effects on the minds of people who make up large populations. Early studies were motivated by the desire to understand war propaganda and the impact of television. A raging debate continues regarding whether televiewing positively or negatively influences cognitive processes and personality. Does viewing violent programs make people, especially children, more violent? Does viewing fast-paced television programming make children more frenetic and less diligent? Do programming and advertising shape culture and perceptions of reality? Concepts such as memory and recall are vital to understanding how people respond to mediated communication.

When researchers discuss persuasion, they become keenly interested in the cognitive processes of communication. They want to know how people receive (if they do) and respond to messages. Persuasion researchers have tried to unlock the relationships between attitudes (or other cognitive elements) and behavior. Even intuitively, we know that people may be predisposed to do something, but not do it. People do not act on all of their attitudes. The attitude–behavior equation frustrates advertisers, who seek to influence buying behavior, and program executives, who risk fortunes in their attempts to guess audience dispositions toward new programs.

Research and theory have evolved to the point where they can explain the processes involved as people create messages, including motivations behind the message design and other strategic choices. Current studies reveal that receivers are capable of being relatively passive and quite active in the way they process messages. Think for instance about conversations persons have after seeing movies. Those conversations often focus on the logic of the plot, the quality of character development, the uniqueness of graphics, the photography, the music, and many other aspects of films. Such conversation is hardly the product of mindless, passive viewing.

Cognition is roughly divided into two categories. One approach to cognition centers on our ability to know the world around us, which is achieved through perception, reports of others (including news reports), and scientific investigation (which features arguments about facts and their interpretation). A second focal point of cognition is called social cognition. This line of inquiry seeks to understand how persons involved in communication perceive and come to know one another. It considers whether how people perceive one another influences how they communicate. Studies such as these have expanded the understanding of the relationship between interactants in the communication process.

THEMES THAT GUIDE
COMMUNICATION THEORY AND RESEARCH

As you have had the opportunity to note in this chapter, many themes are central to the efforts of researchers and theorists to unlock the mysteries of the communication process. This inquiry continues to focus on some dominant themes. These themes seem to researchers and theorists to be the ones most promising in the effort to understand how, why, and to what ends people communicate.

To synthesize the discussion of the anatomy of the communication process, we can think for a moment about some of these dominant themes. They are discussed in more detail in the chapters that follow.

- Uncertainty is uncomfortable. For that reason, people communicate in all contexts to obtain and interpret information as a means for reducing uncertainty.
- People use communication to achieve social influence. Because we do not live on this planet alone, we must interact with others. We must coordinate our efforts with their efforts. We must blend our opinions and motives with theirs. We must influence—and be influenced—if we are to live in harmony and coordination.
- Because we are members of many groups, the dynamics of group membership and communication are a vital part of our existence. We belong to family groups, social groups, educational groups, and work groups–to mention only a few.
- People achieve their identity through communication. How they come to think of themselves is in part the way they think others regard them. Their identity is at least, in part, fashioned after the manner in which they see others of their type (e.g., race, gender, education, income) treated in social contacts as well as portrayed in the media.
- Through communication, people identify with one another. Society carves itself into friendships, families, and classes. We identify with persons who share our interests, attend our college, study our major, and act in friendly ways.

- Meaning is a product of culture. Culture is a product of meaning. As we take on language, we adopt a culture, which gives us a view of the world. We can coordinate our actions with others because we share that view of the world.
- Relationships count. We like quality relationships, which are rewarding and beneficial. We seek to end relationships that are too costly in time, emotion, effort, and such. Relationships can be improved by strategic communication. The quality of a relationship can affect the quality of communication between the relational partners.
- The media are vital extensions of people's need for information, shared reality, emotional release, play, and social identity.
- Entertainment counts. All work and no play makes us dull people. Through communication, we can entertain ourselves. We will pay to be entertained. We are gratified when our expectations for entertainment are satisfied.
- Climates and cultures are important aspects of our lives. Climates and cultures differ so much that each family or company has a climate and culture that it uniquely its own. Communication affects climate and cu.ture; they in turn influence the way the members of the family or organization communicate.
- People seek to form useful attitudes, those that lead to positive outcomes, and predict which outcomes would be negative.
- People want to feel self-efficacious. If they believe they can be successful in communication, they communicate differently than if it is a challenging mystery to them.
- We become known to others—as they become known to us—by what we do and say. For this reason, we can strategically decide to disclose information, emotions, and thoughts. We can withhold that disclosure.
- Interaction is the essence of human communication, but that interaction costs. It can cost in time, emotion, effort, identity, and even money.
- Nutritionists like to say that we are what we eat. We say that we are how we communicate.
- Processes of communication are value laden and must not be separated from ethical judgments. Ethical choice is central to the enactment of communication.
- People calculate the costs and rewards of their communication choices, styles, strategies. They also estimate which of several choices, including the attitudes they hold and behaviors they prefer, are likely to produce positive versus negative outcomes.

CONCLUSION

This century witnessed dramatic advances in the study of communication. Much of the early communication research of this century was guided by a transmission–reception paradigm that depended on the simple principle of stimulus and response, often called the hypodermic needle or magic bullet model. The belief was that a sender's message (stimulus) causes a similar (or exact) response (message reception) in a receiver. According to this view, communication is a means for transmitting ideas from one mind to another to achieve understanding and influence.

Many researchers who studied communication in the 1960s adopted that model and used the term *breakdown* to describe what happens when the outcome of a communication effort differs from what the source had intended. Challenging this orientation, D. R. Smith (1970) observed that "*breakdown* implies a disruption or a malfunctioning of an element or part of a mechanical system. To correct a communication breakdown one either repairs the system or replaces one of its parts" (pp. 343–344). "Parts" cannot be replaced or repaired; we can only continue to communicate in the hope that we may be understood more clearly, achieve the influence we desire, improve a relationship, or be newsworthy or entertaining. In truth, the communication process occurs even if it takes routes that are not what the participants intended.

A major contribution of 20th-century research has been to think of communication, not as a vehicle for transmitting ideas, but as interaction in all contexts: interpersonal, group, organizational and mass-mediated communication. Many new theories have come along to correct and advance the assumptions that were fervently set forth during the 1950s and 1960s. Subsequent chapters discuss and evaluate those theories. As you come to understand them, you should be able to draw on the concepts that were introduced in this chapter. The discussion in this chapter should help you appreciate the roles theory and research play in the effort to understand communication phenomena.

An academic discipline grows because of what its scholars share. To this end, scholars need to understand the discipline's history, have a common sense of the objects of inquiry, focus on similar and compatible questions, agree on the best methodologies, and create a common terminology, or lexicon, with which to discuss the discipline. For this reason, its history is important to its future. To understand where the discipline is going, we must have insight into the issues that have been the center of intellectual curiosity. For a discipline to grow, its researchers must agree on what is being studied—the object of the study. What phenomena count most for understanding the nature of communication? What questions need to be answered for us to understand the nature of communication? Scholars need a common and compatible set of questions to build their academic discipline. They need to share a common and compatible set of research tools—methodologies—by means of which they investigate the phenomena under scrutiny. Without a common terminology, or lexicon, scholars cannot agree on what they have discovered and what they want to discover. You probably have a sense—and that feeling will increase—that much of the wrangle in the field centers on the meaning of terms. As unfortunate as that situation is, it characterizes some of the most vital discussions among scholars.

Earlier in this chapter, you were encouraged to define *communication*. If you did so, did it change as you became more familiar with the issues that were addressed in this chapter? If so, don't feel alone. It is a difficult concept to define, but as we continue, you should have a better idea of the concepts and issues that are vital to it.

3

Language, Meaning, and Messages

L anguage, unlike any other aspect of communication, distinguishes the communication of humans from that of other animals. Language is vital to human communication. Other animals can be taught a language; they may even use their own rudimentary language. Evidence has not revealed any other language as complex and rich as ours. That may be good news and bad news.

Through language, people name and evaluate the objects, sensations, feelings, and situations they experience. Through symbols, they create, manage, and share interpretations of the physical world. For society to function, people use words to create and coordinate their social, political, and economic activities. Because of the power of language, people externalize and internalize their thoughts and those or others (Burke, 1961). Social interaction and cooperative behavior occur through social reality or shared reality, the understanding each person has of what other people know (P. Berger & Luckman, 1966).

Language is not only a means by which people interact, but it is also vital to the cognitive processes they use to define and evaluate one another (C. R. Berger & Bradac, 1982). Without knowledge of these cognitive processes, Hewes and Planalp (1987) reasoned, communication theorists would be unable to explain misunderstanding and its effects on other relational variables such as deception, conflict, and failure to coordinate efforts. As Seibold and Spitzberg (1982) concluded, such insights help unlock the mysteries of human communication:

> Communication can hardly be treated without reference to the interpretations actors bring to their attempts to symbolically interact. Without attention to the ways in which actors represent and make sense of the phenomenal world, construe event associations, assess and process the actions of others, and interpret personal choices in order to initiate appropriate symbolic activity, the study of human communication is limited to mechanistic analysis. (p. 87)

Extending this idea, Hewes and Planalp (1987) concluded, "Effective communication requires not only that people share knowledge (intersubjectivity) but also that they know they share knowledge" (pp. 165–166). Language allows people to function on two levels: that of their individual thoughts and the realization that others share similar meanings and interpretations.

From these opening comments, you may have inferred that this chapter does not cover language and meaning by focusing on grammar and vocabulary. Those topics might be discussed in English classes or by linguists or psycholinguists who seek to reveal the basic structure of language. Instead, this chapter examines theories about how people use symbols to define reality, reduce uncertainty, be entertained, coordinate activities, shape relationships, and express feelings. An understanding of language and meaning can explain how people develop an idea (form a sentence or extended comment) and interact by knowing how words are put together in structured sequences, whether of sentence length or an entire communication episode.

Before launching into those topics in detail, we need to frame our analysis. Recall that in chapter 1 we stressed the relevance of a rules meta-theory for the study of communication. Language occurs in rule-bound patterns. These patterns are vital to language because they help people to know how to express their ideas and feelings. Each sentence requires a grammar—a set of conventionalized rules—that guides its development and expression of thought. What is a grammar for one group of people may be seen as being ungrammatical to other people. Knowing the rules of their language lets people recognize that a pattern of words is gibberish, such as "John went along the quickly sidewalk on his knowing that others would." This statement violates the expected rules of grammar so much that a recognizable message cannot be inferred.

Not only do sentences follow rules, but so must conversations, commonly called discourse. Conversations can transpire over time—one word at a time—only because patterns or rules are followed (McLaughlin, 1984). Interactions must be executed by applying rules that eliminate the randomness that would make communication impossible. If you ask someone, "Are you going to class?" and the person answers, "The duck flies only in the dark," you might think the person is stupid, joking, or not listening. Persons are expected to follow rule-based patterns during discourse.

Rules help us to know how to make statements, and how to make them more clearly or emphatically. For instance, intense language increases the persuasiveness of a message and enhances a receiver's perception of a speaker (Bradac, Bowers, & Courtright, 1979). To demonstrate the effect words have on communication, researchers have featured intensity, diversity, and immediacy. Intensity is "the quality of language which indicates the degree to which the speaker's attitude toward a concept deviates from neutrality" (Bowers, 1963, p. 345). Lexical diversity is the extensiveness of a person's vocabulary. Immediacy is a measure of the degree to which a source is emotionally involved with the topic of conversation. To better understand immediacy, compare the degree of involvement exhibited in the following statements: "I like your suit." "That suit is stylish." "You probably get lots of compliments on that suit." The first statement exhibits the most involvement, and the last one the least (Bradac et al., 1979).

Rules offer one explanation for the use of language. They account for the ways people decide to use or not use certain words, compose sentences, enact discourse as a series of words and sentences in a form we call conversation, and create and interpret texts that capture the meaning that is the residue of the interaction.

In addition to rules, cybernetics can help explain the choices and processes of conversation. People have goals and select (or avoid) words, create sentences, and weave discourse to achieve those goals. To the extent that their selections seem successful, they persist in that goal-oriented behavior. If the selection seems to be leading to failure, they make adjustments in vocabulary, sentence structure, and discourse structure or sequence. A logical sequence underpins the strategic process of language use: Set goals, design message to achieve that goal, select words to form the message via sentences, initiate the plan through an array of statements, weave those statements with the ones used by the interactant, assess the success of the words and sentences, and adjust and refine the selection and use of words to achieve the goal.

In either explanation of how people use language—rules or cybernetics—the product of the strategic choices is a sense of shared meaning, or at least some sense that meaning has been shared. Through the give and take of discourse, people create or co-define meanings that influence their opinions and behaviors. As they watch other people, they make sense of the interaction by knowing the rules and behaviors people use for interaction. In this way, reading a novel, listening to lyrics, watching a movie or a TV sitcom constitutes evesdropping on others' conversertions.

Language can be a dependent variable that results from goal and strategy selection. It also is an independent variable that influences communication outcomes. In either sense, language and thought are inseparable. For this reason, words ought not to be viewed merely as means for dressing up the presentation of ideas. According to Blankenship (1974), more than "cosmetic" ornament, the language used to express an idea is inseparable from its meaning.

Three theories can help us examine the nature of language as it operates to assist and frustrate human communication: (a) referential or representational theory, (b) linguistic relativity theory, and (c) a constitutive theory of language that treats meaning as the product of symbolic interaction using rules and strategic problem solving to coordinate social actions through webs of conversation and by attributing purposes to what each of us says and does. This third theory is broadly discussed as discourse analysis. This chapter explains and compares these theories. To examine these theories, you should appreciate how language makes human communication unique.

WORDS: ONE UNIQUENESS OF HUMAN COMMUNICATION

Human communication is unique because people can use complex and powerful symbol systems. Other animals communicate, but in ways quite limited in comparison to humans. Bees use ritualistic movements to tell one another where pollen is located and how far they must travel to get it. Elephants and whales use sounds as social cues to coordinate their actions with members of their species. Bottle-nosed dolphins and apes can be trained to use signs to engage in rudimentary conversations. Researchers are astounded if an animal learns a few hundred signs and uses them strategically.

No matter how novel such studies are, the uniqueness of humans' use of language is demonstrated by the ease with which most human infants obtain a large vocabulary in a few years with a minimum of rote training and imitation. They do so with ease, whereas other kinds of animals (such as apes) require much more effort to learn far fewer words. Humans are the only animals that use words to store knowledge in libraries.

Computers use language to communicate with one another and with people. But computers know only the language they are taught and, as of yet, develop none by themselves. Computers, unlike humans, do not change their language over time. Human language changes constantly, as is demonstrated by comparing modern contemporary English with that used by Chaucer or Shakespeare. You gain insight into this dynamic quality of language by comparing the pet idiomatic expressions of your peer groups with those of people 5 years your senior or junior.

Stressing the unique role language plays in human communication, this chapter focuses attention on language and messages, but the ultimate goal is to understand meaning. Studies of language delve into the nature of meaning by concentrating on relationships between words and things and by examining how interaction transpires in ways that are meaningful to the participants. In this vein, scholars come to different conclusions:

1. Meaning is the response the source's words produce in the receiver's mind. This basic application of stimulus–response assumes that meaning is a reaction to a word. Carried to its logical extreme, this view of meaning assumes that any word's meaning is nothing more than what it elicits.
2. Meaning is the product of the relationship between thoughts and the objects of thought—what people think about. This view of language assumes that people create views of the world through their idioms by having similar experiences to which words refer.
3. Meaning is the impact each idiom has on the perceptions and actions of the people who take for granted the perspectives that are unique to it. Interaction leads to shared meaning as individuals take on words and achieve convergence.

4. Meaning emerges when people follow rules to use language. Rules guide the selection and use of language. People interpret the meaning of what each other says. To do so, they focus on the intentions they think motivate why people say what they say and why they say it as they do.

Each of these conclusions adds insight into the way words have meaning and serve efforts to communicate.

As we think about meaning, we have three major views from which to choose. One features meaning as something that can be exchanged. Another features meaning as the product of interaction. A third sees meaning as being central to the environment through which people experience and enact their lives (Grossberg, 1982). Each of these views reflects a different model of the communication process. Deciding which of these views is most accurate is a challenge that is central to the remainder of the chapter.

WORDS: COGNITIVE AND CONSTITUTIVE VIEWS

Theorists agree that words are vital to perception—how people view and give meaning to the reality that they experience. Words are essential to social cognition and human behavior. People interact with one another based on how they characterize one another, especially by assigning motives to each other's behavior. If you "see" someone as a crook or a bum, you are likely to act differently toward the person than if you think he or she is honest and decent.

These comments suggest that two broad themes guide the discussion of language: cognitive and constitutive. The cognitive function of language explains the role that meaning, thoughts, and judgments play in the relationship between words and "things"—the phenomena to which words refer. Through words, you can imagine things that do not exist, such as unicorns or poltergeists, and talk about them as though they did exist. You also learn the names and characteristics of things that do exist.

The study of the relationship between words and things is akin to epistemology—the philosophical explanation of how people come to know the phenomena in their world. The key question is that of the chicken and the egg. Which comes first in the shaping of cognitions, the word or the thing? Do words shape views of reality, or does contact with things and experiences in reality influence the meaning these things have?

The relationship probably goes both ways. Two examples can help you appreciate this quandary. Recall the first time you ate liver, if you have. When you did so, you may have had some forewarning about how it might taste. That forewarning probably prepared you to enjoy or dislike the taste and texture. When you took your first bite, what you thought of the taste and texture was affected by your direct experience. Both your primary and secondary experience "flavor" your meaning of the word *liver*.

Here is the other side of the coin: Liver is a traditional, although not universally enjoyed, food in our society. Toasted grubs are not. To people in other countries, toasted grubs are a staple or a delicacy, as are the eyes and entrails of goats and sheep. You probably do not eat horse or dog meat, but people in other countries do. To some extent, tastes (the liking of certain foods) are derived from direct contact with reality, and in other cases tastes are "filtered" through words that express cultural biases regarding what is acceptable to eat.

If we compare these views of language at a superficial level, we may note that meaning is at least partially based on our interpretations of the phenomenal world that we name and describe through words. This cognitive view of language features it as a conventionalized code shared by people within each society. The second broad theme in the study of language involves constitutive rules that function during interaction—the conventionalized functional rules of conversation. The constitutive approach to language and meaning is also embraced by the concept of social cognition.

People learn to interpret meaning based on rules that operate during each communication episode. Meaning is shaded by interpretations idiosyncratic to persons involved in each communication encounter and the nature of the encounter. Meaning depends on the situation, the context in which the encounter occurs, the relationship between communicators, and the intent that is perceived to guide the comments each person makes. In this regard, "Drink!" or "Give me a drink!" can have many meanings. The meaning changes if the words are spoken by a thirsty child or by an alcoholic. In this sense, the constitutive approach to language reasons that meaning is not in the words or in what they refer to but in the perceived intentions and interaction rituals that occur during each episode.

People come to know—or at least think they do—one another through the vocabulary and idiom each uses. For this reason, a person who uses the vocabulary of a stockbroker is likely to be a more credible financial advisor than one who does not use that jargon. The words people use can affect how others judge their competence. Through shared vocabularies and meanings, people identify with one another. The words people use during interaction can determine whether they reinforce or change each other's attitudes (Bradac et al., 1979). In this way, words have perceptual and interpersonal outcomes.

If you think words are used only to convey factual or evaluative messages, you can miss the fact that they are also used ritualistically—as scripts. Meaning results from the interpersonal process in content. A "good day" may be rainy. "How are you?" usually does not invite detailed explanation. Words are used to govern and guide the flow of conversation. For instance, "Yes, I know that," can prompt a person to give less detail than intended. Conversely, the statement, "I didn't know that," can lead a person to give an expanded explanation. Comments, such as, "Please tell me about the courses you took in college that most prepared you for this job," are used during a job interview to invite a response from the interviewee.

In business organizations, words are used to define and evaluate, as well as coordinate, inform, and influence. Rarely do people in an organization share an exact meaning for words. The term *labor* means something different to lower level personnel than to executives. To lower level personnel, it means the efforts they expend and tasks they perform in exchange for money with which to exist and even enjoy life. To executives, labor is a cost, an expense that must be borne in an effort to produce a return on investment. Images you have of a company and its products or services are flavored by the words used to describe them. Words are used to coordinate work, make decisions, give orders, exchange information, and give employees a feeling of being involved in the company. Management can use words to reward or punish employees. So can workers reward and punish management through words.

Constitutive rules specify or guide how people interpret verbal or nonverbal cues that occur during interaction. For instance, constitutive rules regarding your relationship with someone (such as spouse, parent, child, or stranger) suggest how you should interpret a statement such as "I love you." Those words mean something different to a couple whose baby was just born than they do when said by a stranger during an initial encounter in a bar. Or the meaning of "that's an interesting outfit" would be different if spoken by a good friend or someone whom you dislike. Regulative rules govern interaction patterns; for instance, when someone greets you, you are obligated to respond in kind (W. B. Pearce & Cronen, 1980). Were you taught to say "thank you" when you receive a gift?

Thus, cognitive and constitutive (social cognition) insights into the nature of language force us to consider the relationship between meaning, words, and messages. Three theories have developed to offer insight into language: referentialism, relativism, and a constitutive view of interaction. Each theory explains how words acquire meaning, influence judgment, shape perception, and serve the processes of interaction. These theories are not mutually exclusive; each makes unique contributions as well as falls short of completely explaining what language is and how it creates understanding and enables interaction. By understanding and comparing these theories, you can obtain a clearer view of how messages, language, and meaning interact.

The first two theories, referentialism and linguistic relativity, offer contrasting views of cognition and perception. Referentialism postulates that words have meaning in large part because they represent or refer to (stand for) things, feelings, or situations people have experienced. This theory builds on the principle that people learn that phenomena have names. Part of the meaning we have of words results from experiences we have had with the phenomena (e.g., the taste of liver). In contrast, linguistic relativity contends that people's views of physical and social reality are filtered through the idiom unique to each language culture. Thoughts and perceptions are shaped by language. As people learn a language, they take on its unique views of reality.

Both theories have epistemological implications because they seek to explain how words help and hinder human efforts to know and understand their physical and social realms and to communicate about them. Language is basic to the human motive to know—to reduce uncertainty. In this way, it can be questioned whether people know reality accurately or merely live a view of reality that is contained in the language they share with others in their culture.

The third category of theory to be discussed in this chapter features a rules-based explanation of how people seek to be meaningful and how they interpret what occurs in discourse. The principles that are discussed in that section of the chapter are used for scholarly investigation called discourse analysis or conversational analysis. This approach to language features the role that purpose plays in people's interpretations of what they say, and what they mean when they make statements verbally and nonverbally. Regulative rules guide the choices they make in what they do and say. Constitutive rules govern how they interpret what occurs in conversation. This theory explains that people become known to one another during discourse by the rules that they apply.

As we set out to consider the three theories that follow, recall that in chapter 1 we offered several criteria by which a theory should be evaluated. Keeping these criteria in mind can sharpen our understanding of what theorists are attempting to accomplish, namely to explain phenomena and to make predictions. This allows us more control over human communication.

A REFERENTIAL VIEW OF MEANING

To explain how words come to have meaning, referential theory relies on a view of learning theory that was popular early in the 20th century. The theory explains how words have meaning. It argues that people learn the meanings of words by associating them with things and the experiences they have with those things. In this way, the word can come to represent the thing—to stand for it. (Note that this view of language can also be called representationalism.)

To appreciate this theory, think about how children learn language. Children learn the names of animals, for instance, by thumbing through a book or seeing the actual object and learning the name of each animal. As someone turns the pages of a children's book, the child learns that a red object with its unique shape is an apple; "A is for apple." The next page might have an object that looks a bit like an apple, but the child is encouraged to note slight differences in shape and use. This page instructs that "B is for ball." "C is for cat." "D is for dog." In this manner, the child can experience the word through pictures and learn that each category of "things" has its peculiar name.

A child also learns the names for things by encountering the thing itself. For instance, a child might touch a hot stove. He or she learns the meaning of the word *hot* as a parent says, "Don't touch that stove; it's hot!" The sensation of pain becomes a thought that is associated with the word *hot*. Later, the word *hot* stimulates some residue of the experience. The word represents or refers to the thing or experience. The process goes in this sequence: Experience results in thought, which becomes associated with words or other symbols, which subsequently are used to make statements about the experience. Likewise, as a person has a sensation, such as touching something hot, he or she thinks, "That is *hot!*" Words have meaning that are shared to the extent that persons have similar experiences, but meaning is not in words but in the thoughts that result from the experience.

This theory of meaning depends heavily on a stimulus–response rationale. The stimulus–response relationship goes two ways. The child sees the object or experiences the sensation stimulus and learns that it is associated with a unique word—a patterned set of sounds or written letters. Seeing the object later stimulates the response—its unique name. Or, hearing the object's unique name, the child may think of the object.

Ogden and Richards (1923), leading advocates of this theory, concluded that meaning cannot be understood without recognizing the relationship between words, thoughts, and things. To explain this relationship, they created their famous triangle (see Fig. 3.1), which consists of three components: experience, or a referent; reference, or thought (the residue created by the experience); and symbols, or words. The relationship between referent and reference is causal, according to Ogden and Richards; contact with the referent (puppy) causes the reference (warm, cuddly animals).

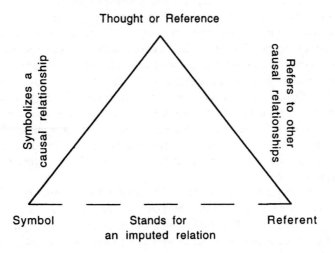

FIG. 3.1. Triangle of meaning,. From Ogden and Richards (1923). Reprinted by permission.

Likewise, these theorists believe that the symbol is causally related to the reference. If you hear or read the word *dog,* you think of the animal. In contrast to these two causally connected relationships, the relationship between words and things is indirect. This indirect relationship they stress by using a broken line to demonstrate that words and things are related only by an intervening thought or reference—the residue of experiencing the reality or by learning the word. Based on this analysis, Ogden and Richards concluded, "When we hear what is said, the symbols both cause us to perform an act of reference and to assume an attitude which will, according to circumstances, be more or less similar to the act and the attitude of the speaker" (p. 11).

This statement—the foundation of the referential approach to language—makes two important points. First, things in reality and encounters with them govern the meaning that people hold. Second, because other people have similar experiences, words can be used to elicit thoughts. In this way, language enables people to communicate. Meanings of words depend on the things and experiences to which they refer. For instance, all people of a unique language culture are likely to become aware of objects, such as a dog, and learn that they are associated with the same word, *dog*. Note also, that each language, such as Spanish, French, Chinese, Russian, or Swahili, will have one or more words for the object *dog*. Those words will sound and be written differently.

In this way, the theory can explain why groups of people use the same word and have similar thoughts when they read or hear those words. This theory explains why people have different meanings for terms. For example, the word *dog* means something different to a person who was attacked by one as a child than it does to a person who has only had positive experiences.

For these reasons, Richards (1925) argued that people can communicate only to the extent that they share experience. Ogden and Richards (1923) concluded, "Communication may be defined as a use of symbols in such a way that acts of reference occur in a hearer that are similar in all relevant respects to those that are symbolized by them in the speaker" (pp. 205–206). By applying this reasoning, Ogden and Richards offered a criterion by which to assess the accuracy of communication: A word is correct if it produces the same reference in the receiver as in the sender, often referred to as isomorphism. This theory assumes that, at least within each group of people who use the same language or idiom, the accuracy of a statement is a measure of the degree to which it corresponds to reality.

Extending this theory, Richards (1936) argued that meaning grows as words are associated with, or modify, one another. Perception is a sorting done in context. Context "is a name for a whole cluster of events that recur together—including the required conditions as well as whatever we may pick out as cause or effect" (p. 34). As Richards concluded, "Language, well used, is a *completion* and does what the intuitions of sensation by themselves cannot do. Words are the meeting points at which regions of experience which can never combine in sensation or intuition, come together" (pp. 130–131). By this analysis, he argued that language can encompass many experiences and offers means by which thoughts in varying degrees of complexity can be created and exchanged. Thus, if a person knows the meaning of the words *big* and *cow,* he or she can then combine the meaning of each to interpret the phrase "big cow."

This theory had—and continues to have—a large following because it is so intuitively logical. It influenced other lines of analysis. In this way, Osgood and his associates (Osgood, 1953; Osgood, Suci, & Tannenbaum, 1957) used learning theory to contend that meaning is the behavioral response a term creates in the receiver. Hearing a word (or seeing the thing) stimulates a thought that mediates between a stimulus and its meaning that occurs in the mind of the receiver. Mediation occurs because the person compares this immediate response to previous ones.

How does mediation work? Osgood (1963) explained, "The greater the frequency with which stimulus events (S–S) or response events (R–R) have been paired in input or output experience of the organism, the greater will be the tendency for their central correlates to activate each other" (p. 741). The meaning that arises in response to a word or the object is a composite of a complex of previous encounters with both the stimulus and our responses to it.

The components of Osgood's (1963) model parallel those commonly used in the 1960s to explain the communication process: encoding (receiving stimuli), associating, and decoding (responding to the association between thought and stimuli). The reasoning is this: When stimuli are received, they become associated with one or more responses such as pleasure or fear. This response to the stimuli—actually seeing the thing or having the experience—constitutes the reaction that becomes the meaning associated with the thing or experience. Once people learn that this thing or experience (stimulus) has a name, the word is associated with the response to the stimuli.

Subsequently, the word can produce the response even in the absence of direct contact with the experience. If the experience has several components or attributes to it, which is often the case, all of them together form the composite meaning of that experience. The meaning of the word that stands for the stimuli contains all of the component attributes. In this way, many component attributes associate together to form the substance of a term, such as *grandmother.* For example, you may associate many attributes with the word *grandmother,* such as kind, warm, good food, big hugs, gray hair, wrinkles, twinkling smiles, and frailty. The word *grandmother* prompts you to bring into your consciousness the component attributes of the meaning of the term.

This reasoning brought Osgood to an important contribution to understanding meaning—the concept of semantic space. He coined this concept to describe two dimensions of meaning and believed that it allowed researchers to measure meaning. One is the several attributes that can be associated with a single term—a featured concept, such as grandmother. The second dimension is the degree to

which any term applies to the featured concept. These degrees are increments
that can be measured between polar opposites. According to the concept of
semantic space,

> each thought or judgment represents a selection among a set of given alternatives
> and serves to localize the concept as a point in the semantic space. The larger the
> number of scales and the more representative the selection of these scales, the more
> validly does this point in the space represent the operational meaning of the concept.
> (Osgood et al., 1957, p. 26)

This analysis led Osgood and his associates to create the semantic differential
as an instrument for measuring meaning by having respondents indicate what
dimensions of various concepts in semantic space they associate with a central
concept (Snider & Osgood, 1969). In this way, the semantic differential allows
researchers to measure meaning. They do that by asking respondents to allocate
a concept to a point in a multidimensional semantic space. As Osgood et al.
(1957) reasoned, "Difference in the meaning between two concepts is then
merely a function of the differences in their respective allocations within the
same space" (p. 26).

Researchers can measure the degree to which any concept is a part of the total
meaning of the central concept, such as grandmother. Many versions of the
semantic differential have been developed as researchers have attempted to
understand and measure meaning. Thus, for instance, product researchers might
measure audience reactions (semantic space) to a product, such as a breakfast
cereal, by having the audience mark the appropriate point in each of the
following differentials. (These researchers want to know which concepts are
associated with the cereal and how strongly each is associated.)

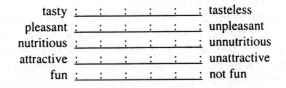

The strength of each concept in semantic space is measured by its location on the
polar scale. If a survey respondent marks the space next to "fun," that indicates
that the attribute is strongly associated with the cereal. Or if the respondent
marks the middle space, that means the attribute is neutral, or essentially
irrelevant. And if the space next to "not fun" is marked, that expresses that this
respondent did not think the cereal is fun. Similar marks for other semantic items
can give researchers a composite view of each respondent's impressions of the
cereal. The data can be analyzed to derive a total view of all respondents'

impressions of the object. These impressions constitute the meaning respondents have of the concept or object being examined. Thus, this group—sample population—of potential buyers of a brand of cereal might believe the cereal is sort of "tasty" and "pleasant," "very attractive" and "fun," but "not very nutritious."

That meaning—measured by a semantic differential—might predict that members of the sample population would purchase the product. Compare that prediction to one based on the following response to a cereal: "Unattractive," "not fun," "not tasty," and "unpleasant," but "very nutritious."

This analysis can help you think about differences in meaning you have in contrast to those of your friends or acquaintances. If you think about dogs, what defining attributes do you associate with them? If you have never been bitten by one, you may have a different meaning than a friend would have if he or she had been bitten. This example illustrates how meaning is a residue of people's experience with the world they encounter.

Drawing on the work of Osgood and his associates, Berlo (1960) applied this theory of meaning to explain the communication process. The key to meaning, he agreed with Osgood, depends on how people learn to connect stimuli to words.

His discussion focused on two types of stimuli. Proximal stimuli are produced by direct contact with the physical world through the senses (e.g., touching a hot stove or tasting an apple). Distal stimuli result in reaction to something with which a person does not have direct contact (e.g., seeing or hearing about a snake). The two kinds of response are paired. Thus, Berlo continued, "People begin to respond (internally) to the distal stimulus, by detaching and internalizing some of their original responses to the proximal stimulus" (p. 183). These internal responses become fixed, or learned. They prompt the individual to make some sort of overt response. "The internal response—and the internal stimulus that comes from it—can be defined as the 'meaning' of the external stimulus, for the person who is responding" (Berlo, 1960, p. 184).

Learning goes through three phases. The first phase is a response to proximal stimuli–direct contact. Distal stimuli, the second stage, provide indirect contact that calls on what was learned from proximal stimuli. The third stage, that which is essential to communication, occurs when individuals learn that words are connected to distal and proximal stimuli. The word *snake* is a linguistic stimulus associated with the proximal stimuli—contact with a snake—and the awareness of what it is (distal stimuli). Affective memories cause emotional responses to the object and to the word; words can elicit these memories.

This line of reasoning was adopted and expanded by another group of researchers, called general semanticists. They believe that by studying language they could help people communicate more clearly. They think that meaning is best when it is derived from the object to which terms refer. To define the word *cow,* for instance, they would have us experience and think about the object COW.

General semanticists worry that miscommunication occurs because people are uncritical of the associations they make between words and things. The meanings people possess may not accurately reflect the nature of the things being referred to. Working to prevent false conclusions and misunderstanding, they stress the need to perceive and refer to reality accurately. They want people to avoid the filtering effects of biases that are embedded in thoughts and words.

A leader in this movement, I. J. Lee (1941, 1952) studied how people use words to name the stimuli they receive. Thus, *table* is the name of an object, *red* is the name of a quality, *run* is the name of an activity, and *over* is the name of a relationship.

This process of naming can lead to errors if people come to believe that words are more than mere references to things, or conclusions about things. To avoid this mistake, semanticists rely on this axiom: Words are *not* things as maps are *not* territories. By this statement, semanticists hope to prevent people from thinking reality is what their words say it is. Thus, Lee pressed for a standard of clarity: "To be most useful, statements must fit, must be similar in structure to the life facts being represented. Words can be manipulated independently of what they represent, and so made false to fact both consciously and unconsciously" (I. J. Lee, 1941, p. 22). The standard of meaning, according to general semantics, is the quality of the thing or other experience to which each word refers.

To help people avoid making false references, semanticists offer several remedies, all of which feature the warning that terms are most accurate when they express one-word/one-thing relationships. They observe that dictionaries are history books, merely reporting what terms meant at the time they were published. They caution that the meaning of words should not be considered as static. If meaning is thought to be static and unchanging, two kinds of problems can occur. One flaw is forgetting that the meaning of words changes over time. Another flaw—"time binding"—is the tendency people have to stop time rather than realizing that the world is in constant flux. This fault can be easily recognized by recalling how surprised you are to see how a friend whom you have not seen for years has changed; your recollection of the person is as you last saw him or her. "Baby" John is now a 6'3" tall teenager. Jan is no longer the high school comic; she is a senior partner in a law firm.

The theory so far discussed in this section relies extensively on the way words refer to things. This discussion can be extended to examine how people make more extended statements about reality. The assumptions of referentialism apply to complex cognitions and statements people make about them.

Many theorists stress how important language is to mentation— thoughtfulness. Such theorists emphasize the impact language has on thought and analytic communication about physical and social phenomena. Accurate and insightful description and analysis of physical and social realities are the criteria that underpin this school of thought.

Part of the referential school, Langer (1951) and Cassirer (1946) went beyond the rudiments of the referential relationship among words, thoughts, and things to argue that words are vehicles for conceiving and expressing complex ideas about reality. Langer reasoned that humans, "unlike all other animals," employ signs or symbols "not only to *indicate* things but to *represent* them" (p. 37). Symbols can be used to think about things in their absence. Words remind us of things and can excite feelings and emotions from past experience.

For Langer (1951), meaning is not merely the reference a term makes to that for which it stands. For instance, the meaning of a dog is not merely a furry, four-legged animal that barks and chases cars. The meaning of the term *dog*, for instance, changes based on its context in each sentence and in the minds of the persons interpreting the sentence. Thus, meaning is the product of abstraction, of thought.

Regardless of its degree of abstraction, the meaning of each word is tested by its ability to make accurate statements about reality:

> This means that as many propositions as possible shall be applicable to observable fact. The systems of thought that seem to us to represent "knowledge" are those which were designed as hypotheses, i.e. designed with reference to experience and intended to meet certain tests: At definite points their implications must yield propositions which express discoverable facts. (Langer, 1951, p. 231)

In this way, Langer concluded that "language is the only means of articulating thought" (p. 81).

She demonstrated how the referential theory of language is the foundation of thought, analysis, and debates about the nature of our physical and social realities. Thus, the study of language is inseparable from problems of epistemology. No matter how abstract terms become, they are to be held accountable for their ability to accurately define and evaluate the objects of thought and analysis. For instance, apple is not very abstract. We can point to one or several of them and easily distinguish them from other kinds of fruits and vegetables. But, if we consider terms such as *freedom, democracy, wealth,* and *joy,* we are dealing with a much higher level of abstraction. We cannot easily point to single, defining examples of each.

Reality serves as the standard or measure against which the accuracy and insightfulness of ideas is tested. Cassirer (1946) reasoned the following:

> Before the intellectual work of conceiving and understanding of phenomena can set in, the work of naming must have preceded it, and have reached a certain point of elaboration. For it is this process which transforms the world of sense impression . . . into a mental world, a world of ideas and meanings. (p. 28)

Naming consists of focusing on key attributes. But naming reality involves more than making a mere copy of it.

In addition to naming the objects, situations, feelings, and events of our physical and social reality, the intellect is capable of evaluation (Cassirer, 1953). His epistemology assumed that pure cognition can translate particulars that exist in nature into universal laws. Individual objects and sensations of reality become joined into categories through the processes of naming and evaluation. Language, Cassirer contended, allows humans to "progress from the world of mere sensation to the world of intuition and ideas" (p. 88). As did Langer, Cassirer believed that language helps us move our thoughts from the concrete representation of things to abstractions about them.

Langer (1951) reasoned that people have an innate desire to make abstract comments about their experiences. This is the essence of rationality. Abstraction is the process of leaving out details about an object, event, or situation. Whether merely a name for a thing or the expression of a more complex and abstract thought, a word is not in a purely one-to-one relationship to things. Words make statements about things and suggest or highlight their properties. Words show the place of things in the culture of those people who use the language being used for the thought. Human brains form ideas. They take in external stimuli that they translate into ideas through language.

With arguments and analyses of this kind, many theorists contributed to our understanding of language and meaning. The essence of this discussion was the referential relationship between words and the perceptions about the physical realm of human existence.

This view of language continues to shed light onto the mystery of meaning. What view of language dominates communication theory? Reflecting on that question, Stewart (1972) concluded, "Speech scholars view language as fundamentally a system of symbols, and meaning as a matter of symbols representing or naming objects, ideas, or behavioral responses" (p. 124). Although no recent survey of texts and articles has updated this finding, referentialism probably enjoys less popularity today because of its limited ability to explain the nature of meaning.

Referential theory is provocative and helps explain how words allow people to communicate. It addresses the difficulty and virtue of achieving accurate references. These theorists want to know how well people use words for naming, abstracting, and sharing meaning. They seek to help people communicate more clearly and accurately.

Referential theory seems intuitively valid for many reasons. But, as critics of this theory contend, it is too simplistic to completely explain how words have meaning that allows people to understand and communicate about reality. Making this point, Cherry (1978) observed that most words do not have a direct relationship to things. To prove his point, he offered terms such as *democracy, freedom, tyranny,* and *happiness.* Even terms that refer to things, he argued, denote categories of things that often ignore many differences of individual things in those categories. Although apples and dogs have certain similarities, there are many species of apples and breeds of dogs. Even apples of a specie or dogs of a breed are different. Extending this analysis, Stewart (1972) observed, "Neither 'abstract' terms like 'democracy' or 'semantics' nor exclamatory utterances appear to stand for or name something else" (p. 126). Articles, such as *a, an,* or *the,* and prepositions are problematic. What is the referent for terms such as *of, in,* or *about?*

Cherry doubted that referential theory can help people use words more precisely. He was aware of the suggestion by the semanticists that one-word/one-thing relationships eliminate ambiguity. Without doubt, if every thing, every feeling, and every experience had its own name, precision could be increased. Cherry added the following:

> Language cannot give precise representation of things or ideas because there are simply not enough different words to express the subtlety of every shade of thought. If we had words for everything, their numbers would be astronomically large and beyond our powers of memory or our skill to use them. (p. 71)

Burke (1969a) added to this criticism by charging that semanticists' advice to focus on specific cases "leaves us with a world of individuals" (p. 251). Once we resort to abstraction to compensate for the impossibility of naming every thing, we move away from the optimal one-word/one-thing standard.

Referential theory explains that meaning results when a word becomes associated with the concept of some phenomenon, a spider for example. Note, however, that an expert on spiders might have a different view of them than would a lay person. Even a moment of thought can suggest that meaning depends on what words impose on reality. For instance, in a delivery room, once the doctor announces "It's a girl!" or "It's a boy!," a lot can be imagined about the different social experiences and customs the baby will enjoy or suffer as he or she grows in a culture that has different meanings for what it means to be a boy or a girl. The terms *boy* and *girl* are not merely descriptive. Men and women are treated according to the mores of each culture; these mores are embedded in the language of that culture, a theme explored extensively by linguistic relativists.

LINGUISTIC RELATIVITY

Instead of assuming that words take their meaning from the things to which they refer, what if we argue the opposite, that the meaning of things reflects the content of the words assigned to them? This line of reasoning concludes that, as people encounter reality, they use that experience to define a term such as *hot,* but they also use words to define reality, whether specific things such as "girl" or "boy" or abstractions, such as democracy. Each word, each idiom imposes a unique view on reality, both physical and social. This conclusion is the heart of linguistic relativism. This section discusses that theory and contrasts it to referential theory.

The central theme of linguistic relativism is that people impose meaning on social and physical reality because each language—each idiom—expresses a different world view. Therefore, reality cannot serve as an infallible test of the validity of propositions because it is perceived through shadings unique to each idiom. For instance, in this culture, a cow is a domesticated bovine of the genus *bovinus*, a kind of livestock that is raised for food. The fate of most cattle is to end up on the butcher block. That view of cattle is embedded in perspectives carried in the American language. Hindus have a different view of cow. They see cattle as a temporary home for the spirit of another human being. To kill a cow, accordingly, is to disturb that spirit. Thus, a cow is whatever each linguistic culture says it is.

Languages are not neutral. They cannot be free from ideology. Ideologies influence perceptions. Each ideology contains one preferred version of physical and social reality. Each ideology prescribes a view of what people see, as well as how they define and evaluate it. Thus, for instance, socialism views labor and workers differently than does the kind of capitalism championed by ruthless robber barons of the past century, who had little regard for the health and well-being of employees.

As an expression of culture, words contain stereotypes that are imposed on reality and through which perceptions are filtered. One of the best expressions of this view was made by Sapir, who observed the following:

> Human beings do not live in the objective world alone, not alone in the world of social activity as ordinarily understood, but are very much at the mercy of the particular language which has become the medium of expression for their society. We see and hear and otherwise experience very largely as we do because the language habits of our community predispose certain choices of interpretation. (quoted by Whorf, 1956, p. 134)

The principle contained in that statement forms a cornerstone for linguistic relativity.

In a similar vein, Whorf (1956) argued that how people name a situation will affect their behavior in that situation. He made this discovery while working for an insurance company. He noted that employees' perceptions of what causes fires had a hypnotic effect on their views of fire prevention in their working environment. He observed how the term gasoline drums caused people to act with more care than they did in the presence of what they considered to be empty gasoline drums. They disregarded (or were unaware) of the fact that empty drums often give off combustible vapors. The formula contained in this view of language is this: "The situation is named in one pattern and the name is then 'acted out' or 'lived up to' in another, this being a general formula for the linguistic conditioning of behavior." He pointed to an instance where a substance that seemed nonflammable, limestone, had its chemical properties altered so that it was combustible. (When limestone is exposed to acetic acid, it becomes calcium acetate, which becomes acetone when heated. Acetone is extremely flammable.) But the employees took no caution around the limestone until a fire occurred.

Alert to how perception is tied to vocabulary, Whorf and Sapir found that the structure of each language gives its users a unique view of reality. To illustrate his point, Whorf compared how Standard Average European (SAE) language and the Hopi (native American tribe in Southwestern United States) language each expressed quantities. Whereas SAE might say "a glass of water" the Hopi would say "water." Standard Average European language might request a "piece of meat" but the Hopi would merely ask for "meat." The notion of modifying collective nouns, such as *water* or *meat,* is not vital to the Hopi way of thinking and therefore not part of their language. Rather than thinking of "a hot summer day," the Hopi would make no such distinction because summer is the hot time, so the day should be hot. Another example of cultural differences is observed by noting that West Africans who speak Ewe use the same word for "yesterday" and "tomorrow." Those words mean "not now."

At this point, the referential theorists might claim that just because people do not carefully use thought and words to accurately describe physical or social reality does not cast doubt on the referential theory of meaning. Indeed, such imprecision could fuel the efforts of referential theorists to help people use language more clearly. But relativists make the point that people think and act toward the world around them and toward one another because of perspectives and biases built into the vocabulary they use. Such biases are unavoidable. Reality is sufficiently ambiguous that no one can truly be sure that he or she accurately understands it. Relativists are willing to acknowledge that because words shape perception, thought and observation can never be free of biases built into each idiom. Each idiom is never free from underlying ideologies and other frames of reference.

For this reason, relativists view language as a conventionalized symbol system. Each vocabulary is a collective property created by a group of people to enable their communication. The meaning of each word is nothing more or less than what the people who use it believe it to mean. As Deetz (1973) concluded, people participate in human interaction by taking on "an already meaningful language through immersion in the stream of heritage" (p. 48). Your language was here when you entered the world. You adopted the idiom of your parents and friends as a conventional and functional means for communicating. As you took on that language, you accepted certain perspectives—values, beliefs, attitudes, ideologies and such. Thus, for instance, if you were raised in a Democratic family, your view of politics is different than if you took on a Republican vocabulary.

As Cherry (1978) said, "Words are signs which have significance by convention, and those people who do not adopt the conventions simply fail to communicate" (p. 69). Each language expresses a culture. As Cherry reasoned,

> a text, when translated from one language into another, may lose or change a great deal of its emotive force. When I read French I need to become a different person, with different thoughts; the language change bears with it a change of national character and temperament, a different history and literature. (p. 72)

For Cherry, "The language of a people largely constrains their thoughts. Its words, concepts, and syntax, out of all the signs people use, are the most important determinant of what they are *free* and *able* to think" (p. 73). According to this view, a translator's dictionary and grammar book may aid a person's efforts to understand a document written in a foreign language, but may not comprehend the ideas of the document if he or she was not reared in that culture.

Symbolic interactionism offers some of the rationale for linguistic relativism. "Symbolic interactionists, among others, believe things have no meaning apart from our interaction with others" (Knapp et al., 1994, p. 15).

To explain the process by which words become conventionalized, Mead (1934) used the principles of symbolic interaction to expand the principles of stimulus and response. The result is one of the richest, most important communication paradigms. The foundation of Mead's model is a gesture made by a "sender," an interpretation of the gesture by the "receiver," and the subsequent development of a shared meaning or interpretation of what that gesture meant. In this way, people come to know the meaning of terms through interaction; meaning is a shared response to each term, which has achieved the status of a significant symbol, the meaning of which is shared by many people.

This theory offers a different rationale for how people come to share meaning than does the referential theory. Recall the story used earlier to describe how a child might learn the word *hot* because it is associated with a stove. The important point is not that the word and the thing become associated, but that the child realizes that in this society that a sensation of pain is associated with the word *hot*. The word is not only important because it can describe a sensation, but also because it can be used to interact (conduct conversations with others). In this way, taking on terms and their meaning allows us to "play" the game of communication that is unique to our culture and society.

To illustrate the basic point of symbolic interaction, Mead noted that communication begins with one entity making a verbal or nonverbal gesture to another. One dog growls at another. The second dog (receiver or interactant) interprets this growl and, henceforth, both dogs have a shared meaning of what that growl means. Similarly, one person may shake a fist in the face of another. Likewise, a vocalization becomes conventionalized as soon as both parties share a meaning for a symbol. As Mead (1934) reasoned, once a "gesture means the idea behind it and it arouses that idea in the other individual, then we have a significant symbol" (p. 43).

Once a symbol becomes meaningful for both partners in a conversation, it is language. In this manner, meaning is conventionalized through symbolic interaction. Meaning is the impact the words have on the communication partners as they engage with one another. This line of analysis has been refined by writers who feature a convergence theory of meaning. Such discussions argue that shared meaning is produced when people publicly share their thoughts and experiences (externalize) as they comment about the experiences and objects they have encountered (Bormann, 1983; E. M. Rogers & Kincaid, 1981). This process leads to shared reality (social reality) that exists in the minds and language of a group of people who use their vocabulary to capture that shared experience.

Simply stated, words are meaningful for humans because they know what the words mean for them. This dynamic and organic view argues that words are not static, nor are meanings easily prescribed. Meaning is the product of interaction—action and reaction. In contrast to those who stress the referential relationship between words and things, Mead (1934) reasoned that

> the meaning of any object depends upon the relation of an organism or group of organisms to it. It is not essentially or primarily a psychical content (a content of mind or consciousness), for it need not be conscious at all, and is not in fact until significant symbols are evolved in the process of human social experience. Only when it becomes identified with such symbols does meaning become conscious. (pp. 80–81)

Meaning is dynamic because what a gesture means to one person is the interpretation and response another person makes to it. The response of the second person is directed toward or related to the completion of that act.

Many of the themes of linguistic relativism were reinforced or amplified by Burke, who produced one of the most complete theories of language created in this century (Heath, 1986). His theory features the concept of dramatism, a model of interaction that views people as actors in a drama; all people act with one another through words. This theme is similar to Mead's contention that meaning is created through symbolic interaction.

Challenging the logic of referential theory, Burke (1966) reversed the basic equation by concluding that, at least to some extent, "things are the signs of words" (p. 363). To justify that point of view, Burke (1966) argued that vocabularies express perspectives. For this reason, he observed, "there will be as many different worldviews in history as there are people" (p. 52). Words, perceptions, and actions are intertwined. Consequently, each person shares perceptions and incentives typical of all other people who use a particular language, with its unique perspectives. Not only do we get a sense of physical and social realities through language, but we also acquire an understanding of the expectations of what constitutes social competence—how to act. "The human animal, as we know it, *emerges into personality* by first mastering whatever tribal speech happens to be its particular symbolic environment" (Burke, 1966, p. 53).

Burke (1966) demonstrated the difference between words and things by reminding us "how easy it is to turn the word 'tree' into 'five thousand trees,' and how different would be the processes required for the similar multiplication of an actual tree" (p. 480). By making this point, however, he does not contend that the universe is nothing more than a figment of our imagination or interpretations. People's characterizations of reality cannot vary completely from "fact" without experiencing a sense of recalcitrance (Burke, 1965). For instance, a stone cannot be made edible by calling it a potato. Thus, "the *thing* tree is not a *word*" (1966, p. 481). Likewise, "*words are mere words*. Nothing could be farther from 'food,' for instance, than a mere word for it" (Burke, 1952, p. 61). We can't eat the word *lunch*.

Words shape people's perceptions of reality, Burke (1964) said, because people "see" through "terministic screens." Words constitute "a kind of photographic 'screen' which will 'let through' some perceptions and 'filter out' others" (p. 105). He was alerted to this phenomenon—which he called *terministic screens*—when he observed how photographs of the same subject matter appeared different when they were taken with different colored lens. Each color of lens produced a different view of the subject matter (Burke, 1966).

A quick illustration shows how terms constitute terministic screens. Think how your view of an adult human female changes if she is called *girl, woman,* or *lady*. In this way, our method for examining the physical and social objects and situations in the world around us *"reveals only such reality as is capable of being revealed by this particular kind of terminology"* (Burke, 1969a, p. 313). This is the case because our instruments for knowing are nothing but structures of terms and therefore manifest the nature of terms (Burke, 1969a). For this reason, people are separated from their natural condition by language, an instrument of their own making (Burke, 1966). This analysis suggests that words join us with wordless nature, while at the same time mediating between us and it (Burke, 1961).

Burke (1966) realized how difficult it is to use our observations of reality to verify the truthfulness of our statements. Problems of verifying truth arise because our conclusions imply *"the particular terminology in terms of which the observations are made"* (p. 46). Because ideologies are imposed through words, our universe appears to be "something like a cheese." People slice it in an infinite number of ways. After each person chooses his or her own pattern of slicing, other people's "cuts fall at the wrong places" (Burke, 1965, pp. 102–103). He cast doubt on the veracity of the referential approach to language when he illustrated how similar events, objects, acts, or feelings appear different when named differently. Thus, Burke noted how "we call *obstinacy* in an enemy what we call *perseverance* in ourselves—or we call another man's frankness 'incaution' and label as 'caution' our own *lack* of frankness" (p. 109). Burke (1952) cautioned, "The last way on earth to transcend the deceptions of *words* is by a mere 'tough-minded' beginning with 'things'" (pp. 62–63). Sheer nonsense can arise if we lose sight of the need to make words correspond to reality as much as possible, but views of reality can never be free from the shadings imposed by idioms.

For this reason, Burke (1958) concluded that people are vocabulary. To manipulate their vocabulary is to manipulate them. Language is "the basic instrument by which social relationships are managed." For this reason, "if there is an 'organic flaw' in the nature of language, we may well expect to find this organic flaw revealing itself through the texture of society" (Burke, 1934, p. 330). Aware that perspectives, and therefore ideologies, are based on language and that flaws in thinking can result, he felt the need to discuss language to help correct the social evils he witnessed. He knew that false and worthwhile ideas can be passed from one generation to the next because language is useful for "inventing, perfecting, and handing-on instruments and methods" (Burke, 1965, p. 276).

Based on his theory of language, Burke (1969b) developed a theory of rhetoric that proposes that, if people identify with one another, they will think and act in similar ways. This theory offers support for believing that language is vital to persons' efforts to share social reality and to be competent in interpersonal activities. Identification is possible because people attempt to minimize their differences by seeing (naming) themselves as similar and sharing views that allow them to act in concert. For this reason, we tend to think that college students identify with one another and act as they do because they "are college students." Why do they go on crazy (or socially responsible) spring breaks? Because they share identities by viewing themselves in similar ways, people are able to persuade one another by ingratiation, by talking each other's language, and by sharing the same speech, gesture, tonality, order, image, attitude, and idea. Identification assists interpersonal interaction because people can enact the perspectives embedded in the idioms they share with others.

Burke's theory is particularly instructive for understanding interpersonal role behavior. Many actions and opinions are implied in terms such as *farmer, laborer, banker, father, mother, teacher,* or *terrorist.* Each term suggests behavioral patterns that prescribe what interaction patterns and beliefs are expected of the persons who hold those titles. These terms play a powerful part in interpersonal attribution. Individuals attempt to understand one another—to reduce uncertainty—by attributing motives to one another. Attribution is predicated on the implications and expectations that are embedded in the terms they use to describe one another. Burke's theory of language helps explain, as does the work by other linguistic relativists, how people make attributions about one another, and why those attributions can be false.

Linguistic relativity reasons that words can serve as propositions. In this sense, they are powerful prescriptions for the roles people play. The term *teacher* is a proposition that those persons who are teachers are expected to teach. Fire and emergency response personnel are expected to fulfill that proposition—fight fire and save lives. In addition to occupations, words hold propositional value for people. "Boys will be boys" is an adage that suggests that boys' behavior is prescribed (and perhaps excused) because they are boys. Similarly children defend their bad behavior by saying, "But I am only a child." *Man, women, child, adult,* and *teenager* are propositional terms. Terms relevant to race, religion, and national origin are propositional. These terms—for good and bad outcomes— guide persons' actions and influence their perceptions of one another. These idioms—sometimes compatible and sometimes at odds with one another—are vital forces that must be acknowledged and negotiated through interaction.

Linguistic relativity argues that, because people tend to live in a world based on shared views of reality, they are wise to wonder what other people use words to mean. However, the choice is not between referentialism or linguistic relativism. Both theories contribute to our understanding of language and meaning. Both have a degree of validity. Words for tangible objects or experiences, such as *bumble bee* or *bee sting,* take on some degree of meaning because of experiences people have with the object or experience. In this way, reality helps people to define terms. But even more importantly, words are conventionalized through social interaction. Meaning is an expression of the ideology and unique world views of the people who create and live that particular language through social interaction.

Linguistic relativism is particularly helpful in explaining the power of language in many contexts. Interpersonally, individuals characterize one another and attribute motives and personality characteristics, in part through applications of prototypes and stereotypes. These are terministic screens people carry that allow them to "know" one another. Internally and externally, organizations create images of themselves and the products and services they provide.

Preferring the relativistic over the referential theory of language, Eisenberg (1984) argued that strategic ambiguity is a reasonable, useful, and normative approach to language used by members of organizations. He believed that it is too much to expect all people in each organization to have the same meaning for terms by expecting or requiring them to have the same experiences. People throughout an organization have quite different experiences. Strategic ambiguity promotes unified diversity, enough consensus for the organization, through its members, to operate successfully, but not so much as to be stifling.

This is not only true for companies, but also for organizations such as churches and educational systems. Each offers different terministic screens based on the words used and their conventionalized meanings. News broadcasts contain perspectives; one year's enemies are next year's allies. Conservative talk show hosts see and report a world where conservatives are good and liberals are bad. Liberal talk show hosts take on the opposite perspectives. Each is a representative advocate for a different ideological and terministic view of the world. Each language of politics, as does each "foreign" language, carries its unique view of reality.

A CONSTITUTIVE VIEW OF LANGUAGE IN INTERPERSONAL INTERACTION

Given what you now know about language, can you explain how people read or interpret each other's comments and thereby know how to participate in communication episodes? If a friend enters your room and says, "What are you doing?," how do you know what that statement means? Imagine for a moment at least five meanings that question might have. Which is the meaning your friend had in mind, if he or she had a meaning in mind? Would the statement be different if it were uttered by a parent or by someone you don't like.

What options do you have to form your answer? You have to interpret what the other person means so that you can respond to the statement. Referential theorists cannot answer this question, nor can the linguistic relativists. What does "I love you" mean? Or "The boss is really angry"? Or "You play the game my way or you'll be looking for a new game to play"? The point that you should realize is that many comments do not refer to any "thing" at all. People use conventionalized, even scripted statements that they understand because they have learned the codes of their society, but how do they know what each statement means at a particular moment?

Questions such as these force us to consider factors more complex than the mere meaning of isolated words and sentences. We have to address the variable of relationship quality and see meaning as something that is codefined and negotiated through interaction. Planalp (1989) offered this challenging guideline for the study of language, social cognition, and interpersonal interaction:

> To study relationships from a social cognitive perspective means to study the representation and utilization of relational knowledge. That is, one is concerned with what people know about relationships, how they come to know it, how they use their knowledge, and how it changes in response to changing events. (p. 270)

Planalp offered three premises to guide the investigation of language, relationships, and meaning. First, rather than the product of passive reception, knowledge of the physical and social worlds entails processes of getting, analyzing, and sharing information. Second, through interaction, people create structured and interrelated bodies of knowledge through cognitive devices such as "schemas, scripts, story grammars, frames, prototypes, and implicit theories" (p. 270). Third, the knowledge people have guides their interpretations of what is said and done during interaction. These interpretations are used to alter their knowledge and the processes of interaction. These processes of modification and adaptation are ongoing and ever changing.

Given the limits of referentialism and linguistic relativity, we need to explain the processes by which meaning is negotiated and codefined during interaction. During interaction, communication partners set limits on what each other can do and say, as well as how what occurs can be interpreted. The desire to create relationships influences which meanings emerge during interaction.

The remainder of this chapter addresses these issues. To do so requires consideration of four theories: constructivism, coordinated management of meaning, ordinary language philosophy, and the inferential/strategic perspective, which is fundamental to discourse analysis. A central purpose of this section is to explain the principles of discourse or conversation analysis.

Constructivism

Partial explanation of how meaning develops through interaction can be found in the work of constructivists, such as Delia et al. (1982). They argued that people can interact with one another because they have the ability to segment experience into meaningful units so that thought and action can be structured and controlled. People are born into a world that is defined by ongoing cultural processes of social organization and interpretation. Interpretive processes develop through interaction with other people who share this social world. For this reason, constructivists contend, culture is (a) an evolving social organization, (b) a conception of reality, and (c) a complex of symbols employed by persons who encounter one another. (Note: This concept of culture is a comfortable application of the theory of linguistic relativity.)

In this way, people create interpretive systems through communication in order to adapt to their social world. Once they acquire these interpretative frameworks, their "action is guided by context-relevant interactions and beliefs produced by schemes of interpretation" (Delia et al., 1982, p. 155). Interaction, therefore, is "a process in which persons coordinate their behavior through the application of shared interpretive schemes; it is a process of implicit negotiation in which strategic choices reflect the emerging consensus about the reality that participants share" (p. 159).

To know the meaning of statements such as "I love you" or "What are you up to?," people employ a set of interaction-interpretation rules that may be complex or simple, depending on the case. One response to this quandary could be merely to ask the other person, "What do you mean by that?" Indeed, that response is possible; however, people often are less direct. Can they trust the answer they receive? How do they reduce uncertainty while showing their own communication competence? One answer to those questions is that people know how to coordinate the management of meaning.

Coordinated Management of Meaning

Coordinated management of meaning theory begins with the proposition, similar to symbolic interaction, that communication enables people to "cocreate, maintain, and alter social order, personal relationships, and individual identities" (Cronen et al., 1982, p. 64). Treating communication as more than a vehicle for conveying thought, this theory views it as "the process of creating the perspectives that give rise to ideas and facts. Communication is not simply one of many things that persons do in relationships; it is the process of maintaining and creating relationships" (p. 65).

During this process, W. B. Pearce and Cronen (1980) noted, people interact with one another in a manner similar to the actions of characters in a play, but unlike a theater production, life is "an undirected play" (p. 120). People learn some scripts from their parents and peers. They learn to say "hello" when answering the phone and "thank you" when receiving a gift. But often, the play of life has no script, and we, the actors, must improvise. This theory postulates that people coordinate activities by managing the ways their messages have meaning for one another because each person knows rule-based interaction patterns.

Burke and other linguistic relativists might explain this process by featuring the terms by which people characterize themselves and thereby give motive to their actions: Terms are propositions. For instance, if a person thinks of herself as mother and the interactant as child, the scripts chosen are motivated by the role-based definitions of mother and child. Coordinated management of meaning depends on interaction rules, message content, and the structure of various kinds of interaction. In this view, communication is "a process in which each person interprets and responds to the acts of another, monitors the sequence, and compares it to his or her desires and expectations" (W. B. Pearce & Cronen, 1980, p. 68). Coordination of what goes on during any communication episode does not require that the participants share mutual understanding. They can coordinate communication episodes even though they assign different meanings to key messages, but without coordinated management of meaning, communication cannot transpire.

To be able to join in meaningful conversation, the actions of each person must be meaningful to their communication partners. All that people can ever know of one another during interaction is what they see and hear; they know one another only by experiencing each other's behavior. In this context, messages produce meaning at two levels: content and relationship (Watzlawick, Beavin, & Jackson, 1967). Meaning occurs because of interpretations each person assigns to the other's actions and statements in the context of the relationship. Thus, "I love you" is interpreted differently if the relationship is romantic rather than platonic. Through these kinds of meanings, people not only interpret one another but also regulate their relationships. One person might want a friendship, whereas the other seeks to be more romantic. The meanings of what they say and do will be shaped by and interpreted according to these goals—and their perception and acceptance of each other's goals.

People interpret messages and know what actions constitute appropriate responses because they can follow rules that guide what they do and say (regulative rules) and how they interpret what transpires (constitutive rules). Rules help individuals to know what behavior is appropriate and likely to be productive (regulative), and what the behavior of others means (constitutive).

W. B. Pearce and Cronen (1980) thought people are able to employ complex, multileveled systems of rules to guide their action and cocreate meaning. These rules help people to understand (constitutive) what others' actions mean and to know how to respond (regulative). To accomplish their communication outcomes, people must be able to interpret what their senses perceive as information and translate this information into actions. To achieve this interpretation, people create theories to explain when their actions are correct.

How do people know how to create these theories of action and interpretation? They learn behaviors that are appropriate to many situations. When they find themselves in those situations, they rely on an interpretative process that consists of six levels: content, speech acts, contracts, episodes, life scripts, and archetypes.

Content consists of "referential cognitive processes by which individuals organize and interpret the world as it is ultimately perceived" (Pearce & Cronen, 1980, p. 130). According to G. Kelley (1955), human behavior is influenced by the perceptual process of each individual, which intervenes between that person and his or her physical and social realities. These perceptions are filtered through the interpretative process that explains the experience. Content consists of the meaning the parties of a conversation assign (cocreate) to what they and their partners say and do. Content can be thought of as the residue of the interaction experience: what people remember of each interaction.

The second level is speech acts. These are what each person does or says (Pearce & Cronen, 1980). This notion is drawn from the ordinary language philosophy of Austin (1962) and Searle (1969, 1976), who argued that the meaning of each speech act is the impact its perceived intent has on communication partners. The question "When are you going to wash the car?" can be interpreted in many ways. Its meaning in a particular conversation consists of the impact it has on the person who receives it. It can be meant (and interpreted) merely as a question used to seek information, or it can be intended (and interpreted) to motivate the receiver to get busy with soap and water. Speech acts include threats, promises, efforts to inform, suggestions, advice, insults, compliments, and such. Each of these speech acts has a set of rules that governs what it means and how it should be executed (Searle, 1969). Rules that are relevant to each kind of speech act regulate social interaction (W. B. Pearce & Cronen, 1980). The meaning of any speech act is a combination of what the interactants thought its content was and what it implied for the relationship.

The third level is contracts, which range from formal agreements (such as legal contracts) to informal social arrangements. People engaged in conversation have a repertoire of contracts (regulative rules) that can be applied. For instance, the repertoire of rules available in an argument can be used to make the argument worse or to lessen the friction. A vital part of any interaction is each participant's recognition of the relevant contracts as well as a willingness and ability to abide by them. Interactants can reward or sanction one another for their selection and willingness to follow a contract. For instance, contracts, as well as rewards and sanctions, are captured in statements such as these: "I like it when you compliment me."; "You are not fighting fair; you told me you would not bring up that issue again."

Episodes, the next level, are definable, recurring communication events, such as having coffee, interviewing for a job, making a date, or planning a family outing. Each episode implies one or more sets of contracts that can be used to guide participants through the event. The conventionalized nature of episodes gives participants the opportunity to know the meaning of specific events within an episode. A greeting at the beginning of a job interview can give participants an idea of what kind of person each other is (as well as perspectives of the self—"I think the person will believe I am a strong person because I shake hands firmly and comment on what a forward-thinking company this is"). Comments at the beginning of an interview serve quite different purposes than do those at the end. The definition the parties hold of the interview, as an episode, will help them interpret what their behavior and the other participant's behavior means. Is a willingness to emphasize your achievements a display of confidence or bragging? Is hesitance to answer questions a sign of deception, falsification, insecurity, or a strong desire to be precise, accurate, and modest when making an important comment? Continuing their metaphor of life as an undirected play, Pearce and Cronen (1980) observed, "The repertoire of episodes known by a particular communicator is analogous to the snatches of scripts known by actors in the undirected play" (p. 136). Participants know which of their communication repertoire to use as they seek to coordinate efforts with each other based on the nature of each episode. You have probably experienced the situation, for instance, of saying something about a person who unexpectedly walks up. You probably switch conversational gears and use statements designed to camouflage the meaning of the statements you were making.

Life scripts, the fifth level, refer to statement options each communicator believes fits his or her self-perception at a particular moment. Life scripts are patterned, repeated series of statements that are used routinely and repeatedly as people engage in each kind of episode. W. B. Pearce and Cronen avoided the term self-concept, which they considered a static concept. They "prefer to think of the self simply as that cluster of episodes defined by the person as those in which s/he does or might participate" (p. 137). A life script is, for example, that set of comments typical of any married couple's routine conversations. Parents and children play out life scripts throughout each day. "Don't go out . . ."; "Be sure to. . ."; "Can I . . . just this once?"; "You don't really understand me." Most of these comments probably sound familiar to you. Note also that we often are not actually interested in the extent to which comments such as these refer to reality. Such statements are not designed to define physical reality. They are used to achieve social purposes within communication episodes. Their meaning is the impact they have on the participants in the episode given the nature of the relationship.

The final level in this hierarchy is archetype, which offers a fundamental logic that interactants can use to frame or define experience. Archetypes are the large organizing patterns of behavior that are so universal to human experience that each culture, no matter how different in other ways, will address these experiences. Every culture has some way of defining and acting meaningfully toward birth, death, pain, agony, leave taking, reunions, marriage, and so on.

These six levels of interaction and the meaning options that accompany them help researchers focus on which kinds of cues and rules interactants use at a particular moment as they negotiate the protocols of interpersonal interaction. This analysis uses the rules of interaction to explain the logics of discourse by which people know how to act and interact. People negotiate and conventionalize communication interactions. As Eisenberg (1986) concluded, "Through communication, individuals over time create, maintain, and transform the social realities they inhabit" (p. 89).

Ordinary Language Philosophy

As does coordinated management of meaning, other action-oriented approaches to the formation of meaning during interpersonal communication draw their rationale from ordinary language philosophy. Whereas other language theories focus on cultural meanings or the relationship between word and reference or referent, speech act theory focuses on the performance of interpersonal relationships through a series of language acts (Austin, 1962, 1964; Searle, 1969).

This theory reasons that meaning is inseparable from the intention people have for making statements. As we interpret the statements our interactional partners make, we focus on the purpose behind the statement. For instance, the sentence, "I love you," can be interpreted in many ways. Each depends on the purpose for which the statement is made. To communicate successfully, each of us needs to telegraph our intentions to our interactional partners. Just as important is the ability of the partners to seek insights into our purpose as they interpret the meaning of what we do and say.

Categorizing statements by what they do (the role they play in interaction), ordinary language philosophy features four kinds of statements.

- The simplest statement, an utterance, is the articulation of sounds, perhaps the vocalization of a single word, such as the greeting, "Hi!"
- A proposition, or locution, states a reference, such as "Houston is approximately 250 miles south of Dallas."
- An illocution is intended to elicit a cognitive or behavioral response because of the way it is framed; for instance one person might say to another, "That sunset is too beautiful for us to pass up." This statement invites a response such as "Let's go for a walk."
- A perlocution is designed to have some consequential effect on the feelings, thoughts, or behavior of the receiver. The sender may state "Please pass the salt" or "No Trespassing." The message leaves no doubt regarding the appropriate response because the purpose for making the statement is obvious, even explicit.

Discerning between each of the latter three types of statements probably requires more cues than those embedded in the sentences themselves. For this reason, interactants often turn to the nature of the episode, along with its typical life scripts and relevant contracts and archetypes, as well as nonverbal cues to determine the content of the exchange.

Messages exchanged between individuals often have the same referential power but differ in terms of what the words mean for each relationship. For instance, directives, a type of illocutionary act, can have at least four effects during negotiation. They can convey levels of politeness, provide relational messages, define participant rights and obligations in dealing with the directive, and indicate the significance of the information requested (Donohue & Diez, 1985).

People may attribute purpose to others by their choice of words and phrases. Some language forms convey powerfulness and others express powerlessness. Kinds of expression often associated with powerlessness include hedges ("I sorta finished my homework"), unnecessary intensifiers ("I'm a good kid"), or tags ("My painting is good, isn't it").

Whether such statements are interpreted as being powerful or powerless depends on the perceived purpose behind the statement, the context in which it is made, and the paralanguage (vocal inflection that accompanies the statement) with which it is delivered. During conversations, people are able to distinguish between powerful and powerless statements. The criteria by which these distinctions are made are quite stable. What could appear as a powerless statement may be spoken in ways to be powerful (Bradac & Mulac, 1984).

Action-oriented theory of meaning argues that meaning is more than a reference to a referent or word (or other symbol). This theory contends that meaning is at least partially unique to each communication interaction, but not so unique that two people cannot know what meaning to assign to the interaction. Meaning is created each moment throughout each interaction. It is not necessarily testable by checking statements against reality, but by seeing their impact on participants. Marriage vows, "I do," or "I pronounce you man and wife," are not referential, but they give meaning to our lives, and help us to know what we need to do and say to be socially competent (Stewart, 1972).

This theory is full of promise. Intuitive and scientific evidence justifies its conclusions. For instance, Bell, Buerkel-Rothfuss, and Core (1987) studied how couples use private idioms in their interpersonal conversation to gain insight into the quality of such relationships. They examined idioms that couples used during confrontation to express affection and for labeling outsiders. Results revealed that for both sexes, loving, commitment, and closeness are associated with an increased use of idioms to express affection, initiate sexual encounters, and refer to sexual matters. Context is a factor. In such relationships, references to outsiders are made in public, whereas sexual invitations are usually made in private.

As Brenders (1987) cautioned, any action-oriented theory of meaning (especially the coordinated management of meaning) can overemphasize the idiosyncratic, intrapersonal rules people use to develop meaning during interaction. This error can lead someone who is analyzing others' communication to mistake conventional or routine functions of language with those that are unique and idiosyncratic. For this reason, researchers and people engaging in conversation can confuse semantic (dictionary or conventional) meaning and pragmatic meaning, which depends on interpreting intentions behind statements to understand their meaning. Pragmatic meanings may differ from semantic meanings. As people interact, they strive to balance semantic and pragmatic meanings. This means that they need to determine when conventional meaning is used and when the perceived intention of the speaker should be applied to interpret the meaning of statements. For this reason, purposive and affective dimensions of meanings often can only be interpreted in the context of each unique interaction. Fathoming this kind of problem challenges researchers and each of us as we interact each day.

During interpersonal communication, people select words that they believe will exert influence. To understand these choices, Giles and Wiemann (1987) reasoned, research and theory should achieve three goals:

1. Integrate the symbolic and referential functions of language for our individual, relational, and multiple group identities.
2. Focus on the creative role of majority and minority collectivities in society while recognizing the dynamic nature of language change and evolution.
3. Feature the interface between the ways that language reflects, builds upon, and determines social reality, as well as highlight the dynamic, skeptical, crafty communicative qualities we all share. (pp. 367–368)

This endeavor is necessary because people use language to define reality (cognition) as well as give them means of interaction (constitutive, social cognition). To understand the role language plays during interaction requires that scholars comprehend the principles people use to generate meanings for statements that are predominantly open ended (Jacobs, 1985).

Such choices can guide individual behavior, what a person says during a conversation. Those choices are also vital to the entire community—all of the people in the community engaged in vital dialogue, what happens between people. Does dialogue bring people together, separate them, or allow one to dominate the other (Buber, 1965)?

Addressing that question, Habermas (1984) conceptualized the ideal speech community where individual interests were subsumed to the greater interests of the collectivity. Dialogue in such communities is best when it consists of a rational discussion of the interests of the people in the community. Capturing the essence of this discussion, Gunson and Collins (1997) concluded that "the realization of such a community involves a process whereby there is a movement from what one might call the I or Us of the particular individual or group interest, to the We of the general interest" (p. 277).

Inferential/Strategic Perspective of Discourse Analysis

Undertaking challenges to describe the structure of interactions such as those addressed in the previous section, Jacobs (1994) observed that the concept of discourse allows us to focus on key elements of meaning in interpersonal communication. As he concluded, "Discourse analysis is an effort to close the gap between conceptions of communication process and language structure and function" (p. 199). Discourse analysis can shed insight into meaning by focusing on parts or all of an interaction. Such is used to explain how people create and interpret the meaning that occurs as they interact with one another. This view of meaning acknowledges that "all language users show great facility in finding the ways in which the elements of language 'hang together' and in seeing to it that their own contributions do so. Such impressions are central to the sense of orderliness, meaningfulness, and appropriteness we find in language structure and use" (p. 201).

Discourse analysis rests on the assumption that people learn the system by which discourse (conversation) units fit or weave together into a sequence so that the parts can be interpreted as such, and so that the entire conversation can be meaningful. Each statement in a conversation can have one or several meanings. Statements individually and in a sequence (the entire conversation) become meaningful. "He/she really makes an issue of my being late" or "We compared our spring break stories and she/he had a much better time than I did." These statements suggest that persons can infer meaning from entire conversations or components of conversations.

The key, then, is to understand the message design and interpretation logics in the context of typical interpersonal communication. Because people understand these logics, they can apply them strategically. They know how to open conversations and close them. They know how to introduce, accept, and reject topics during the sequence of statements that constitutes a conversation. They shift topics and return to topics they were discussing earlier. They ignore topics and dwell on them. They know the conversational choices of hundreds of purposive or intentional outcomes: beg, request, whine, complain, advocate, seek information, give information, flirt, reject (or accept) flirtation, gain compliance, and so forth.

Discourse analysis assumes that sometimes a meaning of what one person says will be quite obvious. Even what seems to be obvious, however, might have basic meanings more central to the relationship. For instance, "Stop bothering me" or "Turn down your radio" can be meant and interpreted in direct and literal ways. Often "the message communicated may not be connected in any obvious way to what is directly and literally said" (Jacobs, 1994, p. 203). "Stop bothering me" might be an invitation by person A for person B to pay more attention. Person A actually wants person B to "bother" him or her. "Turn down your radio" can be a code for "because I am your parent and therefore assert control of this parent–child relationship."

To guide discourse analysis, an inferential/strategic perspective can foster the development and scholarly consideration of several hypotheses, as is explained in the following propositions.

1. *"Linguistic communication requires shared principles for inference beyond information given by a 'surface' reading"* (Jacobs, 1994, p. 203). Support for that generalization is derived from careful consideration of statements typical of the illustrations used to introduce this section.
2. *"Linguistic communication requires generative principles"* (Jacobs, 1994, p. 204). Some statements are scripted, for example, routinely used comments that interactional partners know and even predict each other

will use in various circumstances. Statements are so routine that total strangers can weave conversations because they share generative principles. People may initiate conversation with safe topics such as the weather, but over the course of a conversation may discover and talk about political issues on which they agree or disagree.

3. *"Communicative meaning is context determined"* (Jacobs, 1994, p. 205). The meaning of each word is signalled by its use, which is inferred by the decoder based on the context in which it is used. Context has at least three levels. One level is the topic being discussed. The term *big,* for instance, is relative to the context: A big diamond ring is not the same as a big horse or a big debt. A second level is the modifying role each word performs in each individual sentence. The term *big* can modify diamond ring, horse, or debt and it can be modified by very or not very. A third context is the stated purpose the user has for selecting the word or the attributed intention the decoder believes the user has for selecting that word. Do we trust the statements of a car salesperson or a person selling insurance as much as we trust the statements of our parents or a good friend who is expert on those same topics? Does intent for making one statement as opposed to another shape our interpretations of the meaning of what was said?

4. *"Language structures are functional designs"* (Jacobs, 1994, p. 206). Meaning is intended and can be inferred from the structures that are designed to achieve certain functions. The pattern of each statement and the sequence of statements woven together is designed to achieve some function. If persons join in after-work conversation, they may systematically ridicule coworkers and their place of employment. Each message is designed to that functional end. A person who is asking another for a date engages in a sequence of statements that leads to that functional end. A person who is making a complaint, designs statements—individually and collectively—to achieve that functional outcome.

5. *"Language use is multifunctional"* (Jacobs, 1994, p. 207). Item 4 focuses on each word, statement, and sequence of statements that focus on one function. The point made is that those choices and logics are designed to achieve a function. Principle 5 extends that logic to point out that discourse is multifunctional. A conversational partner may agree with another's opinion of a purchase, such as a new car, because he/she wants to demonstrate love for the other, to achieve being loved by the other, to confirm the self-concept of the other as a wise shopper, and to confirm the other person's cognitive decision-making style. That's a lot to do with a sequence of statements. But, any analysis of language meaning in interaction has to be prepared to deal with that level of complexity.

A combination of interaction rules, desired outcomes, and strategically applied message design logics may account for some of the dynamics of conversation. They may explain how conversations grow topically and coherently as people work to solve various problems that are at play during each conversation. Investigating conversational coherence, Planalp, Graham, and Paulson (1987) found that connections between turn taking in conversations are based on cues that one segment of a conversation provides for the next. Using these cues, participants connect their comment to the preceding ones. Syntactic cues result from the use of pronouns, substitutions, ellipses, and conjunctions. For instance, one person might say, "He saw your car there," and the interactant might say, using the pronoun as a cue, "He who?" Pragmatic cues are conversational pairs, such as questions and answers. (In the previous example, the question "He who?" cues a reply, "John.") Lexical cues are based on meaning relations; for instance, the flow of conversation might center on the development of an idea, such as sports or flowers, until one person says something about a related topic prompted by what someone else said. The discussion of sports (including comments on aggressiveness) might lead to comments on aggression in international relations; aggression is the conversational theme cue. Or a discussion of flowers might shift into a discussion of colors cued by a comment about a flower of a particular color. The researchers compared the use of syntactic, pragmatic, and lexical cues in conversations. Only lexical cues were found significantly more often in coherent conversations. This research emphasizes that meaning is vital to conversational coherence, not just syntactics or pragmatics.

Studying this issue, Villaume and Cegala (1988) concluded that people mesh comments during conversation to achieve coherence as a form of collaboration. Cohesive devices explicitly connect comments. Three grammatical cohesive devices are prevalent in conversation: reference devices such as pronouns, indefinite articles, demonstratives, and comparative forms; substitution devices based on the use of counters or marker words (e.g., "Who wants gum?" "I'll have some." *Some* is a marker standing for *gum*.); and ellipsis, a kind of substitution, where a respondent replies without being explicit (e.g., "Is that your book?" "Yeah," implying that is.) A key factor in the flow of conversation is the extent to which each person is sensitive to a conversation's evolution and is able to integrate his or her thoughts, feelings, and behaviors into the flow. In conversation, communicators differ in their use of various communication devices based on their relative certainty that appropriate means are being used to develop conversational topics. If people are highly involved in a conversation, they are more likely to feel certain in their ability to use the appropriate means for interaction. Reference devices are more difficult to execute than are ellipsis and substitution; the former requires that respondents interpret the meanings of their communication partners' statements. Partners may use interactional direction to tie their talk to each other's statements. The degree of involvement in the conversation is a powerful indicator of the kinds of communication tactics persons use. A speech accommodation explanation of this strategy is that a low-involved person interacts with a high-involved person by attempting to adjust to the socially approved and powerful style of the high-involved in an effort to manage impressions and seek social approval; the second explanation for the reaction is uncertainty/certainty differences. Perhaps low-involved persons are uncertain about how to track conversations and take appropriate turns. In this way, interactions are a product of the chemistry between the interactants and each person's communication competencies (their ability to accommodate themselves to others to be seen as socially competent).

The inferential/strategic perspective helps discourse analysts provide explanatory and predictive power for a theory of meaning in interaction. The key to this perspective is its ability to correct and extend the analysis provided by the normative code model of discourse analysis. This normative code model features the code that interactants learn and use to guide their encoding and decoding processes. It reasons that people could not communicate if they did not share a set of codes that guide the design and interpretation of individual and collective statements. If we think of discourse as an undirected play, this code is a set of themes that the actors use as they "ad lib" their individual and conjoined statements.

According to Jacobs (1994), "A code is a system of rules that specifies derivational relations between the elements at various structural levels (thus connecting meanings with public signs, or signals) and combinatorial relations among the elements at any given structural level (thus providing coherent configurations in the arrangement of signs)" (p. 212). A code is a set of rules. It tells conversationalists what they can and cannot (should and should not) say and do at a particular time (syntactic context, conversational context, and relationship context). A code is functional. It indicates the structural options that are available and appropriate if the user of the words, statements, and conversation sequence wants to achieve his or her functional ends.

What then are norms? Jacobs answered, "Norms are stating social expectations known and adhered to by members of a linguistic communication, or internalized dispositions shared by members of that community" (p. 212). Norms are standards of performance than can be rewarded or sanctioned depending on their appropriateness, in the eyes of the interactional partner, at a given time and under the functional circumstances that are guiding the conversational logic. Statements such as "Don't talk to me that way" or "I like the way you talk to me" indicate sanctions and rewards for the normative code selection of the conversational partner.

How does this model operate? According to Jacobs (1994), "Normative code models predict that communication will be successful just in case the receiver employs the same rules to decode the message that the sender employs to encode the message" (p. 212). In this way, interactants co-define and negotiate meaning at the level of words, phrases, sentences, conversational units, and relationship units. The meaning of language is a product of moves and countermoves. The moves initiate conversational directions, and the countermoves affirm or disconfirm those directions. Countermoves can initiate directional shifts (topic shifts).

Extending and correcting the normative code model, the inferential/strategic perspective reasons that people select words, sentences, and conversations as being problem-solving behavior rather than the normative use of codes. As Jacobs observed, this problem-solving activity involves "the assessment of mutual knowledge in the generation of speaker plans and hearer inferences as to the most plausible solution for what that speaker plan might be" (p. 222). A choice might, this perspective argues, violate a norm but be seen as a logical solution to some conversational problem. This analysis brings us to the current status in discourse analysis:

> Expression and interpretation are not matters of encoding and decoding meaning by determinate rules applied to signals, and language choice is not something dictated by normative regulations. In place of this model has emerged a view of linguistic communication as a process of strategic design and constructive inference. Messages are located in the interplay of text and context. Rather than a process mechanically played out by rule, discourse analysts have come to see linguistic communication as creative problem solving. (p. 225)

Meaning is oriented to the efforts each individual makes to solve the problems attached to the functional reasons for the conversation and functions that the conversation generates.

Constitutive meaning is the product of interpretations and counter plays that become the rationale for the conversation. This social meaning consists of residues that linger as the memory each interactant has of the conversation, the interaction, and the relationship.

CONCLUSION

This chapter demonstrates how language and meaning are inseparable from people's cognitive processes and their efforts to create relationships. Words are a useful vehicle for interacting, reducing uncertainty, entertaining, achieving identity, and exchanging thoughts. A unique human capability, language plays many roles in all communication contexts and domains. Language is a conventionalized code system that consists of symbols, structures, rules (regulative) and interpretative schemata (constitutive).

Cultural studies reminds us that analysis of language gives insight into power. This power may occur at the level of an entire society or be as local as the relationship between parents and children. As Nelson et al. (1992) observed, "Cultural studies demonstrates the social difference theory can make. In cultural studies, the politics of the analysis and the politics of intellectual work are inseparable" (p. 6). By understanding meaning and language, we shed light onto politics as we become convinced that language is not neutral. It influences perceptions of reality, including other people and our relationships with them. Words count for some substantial amount of the dynamics of interaction as well as our feelings of being satisfied by how we relate to others.

People follow patterns of behavior and employ words that are contextually and strategically meaningful. Meaning results from interaction and is not merely based on references between words and things. Nor is meaning limited to the expression of idioms. As people learn about their physical and social worlds, they become members of various zones of meaning. A zone of meaning is a shared understanding or view of some phenomenon. A zone is the meaning structures that people create and share as they attempt to create meaningful bases for shared thought and interaction. Parents share zones of meanings with their children, but both groups also have zones that are not shared. Academics on a college campus have zones of meaning called academic disciplines. Persons in one discipline may not share that zone of meaning with faculty members in other disciplines. All groups of faculty, however, share a zone of meaning about instruction, students, and the academic side of the college or university. Students have zones that are not shared with faculty, such as their idioms and favorite tastes such as the latest musical groups. These zones are shared meaning. They are the residue of interaction in all forms. They lay the foundation for collective action because they provide a shared view on relevant matters.

These and other concepts will help people gain insight regarding how words are used to create meaning and coordinate interaction. With this insight, we better understand why communication can reduce uncertainty, regulate social interaction, foster or impede individuals' sense of self-efficacy, and entertain.

4

Information and Uncertainty: Concepts and Contexts

C ommunication studies have been substantially affected by the concept of information. Few concepts have been as important or as troublesome. A moment's reflection can help you realize how central information is to your communication activities. When you read a newspaper or tune into radio or TV news, you are probably seeking information on some topic (perhaps a ball game score, a fashion change, or a new album by a popular group) or your community and the world in general. As you engage in conversation with a friend, you seek and provide information. You may ask a friend whether someone in whom you are romantically interested likes you. When you watch sitcoms, you are likely to gain information about interaction styles, scripts, and fashions, for instance. Advertisements provide information. You probably watch some ads because you are interested in the product. Other ads might merely amuse or annoy you.

These illustrations hint at a central motive in communication, the desire people have to seek to reduce uncertainty. People do not like to feel uncertain; it produces emotional and cognitive discomfort. For that reason, they seek and remember information to help them cope with their social and physical worlds.

Information is important because it lets people know who they are and how well they are doing. It tells them how well they fit into social circles. People acquire information about others. It also comes from their direct experience with their environment. Information is a basic ingredient in individuals' effort to adapt to their physical and social worlds. A systems meta-theoretic perspective should remind you that information obtained through interpersonal contact in an organization or through mediated communication can help you adapt to your environment and monitor whether your actions are meeting with success. Without information, people cannot make good decisions; they cannot know who their friends (or enemies) are, how they need to perform in an organization, who won an election, or what the weather forecast is.

Some information is sought, but it can come to you without your having to exert much effort. The front page of the newspaper or radio or TV news announces that someone was murdered or three persons died in a car accident. These persons are strangers to you, so how does that information affect your feeling of certainty? One answer is that it helps you to confirm or disconfirm premises you hold about the world around you.

As is typical of most persons, you carry many propositions or hypotheses that you continually test: "Crime is a problem in our town." "People die in car accidents if they drive recklessly." "Pollution is killing wildlife." Information acquired through conversations or news stories confirms or disconfirms propositions that people test to understand events, other people, and themselves. By testing these propositions, they estimate how secure and competent they are or what the nature of the world is. People acquire information, sometimes aggressively and other times passively, with the goal of increasing the certainty that they know what is going on and how to cope with the events and requirements of life.

Information exchange can be viewed as the basic communication paradigm, that is, people seeking, giving, or exchanging information to reduce uncertainty. However, more than describing how information is sent from one person to another during communication, information theory supplies a rationale to explain how people make meaningful contact with others and their environment. Information has been described as the means by which people come to know one another as well as physical and social realities (Watzlawick et al., 1967). Rather than focusing on information as being exchanged, researchers tend to think that what one person does or says can be interpreted by other persons as being informative.

Information as a concept was popularized in the 1950s and 1960s by researchers who were influenced by the work of Shannon and Weaver (1949) and N. Weiner (1948). In that period, cybernetics developed as the science or study of regulation and control via the use of feedback to determine whether strategies were achieving desired goals. Cybernetics seeks to explain the processes by which people or other systems (such as the thermostat in a house or apartment) receive information in regard to the means they have decided to use to achieve their goals.

People employ feedback when they use information to decide to continue or abandon those strategic means or to change their goals. For example, a person might shoot a free throw so hard that the basketball bounces back from the backboard without touching the rim. The second attempt to shoot the basketball so that it goes through the hoop would be guided by the information (feedback) gained from the first. The second attempt might fall short because it was shot too easily. Using information gained from the first two attempts, the third shot might be made in such a way that it goes through the hoop.

If strategic efforts help people to achieve their goals, these attempts are likely to be repeated. If those strategies are unsuccessful, they will probably be abandoned. That simple premise demonstrates why an understanding of information is valuable to efforts to explain and improve the communication process. Information acquisition is basic to communication as a motive, as a crucial element in the process, and as an outcome.

This chapter emphasizes the need humans have to seek, obtain, provide, and use information to reduce uncertainty about the physical and social world they encounter. How they select their communication actions and use them can influence whether they achieve social competence, a powerful human motive. This discussion demonstrates how information is vital to messages and meanings. The chapter compares two views of information, defines key concepts, and discusses research findings regarding the role of information in interpersonal, organizational, and mass-mediated contexts. In this analysis, information is defined as the aspect of messages that increases or reduces uncertainty.

INFORMATION: FOUNDATION
FOR COMMUNICATION THEORY AND RESEARCH

Despite its popularity in the 1960s and 1970s, information has had an uncertain status with communication theorists. Part of the trouble information has encountered comes from unsound assumptions. Let's examine three of these assumptions.

One of these faulty assumptions is that information and persuasion can be treated as mutually exclusive. Evidence of this faulty assumption is the belief that a source can inform or persuade, as though the processes were independent of one another. Often this faulty assumption results from the mistaken belief that information and persuasion are enemies. People who dislike persuasion and believe that it is unethical fail to realize, one might assume, that in making that point they too are trying to persuade others to agree with them. Also, efforts to separate information and persuasion ignore the reality that the person who obtains the message may or may not be persuaded—the choice of the receiver.

The division between information and persuasion has led to unfortunate battles. Some writers have argued, for instance, that some aspects of the communication industry—journalism, for instance—provide information, but do not persuade. Those who adhere to this belief often suggest that in contrast to providing information (which somehow seems to them to be "pure"), others, such as advertising or public relations personnel, persuade—dealing in the "impure." In this sense, persuasion is equated with manipulation, deceit, and lies. This distinction fails to realize that readers may or may not be persuaded that reporters' accounts of events may be complete, accurate, and believable.

Careful and thoughtful analysis suggests that information is a major part of persuasive influence. What the person who is persuaded treats as information is likely to influence her or his conclusions. Addressing this issue, Danes (1978) showed that if receivers accumulate information that differs from their beliefs, they are likely to eventually change those beliefs. Reviewing 50 years of persuasion research, Reinard (1988) concluded that evidence (information) influences opinions (attitudes), especially when it is relevant to topics with which audiences are thoughtfully engaged. Public communication campaign messages can affect opinions when they provide information publics think is relevant to their interests (D. F. Douglas, Westley, & Chaffee, 1970; Mendelsohn, 1973; Winett, 1986).

A second faulty assumption is that information is received and processed independent of other variables. Indeed, research suggests that several variables interact to increase the consistency between the amount of knowledge persons have on a topic, their attitudes on that topic, and the likelihood that their behavior will be consistent with their knowledge and attitudes. One of the most important of these variables is cognitive involvement, which can be operationalized in at least four ways: (a) People who have more involvement (think it affects their self-interest) with a topic are capable of reporting more messages on that topic than can people with less cognitive involvement; (b) people are more likely to receive information regarding those topics on which they believe they have personal risk; (c) people are more likely to receive and think about information when they hold strong positive or negative attitudes on the topic; and (d) information is more likely to influence people who engage in higher amounts of reading—and other forms of information gathering. Two of these variables best predict the consistency between knowledge, attitudes, and behavior: number of messages held on a topic and extremity of attitude position on the topic (Chaffee & Roser, 1986).

A third faulty assumption some researchers have leads them to treat information as being tangible, that is, something that can be seen or touched. As Fisher (1978) observed, it is a mistake to treat information as a thing—an entity that can be transported from one place to another or as having a referent (something for which it stands). A better view, he believed, is to think of it as the means by which people know about one another and their environment. By obtaining what they interpret to be information, people can adjust their behavior—or at least attempt to do so— and adapt to one another. Adjustment and adaptation are vital to the self-organizing and self-regulating activities of systems. As is demonstrated throughout this chapter, information, for instance the informativeness of a message, is subject to the interpretation of the persons who are obtaining and thinking about the information.

Self-organizing and self-regulating activities are central to communication processes in all contexts. The rationale for that conclusion is based on a systems meta-theoretic persuasive. Viewed this way, information is a vital part of a system, and it assists the system's efforts to adapt to its environment. This conclusion can be understood by recalling that energy, for instance, is one of the basic ingredients of a biological or physical system. Animals take in (input) energy in the form of food from the outside and metabolize (process or throughput) it so that it enables them to perform activities (output) such as work or play.

This analogy should help you understand the roles information plays in a system. Social systems, such as individuals, families, businesses, or schools, cannot survive without information. People need information to know one another, to be able to adapt to each other, and to know whether they are achieving their goals. According to systems theory, information is to communication what energy is to biological or physical systems; information flows between systems, giving the systems the means to adapt to one another. In addition to being received and transformed by a system, information can also be created by a system (Krippendorff, 1977).

A fourth faulty assumption is that messages contain information, as opposed to receivers interpreting the amount of informativeness of a message. During the 1960s, information theory helped refine the definition of the concept of message. As discussed in chapter 3, messages are means by which communicators provide and obtain information. Meaning is the interpretation of the information a message contains. It is an interpretation that one communicator assigns to verbal and nonverbal behavior of another. Meaning depends on communicators' experience and language, as well as the context in which it is formed.

By contributing the word *bits* to our vocabulary, information theory added to the understanding of what a message is. A bit is any unit of thought that allows a person to reduce an alternative or choice by half. Viewed this way, we think in terms of either–or, yes–no combinations. The light is on or off. The stock market moved up or down. My friend will come by this evening, or not. Computers think in bits. Each stroke of the keyboard, for instance, is "a" or not "a," "b" or not "b." For instance, you might ask a friend whether you left your coat in his or her closet. The friend can answer this question with one bit of information, "yes" (or "no," depending on the facts). If the answer is "yes," it is there and nowhere else. The decision at the moment is "closet" or "somewhere else." See how "yes" (or "no") reduces the choice by half.

That discussion emphasizes the point that what any person views as information is the result of some interpretation of data that is obtained through a message or by observation of the world and people in it (Ritchie, 1991). Messages contain bits of information (Fisher, 1978). What any bit means depends on the interpretation by the persons involved.

What is information to one person may not be to another. Information is the impact each bit has on a choice or decision being made. This observation raises a theme that scholars have debated. Some researchers have argued that "information must not be confused with meaning" (Shannon & Weaver, 1949, p. 8). In this sense, information refers to aspects of messages that are free of values (Broadhurst & Darnell, 1965).

Disagreeing with the contention that information is unrelated to meaning, Deetz and Mumby (1985) reasoned that all contact with reality provides information. Knowledge and understanding depend on verification via perception. Terms used to define objects, situations, and experiences filter the meaning (the interpretation and importance of bits of information). Bits of information cannot stand as messages separate from the experience, language, or context that gives them definition. For instance, if an expert on snakes heard two children describing the one they had seen in the backyard, the "message" would have different information for the expert than for a worried parent who could not recognize poisonous snakes. $\in \times$.

Another concern is for capacity, the amount of information that can be transmitted given the quality of the sender, message, channel, or receiver. For instance, especially viewed from an engineering point of view, a telephone system is designed to enhance the quality of the signal to be sent and received, not the quality of the content of the information conveyed. Telephones can be used for gossip, financial transactions, medical discussions, or illegal drug deals. The technical problem is to transmit information accurately, efficiently, and correctly. Information theory can address the capacity of channels, messages, systems, networks, and the human mind.

Addressing many correct and incorrect perspectives on the nature of information has led researchers to an enhanced appreciation of its role in the communication process. Discussions of information were largely generated by experts who engaged in technical inquiry regarding the engineering of telephone transmission systems. In its infancy, this topic interested electrical engineers, but not the majority of communication scholars.

Once communication researchers saw how the concept could be applied to everyday communication, its importance increased. Now this engineering concept is important for the entire range of communication situations. For this reason, advances in telecommunications, including those called information technologies, have led to a dynamic renewal of interest in communication—transmission efficiency and systems analysis. It has led to discussions of how information affects societies. For the most part, this line of analysis began to deeply affect communication researchers' views once Porat (1977) and Dizard (1982) proclaimed that many economies, particularly those of Japan, the United States, and Europe, were becoming "information societies."

The industrial worker, according to this point of view, is being replaced by the "information worker." Instead of manufacturing automobiles, this new type of worker generates, stores, transmits, and sells information. Telecommunications offers solutions for communication problems experienced by complex organizations that need to communicate with thousands of people who are in many locations, some a hemisphere away. More and more researchers have begun to study and develop computer-assisted and global satellite communication. Satellite telecommunications links allow millions of people to witness, virtually simultaneously, the same events, whether news, entertainment, or sports. People have become fascinated by the potential of storing and retrieving information from huge databases. Dozens of newspapers can be read online each day by accessing databases through personal computers hooked to telephone lines. Dow-Jones databases offer instant retrieval of information on approximately 750,000 U.S. companies.

Since Porat's (1977) famous proclamation, many studies have only scratched the surface of what the future holds (Dizard, 1982). Many of the subdisciplines in the field of communication, such as advertising and public relations, are busily examining the role new information technologies play in marketing and reputation management of large organizations. These inquiries have largely focused on those new communication technologies that have enjoyed enhanced capacity because they are computer assisted. In addition to the subdisciplinary interest, a new subdiscipline has occurred that is featured in chapter 10.

Influenced by inquiry such as this, researchers have become convinced that information is a medium of exchange that has enormous social, cultural, and political impact. New information technologies, policies, and practices are dramatically changing society (Schiller, 1983). They have helped advance the globalization of economies because they facilitate communication in many forms between people who engage in public and private sector activities through computer-assisted communication. The Internet and the World Wide Web are only some of the more visible aspects of this growth and dramatic change in the way business and government—as well as personal affairs—are conducted.

Included among these changes is the trend toward privatization of information. Information that once was publicly available, such as data from governmental agencies, now has to be obtained through private database companies. Information is power; the people, companies, and countries that control information wield power. Information is changing the nature of society, domestic and global; for instance, with the ability to obtain and process information quickly, physicians can perform complex diagnoses in their offices. Personal credit histories are contained in massive databases. People who have home computers and modems can link into database services to gain instant access to libraries full of information on virtually any topic imaginable. Through the Internet and the World Wide Web people communicate personally, conduct research, and shop for goods and services. Companies and governmental agencies have created intranets to support communication between employees. Banking and other financial transactions can be conducted via computer networks.

In these ways and many more, information is a vital aspect of the communication process and therefore a central concern of communication theory and research. By understanding this theory and research, you can appreciate the principles of message design, transmission, and reception; it explains how communication is affected by several capacities, such as the ability of a channel to transmit information in large quantities and at rapid rates or the mental capacity of people to process information. Information is the "energy" in the communication process. What is information? Although we have offered glimpses of definitions, we need an extended explanation to understand the concept.

Information: Toward a Definition

How do *you* define information? You might define it as facts and figures, that is, statements that are objective, not subjective. An emphasis on objectivity may lead persons to distinguish between information and persuasion. According to this view, persuasion is manipulation, long on emotion and devoid of accurate, factual information.

In keeping with the spirit of the new information age, you may consider information as a commodity that is bought and sold. You might think of it as tangible, a "thing" conveyed from one person to another. But even when a vendor sells information, it still has that information. So, unlike other commodities, such as vegetables, it is not transferred. Moreover, the degree to which data are informative is a vital part of our thinking about information. Not all data are equally informative. Persons will differ on how informative any bit of data is.

Stressing problems involved in defining the concept of information, Ruben (1985) summarized several definitions to show how broadly (and loosely) the term is used. He found it used to refer to data, decision making and problem solving, commodities, and constraints on choices. It is used in conjunction with stimuli, learning, thinking, cognition, memory, knowledge, media, and linkages between a living system and its environment.

To remedy the problems associated with discussing the concept of information, Ruben suggested that it be narrowed to feature four broad topics: (a) data, what it expresses; (b) process, actions and structures by which it is acquired, transmitted, transformed, stored, or retrieved; (c) channel, the technical means by which it is transmitted, stored, transformed, or retrieved; and (d) uses and outcomes, its impact.

Instead of thinking narrowly about what information is, most current definitions approach it in terms of its impact on the persons who obtain and interpret it. In this vein, Devito (1986) wrote that information is "that which reduces uncertainty," as "something that the receiver does not already know" (pp. 155–156). If a person already has the data, according to this definition, it is not information. Information exists only as long as people experience uncertainty. Thinking along these lines, Cherry (1978) concluded that information is valuable (has meaningful impact) only when doubt is present. The amount of information conveyed in a message is always relative; it depends on the amount of doubt a receiver has before and after receiving a message. Viewed that way, information is that component of the communication process that affects the amount of uncertainty (or certainty) that people experience.

Because people must make decisions, they need or desire information. What affects the certainty with which they approach a decision choice is informative. The essence of information is not what it is but what it does as a vital part of the decision process. People get information (input). They think about it (process or throughput). They make decisions (output).

Human cognition is fed by information. Cognition is a computational process—objective and subjective—that handles quantities of information that stem from past experiences as well as fictional accounts, projections, and values. This line of reasoning features the metaphor of the human individual as information processor. Each processor is a system, and all are parts of larger information systems. Information is the medium of exchange between systems, within a system, and between a system and its environment. Viewing information from a systems meta-theoretic perspective, Krippendorff (1977) concluded that

> organizations develop procedures for handling information internally: sorting, coding, selective transmission, storing, deciding on and executing instruction to its executive organs, consulting social memories—explicitly, in the form of libraries and files, and implicitly in the form of net attitudes, etc. (pp. 159–161)

According to this approach to information, a family is an information processing system. Each day, its members obtain and share information (or fail to do so) in ways that affect one another. One member forgets to tell another that the boss called. A note, "I'll be home this afternoon," does not contain sufficient information to reduce the uncertainty about what time the person will arrive. However, as we consider the amount of information in that note we should acknowledge that the degree of uncertainty depends on the information person B wanted or needed to understand what person A would do (arrive) and when. If "when" is not a relevant topic, then person B does not experience uncertainty on that issue.

Viewed through a systems meta-theoretical perspective, information is a basic ingredient in each person's efforts to achieve social understanding, which is needed to produce the self-correction people require to achieve self-efficacy. This perspective explains communication behavior that transpires in social groups, complex organizations, and the media. Information is data an individual (or a social unit such as a family or company) uses in its attempts to adapt to its environment in order to reduce uncertainty and achieve gratification (N. Weiner, 1948).

Daniels and Spiker (1987) defined information as being explicitly linked to meaning, as they observed that

> information includes any kind of pattern that a person can observe or sense in the environment. The significance or meaning attached to the pattern may range from negligible to very substantial. Meaning occurs when information is placed within a

context. The context may be as simple as pattern recognition or as complex as reflective interpretation, in which one piece of information is related to and understood with reference to many others. (p. 24)

Information, then, is the aspect of the communication process that affects individuals' quantitative or subjective estimation (feeling) of certainty. The nature of information is its impact (meaning) on the sense people have between what they want to know and what they believe they know from having obtained and interpreted the data.

Featuring that line of analysis, Ritchie (1991) reasoned that information consists of data and its interpretation, "the *relevance* of data to individual and social purposes" (p. 412). Information is that which informs or tells individuals something they want to know as they interpret data they have acquired.

Entropy

Before turning attention to theories of information and viewing its role in each communication context, we need to examine the concept of entropy. Entropy is the degree of disorganization that exists in any system, whether physical or social. Entropy is the degree of uncertainty that results from the randomness, or lack of predictability, in a situation or message. The relationship between information and entropy is this: When certainty or predictability is present in a situation, no additional information is needed, and no entropy exists. In this way, information is based on the assumptions of probabilities.

We experience entropy, for instance, when we have lost something. Our entropy is greatest when the location of the lost item seems unlimited. "It can be anywhere," we think. Each place where it could be is a bit: It is either there or somewhere else. If we have only two potential locations for where the lost item could be we experience less entropy than if we think, "It could be in a million places." We search for the item one place at a time, concluding that it is/is not there. Our search could appear to be systematic, but it nevertheless has a quality of randomness to it.

Maximum entropy, according to Shannon and Weaver (1949), results from maximum information. This means that entropy is highest when all bits of information are present and equally possible. For instance, you would be uncertain which card would be dealt first from a deck of 52 cards (maximum information equals maximum entropy, unpredictability, and uncertainty). If you kept track of the first 51 cards dealt from the deck, the last card would be easy to predict, which would be low entropy. Randomness would be eliminated because only one bit of information would remain regarding that last card. When people play cards, they shuffle the deck to increase the randomness. If they played with a new deck that had not been shuffled, randomness would be lower and predictability higher regarding the location of each card in the deck. Another example of this point can be made by referring to a maternity room where only one question, "is it a girl or boy?" need be answered to announce the sex of a newborn child. Information theory postulates that certainty is high when entropy is low, and vice versa.

Entropy is concerned with the range of messages (interpretations and conclusions) possible in a given situation. Ambiguity or vagueness is an example of high entropy. It results when a receiver cannot accurately decode a word or statement and know what the sender means. Many possible interpretations lead to uncertainty because of entropy. Ambiguity means that more information exists regarding which interpretation of the message is correct than is the case when a message is clear. It is difficult to predict what the first comment in a conversation will be. If person A does not know person B, that prediction of what will be said is even more difficult to make. In this regard, rules are a means by which people reduce uncertainty in the communication process. If people follow the rules, their communication partners know with greater probability what will and should occur. Think along these same lines of the frustration if television program directors did not schedule programs by date and time.

Unpredictability is maximum when we have unlimited choices regarding what we are going to talk about and what we are going to say about it, and regarding what others are going to talk about and what they will say about it. In this way, entropy refers to the amount of freedom people have in the design and interpretation of messages.

Discussions of information often use the term *randomness.* In the strictest sense, randomness is a dichotomous variable: Something is random, or it is not. Used in this way, we could not talk in terms of degrees of randomness. Because uncertainty is a continuous variable, it is advisable to use terms such as *likelihood, probability,* or *predictability.* These terms allow us to imagine, for instance, that persons are unlikely (or highly likely) to obtain the information they need to reduce uncertainty. Any piece of information might increase (or decrease) uncertainty. In this regard, pieces of information can have large or small effects on uncertainty.

Predictability is a key concept for discussing how information is supplied by media and sought by readers, viewers, or listeners. For instance, when people place news (information) on TV or in a newspaper, they position the information so that a person wanting it is likely to find it. Sports, weather, food, or financial sections help receivers find each kind of information with greater likelihood. Think how difficult a newspaper would be to read if the information were scattered throughout rather than grouped by topic. Likewise, one ad would not stand much chance of being seen or read, even by a target population. Consequently, advertisers increase the likelihood that intended audiences will get the information by placing it in many places on the same day or by repeating it over several days. Many advertisers do both. Advertisers also try to place the information where targeted audiences are predicted to find it.

In an information environment, repetition or redundancy increases the likelihood that people will encounter the message, which, in its own turn, is designed to reduce the audience's uncertainty about the qualities of a product or service. This concept can also apply to interpersonal relationships. For instance, if you want to find information about a friend whom you believe you can no longer trust, you may seek data from the person most likely to have it or ask many people on the assumption that lots of contacts increase your chances of getting the information you want.

Likelihood is the test of information richness. An information environment is rich if many topics are discussed by many people and media. Chaffee and Wilson (1977) used this entropic model to suggest that communities can be media rich or media poor depending on the number of issues people hold to be important. Richness is a measure of the number of media in relation to the range and variety of issues discussed; it is the likelihood that senders will have their messages received and receivers will obtain the information they desire. It predicts that information rich communities are those where individual citizens can obtain the information they want. This is a way of thinking about the difficulty an advertiser faces when attempting to send information to a buyer or when a buyer seeks information he or she needs or wants to make a purchase. The greater the number of messages available on a topic, the more likely the receiver will get the intended message and reduce uncertainty. An increase in sources also enriches the information environment. People in a large organization may have trouble getting information they need due to a lack of information richness (an insufficient number of communication sources people need to obtain the information they want).

Theorists postulate that entropy by its nature tends to increase. Physical systems, such as an iron bar exposed to the weather, tend toward entropy; the bar is likely to rust and disintegrate—iron particles tend to become random. Living organisms are likely to deteriorate if they cannot get needed information and apply it to corrective behavior in order to find food needed to survive. In such a situation, entropy is present, and the organism is likely to perish without appropriate food, if all things are equally likely to be ingested but cannot be equally digested. If you build a sand castle, entropy will eventually set in, and the particles that you have nicely arranged will be scattered in a formless manner along the beach.

This principle of entropy applies to social situations. In a social setting, such as a communication context (whether interpersonal, organizational, or mediated), entropy is present if an individual is likely to generate or receive any message; this means that entropy occurs when no message is more likely to be sent or received than any other. In this way, we might imagine that a child's communication is more unpredictable than is a supervisor's when giving instructions. (Some supervisors may give instructions as unpredictably as a baby babbles.) The concept of predictability increases the understanding of complex systems. Systems theory assumes that entropy will increase unless some force intervenes; physical and social systems tend to become less organized and more random.

In keeping with this view of information, the objective of effective message design is to limit the range of possibilities the receiver has for interpreting the message received, thereby reducing unpredictability and increasing certainty. This view of information explains why communication rules limit, but do not totally constrain, the allowable possibilities of what can be said and what is likely to be meant by what is said. This line of analysis suggests the constraints imposed by policy and tradition within an organization that limit what people can do and say. To offset the principle of entropy, persons who manage media develop schedules and formats to help people get what they want and when they want it.

One argument for a rules perspective to explain communication interaction is that, if appropriate rules are not followed, communication behavior can become increasingly unpredictable and therefore less likely to reduce uncertainty. Patterns, both of interaction and structure of message content, are necessary to mitigate entropy and thereby reduce uncertainty. Similarly, a systems approach to human communication aims to explain the needs and corrective mechanisms individuals require to make systems thrive rather than perish.

During interpersonal communication, the flow of conversation would be very unpredictable and hard to coordinate if persons were equally likely to say one thing as opposed to another, or to imply many meanings rather than one. But conversations are not unpredictable. Each comment, in one way or another, suggests the allowable possibilities that can be used to continue a conversation. People could not conduct conversations if they were totally unpredictable. In similar fashion, organizations could not operate if the people who operated them obtained and provided information in highly random ways.

When we consider the systems typical of a complex organization such as a business or university, unpredictability can mean that people do not have or cannot understand the information they need to make decisions or conduct business. If an employee's search for needed information is random, he or she is equally likely to get needed and unneeded information. Or looked at from the sender's orientation in mass media, this unpredictability can mean that the targeted public is as likely to encounter (or miss) one message as any other.

Such unpredictability is a problem, for instance, for persons who are involved in product advertising or publicity. They work hard to increase the likelihood that their messages will be received from among advertising clutter. For that reason, people advertise in places where they believe they are more likely to encounter people who are interested in the messages. Toys are advertised on Saturday morning television. House cleaning products are advertised during weekdays, but not during sports events. Cosmetics, cars, food, and beer are advertised at night. Women's magazines carry women's products, whereas men's magazines carry products of interest to men. All of this conventional (and social scientific) wisdom follows the proposition that entropy is a measure of the amount of disorganization or unpredictability in a system.

INFORMATION: A FIXED DECISION MODEL

This section explores information by considering a model that features it as means by which a decision can be arrived at accurately and efficiently. The central assumption of this model is that information consists of the bits of data needed to progress through a series of discrete, binary decisions. Each bit of information moves the decision to a certain, predictable conclusion, which results because no additional information is available; persons who are making decisions are certain that the correct decision has been achieved.

This view of information is the result of work on transmission and reception by Shannon and Weaver, N. Wiener's study of cybernetics, and probability theory (Krippendorff, 1977). Probability theory has two distinct branches. One relies on quantitatively derived projections of the likelihood that something is known or could occur. This line of analysis is central to studies such as engineering, natural science, and computer science. The second branch is central to the social sciences; it features subjective probability. This refers to the subjective (nonquantitative) judgments people make as they estimate the likelihood that something will occur or that a positive or negative trait is associated with an objective, situation, or behavior.

Probability is used as the rationale for featuring accuracy and efficiency as two key criteria by which to judge information transmission, reception, and processing systems. This paradigm centers on the likelihood that any bit of data will be accurately and efficiently received or obtained and whether that bit and related bits will reduce the uncertainty people believe is present in a situation. Featuring the role of probability, N. Weiner (1950) wrote that

> it is possible to treat sets of messages as having an entropy like sets of states of the external world. Just as entropy is a measure of disorganization, the information carried by a set of messages is a measure of disorganization. The more probable the message, the less information it gives. (p. 21)

This view of information reasons that as information increases, so does entropy. For this reason, messages need to be designed so that they reduce rather than increase uncertainty. This view of information and message design assumes that the probability that any person will receive a message efficiently and accurately interpret it increases as the available amount of information decreases.

Shannon and Weaver's (1949) approach stressed the conclusion that information is the number of messages (or message units defined as bits) needed to totally reduce uncertainty. Such choices can include the selection of messages, the design of messages, the interpretation of messages, and the information that is offered or obtained with the goal of arriving at a conclusion with certainty. The objective that drives this line of analysis is the desire to understand the problem that produces uncertainty, to estimate the availability of information, and to calculate how much effect each piece of information has on the uncertainty in the situation. Shannon and Weaver concluded that a well-designed message is low in entropy.

Using probability as the basis of their research on message design, Shannon and Weaver (1949) contended that information relates not so much to what is said as to what could be said. That is, information is a measure of freedom of choice communicators have when they select a message. The source's freedom of choice in constructing a message is equal to the receiver's uncertainty about which message will be obtained and knowing what it means. Several factors can limit the choices. One is the strategic design to achieve goals. A second is the rules that prevail that prescribe which of several choices is appropriate or inappropriate.

Viewed this way, information is measured by the logarithm of the number of available choices. The basic unit of measure is the bit, which represents a decision between two alternatives. The number of bits of information in a set of equally probable alternatives is equal to the number of times the set must be divided in half to eventually leave only one alternative. In other words, a bit is an arbitrary unit that serves to quantify the information needed to predict the next symbol to be drawn from a set of symbols. In a fixed decision model, a limited number of bits is known to the person who is making the decision.

For instance, let's think about the amount of uncertainty that exists in knowing which card someone has drawn from a deck of cards. If someone draws a card from a deck, what chance do you have of guessing which card was drawn? Would you bet $50.00 that you could guess which card was drawn? You have one chance to be correct and 51 chances to be incorrect. Those are not very good odds. Would you be willing to gamble (wager that you can guess the card) if the person will answer six questions? You might merely guess six times, but that wouldn't change the odds very much.

Because a deck of cards is a fixed decision (you can only be wrong 51 times), you can know the total number of choices to be made and you have a means by which to make your decision systematically. Approximately six bits of information are required to identify accurately which card was selected from a deck of 52 standard playing cards. This means that a person will need to have six questions answered to determine (reduce the uncertainty of) which card was selected from a deck. Let's think about those six bits of information. The first question could be, "Is the card black?" The answer "Yes" eliminates half of the cards. The next question, "Is the card a club?" could be answered "Yes" or "No" to eliminate 13 more cards. By using these two questions, a person can eliminate 39 cards. Four more questions should be all that are needed to identify the card that was drawn from the deck: (a) odd or even, (b) face, (c) higher than X, and (d) X or Y. This example illustrates the probability approach to information theory, which postulates that for any fixed set of information, there is an optimal method of communicating, based on the probability that the desired information can be conveyed by providing the fewest bits of information needed to reduce uncertainty. The game "Twenty Questions" assumes that skilled question askers who have a good knowledge base ought to be able to solve the problem in 20 or fewer questions.

When a person (Person A) who is designing a message has maximum freedom of choice between independent and equally probable statements or responses, Person B is likely to experience maximum uncertainty about which statement Person A will select and use during communication. Such situations exhibit maximum entropy. Relative entropy is the ratio of the actual entropy in a given situation to maximum entropy. Content (an intended or ostensible message) that does not reduce uncertainty present in a situation contains no information. When Person A and Person B possess the same information, communication can cease. No uncertainty exists. The persons have no need or motive to communicate.

In this way, Shannon and Weaver coupled information and communication. They provided a rationale for message design that argues that, in any situation, the amount of information present is based on the probability that a sender will say what needs to be said and do so in a manner that increases the likelihood that the receiver will get the information and need no further communication. Berlo (1977) advocated a model with which individuals can estimate the probability of something happening, what he calls expectation of occurrence. This model is based on a comparison of the expected versus actual statements or occurrences.

> An expectation set is maximally uncertain when no prediction can be derived from it that is better than any other prediction (i.e., a random distribution of expectations). Given a random distribution, an amount of uncertainty is determined solely by the number of alternatives that are expected. As alternatives rise, uncertainty rises and control and predictability are reduced. (p. 25)

This rationale for making decisions applies to the choices people have in the statements they elect to use or not use when engaging in conversation. In a similar vein, reporters select or avoid certain bits of information in their news stories. Shannon and Weaver postulated that, in a message, each word may or may not help the receiver understand (interpret or decode) what the source of the message means. In this way, information can lead us to be able to predict, to varying degrees of accuracy, what a sentence will lead to in the way of a complete message. The sentence, "I want a 'uh'," leaves a lot of uncertainty regarding how it will be completed. But we know the kinds (however infinite they might be) of terms (reflecting wishes) that the person might use. Context can be helpful, either the context of this term in a conversation, for example, teenagers talking about cars, or the physical context, such as a child standing in front of a sink pointing to a drinking glass. If a young child who is a stranger to you says, "I want blaa," you probably would experience high entropy. You would have the "freedom" to assign many meanings to that sound because you would not know which one is probably correct. If the child approaches you in a kitchen and points to a glass on the sink, entropy would likely be lower as you infer that the child wants a drink of something. If the child makes the same attempt at getting a drink over several days, a pattern (redundancy) is established that reduces the uncertainty regarding the child's request.

Just as you figure out that the child wants a drink, entropy occurs again as you consider, *of what?* Sometimes we offer the child opportunities to give bits of information by holding up the milk, or water, or juice container to see if any of these is what he or she wants. Information, according to this model, is

> a measure of one's freedom of choice in selecting a message. The greater the freedom of choice, and hence the greater the information, the greater is the uncertainty that the message actually selected is the best one. Thus greater freedom of choice, greater uncertainty, greater information go hand in hand. (Shannon & Weaver, 1949, pp. 18–19)

Shannon and Weaver used this principle to define noise and describe its impact on communication. Any bit of information that increases uncertainty is noise. Any addition or omission of a symbol or signal during communication results in a difference between the sender's message and the one received.

When the received signal exhibits greater information, noise is present. Therefore, noise makes redundancy necessary. Shannon and Weaver (1949) wrote:

> If noise is introduced, then the received message contains certain distortions, certain errors, certain extraneous material, that would certainly lead one to say that the received message exhibits, because of the effects of the noise, an increased uncertainty. But if the uncertainty is increased, the information is increased, and this sounds as though the noise were beneficial! (p. 19)

Stated differently, a signal that is received must be selected out of a more varied (lowered probability of accuracy) set of messages than was originally intended by the sender. Thus, Shannon and Weaver (1949) made a key distinction: "Uncertainty which arises by virtue of freedom of choice on the part of the sender is desirable uncertainty. Uncertainty which arises because of errors or because of the influence of noise is undesirable uncertainty" (p. 19).

For these reasons, Shannon and Weaver viewed communication as a process, a series or chain of events, each of which is a choice. During these events, several factors can increase or decrease entropy. One factor is redundancy, where combinations of bits of information work together to decrease entropy. Thus in the English language it is nearly certain that u will follow q in a word. Another factor regarding redundancy is context; the example of the child requesting a "drink" in a kitchen is an instance of context. Realizing that someone knows a piece of information can help increase the likelihood that another piece will be understood. The phrase, "Rm w riv vu," becomes less entropic when it is known to be a real estate advertisement describing a one room apartment with a view of the river. With this kind of analysis, Shannon and Weaver defined what they thought are the key factors of the communication process.

One means for increasing accuracy and efficiency is to employ feedback, the central concept in cybernetics. In this way, N. Weiner (1950) believed that feedback is important to communication; by using it, people, individually or in organizations, can lessen entropy, or uncertainty.

The reasoning is this: Information is sought to reduce uncertainty, and feedback is a means by which communicators can assess the extent (probability) to which their behavior or that of others (such as message design) is producing the desired response. Feedback, in this sense, is a corrective device—in keeping with cybernetics—that allows people to determine whether they are undertaking the actions needed to achieve their goals, which include providing, obtaining, and interpreting information. They want to increase the probability that they have the information necessary to achieve their goals and that they interpret it correctly to make relevant decisions. One way to answer this question is to see whether the information is satisfactory to achieve those goals.

Feedback is the means for answering this question: Test whether information is sufficient by using it to reach the desired goals. Let's think about grades and review answers as examples of this concept. A grade is information that students can use as feedback to decide whether they had studied hard enough to acquire the information needed to pass an exam or score high on it. Obtaining a teacher's reaction to your answers on review questions is feedback that can be used to increase the likelihood that you will be prepared for a test. Getting lost (or arriving successfully) is feedback on a friend's ability to give (and your ability to obtain) directions. In response to your answer on a review question, the teacher might say, "you understand" or "you don't understand," "you understand X" or "you don't understand Y." "What don't I understand about Y?" With this statement, you can get additional information to use as feedback to determine whether you now understand the topic.

Feedback can be used to determine how well you are doing in accomplishing some task. You might ask a friend, "Do you like my car," seeking a binary (either/or) reaction, "Yes" or "No" (even "Not really"). Much of the information you receive under these conditions may not seem binary. In answer to a question about the car you could get comments that appear to fall in a semantic range, "terrific," "great," "good," "OK," "pretty old," "a junker," and "a heap." But this problem is more a matter of precision of thought or response rather than a flaw in the fixed decision conception of information. The binary nature of information exists even in a range. "Really like your car" excludes all other possibilities. What do you think of my car? "I like it because it is a convertible," as opposed to its not being a convertible. "The tires are in bad shape and the body needs work." "The sound system is good, but one speaker rattles." "Is oil dripping from the engine?"

Responses such as these help the questioner get information needed to draw conclusions. The information accumulates or sums to a total, interpreted by the perceptions of the receiver. The value of any bit of information can only be estimated in terms of the goal to which it is being put.

In these examples, we have several key variables: Goals, strategic means for achieving those goals, information as one means for achieving those goals, and feedback, which is the interpretation of the extent to which the strategic means is achieving (or likely to achieve) the desired goal. In making decisions along these lines, note the binary choices. "I could answer X as opposed to Y." I know X." "I don't know Y." Through interaction, the strategic acquisition and interpretation of information is possible. In that way, individuals move toward solutions to problems by reducing their uncertainty through the use of information. The key to the fixed decision model is the knowledge of the total number of decision points that need to be resolved to reach a final conclusion.

Finn and Roberts (1984) claimed that the influence of Shannon and Weaver has reached far beyond the S–M–C–R model often associated with them. Their major contribution is their rationale for using an entropic model to measure the array of observations among variables in a well-defined problem, such as determining which card has been selected from a deck.

This model was extended by Schramm (1955), who postulated that entropy can be a measure of the amount of news in a story, the proportion of news in one story versus other stories, and the amount of information received by readers or viewers. We can think of journalists (reporters and editors) as assisting members of a community in sorting through the maximum available information (high entropy) regarding what events are newsworthy. Reporters and editors reduce the entropy, ostensibly decrease uncertainty, by giving people information about the conditions, events, actions, and people in their community.

To this point we have hinted at an important issue basic to understanding information. The issue is this: Is information something that can best be measured by estimating the likelihood that a bit of data will be available and help reduce the uncertainty through a series of steps that are subject to probabilities?

The first view is basic to the work of Shannon and Weaver (1949). Or, is information something that is best measured by the degree to which the person getting and thinking about the information believes that any piece of it reduces— or increases—his or her uncertainty?

Ritchie (1991) reasoned that two dimensions were central to understanding the concept of information: Data and the means by which people interpret their relevance to any decision. "An event is informative to the extent that it informs a perceiver's representation of the environment and provides a more confident basis for eventual action" (pp. 413–414). The latter view assumes that information is best treated in terms of its impact on each person's judgment rather than as a measure implied in some decision system with a fixed set of choices, such as determining how much uncertainty is decreased when we know something (e.g., what cards have been played out of the 52 that constitute a deck). Keep in mind that Shannon and Weaver said that, as information increases, uncertainty increases. The opposite is also true. The next section discusses a contrasting view.

INFORMATION: A RECEIVER IMPACT MODEL

If you prepare to make a major purchase by getting information needed to buy a new washing machine, car, or stereo, for instance, you probably do not have a fixed equation that can be used to calculate how much each bit of information contributes to a final decision. You begin your effort to make a purchase by going into one store. There you get some information from one salesperson. The salesperson makes statements that contain information that you use to reduce uncertainty about the wisdom of buying one brand as opposed to another. The fixed decision model assumes that at each point (each bit) in the information acquisition process, uncertainty should decrease. That view reasons that as you obtain more information, less remains to be known, and your uncertainty decreases. At least that is the logic of the fixed decision model.

What actually occurs? As we set out to make major purchases we are likely to have incentive to experience greater amounts of uncertainty because we have more at risk in the process of deciding which of several products is best and which one is the best value for the cost. As we speak with one salesperson, we get other bits of information that actually increase uncertainty. If we get conflicting information from several salespeople, uncertainty may increase drastically, or we may find some means to resolve it by focusing on certain decision rules—our decision schema. This case, which is typical in our lives, shows that a "theory of information" must be able to explain everyday events. It must acknowledge that as we get information, our sense of certainty can increase as well as decrease.

This example of making a major purchase illustrates how information can be defined in terms of its impact on the person seeking it. Thus, in contrast to the fixed decision model, the evocative or impact approach to information features the effect any bit of information has on people's need to know, their desire to reduce uncertainty in ill-defined decision circumstances. A situation is ill-defined because the person making the decision has no sequence of questions through which to obtain bits of information that eventually lead to absolute certainty.

Exploring this view, Conant (1979) defined *information* "as that which changes what we know" (p. 177). He made the point that we are constantly bombarded by signals, or stimuli. Some of these messages are sent intentionally, and some are not. He defined *message* as "any input to a system that has, or might have, an effect upon it" (p. 177). He continued, "Every message is potentially a carrier of information in the everyday sense of that word. That is, the receipt and interpretation of a message always entitles the receiver to adjust its knowledge about its environment in some fashion" (p. 177). Conant came to this thesis: "Information is that which changes knowledge, and a message can be said to convey information to a receiver if and only if the receiver's knowledge is changed as a result" (p. 177).

To justify his view, Conant (1979) pointed to several weaknesses of the view advocated by Shannon and Weaver. "For one, viewing the information of a message as dependent only on its probability (in an ensemble of possible messages) makes it extremely artificial, and usually quite impossible as well, to calculate the information carried by real messages transferred in the real world of human conversation" (p. 178). If someone shouts "Fire!" listeners do not calculate the probability of what it means. In this way, he reasoned, the importance of a message is its effect on those who hear it. If a person in the room shouts "Aklee!" instead of "Fire!" the information content of "Aklee!" in the view of Shannon and Weaver would be higher than that of "Fire!" This is true, Conant reasoned, because of Shannon and Weaver's formula, which assumes that each bit reduces uncertainty by half, and that information is greatest when uncertainty is highest. But we know intuitively that a nonsense message carries virtually no "information." Conant argued that Shannon and Weaver's theory provides little help in understanding communication because it assumes that probabilities involved in decisions are stable and do not change over time. Consequently, this model of information, and its implication for communication, is limited.

Information is not stable or fixed. The need to communicate and the value of any piece of information fluctuates over time. A theory of information should take into consideration the impact information has on people who use it. Conant preferred not to define information as "a property of the message stream" and argued that "information is associated with the *relation* between message and receiver. The perspective here is that the *effect* of the message on the receiver is more basic and fundamental than the message itself" (p. 179).

In light of this reasoning, Conant proposed a model that treats the impact of information as belief strength measured on a scale between 0 and 1—a measure of percentage or subjective probability. He reasoned, "When a message induces a receiver to modify its knowledge, the result is a change in the vector (but not, we presume, in the *interpretation*). The *meaning* of the message consists in the change in the vector, along with the associated interpretation" (p. 180). The likelihood of rain would move from 0.4 to 1.0 when rain drops began to fall on one's head. "A message is meaningful if the receiver's knowledge is a result of it." He continued, "a message conveys information if and only if it causes movement of the receiver's knowledge in knowledge-space" (p. 181). People want information to reduce uncertainty and increase their sense of control.

The major feature of information is, according to Conant, the effect a message has on the belief strength of the person obtaining and using it. (The concept of subjective probability as the basis for people's belief strength will be further explained and applied in chap. 5.) It is not a measure of how any bit "should" resolve a decision, such as figuring out which card was drawn from the deck. The impact theory of information has the advantage of treating people as being different. People need more or less information under different circumstances and have different levels of self-confidence. This theory assumes that the information contained in a message is not the same for all people. It acknowledges the cognitive complexity, prior knowledge, and self-confidence of the receiver. This definition of information explains how information has market value. Value of information is a function of the effect it can have for a person who wants to reduce uncertainty and is willing to pay for the information.

To illustrate this view of the concept of information, Krippendorff (1975) noted that the amount of information conveyed by a message is the difference between the amount of uncertainty before a message is received and the amount of uncertainty that exists after it is received. This definition is consonant with Krippendorf's (1977) contention that "*information* is equated with making choices" (p. 157). He explained that "a message conveys *information* to the extent that it is, in fact, and is perceived as the *product of choices*" (p. 157). Senders make choices in regard to what they say, and receivers use information to reduce uncertainty—about what is said or about some choice, or both. This view assumes that people seek and share information to reduce uncertainty produced by choices they must make.

In a similar way, Kennamer and Chaffee (1982) called for media effects studies based on "collective" and "individual" levels of uncertainty. A society can have too little or too much information for its needs. Examining this hypothesis, they concluded that the level of uncertainty in each political campaign is positively related to the number of candidates and the extent to which they are equally likely to be elected. They concluded that the audience that is exposed to the most political information will (a) hold more information than the low exposure audience, (b) add to its information more quickly, and (c) have the lower level of uncertainty as the media indicate how well each candidate is faring in the campaign.

The impact approach to information fits comfortably with research that has examined how well people use data for probabilistic conclusions, such as those involving risk. A risk could be their chances of winning at the lottery or suffering some accident. Research has revealed that people are notoriously bad in their judgments of the likelihood or probability that something will occur (Fischhoff, 1985; Tversky & Kahneman, 1986). Slovic, Fischhoff, and Lichtenstein (1987) noted people's tendency to simplify issues (such as risks they encounter), to ignore evidence that contradicts their current beliefs, and to base their perceptions of risk on what they see in the media and observe in their daily lives.

Reasoning that the interpretative view of information (data plus interpretation) provides the best explanation of how people think about and use data, Ritchie (1991) concluded that schema theory explains how people make sense of the data they obtain. These data can be obtained from observation (perception), interpersonal contact, organizational networks, and the media. Once obtained, they must be interpreted. "According to schema theory, an individual's knowledge of the world can be described as a complex set of schemata for interpreting perception and for initiating action" (Ritchie, 1991, p. 414). Information results when data are interpreted through schemata that are individually and socially derived. Viewed this way, information theory fits with the classic paradigm that people obtain evidence and use it to reason to conclusions based on premises that they hold dear.

The value of information is measured by the impact it has on a person's degree of uncertainty. This perspective adds insight into how information relates to communication and motivation typical of interpersonal, organizational, and mediated communication contexts. The next three sections show how information applies to these contexts. The view of information that will be found to operate in human discourse is one that features subjective probability as a means for reducing uncertainty as a motive for the communication process. Uncertainty is uncomfortable. People need information as a means for adapting to their physical and social worlds.

INFORMATION IN INTERPERSONAL CONTEXTS

As people create interpersonal relationships, they encounter substantial amounts of uncertainty. If uncertainty is uncomfortable, it motivates people to obtain information with which to reduce this uncertainty. For this reason, one of the motivations underpinning interpersonal communication is the acquisition of information with which to reduce uncertainty. This uncertainty can result from persons' effort to know one another. It also occurs as people consider whether their communication partners see them as competent and desirable.

Through contact with others, people create social reality (Berger & Luckman, 1966; Watzlawick et al., 1967) and seek to know one another and to predict how competent they are as communicators (C. R. Berger, 1987; C. R. Berger & Bradac, 1982; C. R. Berger & Calabrese, 1975; Roloff & Berger, 1982). This theory of interpersonal communication, called *social cognition*, predicts that uncertainty motivates the processes individuals use to obtain and interpret information as they scrutinize others, themselves, and reality. Efforts to obtain and process information become more pronounced when habitual or scripted thoughts, cognitions, and patterns of interaction do not satisfy the persons involved.

Crediting Shannon and Weaver (1949) with starting the uncertainty reduction paradigm, Pavitt and Cappella (1979) reasoned that uncertainty is present when people do not know each other and therefore cannot predict their motives, actions or goals. Uncertainty results when communication partners are as likely to engage in one set of communication or evaluations as they are another. Uncertainty occurs when communicators doubt that they can correctly describe each other or when they want to predict some communication strategy or evaluative choice the other person will employ. The desire to reduce the uncertainty motivates people's communication behavior to obtain information about each other, about physical and social reality, and about their own social competency.

Feelings of uncertainty produce a state of emotional or cognitive arousal (a desire to achieve certainty) in many but not all cases. People may not want to know really bad news that has personal, negative consequences, and at least for a while may even deny such information. But in most cases, uncertainty leads to information-seeking communication (C. R. Berger & Calabrese, 1975; Pavitt & Cappella, 1979).

Interpersonal communication patterns change as a consequence of the desire for specific kinds of communication people want in order to reduce uncertainty. For instance, as they get closer to voting age, citizens seek political information to become competent voters. They often ask friends and relatives about candidates (Woelfel, 1977). According to Kellerman (1987), information is the only means by which people involved in an interaction can determine whether they want to continue a relationship and get to know one another or to terminate a relationship. Without information, a relationship cannot progress.

In an attempt to build consensus, people prefer to talk with people with whom they agree and avoid those with whom they disagree. By which dimensions do people estimate the extent to which they and others hold compatible opinions? To partially satisfy this problem, McLeod and Chaffee (1973) postulated that the success of persons engaged in communication can be measured by the degree to which they achieve coorientation, which is the extent to which their perceptions of each other are accurate, satisfying, and based on mutual understanding. Coorientation features three key ingredients in a relationship: mutual understanding (agreement), accuracy, and congruency (satisfaction). Agreement is a measure of the similarity between the views of Person A and those held by Person B. Accuracy is high if Person A's perception of Person B's views corresponds with what Person B actually believes. Satisfaction is a feeling of ease or pleasure that mutual understanding or agreement exists. If Persons A and B both like the same music group, agreement exists. If person A can accurately name Person B's favorite music group, accuracy is high. If Persons A and B are pleased with their choice in music groups, satisfaction exists. This line of reasoning gives structure to people's social cognitions.

Despite their desire to obtain and use information to get to know one another, people's perceptions of one another are rarely accurate beyond chance (Sillars, 1982). This means that their perceptions of each other are not accurate and they do not actually understand one another. A great deal of communication theory and research explores how people try to understand one another, and, using the coorientation model, it measures the extent to which they do.

Pavitt and Cappella (1979) stressed the importance of examining the factors that affect the accuracy of judgments people hold of one another, especially in light of various context variables that operate in interpersonal relationships. To advance research into factors and motivation affecting accuracy and uncertainty, Pavitt and Cappella advised researchers to examine "within-dyad accuracy," "outside-dyad accuracy," and "consensus-task accuracy" (pp. 124–125). A dyad is two people communicating. Within-dyad accuracy refers to the ability of each participant to accurately know the other's views on relevant topics. Outside-dyad accuracy refers to each participant's ability to be accurate about the other's views regarding a person, group of persons, or the nature of the physical world. Consensus-task accuracy refers to participants' ability to use communication to reach agreement on some issue.

A purely cognitive approach to information theory would discount the role that interpersonal attraction might play in this process. On the other hand, social cognition predicts that if people like one another and believe that they have the same attitudes as their interaction partner, they will agree rather than disagree on all major issues. Following this reasoning, Pavitt and Cappella postulated that liking and amount of communication will influence within-dyad accuracy. People who like one another are likely to seek information from one another and therefore get a more accurate picture of what the other person knows and believes.

This analysis is problematic. Liking distorts perception of agreement; people tend to believe that they agree with persons they like and disagree with those they dislike. Perceived disagreement increases the likelihood of disliking. Disliking increases the likelihood of disagreement. People tend to like the ideas of persons whom they like. This analysis assumes that people strive to keep their perceptions of their relational partners and feelings about them in harmony.

Thus, Pavitt and Cappella reasoned that accuracy of judgment is likely to exhibit a U-shaped (curvilinear) relationship with liking, because when people like one another they tend to have unrealistically high perceptions of the amount of agreement, whereas those with extreme degrees of disliking tend toward exaggerated perceptions of disagreement. If people like each other, they may tend to agree with their judgments rather than seek information that could disrupt that liking; and they may ignore information that could diminish disagreement with persons they dislike.

Because liking is such a strong motivation, people tend to be open to increased amounts of information sharing with those they like. This increased communication may lead them to be similar in their opinions of the object, but not necessarily accurate. Agreement or understanding has little to do with whether opinions about some object or situation are accurate, but agreement or understanding is a measure of the accuracy of perception regarding the other communicator's opinion on the object. Thus, Pavitt and Cappella (1979) postulated, "Actual agreement between two communicators about a relevant object is a monotonically increasing function of amount/time spent in communication with each other concerning the relevant object" (p. 129).

This contention predicts that interactants will change toward each other's expressed attitude as interaction continues. Closely related is another hypothesis: "Accuracy in judgments concerning another person's view toward a relevant object is a monotonically increasing function of amount of communication with the other person" (p. 129). Pavitt and Cappella added a third postulate: "Under conditions of actual agreement, accuracy in judgments of another's view concerning a relevant object is directly related to perception of agreement with the other concerning the relevant object. The greater the actual agreement, the more an increase in accuracy will lead to an increase in perceived agreement" (pp. 129–130).

This line of analysis has many implications for interpersonal communication, liking, information seeking, and agreement. When persons are engaged in within-dyad tasks, accuracy is a function of A's knowledge about B's views about the details related to a task. If A is uncertain about B's information, the task cannot be completed until more information is obtained in order to increase confidence. In regard to outside-dyad tasks, A's success does not rely only on knowledge of B's views, but also on information and assumptions acquired independent of B. Other sources of information and direct contact with the object can supplement information acquired from B. Some of the factors influencing judgments in this case will be confidence in one's own opinion and the opinions of others. For these reasons, information is a key factor in the development of interpersonal relationships.

Information is important to communication and cognitive processes that occur during negotiation. Investigating the factors that affect exchange of information during negotiation, Donohue and Diez (1985) found that negotiators need information to coordinate their expectations and identify expected outcomes. In their study, Donohue and Diez defined *information* "as any statement or set of materials that may provide knowledge of the opponent's expected outcomes" (p. 309). Negotiators strategically increase or decrease the amount of information they supply to one another. They use directives to get one another to reveal information, for instance "Tell me about . . . ." Face-threatening directives are used to challenge or force the partner to comply. Negotiators use more face-threatening directives when their goals are different, when they are unwilling to cooperate, when procedures for conducting the negotiation are not rigid, when participants have a substantial relational history, and when participants feel personally involved with the negotiation content. During combative negotiation, information is strategically used on a win–lose basis. In integrative negotiation, participants are more willing to share information. During combative negotiation, participants attempt to impose rigid obligations on one another to respond to directives.

This analysis suggests that several factors are basic to information seeking in interpersonal contexts, its impact on judgments by the relational partners, and degrees to which the interactants like each other and have the same tastes. The value of the information that is at play during interpersonal communication is determined by its impact on persons involved, given a variety of factors such as interpersonal attraction, as well as willingness to seek information and to allow it to affect judgment and self-confidence.

Individuals can manipulate information, trying and even succeeding in their efforts to deceive one another. They may give biased reports about themselves and others. They have direct and indirect strategies, as well as proactive and retroactive strategies, to seek information about persons who are important to them. They manage impressions in an effort to be seen positively by those persons whose regard they desire. They disclose information as a means for demonstrating regard for a relational partner and they receive information their partner discloses. Such information exchanges are strategic, as is predicted by social penetration theory.

This kind of reasoning explains why you estimate whether you like the salespeople you meet and calculate whether their statements match your perceptions. You should be able to understand even better why you behave differently if you are confident in your judgment about the purchase regardless of your relationship with the salesperson. In friendship situations, people seek information from persons they like, and they prefer information that helps them to build and maintain the relationship, which includes knowing the other person's opinions about the relationship. If they find information that can harm their liking of a friend, they tend not to want or believe the information; they require additional information to decide about the friendship. Many applications of this theory are likely to come to mind, but this brief summary suffices to show some relevant variables involved in information-seeking and interpersonal communication. This theme is expanded in chapters 6 and 7.

UNCERTAINTY REDUCTION—SEEKING INFORMATION IN ORGANIZATIONAL CONTEXTS

A great deal has been written about the role of information in organizations. Organizations are typically defined as collectivities that seek to survive by obtaining, processing, and using (outputting) information. As was discussed earlier in this chapter, information theory and systems theory became closely allied in the 1960s and 1970s. Together, they can account for how systems, large or small, need and obtain information to adjust dynamically to their environment. One standard view of an organization is that it obtains input, which it processes (throughputs) to create various outputs. The best metaphor for understanding a system is to think of it as a dynamic organism, a living creature that takes energy from its environment by eating. Through dynamic interaction with its environment, an organism takes in the energy needed to survive. In a similar way, an organization takes and uses information. Information is the energy of the organization.

Underpinning organizational communication research is the theme that the desire to reduce uncertainty motivates people within and outside organizations to obtain and share information. A desire to reduce uncertainty motivates individuals to seek, share, and use information during interactions with other members of organizations and key persons outside of the organization. This hypothesis applies to all aspects of systems: interpersonal interaction; networks; and contact with external communication through public relations, marketing, and advertising.

In organizations, communication flows through networks, pathways through which information flows from one person to another throughout an organization. Fisher (1978) believed that network research "expanded the 'connectedness' dimension from that of merely a message-exchange channel to a broader concept of relationship or kinship" (p. 95).

Communication can be used to transmit and receive information, and to use feedback to determine whether communication and other activities are achieving the goal of adapting to the environment and other systems (Fisher, 1978, 1982; Krippendorff, 1977; Schramm, 1955; N. Weiner, 1948). Information theory, once it became augmented by cybernetics, gave the rationale needed to understand organizations as dynamic information-processing organisms.

Information, coupled with other cybernetic, adaptive behaviors, gives organisms the means to steer a course by which to achieve their objectives. Open systems let in information that helps them adapt; closed systems do not. Rather than thinking of systems as either closed or open, it is best to think in terms of degrees of openness. Open systems take in information to assess whether their actions are moving them toward their goals. For instance, marketing studies are conducted to determine whether companies are selling the right goods or radio stations are playing the music that key segments of the public want to hear. Through the influence of cybernetics, terms such as *intelligence, adaptation,* and *growth* have become key variables for explaining how communication networks operate and how organizations achieve self-modification.

Placing cybernetics in context, Krippendorff (1977) reasoned that "systems theory emphasizes properties of *wholes* and *parts, relationships* and *hierarchies,* while cybernetics focuses on *behavior, processes,* and *circular communication*" (p. 152). Systems theory describes the components of an organization, whereas cybernetics offers a rationale for how it adapts to its environment. Krippendorff believed that information theory expands the basic stimulus–response paradigm, which only links incoming stimuli and triggered responses to explain how organizations adapt. Beyond this foundation, he explained, "the information processing approach considers cognition as a computational process that involves possibly large quantities of information stemming from past experiences, including fictional accounts, future projections, values, and purposes" (p. 159). People are information processors, and social systems are means for handling information. Information theory linked to cybernetics enriches the explanation of how people in complex organizations, through their abilities, adapt to their environments to think and use information for strategic decision making.

Explanations of how communication supports organizations feature the defining characteristics of a system. One characteristic is homeostasis, the tendency for the system to adapt dynamically to survive and prosper by achieving balance with its environment. Another characteristic is equifinality, the ability of systems to reach the same goal even though they employ different means. Wholeness means that a system is a collection of parts, but it is nonsummative; it is more than the sum of its parts. Openness refers to a system's ability to interchange information dynamically with its environment to adapt and survive, or the ease with which information can flow into and from the organization. Complexity means that systems are not simple and tend to become more complex and differentiated over time. Systems exhibit the characteristic of self-regulation, the ability to set goals and guide their actions using feedback to evaluate whether their strategic efforts achieve those goals. The parts of a system are interdependent on one another; a system is interdependent with the environment in which it exists. Interdependence exists because any factor in a system that changes or is affected results in all other parts of the system being affected. That which affects part of a system affects the entire system. Systems are characterized by hierarchy, which means that an organization is a suprasystem that consists of layers of subsystems, which are in turn divided into sub-subsystems and so forth. By understanding hierarchy, we should be able to better understand systems' tendency to become increasingly complex (Fisher, 1978; Krippendorff, 1977).

Each of these characteristics has implications for how communication and information exchange occur in an organization and between it and its environment. A company publishing a newspaper is a good illustration of the traits of a system. A newspaper strives to maintain homeostasis by establishing and maintaining a balance among its component departments and with its environment. One means for achieving homeostasis is to get information that is interesting to and desired by readers; the size of the newspaper will be influenced by the number of readers, the amount each is willing to pay for each day's copy, and the willingness and ability of advertisers to spend money that defrays printing costs and increases profit. A newspaper must balance itself with other news sources in a community, such as radio and television. Two reporters exhibit equifinality by getting their stories in different ways; one reporter may be subtle and the other very aggressive. All of the systems of the newspaper constitute its wholeness; a newspaper must have reporters, printers, accountants, editors, procurement, maintenance, sales, and distribution. Reporters help the paper to be open to the environment, and readership surveys are another kind of openness by which the newspaper management attempts to understand and adapt to its environment. A small town newspaper may have few people who do many tasks (low complexity), whereas a major city newspaper may have many people, each of whom does few tasks (high complexity). A newspaper must self-regulate; if circumstances change, so must the paper. For instance, legal interpretations of libel may make reporters and editors more cautious in regard to what they print about people. The components of a newspaper are interdependent. If a news print shortage occurs or the presses break, the printing department cannot produce the paper. Thus, what the reporters write cannot be printed or distributed to customers. Hierarchy refers to the organizational structure of a system. You might immediately assume that hierarchy follows the patterns of the organizational chart with management at the top because it is most important. Hierarchy in systems terminology refers not to importance but to levels of complexity, because each part of the system is important; take one part away and the entire system changes. If reporters do not report well or maintenance does not keep the presses operating, the paper will not be produced despite the "power" of management. Hierarchy refers to levels of specificity; a system is divided into subsystems, and sub-subsystems. One system is reporters, which is divided into subsystems such as local news, sports, business, and fashion.

This illustration portrays the routine efforts individuals use to bring an organization to life by helping it to adapt to its environment. Changes in the environment are likely to affect the organization. Dynamic changes occur when information becomes more complex, the information environment becomes turbulent, or people experience information overload. Under these conditions, companies use scanning and probing to acquire information (input) from the external environment. This information is throughput (processed and used to reduce uncertainty) and output (the product of the throughput is sent to the appropriate personnel). Once information has been acquired, several factors affect what is done with it. For instance, information can be routed from people in one part of the organization to people in another part. During this process, the information may be altered, summarized, or delayed at each point where one person has access to it before passing it on to others.

Huber and Daft (1987) explained this process by featuring several concepts. Complexity is a measure of the number of variables that must be considered when processing information about an organization's environment. A situation is complex if it requires attention to many variables. A crash of a major airline might be complex if variables such as terrorism, pilot error, or structural flaws are equally probable as causes. Turbulence refers to the degree of stability or instability in the environment; maximum turbulence results in maximum entropy, randomness, or uncertainty. Turbulence results from two factors: instability (frequency of change) and randomness (unpredictability of frequency and direction of change). Information load is the amount of information and the difficulty of obtaining and processing it in meaningful ways within the organization to adapt maximally to the environment. A student who has too many difficult classes in a semester may experience information overload. Add to this load the problems of a family member who is suffering from cancer and the load increases.

In times of turbulence, Huber and Daft (1987) reasoned, organizations seek to protect the basis of their business and increase their means for adapting to their environment. Huber and Daft predicted that information load, complexity, and turbulence will increase in correlation to one another. These changes will have dramatic implications for organizational communication and organizations' abilities to reduce uncertainty. How quickly and effectively any person handles information in an organization depends on many factors, especially workload and competence. Thus, Huber and Daft concluded, if the sender is either cognitively or logistically overloaded, it is likely that messages will be modified (distorted or abbreviated).

Applying the uncertainty-reduction paradigm, Huber and Daft (1987) studied how companies monitor their environments to discover problems or opportunities and how they extract, process, and act on information from those environments. One problem, information overload, occurs when information processing becomes difficult due to its quantity, ambiguity, and variety. Quantity is the number of messages received per unit of time. If a person gets several conflicting reports on the same topic, he or she is experiencing quantity. Ambiguity means that symbols or messages can have multiple interpretations. A company that manages solid waste is likely to be confronted with ambiguity as local residents proclaim that they want to be rid of their garbage, but they do not want it deposited near their homes. Variety refers to the complexity and turbulence of the information stream. Companies experience variety when they are attacked by activists or when a crisis occurs and they are the subject of intense scrutiny by the media.

Complexity can be subdivided into three components: numerosity, diversity, and interdependence. Numerosity is the number of components in the environment. For instance, if you try to understand and accommodate to the purchasing preferences of a few buyers or ones that are quite similar they have less turbulence than when they have many kinds of buyers who are also quite different in their tastes. Diversity refers to the differences among markets served; for example if a company provides one line of clothing for men only, getting and making sense of customers' reactions to the quality and style of the clothing is different than if the company produces ten lines of clothing for different age groups of both sexes. Interdependence refers to the relationship that exists when many companies share the same environment and develop complex relationships and dependencies on one another. As an example of this last variable, you might think how buyers and sellers of used homes are both interested in the current market values of homes, but for quite different reasons. Buyers want to be able to see how little they can pay for a piece of property, whereas sellers want to use those data to maximize their profits. Using these constructs, Huber and Daft (1987) postulated that the more complex the environment, the more resources the organization will have to commit to scanning for information that can be used to take advantage of opportunities and avoid problems. In this way, Huber and Daft defined perceived environmental uncertainty, which consists of several factors: amount of information, specificity of messages about the environment, and the quality of messages about the environment.

Organizations need the ability to change; to do so requires effective means for the acquisition and processing of information. How well organizations obtain and transmit information internally and externally is vital to their ability to innovate. Innovation within an organization is influenced by the degree to which management encourages it, the number of channels used to transmit information about it, and the degree to which supervisors personally seek information about the innovation. Impetus to adopt any innovation correlates with management's encouragement to be innovative (Hoffman & Roman, 1984).

In this way, companies vary in their abilities to obtain and utilize information. The same can be said about the departments or subsystems of those organizations. Depending on how cybernetics is used, an organization's adaptation can be mechanistic or dynamic (Morgan, 1982). The mechanistic view of cybernetics features the selection of those activities that are most likely to achieve an organization's goals. A classic example of this mechanistic approach is a thermostat, which regulates the comfort of a room by reading its temperature and making the appropriate signals to the heating or cooling system. Adaptation occurs within a limited range of goals and activities. In this view, systems are designed and set into operation to satisfy a narrow range of goals that may ignore many others that are not noticed because they are perceived to be outside of the immediate system.

In contrast to this mechanistic view, Morgan (1982) argued that cybernetics should be approached as an epistemology, a way of thinking about an organization as the means for looking for new and better goals by which to guide its actions. This, he believed, is a constructive way to seek information, in a sense by looking for uncertainty that needs to be reduced. To illustrate the point, recall the story of the fellow who felt successful that he had cornered the buggywhip market only to discover that there no longer was a market. The point is this: Cybernetics can be applied narrowly to argue that a company is in harmony with its society because it is at peace. Cybernetics can be viewed too narrowly in this regard. The search for information must include surveillance of the environment to see how it is changing and why. A cybernetic device such as a thermostat does not draw information from the environment to determine how and why changes are occurring; it knows only that they are, that is, the temperature is warmer or colder. Reading this information, a thermostat instructs the heating or cooling system appropriately. Cybernetic adjustment to the environment must include the possibility of establishing new goals, developing new criteria for evaluating success, and being sensitive to change and turbulence. A cybernetic system that does not include these features can become static and close itself to its environment.

Individuals are prone to increase their ability to obtain information as part of their effort to make organizations more effective. New communication technologies are designed and produced to help people in companies obtain, store, share, and interpret information more successfully within and outside of their corporate confines. Such innovation may be implemented with disregard for the humans who are expected to create, store, and transmit the information. For that reason, assumptions regarding which information systems to implement and their consequences on the people in organizations pose major challenges to people who manage these organizations (Walton, 1982).

In these ways, systems theory and information theory have made important contributions to efforts to explain how and why people communicate in their capacity as members of organizations. Topics of these sorts are the basis for discussions that occur in chapter 8.

UNCERTAINTY REDUCTION—SEEKING INFORMATION
IN MEDIATED CONTEXTS

To apply information theory to mediated communication seems almost too obvious to require explanation. After all, don't the media exist to provide information and entertainment? But the issue is more complex than that. Developed in its "bare bones" fashion, the role of information in media might be described in terms of who observing who is saying what to whom under what circumstances and with what effect (Lasswell, 1948). This linear model is typical of the views expressed by Shannon and Weaver (1949), Westley and MacLean (1957), and to a lesser extent Schramm (1954, 1955). What can be said of information in mediated contexts?

How this question is answered depends largely on whether a receiver of information is viewed as a passive receptacle into which a sender injects information or as an active participant who seeks information. Reinforcement (selective exposure) theory and uses and gratifications theory, as well as other theories of mediated communication, challenge the sender-to-receiver paradigm.

Reinforcement theory rests on research findings that the media have limited effects because viewers, readers, and listeners select programming and information to which they want to be exposed. The hypothesis that people seek information that serves their needs is fundamental to the selective exposure rationale for this theory. For instance, participants who experienced high threat by hearing about a violent crime that occurred near them (on campus) or low threat (hearing about a crime across town) expressed preference for film clips containing retribution, but they did not want to view film clips regarding information on attacks, or comedy, or romantic sequences (Boyanowsky, 1977).

Uses and gratifications theory contends that receivers are dynamic because they can and will seek sources of information and entertainment to satisfy their needs. This theory makes the following prediction: Needs that have psychological and social origins lead individuals to have expectations of the mass media and other sources, which lead to differential patterns of media exposure to gratify those needs. That means, for instance, that if we are tired we might chose a sitcom to watch. If we want to be intellectually challenged we might decide to watch a program on one of the educational television channels.

Researchers have debated which list of needs is most accurate. One list of needs features diversion or escape, personal relations and affiliation, personal identity and self-esteem, and surveillance (E. Katz, Blumler, & Gurevitch, 1974). In a study of students (middle school, high school, and college), three categories of gratification behavior were found to influence selection of communication channels: surveillance/entertainment, affective guidance, and behavioral guidance (Lometi, Reeves, & Bybee, 1977). The first category is oriented to information seeking, whereas the latter two reflect the desire to learn the norms that indicate which feelings and behavior are appropriate.

Preferences regarding kinds of information and gratification sought are used to predict media use. Media selection and use behavior are not merely influenced by the gratification to be received by watching a specific program (a favorite newscast) or that type of program in general (news). An estimation of the amount of gratification that will be derived by watching one program is meaningful only by comparing it to other programs that could be watched or other activities in which the person could engage. Viewers may monitor their behavior to infer that they must like a certain kind of program because they watch it often (Palmgreen, Wenner, & Rayburn, 1981).

People seek information in product purchase situations (e.g., buying cosmetics) for social comparison as well as personal reasons. Interpersonal-social influence variables are as important for predicting the types and amounts of information sought as are personal variables, such as education or desire to reduce uncertainty. Social comparison influences operate when individuals are uncertain whether their judgments about a product are correct and when they need social approval (Moschis, 1980).

Entropy is a valuable concept for discussing information in mediated contexts. If an audience experiences needs and desires gratification, and if the number of media is large or the amount of information is rich, then individuals are more likely to satisfy their needs. Applying the concept of entropy, Chaffee and Wilson (1977) found a significant relationship between the number of local mass media institutions and the ability to diffuse diverse ideas in a community. When many media outlets discuss a wide array of topics, the information environment is "rich." The amount of information being provided by the media can be described as constituting a news hole. The amount of news space and time is fixed: Each day approximately the same amount of time is given to all news on TV and radio, and newspapers are approximately the same length each day, except Sunday. The importance of each topic discussed by the media depends on how much time and space it receives in proportion to all other news topics.

Entropy is used to refer to the likelihood that people will find information they want and that the media will get the information to them. A long-standing assumption of media effects is that if a public's knowledge is to be increased on a topic, then media have to provide more information to increase the public's chances of being exposed to it. In this regard, the number of media outlets in a community can remain constant, and the amount of information can increase if the proportion of media space or time devoted to an issue increases. If more time or space is devoted, the probability of people encountering the information increases. During an information campaign, the proportion of time or space given to one bit of information increases at the expense of another. Thus, Salmon (1986) concluded, the impact of an information campaign probably depends on the extent the information being disseminated relates to people's self-interest, the amount of information available in the environment prior to the campaign, and the magnitude and duration of the campaign.

In addition to using entropy to discuss information diffusion throughout a large population, the concept is used to analyze the content of individual programs, for instance the degree of abstractness present in a television program. Age and education level of viewers correlate with tolerance for entropy (amount of complexity). Older and better educated viewers can understand more abstract television programs than can their younger or less educated counterparts (Krull, Watt, & Lichty, 1977).

Diffusion of innovation theory predicts that media as well as interpersonal contacts provide information and influence opinion and judgment. Studying how innovation occurs, E. M. Rogers (1962) argued that it consists of three stages: invention, diffusion (or communication), and consequences. Diffusion means that an idea spreads from a point of origin to others and eventually achieves general or limited acceptance. The information flows through networks. The nature of networks and the roles key people play in them determine the likelihood that the innovation will be adopted. Networks are more than simple information linkages among people. The key is the extent to which convergence occurs where people who could adopt the innovation begin to get the same information from credible sources. The process by which innovation spreads throughout society is not linear (E. M. Rogers & Kincaid, 1981). Although promoters of an innovation try to channel information to adopters, to a large extent the information is randomly diffused. Information is sought primarily by persons who adopt innovation more quickly than others do.

Innovation diffusion research has attempted to explain the variables that influence how and why users adopt a new information medium, such as the Internet. Adoption of a new medium depends on adopters' information needs, which medium adopters prefer, availability of the medium, and familiarity with it. Adoption of a new medium depends on the extent to which it is perceived to be more effective, convenient, or gratifying than old ones. A new medium has its greatest impact on media or leisure activities that are its closest equivalents. For this reason, movie going declined after the adoption of television (Heikkinen & Reese, 1986). Media use preferences depend on availability and accessibility more than content. The most useful and gratifying media are television, newspapers, and books, in contrast to radio, magazines, and films (Kippax & Murray, 1980). Findings such as these vary according to the kind of audience that is studied.

One of the key questions that motivates mass-mediated communication research is the way people use information to form opinions. When many people hold the same opinions, we think in terms of public opinion or at least the opinion of key publics. The current analysis of public opinion begins by recognizing that far more information exists than people are willing to or capable of obtaining, absorbing, interpreting, or recalling. For this reason, people create or adopt schema, cognitive structures that allow them to draw conclusions with substantially reduced amounts of information. This theory of public opinion is called *schema theory*. Schema are views of life (and key issues related to it) that people form collectively so that they can interpret the key information they need to make relevant, important decisions. One salient example of this is the need for what we can call public opinions, those widely shared opinions that allow groups of people to form their particular opinions on political and other public policy issues.

Advancing the research relevant to schema theory, Graber (1989) found that people use schemata, which are schemas that offer serviceable cognitive patterns with which to cope with the complexity of their physical and sociopolitical world. Schemata may suffer serious flaws in accuracy and soundness, but they nevertheless provide premises by which people interpret information and draw sociopolitical conclusions. The schemata are learned and shared by individuals with similar zones of meaning. As groups of individuals share schemata, they interpret information and draw conclusions that are similar to others in their zone of meaning. Thus, to understand public opinion, or the opinion of any key public, requires an examination of the schemata that they use to interpret information and reduce uncertainties. In this way, relatively uniform patterns of agreement and disagreement can be found in society. The media provide some information and at times shape the schemata people use to interpret that information. But people also seek and interpret information that conforms to their schemata. Public opinion results from similar patterns of cognitive processing of information that is available in a society.

Issues and theories that were treated briefly in this section are expanded in chapters 9 and 10.

CAPACITY: THE ABILITY OF A SYSTEM TO OBTAIN, STORE, AND PROCESS INFORMATION

Another variable that influences how people accept and use information is capacity. In 1955, Schramm encouraged researchers to investigate the relationship between channel capacity and audience capacity. In this tradition, the term capacity is used to address the extent that the parts of the communication process can handle information.

Sender capacity refers to the amount of information that a source (person or object such as a computer or a library) can supply at a given time vis-á-vis the receiver's needs. Message capacity is the amount of information that can be contained in a single message, such as a specific combination of words (the space of a memo, or duration of a conversation). Some messages efficiently deliver the content; others, for instance, are "too wordy."

Channel capacity is "equal to the maximum rate (in bits per second) at which useful information (i.e., total uncertainty minus noise uncertainty) can be transmitted over the channel" (Shannon & Weaver, 1949, p. 21). Such measures could apply to the kind of conductor involved; for instance, fiber optics has more capacity than does standard transmission cable.

Time capacity is a measure of how long communicators have or take to transmit a message as well as process it. If time is shorter, the message must be more brief or efficient or information must be omitted, or other types of capacity must be increased.

Receiver capacity refers to the ability to receive and process information. This capacity can be a function of each individual's cognitive ability or experience with the information. It could refer to the person's need for information. The human mind files and retrieves information based on associations (which ideas, thoughts, objects, feelings, or concepts go with one another), as well as the level of interest the person has for the information (Anderson, 1985). To illustrate sender and receiver capacity, imagine a small computer drawing information from (or sending it to) a large one. A small computer has less capacity and therefore sends or receives at a slower rate, measured in bits per second.

This brief discussion of information in mediated contexts demonstrates that an interactive, reciprocal relationship exists between the audience that wants information and the media that provide it. Key factors in this process are the probability that people will encounter and be satisfied with the information. People seek and use media and message content to reduce uncertainty and achieve social competence.

CONCLUSION

Information is basic to communication in all contexts. Craig (1979) urged communication researchers to study cognitive processes to understand the content of what people say and the effect it has on interaction. Cognitive science addresses information as a key variable that helps explain that people communicate about something. This view requires understanding the role and effects that perception, forgetting, memory, and recall have on communication.

Information is a key concept in many topics of discussion. It can be manipulated during interpersonal communication; we call this deception or biasing. We discuss information overloads and underloads as being vital to organizational communication. Information is a factor in social, economic, and political control; the ability to control information is one element of power. We have information networks and information technologies. If we are going to truly define and understand our information society, then we need as a starting point to understand the nature and dynamics of information.

During interpersonal communication, people lower or raise certainty by asking questions, eliciting responses, and attributing personal characteristics to one another. People communicate by using conventional patterns or interaction rituals to lower entropy. In organizations, information is a medium of exchange that can be used to correct activities of individuals, groups, or companies. Individuals use media to reduce uncertainty even though they seek information selectively. Prior to finalizing decisions, people seek information that reinforces the decision they want to make, and after they make a decision, they seek information to reduce the dissonance associated with the decision (Wheeless & Cook, 1985). An understanding of information supplies additional rationale to explain how and why people communicate to come into meaningful contact with one another and their environment.

5

Persuasion: Concepts and Contexts

S ociety cannot exist without people influencing one another's opinions and behavior through discourse. People seek influence as well as exert it. Those practices explain why persuasion theory and research command so much interest. They deal with social influence, that is, people communicating to affect one another and to form useful opinions.

In interpersonal communication, people influence each other's judgments and behaviors; they are affected by each other's actions and statements. Corporations influence employees' opinions and behaviors, shape images each external public has of them, and create customer preferences for their products or services. The opinion climate inside companies results, at least in part, from management's influence on employees and of employees' impact on management. Persuasion, media effects, advertising, marketing, political campaign communication, and propaganda are terms that have become so entwined they are often used synonymously.

More than 2,000 years ago, Aristotle (1954) studied rhetoric, the art of creating situationally relevant persuasive arguments. His interest centered on strategies a rhetor could use to persuade audience members. As Petty and Cacioppo (1986b) noted, "After accumulating a vast quantity of data and an impressive number of theories—perhaps more data and theory than on any other single topic in the social sciences," researchers do not agree "if, when and how traditional source, message, recipient and channel variables affect attitude change" (pp. 124–125).

Persuasion research is complex and problematic; generalizing about the influence process can be misleading, if not downright incorrect. Efforts to study persuasion are frustrated by the complexity of the human mind, which is capable of receiving and weighing many influences simultaneously. Moreover, persuasive impact can result from interaction of many factors such as message variables, especially content, structure, and style. This list of variables includes those related to sources, especially credibility, interpersonal relationships (such as liking or conflict), channels, and idiosyncratic characteristics of receivers (including the extent to which people are self-interested in outcomes and expect to obtain rewards or avoid punishments by taking one action instead of another).

Research and theory are hard pressed to explain how these variables interact and thereby predict the factors that result in persuasive influence. For these reasons, this chapter cannot encompass all you need to know to understand the process of persuasive influence, but it reviews major concepts, theories, and research related to social influence in interpersonal, organizational, and mediated contexts.

TOWARD A DEFINITION

Should the definition of persuasion acknowledge a role for coercion? Persuasion, G. R. Miller (1980) reasoned, is the use of messages to modify behavior by using some combination of coercive force and message appeals that affect reason and emotion. Emphasizing the role that threat and coercion can play in persuasion, he recognized the influence that can result when, for instance, a child threatens to run away from home rather than eat vegetables or when terrorists hijack a plane demanding release of their compatriots.

Should your definition of persuasion distinguish between emotion and reason? Quite accurately, G. R. Miller (1987) did not view reason and emotions as qualitatively different concepts that can be easily separated. Some researchers believe reason is the logical, analytic part of judgment, whereas emotion involves feelings that influence judgment and behavior. Other researchers acknowledge that each plays an important role in social influence, and both can account for shifts in opinion and behavior.

Research and theory might assume that persuadees are passive and influenced only by what others do and say. Rather than being passive, persuadees often seek persuasive influence. Is that not what people do when they look through a catalog, enter a car dealership, or go to a political rally with an open mind to have their voting preference influenced? Persuadees ignore, resist, and refute messages with which they disagree. They can be dynamic and may distort messages through selective perception, interpretation, and retention.

Instead of using reason and emotion as key terms, most researchers prefer concepts such as attitude as the central cognitive process in the process of receiving and considering messages. By 1935, in the judgment of the esteemed psychologist Allport (1935), attitude had become the most important term in social psychology and persuasion research. In this intellectual tradition, persuasion studies feature attitude and attitude change; Devito (1986) defined *persuasion* as "the process of influencing attitudes and behavior" (p. 225).

The dominant paradigm behind persuasion studies is this: Attitudes and attitude changes precede behavior and behavior change. Such research can lead to the conclusion that thoughts are neat and orderly and people receive and process persuasive messages mindfully. Many people involved in advertising believe, naively, that a message containing an appeal will necessarily stimulate a favorable attitude response and guide behavior.

Studies challenged the attitude-to-behavior paradigm. One challenge was issued by LaPiere (1934), who toured the country with a Chinese couple who ate at cafes and stayed at hotels. Afterward, LaPiere sent a postcard to the establishments asking whether they would serve Chinese customers. The vast majority said they would not even though they had. Even though his research suffered methodological flaws, LaPiere led many to question seriously whether behavior necessarily follows attitudes.

A second conceptual breakthrough in the attitude-to-behavior paradigm was produced by Bem (1965, 1968, 1972). He noted that people often infer their attitudes from their behavior rather than basing their behavior on their attitudes. An illustration of his classic principle is this: "I must like (attitude) brown bread because I often eat it (behavior)." The paradigm behind this statement differs from the attitude-to-behavior paradigm reflected in the following statement: "I should buy brown bread because I like it." You may intuit that both models work in your life. But, the first one is a conceptual counterbalance to the traditional one. It allows researchers to discuss the relationship this way: At times people change their behavior and then their attitudes.

The attitude-to-behavior model can be expanded to include one more variable: knowledge. Thus, a traditional view is knowledge–attitude–behavior (KAB), which assumes that people acquire information, which they use to form an attitude, which guides their behavior. Research suggests several variations on this basic model: AKB (affinity), KBA (rational), BKA (grudging), BAK (dissonant), and ABK (emotional). KAB is a learning model; knowledge helps people form attitudes that justify their behavior. AKB suggests that through social contacts people form attitudes and acquire knowledge that prompts their actions. A rational model (KBA) postulates that people acquire knowledge, which they test through behavior to see whether it justifies a positive attitude toward the behavior. People take actions, which they learn (BKA) leads to positive or negative outcomes from which people infer the best behavior. A dissonant or disharmonious cognitive feeling occurs when people engage in action (BAK), which encounters counter-attitudinal messages from which people learn to refine their behavior. And ABK occurs when people like their behavior and discover supporting knowledge (Valente, Paredes, & Poppe, 1998).

Such is the case because people want their attitudes and behavior to conform to each other. Many employees experience this phenomenon when, after working at a company for several years, they say they like their jobs to rationalize why they have worked there so long. People feel cognitive discomfort when their behavior and attitudes do not coincide; if behavior cannot change, then attitudes may. This approach to the attitude–behavior relationship argues that people monitor their behavior to know what their attitudes are and act in ways (manage impressions of themselves to others and themselves) so that their attitudes and behavior are consonant.

One explanation of how behavior change can lead to attitude change was supplied by forced compliance research (Festinger & Carlsmith, 1959). Parents "force" children to brush their teeth, take baths, and eat proper meals. Eventually, these behaviors become the norm, and attitudes are formed to correspond to them. Likewise, social change can be created by requiring people not to discriminate on the basis of race, gender, age, handicap, or religion. Eventually, such behavior may become ingrained and result in new, adjusted attitudes.

Processes relevant to information acquisition and persuasive influence are compatible lines of analysis. Chapter 4 demonstrated how people seek and cognitively process information to reduce uncertainty. As is demonstrated herein, people work to form useful attitudes that can lead them to make rewarding decisions and avoid unrewarding ones. In that regard, they want to reduce their uncertainty about which attitudes are most likely to result in favorable choices. If that is true, then we can argue that the processes of forming attitudes are parallel to and supportive of those devoted to obtaining information to reduce uncertainty.

A definition of persuasion must acknowledge that people sometimes persuade themselves. It should account for the impact of many kinds of communication stimuli, including words, other symbols such as numbers and pictures, nonverbal cues, veiled and overt threats, and coercion. It must deal with opinions that result from careful consideration, based on reasoning and evidence as well as nearly mindless responses to clever ads—nearly devoid of information—that claim products to be "new and improved."

Views of persuasion need to be comfortable with a critical perspective. One critical perspective, feminism, challenges persons who study and employ persuasion to avoid a paternalist approach to persuasion—rhetoric—in favor of a feminist approach. Advocating an invitational view of rhetoric, Foss and Griffin (1995) argued against persuasive strategies that "constitute a kind of trespassing on the personal integrity of others when they convey the rhetor's belief that audience members have inadequacies that in some way can be corrected if they adhere to the viewpoint of the rhetor" (p. 3). This trespassing view of persuasion, one that is patriarchal, reflects the values of change, competition, and domination. In its place, a feminist view of persuasion features equality, immanent value, and self-determination. It assumes that the best relationship between persuader and persuadee is characterized by equality, rather than change, competition, or domination. To base a theory of rhetoric or persuasion on immanent value is to accept the ethical principle that all beings are a unique and essential part of the universe. Persuasion should not be based on control or domination but assume that messages allow individuals the power of self-determination. This critical perspective challenges you to hold the theories and research that follow up to the standard of invitational rhetoric.

What is unique about persuasion, a domain that has been studied for centuries? We could claim that all communication is social influence, and therefore because persuasion deals with influence, communication and persuasion are identical. Berlo (1960) made communication and persuasion synonymous by concluding that "we communicate to influence—to affect with intent" (p. 12).

Based on this short review, can we define persuasion as those communication processes that focus specifically on social influence? That influence occurs between persons, between people and organizations, and within each person as he or she proactively or passively forms attitudes that are intended to distinguish rewarding from unrewarding outcomes.

AN OVERVIEW

Many misconceptions about persuasion result from incorrect assumptions about the ways receivers are influenced. Communication students, particularly those interested in advertising, public relations, and mass media effects, often overestimate the impact that messages have on receivers. Some of these students defend their bias by saying, "Advertisers would not spend all of that money if their ads did not work." This view can be corrected partially by recalling how many hundreds of ads each of us watch, listen to, or read that do not create a favorable attitude or lead to action. Think of the havoc you would wreak on your home and budget if you purchased everything you saw advertised. Many ad campaigns with enormous budgets have failed; some have backfired. Many messages designed to influence opinion or behavior do not.

Before analyzing the major theories of persuasion, we should examine some factors that are basic to persuasion theory. This foundation will increase your insight into how people receive and process persuasive messages.

1. Receiver exposure, attention, perception, and retention are selective. Selectivity is based on a vast array of idiosyncrasies of the persons involved: messages, type of decision, circumstances, and values people believe to be situationally relevant (Heath, 1976). Receivers of the same persuasive message often perceive and interpret it differently; what one receiver sees as an attractive item, for instance, may be viewed as wasteful by someone else. Some research finds that people prefer messages that are consistent with their existing opinions; other research finds just the opposite. People may pay more attention to ads and statements about a product after, rather than before, they purchase it. This information is used to confirm the purchase, exemplifying a postdecision rather than predecision attention model. People tend to ignore, forget, or downplay information that conflicts with their purchase decision. They attend to messages provided by people who are similar to them more than by persons who are dissimilar, unless dissimilarity is overridden by other

circumstances, such as status or competence. You might seek advice on making investments from someone who is different from you, someone who is rich and therefore of different status. When you ask strangers for street or road directions when you are lost in an unfamiliar town, you probably check to see if they are competent more than if they are similar to you. A message may gain attention because the audience is self-interested in its usefulness, or attention can have nothing to do with self-interest but result from other stimuli, such as novelty (Wheeless & Cook, 1985).

2. Reactions to persuasive messages depend on the extent to which receivers are self-interested and whether holding opinions or taking actions can help to achieve rewards or avoid undesirable outcomes. These two powerful variables affect how people receive, process, and act on messages (Ajzen & Fishbein, 1980; Petty & Cacioppo, 1986a; C. W. Sherif, Sherif, & Nebergall, 1965).

3. The message-impact model must account for simple and complex relationships. Some messages have a lot of impact even though the persuadee expends minimal effort in the process of receiving and thinking about them. Advertisements for soft drinks are good examples of how people make some decisions based more on glitz than fact. In other instances, the message alone cannot influence judgment or behavior. In such multiple-factor situations, many variables interact to produce acceptance or resistance to the message. For instance, peer approval may increase or decrease message impact, and receivers may have conflicting pieces of evidence that need to be incorporated into the final decision.

4. People are capable of resisting persuasion. Resistance can result from reactions to message content, but it can be the product of a negative reaction to the source. Resistance is likely to occur when people need to comply with group norms that are contradictory to message content or advocated behavior. People who do not see the benefits of action, or think it fraught with liabilities, are likely to resist messages.

5. To some extent (probably varying with circumstances and individual differences), people are capable of self-persuasion. They solicit and accept information and influence, sometimes from many sources, and weigh it to reach conclusions, form attitudes, or decide on behaviors to achieve goals they have derived for themselves.

6. Some social influence occurs so subtly that people do not think of it as persuasion. This is the case when people acquire norms, values, judgments, preferences, and behavioral intentions merely by adopting the idiom used by those with whom they associate. Language is loaded with attitudes, many of which are so much a part of their thoughts that people

do not recognize them. Idioms contain social reality; with the words we learn, each of us takes on attitudes toward people of other nationalities, ethnic groups, or religions.

7. Attempts to separate persuasion from information create an inaccurate division. Information is invaluable to persuasive impact. For instance, beliefs can be held with a high degree of certainty despite the lack of information to support them. However, beliefs that are based on accumulated information are more resistant to change than are those merely held with a high degree of certainty (Danes, 1978). When attitudes are stable (held for a long time), they reflect increasingly the information (number of messages) that the individual knows supports them (Saltiel & Woelfel, 1975). Studying media impact, Alper and Leidy (1969) concluded, "Information need not lead to attitude change, but attitude change is improbable without any input of information" (p. 556). When people receive messages that contain conflicting information, they are less likely to recall that information or to have a favorable attitude toward the message than are people who do not receive conflicting information (Burgoon, 1975). Examining the impact of information on persuasion, J. K. Morley and Walker (1987) found that it produces belief change only when it is very important, novel, and plausible. Information acquisition and processing is a vital part of influence through which people form attitudes that help them make rewarding choices.

8. People want useful and "accurate" attitudes because a major function of an attitude is to help them adapt their behavior to circumstances. Information helps people understand reality and reduce uncertainty.

9. People have implicit theories of persuasion that they use as they attempt to exert social influence in their daily lives. Individuals' use of such models is guided by (a) the extent to which they feel well informed and have internalized opinions, and (b) the social acceptability of strategy in light of the target of social influence and the situation (Roskos-Ewoldsen, 1997).

CONCEPTUAL AND RESEARCH FOUNDATIONS: LEARNING THEORY

Persuasion research has been driven by a paradigm of human thought and behavior that places attitudes central in the cognitive system. Communication, often in the form of messages, is viewed as the independent variable, and attitudes and behavior were dependent variables.

One view of persuasion is the drive-motive paradigm, which assumed that people have many drives that can be tapped by persuasive messages. The reasoning was this: Attach an action to a motive and people will respond accordingly. By this logic, many people thought that anything could be sold if attached to a drive-motive. But what happens if all perfume or cologne is marketed by appeals to sex, or food is marketed by appeals to taste? What distinguishes one product from another? The drive-motive model was too unrefined to be helpful.

Although some students of advertising and marketing continue to believe that behavior is largely an outcome of inherent and learned drives and motives that can be tapped by persuasive messages, most researchers look more deeply for at least two reasons: (a) People do not always respond in singular, causal ways to satisfy motives. Motives often conflict; all cannot be satisfied. Much of our behavior is not merely a response to inherent or learned motives: (b) Even if people respond to motives, it would be impossible to list all of them and connect them to all behaviors in ways that would allow persuaders to move receivers to act like a puppeteer moves marionettes.

To advance theory beyond the drive-motive paradigm, a major series of persuasion studies was conducted at Yale in the 1940s and 1950s. This work also grew out of efforts to understand the impact of "propaganda" on society and individual beliefs and behavior. This research project was especially important given a desire to build public commitment during wartime and divert public opinion away from "foreign" propaganda that many believed could subvert the United States war efforts. This research relied heavily on learning theory, which was very popular and subscribed to Lasswell's (1948) linear model: Who says what to whom with what effect.

Yale researchers reasoned that stimuli-data (messages) lead to learning through repeated actions (including statements made to oneself) and rewards. The research led to this proposition:

> A major basis for acceptance of a given opinion is provided by arguments or reasons [obtained from a message] which, according to the individual's own thinking habits, constitute "rational" or "logical" support for the conclusion. In addition to supporting reasons, there are likely to be other special incentives involving anticipated rewards and punishments which motivate the individual to accept or reject a given opinion. (Hovland, Janis, & Kelley, 1953, p. 11)

The task, the Yale group thought, was to understand how people accept and comprehend messages that subsequently guide behavior. Relying on learning theory, the researchers proposed to demonstrate how people obtain and think about messages that can inform them on which attitudes are rewarding and which ones are not.

To explain this learning process, the Yale team created several models of the stages of the influence process. One model featured five steps thought to occur in this order: A message is received because it captures attention, and if it is comprehended, it will lead to acceptance, yielding to the message by deciding that it is reasonable. To have impact, a message must be retained, requiring that the receiver have the ability and motivation to remember the information. If all of these factors are present, the message leads to action.

The number of variables featured in the Yale model changed over time. For instance, it was reduced to four components: attention, comprehension, anticipation, and evaluation. Attention, comprehension, and anticipation are learning factors, whereas evaluation is an acceptance factor. If individuals are motivated, they are likely to pay attention to messages, devote energy to comprehending them, and anticipate the potential each message has for predicting which attitudes and behaviors are rewarding. Persuasibility was thought to be a product of ability factors, such as intellectual capacity and training in thinking about persuasive messages, and motive factors, such as temperament and habits of processing messages.

These researchers concluded that the variables that influence learning are facilitating factors, whereas evaluation is an inhibiting factor. If motivating factors increase evaluation, a person is unlikely to be persuaded because flaws will be discovered in the message. Persuasibility was thought to result from the interaction of facilitating and inhibiting factors. For instance, when persons are low in motivation to use facilitating factors, persuasibility will decrease. Low motivation to use an inhibiting factor increases persuasibility. Low motivation is likely to lessen the effect of all four factors, which has the same effect on persuasibility as does deficiency in those factors (Janis et al., 1959).

To further refine the Yale model, McGuire (1968a, 1968b) reduced it to two variables: reception and yielding. Reception entails those processes by which a person is attentive to and considers a message. Yielding refers to the stage when the person allows the message to influence his or her attitudes or behavior.

Cast as a formula, the model postulated that the probability (Pr) of opinion change (O) equals the product of reception (R) and yielding (Y), which he expressed in the formula, $Pr(O) = Pr(R) \times Pr(Y)$. McGuire's study produced the compensatory assumption that receiver characteristics, which increase reception, will decrease yielding. For instance, the ability to comprehend, as a part of reception, will decrease yielding. McGuire argued that anxiety usually lessens reception but increases yielding. Self-confident people will let in information (reception) but are willing to disagree with the source (not yield). The second major principle that McGuire contributed was the situational weighting assumption. If a message is easy to comprehend, reception is unlikely to be as important as yielding. When messages are complex, reception and comprehension are at least as important as yielding.

Without abandoning his commitment to reception and yielding as central concepts, McGuire (1981) saw them as two of several stages of persuasive influence. Presented in the sequence in which they are likely to occur, the variables follow:

1. Being exposed to the message.
2. Attending to it.
3. Liking it and becoming interested in it.
4. Comprehending it.
5. Learning how to process and use it.
6. Yielding to it.
7. Memorizing it.
8. Retrieving it as required.
9. Using it to make decisions.
10. Behaving in accord with the decision.
11. Reinforcing the actions.
12. Consolidating the decision based on the success of the action.

Persuasive influence is possible at each stage.

In addition to striving to define the steps of the persuasion process, Yale researchers examined how each component of the communication process (source, message, channel, and receiver) figures in persuasion. These components were a popular way of thinking about the communication process and for that reason offered researchers an opportunity to dissect the process by examining what each part contributed to the final outcome.

Source Variables

By focusing on source variables, the researchers spawned decades of research into the effects source credibility has on attitude and behavior. The argument is that receivers' perceptions of the speaker affect the impact of the speaker's messages. The Yale group argued that credibility depends on whether the source is perceived to be expert, trustworthy, or affiliated with groups the receivers view positively. High credibility sources are more likely to create opinion change than are low credibility sources. The assumption is that information is more accurate and opinion is more useful if they are provided by credible sources.

Credibility counts in the influence process. However, over time receivers dissociate the source from the message so that opinions received from a low credibility source can increase and those from a high credibility source may decrease in impact (Hovland et al., 1953).

Many traits are used by receivers to attribute credibility. For instance, fast talking sources are more credible than slower talkers. Although experts have high credibility on topics related to their expertise, the ideal source is one that is similar to but slightly higher in status than the receiver (P. L. Wright, 1981). Nonverbal cues are vital to receivers' assessments of speaker credibility. Speakers are perceived to possess competence and composure when they exhibit greater vocal and facial pleasantness. Facial expressiveness increases perceptions of competence. Speakers who exhibit naturalness, dominance, and relaxed posture are viewed as sociable, especially when they have a pleasant voice. Speakers are thought to be more persuasive when they exhibit naturalness, facial expressiveness, and relaxed posture (J. K. Burgoon, Birk, & Pfau, 1990).

In recent years, the debate regarding source credibility has centered on which characteristics (such as dynamism, expertness, intelligence, trustworthiness, safety, or qualification) constitute credibility (Berlo, Lemert, & Mertz, 1969). Studies such as these are problematic for several methodological reasons; for instance, the categories used to define credibility are generated by researchers and may not be those of participants (Cronkhite & Liska, 1980).

Although researchers differ about which factors are most important, they agree that receivers hold standards of credibility against which the source and his or her presentation are compared favorably or unfavorably. What constitutes credibility changes according to situations and specific receiver needs and expectations. Factors leading to credibility are dynamic and interactive, not static or singular. People use the situation and the goals they have in that situation to construct their list of attributes of credibility relevant to those goals in that situation (Cronkhite & Liska , 1980). The credibility of a physician, for instance, regarding a medical problem might not be the same as his or her credibility regarding playing golf or buying an automobile.

As additional evidence that credibility is not static, research indicates that if the qualifications of a source are presented late in the message, credibility has less effect than if that presentation of credentials occurs prior to presentation of the message (D. J. O'Keefe, 1987). People decide credibility on an ad-by-ad basis. Attitudes toward advertising do not significantly influence attitudes toward content of specific ads (Muehling, 1987).

Credibility is not static in the course of conversation. G. R. Miller (1987) argued that as conversations progress the need for credibility may change. On one topic, one conversational partner may be more credible than another; this relationship can reverse as conversational topics change. Interpersonal credibility depends on communication style and other tactics people use to induce others to like them.

This logic can apply to corporate or organizational communication. Not only do companies have high or low credibility, but the same can also be said for various persons who communicate on behalf of the organization. Companies must be aware of the consequences of the credibility of their claims regarding products, services, or their images. Their credibility changes over time. Regardless of the context, credibility is multifaceted, dynamic, and constantly changing.

Message Variables

In addition to source variables, the Yale research group studied how message variables affect opinion change. Their findings in regard to fear appeals are particularly instructive. A fear appeal is a component of a message that contains information that directly relates to some dreaded effect that could be suffered by the persuadee or by persons for whom this person is responsible, such as a child. Television advertising routinely employs fear appeals, such as ads related to automobile safety or dental hygiene.

Learning theory researchers were keenly interested in how attention could be gained as a first stage in the persuasion and attitude change process. They found that fear appeals increase attention. People are more likely to pay attention to messages that relate to their well-being. Message impact increases if the threat applies to persons for whom they are responsible; for instance, parents are likely to pay attention to messages that alert them to safety hazards faced by their children. Although fear increases persons' willingness to pay attention to messages, if the appeals are intense, they can be so arousing that they can inhibit attention and increase distraction, which impairs comprehension and leads to avoidance (Hovland et al., 1953). If they encounter information that is too threatening, they are likely to experience some denial and avoidance.

Fear appeal research opened a provocative line of research, especially when it went beyond attention to focus on attitude change. How much fear is too much to be appealing? Before attempting to answer that question, we must understand that the amount of fear in a message depends not on the message as such, but of its interpretation. Even a gruesome message is not fear inspiring if it is not interpreted to suggest that dreaded outcomes will occur.

Examining the impact of fear appeals, some studies concluded that high amounts of fear produce attitude change, but other studies found low amounts to be more effective. Evaluating the relationship between fear appeals and attitude change, Boster and Mongeau (1984) suggested that when fear is experienced it is likely to enhance the impact of the message. This impact is influenced by the age and degree of anxiety felt by persons who interpret the fear message. Persons who are less comfortable in coping with fear are likely to find that it enhances messages most.

Three factors appear to be important in regard to the impact of fear appeals: (a) the extent to which the object of fear is presented in extreme or noxious language, (b) the likelihood that the fear event will occur, and (c) the persuadee's ability to make a protective response. An assumption is that fear appeals are powerful because they are associated with negative outcomes, a prediction based on expectancy value theory (R. W. Rogers, 1975).

This line of analysis helps explain the impact of fear appeals. D. J. O'Keefe (1990) reasoned that fear appeals are likely to have more impact on attitude and behavior if they stimulate a cognitive rather than more emotional reaction. If an emotional reaction occurs, denial may work against attitude change or behavior change. If a person cannot think of ways to prevent the harm from occurring, then he or she is likely to deny or avoid the message. If the person cognitively thinks about the threat and sees advantages in different attitudes or behavior, then change is likely to occur. Giving further support to this line of analysis, Witte (1992) concluded that "threat determines the degree or intensity of the response, whereas efficacy determines the nature of the response" (p. 345). When people experience a threat and believe they have the self-efficacy to deal with it constructively, they will.

In addition to focusing their research on fear appeals as a message factor in persuasion, learning theory researchers have also considered the effects of presenting one or two sides of a message. Studies of message effects compared two-sided versus one-sided presentations. One-sided messages can include the pros of one point of view or the cons of the opposing view. Two-sided messages can support one message (proattitudinal) and oppose the contrary point of view (refutation). It can acknowledge the strengths of one point of view and counter refutation against that point of view. It can indicate that although an opposing point has merits, the preferred message in general is stronger than its counterpart.

Two-sided messages (those that present pros and cons) are more likely to be effective for receivers who are initially opposed to the arguments, who will hear the opposing side later, or who are better educated. One-sided presentation is best for people who initially support the message. Messages that are used to refute other messages are more effective when they present two sides rather than only one side. However, one-sided refutational messages are more persuasive than two-sided nonrefutational messages (Allen et al., 1990).

Since the Yale studies, other researchers have determined that sidedness may not operate alone. Persons who believe that an issue relates to their self-interest are more persuaded by two-sided arguments than by one-sided arguments. This is particularly true for persons who are more able to cope with uncertainty. The opposite is true for people who are less comfortable with uncertainty (Sorrentino, Bobocel, Gitta, Olson, & Hewitt, 1988).

Continuing the work of the Yale researchers, recent attention has been given to sidedness in advertising research. After years of avoiding comments about other products and assuming that only good news should be presented, researchers have discovered that two-sided presentations achieve higher commitments to purchase products (Golden & Alpert, 1987). Sidedness in advertising can include making negative comments about competitors' products as well as acknowledging limitations of the sponsor's products or services.

A third major line of message impact research focused on the order or sequence in which message points are presented as part of a total message. That line of research asks us to consider which messages we put in which order of presentation. For instance, if you have a particularly strong point to make, do you present it at the opening of your message or do you wait to use it at the end? To answer this kind of question, research compared the impact of arguments heard early in a message or campaign (primacy) versus those heard at the end of a message or campaign (recency). Primacy refers to points that are presented early in a message or campaign. Recency refers to the points that are received at the end of a message or a campaign. Political campaigns often wait until the end (recency effects) to make some of the most damaging claims about opponents. This gives little time for the opponents to refute the claims and is expected to still be on voters' minds as they enter the voting booth.

Primacy is superior when it creates an incentive to learn, to take in the message. Strong arguments presented at the beginning of the message have more impact on those who are initially disinterested. Anxiety-arousing arguments can disrupt the comprehension process and be counterproductive (Hovland et al., 1959). Primacy may have more impact when particularly strong messages set a tone for the interpretation of all messages that follow. For instance, if you receive strong arguments that convince you early that a candidate is worthy or unworthy of your vote, you are likely to interpret subsequent statements about the candidate by considering it against this attitudinal position. If the last thing you hear in a message has strong impact, it is likely to have a predominant effect until another message challenges it.

Message order effects can be viewed in another manner. An individual's attitudes may change if he or she is induced to make a statement or take an action that is contrary to his or her attitudes. Making a statement or taking an action (such as eating grasshoppers at survival school) is likely to change attitudes so that they conform with those expressed in the statement or so that they agree with (are consonant with) the action. The outcome is more likely to occur if the action is taken or the statement made with minimal reward or to comply with the request of an unattractive person. G. R. Miller (1987) said that this result occurs because individuals persuade themselves. G. R. Miller and Burgoon (1978) characterized this as an active participation paradigm rather than passive reception.

Two broad explanations can be given for this outcome. One line of analysis reasons that people attempt to avoid or reduce dissonance (an uncomfortable feeling) when confronted with conflicting attitudes, information, beliefs, or choices (Festinger, 1957). To reduce dissonance experienced by stating something contrary to existing beliefs, an individual may adopt the new attitude. The second explanation is predicated on individuals' tendency to manage their impressions. Impression management, particularly when it is associated with self-monitoring can lead an individual to believe, as Bem (1970) reasoned. An illustration of Bem's point is the typical self-reflection: "I must believe what I am saying otherwise I wouldn't be saying it." Bem observed that people often monitor their behavior to determine what their attitudes are. For example, people reflect on their behavior to infer their attitudes: "I must believe this statement (or approve this behavior) because I just said (or did) it."

If people can be prompted to make a minimal proattitudinal commitment, they are likely to agree subsequently to an even larger request on the same subject.

This is called the *foot-in-the-door* phenomenon. People can also be persuaded if a large request is made of them, followed by a smaller request. This is called *door-in-the-face*. These are strategies often associated with a sales scenario. A salesperson gets a potential buyer to make a small commitment. This kind of strategy may be employed when the car salesperson gets you to take a test drive. Even if you don't buy that car, you at least are in position to persuade yourself that you must want a new car otherwise you would not be test driving them. Sales people like to get a public commitment to a minor request, "Do you like the color?"

Door-in-the-face tactics occur, for instance, when a solicitor for an environmental or humane society group asks for a $100 donation for a worthy cause. The solicitor will gladly accept this amount but is willing to settle for less. Likewise, most sales people "sell down," starting with expensive merchandise and going to less expensive. As typical as these examples are, research suggests that neither strategy has a very strong relationship to eliciting a final response. The final request in the door-in-the-face situations must be made soon after the first one, whereas time does not seem to have an effect in the foot-in-the-door situation. Researchers explain these phenomena by using self-perception and reciprocal concessions theories (Dillard, Hunter, & Burgoon, 1984), as well as guilt reduction. If refusal of the first request creates a sense of guilt, then the person is prone to make a lower request as a means for eliminating this feeling (D. J. O'Keefe & Figge, 1997)

As well as the order in which points are made, language is a vital part of message design. Messages can be framed in effective or compelling language, or bland terms. Striking language is likely to enhance the persuasiveness of a message. Language and source credibility have been found to interact; sources that use extensive figurative language are seen as being more authoritative (Reinsch, 1974).

Another instance where message and credibility interact is the effect evidence has on credibility. Factual evidence increases the impact of persuasive messages, at least in part because it enhances source credibility. Although statistics increase persuasive impact, they have no greater effect than do other kinds of evidence. The quality of evidence is less a factor with disinterested audiences; for this reason, more arguments, regardless of their quality, will have more impact with less interested or uninvolved audiences. This is not the case for involved receivers; they are more discriminating in their reception and use of evidence (Reinard, 1988; Stiff, 1986). In fact, when people are cognitively involved with an issue, relevant information can change their opinions (Petty, Cacioppo, & Goldman, 1981).

Channel or Medium Variables

Persuasive influence can occur through all channels, or media: interpersonal, written (print), aural (radio and telephone), and aural/visual (film, television, video, and CD-ROM). Studies have produced predictable findings that suggest that media that give most information about the sender may be the most influential, for instance interpersonal. Some persons are heavily influenced by messages that are presented in print. They are prone to think, and even say, that if they can read something it has to be "true." Television is powerful because it allows people to receive information by two receptors; they can hear and see, not only the object being discussed but the persons who are presenting the persuasive messages. Television, and even radio, can be powerful because of their ability to capture attention. You probably view and listen to messages about products and services you don't want, but you are attracted to the presentation of the message anyway.

Helpful in understanding these influences, one study examined the different impact four channel modalities had on perceptions of presidential candidates. The study used the 1984 debates between presidential candidates Ronald Reagan and Walter Mondale. Messages were presented to participants through four channels: audiovision, visual only, audio only, and print. Reagan was rated more favorably than Mondale in all four treatments. He gained the greatest advantage in the television or audiovisual modality (Patterson, Churchill, Burger, & Powell, 1992).

We also need to consider that channels are often multidimensional. If someone you like or admire communicates with you interpersonally or via television, for instance, which are the source effects and how much influence results from the medium itself?

Receiver Variables

Interested in how all elements of the communication process affect persuasion, Yale researchers also examined the receiver by looking for factors that influence persuasibility, the extent to which receivers can be readily persuaded. Believing that demographic factors (such as age or education) are unrelated to persuasibility, they concluded that it is a function of several factors that are situational. Females are not always more persuasible than males; nor are older people always less persuasible than younger people. People are more persuasible when they need information and when the information they receive does not conflict with what they know about the topic. When evaluating incoming messages, people rely on information with which they are familiar (Janis et al., 1959). Rather than focusing narrowly on demographics, more sophisticated research sees beyond that level of analysis to stress that messages have more impact when persuadees believe they can use the information to form attitudes and take actions that lead to rewards and help them avoid negative outcomes.

In addition to the typical demographic factors that might predict persuasibility, the Yale research group also studied the effects of group affiliation on opinion change. They discovered that people who desire to belong to a group are most likely to accept the opinions of that group. Self-confident individuals who are less needful of a group are likely to be more independent in forming opinions (Hovland et al., 1953). One theme that runs throughout the study of communication is the connection between attraction and attitude similarity. People seem to prefer to hold attitudes that are similar to those with whom they identify.

Examining what makes people resist persuasive messages, McGuire (1964) studied whether forewarnings (telling persons that a countermessage is coming) prepare them to resist the message. Parents, for instance, may prepare their children to resist messages by warning them that such is likely to occur: "Other kids will offer you cigarettes, saying that you should try one. We think cigarettes are unhealthy and hope you never smoke." McGuire based his analysis on an analogy to medical inoculation; a small dose of a disease is injected into a patient to stimulate the body to develop immunity to it. He reasoned that if people feel a mild threat from learning that someone is going to challenge their opinions, they will increase their resistance. He examined the efficacy of preparing people to resist by giving them proattitudinal statements to reinforce their existing attitudes or refutational statements to challenge the espoused statements. Two kinds of refutational arguments are viable: those that are similar to the espoused argument and those that directly challenge it.

Following McGuire's lead, P. L. Wright (1973, 1974, 1981) argued that individuals respond to message content by comparing it to their existing opinions. This comparison occurs in three forms: counterargument, source derogation, and support argument. Counterargument consists of spotting discrepancies between existing opinions and those contained in the espoused message. Source derogation attacks the credibility of the message source. Support arguments are generated in behalf of existing opinions. Wright observed that counterargument is the most powerful mediator of content expressed in advertisements. When people heard an audio version of the ad, they were more attentive and therefore more likely to generate support arguments and resort to derogation than were those who read the ad. When individuals are involved in the decision outcome they are likely to participate in these three mediating processes.

Expectations of how a persuader will communicate affects how a persuadee responds to the message. When a persuadee expects an intense attack on an attitude and this attack is more moderate than expected, the persuadee is prone to favor the position espoused in moderate terms, but will eventually return to the previous level of counterargument. In contrast, people who receive intense messages after expecting low-intensity messages are initially negative toward the espoused message but become less likely to counterargue. Derogation of the source seems to reduce the need to counterargue.

Inoculation may be more effective with some persons than it is with others. One study learned that adolescents who have lower self-esteem are more likely to experiment with smoking than are their counterparts with higher self-esteem. Will inoculation reach persons with lower self-esteem and, for instance, help resist messages that lead to initiation into smoking behavior? In this experiment, antismoking messages were presented through peer presentations and through video. Messages included reinforcement for not smoking and refutation messages persons might use to encourage others to experiment with smoking. Results revealed that inoculation can lead to less positive attitudes toward smoking, increased resistance to initiate smoking, and reduced likelihood of actually starting smoking (Pfau, Van Bockern, & Kang, 1992).

Inoculation increases when the forewarning message elicits a sense of threat in the target of the message. Threat leads to resistance, as people want to resist what appears to be potentially harmful to their interests. This sense of resistance increases as people are more self-interested or involved in the topic (Pfau et al., 1997). We discuss the topic of involvement in one of the sections that follow.

The impact of the threat is increased when persons already believe that the topic of the message relates to their self-interest. In this way they are thoughtfully involved with the topic (Pfau et al., 1997). The concept of involvement will be discussed in more detail in the section devoted to cognitive-involvement theory. The important point to note here is that a threatening forewarning has more impact when persons already believe they need to be attentive to and mindful of messages that help them form useful opinions on topics that are vital to their self-interest.

Research such as this demonstrates that many factors influence how individuals receive and process persuasive messages. Although some messages prepare people to resist new messages, others do not. People's involvement with some issue or choice, as well as their personal disposition toward the topic are likely to affect their willingness to accept or reject new messages.

Even though the Yale studies relied on a sender-to-receiver paradigm and learning theory, they made a major contribution to persuasion research. Their research project was comprehensive, noting that influence is subject to many factors at each point in the communication process. The work of the Yale researchers set an agenda others have followed. Despite the comprehensive approach of this research team, many questions remained to be answered by other theorists. Several of these are featured in the sections that follow.

Much of the research that built on the Yale project focused on the individual who is being persuaded. The key question that drove those studies was why people form, change, and use attitudes. That is conceptually a different research point of view than asking what can persuaders do to influence persuadees. Many new explanations have come forth because of this different research perspective. Whereas much persuasion research is oriented toward antecedent–outcome relationships, some theorists have even used a rules perspective to explain how cognitions and behavior are influenced. By that logic, a person might argue that if a goal is sought that requires a specific set of attitudes, then those attitudes need to be adopted to achieve the goal (Reardon, 1981).

SOCIAL LEARNING—SOCIAL COGNITIVE THEORY

The Yale researchers wanted to know what tactics could be used by the persuader to influence persuadees. Placing the focus on the persuadees, other researchers asked how they form, change, and use attitudes. To modify the orientation taken by Yale researchers, social learning—social cognitive theory—developed to show how people actively participate in their own persuasion. Its major proponent, Bandura (1986), concluded, "Social cognitive theory embraces an interactional model of causation in which environmental events, personal factors, and behavior all operate as interacting determinants of each other. Reciprocal causation provides people with opportunities to exercise some control over their destinies as well as set limits of self-direction" (p. xi). The key terms in that statement are *some control.* The central assumption of this approach to persuasion is that individuals are not passive receptors of persuasive messages. People have goals. They realize that they must have attitudes and behaviors that help them achieve those goals. Individuals not only can decide on their goals, but they can select the attitudes and behaviors they believe are best suited to achieve those goals.

Like the Yale research project, this theory is based on a learning theory paradigm. The theory reasoned that people want to learn which goals are satisfying and which are not. In addition, they want to learn which attitudes and behaviors help them achieve satisfying goals and allow them to avoid or minimize negative outcomes. Thus, this theory argues that people seek to learn how to achieve rewards and avoid punishments.

The theory features three processes: acquisition, generality, and stability. The theory is interested in how people acquire beliefs and rules for obtaining rewards and avoiding punishment. It studies the extent to which beliefs about reward behavior generalize to various circumstances. It attempts to determine which factors cause beliefs and behaviors to be stable predictors of the means for achieving goals.

Although acknowledging humans' biological nature, the theory proposes that most motivation is not the result of internal drives but of preferences people create in their efforts to maximize rewards and avoid punishments. Preferences for action grow, at least in part, out of internal standards and evaluative reactions to one's own ability to perform to achieve rewards or avoid punishments.

This theory relies on the learning process. "Learning," Bandura (1986) observed, "is largely an information-processing activity in which information about the structure of behavior and about environmental events is transformed into symbolic representations that serve as guides for action" (p. 5). People acquire information—of many kinds—and translate that information into generalizations about means to achieve rewards and avoid unfavorable outcomes. For this reason, people are neither driven by inner forces nor helplessly shaped by external ones. People can set goals and reward themselves; they are insightful as well as foresightful and do not rely exclusively on external forces for rewards. Social learning theory views people as capable of self-regulation, through self-reward and self-punishment.

This theory views behavior as being directed toward achieving goals and outcomes projected into the future. People have some say over which of these goals they prefer and, based on that decision, they explore their options to achieve reward and avoid punishment. Projections into the future coupled with self-motivation encourage people to acquire knowledge through communication, forethought, vicarious experience of others' successes and failures, self-regulation, and self-reflection. Individuals receive information from their environment that is used to create motivation. From this information, they learn the consequences of certain opinions and behaviors and select those that seem most likely to produce reward and avoid punishment.

Reasoning in this way, Bandura featured the individual as problem solver as the essence of the persuasion process. He then was challenged to explain how people obtain information and how they use it in making rewarding decisions.

At least four means are featured to explain how people learn which opinions and behaviors are likely to produce desired results. At first glance, you might think that learning entails receiving informative information prepared by someone else. That counts, but the process entails four well-defined means by which people obtain information: information acquisition, direct experience, role playing, and modeling.

By acquiring information, individuals learn what attitudes and actions to adopt to achieve rewards and prevent negative consequences. If we read or hear a message that provides information about some attitude leading to rewarding behavior, we have acquired information.

By direct experience, people learn the consequences of opinions they hold and the behaviors they employ. You want to eat to be satisfied. You like food that tastes good and try to avoid food that tastes bad. How do you know which tastes good, and which tastes bad: direct experience. You taste it. Does ice cream taste good? Does liver taste good? Watch a small child test taste food. Some they like and some they do not. They learn that by the direct experience of pleasant and unpleasant taste. That is one example of direct experience.

Role playing allows them to try out opinions and behaviors without direct experience. For instance, children can play the role of "adult" to see how the attitudes and behaviors of adults are rewarded. Role playing can entail thinking about doing something and imagining whether it would be rewarding. Some people think about bungee jumping. Many more think about it and don't try it than do. As well as merely role playing by thinking about using certain attitudes to achieve positive goals, people may experiment as a form of role playing. People may use an internship or engage in student teaching to determine whether they will find the role positive or negative. Do they have the skills and attitudes needed to be successful? Role playing allows people to learn that answer without a full commitment to the activity.

Modeling is observational learning. Other people (including actors who appear in ads) are used as models. If an individual believes that he or she can perform as the model does, then action is likely, given the assumption that action will produce the same rewards (or avoid punishments) as it did for the model. People learn from experiences of models to the extent that the model is similar and to the extent that each person believes himself or herself able to perform as the model does. (For this reason, extremely attractive models in advertisements may not be as persuasive to average receivers as are models more similar to receivers in attractiveness.)

Modeling can teach cognitive skills and processes as well as supply opinions, behaviors, preferences, and rules. Models' behavior not only sets examples to be followed, but it also directs the observers' attention to objects and circumstances to be sought or avoided. This behavior establishes examples of thought processes observers can use to guide their choices. Not all thought or behavior that is observed leads to immediate imitation, but it can establish patterns or rules that are cognitively stored for retrieval under appropriate circumstances. Individuals learn rules that have led themselves or others to obtain rewards and avoid punishments. A cybernetic principle underpins this theory; it reasons that people use feedback to assess their success in obtaining rewards and estimating the extent to which certain actions and opinions are satisfying.

Whereas other theories assume that messages created outside of each of us lead us to form attitudes, this one is less reliant on that explanation. People receive information (as well as obtain it through direct and indirect experience) from others that is used to create beliefs. Beliefs take the form of assessments of which opinions and behaviors produce rewards and avoid punishments. In making assessments, self-esteem is vital, Bandura (1977) argued, because it is an estimate of how highly individuals value their own opinions. Learning creates "if–then" rules that guide behavior: "If this behavior is taken, then the desired consequences will result."

One last major variable needs to be included in this theory's explanation of the persuasion process. That variable is self-esteem, the extent to which individuals have confidence in their ability to use attitudes (those that they have learned) to achieve their goals. This variable is particularly important in experiential learning, or modeling. If people think of themselves as being capable of doing what models do to achieve the goals models achieve, then the attitudes acquired are likely to predict the actions the individual will take. If people perceive themselves to be inefficacious, they are less likely to use modeling as means for guiding behavior; they feel that even though others can obtain rewards, they will be unable to do so.

Let's think for a moment about how this works. If a person sees a highly attractive person use a fragrance to enhance her or his attractiveness, leading others to be attracted to the person, that person might demonstrate that if others use this product they too will be attractive. Now, the individual who is engaged in social learning, based on her or his sense of self-esteem, is likely to reason "that fragrance will not make me attractive so I will not use it," or, "I'll use that fragrance because it will make me even more attractive."

Bandura (1986) concluded that the closer the reward is to the action taken, the more impact it has on the learning curve. He pointed out that what people expect to get out of behavior is more likely to serve as motivation than is what they actually obtain. Because monitoring of behavior–reward relationships is quite complex, individuals do not always accurately estimate what factors cause rewards or punishments. Typically, they rely on factors most immediately associated with the rewards in attributing the reasons for success or failure. Cues that can be used to predict outcomes sometimes are complex. In the formation of beliefs about which actions are preferred, people often have to weigh some factors more heavily than others. Estimating what the factors of success are and how much each contributes to success can be bewildering. The model assumes that people estimate the likelihood of achieving desired outcomes in terms of a probability model. The beliefs they hold about outcomes are largely a function of how well they think they can function in a situation.

Social learning theory is powerful because it captures the interaction between people and their environment, and it features foresightfulness, self-direction, and self-esteem. Building on learning theory, it can explain how and why people adopt beliefs and behavior rules. Its weakness is its inability to indicate which variables go together in what circumstances. It tells us more about beliefs in the context of rewards and punishments than it does about them as factors of knowledge or judgment.

In its own way, social learning theory helped solve some of the issues surrounding persuasion. It has even played a major role in explaining and predicting media effects. As is seen in chapter 9, this theory has offered insights into why people are attracted to advertisements and programming and why they pay a vital role in individuals' opinion formation and behavior.

SOCIAL JUDGMENT–INVOLVEMENT THEORY

Persuasion research has always focused on the relationship between message and opinion change. Intuitive evidence suggests that sometimes people knowingly change their opinions based on attention to a message's content. At other times, people resist the influence of the message. Thus, researchers ask, what makes some messages effective, whereas others are not. As a companion question they ask, why are people sometimes willing to yield their opinions to some messages but not to others?

Social judgment–involvement theory offered some interesting answers to these questions. This theory improved on earlier studies by emphasizing the roles that self-concept and prior attitude play in persuasion. This theory takes the tack that "attitudes are not discrete elements in human psychology, but are, on the contrary, constituents of persons' self-esteem" (M. Sherif & Sherif, 1967, p. 4). Consequently, the theory postulates that any attitude change results in a new "self-picture." This change also can result in uncertainty, disturbance, instability, and puzzlement.

Viewed this way, attitudes are part of the "ego constellation" and remain stable until disrupted by communication that challenges them. They are "the stands the individual upholds and cherishes about objects, issues, person, groups, or institutions" (M. Sherif & Sherif, 1967, p. 4). Because people prefer not to continually change their sense of who they are (their self-concept), they are prone to resist change. They prefer not to adopt new attitude positions.

Ego-involvement is a perception that an attitude in a message is relevant to a person's sense of self (her or his self-concept). That means that a person is ego-involved if changing a topic would require alterations in the person's self-concept.

Ego-involvement is topic specific. A person is likely to be ego-involved with some topics, but not all. Ego-involvement is likely to change so that a person may not be involved with a topic today but may become involved at a later time. Also, ego-involvement can wane. At one point in your life, you were probably ego-involved with topics that today seem pretty trivial.

Ego-involvement increases as the attitude contained in a message is thought to be relevant to a person's self-concept. If the message expresses an attitude that would dramatically affect a person's attitude, the person is more likely to be more ego-involved. The greater the difference between the opinion a person holds and the one expressed by the persuader, the less likely that the new opinion will be accepted, especially if the change would require alterations of the self-concept. If ego-involvement is high and the message dramatically challenges the attitude position preferred by the individual, she or he is even more likely to reject the view expressed in the message.

As people encounter a message that expresses an attitude, they compare the attitude in the message against the attitude position they hold (an anchoring attitude). These anchoring attitudes are present in the mind whenever a person receives a new message. Each new message is compared to this existing attitude and is evaluated by considering the extent to which the two are similar or dissimilar. This theory reasons that individuals' willingness to change their opinions depends on the proximity between the opinions they hold and the opinion in the message, and to the extent they are ego-involved in their judgment.

According to this theory, an attitude is "a range or latitude of acceptance" (C. W. Sherif et al., 1965, p. vi). To better understand this view of the concept of attitude, let's see how Sherif and his research associates might have measured it. They believed that each person's attitude on a topic fell at a measurable point along a continuum from one point of view to its opposite. Let's use the following scale as an example.

_____ (A) The XYZ political party is the only one that will be able to ensure economic prosperity and therefore deserves my vote.

_____ (B) The XYZ political party is likely to be able to ensure economic prosperity and therefore most deserves my vote.

_____ (C) The XYZ political party usually leads to favorable economic prosperity and therefore might deserve my vote.

_____ (D) The XYZ political party and the ABC political party have mixed records on economic prosperity and therefore neither absolutely deserves my vote.

_____ (E) The ABC political party usually leads to favorable economic prosperity and therefore might deserve my vote.

_____ (F) The ABC political party is likely to be able to ensure economic prosperity and therefore most deserves my vote.

_____ (G) The ABC political party is the only one that will be able to ensure economic prosperity and therefore deserves my vote.

Let's imagine that Voter 1 holds attitude position B as her or his anchoring attitude. What is the reaction Voter 1 will make to Candidate Dud who takes the following issue stance: I represent the XYZ party; vote for me because I will ensure economic prosperity. One could predict that Person 1 will support Candidate Dud, whose position is comfortable with hers. The prediction is based on the proximity between the expressed attitude position of the candidate and the voter.

We can better understand that prediction if we look a bit deeper. Let's ask potential voters to place two As (A = accept) on the measure point most acceptable and one A on those measures that also express the person's attitude position, but less strongly. The two As would indicate the anchoring attitude. One A would mark that acceptable attitude position. What if we also asked the person to use an N (N = noncommitment) to mark positions that are irrelevant—neither accept or reject? And, following this logic, we could ask the person to mark attitude positions that are unacceptable by using an R (R = reject).

People use anchoring attitudes to assess what is said and done by others. Using the measurement we just outlined, we now have the logic to explain the following. How closely an espoused attitude agrees with an anchoring attitude can affect one of three latitudes: acceptance, where the attitude being espoused is close enough to the anchor to be accepted; rejection, where the espoused attitude is objectionable and is therefore rejected; and noncommittal, where the new attitude is seen as neutral or produces "no opinion." The range of acceptance is its latitude. So too, do we have latitudes of noncommitment and of rejection.

With this explanation, you should now understand social judgment's partial explanation of how people respond to messages. They accept those messages as valid that fall within the latitude of acceptance, ignore those in the latitude of noncommitment, and reject those in the latitude of rejection. By this means, we can explain how people resist, ignore, or accept message positions, but we can't explain how attitudes change.

How is change possible, according to social judgment theory? To change an attitude, a source can express an attitude that is slightly different (within the latitude of acceptance) from the anchoring attitude, but not so different as to be rejected. If it is close enough, it is accepted and shapes the anchor attitude.

Thus, attitude change is the product of assimilation effects, the tendency to subjectively minimize the difference between an anchor attitude and attitudes that are similar to it. Attitudes that differ from an anchor attitude and are not close enough to be acceptable suffer rejection because of contrast effects. Contrast effects result when persons maximize the difference between their attitude and those that are objectionable (M. Sherif & Hovland, 1961).

To change an attitude requires alteration of self, a change in the person, thereby producing ego-involvement and resistance (M. Sherif & Cantril, 1947; C. W. Sherif et al., 1965). Persons who are highly ego-involved have narrower latitudes of acceptance than uninvolved persons do. Ego-involvement increases the tendency to evaluate messages, even when participants are instructed not to do so. When people are ego-involved, they use their attitude position to evaluate other positions (M. Sherif & Sherif, 1967).

The amount of change depends on the degree to which attitudes are structured and familiar. When they are neither structured nor familiar, they are more likely to be changed, especially if the message is stated by a high credibility source. In cases where involvement is high, information is sufficient, the source is credible, and discrepancy is great, the anchoring attitude may change, but if it does not, a boomerang effect is likely to occur and increase resistance to change (C. W. Sherif et al., 1965).

Social judgment–involvement theory was popular for several years, but it was criticized for relying too heavily on single, anchoring attitudes as the factor for predicting message influence. It does not take into account the likelihood that, in most important decision situations, many attitudes are involved, not just the one provided by a source and the anchor against which it is weighed. Decisions often require weighing several conflicting attitudes. Social judgment–involvement theory does a better job of accounting for the impact messages have on judgment than it does of explaining how attitudes relate to behavior. Despite its limitations, it contributed the concept of ego-involvement.

COGNITIVE–INVOLVEMENT THEORY: ELABORATION LIKELIHOOD MODEL

Previous sections of this chapter have addressed many points, three of which need additional attention: (a) Not all persons react to the same message in the same way, either in terms of being thoughtful about it or being influenced by it; (b) Not everyone pays as much attention to a message or works as hard as others do to obtain and think about information in order to form an opinion on a particular matter; and (c) Not every matter receives the same amount of effort by each individual who must form many opinions on a wide range of matters, important and unimportant. Opinions are not passively created, at least those that count most. Opinions that count most receive more cognitive time and effort. Given these generalizations, we turn to a theory that has largely been created to refine them.

Let's begin this review by recalling the discussion from the previous section: social judgment–involvement theory fostered research into the cognitive processes that operate once a person receives a message that advocates an attitude position. One of that theory's predictions was that high amounts of ego-involvement reduce the likelihood of attitude change. When a message differs from an attitude position the person holds, it threatens the individual's self-concept, and resistance to change sets in.

To refine this line of analysis, investigators examined the cognitive processes people use, whether complex or simple, when they desire information about objects and issues related to their personal interest. Advancing cognitive–involvement theory, Petty and Cacioppo (1979) discovered, in contrast to social judgment–involvement theory, that high levels of involvement do not invariably decrease persuasion. Indeed, high involvement can enhance persuasion if the message contains cogent arguments and if people have enough knowledge regarding an issue to enable them to process issue-relevant statements.

Cognitive–involvement theory defines cognitive response as "a unit of information pertaining to an object or issue that is the result of cognitive processing" (Cacioppo, Harkins, & Petty, 1981, p. 37). An argument is any bit of information that is "relevant to a person's subjective determination of the true merits of an advocated position" (Petty & Cacioppo, 1986a, p. 16). Persons use cognitive processes to reduce each persuasive argument to its component parts (the information contained) and compare them to opinions they hold.

This approach to persuasion begins by acknowledging that individuals set out to receive, obtain, and process information in an effort to form correct and useful attitudes. Cognitive–involvement theory assumes that people want correct and useful attitudes and will expend the effort needed to obtain and process information to do so (Petty & Cacioppo, 1986b). Attitudes allow individuals to know, in their judgment, which opinions and actions are rewarding. Individuals are confronted with evaluating their physical and social world. They make choices. They want those choices to be rewarding. They know that they need well-founded attitudes to make those choices.

People are willing to expend more effort to obtain and think critically about information when they have choices they want or need to make. Persons who experience high levels of involvement are willing to read, talk, and teleview to obtain information on those topics. They also have more messages on a topic than do their low-involved counterparts (Heath & Douglas, 1990).

According to Petty and Cacioppo (1986b), individuals progress from mere positive or negative associations in regard to a topic, action, or object to the point where "the formation and change of some attitudes become very thoughtful processes in which issue-relevant information is carefully scrutinized and evaluated in terms of existing knowledge" (p. 131). When people encounter a topic that relates to their self-interest, they elaborate on it by receiving and storing messages relevant to it. Elaboration is a continuous, not a dichotomous variable. Thus, in contrast to social judgment–involvement theory, this theory predicts that high involvement increases the likelihood of receiving a message, thinking about it, and changing attitudes or behavior when that change is in the self-interest of the individual.

Self-interest is a central concept in this theory. Once they believe their self-interest is affected by the content of a message or some event, including choices, in their lives,

> people are likely to attend to the appeal; attempt to access relevant information from both external and internal sources; scrutinize and make inferences about the message arguments in light of any other pertinent information available; draw conclusions about the merits of the arguments based on their analyses; and consequently derive an overall evaluation of, or attitude toward, the recommendation. (Petty & Cacioppo, 1986a, p. 7)

The more people are prompted to think about any set of arguments, the more likely their opinions will change. Persuasive messages change opinions, according to this theory, because thought is devoted to arriving at satisfying conclusions.

People can only think about so much at a given time. In light of their limits, people cannot and do not spend a lot of effort forming opinions on every matter. They work harder for useful attitudes on the matters that are more important.

Thus, some opinions require a high level of cognitive processing and some do not. The difference is the degree of involvement, or the extent to which individuals believe that they need to make a choice, based on a well-formed attitude, on matters that affect their self-interest. Cognitive involvement is a product of how important an individual believes any message's content is and how aroused that person becomes.

Level of involvement depends on the extent to which people believe their self-interest is affected by a message, purchase, issue, situation, or such. If they feel their self-interest is affected, they experience a high level of arousal and become involved. Involvement is a mediating variable that influences how a message will affect attitudes or behavior. Thus, for instance, advertising messages that associate soft drinks or beers with enjoyable activities require a different kind and degree of cognitive processing than do those that address solutions to the problem of illegal drugs or nuclear arms reduction.

Acknowledging that high and low levels of involvement are typical of individuals' decision making, Petty and Cacioppo offered the elaboration likelihood model (ELM), the heart of cognitive–involvement theory (Petty, Kasmer, Haugtvedt, & Cacioppo, 1987). This model features two routes of persuasive influence: central and peripheral. When people experience high levels of involvement, they pay attention to messages and scrutinize them by comparing them against existing information and arguments. This central route requires mindful cognitive processing that includes evaluation of message content. This route is likely to lead to lasting cognitions and predict behavior, until these cognitions are challenged by other cogent arguments.

The peripheral route is based on pleasant or unpleasant associations, requiring only a relatively mindless consideration of affective responses to extra-message cues such as source credibility, context in which a message is received, or attributes of the object. For instance, soft drink or beer ads typically associate the beverage with refreshing scenes, happy and fun-loving people, rich and vivid colors, warm puppies, and the like. Ads for these products feature ice sliding down the sides of the bottles. Pleasant embellishments, such as accompanying up-beat music, help reinforce a positive impression that remains in affective memory. This kind of influence is not cognitively involving and therefore not particularly powerful, enduring, or predictive of behavior (Cacioppo et al., 1981; Cialdini, Petty, & Cacioppo, 1981; Petty & Cacioppo, 1981, 1986b; Petty, Cacioppo, & Schumann, 1983; Petty et al., 1987). These two cognitive processes are diagrammed in Fig. 5.1.

The ELM accounts for the differences in persuasive impact produced by arguments that contain ample information and cogent reasons as compared to messages that rely on simplistic associations of negative and positive attributes to some object, action, or situation. The key variable in this process is involvement, the extent to which an individual is willing and able to "think"

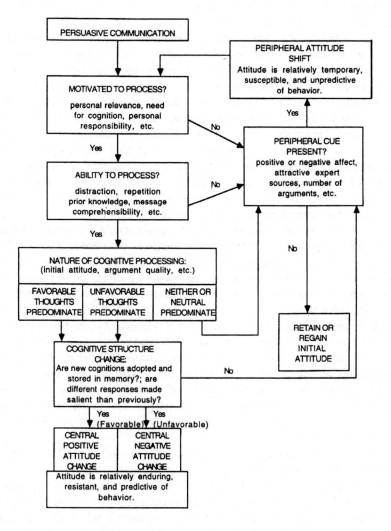

FIG 5.1. Schematic depiction of the two routes to persuasion. From Petty et al. (1987). Reprinted by permission of the National Communication Association.

about the position advocated and its supporting materials. When people are motivated and able to think about the content of the message, elaboration is high. Elaboration involves cognitive processes such as evaluation, recall, critical judgment, and inferential judgment. When elaboration is high, the central persuasive route is likely to occur; conversely, the peripheral route is the likely result of low elaboration.

Studying receivers' ability to process information in an advertisement for disposable razors, Petty et al. (1983) discovered that strong arguments had more persuasive impact than did weak ones. High involvement increased recall of brand names but had no effect on recall of ad content. Participants who were more involved were more critical of arguments than were low-involved participants; high-involved respondents were more persuaded by strong arguments than were low-involved respondents and were more critical of and less persuaded by weak arguments. Low-involved respondents were more likely to use peripheral cues, such as source credibility, rather than issue-specific argumentation, whereas the opposite was true of high-involved people. When individuals are prepared to deal with more information, they will be more likely to act on those arguments and resist later change than will individuals who receive many arguments but are not involved (motivated or skilled) to assess the accuracy and worth of the messages (Petty et al., 1987).

The ELM holds that variables, such as messages, source attributes, or situation attributes, can play any of three roles in cognitive involvement: They can be an argument, a cue, or a factor, each of which can influence the extent to which people will process the information. For instance, a source can serve any of the three roles. A person who is ill from excessive smoking is an argument or a message about smoking. For instance, the famous "tough guy" actor Yul Bryner made an antismoking commercial that was aired only after he died from cancer that he believed was related to smoking. His apparent physical ill health was a cue to listeners that if they wanted to avoid a similar condition, they should be involved or self-interested in what he had to say. The fact that Bryner had been a "tough guy" actor was a factor that could have influenced people to be more involved in the ad because it said that even tough people can be killed by cancer. All three variables (argument, cue, and factor) can operate at the same time (Petty et al., 1987).

One factor relevant to persuasive impact, according to ELM, is message repetition. An evening spent watching TV or listening to the radio will convince you that advertising sponsors believe that repeated messages increase the likelihood that persuadees will recall messages and use them when formulating opinions about a product. Parents also seem to believe that repeated messages "drive their point home" because they give their children the same instructions over and over. Studying the power of repetition, Cacioppo and Petty (1979) found that a persuader can use repetition to increase the likelihood that a message will be recalled. When people receive repeated messages, their agreement first increases and then decreases. This occurs because counterargument at first decreases, then increases, as messages are repeated.

A high level of cognitive involvement and the need to know predicts the impact information received from a public information campaign has on receivers' knowledge, attitudes, and behavior. The need to know motivates information seeking on topics such as those related to health. When situations produce little involvement, behavior is likely to be a product of situational factors rather than attitudes or knowledge. When involvement increases, behavior should be a product of attitude and knowledge. Under low involvement, people are likely to respond to cues such as the likability or credibility of sources; high involvement is likely to produce careful analysis, thought, and consideration. Perceived risk produces erratic relationships among knowledge, attitude, and belief and does not always lead to a desire for more knowledge (Chaffee & Roser, 1986). A curvilinear relationship exists between the degree to which a persuadee is involved in a persuasive topic and the effects of source credibility on that person's attitudes. As involvement increases, so does the impact of source credibility to a point, after which further involvement can actually reduce attitude change (Stiff, 1986). One explanation for these findings is that when people are worried about some matter, such as their health, even though they have high levels of involvement, they ignore information on the topic because they want to avoid increases in their level of fear.

You can provide intuitive support for these findings. When you first discover information on some topic, it is likely to influence your opinion even if it is incorrect. This is the case because you have no information against which to evaluate the new information. As you become more involved in a topic, you can evaluate information more thoroughly and accurately. Thus, the central route leads to attitude positions that resist change. Behavior is based on information that the individual decides is the most reasonable (Reinard, 1988). Lacking knowledge, people rely on peripheral cues, which result in less lasting persuasive impact (Wood, Kalgren, & Priesler, 1985).

This theory is promising because it integrates an array of variables into a single explanation of persuasion. It addresses factors that explain why and when messages and self-motivated efforts are more or less likely to lead to attitude formation (D. J. O'Keefe, 1990). It stresses the serious efforts people make to form what they believe to be wise attitudes on matters central to their self-interest. It also accounts for the sort of passing or peripheral attitudes that people form. It sees attitude formation as choice-driven efforts that result from interaction between people, and between them and the world around them.

INFORMATION INTEGRATION–EXPECTANCY VALUE THEORY

Each of the theories discussed in the sections above contributes to the understanding of persuasion. The Yale research program attempted to explain how each part of the communication process affects the learning that leads to attitudes and behavior. Social judgment–involvement demonstrates the ego-involving interaction between anchoring attitudes and self-concept, as they affect reception and response to persuasive messages. Social learning–social cognition features people as dynamic participants who help to form their own opinions regarding which opinions and actions achieve rewards or avoid punishments. Elaboration-cognitive involvement distinguishes between complex and simple persuasive efforts—thoughtful versus relatively mindless processes.

Although each of these theories makes contributions, none describes how attitudes interact and people assess the expected value of holding opinions or decide to act. To remedy that deficiency, information integration–expectancy value theory was developed. It explains how each attitude is composed of several, and often conflicting, components. It reasons that behavior is a product of two factors: (a) attitude toward the action, and (b) belief about the subjective norms held by significant others who favor or disapprove of the action. In other words, this theory argues that behavior results from a colinear interaction between the attitude that a specific action is rewarding—or not—and awareness of social pressures or norms favoring or disfavoring it (Ajzen & Fishbein, 1980). The theory reasons that what we do (our behavior) is the product of what we want to do—or not to do—considered against what we think others who are important to us want us to do—or not to do.

In the most simple terms, we can conceptualize an attitude as learned likes and dislikes, evaluations that predispose behavioral choices. Thus, a person might like (positive attitude) ice cream and dislike (negative attitude) liver or spinach.

Emphasizing this notion, Fishbein and Ajzen (1975) defined *attitude* as *"a learned predisposition to respond in a consistently favorable or unfavorable manner with respect to a given object"* (p. 6). In fact, anything that can be perceived can have an attitude assigned to it: an object, taste, sound, idea, behavior, situation, and so forth. It can be evaluated.

Building on this foundation, this theory makes two basic arguments. First, once they are acquired, attitudes provide consistency for judgment and behavior because they reflect patterns of preferences that each individual has established. Second, attitudes are not singular or undifferentiated evaluative cognitions. Rather, each attitude is the product of several affective (evaluative) qualities that are combined into a singular expression of opinion. Thus, for instance, a person might like the taste, texture, and temperature of ice cream—three positive attributes. That person's attitude toward ice cream may also include two negative attributes: animal fat (dislike for health reasons), and sugar (dislike because of desire to maintain lower body weight).

Attitudes are not only affective; they also have cognitive dimensions that can be measured as degrees of certainty—the extent to which people hold some idea or opinion to likely be "true." A belief is the cognitive dimension of an attitude that expresses the extent (subjective probability) to which an evaluation (positive or negative attribute) is associated with an object, concept, situation, or action being evaluated. Thus, an attitude such as "harmful to health" is a negative evaluation. The weight of this evaluation in the total attitude depends on how strongly (belief) each person associates that attribute, "harmful to health," with an object such as cigarettes. A person who does not believe they are harmful would have a different attitude than one who believes cigarettes are harmful. But both persons would agree that "harmful to health" is a negative evaluation.

This concept of belief is the same as the one discussed in chapter 4 regarding the impact data have on degrees of certainty measured in percentages. A belief, measured as a percentage of certainty, can be increased or decreased with information. For example, a person who plans a picnic might look at low, menacing clouds the morning of the picnic and have a relatively strong belief (based on apparent information) that rain is likely. That belief (percentage) will lessen if the clouds begin to lift and sun pops through periodically. The belief, "We'll have good weather," replaces its opposite as the clouds clear and the sun shines continuously. In this way, beliefs are conclusions that are affected by information.

For this reason, Fishbein and Ajzen (1975) concluded that beliefs are the building blocks of the cognitive structure, the information base that supports evaluative systems as well as intentions and behaviors. One strength of this theory is its ability to show how attitudes are comprised of many components. Each component has a positive or negative evaluation associated with it. That evaluation can be strong or weak. And the evaluation can be associated with the object, action, or situation that is being scrutinized. To express this integration, Fishbein and Ajzen used the following formula:

$$A_o = \sum_{i=1}^{n} b_i e_i$$

This formula consists of A_o, the attitude toward some object (O), situation (S), or behavior (B); b_i, belief i about O, (the extent to which any attribute i is related to the object); e_i, the evaluation (positive or negative) associated with the object; and n, the total number of beliefs involved in the attitude, expressed as a summation (Σ).

To understand how an attitude is a composite of many evaluations of different strengths and valences (– or +), imagine the following analysis. Let's imagine that a married couple (in this case the mother and father of a family) is shopping for an automobile. As you go through this illustration, remember that belief is calculated by obtaining a degree of certainty, a percentage expressed in a range from 0 to 1, and that evaluation is a response on a continuum from –3 to +3. The interaction of the belief and evaluation is the product, be.

Imagine that the couple have looked at several other cars before they stop to consider Brand X. Keep in mind that Brand X is evaluated by comparing it to all other brands (Brands A, B, C). A similar matrix must be created for each competing brand, and the final preference should be based on the comparison of all A_o's.

Imagine that this decision is being made by a family that has a limited budget and consists of six members. The attitude they hold is one that is expected to achieve the most rewards and avoid negative outcomes. The components of the attitude of the mother and father toward Brand X are provided in Table 5.1. Note how this decision reflects the unique circumstances of this family. Comfort and size are important, as are serviceability, economy, and reliability; style is unimportant. Another family might use a completely different matrix.

Before you can predict the behavioral outcome of the buyers' attitudes toward Brand X, you need to know that their attitudes regarding other automobiles are as follows: Brand A, 1.35; Brand B, 1.87; and Brand C, 2.12. Based on the integration of beliefs and evaluations, you should predict that the family would buy Brand C.

This theory is useful because it helps the persuader to know what decision ingredients might be changed by a persuasive message. For instance, a salesperson could convince the potential buyers that Brand X is larger than they originally thought. If "small and uncomfortable" could be changed to "large and comfortable," by informing the buyers of the internal passenger space, the decision should change. The relevance of the criteria "small and uneconomical" could be lowered by reminding the buyers that the two oldest children of the family (twins) will soon be away at college so the family car needs to be only large enough to carry four passengers instead of six. This illustration should help you understand how this theory manages judgments about objects and predicts behavior.

Information integration–expectancy value theory can help you to appreciate the relationship between judgments and behavior (Ajzen & Fishbein, 1980; Fishbein & Ajzen, 1975). The theory suggests that behavior is a product of attitude toward the behavior (especially its expected reward value) and the subjective norms involved.

TABLE 5.1
Illustration of Components of Attitude Toward Brand X

	b	e	be
Brand X is reliable	.75	+3	2.25
Brand X is economical	.70	+3	2.10
Brand X is small	.99	−3	−2.97
Brand X is uncomfortable	.99	−3	−2.97
Brand X is hard to service	.65	−1	−0.65
Brand X is stylish	.80	0	0.00
The total A_o regarding Brand X is			−2.24

The theory predicts that people's actions take into account two kinds of information: (a) a desire to behave so as to obtain the most rewards, and (b) a desire to conform to the norms of individuals who are valued by the person who is making the decision. Subjective norms consist of actual and assumed opinions that valued others (persons whose opinions are important) have regarding a decision. The formulation of this norm is based on a decision maker's beliefs that specific individuals or groups think he or she should or should not perform the intended action. (Note how beliefs about the subjective norm can explain why people sometimes do what they don't want to do, and why they don't do what they want to do.)

Let's return to examine the car buying illustration. Recall the key subjective norm that supported the parents' purchase decision: This family should buy an economical and roomy automobile that is reliable and easy to maintain. Where did those decision criteria come from? They came from the decision maker's experience as well as the opinions of others. The person who is making the decision may have a normative belief about the intended action that can be calculated to be +2. (The figure could be +3, but we believe that in the back of each car buyer's mind is a "lust" for a small and racy car.) This motivation to act depends on each buyer's perception of the opinions other people hold in regard to this decision. The opinions of others, their normative beliefs, is a calculation of each person's agreement/disagreement with the norm (+3 support the norm and −3 oppose it).

The extent to which each person agrees or disagrees with a decision criterion is a normative belief. So, as we think about making a decision we can recall the norms others have expressed. Or they may express these norms as we discuss the choices we are preparing to make. As the couple considers buying one car as opposed to another, they may think about the norms expressed by others: the spouse, a respected friend, a respected coworker, the sales person, and other members of the family—the children in this illustration.

So, as we consider choices, we think about what others would want us to do, and we weigh the extent to which we want to comply with their wishes. Sometimes our choices are heavily influenced by a desire to know and conform to what others want us to do. At other times, we do the opposite of what others want us to do. If we like and respect others, we are more likely to conform to their expectations. If we dislike them, we stand a good chance of doing the opposite. Thus, a second measure predicting actions is the extent to which the person making the decision wants to comply with the advice or wishes of other persons (+3 to 0). Because we may be making decisions about which many people hold opinions, we may have to integrate those expressions.

This phase of the decision process, development of subjective norms of behavior (SN), consists of the sum of the norms others favor (NB) coupled to motivation to comply (MC) with those persons' norms. Expressed algebraically,

TABLE 5.2
Illustration of Components of Behavioral Intention

Valued others	Normative belief		Motivation to comply	Product
Spouse	+3	x	+3	= +9
Respected friend	+2	x	+2	= +4
Respected coworker	+2	x	+1	= +2
Salesperson	-3	x	0	= 0
Oldest boy in family	-3	x	+1	= -3
Oldest girl in family	-3	x	+1	= -3
Total estimation of prevailing normative belief				+9

this relationship is $SN = \sum (NBi)(MCi)$, as is illustrated in Table 5.2. The normative belief is favored by the individual (+2) and by the others (+9). The +9 should give the person making the decision confidence that it is proper. This decision matrix is sensitive to the valued opinions of the spouse, a neighbor, and a co-worker. The opinion of the salesperson, who wants to sell a car that is small, uncomfortable, and expensive is disregarded (0). The two oldest children in the family prefer a small and sporty automobile to a "tank." Although given positive regard (+1) by their parents, their opinions on the normative belief do not overweigh others' opinions. These kids argue for style and against the criteria preferred by their parents. Note that this argument lessens the parents' commitment by a total of (6). If not for the kids' arguments (attitude position), the parents' commitment to the criteria of comfort and economy would be +15 instead of +9. See how others' opinions have a measurable effect on each of our judgments and behaviors.

In this way, we can estimate (a) a person's attitude toward an object (situation or behavior) and (b) the normative belief regarding the intended behavior, which can be expressed as $BI = (A_o)(SN)$. Both factors influence behavior. This theory explains how people often must balance conflicting information and opinions as they consider making choices. This theory can explain why people do not buy every product or service they see advertised. Even if they have a positive attitude toward the product, they do not intend to buy it now or at all because of personal intentions or because they yield to the prevailing subjective norms perceived to be held by others whose opinions they respect.

Refining this theory, Shepherd (1987) discovered that the degree of colinearity between attitudinal and normative beliefs differs, depending on how clearly each person who makes a decision differentiates the issues or choices involved and how much information he or she brings to the situation. For instance, people with undifferentiated opinions on political candidates evidence substantial colinearity, whereas people with differentiated opinions do not. Insight into the decision leads the individual to prefer either the attitude toward the action or the prevailing normative belief. The key to the decision is which of the two seems likely to result in the most favorable decision (expectancy value).

This theory is instructive for those who wish to be persuasive. It allows them to see that they can change one or several components of an attitude by changing the evaluation or the belief (degree of certainty). They can also change a person's intention by focusing on the goodness or badness of the decision or by influencing a person's perception of the prevailing subjective norm. All of this is founded on research that supports Fishbein and Ajzen's (1981) belief that "information is the essence of the persuasion process" (p. 339).

INTERPERSONAL CONTEXT

The earlier sections have focused attention on major theories that have guided persuasion research for 50 years. Such theories tend to focus attention on basic issues and do not address persuasive processes that are at play in key contexts. This section examines persuasion research regarding the dynamics of influence in interpersonal contexts.

Let's begin by examining a gender-based issue. Are men—or women— typically more persuasive than their counterparts? Examining how men and women view themselves as persuaders in interpersonal settings, Andrews (1987) found that women are less confident of their ability to be persuasive than are men. This self-consciousness is unwarranted because trained coders who observed interactions as part of this research project did not detect that women are less competent. Nevertheless, some gender-based differences do appear. Men use different kinds of arguments than do women. Men use more criterion-based arguments (arguments that are based on criteria unique to the message under consideration). In contrast, women are prone to invent their own arguments. As they do so, their arguments tend to be based on principles of social responsibility. When men succeed in being persuasive, they take personal credit but blame failures on the situation. Women believe that their success as persuaders results from hard work in preparing strong arguments.

In addition to gender, one topic that has fascinated researchers is compliance gaining. Every day, each of us makes requests of persons whom we encounter. In a typical day, how many times do you and acquaintances or family members ask "favors" of one another? "Please pass the salt." "I will let you have my calculus notes if you will share your communication theory notes with me." "Because you are my best friend, I'm sure you will loan me $10 for a couple of days." "Remember yesterday when I worked overtime for you? Now I need a favor; will you work late for me today?" Do those sorts of statements sound familiar? We expect that they do.

Some requests are scripted and routine; others may be carefully planned and require skilled execution. However scripted or strategic, the processes of compliance gaining characterize interpersonal communication. People request and yield to or deny the requests others make of them.

The concept of compliance gaining has been used to explain how people in interpersonal contexts attempt to influence each other through the use of requests. The basis of compliance gaining research is this: Messages can induce compliance because of expectations, relationships, or consequences of actions by or in behalf of the person who receives the request.

One means for studying compliance utilizes categories of statements people use when making requests of one another. This research assumes that people are more or less familiar with the kinds of statements available to be used for making requests and seeking compliance. Researchers are interested in the kinds of statements people select to use.

The list created by Marwell and Schmitt (1967) contains 16 types of messages. The list includes promises and threats, as well as recommendations based on positive expertise (do as I say and you will gain rewards) or negative expertise (if you follow my recommendation you can avoid negative consequences). Compliance-gaining messages can be based on liking, debt, moral appeal, pregiving (whereby the source gives the reward in advance of the requested action), and aversive stimulation (a request which promises to discontinue punishment if the request is granted). The list of compliance-gaining strategies includes requests based on positive self-feeling (compliance will make you feel good) and negative self-feeling (noncompliance will make you feel bad). Positive altercasting bases a request on claims that a person of good character will comply, whereas negative altercasting claims that persons who do not comply are of bad character. Altruism is an appeal to comply because the person is altruistic. Compliance messages can claim that people will like the person if he or she complies (esteem-positive) or will dislike the person if he or she does not comply (esteem-negative). These statements probably sound familiar to you. You probably use some or all, and perhaps you have acquaintances who use some of these all of the time.

Marwell and Schmitt's research consisted of having participants read the list of 16 strategies and check which ones they use when seeking to gain compliance in different situations and in the face of different kinds of counter moves. This sort of research is designed to determine the conditions under which people choose one kind of compliance strategy as opposed to others that are available.

Other researchers claim that this methodology lacks validity because people do not actually communicate that way. It is rare, if ever, that people consider all of the available strategies relevant to a situation or desired outcome. Giving participants a list from which to choose involves a methodology that truly puts "words" into the "mouths" of participants that they otherwise might not have.

For this reason, Marwell and Schmitt's approach to studying compliance should be used with extreme caution or avoided completely (Burleson et al., 1988).

Another line of analysis has asked whether the list can be shortened to fewer than 16 items. G. R. Miller (1987) believed that the list only needed to include four (instead of 16) compliance strategies:

1. Reward-oriented statements (one or both parties can receive rewards from compliance).
2. Punishment-oriented statements (compliance helps avoid punishment).
3. Communicator onus (threat, negative expertise, aversion, or negative esteem).
4. Recipient onus (negative moral appeal, negative self-feeling, or claims of indebtedness).

This model employs expectancy-value theory, which predicts that people prefer to comply with requests that produce positive outcomes (or avoid negative ones) and that conform to their norms of behavior.

Along with an interest in the kinds of compliance messages that can be selected, other research featured relational variables as the basis of compliance requests. Cody and McLaughlin (1980) claimed that six relational factors influence which message type a person selects when trying to gain compliance:

1. Amount of intimacy that exists between the person making the request and the person whose compliance is being requested.
2. Extent to which compliance will personally benefit the person making the request.
3. Consequences of the compliance-gaining effort on the relationship.
4. Rights of the persons involved in the relationship.
5. Extent to which the person making the request typically dominates the other.
6. Degree of resistance the person initiating the request expects from the other during the compliance-gaining effort.

Even though relational variables such as this are important, Hunter and Boster (1987) argued that the person seeking compliance is unlikely to use a request type that would make him or her uncomfortable.

As well as the quality of relationships, people tend to select compliance strategies that they believe they are justified in using. If people believe they are justified in making a request, they are more likely to use verbal aggression as a message tactic. If people think they have lots to gain from the request, they are likely to use many strategies. If the person making the request senses a high degree of intimacy in the relationship, he or she is less likely to use verbal aggression or harsh messages (Dillard & Burgoon, 1985).

Compliance-gaining strategies differ depending on the kind of request. A person who is seeking to borrow something is likely to make contractual statements designed to reduce the cost of granting the request. When people request favors, they inquire about the cost of the target's compliance, ask about the ability of the target to comply, and offer compensation. When borrowing requests are denied, the person seeking compliance is unwilling to express forgiveness and seeks to persuade the person to comply. In contrast, when favors are denied, the person seeking compliance is prone to be forgiving (Roloff & Janiszewski, 1989). As is seen in chapter 6, this view of compliance gaining depends on the basic assumptions of social exchange theory. For that reason, people select messages that will lead to compliance, but they will not harm the relationship in the process.

Some people are more sensitive to the presence of compliance-gaining tactics than are others. How they view the use of such tactics differs depending on the focal point from which people view them. People think about the person who is using them, the person who is the target of them, and in terms of how others use the tactics or are the target of them. This research suggests that how people employ tactics and respond to them is based on how insightfully they observe them and their judgment of whether the tactics are appropriate or inappropriate given the nature of the relationship (Wilson, Cruz, & Kang, 1992).

When compliance tactics fail, people may turn to physical threats, even force, to gain compliance. The quality of interpersonal relationships influences which compliance-gaining strategies are used. Also, gender differences exist. Males are more likely than females to use force against noncompliant males in situations when a relationship is not at stake. Males are more likely than females to use force in interpersonal situations, especially those with short-term consequences (deTurck, 1987).

Some interpersonal relationships, because of their archetypic nature, reveal unique patterns of compliance gaining. Marriage is one of those archetypic relationships. Married couples differ in their use of power to achieve compliance. For instance, "traditional" couples state their expectations of one another to gain compliance; their interdependency is the basis of their marriage. They discuss the positive and negative outcomes of the requested behavior and use their relationship as a basis of power. "Separates" (people who are less committed to interdependence) avoid messages that express relationships or lead to conflict to gain compliance. They use open appeals to influence their partners. "Independents" hold less traditional relationship values and are mildly committed to interdependency. They appeal to obligations and the values of their partner (Witteman & Fitzpatrick, 1986).

Some strategies seem to work better than others. For instance, people seek compliance by indicating that they need someone's help or by expressing hostilities toward persons other than the other participant (seeking to gang up against someone else). When people recognize that these tactics are being used, they respond with positive messages and report a positive attitude toward the request and the relationship with the person making the request. However, such strategies do not increase willingness to comply (Shimanoff, 1987).

What motivates people to yield to compliance strategies? Willingness to comply (or not) is governed by contingency rules that are selected to achieve anticipated consequences. These rules depend on the self-identities of the participants, their personal values, and the image-maintenance rules they feel comfortable in using. How these rules are used depends on the circumstances of the moment, rules governing the particular relationship, salient social norms, and the person's desire to present her- or himself in a favorable manner (M. J. Smith, 1984).

One major compliance-gaining rule is equity. People are concerned that others are treated fairly (as they themselves wish to be treated). Thus, people will work harder to persuade another if they believe that person can benefit from the outcome (Boster & Stiff, 1984).

Compliance strategies are sensitive to situations. For instance, self-oriented credibility statements are used when seeking compliance, at least by proponents of environmentalism. In such cases, persuaders seek to demonstrate the negative expertise of opponents and the positive expertise of proponents. Altruism is an effective appeal for addressing persons who are socially oriented, whereas aversive comments are effective when targets of the request are self-oriented (Baglan, Lalumia, & Bayless, 1986).

Studies such as these demonstrate that progress is being made toward understanding how people seek to gain compliance in interpersonal contexts, but more work remains. As is the case in all communication studies, many factors interact to influence the outcomes of compliance tactics. Research is needed to consider the weighted interaction of several factors:

1. Motivation and cognitive factors relevant to requests.
2. Relational and identity goals and the ways participants use messages to manage them.
3. Characteristics of influencers and targets.
4. Message tactics.
5. Factors related to relationships and reciprocation (G. R. Miller, Boster, Roloff, & Seibold, 1987).

This section has reviewed compliance-gaining research and its connections to the major theories of persuasion. The attention this section gives to that topic could leave the impression that interpersonal communication researchers are only interested in compliance. Many other topics discussed in chapters 6 and 7 deal with the processes of social influence that characterize interpersonal communication. We form attitudes toward relational partners. They persuade us to like them. We seek to persuade them to like us. We tend to like persons whose attitudes are similar to ours. We gather data that help us to reduce uncertainty regarding whether others like us. Applying the principles of social learning, we acquire attitudes and behaviors, by processes specified by the theory, to help us to be effective in the creation, maintenance, and dissolution of relationships. This section only previews topics that are explored in more detail in subsequent sections.

ORGANIZATIONAL CONTEXT

Throughout the chapter, references have been made to organizations' use of persuasion to influence opinion and behavior, especially through advertising. Rather than go into additional detail, it will suffice to say that as a source of persuasive messages, an organization is similar to a person, being assessed according to criteria of source credibility and being met with varying degrees of receptivity and resistance. Organizations attempt to create social realities that influence how their members and outsiders perceive them. Organizations use compliance-gaining messages. As receivers, organizations are subject to influence whether through information, other types of appeals, or coercion and forced compliance such as that exerted by governmental regulatory agencies.

Chapter 8 offers opportunities to explore many of these topics in detail. Here we offer a mere glimpse of issues that need much further discussion. We become interested in how superiors (bosses) influence their subordinates' attitudes and behaviors. Subordinates also influence the attitudes and behaviors of their superiors. Persons persuade organizations to allow them in. We examine the processes by which people are attracted to, think about, try to enter, successfully enter, and decide to stay with organizations. These are assimilation processes, vital to understanding how people successfully become employees or other members of organizations. We know that people in an organization influence each other's views of the organization, the priorities and beliefs, values, and attitudes that guide the organization. Each organization operates to persuade others to support it. For instance, businesses persuade consumers to buy goods and services. Without this ability to persuade, the organization fails.

MEDIATED CONTEXT

Many persuasion tactics are employed through the media. Television, radio, and print advertising bring claims about many wondrous goods and services to homes around the nation. Many of the studies cited in this chapter help explain the impact of persuasion in mediated contexts. According to social learning theory, people use the media as means for formulating attitudes and adopting behavior. Media form opinions primarily by portraying successes or failures of persons whom others use as models. People attend to media content to learn which opinions and behaviors produce rewards and punishments, lessons they want to learn. Advertising can have central or peripheral influence on the cognitive system. Marketing research can operate on the assumption that satisfaction occurs when the attributes of products coincide with those desired by buyers (Oliver, 1981).

Relevant to persuasion theory in mediated contexts, Chaudhuri and Buck (1995) discovered that cognitive processing of advertising messages occurs independent of affective processing. One response to advertising is to be thoughtful, critically analytic of the message content. The other response is to be affectively moved by the advertisement itself. These processes account for why a person might like a product and not respond to an advertisement, or vice versa. Most of us experience a reaction whereby we might like (find appealing) an advertisement, but we know that it does not influence our choice of products or services.

One line of analysis joins persuasion theory, especially expectancy value, to uses and gratifications research (Palmgreen & Rayburn, 1982, 1985a, 1985b). The argument is that people select and watch television programs because of the interaction between gratifications sought and obtained. People select television programs that produce the gratification they desire and based on their perception that others would approve or disapprove of the selection. Viewing behavior is guided by desire for information and entertainment, as well as creation of a social bond or dependency with a prominent media personality or entertainment program character. Each of these factors constitutes an expectancy value for watching television (Babrow & Swanson, 1988).

Chapters 9 and 10 dig more deeply into issues introduced in this section. Social learning and information-integration theory are vital underpinnings to explain why media influence key segments of the public. But we know that people convince the media as well. If the media meet the expectations key segments of the public have to be entertained or informed, those media thrive. If they fail to gratify expectations, they fail. In these ways, media influence key segments of the public. In turn, the audiences influence the media. So the cycle goes.

CONCLUSION

This chapter concentrates on several major theories and research that shed light on the processes of social influence. This aspect of communication study concentrates on the means by which people construct and live a social reality in coordination with one another. The ability to influence others and in turn be influenced by them assumes that each of us wants to reduce uncertainty about the opinions and actions that lead to rewards and avoidance of negative outcomes. People work to hold opinions and behave in ways that are rewarding. For this reason, people expose themselves to others' persuasive influence, but they are also capable of self-influence (self-persuasion).

When people encounter messages, they pay attention and respond to them with varying amounts of interest and degrees of willingness to believe those messages. For instance, each day, we encounter hundreds of ads. We pay little attention to most ads, but some we find agreeable and others we disagree with. According to social judgment–involvement theory, people reject messages that conflict too greatly with attitudes central to their self-concept. Sometimes people accept almost any information uncritically; at other times they are quite critical. The difference, at least according to ELM, is due to the degree of involvement, the ability and willingness to pay attention to and process useful information and strong reasons.

Influence requires information, albeit of varying amounts and interpreted by each person in his or her own way. People seek and receive information and compare it against what they already know in their effort to achieve accurate views. To maximize rewards and minimize losses, people acquire information by watching the behavior of others, obtaining messages, and monitoring their own behavior. They draw conclusions about which behavior produces rewards under various circumstances. As they observe the outcomes others achieve, individuals estimate their ability to acquire rewards and avoid punishments by considering whether they too could use those attitudes or behaviors in rewarding ways. In the process of participating in social influence, people are sometimes active and sometimes passive. In these ways, people communicate to exert social influence.

As we reflect on these processes and engage in them, we are wise to be guided by the challenge issued by Foss and Griffin (1995). We should prefer an invitational approach, rather than a manipulation and control approach to persuasion.

6

Interpersonal Communication: Relationships, Expectations, and Conflict

A desire to understand how to improve relationships has fueled the study of interpersonal communication. People assume that if they better understand the processes of interpersonal communication, they can explain how relationships grow, remain static, or deteriorate (Knapp, 1978). Ever since Mead (1934) demonstrated that people grow personally and relationally through communication, scholars have been sensitive to the importance of interpersonal interaction.

Few if any aspects of communication receive more attention than the quality of relationships. Popular culture abounds with discussions of building, maintaining, and dissolving relationships, including countless poems, songs, stories, television programs, and movies. In the past two decades, thousands of popular books, articles, and advice columns have advised people on myriad ways to get along better, be assertive, think well of themselves, and enrich their lives through communication. By the time you reached adolescence, you acquired a long list of rules by which to guide relationships. You were told how to be polite, to defend yourself verbally, to get along with others, to ingratiate, to resolve conflicts, and to enhance relationships.

Interpersonal communication research and theory address a wide array of topics, especially five major themes: meaning that is cocreated during interaction, quality of relationships, social conflict, accuracy of people's understanding of one another, and communication planning and competence. Uncertainty reduction is a central motive to interpersonal communication because people make substantial efforts to gain and share information to understand one another as well as themselves. To bridge separateness requires interpersonal competence, one's own as well as that of relational partners.

Relationships are sometimes taken for granted. At other times they are strategically created and groomed. In either sense, relationships cost. They have an "economic" dimension; as people negotiate relationships, they calculate the costs and rewards of compliance, conflict, disclosure, and relational commitment. A lot of research assumes that people seek to maintain and negotiate relationships so that rewards outweigh costs.

How people communicate affects and reflects the quality of relationships. For instance, although all couples seem to voice the same number of complaints to one another, the quality of their relationship influences the types of complaints they voice. Couples who enjoy a good relationship complain about each other's behavior, make complaints that carry positive affect, and deal agreeably with their partner's complaints. In contrast, maladjusted couples complain about one another's personal characteristics, voice negative feelings, and make counter complaints in response to complaints made by partners (Alberts, 1988).

Relationships depend on how individuals manage meaning. As discussed in chapter 3, some meanings are referential; participants recall experiences they have had with objects, situations, and feelings. Of greater relevance is linguistic relativity that explains the linguistic environment in which people enact relationships; through shared language cultures, people identify with one another, such as "members of this company," "my best friend," "university students," or "our family." Central to the meaning in interpersonal relationships is the process of interaction through which people seek to solve communication problems and cocreate an understanding (meaning) of themselves and their relationships. People attribute causes to what others do and say, for instance, "Nobody but a 'scumbag' would do that." Meaning is influenced by perceptions of the intentions behind statements people make. For instance, the statement, "You're a good kid," takes on meaning more from context and the intentions of those involved than from any reference to "good kids."

Prior to the 1970s, little research was done to understand the processes of interpersonal communication, despite its prevalence in people's lives. In the 1960s, several trends heightened interest in the study of interpersonal communication. Seminal work in psychiatry considered how personality shapes and is shaped by relationships; people's psychiatric problems are not only the result of personal problems, but also the product of interpersonal problems. Humanistic psychology, European philosophy (particularly existentialism), and the peace/love movement of the 1960s popularized the notion that lives and relationships could be improved through effective communication. Rules theory, speech act philosophy, linguistic relativity, and systems theory, supported by the concept of cybernation lent perspectives that fostered research on interpersonal communication. Interest in negotiation and cooperation gave insight into how interpersonal communication could be studied without focusing narrowly on concerns such as how one person affects the attitudes of another (C. R. Berger, 1977b).

In that tradition, this chapter examines how people communicate to create, maintain, and dissolve relationships. Insight into relationships can be gained by understanding that how people communicate affects their relationships—and vice versa. Research has demonstrated that people reward or punish one another through verbal and nonverbal communication. By those means, they negotiate and shape relationships. During relationships, people seek and share, as well as hide, information from one another. They are concerned whether they are competent in creating and sustaining relationships. They weigh the costs and rewards of creating, maintaining, and dissolving relationships. All of these issues need further investigation under the heading of interpersonal communication.

WHAT IS INTERPERSONAL COMMUNICATION?

Let's start by seeking a definition of *interpersonal communication.* Can we accurately use this definition? Interpersonal communication is dyadic interaction in which people codefine and negotiate relationships by using communication styles, content, and strategies that become personally meaningful in their attempts to reduce uncertainty (about themselves, their partners, and their relationships), to be self-efficacious, and to maximize rewards from creating, sustaining, or ending the relationship.

What is a dyad? It consists of interaction between two people. However, we must be cautious that by featuring the dyad as a basic unit of analysis, we do not ignore how each dyad exists in a network of other dyads. Thus, if you find that you are romantically interested in someone, you are likely to be interested in knowing whether that person is also interested in someone else. What if you are in a romantic relationship with someone else? Do you talk to your friends (platonic relationships) about persons with whom you are romantically interested or involved? Might you ask a friend of the person with whom you have a romantic interest whether that person talks about you as a romantic partner? Our lives are dyadic moments in a web of multiple relationships. One study discovered that one of the factors that makes a marriage partner more attractive is his or her ability to use social networks to product positive outcomes (Canary & Stafford, 1992).

What is a relationship? Typically, a relationship exists—or is the objective of one or both parties—when persons move from independence to dependence or interdependence on one another. People often think of a relationship as romantic and even sexual: "I entered into a relationship, but it is over now." That sense of relationship is too limited. We need to acknowledge that relationships can be platonic (e.g., acquaintances) and romantic. We know that romantic means love. Is a relationship with a parent, grandparent, best friend, or sibling likely to involve love? Is it romantic or platonic? Is communication between boss and employee interpersonal—having an effect on their relationship? Is a purely business interaction (e.g., talking to a bank teller) interpersonal communication? What is the relationship? A successful business transaction?

Let's dig more deeply. To understand interpersonal communication requires insight into how relational partners interact to provide and obtain information about each other, themselves, and their relationship (Cappella, 1987). *"Mutual influence is the defining characteristic of interpersonal communication"*

(Cappella, 1994, p. 409). In this sense, then, one purpose of interpersonal communication is to understand and be understood. Another is to move from independence to dependence or interdependence. G. R. Miller and Steinberg (1975) argued that the primary content of interpersonal communication is psychological, rather than sociological or cultural information. People can only know one another by experiencing each other's behavior—what they do and say. The key to understanding psychological information is not to focus only on the content of conversations (what people say to one another) but also to examine the effects of what they say and do during interaction.

We can get a better sense of what interpersonal communication is by understanding why people engage in it. First, they actually can't avoid such contact because they continually encounter other people. As they encounter one another, interpersonal communication is a means by which other objectives are sought and obtained. Thus, interpersonal communication is a process by which people influence one another and are in turn influenced by the actions and statements of each other.

What is interaction? The essence of interaction is action and response to that action. When we interact with others, each affects the other, sometimes simultaneously, such as occurs during conversations. At other times, we alternatively affect one another. A good example of alternative effect is when we write letters (or fail to respond to someone's letter.) Interaction transpires over time through a process that involves turn taking, interruptions, topic shifts, disclosures, and confirmations. How interaction occurs is fostered or hindered by variables such as complementarity (how what one person does complements the other), divergence (moving apart) or convergence (coming together), and compensatory reactions (making up for what the other person fails to do).

We must be cautious when we think about the objectives and intentions people have in interpersonal communication. In the most general sense, we know that the process is motivated by uncertainty reduction and the desire to maximize rewards and minimize losses. This paradigm, C. R. Berger (1977b) believed, differs substantially from a rules-based approach, which assumes that people prefer rule consensus (participants playing by the same interaction rules) to achieve agreeable communication outcomes. Stressing the differences between the two positions, C. R. Berger agreed with G. R. Miller and Steinberg (1975) that people may break rules to gain rewards, even for the short term. Based on this view of interpersonal communication, Berger advised that the key concepts needed to study interpersonal communication are communicator style, communicative competence, and communication process.

One challenge in the study of interpersonal communication is to gain insight without coming to believe that people are mindful of each comment they make. Some people are more mindful of what and how they communicate than are others. People are more mindful at some times than others. But none is aware of what he or she is doing and saying all of the time.

Part of the challenge of studying interpersonal communication is deciding which variables account for the differences in relationships. Several variables seem characteristic of successful and rewarding relationships. Terms such as *trust, openness, conflict, harmful,* and *supportiveness* come to mind when people think about the qualities that characterize relationships. Like you, researchers are faced with trying to determine which variables account for the quality of relationships and how those variables interact. Before examining that kind of research, we should stop to define *interpersonal communication.*

Interpersonal communication is sensitive to context. Some contexts are physical, for example, sitting next to one another on a bus or airplane. Role contexts exist, such as doctor and patient or boss (superior) and employee (subordinate). Context can be public (persons in the company of others) or private (persons alone). We have temporal contexts where we move from initial interaction, to getting to know one another, to maintaining or dissolving a relationship. We have outcomes context in which the actions of individuals are shaped by the goals they have for the interaction. We are interested in parent–child and male–female contexts. Chapter 8 features relationships in a work context. Chapter 9 examines the portrayal of interaction in entertainment media. Entertainment portrayals affect people's views of family, friendship, romance, love, intimacy, and sexuality (Denzin, 1992). Chapter 10 investigates how new communication technologies mediate the interactions. Today, for instance, many relationships are shaped by the use of the Internet.

Interpersonal communication theorists are interested in the role that social cognition plays in our relationships. Key elements of social cognition include roles, contexts, sensitivity, meaning, history, self-awareness (self-monitoring), language goals and strategies, meaning, attributions, uncertainty reduction, communication planning, script learning and recall, and problem-solving ability. Each of these themes emerges in more detail in this chapter and the next.

Meaning is the residual sense each person in a relationship has of the relationship, the actions of the other person, the actions of oneself, and the reactions each person makes to the other. Meaning has its referential dimensions, but more importantly, interpersonal communication occurs in language cultures. Idioms of each culture influence people's efforts to initiate, build, maintain, and dissolve relationships. As argued by linguistic relativists, we are hostage to our thoughts and to the language of our culture. For instance, then, terms for man and woman may imply a myriad of communication rules and roles. The ordinary language philosophers stress the role that perceptions of purpose play in our choice of words and statements, as well as the rules we use to interpret them. Through rules and problem-solving strategies, people weave conversations, interactions, and relationships. Through intersubjectivity, people come to know and share social realities that govern what they think, how they act, and what they do as they negotiate relationships.

Interpersonal communication involves a high degree of direct contact. It need not be face to face; many relationships rely on letters or telephones as communication media. Today, people spend many hours of contact via the Internet with persons around the country and the globe. Many of these people never meet. Nevertheless, they form strong platonic, and even romantic relationships.

Interpersonal communication is that form of communication where people are immediately interdependent and interlocked; what each does affects the other and the outcome of the interaction. Persons involved in interpersonal communication codefine the dynamics of relationships. For instance, it is impossible to fight if a relational partner does not want to fight.

Interpersonal communication research begins with the premise that people perceive and respond to one another based on what they experience each other doing and saying. This entails all behavior, verbal and nonverbal, that participants perform during interactions. J. K. Burgoon (1994) underscored the importance of nonverbal cues by contending that anyone who fails to note their important role is likely to misunderstand the true nature of interpersonal communication. Not only is behavior essential to a relationship, but so is the way participants cognitively process what that behavior means to them and the relationship. People come to know one another only through exchanges that have content and relational characteristics.

Critical theorists have examined research and approaches to the study of interpersonal communication. As is true of each context that is studied, they doubt that insights into interpersonal communication can be reduced to mere fact (empirically based observations and conclusions). In this vein, Bochner (1994) challenged theorists and researchers to realize that interpersonal communication is the enactment of culture narratives. People live their lives by telling stories, and as stories our lives consist of interactions with characters. Plots and themes govern what we say, how we say it, and who we conclude we are as part of our interaction. Thus, interpersonal communication is a means by which actors (coparticipants) in life's drama enact texts with one another. Interpersonal communication is a means by which people participate in the crafting of relationships.

Concepts such as these are central to this chapter and the next. This chapter concentrates primarily on variables that advance or harm relationships; the next chapter examines social cognition (how people "know" one another) and communication competence (how well people interact). Both chapters address two overriding themes central to interpersonal communication and the development of relationships. People prefer positive to negative relationships and select interpersonal partners on that basis. Because of the desire to know which people and communication styles and strategies foster positive relationships, people are motivated by the discomfort of uncertainty to make attributions and seek information that helps them make satisfying choices while accommodating others.

INTERPERSONAL COMMUNICATION:
PEOPLE AND THEIR VIEWS

Who are your friends? Your enemies? How do you know that friends are friends and enemies are enemies? Who can you trust? What do you do to get people to trust and like you? Do you know when other people are trying to control you? Do you let some people control you more than others? How do you exert control or counter the control moves others employ? What nonverbal cues are most important to you in getting to know someone? Questions such as these should help you focus on some issues basic to interpersonal communication. The objective is to address the variables that account for the qualitative differences between relationships and affect growth, stability, or decline of relationships.

Questions of this sort may help you focus on two dimensions of interpersonal communication: communicator characteristics and definitions, the views with which people approach one another and each relationship. People engage in interpersonal communication to define their relationships. How they interact (act and react) reflects their definition of each relationship and the problems they are trying to solve in its management. "At the core of this definitional process are the relational messages exchanged between participants" (J. K. Burgoon & Hale, 1984, p. 193). The meaning a relationship has for its participants exists in their minds rather than in the relationship per se.

Communicator variables are studied to help explain and predict how and why people communicate as they do. To advance this line of analysis, Giles and Street (1994) discussed several key characteristics of communicators.

1. *Self-monitoring:* People differ in the degree to which they are sensitive to how they present themselves. Sensitivity affects what they think is appropriate behavior and which means are appropriate to express themselves.
2. *Extraversion–introversion:* Some people are outgoing. Others are not.
3. *Dominance–submissiveness:* Some people are confident and assertive. Others are not; they are more likely to yield to influence than to exert it. As is noted later, people can be too dominant for the health of the relationship.
4. *Machiavelianism:* People influence one another. Do they manipulate one another? The concept of Machiavelianism refers to the extent that one person will seek to manipulate another for her or his personal objectives.
5. *Reticence/apprehension/unwillingness to communicate:* Some people communicate freely and openly. They do so with ease. Others are reluctant to communicate; they may be less open, responsive, and involved with others.
6. *Anxiety/cognitive stress:* This is an age that thinks of itself as being "stressed." Anxiety can be defined as a visceral sense of fear of failing to

cope. Stress results from this fear of failure to cope. These factors can affect how, why, and when people communicate.

7. *Cognitive complexity:* Starting in chapter 1, we emphasize this concept. It refers to individual differences in the ability to think in complex rather than simple terms, to develop complex rather than simple plans, to have multiple interpretations of what others do and say rather than to have few interpretations.

8. *Field dependence:* Persons are field dependent when they are responsive to external cues. If they respond to internal cues, they are field independent.

9. *Need for affiliation and approval:* Some people have a high need for affiliation and approval. Others do not.

In addition to these communicator characteristics, Giles and Street (1994) stressed many others, especially demographic characteristics such as age, gender, race, verbal behavior, nonverbal behavior, status, race, culture, and handicap. How people communicate can be affected by dialect, accent, and language. Communication style may exhibit patterns such as speech rate, pauses, vocal intensity, vocal pitch, vocal attractiveness, talk duration, self-disclosure, and language intensity. Even passing reflection is likely to help you think about such patterns that you have witnessed in the persons with whom you interact. Some have pleasant voices. Others do not. Some speak with intensity—vocal and language. Some disclose a lot. Others disclose very little.

Centering on communication variables such as these, studies of interpersonal communication analyze the characteristics of people as means for explaining how and why they interact as they do. Of related interest, we cannot ignore the impact their perceptions of themselves and one another have on the dynamics of relationship growth, maintenance, and deterioration. Communication styles, strategies, and competencies are important. What transpires in a relationship depends on what the participants think occurs and the impact those thoughts have on the relationship.

Examining the role their view of a relationship plays in each person's actions, Morton, Alexander, and Altman (1976) offered several propositions to stress the relationship between action and definition. Central to their analysis is the proposition that relationships change; they may progress to the point where both parties have the same view of their relationship.

1. Viable relationships occur when persons have mutual control over one another. For instance, Person A is either satisfied or dissatisfied by the amount of control Person B exerts in the relationship. Person A is either satisfied or dissatisfied by the amount of control Person B allows Person A to exert. These illustrations suggest that control is negotiated,

codefined, and a result of each person's desire to control and to be controlled.

2. Relationships are defined by multiple modes of communication (verbal, nonverbal, time, context, and occasion) that occur at multiple levels (superior–subordinate, formal to informal).

3. As a relationship develops, modes of exchange increase and diversify. For instance enemies find more ways to fight, as lovers find more ways to express affection.

4. If a relationship lacks a sense of mutuality, it is likely to suffer crisis. Most lopsided relationships do not last, or if they do, they rarely produce happiness.

5. Individuals negotiate the relationship. They like to know the ground rules of their relationships. For instance, they want to know when and how to be open, or whether they can be open or are expected to be open. They share an understanding of the rewards (or their withdrawal), punishments, and coercions that are appropriate for influencing how each other performs in that relationship. For example, they know that if they talk too much, other people might tell them to be quiet; if they do not listen, they may find their relational partners unwilling to listen. The parties also seek consensus regarding whether specific communication tactics can be used and how they can be used. Is it okay for you to lose your temper during a conversation; can your friends lose their tempers with you? Parents may tell their children which tactics may or may not be used: "Don't talk to me in that tone of voice." Sometimes parents "scream" at their kids or "whine" to show them they too can use those control tactics.

These premises suggest that the styles and content interactants use in interpersonal communication are vital to the needs, interests, and definitions each interactant brings to the relationship. They think about (define) themselves as relational partners as they think about (define) their partners.

This brief summary emphasizes how interaction follows a cybernetic model whereby people use positive and negative responses to influence each other and guide interaction. Through interaction, participants act and react. They define, refine, and negotiate the meanings they assign to one another, to themselves, and to their relationship. Participants calculate the rewards and costs of the relationship and reflect on their ability to improve it. Featuring a rules perspective to explain this process, Millar and Rogers (1976) concluded, "A transactional perspective of communication behavior tries to look directly at the combinatorial rules characterizing the system's message exchange process and not at the individual characteristics brought to the situation by the individual participants" (p. 90). Cultural rules guide such displays (K. S. Aune, Buller, & Aune, 1996).

The study of interpersonal communication, therefore, centers on the nature of people, their interaction motives, content, and styles. It seeks to understand and explain the dynamic processes that foster or impede the growth of quality relationships that are rewarding to the participants.

SOCIAL PENETRATION THEORY: THE ROLE OF DISCLOSURE

As you think about the quality of relationships, you may conclude that they are best when people feel free to disclose, to be themselves and to speak openly about their important experiences and thoughts. All people are not open about all details in their lives to everyone all of the time. Thus, disclosure is strategic. How and when people disclose is likely to reflect the principle of cybernetics. People disclose a bit of information and wait to see how another person responds. They weigh the cost of disclosure against its benefits.

This line of inquiry addresses several broad questions. Some answers to these questions have been provided by social penetration theory (Altman & Taylor, 1973; Taylor & Altman 1987). This theory reasons that people determine the amount of disclosure they need to use or are comfortable using to get to know one another. By disclosing, people indicate that they trust the person to whom they disclose and they trust themselves to cope with negative consequences that can result from disclosure. They share experiences and thoughts because they like one another and like being known and liked by others. The theory focuses on the processes whereby people come to know one another in varying degrees of detail as the foundation for a solid relationship.

Social penetration theory views the quality of communication (what and how much is exchanged between relational partners) as vital to the development and maintenance of relationships. A central premise of this theory is that positive communication produces positive relationships, whereas negative communication results in negative ones. People prefer positive to negative relationships.

In positive relationships, people are willing to disclose (communicate openly). Disclosure is gratifying to most people. Being closed to others produces negative outcomes. Relational partners tend to be flattered when others are willing to disclose to them. This willingness asserts that the person is worthy of being trusted with the details that are disclosed. However, too much disclosure can become negative, a burden on a relationship. Relationships grow through overt interpersonal behaviors and internal cognitive processes whereby participants create messages, select message strategies, and think about how those messages will affect the quality of the relationship.

Social penetration theory argues that relationships grow or dissolve by passing through developmental stages. The metaphor of penetration is used to emphasize how people "get into" each other, come to know and willingly disclose to each other. Each disclosure allows the partner to know another "layer" of who you are.

As viewed from a systems meta-perspective, disclosure occurs in stages; using the cybernetic principle, people see how some disclosure produces positive results as they decide whether to give more details or decide not to disclose any more. For this reason, relationship growth is gradual and relatively orderly, moving from superficial awareness, to recognition, understanding, and appreciation of one another. Deterioration of relationships follows the opposite path. In a deteriorating relationship, people become increasingly closed. As well as following a systems explanation, disclosure seems to follow cultural rules. Persons display more emotion after they are comfortable with a relationship, and men display less emotion than women (Aune et al., 1996).

Before we consider the stages of disclosure, we need to stop to understand the different kinds of information that might be disclosed. Think of what you say (topics you discuss) when you first meet someone, especially someone whom you are trying to impress. You probably share a lot of public information, that which is well and widely known about you. That kind of detail is not threatening. No one can use it in ways that harm your interests. Semiprivate information is more personal. You will tell it to some people, but not to all. The kind of information that is most difficult (costly) to disclose is private personal. This is the sort of information that you only tell to your best friends, who may be someone with whom you are romantically involved. Can you imagine telling something to your best friend that you would not tell to a girlfriend, boyfriend, husband, or wife? Thus the amount of disclosure is a key variable. The risk of betrayal is the cost weighed against the rewards of disclosure.

We can think of the amount of disclosure by focusing on two more dimensions. Amount of disclosure can be conceptualized in terms of quantity (number or breadth of topics that can be shared) and quality (depth of intimate detail on each topic). Change can be quantitative, more topics become open for discussion, and qualitative, disclosure deepens on each topic. Dissolution of relationships assumes that the opposite processes occur: less depth and fewer topics. You probably recall how you spent time talking about topics with a relational partner when the relationship was good, but found that you really did not have much to say as the relationship became less satisfying.

This theory postulates that relationships progress through four stages: Orientation, exploration, affective exchange, and stable exchange (Taylor & Altman, 1987). Orientation occurs in public areas. At this stage, the level of intimacy is that typical of initial interactions when people first meet and start to become acquainted. The tone of conversations at this stage is likely to be cautious and exploratory. Initial, superficial efforts are made to reduce uncertainty and forecast the reward/cost ratio of getting to know the other person.

A relationship progresses to the second phase if participants become willing to have exploratory affective exchange. This stage involves preliminary attempts to reveal aspects of personality and more private thoughts. The tone of this stage is more friendly and relaxed. An exchange of feelings and emotions is vital at this phase. This reveals information about the person who volunteers it that the partner would not otherwise have. A level of trust is developing because each person is willing to share intimate details and to be more expressive and less guarded. This stage may be characterized by "what do you think (or feel) questions." It may involve open expression of feelings, "You're nice" or "I enjoy your company."

The third stage, affective exchange, is a continuation of the previous stage. It is typical of close friendships and romantic relationships, in which intimacy increases because participants disclose to each other in more casual and free-wheeling ways. The final stage, stable exchange, is characterized by continuous openness. Because of disclosure at previous stages, participants have come to know one another sufficiently well to reliably interpret and predict feelings and behavior of each other.

Relationships change because mutual exchange of disclosure occurs. Van Lear (1987) investigated whether relationships show incremental increases in depth (quality) and breadth (quantity) of disclosure topics (public, semiprivate, or private personal) and, if so, by what pattern. This research found that levels of disclosure tend to follow norms of reciprocity; intimate disclosure is matched by intimate disclosure. This reciprocity was strongest for semiprivate disclosures. Development of relationships seems to follow a cyclical model of self-disclosure reciprocity. One person's disclosure may prompt the partner to reciprocate at least for a short time, but intimate disclosure is difficult to maintain for very long. Although this progression is cyclical in some dyads, it does not occur in all.

Participants cannot progress through these stages without using verbal and nonverbal communication, as well as situationally oriented behaviors, including nonverbal cues of space, distance, and physical objects. As relationships become more intimate, participants can make transitions through space—even into intimate space—easier and with a prediction that the outcome will be positive. We allow friends to get physically closer to us—including hugging—than we do strangers. This phenomenon is easy to appreciate as you recall how you become "closer" to others physically as well as psychologically. It is uncomfortable for most people to put an arm around a stranger. Most people have encountered the awkwardness of initiating, accepting, or repelling a kiss, which is a good example of the penetration of intimate space.

Taylor and Altman (1987) acknowledged that few relationships can grow without conflict and strains. If crisis and conflict lead to forecasts that costs will outweigh rewards, the relationship is likely to dissolve or at least become less intimate. This outcome could result from failure to manage conflict effectively.

According to this theory, all relationships entail costs. To understand interpersonal relationships requires insight into this formula: Relationship outcomes = rewards − costs. Taylor and Altman (1987) presented five propositions in this regard.

1. When rewards outweigh costs, a relationship is satisfying.
2. In assessing the reward/cost ratio, people estimate an absolute reward/cost ratio yardstick against which to measure each specific relationship.
3. As interaction transpires, critical moments are assessed in terms of the absolute reward and cost ratio of the relationship.
4. As the relationship continues, participants forecast rewards and costs based on apparent progress, given its history and immediate rewards.
5. Participants calculate the cumulative rewards and costs over the duration of the relationship.

For these reasons exchange at superficial levels allows people to test the relationship before progressing to more intimate levels.

If rewards are present, relationships are either stable or change in positive ways. If the relationship is not positive, it is likely to change for the worse. This tug-of-war between stability and change occurs between polarities such as closeness–openness, acceptance–rejection, or disclosure–secretiveness. Change is necessary if relationships are to develop. They must have sufficient stability to justify subsequent levels of intimacy.

Whether the quantity or quality of openness or closeness remains stable or changes depends on four factors: frequency (how often a person is open or closed), amplitude (the degree of openness or closedness), regularity (the patterns of openness or closedness), or relative duration of either state (how long a person is in either state).

Change and stability occur because people seek to maintain balance, a concept consistent with the cybernetic, systems approach to communication. As people interact, they seek a balance between closedness–openness and stability–change in an effort to achieve comfort in each relationship. Tensions result from efforts to achieve balance. How the dimensions of closedness–openness and stability–change operate in an interaction depends on timing and synchrony. Timing refers to the moments when each party is open or closed on a topic. Synchrony occurs when interactants are in complementary states at the same times so that their efforts match one another (Altman, Vinsel, & Brown, 1981).

Positive change occurs, Taylor and Altman (1987) predicted, when the ratio of rewards to costs is high. One reason for relationship change is the norm of reciprocity. Disclosure by one person invites disclosure by another. This exchange process is regulated by norms of equitable exchange, implying that each person is obligated to achieve the same degree of disclosure. These processes are influenced by the ability of people to perceive the degree to which others are disclosing and their willingness to match that disclosure.

As strategic behavior, disclosure is sensitive to at least four factors: setting, self, interpersonal partner, and relationship. To decide whether to disclose, women tend to rely on their and their partner's characteristics more than men do, and they place more importance on prerequisite conditions for disclosure on all topics than men do. Women are more willing to express empathy than men, have greater need for affiliation, and are more responsive (Petronio, Martin, & Littlefield, 1984).

Comforting is a vital form of strategic behavior in the face of disclosure. Highly apprehensive individuals do not engage in as much comforting behavior as do their less apprehensive counterparts. Comforting behavior is unrelated to empathy or locus of control (Samter & Burleson, 1984).

What each person is likely to disclose at any moment in a relationship tends to depend on the history of the relationship. Each moment in a relationship has a past. As well, participants can imagine its future. Whether a person is willing to trust another depends in large part on whether trust was violated or accepted in the past. If all is well with the relationship, it can progress to a new level: a mix of cyclical and linear patterns (Duck & Miell, 1986). The cyclical nature of disclosure occurs when people constantly test their partner's reactions to certain topics. Linear patterns mean that the amount of openness by one partner is reciprocated by the other and the ability to discuss that topic becomes easier and in a linear progression.

The history of a relationship is a vital part of what occurs at each moment. How well do people remember the events that define their relationship? Contrary to what most people think, they are able to recall relatively little (about 10%) of what was said in a previous conversation. And they remember selectively (Stafford & Daly, 1984). What people remember is likely to be behavior specific (what other people did) rather than the qualities of the relationship (such as control) or the situation in which it occurred (Planalp, 1985).

What people remember about their interpersonal encounters is influenced by what they think are prototypical interactions. People remember relational history by categorizing events according to what they think a typical relationship should be. They create their interaction plans according to a similar set of expectations (Honeycutt, Cantrill, & Greene, 1989). For this reason, two people in an encounter might remember differently what happened. They focus on different features of their encounters because of their unique expectations of what should happen in interpersonal communication.

Disclosure is vital to the process of inclusion and exclusion. If we tell personal details to someone, we include them in our life. If we refuse to give those details we exclude that person from that dimension of us. Viewed that way, disclosure "invites the partner into an exclusive relational club where the most important issues of the day reside" (Duck & Pittman, 1994, p. 691).

Does disclosure go on indefinitely? Uncertainty reduction theory postulates that disclosure should diminish over time as each partner feels that enough uncertainty has been reduced for the relationship to be maintained (C. R. Berger & Calabrese, 1975). If uncertainty is reduced, the partners can use that as a foundation for further exploration.

In this way, social penetration theory offers insight into interpersonal communication as a basis for relationship development or deterioration. This theory features a dimension, estimations of costs/rewards, that is featured in the next section. That section explains how people decide what makes a good relationship and how people know and follow rules to negotiate its boundaries and define its obligations.

SOCIAL EXCHANGE THEORY: BALANCING COSTS AND REWARDS

How do you know what is required of you as you attempt to achieve and maintain a friendship or some other relationship? As we have discussed in other sections, each of us learns rules of interaction that we can apply during interpersonal communication. However, each friendship is different. A platonic one differs from a romantic one. Each romantic relationship is different. You may have one relative who demands a lot of you, whereas another gives more than he or she receives. You might have a good relationship with someone based on the mutual willingness to disclose, as social penetration theory suggests. What do you do or expect of others with whom you have ongoing relationships? What happens if someone asks more of you and your relationship than the person gives in return?

Rules metatheory and its offshoots can answer some of these questions. However, other answers focus attention on the willingness and ability of relational partners to know, negotiate, and comply with obligations of relationship building. Exploring this phenomenon, social exchange theory postulates that people negotiate the "rules" and "requirements" of each relationship. As do other theories, social exchange theory assumes (a) that people prefer positive to negative relationships and (b) that positive communication leads to positive relationships.

Social exchange theory features a process that is analogous to monetary exchange. In situations regarding monetary reciprocity, people are interested in giving and receiving fair value for their efforts. If one person gives something of value to another, according to social exchange theory, reciprocation of equal or sufficient value is expected. Rules based, this theory suggests that individuals— separately and as relational partners—have goals that they can obtain by selecting and applying appropriate strategies.

What is fair value? What is "fair" exchange to one relational partner may be too much (or too little) in the estimation of another. One goal of the theory is to explain how people negotiate how much relational reward is sufficient, and how long a person can take before repaying a reward received. Resources in this context can be many: kindness, regard, love, compliments, and requests to be involved (inclusion). They can be verbal or nonverbal. A smile, for example, is a valuable resource, as is a kind touch. Rewards can be as tangible as a dinner invitation or as intangible as willingness to listen attentively.

According to social exchange theory, individuals learn, define, and negotiate what constitutes positive and negative communication and which rules must be followed to nurture a relationship. Which actions build a relationship are defined by each person's expectations and needs, as well as by what each person is able and willing to perform in behalf of the relationship. Capturing the essence of this process, Roloff (1981) concluded, "Interpersonal communication is a symbolic process by which two people bound together in a relationship provide each other with resources or negotiate the exchange of resources" (p. 30).

The central issue in this theory is the process of exchange. Roloff (1987) shed insight into the exchange process—action and reaction—that occurs when people negotiate the means for improving or harming their relationships. Everyday rewards that people give to or withhold from one another constitute "payments." How well relational partners define, negotiate, and comply with the responsibilities and limits of "paying" for what they receive from a relationship predicts the relationship's likelihood of surviving.

Relational partners set limits on the activities needed to foster each relationship. If one person discloses too much (or too little) or interrupts too often or does not listen attentively, the partner may think the cost too high. As a consequence, she or he may demonstrate that the behavior is inappropriate.

Through communication resources, the partners negotiate the amount of each kind of action (e.g., how much disclosure is enough) each believes is necessary for the relationship to grow. In this way, a partner might believe that an amount of disclosure is sufficient, but if the other person says, "Tell me more about yourself," the amount was insufficient. Conversely, the other person might say, "Stop. You've told me more than I want to know."

By defining and meeting obligations, people demonstrate to one another which goals are appropriate and which means can be used to achieve them. For instance, marital happiness is positively correlated with the number of positive communication exchanges received each day. These communication exchanges cover a wide range of activities too long to list here. Some examples are helpful: Kind looks (eye contact), a pat on the back, listening or disclosing at appropriate times, including the other in a conversation, or introducing that person to one's friends. People seem to be happiest when others whom they like perform positively and avoid negative jabs. These kinds of communication acts are the basis of social exchange. Each person uses the other person's behavior to gather data needed to reduce uncertainty and define rewards (and costs) to enhance relationships. People tend to use fewer maintenance strategies when they believe a relationship is not beneficial to them or others.

People believe that equity of exchange (giving positive input in proportion to receiving positive output) depends on the strategies their partners use, each person's perception of the strategies and rewards, and a mutual commitment to maintaining positive exchange. When assessing the equity that exists in their relationships, people prefer to share control, to like and be liked, and to achieve mutual commitment to the relationship. Such balances help define satisfying marital relationships and are central to equity theory. This theory is based on the principle of distributive justice: "Fairness is determined by comparing partners' outcome–input ratios" (Canary & Stafford, 1992, p. 244).

Throughout the discussion of social exchange to this point, we have noted the role of norms—the rules for exchange. Pursuing this issue, Roloff (1987) discussed some typical norms that are basic to social exchange.

- First, norms of reciprocity govern whether resources must be the same or merely similar. Homeomorphic exchanges require returns of the same benefits. That is, if one person compliments another, a similar compliment is expected to balance the exchange. A return of an equivalent but different resource is heteromorphic. A sincere compliment by one person may be exchanged for a heartfelt "thank you" by another. If you receive a greeting card, do you feel compelled to reciprocate?
- The second norm features the length of time allowed or required between the gesture and the reciprocation. If too much time passes between gesture and reaction, the exchange may not be satisfying. Sometimes people feel obligated to perform an exchange immediately (or expect an immediate exchange). Others who are "laid back" may be in no hurry to exchange. (Do you send greeting cards to persons who do not send them to you? How many years can a person not reciprocate before you take them off your list?) People who expect an immediate exchange may get the response but interpret it as being "late," that is, payment took too long. In this case, failure to respond as expected constitutes negative communication that can be used to decide that the partner does not desire to achieve or maintain a friendship. It is possible that no such slight was intended, but in interpersonal communication, people interpret each relationship through the behavior of the other parties and judge them based on criteria that may not be voiced.
- A third norm refers to whether the exchange must be of equal value or whether it can be of equivalent value. A rich friend could invite a poor friend to an expensive lunch and be satisfied by a sandwich in exchange; this is an equivalent rather than an equal exchange but could serve nicely as a fair exchange of friendship.
- A fourth norm relates to whether a clear link must be made between the resources exchanged. Do you ever tell someone why you are doing something nice for them? If a link is not expressed, but it is required, the person may have received the exchanged resource but did not know it.

This means that one person thought the exchange had been made, but the other person did not. One person is satisfied and expects further reciprocation, whereas the other is dissatisfied and may withhold reciprocation. Misinterpretation can lead to relational conflict.

Norms specify whether and in what ways resources are transferable. A resource is transferable when it is given beyond the relational partner to someone who the relational partner owes resources. For instance, you may need to be friendly with a friend of your relational partner. An exchange may require that resources not only be returned to the original giver, but also be given to persons close to that person. Other people associated with the person who receive the resource may be obligated to return the same or similar resources to the original giver. Noting this network of relationships and norms of exchange help us understand how normative obligations extend beyond the dyadic relationship itself. One strain on a marriage partner results from taking on members of his or her spouse's family. A wife may like her uncle, but her husband might not. She may believe that her marriage is not strong if her husband cannot be nice to her uncle. Being nice is a resource, and giving or withholding it is relevant to the norm of transferability.

Norms of reciprocity refer to how the initiation of giving resources starts. People may initiate a relationship and give resources (a) without any expectation of return, or (b) because a specific response is expected or desired by the original giver. For instance, in the initial stages of a romantic relationship people give signs of affection (e.g., flowers or a card) in hopes of receiving a similar or the same exchange. If the exchange is given, it may signal that the other person also wants a relationship to grow. If the exchange is not given, the relationship may not change or mature.

Norms imply that one person may invoke sanctions against his or her communication partner if that person does not give fair exchange in return. Thus, for instance, if you did not listen to a good friend the last time he or she had something to say, that person might avoid listening to you the next time you are together. The person may actually tell you that he or she is not listening because you did not listen. That is an explicit sanction. Sanctions that are not explicit are much more difficult to identify and, therefore, are more difficult to resolve. Sometimes people use questions to reduce uncertainty as to whether a sanction has been placed on them. We have all asked, "Are you mad at me?" Our partner might say, "No" or "I'm sorry to be distracted, but don't think that I am ignoring you because I am mad." In these ways, people link their statements to solve problems related to relationship growth and maintenance.

People who do not return resources (of equal or equivalent value or in a timely fashion) may experience various sanctions. Norms may prescribe how many resources can be given without reciprocity before sanctions are permissible.

They may also prescribe the kind and degree of the sanction and the amount of time that must elapse before sanctions are appropriate.

Partners in intimate relationships may be better at knowing and following norms; they may be superior in their ability to perceive when certain exchanges are needed and have the communication competencies to perform appropriate exchanges. People who are not so competent, either in perception or exchanged, may find that creating intimate relationships is difficult. To achieve relational growth and positive stability, both partners need to be able to know what resources need to be exchanged, what actually constitutes a resource, which norms apply at a given moment, and how effectively each party meets the norms.

Drawing on these assumptions, Roloff (1987) offered several hypotheses that could advance the understanding of social exchange theory. He speculated that as the degree of intimacy increases, several factors are at play:

1. As a relationship matures, it will exhibit more heteropathic responses, because intimacy allows, perhaps even warrants, greater latitude of exchange. As intimacy increases, people come to have more knowledge of one another and can better appreciate the value of each resource in the perception of their communication partner. Thus, as a relationship grows, exchange does not need to be equal or the same but can be equivalent and similar.

2. As intimacy increases, the time expected between the giving of one resource and the exchange becomes more variable. As a relationship matures, partners grow to trust each other to repay resources and, therefore, need not exchange so quickly to demonstrate that a norm of reciprocity has been fulfilled.

3. As a relationship matures, partners are less likely to use a resource merely to get one and are less likely to expect or state explicitly that a resource is given in specific payment for one received. People need to do less to be sure the other person knows that a resource has been repaid. Trust and understanding, as well as ability to reduce uncertainty, increase as a relationship becomes more intimate. Indeed, one of the tests of increased intimacy may be that the level of regard remains high even though explicit exchanges are not made. But partners must guard against "taking the other for granted."

4. Increased intimacy makes more resources available for exchange.

5. Increased intimacy requires more transferability of exchange.

6. Increased intimacy obligates partners to initiate and fulfill exchanges.

7. Increased intimacy allows partners to be more tolerant of asymmetrical relationships, whereby one person gives more than the other does without harming the relationship.

8. Intimates are less likely to be upset and willing to impose sanctions if exact reciprocation does not occur.

Focusing on factors that can affect relational growth, Roloff (1987) suggested that, as individuals sense or desire that a relationship is becoming more intimate, they are more likely to engage in reciprocation. To foster the growth of their relationships, participants may talk about exchanges. During such discussions, they inquire about the other to see which resources are needed and whether "the ledger" is balanced.

Increased intimacy prompts interactants to be more disclosive because they know that their partner is capable of reading the need for reciprocity and will know what to do. Increased intimacy is associated with willingness of participants to accept an offered resource and to be less likely to express gratitude for receipt of a resource.

As the quality of a relationship increases, participants feel more comfortable in using it to solve resource problems. They know that their needs will be met, and that they can pay the exchange that is needed to reward the person for giving the needed resources. Thus, if we are having a bad day, we may turn to a friend for comfort; we also know, and the person knows, that we will give comfort on those days when our friend needs it. Thus, as intimacy increases, people become more willing to seek needed resources from the other, and less explanation is needed for why requests are made. Fewer inducements are given for these requests.

Prior to development of intimacy, partners desiring intimacy may have to work hard to achieve appropriate exchanges. Dating behavior, for instance, may in the beginning be characterized by lots of effort on the part of one or both partners. As a relationship continues, it is likely that at various times one or both partners will fail to give the desired exchange and may suffer some sanctions. Statements indicating the presence of imbalance might include, "You did not call me," "You do not call me enough," "Tim gave Susan flowers," or "Joanne doesn't flirt with other guys the way you do." These comments probably sound familiar. If so, you probably have pretty good insight into the presence and operation of social exchange.

Social exchange theory offers a powerful explanation of why each relationship is different and how those differences are negotiated. In keeping with our central themes, this theory emphasizes the importance of social competence, rests on the principle of uncertainty reduction, suggests that people persuade others to be friends by what they do and say, and features rewards and costs of building relationships.

WHICH VARIABLES SHAPE RELATIONSHIPS?

To this point in this chapter, we have discussed two theories that reason that people seek positive relationships and use disclosure, as well as the exchange of resources, to create or dissolve them. This discussion has implied, and sometimes stated, that certain variables are vital to explaining what makes a relationship good. That discussion suggests that lots of factors come together as people codefine, interpret, manage, and negotiate relationships.

As we think about the dynamics of interpersonal communication, we become pressed to decide which variables count most for explaining why one relationship is better than another and why interpersonal communication transpires as it does. As individuals, as well as researchers, people want this insight so they can predict which variables will lead to positive or negative outcomes. This intellectual effort strives to meet the challenge C. R. Berger (1977a) issued to discover the variables that are essential to understanding a relationship as opposed to those that are not (those that constitute irrelevant variety).

A review of interpersonal communication research and theory suggests that such variables can be divided into many categories, which include the following:

- Personal variables (those that affect how people design, execute, and respond to interpersonal messages and nonverbal cues, as well as reflect personal attitudes, self-identity, and self-monitoring).
- Process variables (such as mutual disclosure, norm compliance, turn-taking, and synchronicity—ease of interaction).
- Meaning variables (those that guide interpretation of what is said and done as well as the linkages of statements into a coordinate and coherent conversation).
- Context variables (such as superior–subordinate, doctor–patient, or parent–child conversations).
- Temporal variables (such as how long each person talks during a conversation or when certain kinds of conversation transpire).
- Outcome variables (such as control, trust, and intimacy).

Which variables actually should be studied because they account most for differences between rewarding and unrewarding relationships? To help answer this question, Knapp (1978) suggested the following list: Depth, breadth, evaluation, smoothness, difficulty, spontaneity, flexibility, and uniqueness. The first two of these concepts are featured in Altman and Taylor's (1973) social penetration theory that argues that relationships depend on the breadth (quantity) of topics and depth of detail (quality) participants share with each other.

Smoothness refers to the degree to which the efforts of conversational partners synchronize and their conversational styles are similar and free of strain. Difficulty is an estimate of the extent to which interactants are able to accurately understand one another. Spontaneity relates to the amount of strain or tension present in interactants' efforts to get to know one another. Flexibility and uniqueness refer to the variety of channels participants use to communicate and their ability to adapt messages to each other as unique personalities.

These eight factors, Knapp, Ellis, and Williams (1980) argued, can be reduced to three:

1. Personalized communication refers to the degree of intimacy or disclosure, such as private conversations, expression of feelings, and sharing of secrets.
2. Synchronized communication relates to conversational styles that affect how easily people interact.
3. Difficult communication is the opposite of synchronized communication.

J. K. Burgoon and Hale (1984) criticized Knapp's taxonomy for featuring communication styles or relationship quality rather than the message content that fosters or harms the quality of relationships. Featuring message content, Burgoon and Hale reasoned that the best taxonomy should include the following:

1. Dominance–submission, comments participants use to exert and share control.
2. Intimacy, statements that convey affection–hostility, intensity of involvement, inclusion–exclusion, trust, and depth–superficiality,
3. Immediacy, verbal and nonverbal behavior that fosters and signifies intimacy, such as touching, eye contact, rapport, physical closeness, and vocalizations of closeness such as the use of the pronoun we. Immediacy has been a featured variable to emphasize the means by which people approach and get involved with appealing or pleasing people and avoid those who are not (Mehrabian, 1981; M. Weiner & Mehrabian, 1968).

From this base, J. K. Burgoon and Hale (1987) expanded their taxonomy to include dominance, similarity/depth, immediacy/affection, formality, task-orientation, equality, receptivity-trust, and composure. Part of the usefulness of Burgoon and Hale's taxonomy results from its emphasis on nonverbal cues. Demonstrating this point is a study that investigated the kinds of messages physicians use to gain compliance and satisfy patients' health needs. Patients are more satisfied when physicians exhibit receptivity, immediacy, composure, similarity, formality, and low levels of dominance (J. K. Burgoon et al., 1987). Patients are more satisfied when their doctors exhibit nonverbal communication styles that are similar to those of the patients. Doctors tend to match or reciprocate patients' nonverbal patterns, such as response latency (time between statements), pauses during speaking turns (hesitance), body orientation (such as turning toward someone instead of turning away), and interruptions (breaking into statements by one another) as well as duration of turns (how long one person speaks) and gestural patterns. Doctors are less domineering and more responsive to patients over 30 years old. They are responsive to patients who experience anxiety (Street & Buller, 1988). Many of these relationship cues are nonverbal.

Studying romantic relationships, Baxter (1990) featured three relationship pairs: autonomy–connection, openness–closedness, and predictability–novelty. As respondents reflected back on a romantic relationship, they recalled all three variables and could indicate the communication strategies they used in response to each. Openness-closedness is the dominant pair at early stages of romantic relationships, and the other two dominate later stages. How satisfied partners are with a relationship correlates with their use of strategies: Selection, separation, neutralization, and reframing. Selection entails deciding to use strategies that feature one end of the continuum, such as becoming more open or closed. Separation involves assigning one of the polar concepts to topics or events, such as saying that the two partners should spend Friday evenings together, a loss of autonomy for the good of the relationship. Neutralization occurs when the parties lessen the emotional intensity associated with one of the polar terms, perhaps by agreeing to be less upset by their partner's closedness. Reframing results when one of these three concepts is redefined through interaction. For instance, one or both partners may decide not to view autonomy as the opposite of connection, but its enhancement. Thus, a person may feel that the romance is strong because he or she feels even more connected during absence and that absence proves the strength of the romance (Baxter, 1990).

Two researchers, Millar and Rogers (1976, 1987), helped discover which variables predict the quality of interaction and relationship development. Their taxonomy featured control, trust, and intimacy. Their work assumed that if complementarity exceeded contradiction, the relationship would likely be satisfying. That means that each relational partner approaches a relationship with a sense of what is a good relationship and what must be done to foster relationships.

Such decisions can be made by one of the interaction partners, but eventually individual choices affect mutual decisions and communication styles. Thus, interpersonal communication consists of actions that are redundant, interlocked, and codefined. Each partner helps define what is needed for a particular relationship. Patterns of communication behavior are played over and over (redundant). What one person does in turn produces a reaction (interlocked). Partners codefine their relationships; for example, if you ask one person to describe a relationship, he or she is likely to say what he or she thinks of its quality and what he or she believes the partner thinks of the relationship. If the same question were put to a relational partner, he or she would have the same two perspectives (what he or she thinks and what he or she thinks the partner thinks).

Another way to realize that relationships are interlocked is to recall that one person cannot carry on an argument if the other person is unwilling to argue.

(Most of us know how to bait someone into an argument, but it takes two to argue.) Trust is codefined by what each does for and to the other. With these principles in mind, we can examine what Millar and Rogers believed were the variables that have the most effect on relationships.

Control refers to the right and ability each participant has to define, direct, and delimit the actions that transpire during interaction. Control often varies, at least by topic and context, between participants. For instance, in a marriage, one partner might exert more control over budget matters, whereas the other might exercise more control over recreation. In some relationships, control is distributed relatively equally between partners, and in other relationships it is disproportionate (one partner exerts more control over a broad range of topics, matters, and conversations). Although researchers assume that control is best when it is equally distributed, they recognize that a good relationship can exist with one person exerting disproportionate amounts of control (as long as the partner willingly yields to this control). A key in a relationship is the extent to which partners support each other's role identity. A dependent person can be supported by another's strength. That person is rewarded for having strength by the other person's need for guidance.

Control is the most basic of the three concepts. It is exerted through commitments, norms, rules, promises, threats, and contracts. During interactions, people estimate the probability of how their partners will behave under control constraints. If they exert control in a particular situation, will their partners yield or resist? What will happen if one person seeks to change the dynamics of a relationship by attempting to exert control, whereas before that person yielded to the partner's control? If one person withholds control, will the partner exert control?

One way this issue can be framed is to consider the relationship between dominance and affiliation. One study argued that the two key variables individuals use to estimate relationship satisfaction are dominance and liking. If people like one another, they tend to become involved. Increased amounts of dominance decrease the perception that the relational partner is polite (Dillard, Palmer, & Kinney, 1995).

To answer questions such as these, Millar and Rogers (1987) offered three measures of control. Redundancy refers to the amount and kind of control tactics each person exerts, the kinds of constraints they use to wield control, or the tactics they use to negotiate the rights to define the relationship. If one or both parties repeatedly use the same patterns of control, redundancy is high. High redundancy equals high rigidity, the unwillingness or inability to change tactics. Dominance is the amount of influence or control exhibited by A relative to B. To measure how control is distributed in a relationship, all of the control can be divided by the amount of control A exerts. The result of this calculation is the extent to which dominance is distributed. If one person has all of the control, he or she is dominant. Keep in mind that relationships are codependent; one person can dominate only if allowed to do so by the other person. The last measure of control, power, refers to the degree to which one person can influence or constrain another's opinions or behavior. Power also is the ability to resist the control efforts others are attempting to exert (C. R. Berger, 1994).

The second major variable affecting a relationship, Millar and Rogers (1987) contended, is trust, the extent to which participants experience uncertainty in regard to the amount and kind of control exerted in a relationship. Trust is a counterpart of control; it refers to the control persons exert over themselves and their partners. They consider whether they can trust one another to handle control responsibly, that is, in ways that produce rewards rather than costs. Because people are interdependent, their actions influence one another, and outcomes depend on what each one does regarding the other. Trust is contingent on the extent and ways one person can depend on the other; in this regard, trust involves predictability and obligation. Based on the assumption that people seek rewards during relationships, trust involves attempts to increase predictability and reduce uncertainty.

Trust has three indices: vulnerability, reward dependability, and confidence. Vulnerability is an estimate of the frequency that A is willing to be vulnerable to B. Vulnerability depends on the difference between the subjective cost of risking and the reward to be derived from risking. Person A is vulnerable to Person B if B can deliver or withhold rewards to A. Vulnerability is a function of the cost of getting the reward and occurs when cost may not equal reward. The parties in a relationship must be vulnerable for it to grow. A second factor of vulnerability is reward dependability, a score based on the frequency that A has been (or will be) rewarded for being vulnerable to B. Reward dependability is high if one partner can depend on the other for rewards. Trust results when reward dependability is high, or the extent to which the relationship of A's need for reward is met by B; A's need for reward divided by B's giving reward equals 1 when trust is high. Confidence is the extent to which people believe others will not betray them. This estimate is set against the vulnerability score, which is an estimate of the ratio between costs and rewards.

Intimacy, the third major construct in this model, depends on one person using the other for self-confirmation. It refers to the extent that relational partners have depth of attachment. Intimacy is high if partners are exclusive with one another, meaning that only the partner can provide some need or satisfy some part of the relationship. Statements such as "I can't live without you" or "I really miss you when you are away" characterize intimacy.

What are the factors of intimacy? One is transferability, which refers to the number of persons who can confirm Person A. If transferability is high (many people can satisfy Person A), the amount of intimacy and confirmation any person has for Person A is low. Attachment refers to subjective feelings (liking) partners have for one another. If one person likes the confirmation the other can give, attachment is high. Knowledge is vital because it refers to what one partner knows about the other's transferability and attachment. Person A's attachment for Person B depends on the extent to which A believes B views A as a relational partner.

Based on this model, Millar and Rogers (1987) defined dominance in marital relationships as occurring when reward dependability and knowledge ratios are small. If the control system is flexible, dominance is low; rigidity means that dominance is high. If B's needs are not transferable beyond A and if B is attached to A, A is dominant.

Defined in this way, Millar and Rogers distinguished between domineeringness and dominance. Dominance assumes that one partner must reciprocate or yield control to the other. If neither wants to yield and both want to control, domineeringness occurs and results in neither partner being pleased by the relationship. In keeping with this line of research, Warfel (1984) discovered that people use communication style (how they communicate) to determine which person is powerful. People who use "powerless" language are viewed as less dominant but more competent as communicators because they employ a wide range of relationship-building strategies and do not force relationships.

Research such as that reported by Millar and Rogers is intuitively interesting but it has been criticized from a research methodology standpoint (Folger & Poole, 1982). The difficulty is that the research is often conducted by having coders listen to conversations between subjects. The coders are asked to code the kinds of statements they perceive and estimate the depth of feeling expressed in the statements. Knowing, as an outsider, whether a statement exerts (rather than exhibits) dominance, control, trust, or intimacy can be difficult and judgment can be inaccurate.

Each of us has experienced this research methodology flaw during everyday conversations; many times we misjudge intensity of feelings or relational meaning of comments we hear exchanged among our acquaintances. A statement such as, "I thought you were really mad at her," exhibits how we can be wrong; such a statement might be found to be in error when our friend says, "Oh, I always talk to her like that. She knows I don't mean that. We've been friends for years." Such misperceptions not only plague researchers, but they also have implications for how each person interacts with others. Some people seem to be more competent than others in telegraphing the relational meaning of comments and in interpreting the relational meaning that others' comments contain.

This section has discussed efforts to determine which variables explain why some relationships are superior to others. Throughout this chapter, one theme is central: People favor rewarding relationships and avoid those that cost more than they offer in exchange. Such observations are almost too facile to be helpful. By digging into the nature of relational communication, researchers are slowly discovering which factors of communication content and style influence how people understand and relate to one another in interpersonal communication. We must discover exactly what variables stand the test of describing satisfying relationships.

EXPECTATIONS IN RELATIONSHIPS

As you communicate with other persons, you probably think about whether they meet or violate your expectations of how they should interact. The study of interpersonal communication rests on the principle that people are more satisfied in relationships when they and their interpersonal partners know and meet expectations required for rewarding interactions. This principle regulates when, where, and how people disclose. It is central to their efforts to know and comply with norms of reciprocity. Such violations may result from inappropriate nonverbal cues even more than verbal cues. For instance, you might conclude, "Well, I never expected her (him) to react that way." Or you might think, "Do you need to stand so close to me?"

People expect one another to communicate in certain ways. Without such expectations and the ability to meet them, communication would be chaotic. People have expectations in regard to which communication styles, strategies, and messages should be used at various points in a relationship.

People may misinterpret one another because they have difficulty knowing what each other means or why the other acts as he or she does. Moreover, some people are more competent at sensing which communication behaviors are expected and in performing the appropriate behaviors. Usually, when expectations are met positively, the relationship is rewarding.

What happens when expectations are not met? This section explores that question, giving attention to the roles nonverbal communication plays when individuals satisfy or violate expectations. The section stresses the role nonverbal cues play in strategic self-presentation, impression management, relationship management, roles, gender, affect arousal (feelings), and compliance gaining.

Important to all contexts of communication, nonverbal cues are vital for interpersonal communication. As much as 65% of the social meaning that occurs during interpersonal communication results from interpretations of nonverbal cues (J. K. Burgoon, 1994). Differentiating the role of nonverbal cues by type of communication process, J. K. Burgoon (1994) concluded that "verbal cues are more important for factual, abstract, and persuasive communication, whereas nonverbal cues are more important for relational, attributional, affective, and attitudinal messages" (pp. 235–236).

Most people believe that they and others should conform to communication norms to be successful; this assumption is basic to the rules perspective, as well as theories that postulate that violations produce arousal that leads to negative consequences (Andersen, 1985; Cappella & Greene, 1982; Patterson, 1982, 1983). Some violations of expectations harm communication, but some violations, whether verbal or nonverbal, enhance communicator effectiveness (J. K. Burgoon & Hale, 1988).

Nonverbal patterns of relational partners should complement one another if a relationship is positive and likely to progress. Nonverbal patterns that do not match may prompt interactants to abandon a relationship. For instance, one might assume that the more supportive someone is, the more he or she will be liked. C. R. Berger, Weber, Munley, and Dixon (1977) examined five types of relationships: formal, acquaintance, friend, close friend, and lover. Three factors (sociability, character, and supportiveness) affected interpersonal attractiveness. Across the five relationships, supportiveness showed the greatest difference. A substantial amount of supportiveness is interpreted from the nonverbal cues that occur during interaction. What individuals do in regard to one another at each moment in an interaction can affect whether the relationship improves, remains static, or declines. People who adapt or accommodate to one another are likely to be acceptable and attractive conversational partners (Giles & Powesland, 1975). Liking tends to increase when people see their communication partners as being supportive and similar (C. R. Berger et al., 1977).

Interaction participants use nonverbal cues to give and gain information about each other. People interpret nonverbal communication to reduce uncertainty about the people with whom they communicate and the likelihood that a relationship is rewarding. The most important nonverbal cues are those used intentionally and regularly within each social community (J. K. Burgoon, 1994). Those cues become a routine and stable part of the communication repertoire of members of that community.

How nonverbal cues accompany what is said can have a lot to do with the interpretation the receiver makes of what he or she thinks is said. You might say something to a friend that you do not intend to be interpreted as unpleasant, but if you say it the "wrong" way, your friend can be hurt or angry. A statement, for instance "You know what I mean, don't you," can be said so that it is interpreted as an expression of uncertainty or as a threat. Vocal qualities modify the statements they accompany. The context in which a statement is made can modify the meaning of nonverbal cues. Nonverbal cues are so subtle and situational that people often use one set of nonverbal displays in private and a different set in public (J. K. Burgoon, 1994).

Nonverbal cues either complement or contradict what is said. That principle is central to persons' effort to spot deception. Despite the tendency to believe that they can spot deception, people may not be very skillful, at least according to some research results (Bauchner, Brandt, & Miller, 1977; Ekman & Friesen, 1974; Hocking, Bauchner, Kaminski, & Miller, 1979). Other researchers would disagree with those findings (J. K. Burgoon, Buller, Dillman, & Walther, 1995).

Researchers who contend that people can spot deception with reasonably high levels of accuracy suggest that such detection focuses on interpersonal partners' language choices, strategic statements, and various nonverbal cues. People who are attempting to deceive may become more emotionally aroused and experience cognitive difficulty that comes from having to "make up" a story or facts rather than merely report them. Persons who seek to be deceptive are likely to attempt to exert more control over the conversation, such as keeping the floor and changing the subject. People who engage in deception are likely to respond more quickly, have shorter periods of eye contact, and restrain or inhibit the display of nonverbal cues (Greene, O'Hair, Cody, & Yen, 1985).

Deception is a vital aspect of interpersonal communication research. It forces us to address topics such as trust and uncertainty. People want to assume that relational partners tell the truth. When they do not—or appear not to be telling the truth—uncertainty is likely to rise. Uncertainty is uncomfortable. Too much discomfort can strain a relationship.

Interpersonal deception theory has been developed to address the communication styles and interaction patterns that are central to deception, deception detection, and counter moves by the deceiver who believes that his or her efforts at deception are failing (J. K. Burgoon et al., 1995). Researchers are interested in the communication activity that deceivers use to avoid detection, the cues persons use to spot deception, and the cues those persons give off that can lead their partners to take countermoves to avoid getting caught in their deception. All of that sounds complicated, but a moment's reflection can bring to mind many experiences where each of us tried—perhaps succeeded—to deceive someone and to spot deception. Do people engage in deception planning? Have you ever practiced your "deception story" to polish your delivery to make it sound true? Have you used conspirators—friends in crime—to help you "pull off a deception"? Have you ever tried to sound really sick as you call your professor to explain why you can't take an examination?

Studies have discovered that individuals have expectations of how people will behave when they are telling the truth and when they are deceiving. They compare these expectations against the cues they receive during the encounter. Interpersonal deception theory postulates that cues are strategically managed by persons who are seeking to deceive. Such efforts are tested and altered if the deceiver believes the partner is becoming suspicious of the "story." Thus, we have relevant categories of analysis: impression management, emotion management, identity management, self-presentation, conversation management, uncertainty reduction, and social influence (J. K. Burgoon, 1994). Such cues include many signs of impaired communication performance:

1. Less contact (such as avoiding eye contact).
2. More control of what is said and how.

3. Less smiling.
4. More postural shift (such as rocking and twisting).
5. Longer pauses (response latencies) between what one person says and the other's reply.
6. Slower speech rate.
7. More speech errors (such as wrong word selection).
8. More hesitancies (uhs and uhms).
9. Less immediacy (less gaze, leaning, and facing).
10. Higher vocal pitch (signs of nervous arousal).
11. More nonverbal adaptors.
12. Less time spent answering questions (trying not to incriminate oneself).
13. Decreased use of illustrators, that is, gestures used to illustrate comments such as the length of "the fish that got away" (J. K. Burgoon, 1994; deTurck & Miller, 1985; Zuckerman, DePaulo, & Rosenthal, 1981).

Expectations that differentiate truthful and deceptive communication are vital to efforts to detect and achieve deception. If conversational partners know one another well enough and have a conversational history, they are more likely to spot deception because they perceive discrepancies between what is said, how it is said, and what is expected (verbally and nonverbally). However, in intimate relationships, familiarity may not necessarily increase the ability to recognize deception but produce a level of trust sufficiently high that partners do not expect and therefore do not look for cues of deception. In such situations, ability to spot deception is enhanced by a general suspicion of others and because events or situational circumstances arouse suspicion (McCornack & Levine, 1990).

When a person who is deceiving believes her or his relational partner is "wise to the game," the communication behavior is managed more closely. Clues that deception may have been spotted include nonverbal cues of suspicion and the use of probes. Once deceivers spot these strategies, they mask their arousal cues and take on a "nondeceptive" demeanor. Probes can help people force deceivers to stop their efforts to shade the truth (Buller, Strzyzewski, & Comstock, 1991).

Deception theory is a vital area of study. One primary reason for communication is to reduce uncertainty. For that reason, people want to know others, want to know what others think of them, and want to know what others know. People have an incentive to deceive in order to manage impressions and exert control through strategically giving and withholding information. Thus, we have expectations that people might engage in deception, even though we prefer that they tell the truth. A key to spotting deception is to compare how we think persons should act under the circumstances; we compare that to how we believe they are acting. Differences between actions and expectations can be used as the rationale for concluding that deception is occurring.

People have other reasons for determining the extent to which others meet or exceed their expectations for appropriate behavior under the circumstances (in the specific context). To further explore that premise, the remainder of this section focuses on expectancy violations theory. This theory has developed to explain when violations of nonverbal behavior will lead to positive or negative evaluations of the relational partner making the violations.

Before explaining that theory, a review of key terms used to describe nonverbal cues can be helpful. Each category of nonverbal cues offers an opportunity for expectancy violations. The study of body movement, posture, and gestures is called *kinesics*. Kinesics can involve studying whether leaning toward a person during a conversation shows signs of liking for that person, or whether leaning is a threat.

Paralanguage, or *vocalics,* refers to vocal elements that accompany, complement, contradict, or substitute for vocalized words. These elements include vocal qualities, characterizers, qualifiers, and segregates, or hesitancies. Qualities refer to factors such as pitch, rate, articulation, and rhythm. Characterizers are sounds that signify, for instance, whether a person is happy or sad. Qualifiers are vocal cues that vary from the norm, for instance, by being too soft or too loud. Hesitancies include sounds such as uhs or uhms and pauses. Paralinguistic cues are important to the ability to interpret feeling. They more accurately indicate feelings than does verbal disclosure. People use their own feelings as reference points against which to interpret feelings others express through paralinguistic cues (Sillars, Pike, Jones, & Murphy, 1984).

How vocalics accompany compliance-gaining requests influences whether those requests will be granted. Positive violations increase the likelihood that requests will be granted, whereas negative violations lessen the likelihood of compliance (Buller & Burgoon, 1986). For example, a child's request to be taken to the zoo should be accompanied by vocal cues showing a desire to go. If the child is very excited (positive violation), the request is more likely to be granted because of the person's desire to please the child. If the request is made in vocal tones that suggest the child is not actually interested (negative violation), the request is unlikely to be granted because of the belief that the effort will not be rewarding because the child does not truly want to go.

Proxemics is the study of how people communicate with distance and space ranging from architecture (design and lay out of a building or selection and arrangement of furniture) to the positioning of one person's body in relation to another's during interaction. Proxemic distance includes touch, closeness, eye contact (gaze), and thermal factors (warmth of the body) resulting from proximity. Through proxemic adjustments, for instance, people welcome others and move close to show signs of greeting through eye contact. In contrast, people can turn away and ignore others, avoiding eye contact or glaring. Elevator "politics" give you many opportunities to see how people act with space; the dynamics between two friends alone in an elevator change, for instance, once their space is invaded when others enter the elevator.

Touch can be studied by itself, under the taxonomic heading, haptics. Chronemics refers to the use of time in communication; for instance, some party guests show up late to give the impression that they are busy and therefore socially important and attractive. This kind of expectation depends on culture and context. Physical appearance can include how people dress or groom themselves to manage impressions. Appearance can include cues derived from size, body shape, age, sex, race, or ethnicity; each of these factors can affect communication interaction. Artifacts is a category of nonverbal cues that consists of things with which people associate themselves. A person might wear a particular kind of watch or drive a particular model of automobile to make a "statement" about who she or he is.

When people interpret one another's nonverbal cues, they tend to do so by using them in combination (multidimensional). For instance, high amounts of eye contact, close body proximity, forward body lean, and smiling combine to indicate intimacy, attraction, and trust. In contrast, the combination of little eye contact, turning away, leaning backward, and absence of smiling and touch combine to indicate detachment. People who display high amounts of eye contact, close proximity, and smiles are seen to be calm, not aroused, and composed. High amounts of eye contact and close proximity are interpreted together as signs of dominance (J. K. Burgoon, Buller, Hale, & deTurck, 1984).

In a similar fashion, estimates of how involved a communication partner is with a topic of discussion are calculated by looking for combinations of kinesic/proxemic attentiveness (leaning forward), smiles, laughter, synchronized speech, few silences and latencies, and less toying with objects. Other indicators of involvement include facial animation, vocal interest, deeper vocal pitch, less fidgeting, and vocal tones indicating attentiveness (Coker & Burgoon, 1987).

Nonverbal cues serve many functions. They illustrate (clarify), point, and highlight. They serve as emblems, behaviors that have direct verbal translations such as a hushing sign. Nonverbals are a vital part of affect displays. They regulate; people signal to others to speed up or slow down during conversation. Nonverbal cues are used for greetings and to end conversations. For instance, a teacher may stand up to signal the end of a conference once a student has taken long enough to discuss a problem or complain about a grade. People may use nonverbal communication to show relational harmony or disharmony, that is, relational messages. They may match one another's nods in synchrony to signal approval or avoid synchrony to indicate displeasure. They constitute adaptors, such as fidgeting, rubbing, and other "idle" or "nervous" displays. They can be rituals, typical of cultural conventions, for example displays that are typical of gender, roles, race, religion, age, region, or occupation.

One key regulator is turn taking, an important part of conversation management. Turn taking includes allowing the other person to finish a statement rather than interrupting. This nonverbal pattern can affect rapport during a conversation; thus, researchers are interested in patterns of who interrupts and who allows interruptions. It might be assumed that men interrupt more during conversations than women do. However, Dindia (1987) discovered that some people, regardless of gender, interrupt more than others do. Interruption patterns cannot be predicted by gender; men do not interrupt more than women, and women are not interrupted more than men. People who interrupt more than others do so in same and other gender interactions. Women are less likely to interrupt supportive comments, whereas they tend to interrupt informative statements more than men do.

Amount and kind of eye gaze can affect rapport between persons joined in conversation. People watch conversational partners to regulate and adjust to them; gaze is used to determine when a partner's conversational turn is ending. While communicating with one another, women use more mutual gaze/mutual talk and mutual gaze/mutual silence than occurs in male-to-male or male-to-female interactions. In mixed-gender dyads, women tend to adopt patterns of eye gaze used by their male partners, whereas in those dyads men do not adapt to women but use patterns typical of male-to-male interaction. Women tend to accommodate to one another and to men in interpersonal communication, but men do not accommodate as much to women. Women, more than men, seem sensitive to the importance of accommodation in interpersonal communication and have more skills to accomplish it (Andersen, 1985).

When people violate eye gaze expectations, the results will be evaluated differently if the violator is thought to be able to reward the partner. Eye gaze patterns can affect impressions of attraction, credibility, and communication style. Eye gaze aversion (not making eye contact) harms the relationship (J. K. Burgoon, Coker, & Coker, 1986).

People use nonverbal cues to define relationships. Although partners periodically discuss their relationships, for instance, "We are good friends," they continually make nonverbal "comments" about the relationships. Relationships are defined by several key nonverbal patterns, such as composure, dominance–submission, immediacy–nonimmediacy, and intimacy–similarity. Nonverbal cues can indicate trust, liking, attraction, and friendliness. They can suggest how much one partner is involved with the other. Distance and use of space are particularly important in this regard. Communication reticence or uncommunicativeness gives an impression that a person is disinterested or uninvolved in a relationship. When communicators are reticent with friends, the quality of the relationship is perceived to be more positive than negative. Such is not the case when reticence occurs between strangers, where uncommunicativeness is a sign of disinterest. Strangers often match reticence with less facial pleasantness while displaying tension, disinterest, or anxiety (J. K. Burgoon & Koper, 1984).

These research findings demonstrate that nonverbal communication is guided by norms. People who comply with norms are thought to be more competent and attractive communicators than are those who violate them. However, nonverbal expectancy violations theory posits that under certain circumstances violations of social norms and expectations can enhance communication rather than harm it (J. K. Burgoon, 1994; J. K. Burgoon & Hale, 1988).

People use their expectations about nonverbal communication to evaluate the communication competence of others. Violations, whether positive or negative, can influence the communication outcome and the perceptions that the interactional partners form of one another. Expectations follow social norms unless communication partners know one another quite well. Under that circumstance, partners tend to ignore each other's idiosyncrasies.

How norms are used may be a function of gender, age, or personality; they can be triggered by relational characteristics such as degree of acquaintance, status, or liking. These variables interact in a matrix that makes predictions about communication strategies and outcomes difficult, but norms, expectations, and known idiosyncrasies help to make communication systematic and predictable. In terms of nonverbal distance, for instance, communicating at moderate distance is preferred to being far apart or too close. Whereas you might find a friendly person invading your space on first meeting (norm violation), you might become comfortable with the person's use of distance as a friendship develops. Some of your friends are likely to get physically close to you and even touch you, whereas others will not. You might be offended if a stranger touched you the way a friend might touch you.

Some violations are positively evaluated. You know this because you think that some persons you meet are "phony" or "syrupy" in their efforts to be warm; whereas others who are more competent leave you thinking of them as "warm" and "cordial." Both may have violated the same norms of nonverbal communication by being "extremely" friendly during greeting phases of acquaintanceships. But the consequences are different: liking versus disliking.

People assume relational partners will comply with expected communication behaviors, including nonverbal cues, such as amount of distance between people. Violations may produce negative reactions, but that is not always the case, especially when the violator can reward the partner. Deviation from the norm by moving closer can communicate attraction, interest, and affiliation, whereas deviation from the norm by being further away can communicate the opposite. Violators are likely to be seen as insensitive if they lack the potential to reward their partners (J. K. Burgoon & Aho, 1982).

To explain these different outcomes, J. K. Burgoon and Hale (1988) advanced the nonverbal expectancy violations theory that, like the social exchange theory, reasons that people continue to communicate as long as benefits outweigh costs. A key factor in this theory is the reward relationship between participants. If a person who can reward another violates a norm or expectation, that violation is disregarded or in some instances increases the positive regard of the other person. If a violation carries with it the possibility of high reward, it may increase attraction and credibility. Once a person spots a violation on the part of another communicator, the person asks, "Do I like/dislike this violation?"

Because immediacy is a vital part of communication, friends and strangers are evaluated positively as being credible when they show the expected amount of immediacy. The opposite is also true. Failure to achieve the minimum amount of immediacy communicates detachment, nonintimacy, dissimilarity, and dominance. Whether the violation results in negative or positive evaluation is mediated by the ability of the violator to reward the communication partner (J. K. Burgoon & Hale, 1988).

Expectancy violations theory (supported by findings such as these) was created in response to discrepancy arousal theory proposed by Cappella and Greene (1982). This theory views the communication process as consisting of moment-by-moment occurrences by which each communicator affects and is affected by the other. Positive or negative feelings result when a discrepancy occurs between actions one person expects of another and what those actions are. Levels of arousal correspond to amounts of discrepancy; the greater the discrepancy, the higher the arousal. Persons can expect one another to exhibit certain feelings or to perform certain activities; when they do not, discrepancy and arousal occur.

Responses to violations can take the form of reciprocity or compensation. Reciprocity is characterized by matching sequences. Compensation is characterized by approach-avoidance or avoidance-avoidance sequences. Patterns of reciprocity and compensation are accompanied by physiological, cognitive, and affective reactions. Whether an interaction is going well or poorly, individuals tend to reciprocate or compensate in response to one another.

Reciprocation and compensation exhibit levels of intensity, duration, or frequency. How each person responds depends on the affiliation he or she feels toward the other person in the situation. Expectations and reactions to arousal are personal and produce responses that are signaled through actions such as vocalizations, pauses, response latencies, loudness, eye gaze, distance, body orientation, smiling and laughter, touch, body lean, and verbal intimacy. When expectations are met, participants enjoy a sense of pleasantness.

Arousal occurs because individuals depend on one another. When dependency is mutual, interdependence, actions, and reactions are likely to be compatible. When people are compatible, each makes appropriate positive responses to the other's actions. Responses can be immediate or delayed as well as positive or negative and abstract or concrete. Violations of expectations are likely to occur, but when they do, they are interpreted less negatively when partners are compatible and possess social competence. How these violations affect the relationship depends on whether the partners see one another as attractive and if they have empathy for each other (Cappella & Greene, 1982).

As you think about adjustments by persons with whom you communicate, imagine that the kind of response each makes fluctuates during a series of interactions. At times each person compensates or reciprocates. Patterns that are pleasing prompt pleasing patterns as interactants match one another's efforts to be seen as pleasant and competent. If the patterns violate expectations and are met with compensation, a downward spiral of disliking and lowered attraction occurs. Interactions that suffer this downward spiral are seen as unrewarding and therefore are likely to be terminated or at least viewed negatively. In this way, discrepancy arousal theory predicts that violations lead to negative feelings and a strained or terminated interaction.

Expectancy violations theory offers a correction to that theory. If people can reward one another, they overlook violations. Moreover, toleration for discrepancy is greater when one or both persons like each other (J. K. Burgoon & Hale, 1988). In these ways, people engaged in interpersonal communication use expectations to evaluate the competence and attractiveness of one another and decide whether to maintain interaction and a relationship or terminate them.

INTERPERSONAL AFFINITY, CONFLICT, AND RELATIONSHIP DISSOLUTION

Throughout this chapter, theory and research have focused on the creation of relationships through interpersonal communication. The chapter ends by addressing three concepts that capture the historical stages of a relationship. After initial interaction (meeting another person), effort may be devoted to seeking affinity. From this foundation, relationships need to sustain periods of conflict. Relationships that cannot establish a foundation where rewards outweigh costs are likely to dissolve. This section features "good, bad, and ugly" dimensions of interpersonal relationships.

As a preview to this section, we adopt the principle of dialectic as a defining characteristic of interpersonal communication. The concept of dialectic can be grounded in a critical perspective by drawing on the work of Kenneth Burke, whom we cited extensively in chapter 3. His view of dialectic featured the process by which merger could result from division. Two people through communication merge toward one. The ultimate transcendence of division is a merger that transcends separation so that two become one. That ideal is captured in terms such as good friends, buddies, or happily married couple. Relationship assumes similarity and compatibility. Thus, Burke (1966) noted that each of us becomes ourselves through actions with others: "The very essence of a character's nature is in large measure defined, or determined, by the other characters who variously assist or oppose him" or her (p. 84). Each of us acts, others react to that action, and growth results from what we learn from that counteraction (Burke, 1969a).

Interpersonal communication and relationship building, maintenance, and dissolution are dialectical processes. Making this point, Werner and Baxter (1994) concluded that "the total autonomy of parties precludes their relational connection, just as total connection between parties precludes their individual autonomy" (pp. 351–352). If people are separate (independent), they cannot have relationships. Relationship building is a dialectic of moving from autonomy to interdependence. If we achieve interdependence, we have a lasting relationship. If we fail, conflict and an imbalance of reward to cost will cause the relationship to terminate.

Affinity is a goal of persons' interpersonal strategies as they move from separation to interdependence. Getting others to like us is a vital communication goal, as is demonstrating that we like them. People employ affinity-seeking behaviors, verbal and nonverbal, to lead others to like them. Affinity-seeking strategies can employ nonverbal cues as basic as smiling, demonstrating similarity through apparel, and listening. Verbal message strategies include supportive question asking, compliments, norm reciprocity, and disclosive sharing.

Affinity seeking motivates individuals to manage impressions so that one person can be an attractive relational partner to another. One taxonomy that explains this behavior features four interrelated units:

1. Antecedent factors (interaction goals, motives for seeking liking, and level of mindfulness). Studies of affinity seeking acknowledge that it is a goal that is the product of related motives. Some people more mindfully than others do what is needed to foster relationships.
2. Constraints (dispositions and social skills) and characteristics of the communication partner. Not every attempt to achieve affinity works. Sometimes constraints such as distance are a problem. People may enjoy romantic relationships until they go to separate colleges. Distance usually does not make the heart grow fonder. Parents and friends may foster or hinder relationship development. Factors such as race or religion can support or hamper people's ability to achieve affinity. Similar conclusions can be drawn regarding social skills. Some people achieve affinity easily. They enjoy a repertoire of communication skills and strategies that make them "popular." Other people do not have those same social skills and for that reason may take longer to accomplish affinity.
3. Strategic activity (strategy selection, integration, and quality of enactment). Part of affinity seeking is to have social skills. The other part is how well and wisely those skills are used. We know that on first meeting too much disclosure and too intense an expression of feelings may hamper affinity seeking. Ingratiation and positive question asking

may be the right combination of integrated strategies to lead individuals
to feel that they have made progress toward affinity.
4. Responses by the person whose liking is being sought. Affinity-seeking
   strategies involve control, trust, politeness, involvement with the other,
   self-involvement, and commonality. Many affinity-seeking strategies
   can be employed such as altruism, control, equality, openness, nonverbal
   immediacy, similarity, supportiveness, and trustworthiness (Bell & Daly,
   1984).

As we think about the role attitude similarity plays in affinity, we may note that
interaction style is also a factor. More important than similarity of attitude,
similarities in social-cognitive and communication skills are key factors in
predicting which relationships (especially marriage) will be rewarding. Although
people like those with similar attitudes, they are even more interested in people
whose interaction styles are rewarding. The bottom line is that we tend to like
people more if we enjoy interacting with them (Burleson & Denton, 1992). Part
of that interaction is the pleasant feeling that results from what is typically called
small talk: chatting, making plans, gossiping, joking, and recapping daily
activities. Interpreted constitutively, such conversation signals mutual
knowledge, trust, and relational continuity (Goldsmith & Baxter, 1996). By such
communication message design logics, relational partners persuade one another
that a relationship is worth maintaining. Thus, each relationship is a work in
progress (Duck, 1990).

Emotional displays are a typical part of interpersonal communication. Liking
is affected by the display of negative and positive emotions. For this reason,
people temper the display of emotions. They are less likely to display negative
emotions early and later in a relationship. Although emotional displays become
more appropriate as relationships mature, males are more likely to mute these
displays than their female counterparts are in dating, marriage, or cohabiting
relationships (K. Aune et al., 1996).

Affinity seeking assumes that people have many incentives to accomplish a
positive integration of attitudes and interaction styles. Even a moment's
reflection reminds us that relationships must be sufficiently strong to weather
periods of conflict. Social conflict can be defined as a contest for scarce
resources or positions in which participants are ego-involved. This means that,
when people can grant or deny each other some position or resource, conflict can
result if both participants truly want the position or resource. For instance, no
conflict exists in a game if everyone who plays can win or if no one cares
whether he or she wins. As long as lots of cookies are in the jar, no conflict exists,
but once the cookies are nearly gone, a contest for scarce resources can produce
conflict.

Beyond that traditional but somewhat narrow resource view of conflict, it can
be defined as the communication strains that occur when people suffer actual or

even perceived incompatibility of objectives. Conflict can include perceived interference with communication partners' efforts to achieve relational or other personal goals. It may result from loss of potential payoffs, rewards, or benefits. It may occur when communication partners have incongruent or incompatible behaviors.

Viewed this way, conflict is not misunderstanding. Misunderstanding can be remedied by communicating more completely or clearly. However, conflict is not necessarily resolved by clarity. In fact, persons in conflict may understand one another quite clearly. Even though conflict elevates emotions and produces distortions, persons engaged in it often know what is going on and what each other means. The problem is not clarity but incompatibility of objectives.

Despite the fact that it can generate substantial emotion, conflict is not inherently harmful to relationships. If conflict occurs because of honest differences that can be resolved, it can even strengthen a relationship. The quality of each relationship (trust, control, and intimacy) predicts the likelihood participants will resolve conflict constructively.

Conflict resolution tactics involve rules and compliance behaviors people use to create and manage conflict, as well as contexts in which it occurs (M. J. Smith, 1984). To resolve conflict, people may employ collaborative decision making, compromise, competition, accommodation, and avoidance. Collaborative decision making entails identifying and solving the mutual problem that has led to the conflict. To compromise, participants exchange (give and take) resources in an attempt to maximize their own and each other's outcomes. Competition is predicated on a win–lose paradigm, but even under that condition, it may not be harmful if participants believe the conflict will lead to positive relationship outcomes. For instance, friendships can tolerate, even depend on, healthy athletic competition. Accommodation means that one person tries to resolve conflict by smoothing the feelings of the other. This tactic can be helpful, especially when ego-involvement leads to competition rather than other resolution strategies. Avoidance is the tactic of leaving the area of combat. Sometimes a conflict resolves itself merely when combatants have time to cool. You probably have been engaged in many conflicts that a day or two later seemed so trivial that you and your partner had a hard time recalling why the conflict became emotional. Each conflict resolution tactic can be used constructively or it can be inappropriate.

Examining how college roommates resolve conflict, Sillars (1980) found that they often employ passive (indirect) strategies, including withdrawal. Distributive strategies are those that promote individual over mutual outcomes, whereas integrative strategies feature information exchange and mutually beneficial outcomes. When roommates think their partners will select positive strategies, they reciprocate with integrative strategies. This kind of strategy is likely to be used when a party believes that he or she is responsible for the conflict. Once a roommate relationship becomes stable, integrative strategies are more likely, and passive ones are less likely.

How people in conflict perceive one another can affect how they resolve conflict. Likewise, beliefs relational partners have about relationships in general influence how they solve problems, or whether they try to solve them rather than merely ending a relationship (Metts & Cupach, 1990). If we see others as valued and believe that relationships need to be maintained, we are more likely to work for appropriate modes of conflict resolution than if we don't value the other persons or the relationship.

One factor central to conflict is power: the ability one person has to affect the behavior or feelings of another. Power may be symmetrical or asymmetrical; it is enacted through moves and countermoves. These moves involve choices: approach–avoidance, positive–negative, and direct–indirect. In a symmetrical relationship (one that enjoys mutual influence and compatibility) approach will be met with approach, and positive moves are met with positive moves. If one person begins by using positive tactics and they enjoy positive response, that mode will continue. If a response is negative, the countermove is likely to be negative. Moves are employed to the extent that each participant is able and to the degree that the tactic produces desired results (C. R. Berger, 1985).

Several communication strategies are typical of conflict situations: apologies, explanations, inducements, contingencies (limitations placed on a request or offer), counterpersuasion, and coercion. How requests are made and conflict is resolved depends on the degree of intimacy between participants. When people make requests of others with whom they are relationally close, they assume that the requests will be granted, as much out of obligation as for any other reason. This generalization can be explained by a rules approach, which prescribes that requests are to be granted if the partner is able. Or it can be explained by a systems perspective, whereby each participant knows that what is done to, or granted for, the other will affect how the conflict is resolved. Requests made in intimate situations require less elaboration to justify why they were made or whether they should be granted. If their requests are denied, people seem less inclined to be polite in their reaction if they are involved in an intimate relationship. Relational intimacy is characterized by contrasting communication styles: cooperative/friendly versus competitive/hostile, equal versus unequal, intense versus superficial, and socioemotional/informational versus task/formal (Roloff, Janiszewski, McGrath, Burns, & Lalita, 1988).

How people approach conflict is vital to whether it is likely to be resolved. The use of decision rules can help persons engaged in conflict to focus on issues and the decision process rather than on each other's personality. If conflict becomes personal, it may be more difficult to resolve because people defend their feelings and self-concept rather than attempt to resolve the conflict. Decision rules appear to have less inhibiting effects on men than women involved in conflict (Donohue, Weider-Hatfield, Hamilton, & Diez, 1985).

If following decision rules can help, should people learn goal management strategies? According to B. J. O'Keefe and Shepherd (1987), communicators' ability to resolve conflict depends on their skill in devising goal-management strategies. Strategies include selecting one goal outcome in preference to others, separating the issues basic to the conflict, and integrating or reconciling competing aims. If a person uses a message strategy that features positive outcomes for both parties (integrative) then the other person is more likely to be persuaded. The person who uses that message design option is viewed as being more credible and likable. Persons who are able to see many issues and strategy options and who rely on integration and face-saving tactics are likely to resolve conflict. Effective conflict resolution depends on the ability to recognize the relevance of, and simultaneously pursue, multiple and competing objectives.

Burggraf and Sillars (1987) observed that communication styles that married couples use during conflict are negotiated and do not differ by gender. This conclusion suggests that the tactics married couples use during conflict are determined by how they have taught each other to communicate (negotiated and reciprocated). In this vein, conflict is a relational process that may be ambiguous and improvised or culturally defined and regulated (Sillars & Weisberg, 1987).

Evidence indicates that conflict management by married couples depends on their definitions of conflict and marriage. Married couples, Fitzpatrick (1977) reported, base their conflict-resolution tactics on the kind of marriage they have: independents, separates, and traditionals. Independents consider themselves less restrained in the use of verbal tactics than do other types. They use contracts as the basis for creating obligations and resolving conflict. Separates show very little willingness to share and therefore tend to avoid conflict. Traditionals rely on stereotypes of a traditional marriage. Their view of the rules and values of a traditional marriage influence their strategic choices for resolving conflict. Traditional married couples tend to use communal (togetherness) themes. Individualistic themes are typical of conversations by separates. Communal themes are more satisfying than are individual themes (Sillars, Weisberg, Burggraf, & Wilson, 1987).

One principle that runs throughout interpersonal communication research is that people select strategies to obtain communication goals, and they do so with varying degrees of insight or mindfulness and employ them with different degrees of skill (B. J. O'Keefe & Shepherd, 1987). Strategy selection can include choice of words, as well as a decision to attack the other person's self-concept. In such instances, interactants need to realize that conflict management is sensitive to the adage, "It's not what you say, but how you say it." Exploring this principle, Infante, Rancer, and Jordan (1996) discovered that argument becomes aggression when people attack each other's self-concepts or fail to confirm the other's self-concept during an argument. This effect seems to be more noticeable in women than in men.

How people communicate during conflict is likely to reflect their views of conflict as such. Exploring that theme in family and work settings, Buzzanell and Burrell (1997) reasoned that as few as three views of conflict may operate. They discovered that people see conflict as WAR, as RATIONAL, and as IMPOTENCE, which convey a sense of imbalance and inability to work through conflict constructively. Most people see conflict as war or impotence; far less view it constructively as a rational process by which people reconcile differences of opinion, resource management, and objectives. Men tend to see conflict as war, whereas women are prone to view it as impotence.

Conflict can be rewarding (if it is positively solved) or destructive. That factor, along with many others, emphasizes how relationships that enjoy positive interpersonal communication grow and maintain themselves. When the costs of a relationship outweigh what one or both partners think are its rewards, the relationship is endangered. When people begin to realize that a relationship costs more than it produces in rewards, they consider dissolving it.

Does conflict resolution end quickly, or is it a process that typically goes through several stages? Researchers believe that it progresses over time as one or both partners engage in thought and interaction strategies. One model of that process features four stages.

The first stage, intrapsychic, occurs when one or both partners think about the cost–reward ratio associated with the relationship. At this point, partners consider one another's behavior and assess the partner's willingness and ability to perform in ways that meet expectations. If the discomfort associated with the relationship is high and the person believes that communicating with the partner might correct the cost/reward imbalance, that person is likely to enter the dyadic phase, which consists of talking with the partner. This talk can take many forms: confrontation, negotiation, attempts to repair damage, and joint assessment of the future of the relationship.

Depending on the success of the dyadic phase, a person considering ending a relationship is likely to enter the social phase, which involves conversations with others (friends and relatives) about the relationship. Such conversation takes many forms: efforts to repair it, calls for intervention, face saving, and blame placing. These efforts may not save the relationship. Once it ends, the partners move to the grave dressing phase. They communicate to get over the relationship; to do so, they engage in retrospection, and present the "breakup" story to their acquaintances (Duck, 1982).

Baxter (1982) discovered that persons who suffer relationship breakups like to think of themselves as the person who made the decision to end the relationship. Such situations are likely to incur four kinds of strategies: withdrawal/avoidance, manipulation, positive comments, and open confrontation. Efforts to end relationships often begin with (a) direct statements that the relationship is over; (b) indirect statements that avoid asking about and involving the partner in conversation or activities; and (c) nonverbal withdrawal, for instance, avoiding touching, standing less close, or seeing the other less often (Wilmot, Carbaugh, & Baxter, 1985).

In these ways, people use communication to demonstrate liking, to fight, and to dissolve relationships. Communication styles, strategies, and content are important to the initiation, growth, maintenance, and dissolution of relationships. Part of the success of each relationship depends on the interpersonal communication skills partners have and are willing to employ. This is especially true as they find themselves in conflict and seek to resolve it.

CONCLUSION

Relationships seem to endure because participants find them satisfying; rewards outweigh costs. People in good relationships communicate differently than do people in bad ones. With these basic observations in mind, you might ask, "But how do I know when I am in a good relationship and what can I do to make it better?" The need to reduce uncertainty about the people with whom you communicate and about relationships you create is the theme of the next chapter.

7

Interpersonal Communication: Social Cognition and Communication Competence

Through interpersonal communication, relationships begin, grow, remain static, or deteriorate. People seek to create and maintain rewarding relationships. They prefer to avoid or terminate those that are not rewarding.

That overview challenges us to consider how people know whether a relationship is sound or souring? Chapter 6 discusses variables that predict and explain relationship quality. As people communicate, they have expectations, of themselves and others, about which interpersonal action is appropriate and what is not. When communication partners do not meet each other's expectations, they are likely to experience arousal that can affect, negatively or positively, their attractiveness as relational partners. People negotiate and codefine the limits, conditions, and obligations needed for a positive relationship, including how much disclosure is sufficient or excessive. Obligations in a relationship are discussed and negotiated through norms of social exchange. Given these conditions, each participant experiences the need to obtain information that will help him or her assess the quality of each relationship and better understand each relational partner.

Because people cannot know others directly as they actually are, they do the best they can to know them through communication. We only know each other by what we do and say. We are aware that people can cleverly manage impressions thereby leading us to conclude that they are different—usually more attractive as a relational partner—than they actually are. Thus, people seek information to reduce uncertainty about their relational partners. They also want to know how their partners view them.

This chapter addresses how this desire to obtain information and to be seen as being competent influences the communication plans people develop and employ. To understand how people strive to reduce uncertainty during interpersonal communication, we need insight into the processes of interpersonal attribution and uncertainty reduction. These concepts and relevant theories help explain how people get to know each other and how they perform competently. This discussion shows why and how individuals attempt to reduce uncertainty (about others, themselves, and relationships) during interpersonal communication. This analysis pursues the theme that people select, with varying degrees of mindfulness, those communication strategies most likely to achieve goals. One goal is to be a competent, desirable communication partner.

This chapter builds on the realization that we cannot let others into our minds to know us nor can we get inside their minds to know them. Because of these limitations, some amount of uncertainty exists in relationships. Uncertainty tends to be unpleasant and, therefore, motivational. People want to reduce uncertainty they feel toward others (getting to know who they are), and they want to know what others think about them and why other people act as they do. "Does he/she really like me?" "Do people see me as a nice person?" "Does my boss think I am a competent worker?" "Will I be able to say the right things to get a date (or make a sale)?" "Am I a competent communicator?" During interpersonal interaction, people seek to answer questions of this type. As you were cautioned in the last chapter, you need to guard against coming to think that people are always mindful of what is happening during communication. But, by gaining insights, they increase their chances that when they are mindful of what is going on they will be more competent.

The quality of each relationship tends to be affected by being open; balancing costs and rewards; complying with communication rules or norms; defining control, trust, and intimacy; meeting expectations; achieving affinity; and managing conflict. Chapter 7 describes the processes by which individuals attempt to figure out each other and each relationship. This chapter stresses the role information plays in building relationships, factors associated with communication accommodation, and plans people develop and use to manage relationships.

GUESSING AND SECOND GUESSING

The process of getting to know others may be short circuited. When people communicate interpersonally, they often assume they know who the other person is and why he or she is acting in a particular manner. This process of characterizing others (and oneself) is called *attribution,* assigning motives to explain why people act as they do. This is the basic process of social cognition.

Even though people do not actually know why their communication partners act as they do, they speculate about or attribute causes to that behavior. They do this to feel comfortable that they know what is going on. For instance, as you communicate with others, you may think, "He/she likes me because he/she smiles and looks at me (as opposed to averts eye contact) when we talk," or "No one really listens to me; I guess I'm not the sort of person that people like to be friends with." You make self-attributions based on your involvement with others. "I would have done better in that interview if the interviewer had not tricked me." "I should get a raise because I work hard and my boss knows it." "I would have done better on that test if my roommate had not persuaded me to go to a movie instead of studying."

Giving perspective to this discussion, C. R. Berger (1987) observed that when rewards for being in a relationship exceed costs, the relationship is likely to improve. Thus, people set out to determine whether their relationships are rewarding. Via processes of social cognition, C. R. Berger argued, "interactants determine which stimuli are rewarding and which are costly to their partners" (p. 57). When costs exceed rewards, the relationship is likely to deteriorate, or at least one person will blame the other or him- or herself for this failure.

Much of what goes on during interpersonal communication is aimed at reducing uncertainty about the persons engaged in communication, the quality of relationships, and communicator competence. "Hence," C. R. Berger continued, "uncertainty reduction is a necessary condition for the definition of the currency of social exchange, and it is through communicative activity that uncertainty is reduced" (p. 57). Why do people want to know when rewards justify costs? Berger answered, "What gives individuals the ability to exert control in relationships is the knowledge of what is rewarding and costly to their interaction partners and to themselves" (p. 57).

Attribution and disclosure are interrelated. When people disclose positive details about themselves and their relationship, their partners are likely to reciprocate this self-disclosure. If negative attributions result from what a communication partner discloses, that disclosure is unlikely to be reciprocated and the relationship may even terminate. Disclosure has a positive effect on attribution because it suggests that the person who makes the disclosure likes the person to whom it is made. This analysis adds credence to social penetration theory, but also suggests that disclosure alone is not the key. Attributions made about what people disclose and why they disclose those details affect whether the relationship seems rewarding (Derlega, Winstead, Wong, & Greenspan, 1987). Attribution affects how people make sense of what others disclose to them.

Social cognition assumes that persons who are engaged in interpersonal communication do so with varying degrees of mindfulness. Most routine communication consists of scripts, which are comments made with little thought. Thought focuses on the interaction and participants (self as well as others). To make these assessments, people create or adopt schemata, which are patterns of thought and assumptions that constitute the social reality they share with persons with whom they interact. Interpretations of our physical and social worlds are designed to achieve accurate representations of self, others, and relationships (Roloff & Berger, 1982).

Although the goal is to form accurate assessments of interactional partners, people often fail in that regard. Either their schemata may be faulty or the information supplied by others may not be accurate. Information may be fabricated through deception or it may be biased, shading the truth. To reduce uncertainty about persons whom they encounter, people want to solve riddles of this kind. With varying degrees of mindfulness, people attempt to spot deception and debias or second guess what each other says.

Deception is not telling the truth or telling something other than the truth—mindfully and strategically—to achieve a goal that could not be accomplished by telling the truth. People are likely to experience uncertainty and employ a variety of strategies when they believe that they have spotted deception at work. Even when people are not attempting to deceive, they may be misreporting information and therefore prompt their interactional partners to become more focused and mindful of what is being said (Hewes, Graham, Doelger, & Pavitt, 1985).

Once people suspect that they cannot wholly trust the information they are receiving, they resort to alternative interpretations. Contrary to the notion that people are gullible and easily misled, research finds that they are skilled at debiasing when they sense the need. People frequently employ this strategy. When people are trying to determine whether others' comments are biased, they watch for some or all of the following:

- Inadequate sampling (generalizations made from too few instances).
- Inaccurate reports (ones that differ from facts known to the communication partner).
- Inconsistencies.
- Self-serving bias.
- Opportunity to adequately know the truth.
- Lack of information the partner should know if the story is not biased.
- Errors in attribution.
- Diagnostic errors (inaccurate analyses of circumstances).

In the process of debiasing, people look for explanatory cues, those that suggest that the source is biased due to motivational or cognitive processing patterns, or warning cues, the way the message is constructed or delivered nonverbally (Doelger, Hewes, & Graham, 1986).

People reinterpret messages to achieve a more accurate picture of what is going on. Mindfulness increases as persons have a self-interest to look for bias. Persons who have a high need for information are likely to seek information to assist their debiasing, particularly if it is not difficult to obtain. If people have a high need to assure themselves that information is accurate, they are likely to interpret it in many ways. If many interpretations exist, people experience uncertainty and tend to avoid looking for additional interpretations (Hewes, Graham, Monsour, & Doelger, 1989). Mindfulness increases until the cognitive strain exceeds the likely reward for debiasing the information. These conclusions conform to the principles of cognitive-involvement theory discussed in chapter 5.

Social cognition, in this way, constitutes processes by which people seek information, receive what is available to them, and interpret it with varying degrees of mindfulness. Information is important to relationships but may not be enough to maintain them. Indeed, Duck (1985) contended, new information may actually harm rather than help relationships. Uncertainty has its place in the management of relationships, but what also counts is the ability of persons to persuade one another to improve, maintain, or dissolve a relationship.

The ability to know each other as well as develop and execute successful communication plans is vital to being socially competent. To understand this process requires an understanding of uncertainty reduction theory, which builds on the intellectual foundations of social cognition.

INTELLECTUAL ORIGINS OF SOCIAL COGNITION

This chapter deals with attribution processes. That means, essentially, that people judge one another. Judgment includes attempting to explain why they act as they do, largely by cuing on one or more key traits about the individual. For this reason, this discussion has implications for what are commonly called stereotypes. As people become more enlightened, they try to avoid using stereotypes. We may say, "Don't stereotype me," but the reality is that humans cue on key aspects of one another as they quickly attempt to make sense of one another. We can't deny the fact that we don't start from scratch or accurately get to know someone at first glance: We generalize and categorize. Some stereotypes are quite positive. For instance, you may use the stereotype that people who do not stereotype are good. That is a stereotype, although probably a good one. Certainly, at minimum, we would ask each other not to jump to easy conclusions, every time, without giving us a chance to be more than a stereotype. Nevertheless, we have limited cognitive capacity and therefore make many generalizations about the people we encounter. As a critical perspective, let's challenge ourselves to avoid allowing stereotypes from leading to unfortunate and unnecessarily negative conclusions and reactions to each other.

One intellectual ancestor of social cognition is information theory, which is discussed in chapter 3. That discussion explains that a motive for obtaining and using information is to reduce uncertainty. Uncertainty is unpleasant, isn't it? If you take a hard and very important test, don't you hate waiting to learn the results? Don't you want to reduce the uncertainty? Information increases or decreases the degree of uncertainty, or entropy, a person feels in a given situation.

Another intellectual foundation of social cognition was provided by attribution theory, which originated in the work of Heider (1958). He reasoned that, in everyday activities, people engage in a relatively unsophisticated version of the kind of observation and analysis that social scientists use when conducting laboratory experiments. This activity he called *naive psychology*. He reasoned that people make their way through life as naive psychologists. They gather facts and use them to generalize about the character and motivation of one another. His point was that people attempt to assign causation and meaning to the actions of others as well as of themselves.

Social cognition assumes that people desire a causal explanation of the world. They like to believe that human nature is regular and knowable from the behavior they observe. People like to believe they can understand (make sense of) the physical and social world they encounter. They think the world is rational and adheres to fundamental principles, the most essential of which is causation. "Things" happen for a reason. People do what they do for a "reason."

As people interact, they attempt to make sense of each other's behavior so that they can know who the other person is, why the person acts as he or she does, and what those actions (verbal and nonverbal communication) mean for the relationship. Thus, they attempt to explain their own behavior and that of others by assigning causes to it. These means are used to assign motives to people and to make judgments about relationships. This frame of mind assumes that what each person does is purposive, the result of the kind of person he or she is and the circumstances that influence how the person behaves.

Advancing the principles Heider established, H. H. Kelley (1972) argued that insight can be gained into the process of interpersonal perception and interaction by looking for the cognitive schemata or cognitive rules people use when attempting to infer the causes of behavior. When people assign one cause rather than its alternatives to explain behavior, they make assumptions. These assumptions constitute their cognitive schemata. As individuals, as well as scholars, gaining insight into these schemata help to explain why people do what they do during interpersonal communication.

Following this line of reasoning, Kelley cautioned that it is easy to assume that people are better at attribution than they actually are. They often make incomplete analyses, use small data samples, and are incomplete when looking at trends of data. For instance, a person might attribute personality characteristics to another person based only on the clothing the person wears and his or her appearance. If the clothing is expensive and the person is well groomed, the conclusion could be made that the person is wealthy; based on that reasoning, other conclusions could be drawn. A more complete review of the data could reveal that the person borrowed the trappings of affluence and is a dishonest, untrustworthy fraud.

Observational patterns, H. H. Kelley (1972) reasoned, follow a covariation principle: *"An effect is attributed to one of its possible causes with which, over time, it covaries"* (p. 3). Sometimes an individual will be certain that an attribution is accurate because only one reason seems to explain why someone is behaving in a particular manner. (At least the individual can think of only one reason for the behavior.) At other times, the attribution may not be as certain, especially when several causes are present. H. H. Kelley (1973) called this the discounting effect: *"The role of a given cause in producing a given effect is discounted when other plausible causes are also present"* (p. 113).

Social cognition assumes that as people witness events, situations, and actions occurring at the same time, they conclude that some principle of causation is operating. How people attribute causes in each situation is a product of the heuristics or schemata they routinely use to make attributions about their world and the people they encounter. For instance, if they stereotype people and have acted on those stereotypes, they are likely to continue to use those stereotypes to make attributions. Each instance they witness that confirms the stereotype will be used as evidence that specific traits fit the stereotype; each instance that occurs that could disconfirm the stereotype is likely to be dismissed or ignored.

This kind of analysis brought H. H. Kelley (1973) to argue that a few principles predict each person's efforts to attribute causes of behavior. Even if beliefs and judgments are not veridical, they are servicable because people know that they know. He reduced these principles to key combinations: When attributing, people rely on other people's qualities or perceived intentions, to the time (situation) when the action occurs, to the entities involved in the action, to the interaction between person and entities, or to the circumstances surrounding the behavior.

When assigning causes to what occurs to them and around them, individuals employ causal schemata, beliefs about which factors cause events to turn out as they do, or at least appear to turn out (H. H. Kelley, 1973). Some examples can help you understand the attributions that result from these thought processes. If a person you know well does something, you will probably use your knowledge of him or her to attribute the causes for the action or outcomes. If the person is a good friend, you might focus on his or her good traits to explain a good test score. If the person is someone you don't like, you might reason that he or she cheated or that the test was quite easy. If you do well on a test, it is because you studied (attribution to self). If you get a bad grade, you may blame the teacher for being too hard, too vague, or tricky (attribution to circumstances). Most people take credit for good outcomes and blame circumstances when things do not go well.

In this way, people focus on a combination of personal and situational traits when attributing causes. If we know someone well and like that person, if we see him or her in a situation (such as being ticketed for speeding) we assume the person had a good reason, got unlucky, or was unjustly accused. If we see someone being arrested whom we don't like, we believe they are guilty and got what they deserved. If we don't like police, we side with the person who is receiving the ticket. If we like police, we support the officer against the offender.

In addition to personal and situational traits, we focus on the things (entities) with which people associate themselves. Entities could include watches, clothing, cars, CDs, houses, books, an infinite list of things that people can use to manage impressions. Thus, if we see someone we don't know very well listening to a kind of music (entity), we may infer that he or she is the kind of person who likes that style of music. If the person is someone we know well and know they don't like that kind of music, we make attributions to explain away that apparent inconsistency. In making attributions based on the sort of music a person is listening to, you might ignore the possibility that the person is trying to like or understand the music for a test or to impress someone. If you see classmates in the library during most of the semester, you are likely to assume that they are good students. If you see them there only during finals, you are likely to conclude that they are bad students cramming for tests. A person driving an expensive automobile is assumed to be prosperous and to like other expensive things. See how attribution works? If you stop to think for a moment, you are likely to recall many times when your inferences were incorrect.

This view of attribution assumes that people manage their impressions. It also postulates that people operate as naive scientists, observing behavior, learning interpretive schemata, and using them to make attributions. How are categories and the attributions drawn from them influenced by communication? To answer this question, constructivism explains attribution by drawing on different assumptions than those made by Heider and Kelley.

Rather than believing that people observe behavior, create interpretative schemata categories, and make attributions experientially, constructivists believe the process operates in a different manner. They reason that people form attributional categories through communication with one another. They are most likely to share views with persons with whom they must accommodate or with whom they associate. In this sense, people take on perspectives as they learn the language of the people with whom they associate. People who associate with one another come to have similar views of each other and the world they encounter. Constructivism reasons that people can communicate with one another, and make attributions, only because they have learned interaction and attribution patterns that are relevant to their encounters.

Constructivism assumes that individuals are creative and dynamic. They act dynamically to affect changes based on how they think and regulate their activities (Delia et al., 1982). People can coordinate activities with one another because they recognize and employ strategies that lead to certain shared goals. Each of us can talk to one another easier, with greater accuracy and insight, when we share similar thoughts that can be used to coordinate social interaction.

One central goal of constructivism is to discover the interpretative schemata people use to characterize, and therefore understand, their physical and social realms. To this end, the theory reasons that by imposing meaningful categories on these realms, individuals make sense of what they perceive. For example, if someone flunks a test, breaks a date, or wins an award, the people who need to understand this behavior do so by interpreting it according to schemata that make sense to them as members of social groups.

Once interpretative patterns have been formed and shared by interactants, they guide human action. For this reason, people who share the same sense of the world and social expectations are likely to act in similar ways. This does not mean, however, that everyone acts in exactly the same way in the same situation.

People may act differently from one another if they perceive the situation (make attributions), the people in it, and the strategies that are relevant to it differently. As they become more aware of the schemata each is using to guide actions and interpretations, they tend to become more similar. Any moment of interpersonal behavior reflects both partners' histories regarding the behavior relevant to the situation and the parties who are involved in it. Behavior follows schemata that allow people to interact because they know which action is appropriate to each set of circumstances. Because individuals share schemata, they can coordinate activities. Even when interpretative processes differ in significant ways, enough overlap exists for them to be able to coordinate their activities. Through attribution and communication, people join together into a society that is meaningful for them (Delia et al., 1982; B. J. O'Keefe & Delia, 1982).

How people make attributions and use them to try to know one another and act in coordinated ways are important factors in interpersonal communication. During interpersonal communication, many attributions are likely to occur. For instance, if a person talks about a topic, you probably assume she or he likes and may even be knowledgeable about it. If someone appears to like you, you might conclude that (a) the situation calls for "liking," (b) the person is just being polite, or (c) the person should like you because you are likeable. If you are a good student, and a classmate shows unusual interest in your ability in a class, you may conclude that you have a positive effect on others, and that the person is like you and is a good student. If you doubt that the person's interest lacks positive motives, you may reason that she or he is merely trying to be nice to get your help in class. Thus, whether attributing positive or negative motives, you are likely to share a sense of which motives and attributions are relevant. And, you are likely to share a relatively similar set of interpretations because you and the other person construct, or interpret, the world in similar ways.

The schemata you employ regarding such matters, and the questions or comments you use to seek additional information, are used to reduce uncertainty about the person's interest in you. Does the person like you for yourself or because you take really good class notes? These interpersonal quandaries motivate each of us to gain insight into the processes of attribution.

Attribution is a good starting point from which to study interpersonal communication because all people have to go on is what they think others do and say. H. H. Kelley (1973) believed that people make attributions even if they are inaccurate. How good are people at attributing causes of behavior? People assume they are quite accurate. What do you think?

Addressing this question, Sillars (1982) cautioned that people are not naive scientists, using primitive covariation to make attributions; rather, they are just naive. His list of reservations about people's ability to make attributions is enlightening because of what the list says about the difficulty or impossibility of making accurate attributions. A brief review of his criticisms will sharpen your insight into the difficulties of understanding how people go about reducing uncertainty.

One significant flaw in attributional schemata results because prior expectations cause people to imagine relationships between personal traits, situational circumstances, and entities even when no correlation exists. People may overlook or ignore crucial relationships of this sort that do exist. Sillars made this point to defend his reservation that people actually operate out of schemata that contain stereotypes and other faulty expectations of why people do what they do.

Whereas H. H. Kelley (1972, 1973) argued that people use consensus as a vital part of their attribution processes, Sillars contended that they make little use of this principle. They often ignore consensus data and base their attributions on nonnormative actions or traits that they observe in others, an inferential bias. Instead of searching for the best explanation, people usually settle on the first sufficient explanation that comes to mind. Stereotypes are typical examples of this kind of bias. This tendency to settle on the first sufficient explanation is likely to result when some degree of emotion is associated with the explanation. For instance, an egocentric athlete may believe a victory was the result of his or her exceptional effort, whereas a player who believes in the importance of team effort may credit that factor for producing victory. Or people who are fearful that they will be cheated are likely to use this as the basis of attribution and therefore find more cheating than do persons who use different schemata.

H. H. Kelley's approach to attribution assumes that each day is relatively new and that people are constantly alert to refining their attributional schemata. Sillars disagreed and contended that people do not adequately reevaluate attributions in light of new data. Even when people are aware that new data do not agree with their attributions, they are not likely to be objective. When new information is received that contradicts an attribution, the information is likely to be critically evaluated; however, when information is received that confirms the attribution, it is likely to be accepted uncritically as confirmation.

Sillars contended that the attributional schemata that people use produce many biases. Some of these result from traits that are salient about the person toward whom attribution is being made. A self-serving bias exists because people prefer to deny responsibility for bad outcomes and take credit for good ones. People tend to overestimate the extent to which they have control in a situation. Many people hold a just "world view" that people get what they deserve; this bias would occur if you say that a person who wrecked a car because of careless driving deserved to suffer the accident, but you may not think how unjust the world is to the innocent persons hurt in the accident.

An important bias results from the belief people have that others are like them and thereby have similar feelings and opinions. Often people expect that others think and behave for the same reasons they do. In making attributions, most people prefer to use a linear model of causality, rather than assuming that many "causes" could have operated to lead a person to a particular opinion, judgment, or behavior. Bias in attribution becomes greater during conflict or when the person making the attribution is emotionally involved with the other person. These observations are intended to lead people to be cautious in their efforts to explain attribution processes.

The starting point to understand and appreciate how people reduce uncertainty, in part through attribution, is to realize the shortcomings in the attributional schemata that people use. This kind of analysis reveals the difference between uncertainty reduction and accurate attribution as vital parts of interpersonal communication. The incentive to reduce uncertainty may lead people to make false attributions. If uncertainty reduction (as a part of social cognition) is essential to knowing whether relationships are good or bad and why relational partners act as they do, then caution must be used when examining and explaining the processes of social cognition. This line of reasoning asks us to cautiously answer the question, can people ever really know one another?

The standards for accuracy may have to be derived through conversation and observation by the parties involved. Can attribution be accurate if the parties involved hold different opinions about what their own traits and actions mean? Person A may think Person B is aloof, whereas B thinks of him- or herself as quiet and unassuming. Person A may think of B as irresponsible, whereas B prides his or her carefree spirit in an uptight world.

Accurate attribution would seem to require that relationships and the efforts of relational partners depend on whether the partners agree on which elements are salient to the attributions and what these attributes mean. Many relationships struggle because Person A wants B to be "open," whereas Person B does not want to burden A with "all of my thoughts and feelings." Relationships are harmed by one partner who believes in saving for the future, whereas the other does not want to be so frugal. As people date, how can they know with any degree of certainty what their partners will be like in 5, 10, 20, or 40 years? How can relational partners be less uncertain (or more certain) in regard to what each other really is like?

These concerns are brought into perspective by applying a coorientation model. It forces us to acknowledge that perspectives held by communicators flow both ways (McLeod & Chaffee, 1973). Coorientation features matching sets of perceptions that fall into three categories: mutual understanding (agreement), accuracy, and congruency (satisfaction). Agreements exist when the views held by Person A are similar to those held by Person A's perception of Person B's views corresponds with what Person B actually believes. Satisfaction is a feeling of ease or pleasure that mutual understanding or agreement exists. Accuracy refers to the extent to which the partners in a relationship see each other in the same way. What each person thinks of the other and how accurately each person knows the other as that person knows him or herself determines whether people deal with each other in similar or dissimilar ways. Satisfaction refers to the extent to which the participants are pleased by what they know about each other and about the relationship. People could agree and be dissatisfied; both parties might agree that one of them is selfish, but only one person might be satisfied by this fact.

After this summary of the origins of attribution theory and problems that are inherent in the processes of social cognition, it is useful to discuss whether some people are better at cognition than others. If all people were equally good or bad at making attributions, the study of communication would be quite different. How do people make attributions, and how skilled are they?

Research indicates that some people are better (more accurate) at making attributions than others are. Sensitive people listen differently than do less sensitive people. Sensitive listeners make more high-level inferences; they divide conversation elements into small units, store conversation characteristics in their memories, and make more self-references about conversations. Sensitive listeners are more likely to self-monitor, be self-conscious, be perceptive, have higher self-esteem, be assertive, exhibit empathy, and enjoy better social skills. Sensitive listeners are less likely to suffer communication apprehension, receiver apprehension, and anxiety about social relationships (Daly, Vangelisti, & Daughton, 1987).

This review of the intellectual origins of social cognition emphasizes the important role information plays in the process of getting to know one another. This review demonstrates that how each person makes attributions (applies idiosyncratic schemata) may produce inaccurate and biased attributions. Moreover, the individual is likely to be blind to those attributional problems. Patterns of attribution exist; they are useful in the efforts people make to get to know one another. Biases indicate patterns that can be observed and compared. These biases become topics of conversation between interactional partners. In the effort to make attributions, some people are more competent than others, and coorientation supplies a model by which each of us can look on our communication partner's patterns of attributions as we look on our own. We are reminded that "thoughts about self, other, and situation are the designated units for investigation" (Knapp et al., 1994, p. 13). To get to know one another is a person's incentive to reduce uncertainty, which is a motive for communication.

UNCERTAINTY REDUCTION

Chapter 3 explains how information affects uncertainty. Because uncertainty is uncomfortable, people seek and process information. Sometimes information comes when it is unexpected; even so, it can increase or decrease certainty. This quick review shows how information is vital to social cognition.

Stressing the importance of this line of research, Werner and Baxter (1994 concluded "that intimacy is facilitated when the parties have certainty and predictability about one another, their interactions together, and the state of their relationship" (p. 359). Too much certainty and predictability can deaden a relationship; too much uncertainty raises its cost to an unacceptable level. Relationship building is a dialectic of stability and change, certainty and uncertainty.

As people interact, they try to get to know one another. People "read" nonverbal cues to assess personality and behavioral traits. They want to know why persons behave as they do. Not only do they obtain information from and about others, but they also want information about themselves to help reduce their uncertainty about whether they are socially competent. They want to know what others think of them. Each of us is something of a mystery to others. Sometimes we are a mystery to ourselves.

Thus, uncertainty refers to "the number of possible alternative ways of behaving and believing when strangers meet." Uncertainty can increase or decrease throughout a relationship. It also "concerns the ability of each interactant to explain his own and the other's behavior. Each interactant must develop a set of causal attributions in order to answer the question of why he and the other are behaving in particular ways or believing certain things" (C. R. Berger, 1975, p. 33).

As you encounter others, you may wonder, "Is this person friendly?" "Does the person like me?" "Can I talk this person into helping me with my homework?" "Is this person hostile toward me?" If you become romantically interested in a person, you might seek information, such as asking a mutual friend whether the person says nice things about you and likes you. Despite your efforts, you may not get information you seek it. Some comes accidentally, such as seeing a person you like holding hands with someone else or when a mutual friend comments on how fickle that person is or that the person is involved with someone else. As you encounter others, you only know them from what they appear to be and what they do. This information is used to attribute motives and personality traits that affect how, whether, and why you communicate with them.

Uncertainty reduction, as a theoretical perspective, originated with C. R. Berger and Calabrese (1975) who drew on the work of Heider (1958). They reasoned that people seek to make sense of their environment, including the people in it. Uncertainty-reduction theory is a powerful explanation for communication because it operates in all contexts to help explain why people communicate as they do. Uncertainty is unpleasant and therefore motivational; people communicate to reduce it. But people also create uncertainty. They withhold information from one another and act mysteriously. They provide information that is biased, untrue, or partially true. They mislead, distort, and tantalize.

C. R. Berger (1987) observed how difficult it is to interact with a stranger who we know can choose to behave in many ways, some of which might be quite unpredictable. As people begin to interact with strangers, they may encounter personalities, opinions, and communication styles that can be disconcerting.

Uncertainty-reduction theory has helped explain how individuals obtain enough knowledge about one another to increase the predictability needed for conversations to be conducted smoothly. As people are able to predict how they and others will behave, they are more confident in deciding which of their communication repertoire to use in each situation to obtain the goals they have in mind. During this interaction, the quality of information exchanged is more important than its quantity.

By using context as a starting point to reduce uncertainty and to attribute opinions and judgments, people may be able to decrease uncertainty more quickly. People use many other cues to reduce uncertainty: person prototypes (a version of stereotype), roles, schemas, scripts, and conversation sequences. As you interact with others, the biases they exhibit will be used to figure out who each person is and what he or she likes or dislikes. The role the person assumes can be the foundation of attributions. How the person thinks, what scripted conversational patterns the person uses, and how he or she joins (or does not join) in conversations serve as information that persons use to make attributions about one another.

As postulated by C. R. Berger and Calabrese (1975), uncertainty reduction follows a pattern of developmental stages. This pattern is especially likely to occur during initial interaction, when people first meet or when new topics are introduced later in a relationship. The entry phase typically consists of information exchanges of demographic information and expressions of attitudes on topics of minimal consequence or low involvement. After this phase, one or both interactants decide whether a relationship seems worth pursuing. The personal phase occurs when participants disclose intimate information and discuss topics that involve personal attitudes, feelings, and judgments. This phase is likely to exhibit conversation patterns that are freer of scripted comments and social norms than are typical of the initial phase. The exit phase occurs if one or both parties decide to terminate the relationship. As is true of the first two phases, this one is shaped by norms that guide individuals' efforts to signal that a relationship is terminating. In all phases, verbal and nonverbal communication is important, but the last phase may be characterized by nonverbal terminating or leave-taking behaviors, such as refusing invitations, avoiding, or ignoring the other person. This pattern assumes many of the characteristics of social penetration theory, which postulates increased disclosure if the circumstances are right. The pattern also is predicted by social-exchange theory, which features the rewards/costs decision regarding whether a relationship is worth pursuing.

At each of these three phases, uncertainty reduction is a primary motive behind communication activities. As C. R. Berger and Calabrese (1975) suggested, "When strangers meet, their primary concern is one of uncertainty reduction or increasing predictability about the behavior of both themselves and others in the interaction" (p. 100). One goal of researchers is to determine what norms and schemata guide attempts to obtain information about the communication partner and about one's own competence in the interaction. What do interactants look for in the comments and behavior of others and themselves as they work to reduce uncertainty about the worth of the relationship? The answer to this question needs to be revealed by research.

In keeping with the tenets of attribution theory, we can reason that people will make judgments about their performance and that of other participants even if those judgments are inaccurate. In response to the kind of reservations Sillars (1982) raised in regard to people's ability to make accurate attributions, C. R. Berger and Calabrese (1975) stated that "attribution theorists have been quick to point out that such predictions and explanations generally yield imperfect knowledge of ourselves and others. However, it is significant that such imperfect knowledge does guide our total behavior toward others" (p. 101). Regardless of their ability to attribute accurately, people do so, nevertheless, and act accordingly.

We may be wrong in our judgments of who other people are and why they act as they do. Nevertheless, we tend to persist in our patterns of attributions about them until we have reason to change. We tend to confirm, rather than disconfirm, our attributions. For this reason, misperception is likely to be a lingering factor in relationships.

Given this problem, uncertainty-reduction theorists have been motivated to conduct a systematic investigation of these crucial interpersonal processes. To guide research into the ways people attempt to reduce uncertainty, C. R. Berger and Calabrese (1975) offered several axioms and theorems.

Axiom 1. *"Given the high level of uncertainty present at the onset of the entry phase, as the amount of verbal communication between strangers increases, the level of uncertainty for each interactant in the relationship will decrease. As uncertainty is further reduced, the amount of verbal communication will increase"* (pp. 101–102).

Axiom 2. *"As nonverbal affiliative expressiveness increases, uncertainty levels will decrease in an initial interaction situation. In addition, decreases in uncertainty level will cause increases in nonverbal affiliative expressiveness"* (p. 103).

Axiom 3. *"High levels of uncertainty cause increases in information seeking behavior. As uncertainty levels decline, information seeking behavior decreases"* (p. 103).

Axiom 4. *"High levels of uncertainty in a relationship cause decreases in the intimacy level of communication content. Low levels of uncertainty produce high levels of intimacy"* (p. 103).

Axiom 5. *"High levels of uncertainty produce high rates of reciprocity. Low levels of uncertainty produce low reciprocity rates"* (p. 105).

Axiom 6. *"Similarities between persons reduce uncertainty, while dissimilarities produce increases in uncertainty"* (p. 106).

Axiom 7. *"Increases in uncertainty level produce decreases in liking; decreases in uncertainty level produce increases in liking"* (p. 107).

By reviewing these axioms, you should understand better the relationship between the quality of relationships, degrees of uncertainty, and communication activities that transpire.

Two primary attribution processes occur during attempts to reduce uncertainty. The first, proactive attribution, occurs when individuals use information received verbally and nonverbally during interaction to interpret who their partner is and why he or she acts as is the case. Such data are considered in the context of a particular situation. As individuals receive information early in an interaction, they make attributions that are tested, as hypotheses, during the conversation. This process includes estimates of opinions the other person has not revealed but may do so as the conversation progresses.

The second process is retroactive attribution. It occurs when individuals use information they acquire, whether verbal or nonverbal, to explain comments and behaviors that occurred previously in the relationship. We think back onto statements, actions, and relationship developments to explain to ourselves why they turned out as they did. One obvious occurrence of retroactive attribution is when a person thinks, "So that is why the person said (or did) that."

These processes occur throughout interactions. Retroactive processes often occur when proactive predictions are not affirmed. Retroactive attribution is used when people need to confirm or disconfirm attributions they made earlier in the relationship. One schemata that is used in proactive attribution is that when individuals perceive they have similar backgrounds, they will predict they also have similar attitudes. Attitude differences appear to be attributed to personality, whereas agreements are attributed to similarities of communication style. When persons are engaged in conversations where they experience attitude dissimilarity, they characterize the situation in negative terms, such as unpleasant, cold, active, honest, awful, and complex. Attribution in such situations is problemmatic. Are people being honest and truthful when they express opinions that differ from those of their interaction partner? Expressions of attitude similarity can be truthful or merely attempts to manage impressions (C. R. Berger, 1975). Studies such as this provide keys for unlocking, not only the attribution process, but also the communication strategies employed to reduce uncertainty.

Postulates by Berger and Calabrese prompted more than two decades of research to prove, clarify, and critique uncertainty reduction's explanation of how people communicate interpersonally. One assumption is that people are more likely to engage in question asking to reduce uncertainty when they expect to meet again. A test of low, intermediate, and high levels of anticipation revealed that people in the intermediate treatment did more question asking than did their counterparts. People seem to avoid negative conversational outcomes (W. Douglas, 1987).

People appear to experience different levels of apprehension toward the perils of engaging in interactions for the first time and about forming relationships in general, what can be called global uncertainty. Analyzing that concept, W. Douglas (1991) discovered that people who experience high global uncertainty think of initial interactions in negative ways, prefer to avoid them, and develop less satisfactory long-term relationships. Such persons feel less self-assured and more awkward. During the first moments of interactions with strangers, those persons ask fewer questions and disclose more than persons who do not suffer from global uncertainty. Their more assured counterparts rate them to be less competent communicators.

Uncertainty-reduction theory has predicted that during initial interaction, information seeking will occur whether the relationship appears likely to produce negative or positive outcomes. Contrary to that prediction, research findings indicate that information seeking increases when individuals predict a positive outcome from initial interaction, whereas a negative prediction leads to less information seeking. The assumption is that people seek information to support their predictions that a relationship will be rewarding. No similar attribution seems to occur when initial predictions are negative (Sunnafrank, 1990).

Do people handle initial interactions differently and, if so, why? One explanation focuses on different levels of self-monitoring (paying attention to oneself as a communicator). High self-monitors are better at initial interactions than are low self-monitors. High self-monitors are more aware of situational demands and use more information-seeking strategies than do low self-monitors. They do more to direct the flow of conversation. High self-monitors use more extensive and strategic verbal communication, and they use more conversation topics than do low self-monitors (W. Douglas, 1984).

Tensions exist between persons involved in a relationship because each partner seeks more information than he or she wants to give. How this relationship is negotiated is influenced by the form, content, and value of the information exchanged. Form relates to the methods of giving and obtaining information. Form results from desires to interrogate, disclose, demonstrate affect, be involved, and elaborate on matters relevant to the relationship. Content includes polarities such as ambiguous–clear, general–specific, personal–nonpersonal, descriptive–explanatory, atypical–typical, accurate–inaccurate, or negative–positive. Each polarity reflects choices made by the person giving information.

Value refers to factors related to self-evaluation, evaluation of partner and the relationship; this category includes liking, perceived similarity, uncertainty, outcome, and the personality of the people involved (Kellerman, 1987).

This theory has been criticized because the stages for reducing uncertainty are not well defined, the causal mechanism that produces changes in levels of certainty has not been specified, and it appears to ignore the environment or context in which relationships develop. However, Gudykunst, Yang, and Nishida (1985) added support for the postulates by C. R. Berger and Calabrese (1975) by comparing uncertainty-reduction tactics in acquaintanceships, friendships, and dating relationships in Japan, Korea, and the United States. Under these conditions, uncertainty reduction postulates for initial interaction hold up across different cultures.

Cross-cultural settings offer an opportunity to test uncertainty-reduction theory. Special problems may result when people encounter persons from other cultures. When people make positive comparisons of persons from different ethnic groups, they are likely to employ typical uncertainty-reduction processes. When people feel good about their own ethnic group, they are more likely to be confident when dealing with persons of another ethnic group. Perceived intimacy level in a relationship will influence the willingness of partners to disclose. These tendencies are more likely to occur when the partner is thought to be typical rather than atypical of his or her ethnic group. These findings not only support uncertainty-reduction theory but also social penetration and social identity theories.

Social-identity theory posits that people make sense of their world by seeing themselves and others as members of groups. Such identities are vital to the self-concepts of persons who engage in interpersonal communication and relationship construction. When persons encounter others who are typical of a social group, they experience less uncertainty about them. When people feel better about persons from other ethnic groups, they should be more willing to disclose, as predicted by social penetration theory. Such disclosure should eventually improve the quality of the relationship because of the rewards gained from increased quality and quantity of insights about the persons involved (Gudykunst & Hammer, 1988). According to social-identity theory, each person's self is defined by sociocultural features, such as age, gender, race, or occupation.

The identity each person uses in regard to self and others constitutes a basis for their attribution of motives as to why others do what they do (J. K. Burgoon, 1994). People's sense of themselves (self-construal) is a product of their culture and influence, whether they prefer independent or interdependent communication styles (Singelis & Brown, 1995).

How people communicate, as well as what they say, appears to be a crucial part of the attribution process. Two indices seem useful in attempts to understand this process. One is the richness of the vocabulary used. The other is verbal immediacy, a product of the directness of the language (the psychological closeness of the speaker to the topic). As individuals experience uncertainty, they look for signs that can help them know whether the interaction partner is being honest and open. Honesty and openness are signalled by a richer vocabulary and by more verbal immediacy. When people speak with conviction and have a richer vocabulary, they are perceived to be more open and honest (Van Rheenen & Sherblom, 1984).

Relevant to uncertainty-reduction theory is people's ability to detect deception, a topic discussed in detail in chapter 6. If people want information and other people have it, those in the latter category have motives to control the flow of information. They also have incentives to create, withhold, and distort information. As noted in chapter 6, nonverbal cues play a major role in deception detection. People who are being deceptive pause to prepare their statements for shorter periods of time than those who are telling the truth. Deceivers maintain less eye contact and inhibit or control themselves in order not to display behavioral cues of deception. A high degree of control is a sign of deception. Whether or not people are good at spotting deception, they want to believe they are (Greene, O'Hair, Cody, & Yen, 1985).

To increase understanding of processes people use to reduce uncertainty, researchers need to examine more than strategies employed by strangers. Much of the communication in which each of us engages occurs with people we know and toward whom we have various feelings of regard and similarity. As we first encounter others, we may actually have less reason to attempt uncertainty reduction than is the case as we seek to negotiate and codefine ongoing and changing relationships. What happens when events or actions change within existing relationships that cause people to have to deal with new levels of uncertainty?

To better understand the dynamics of established relationships, Planalp, Rutherford, and Honeycutt (1988) examined how key events can affect relational knowledge when taken-for-granted knowledge is disrupted. These researchers had respondents report their feelings and communication activities following an instance when someone close to them changed in ways that introduced uncertainty into a previously stable relationship. For instance, one of your "best" friends, whose friendship you thought you could take for granted, begins to show less interest in doing the sorts of things that are required to maintain the relationship. Relationships may go along for some period of time without producing uncertainty. Then something changes to disrupt what had been taken for granted. (Many topics of disclosure were reported in this research, including an announcement that a person was no longer interested in dating the respondent and that the person had betrayed a confidence.)

The researchers elicited respondents' reactions to this kind of announcement and event. New information increased uncertainty. Although it decreased after a while, the degree of certainty regarding the quality of the relationship never returned to the level prior to the disclosure. Disclosure resulted in respondents' having negative feelings, but events did not produce negative outcomes. Some disclosures resulted in stronger relationships. Disclosed information affected relational variables of trust (including factors of honesty, confiding, and fairness), involvement (such as closeness, companionship, and emotional involvement), and rules (such as rewards, freedom, and duties or responsibilities).

Disclosure of the information led most participants to talk over the information rather than to argue about or avoid the issue or the other person. Respondents who talked the matter over with the other person felt the relationship had strengthened. Suggesting the presence of proactive and retroactive attribution, some respondents (41%) reported sensing that the other person had been leading up to an announcement. Whether they were insensitive to relationship changes or whether their partners were not good at signaling changes, most participants became aware that a serious topic was coming only after it was introduced in conversation. Hints that led participants to suspect the coming information included changes in communication behavior, such as the lack of writing "I love you" in letters. Once the new information was introduced, typical communication reactions to the change included talking, explaining feelings, and information seeking. Some participants reported that they or their relational partners renegotiated the rules of the relationship. Most participants reported talking to someone else about the disclosure; these conversations were used to get more information, to understand what was occurring, or to complain or ventilate about the change in the relationship.

Despite these findings, it is unwise to assume that people can easily discuss the quality of their relationships. It may be easier to discuss aspects of the relationship than the total relationship. People have indirect means for discovering information that can be used to reduce uncertainty about the quality of relationships in which they are involved.

C. R. Berger (1987) suggested that three information-seeking strategies are used to reduce uncertainty: (a) passive strategies, unobtrusive observations of what the target person does and says; (b) active strategies, including asking third parties or creating situations that test the target individual's responses; and (c) interactive strategies, whereby the interested party communicates with the target individual.

C. R. Berger (1987) observed three interactive methods people use to discover information about one another and their relationships: question asking, disclosure, and relaxation of the target. When people attempt to acquire large amounts of information, they are not likely to ask any more questions than persons do when having a normal conversation. Rather than the number of questions asked, the difference seems to be the kind of questions; better information is more valuable than more information. Thus, people may seek more information and sift from it the best information. The objective is to reduce uncertainty. When persons are in a high information-seeking mode, they ask their relational partners more questions designed to elicit explanations for their partner's behavior, goals, and plans. Strategy selection seems to be guided by (a) the efficiency of the strategy and (b) its social appropriateness. While seeking information, persons try to get their partners to like them as a means to obtain more information.

People employ several kinds of interactive strategies to obtain information with which to check the quality of relationships:

1. Direct questioning, whereby one person asks the other about the condition of the relationship.
2. Asking third parties about the relationship.
3. Trial intimacy moves, including becoming physically close or touching, disclosure, or public presentation in which the target individual is put on display or confronted with information to observe his or her reaction.
4. Taken-for-granted strategies to see if the other person reveals something about the relationship or merely takes it for granted. (This category includes joking; structuring the situation so the other must assume or reject the burden for the relationship; self-putdown, which challenges the target individual to counter the putdown or take it for granted; and hinting, where the target individual is expected to take up the hint if the relationship is serious.)
5. Endurance tests, which include forced choices ("Either bring me flowers or admit that you don't like me"), physical separation, and testing limits (e.g., to see what the target individual is willing to give or do to maintain or advance a relationship).
6. Jealousy tests to see if the target individual will respond by showing jealousy. (These tests are created by describing alternatives, such as talking about another boy friend or girl friend or initiating alternative behaviors, e.g., going out with someone else.)
7. Fidelity checks to test whether the person will remain faithful to or violate the relationship.

Females use more tests than males do. More tests are employed in romantic relationships than in platonic ones. Being able to distinguish between these two kinds of relationships is important because people may want platonic relationships to become romantic (or vice versa), or they may want to prevent romantic relationships from becoming platonic. Separation tests and indirect suggestion tests are more likely to be used when relationships have the potential of becoming romantic than in platonic or romantic relationships. Romantic and platonic relationships are most satisfying when they enjoy openness, trust, and shared control. Regardless of the quality of relationships, people have difficulty talking directly about them with one another, particularly about aspects that are traditionally taboo (Baxter & Wilmot, 1984).

One of C. R. Berger and Calabrese's (1975) original propositions was that, as uncertainty is reduced, people become more attractive to one another as relational partners. Reflecting on this proposition, C. R. Berger (1987) acknowledged that evidence actually shows that communication may produce information that increases uncertainty or triggers dislikes. Either can lead to the person's being viewed as a less attractive relational partner. He reasoned that, if levels of uncertainty are high, relationships are likely to be strained, in part because costs of social exchange may outweigh rewards. Strained relationships are likely to dissolve. Initial interactions may be predicated on information that is obtained at, and based on, superficial levels. Subsequent communication may strengthen, blunt, or negate initial impressions.

Although he acknowledged the value of using social exchange as a theoretical underpinning, Berger cautioned that it focuses on outcomes and not on processes. If people are to successfully calculate and exchange what is appropriate to achieve a strong relationship, they must use communication tactics to reduce uncertainty in regard to what conditions produce an equitable social exchange. This process is difficult and fraught with ambiguities and inaccuracies. It is difficult to tell what each relational partner thinks is a fair exchange and whether sufficient exchange has been accomplished. Knowledge of what constitutes equitable exchange can be used as relational power and can lead to conflict.

This kind of research extends understanding of uncertainty-reduction processes beyond the initial stages of a relationship. It gives us insight into the management of communication and of the creation or dissolution of relationships. More skillful communicators have a strong sense of which conversational events can substantially alter the direction and outcome of a conversation (Cappella, 1994). At turning points during romantic relationships, participants are more likely to discuss their relationship than at other times. Whether people talk about the turning points in their relationships depends on the kind of turning point that occurs (Baxter & Bullis, 1986).

Uncertainty can also be reduced when partners (romantic partners, for instance) communicate with their partner's friends and family. Moreover, stronger relationships are characterized by open communication and perceived similarity between partners (Parks & Adelman, 1983).

To understand how people make attributions and use communication to reduce uncertainty, researchers strive to disclose the schemata they use. People acquire schemata that they use before, during, and after interactions to make sense of the information they obtain and the goals they want to achieve. They might, for instance, believe they are more likely to obtain information in social settings rather than formal settings. They use hypotheses as the basis of information seeking and processing. A typical hypothesis might take this logical form: People who . . . (act in a certain way, for instance) during a conversation are X kind of people.

To this point in the chapter, a case has been made that social cognition involves strategic efforts to gain information about others. Uncertainty is uncomfortable. The search for information is strategic. Nevertheless, we obtain a great deal of information by accident, without intending to do so.

Getting information is one matter, interpreting it is another. Information needs to be interpreted in the context of the relationships. Schemata are employed to figure out the character and motives of the persons involved in each relationship. Information is interpreted in ways that are meaningful, given the nature of the relationship and the goals of the persons who are involved in it. For instance, information about a friendship is interpreted differently than in a work, superior–subordinate relationship.

Based on information gained and goals people have for the management of relationships, they create plans to achieve those goals. Communication strategies (plans) are developed and employed to enact communication episodes in ways thought to be rewarding. All of these factors combine to affect each individual's communication competence.

This review of research and theoretical perspectives points to some universal themes in interpersonal communication research. A common element is that to understand how people make attributions about one another and about themselves and how they act in regard to one another requires insights into the cognitive schemata they use. With these schemata, they attempt to interpret the data they have about their relational partners. In this way, they work to understand and make sense of their circumstances, especially the people involved with them. As was discussed in chapter 3, how people characterize one another and the social and physical realms in which they operate depends on perspectives embedded in their idioms, their language. Processes of attribution or characterization are used to understand, that is, to know others, what they know, and the surrounding circumstances. The objective is to create and maintain positive relationships and to terminate negative ones. To negotiate the creation, maintenance, and dissolution of relationships requires shared knowledge. This shared social knowledge helps people not only to know, but to know what others know. The desire to reduce uncertainty motivates individuals to make sense of their physical and social world and to calculate their self-efficacy as communicators.

Part of their skill in creating and maintaining relationships depends on their ability to reduce uncertainty about themselves and others. Another vital skill is to act in ways that lead them to be seen as attractive relational partners. One of the theories that explains this process is communication accommodation.

COMMUNICATION ACCOMMODATION

Three factors that are crucial to interpersonal communication are cognition, planning, and accommodation. Cognition refers to the schemata each person employs to make sense (interpret the meaning) of what occurs during communication. Planning is employed, based on plans learned and schemata utilized, to develop strategies that are needed to interact with and accommodate to communication partners in order to achieve goals, however ill defined. Not all conversations are planned; many just happen. Even when they are planned, much that happens is the result of what transpires as a response to what the partner does and says. For these reasons, an understanding of interactions must encompass a range of actions from the highly planned to the purely spontaneous. Accommodation may occur for other reasons, such as a sign that one person respects the other. To conduct a mock test of this theory, observe groups of students visiting during lunch. Do the students at each table exhibit similar communication patterns (convergence) or divergence?

This theory explains the old adage, birds of a feather flock together. Do members of middle school cliques dress and act the same? Do they talk the same way? Do they walk and act the same way? Do they wear their hair in the same style? Do they use the same vocabulary?

During interaction, some people are more mindful than others. Situations may require people to be more mindful than they would be in different circumstances. For this reason, people might devote more planning to communication events that have important outcomes. Casual conversation may not require much planning, whereas a job interview may require considerable planning.

Although people can be quite complex and mindful in their communication, much communication is automatic and scripted, at least that is the argument made by speech or communication accommodation theory. This theory assumes that communication competence depends on individuals' ability to perform in ways that enhance interactions in order to achieve their goals (Street & Giles, 1982). This theory is a companion to impression-management theory, both of which postulate that individuals act in ways that increase the chances that their partners will make favorable attributions about them as attractive communication and relational partners. When people like one another, their communication patterns are likely to converge, be similar. When they don't like one another, their patterns are likely to diverge, to be dissimilar.

This line of research predicts that, as people interact, they tend to accommodate to each other. To accommodate means that one or both partners tend to adopt nonverbal and verbal patterns that are similar to those of the other person. The assumption is that when people are thought to act in ways that are similar to those of their partners, they are seen as attractive because they have styles that match and share similar attitudes. To the extent they accommodate successfully, they are seen as positive communication partners. Much accommodation occurs through nonverbal cues, such as response latency (time that transpires between a stimulus, a comment, and the response to it), speech rate (how rapidly a person speaks), and turn duration (how long each person talks).

Communication-accommodation theory asserts that communication consists primarily of scripted behaviors that people use to present themselves favorably to their communication partners. People manage impressions by performing acts designed to get their communication partners to see them as desirable, rational partners. How people communicate with and accommodate one another is to a large extent a product of their self-identities, the situation, relationships, goals, and levels of arousal. Throughout interaction, people monitor their behavior and that of their partner. This behavior is evaluated by calculating the extent to which it fits the expectations relevant to the situation (Giles & Street, 1985).

Communication accommodation theory makes quite different assumptions about responses to similar and expected interpersonal behavior than does Cappella and Greene's (1982) discrepancy-arousal theory, discussed in chapter 6. Discrepancy-arousal theory postulates that when interactants act in ways that violate the expectations their partners have of them, arousal is created that can negatively affect their interaction and relationship.

Comparing this theory to communication accommodation, Street and Giles (1982) believed that three causal links are relevant to communication accommodation theory: (a) communication patterns one person expects the other to exhibit (such as speaking at an appropriate rate, taking the appropriate amount of time per turn, or matching responses such as nodding approval); (b) arousal, which leads to affect that is positive or negative; and (c) responses based on the arousal (for instance, if one person speaks too quickly the relational partner might speak more slowly).

Cappella (1985) reasoned that communication-accommodation theory can explain what happens in conversations as long as they are going well, but he doubted that it helps explain why they go badly. He argued that convergence, reciprocity, and similarity of communication patterns (verbal and nonverbal) lead interactants to evaluate one another positively.

Street and Giles (1982) were concerned by the discrepancy-arousal model's prediction that little or no discrepancy can lead to little or no arousal, which is affectively neutral. In contrast to this prediction, speech-accommodation theory reasons that if responses are matched, no discrepancy occurs, but the reaction is positive rather than neutral. Similarity produces positive rather than neutral reactions.

Street and Giles (1982) offered communication-accommodation theory as an alternative explanation because it (1) acknowledges social cognitive processes, (2) has the potential for further scope in those directions, (3) incorporates the social consequences as well as the determinants of speech adjustments, (4) is applicable to many linguistic levels of analysis, from the more intercultural language and dialect switching to the more intracultural conversational and noncontent speech domains, (5) attends to intergroup phenomena and processes, and (6) has had applications to a wide range of speech domain, including those of language and sex. (p. 204)

Seeking to support this theory, Street (1984) examined the extent to which interactants' noncontent speech patterns (speech rate, pauses, pitch, intensity, duration, and accent) converge or become similar to one another. Also important in this situation is the evaluation each person makes of the other in terms of what transpires during conversation. This theory predicts that as a conversation transpires, participants' noncontent communication patterns should change in ways that mirror one another, what Street called speech-convergence phenomenon. If convergence occurs, interaction should be more successful, and partners should form favorable impressions of each other, even though they may be unaware that it is happening. Convergence seems to occur for several reasons: desire for approval, sensitivity to interpersonal cues, perceived attitudinal similarity, communication effectiveness, competence, social attractiveness, communicator warmth, or desire for social identification.

Accommodation theory is based on principles of similarity–attraction, social exchange, attribution, and social identity. According to this theory, people are motivated to adjust their speech styles with respect to one another to foster social identity, shared expression of values, attitudes, and intentions. A key mechanism in the process is the perception one person has of another's speech. Based on what one person perceives as the other's communication patterns, the first person makes evaluations that lead to behavior, further evaluation, and subsequent adjustments. The assumption is that intentions, actions, and adjustments will lead to convergence as an expression of a desire for social integration, seeking or showing approval, social identification, or communication competence. Convergence is employed when one person in an interaction attempts to be like and be liked by another. If convergence is perceived to be intentional rather than accidental, it is likely to be evaluated more positively.

Convergence has positive benefits. It can result in enhanced perceived intelligibility, supportiveness, predictability, intersubjectivity (shared ideas and views), and smoothness of interaction. It may indicate positive feelings toward the other person involved. Convergence can foster warmth, perceived competence, attraction, and willingness to cooperate.

Convergence is likely to occur when rewards for doing so outweigh the costs. It will not occur under the opposite conditions. Convergence depends on participants' communication repertoires and their need for social approval. The social-identity component of this theory predicts that divergence will occur when people desire to reject or dissociate themselves from people who are perceived to be nongroup members (those who are not part of the person's social, ethnic, economic group, etc.). Divergence will occur if Person A desires to dissociate from Person B, and if he or she has the communication repertoire available to accomplish this goal.

Communication maintenance occurs when interactants deliberately seek to maintain social distance between themselves and others. In this way, they establish autonomy and independence. Such patterns occur when communication partners are seen as undesirable socially and when differences are to be maintained. Under such circumstances, communicators may even accentuate differences between themselves and their communication partners.

Accommodation theory predicts that communication styles of interactants must match one another if the persons are going to achieve harmony, be successful, and demonstrate to one another that they are competent communicators. For this reason, people who speak quickly are more likely to influence people who think quickly. Likewise, slow decoders are more likely to comply with requests made by slow speakers (Buller & Aune, 1988). Such accommodation increases communicator attractiveness. Williams and Giles (1996) found that young adults were more satisfied with conversations with older adults when the older adults were more accommodative to the styles of the younger persons.

Convergence is likely to occur when the persons involved in communication desire social approval, want the communication to be efficient, have a high incentive to manage their impressions, and have the repertoires needed to accomplish the accommodation. In contrast, convergence is unlikely if (a) the costs outweigh rewards, (b) the patterns required for accommodation have stigmas associated with them, or (c) if one partner desires to change the other's behavior (Giles, Mulac, Bradac, & Johnson, 1987).

This theory helps explain why persons make communication style choices during their interactions. For similar reasons, they are likely to make similar communication content choices. Accommodating to someone may be a way of yielding power to them. Expecting others to accommodate to us is likely to be a move to exert power (Berger, 1994).

If we want to be seen as likable, we may not want to risk the social exchange costs of taking issue stands with which our partners disagree. We may wait for some while, as a relationship matures, before we feel comfortable in discussing topics with which our partners disagree. In contrast, when we dislike someone, we may disagree with them (divergence) merely for the sake of demonstrating our dissimilarity. When we diverge, we are likely to be seen as unsupportive. When we want to be supportive, we are likely to accommodate to our partners.

COMMUNICATION COMPETENCE AND PLANNING

Some of your friends and relatives are probably quite competent communicators, whereas others might not be. Do you sometimes feel more competent than at other times? This moment of reflection sets the stage to discuss communication competence. "The ability to control conversations, intentionally or unintentionally, depends upon the existence of certain regularities than can be exploited by one or the other conversational partner, and this exploitation depends upon knowledge" (Cappella, 1994, pp. 380–381). Following that theme, Parks (1994) featured control, adaptation, and collaboration to define communicative competence. He offered this definition: "Communicative competence represents the degree to which individuals satisfy and perceive that they have satisfied their goals within the limits of a given social situation without jeopardizing their ability or opportunity to pursue their other subjectively more important goals" (p. 595).

Communication competence requires cognitive and interaction skills needed to exert personal control, the ability to adjust to and affect the environment, including communication episodes. Such skills need not be maximal, merely adequate. Competence occurs at all levels—interpersonal, organizational, and mass-mediated—all of which require the ability to translate thoughts into words from verbal and nonverbal cues. Such cues are organized into sequences ranging in length from sentences to conversational episodes. Control includes the ability to interact in ways that affect relationships and execute programs of action in search of goals. During communication, persons may have to improvise if their initial plans fail (Parks, 1994).

Executing conversational strategies entails managing conversational behaviors, including knowing when to take turns in talking. Conversation may require vocal and kinesic behaviors, as well as verbal behaviors including disclosure and topic management. How skillfully persons execute these challenges is likely to be a function of their timing, appropriateness, and sensitivity to context (Cappella, 1994).

How competent people think they are can affect their willingness and ability to interact with others. Various reasons have been used to explain what impact competence has on the ability to use communication effectively. Studies have concentrated on the communication efforts people make, whether effective or not, to appear competent to others. Three variables are basic to communication competence: motivation, knowledge, and skills. A cost–rewards matrix governs the motives people have to be competent. People are likely to be more competent if they have knowledge (the information and experience needed for interactions). If their skill level is high, they are likely to be less anxious and show more immediacy, expressiveness, and ability to manage interaction, as well as take orientations toward other people (Spitzberg & Hecht, 1984).

A basic issue in the study of communication competence is the degree to which interpersonal communication is strategic and mindful rather than routine and scripted. Rather than performing in ways that are merely mindless and scripted, argued H. E. Sypher and Applegate (1984), people apply communication-relevant beliefs that arise from their definition of each situation and their estimation of which communication tactics are most appropriate to achieve their goals. Strategies are "intended lines of action and general choices in transforming plans into practice so as to accomplish particular goals" (Seibold, Cantrill, & Meyers, 1994, p. 544).

Favoring a mindful interpretation of this issue, B. J. O'Keefe and McCornack (1987) contended that people communicate with one another based on theories of communication. Each person must share in the theory so that they know which actions and statements are appropriate to which goals. In addition to knowledge, people need skill to execute an appropriate theory to achieve his or her goals under constraints of each situation. A theory, in this sense, is a general plan based on how interactants believe communication transpires.

In any situation, each person may have several theories or plans. These are derived from knowledge of how to act to be competent in different contexts with many types of communication partners. As their competence develops, people acquire increasingly more sophisticated rationale that can be used to decide which communication means should be employed to achieve each particular set of outcomes. People watch the communication behavior of others to learn which message-design logics are more or less effective. Messages that convey the users' communication goals and are designed to save face for the other person involved in the communication are likely to be the most effective.

Why do different people use different plans? One explanation is that some communicators are more differentiated that others. People are more differentiated if they utilize more aspects of the communication event when making inferences about the other person, the goals at play in the interaction, and the options that are available. Thus, one hypothesis is that highly differentiated communicators possess more complex schemata when planning their communication. Another hypothesis is that highly and less differentiated communicators employ different plans, especially if they are less cognitively involved in the communication event (Wilson, 1995).

Because many plans are available, communication partners might not employ the same one. B. J. O'Keefe and McCornack (1987) argued that variety in behavior occurs during communication episodes when partners set different goals or use different strategies to achieve their goals. People involved in the same communication episode may operate out of different theories or message-design logics regarding which communication tactics are best. Qualities such as egocentrism, rhetorical sensitivity, and person-centeredness account for why people communicate differently. Three kinds of message-design logics seem to account for differences in behavior. Expressive logic is used when people "dump" their thoughts and feelings on each other. They assume that receivers interpret the messages for what they are. Conventional message logic treats communication as a game played cooperatively via rules and conventions; messages are designed to achieve effects. Rhetorical message-design logic consists of tactics people believe are necessary to portray themselves as they wish to be seen and to influence the outcome of interaction given the circumstances.

B. J. O'Keefe and McCornack (1987) contended that people's perceptions of the effectiveness of various message-design logics influence which ones they select to achieve their goals. In any situation, various message logics can be equally effective. (Recall the concept of *equifinality*, a term used in systems theory to indicate that each system can obtain the same goal by employing different methods.) Communication competence is enhanced when message logic and goal selection take into consideration what the receiver of the message wants to achieve from the interaction. When the message-design logic is well adapted to the receiver, it helps that person to save face and to feel rewarded and competent as a person.

Pursuing the variables central to message-design logics, B. J. O'Keefe (1988) found two major functional differences between message efforts. The first, message goal structure, is a product of the number and types of goals a person is simultaneously pursuing or giving attention to while organizing a message. The second is message-design logic; this logic reflects the beliefs the person producing a message relies on while deciding which tactics to use to achieve the goals. Cognitive processes, particularly cognitive complexity, rather than personality traits, seem to explain the differences in people's abilities to select goals and message-design logics that are appropriate to one another. If people have message-design logics that work in one situation, they are likely to use them in other situations.

The kinds of message-design logics people apply may depend on whether they are task or relationship oriented. Males tend to take a task orientation in conversations; this pattern is also likely to be preferred by people who measure high in verbal aggressiveness and low in interpersonal orientation, regardless of gender. Women prefer a relational orientation, as do people who seek interpersonal harmony and to avoid arguments as well as verbal aggressiveness (Hample & Dallinger, 1988).

Some amount of communication is routine, habitual, and scripted, requiring little conscious processing and planning. However, the most important parts of communication are probably those that result from more active planning and processing. Studying communication interaction, persuasion, and conflict resolution, B. J. O'Keefe and Shepherd (1987) identified four categories of message strategies that reflect the kinds of plans that can be executed during conflict. These feature the communicative roles persons take as they produce messages, the points of view they take during their turns, the extent to which they explicitly acknowledge conflict, and the manner in which they use strategies to protect the face of their conflict partner and maintain interaction. Planning, in this sense, relates to the ability to select one goal or outcome instead of others, to separate issues, and to integrate efforts, as well as to achieve reconciliation.

Message design can include content. It can also feature the message functions that are tailored to the sequence of events that occur during interaction. Such functions are selected based on mappings that occur as individuals think through and enact a sequence of statements over time. Message function is the use of strategies at various points on the map (B. J. O'Keefe & Lambert, 1995). If you think for a moment, you will recall message-design choices you have made where, for instance, you decided to take a "soft" approach, knowing that you could choose to use more harsh words. You might select the soft approach first, because you have the multiple goals of saying "No," while being nice to the person to maintain a cordial relationship. If the soft words work, your message design was successful, such as saying "I want to study tonight," rather than merely saying "No" to a proposal made by a communication partner. If the soft approach does not work, your map of such conversations lets you know that you have a more firm way of denying the proposal. And you can merely walk away from the person. So, you have message-content and message-function choices that are selected based on your communication goal and executed according to your map of the situation.

To what ends are logics applied? One end is to be supportive. Another is to have others be supportive. "Supportive interactions can result in such outcomes as lessened sorrow or distress, improved recovery from trauma and illness, and resolutions to conflict" (Albrecht, Burleson, & Goldsmith, 1994, p. 419). What is supportive communication? It is "verbal and nonverbal behavior that influences how providers and recipients view themselves, their situaitons, the other, and their relationship" (Albrecht et al., 1994, p. 421).

Supportive messages offer and seek help. People can seek support by employing many communication plans, ranging from requests for assistance to using strategies that suggest the person is having trouble coping. Giving of support can include offering advice, reassuring, offering assistance, and sympathizing. Supportive messages can encourage as well as scold. We might, for instance, attempt to guide someone to more positive conditions, such as improved health, by scolding them for an unhealthy diet. Supportive communication typically features a genuine two-way interaction. It can entail collaboration whereby both parties engage in solving the problem of one of those persons (Albrecht et al., 1994). Supportiveness is a crucial process in people's lives, as they take or are asked to take on caretaker roles. People also learn to use strategies and employ communication plans to elicit support. As we can easily imagine, children seek and give support. Teenagers seek and reject support. Elder members of society suffer the transition from support givers to support seekers. Children seek support, only to find themselves giving support to elderly parents and other members of society. Communication planning ranges from thinking of the words needed to encourage a child to try to ride a bicycle as compared to the words and interaction sequences needed to steer an elderly parent into a rest home.

From discussions such as this, it can be assumed that all communication is mindful rather than scripted. Indeed, it is likely that interactions exhibit combinations of both. Action-assembly theory has been advanced to explain why communication is patterned and repetitive as well as unique and creative. During a conversation, you may find yourself repeating scripts (words, phrases, or entire conversational passages) that you have used in similar interactions. You may also find that some statements are unique and creative; you may make comments different from any you have made before. Life requires that we periodically create, practice, and employ new communication plans. Such efforts require people to recall scripts used in previous conversations. Factors that influence this process include memory storage, retrieval, and utilization (the ability of communicators to remember, know when and what to recall, and competently utilize what is recalled). Because previously used scripts may be unsatisfactory to achieve an immediate communication outcome, unique versions of conversation may be required (Greene, 1984).

What is recalled and required for each person to participate in a conversation consists both of content (what is or can be said) and procedural protocols (tactics needed to progress through a conversation). These may be stored and recalled in units based on a combination of actions and outcomes (strategies, situations, and goals). Which actions are needed (and perhaps recalled or invented) to achieve the outcomes required in a particular conversation? One of the quickest ways to intuit the process we are discussing here is to recall how, after a conversation, you may think, "I wish I had said . . ." or "I'm glad I remembered to say . . . ." In the course of conversation, an individual is expected to recall or invent a wide array of content and procedures. A conversation entails knowing procedures, selecting words and nonverbal cues (to the extent that these are selected rather than merely spontaneous or purely habitual), and identifying conversation goals (Greene, 1984).

This process consists of combinations of actions and outcomes associated with them. How likely a person is to recall any action–outcome unit depends on the recency and frequency with which it is utilized. Activation of any content or procedural script depends on the extent to which the conversational participant recognizes a goal and makes the connection between the goal and a specific message or procedural tactic. Each procedural record is unique to the extent that it relates to one or a combination of outcomes:

1. Interaction to achieve outcomes specific to a situation, relationship, or identity of the participants.
2. Content.
3. Conversational management—the steps and connections between statements that move the conversation along.
4. Utterances, including word choice, syntax, and articulation.
5. Regulation of the conversation through turn taking and response matching.
6. Need to regulate physiological requirements to participate in the conversation (e.g., keep one's temper under control).
7. Coordination of vocal and other nonverbal behaviors needed to affect the conversational partner.

Components of any conversation are not entirely unique, nor are they free from the unique ways participants perceive and characterize themselves and the persons with whom they interact. Each participant is reasonably mindful of what to say and the consequences of what is said (Greene, 1984). The theme of this theory is that individuals "assemble" their conversational "actions" based on predictions of expected or required outcomes.

To explain the action-assembly process, Greene postulated that lower motor and autonomic processes support higher order skills such as communication and cognitive processing. This model assumes that several factors are interrelated: (a) expected interaction success, (b) projected self-image, (c) importance of interaction, and (d) interaction success and importance. Action assembly postulates that individuals usually can think of social behaviors (especially communication) needed to achieve communication goals, but a problem exists when they think that they have low personal competency and, therefore, anticipate they will be affected negatively by communication outcomes. When they cannot automatically or easily think of the needed behavior, they are likely to experience anxiety. By comparing the communication efforts of high- and low-communication apprehension individuals, Booth-Butterfield (1987) added support to the action-assembly theory, thereby giving additional insights into factors that affect communication planning and competence.

Action-assembly theory gives researchers the challenge of seeing how individuals select strategies from their repertoire when confronted with multiple functions. Each communication situation has many features that allow choices regarding strategic responses. Under these pressures, which are augmented by the choices communication partners select, each person is confronted with making quick strategic choices. These choices can exceed the capability participants have to devise and execute their plans (Greene, 1995).

Although communication accommodation and nonverbal convergence may improve rapport between communicators, Hewes and Planalp (1987) argued that shared knowledge is also vital to communication. This view stresses a model of interpersonal communication that assumes more cognitive activity than is typically associated with speech accommodation. To understand communication, insight must be gained into the cognitive processes by which influence and social knowledge are managed. Attributions people make of one another are crucial to explanations of why they act as they do.

Planning results when people seek to know what others know, how they process information, and what their goals are. Such estimations constitute the heart of the planning process by which people seek to achieve communication goals. This process is summarized as follows:

> Speakers are better able to assess and optimize the impact of a message if they know what listeners are focusing on, how they are likely to integrate information and draw inferences from it, what they are likely to remember, and how they will select and implement their responses. But impact also depends on what the listeners think speakers are focusing on, what inferences they are inviting, and so on. (Hewes & Planalp, 1987, p. 168)

At least to some extent, efforts to reduce uncertainty involve plans and are strategic. When people encounter one another, they formulate and test hypotheses about each other. Reasoning that people gather information out of curiosity and to increase self-efficacy, Hewes and Planalp (1982) contended that efforts to reduce uncertainty require knowledge of prior interactions and attributions. Four factors influence how people go about reducing uncertainty: goals they have for reducing it, communication tools they employ such as asking questions, cognitive functions they utilize to process the information they obtain, and their cognitive capacities. Goals people have for reducing uncertainty in each case guide how they go about doing so. Goals, whether interpersonal or cognitive, are specifiable, even if not explicitly, as part of the process. When people encounter one another, whether for the first time or on subsequent occasions, they do so with a set of goals that govern the kinds of attributions they make. These goals, along with the cognitive capacity of the person who wants to reduce uncertainty, constrain the process of uncertainty reduction. "Interactants' goals determine what social knowledge will be brought to bear, what inferential tasks are needed to reduce uncertainty about the social events, and what cognitive functions and communication tools are needed to accomplish the goals" (Hewes & Planalp, 1982, p. 112). This approach assumes that efforts to reduce uncertainty and to interact depend on strategic and cognitive abilities. Thus, for instance, as you encounter a store clerk for the first time, you estimate the person's ability to help you achieve your purpose for shopping in that store. Is this person competent, as compared with other clerks you have encountered?

The cognitive processes involved in uncertainty reduction follow plans. Employing the metaphor of people as naive scientists, Hewes and Planalp argued that the information people receive is meaningless if generalizations ("theories" or "hypotheses") are not used to make sense of it. Four kinds of cognitive processes seem to be employed during efforts to reduce uncertainty: correlation (what factors about the other person occur at the same time); generative (theories of how stories are structured—interaction happens in narrative form: "I said . . ." and "He/She replied . . ."); temporal (in what time order events are observed and what that order says according to the theories individuals hold about others' behavior); and causality (assumptions people make about which factors cause what outcomes). All of these factors give interactants a sense of expectation regarding what attributes co-occur, how parts of an episode work together, what events follow one another, and what events are or will be produced by others. Cognitive processes involved in uncertainty reduction are focusing (what people pay attention to), storage/retrieval (how people "file" and recall information about the targets of their attributions), integration and inference (specific cognitive processes people use to process data), and selection and implementation (choice and use of specific communication tools and cognitive processes).

Ability to create and execute communication plans is vital to each individual's efforts to initiate and maintain social relationships. "A plan," C. R. Berger (1988) claimed, "specifies the actions that are necessary for the attainment of a goal or several goals. Plans vary in their levels of abstraction. Highly abstract plans can spawn more detailed plans. Plans can contain alternative paths for goal attainment from which the social actor can choose" (p. 96). Some plans become scripted, habitual efforts to conduct routine interactions, such as asking about a friend's health, welfare, or weekend activities. As long as the plans used by interactants are appropriate, compatible, and skillfully employed, successful interaction is expected. Plans are likely to reflect not only the means by which to execute an interaction, but also a larger plan as well—the purpose of the interaction. A person applying for a job may have a plan for being successful during an interview, but the larger goal is getting a job and being successful. When plans do not succeed as intended, the individual has to improvise, depending on alternative plans that can be created. This kind of adjustment is likely to require people to have plan repertoires; some will have more plans and be better at improvising than others.

Plans may call for use of various communication activities at different times during a conversation. A person might plan to start a conversation with small talk. This tactic could be used to see if the partner has any interests that can be used as the basis of further discussion, perhaps with the purpose of finding out that both parties share similar tastes in rock music. All of this conversational sequence could be a means one person uses to build up to asking the other for a date (or making oneself available to be asked for a date).

In this process, each individual's perception of self and of the communication partner influences the planning and execution process. Supporting this analysis,

C. R. Berger and Bell (1988) discovered that plans created to initiate social relationships are better when they are longer and demonstrate greater breadth, thereby offering more possibilities for creating the relationship. Shy and lonely persons are hampered in their ability to create plans to create social relationships.

People are more likely to achieve positive relational outcomes when they have plans that include a wide variety of actions (C. R. Berger & Bell, 1988). However, if a plan is too complex, the person employing it may suffer a loss of fluency because he or she cannot decide which variation of the plan to employ at a given moment (C. R. Berger, Karol, & Jordan, 1989).

If people obtain more information about their partners and the situation in which a plan is going to be employed, they tend to form more elaborate plans. The diversity of information about the partner and the situation seems to be more useful for planning than does the quality of the information (C. R. Berger & DiBattista, 1992).

Let's imagine that you have a very important communication objective. You get to choose. If you really want to achieve your goal, you might develop many plans to use during your attempt to achieve your goal. Let's imagine that you have six plans, and they fail. How difficult will the task be of developing another? To explore that kind of problem, Knowlton and Berger (1997) discovered that if a person only had one plan or had as many as six, he or she would have a difficult time thinking up additional plans if the first ones failed. This curvilinear relationship suggests that you can have too few or too many.

Narratives, stories if you will, seem to be part of the planning and communication process. People talk about themselves in narratives. We tell stories about ourselves. Such stories reveal our sense of who we are, our self-concept. We present this narrative of our self-concept in ways that we believe manage impressions of who we are. Others, such as friends and relatives, use narratives to talk about us. In doing so, they also reveal what they think our self-concept is. Thus, these narratives are a vital part of planning and serve an impression-management function (C. M. Shaw, 1997).

This section has demonstrated an array of views of how people develop and employ communication plans. Such plans are tailored to the situation, the communication partner, and the desired outcomes. They are employed to reduce uncertainty. Although some communication is purely routine and scripted, some of the most important moments require individuals to be competent in their ability to determine what plan is appropriate and to be able to execute it successfully.

CONCLUSION

The research and theory reported in this chapter emphasize cognitive and interactional processes of interpersonal communication. How and why people communicate are influenced by the ways they characterize or make attributions about one another. This theme underpins the social cognition approach to interpersonal communication. Interaction is, in various ways, motivated by uncertainty reduction, which relates not only to others but also to one's own social competence. One of the ways people show their willingness to identify with one another is through communication accommodation. To some extent, such behavior is strategic and mindful. However, higher level and more complex plans seem essential in efforts to communicate strategically in order to achieve communication goals, especially when scripted patterns are inadequate to achieve them.

8

Communication in Organizations

S ince the dawn of human existence, people have worked and played together. You probably cannot remember a time when you were not part of several organizations. This book was the product of many individuals in many organizations working together, many of whom never met or communicated with one another.

Humans spend their lives in organizations of all sizes and kinds. They include businesses, nonprofits, and governmental agencies. They range in size from a single family to educational institutions and companies with dozens, hundreds, even thousands of employees located around the globe. Our families are groups.

Organizations communicate with people outside and inside of them. Organizational networks bring us news from around the globe. People communicate inside of them through conversation and by using professionally prepared documents, such as newsletters.

Organizations serve many tangible and intangible needs, but always at a cost. Through organizations people are more efficacious than if they work and play alone. They help us to achieve our goals, but they do so at a cost. Our membership is obtained at the cost of our freedom to act as we chose. To be in an organization requires that our communication support its efforts so that it in turn helps us achieve tangible and intangible rewards.

Members of organizations attempt to make rational decisions about their performance; they seek to maximize the rewards for their efforts while minimizing the costs. Members of organizations communicate to perform tasks and enact roles on behalf of those organizations. Individuals negotiate with other organizational members, including management on how those tasks and roles will be performed.

The study of organizational communication centers on means by which people gain information, shape opinions, make decisions, coordinate efforts, voice expectations, assimilate into the organization, leave the organization, and create rapport with one another. Through communication, people coordinate their actions to achieve individual and collective goals. This process begins early in people's lives and continues as they mature. People learn communication styles and content at an early age from other family members, educational institutions, media, and work experience.

The study of organizational communication focuses on processes of interaction, means by which members create shared meaning, and strategic coordination of goal-oriented activities. Organizational communication is not something that transpires within a "box" (the organization) but rather what happens between people who are members of an organization or outsiders who interact with them. Rather than thinking of an organization communicating, it is best to think of people communicating within and on behalf of an organization. This action is not random, but coordinated; it requires that members acquire and share information as well as persuade one another on an array of matters. Actions and statements of individuals bring the organization to life. Meaning (individual and shared opinions) influences what people do and how they do it. Actions are affected by the "culture" and "climate" of each organization.

This chapter examines variables and theories to explain why people communicate as they do as a consequence of their membership in organizations. Themes address the unique nature of organizational communication, organizations as systems and as shared meaning. The chapter focuses on units of analysis: interpersonal, especially superior–subordinate interactions, task-group interaction, and the organization communicating inwardly and externally to foster mutually beneficial relationships with key stakeholders.

As we consider the issues discussed in this chapter, we are challenged to keep in mind that because people mature into and through many phases of organizational membership we should adopt a "life-span" perspective (Jablin & Krone, 1994). Members of organizations, especially those where they work, struggle to balance multiple identities because they identify with many organizations (Cheney, 1991). Communication in organizations is not neutral; managements attempt to use it for purposes of domination and control, a tendency that may damage organizational effectiveness and human relations, as well as harm the human spirit (Mumby, 1988).

UNIQUENESS OF ORGANIZATIONAL COMMUNICATION

Early studies of organizational communication featured four key variables: organizational structure, messages, media, and communicators (Farace, Stewart, & Taylor, 1978). Those studies were underpinned by the spirit of Lasswell's (1948) questions: Who says what to whom through which channel and with what effect? Researchers wanted to help executive managements understand to communicate so they could improve employee performance and thereby increase their organizations' effectiveness. The goal was to make organizations effective, by taking a top-down perspective from management to employee. Organizational effectiveness was the goal, and individual effort was the means to accomplish that goal.

Out of this tradition, scholars struggled to define the field of organizational communication (Redding, 1985). The pursuit was necessary because organizational life is an inescapable part of human experience (Wiio, Goldhaber, & Yates, 1980).

Advancing beyond its limited origins, organizational communication analysis began to focus on the collective opinions and coordinated actions of organization members. The dyad became a focal point of analysis. Researchers learned that employees contribute to the shared meaning of the organization as does management. Of critical concern to contemporary organizational communication research is the desire to make organizations better places for members—especially employees—to work. If communication is improved, members will have more commitment to the organization, be more able to achieve their work, and live more enriched lives.

Researchers focused on several themes in their search to unlock the secrets of organizational effectiveness. Central to the best thinking in organizational communication is the premise that organizations are thinking organisms. Taking that view, Weick (1979a) argued that companies seek information, which they strive to interpret correctly and wisely in an effort to maximize opportunities and minimize costs.

Researchers know that personal communication effectiveness is a valuable asset, for the individual as well as the organization. If the ability to climb the organizational ladder is a mark of success, then effective communication skills are helpful. B. D. Sypher and Zorn (1986) found that people who hold positions at higher levels in companies (as well as those who are most likely to be promoted) exhibit better cognitive skills and superior communication abilities, as measured by ability to self-monitor, to understand the perspectives others are taking, and to be persuasive.

Modern research is keenly interested in how shared meaning is created and guides the actions of members of organizations. Even what appears to be casual communication in organizations can have enormous impact on members' thoughts and actions. Members of organizations tell stories, foster myths, call one another by code names, and enact elaborate rituals. These forms of communication convey each organization's culture and reflect its climate, and thereby help members to coordinate their activities.

To explore themes of this kind, two broad competing perspectives have developed: Functionalism and interpretivism. Contrasting these approaches to the study of organizations, Smircich (1983a, 1983b) argued that the key to organizational success is the management of meaning. Functionalist theory "considers organizations as ends in themselves and management as the pursuit of efficiency" (p. 241). "The interpretive perspective recognizes that managers are enactors of their situations; they often contribute to patterns of action that are unnecessarily limiting. Thus managers informed by the interpretive view would develop reflexivity and consciousness of the ways they create their organizational worlds" (p. 241).

Researchers are aware that organizational success depends on two broad sets of functions: task (work activities and role performances) and socioemotional (climate). Job performance functions are tasks required for an organization to achieve its objectives (e.g., to sell a product or keep accurate financial accounts) and for its members to accomplish their private goals (e.g., to earn a living). Task refers to what individuals or groups do, and socioemotional climate is the psychological state that accompanies those activities. How tasks are performed is influenced by what members of each organization sense as its climate. Socioemotional functions affect employees' interpersonal work relationships, job satisfaction, and job involvement.

Researchers focus their attention on interpersonal contexts that are fraught with communication norms, goals, and constraints. When interpersonal episodes occur in organizations (and on their behalf), they are expected to support the purpose for which each organization was created and reflect the reasons persons have for being part of it. Communication in an organization, its groups and dyads, happens because of the dynamics of the system itself, the shared meaning in the organization, and the organization's interaction with other systems.

Researchers know that organizational life is like the enactment of an unwritten drama (W. B. Pearce & Cronen, 1980). Enactments of organizational relationships are episodic; they exhibit dramatic form (Gergen & Gergen, 1988). Similar to interpersonal contexts, a lot of communication in organizations is scripted and results from role expectations. For instance, away from a school, a teacher might not intervene in a fight between two children, but at school, a norm attached to the role of teacher would motivate him or her to intervene. Outside of an organization, interpersonal relationships depend on outcomes that participants create and negotiate themselves, whereas in an organization, relationships are substantially influenced by outcomes and meanings expected by other members on behalf of the organization. Enactment theory offers a powerful explanation of this activity because it

> allows us to use all that theatre, as a performing art, implies. It allows us to think about creativity, to consider the craft of actors playing characterizations, it provides considerations of tragedy and comedy, it suggests all the constraints of situation and history which affect any live performance, it allows for inquiry about the link between performance and what goes on backstage. (Mangham & Overington, 1987, p. 3)

Researchers have drawn heavily on information and systems theories for the study of organizational communication. Organizations are treated as systems that use information to achieve goals and maintain equilibrium. According to this view, members of organizations (as well as subgroups in organizations) obtain (input) information, process it (throughput), and output it. How information flows between individuals and groups in organizations demonstrates the presence and quality of relationships between them.

Researchers know that persuasion influences organizational processes. Through persuasion, individuals in an organization influence people who are outside of it, for instance through contract negotiation, public relations, advertising, or sales. Persuasion is pervasive inside organizations; it occurs when supervisors motivate workers and when workers influence one another. Large organizations employ internal public relations in an attempt to increase employees' commitment to them. Through persuasion, relationships are created, codefined, negotiated, and terminated. How organizational members coordinate their efforts involves persuasion variables such as credibility, as well as message and channel effects. Persuasion theories, especially information integration, involvement, expectancy value, and social learning, explain how people enter, become assimilated, maintain, coordinate, and terminate organizational membership.

Theories help explain why employees hold the opinions they do toward work, themselves, the company, and other members. Through persuasion, members negotiate reward systems, role expectations, and relationships that affect organizational structure and power. Leaders of organizations are influenced by actions and statements of their personnel as well as outsiders, such as customers or governmental regulators and legislators. Compliance gaining and conflict resolution are typical organizational communication activities. Relationships are negotiated to maximize reward/cost outcomes, a concept basic to social exchange theory.

In organizations, managers use persuasion to create social realities that influence the perceptions, attributions, judgments, and activities of the members. This social reality provides unobtrusive control over employees' thoughts and behavior once they adopt its assumptions and identify with one another and the organization (Tompkins & Cheney, 1985). Political influence is exerted in an organization when individuals use stories to define roles and relationships (Mumby, 1987). So influential is shared reality on organizational members' thoughts and behavior that scholars study organizational rhetoric. That mode of organizational analysis (interpretivism) assumes that members persuade one another—as well as persons outside of it—to adopt a particular view of the organization and how to act toward it. Brought to life through acts of their members, organizations are interpretative, adaptive systems that survive by obtaining and making sense of information about themselves and their environment (Heath, 1994).

Researchers work to cut through the complexity of organizations, seeking to isolate the key factors at each level: personal, interpersonal, group, organizational, and societal. Such levels of analysis are easy to conceptualize but, as Jablin and Krone (1987) concluded, "While researchers have long recognized the theoretical importance of organizing their research around such levels of analysis, as individuals, dyads, small groups, intact organizations, and environments, they have had great difficulty accomplishing this task" (p. 711). Mindful of these limits, sections of this chapter address issues unique to these levels.

Drawing on these research trends, this chapter explores the uniqueness of organizational experience by examining the origins and assumptions of organizational communication research. It considers paradigms for the study of organizational communication, the systems perspective, communication networks, organizational climate and culture, and levels of analysis (individual, interpersonal, group, organizational, and interorganizational).

PARADIGMS FOR THE STUDY OF ORGANIZATIONAL COMMUNICATION

The origins of organizational communication are timeless, but in this century, it has been studied by using social scientific methods since at least the 1920s. Early in this century, the paradigm that guided the study of organizational communication was that managers tell workers what to do and when and how to do it; organizational communication was viewed as flowing downward, in an autocratic fashion. The early approach to organizational effectiveness was designed to empower managements. As the study of organizational communication has progressed, the emphasis has shifted to a desire to discover ways to empower employees to better achieve their organization's goals. This section briefly examines four organizational theories and competing candidates for the best approach to study organizations.

Early views of organizational effectiveness reflect the classical management philosophy. It assumes that employees are hired to work, not to think (Morgan, 1986). Although many people have challenged this theory, it persists more than it should. This management philosophy features organizational communication designed to help managers achieve command and control. According to this theory, efficiency is more important than humanity.

Classical management philosophy assumes that employees work only for tangible rewards, such as money and position. This philosophy assumes that workers need to be directed by managers because they are incapable of making wise decisions about their work; with management status comes the prerogatives of directing others' behavior. The theory postulates that people work only because they have to, and they require constant, close supervision to make their efforts efficient. Communication is largely from the top down. Management is not interested in the ideas of workers. Management communication consists of orders that guide work activities. Upward communication is discouraged. Task functions were highlighted, and socioemotional aspects of work were ignored or prohibited.

Scholars looking for an alternate theory got a substantial boost from the classic Hawthorne studies. While investigating how changes in working conditions affect employees' behavior, researchers conducted thousands of interviews at Western Electric's Hawthorne plant in 1927. Even though working conditions were experimentally made unpleasant, such as dimming the lights to determine the effect on workers' behavior, employees worked harder to compensate for poor lighting. Workers were motivated to compensate for such conditions because they appreciated knowing that someone cared enough about their opinions and feelings to ask questions about them.

Following the Hawthorne Studies, management philosophy began to emphasize human relations. If employees worked harder when management talked with them, then communication could motivate increased productivity. Some upward communication was encouraged; downward communication was less a matter of directive and more a matter of giving policy and instruction. This management philosophy fostered activities, such as company picnics, where employees could get to know one another. This rapport was expected to increase their willingness to work. If carried too far, this philosophy can turn companies into "country clubs," where managers worry too much whether employees feel good. Work functions can be deemphasized, whereas socioemotional functions can be over emphasized.

In his discussions of organizational behavior in the 1930s, Chester Barnard, president of New Jersey Bell Telephone Company, emphasized the importance of communication among employees. He proposed that communication is best when it achieves understanding, is consistent with personal and company goals, and supports employees' mental and physical tasks. Following these trends, the 1940s and 1950s witnessed an emerging interest in communication, especially two-way flow and network studies. Drawing on the prevailing interest in information theory, communication studies began to examine how information is vital to organizations, not just in the sense of something sent from one department to another, but as an essential aspect of their survival. Information theory and systems theory combined to form the dominant paradigm of organizational communication research.

In part because of the humanizing spirit characteristic of the 1960s, a third period dawned committed to human resource management. During the 1960s, researchers began to go beyond job satisfaction and motivation studies to explore the intricacies of networks, superior–subordinate relationships, and performance feedback. The 1970s witnessed serious commitment to study climate, culture, patterns of information flow, and message content. That decade felt the influence of humanistic psychology's belief that quality of life could be improved through effective communication. During that era, the relational orientation that began to permeate the study of interpersonal communication spilled over into studies regarding superior–subordinate relationships. Consideration was given to variables such as inclusion-exclusion, similarity, reciprocity, growth, and self-actualization. Relational communication argued for openness in superior–subordinate relationships. Terms such as acceptance, openness, and reciprocation became popular for explaining employee motivation, job satisfaction, and productivity.

The 1980s extended human resource development by giving even more attention to organizational climate and culture and by placing less interest in communication networks. The trend is to explore how people negotiate relationships and share meanings needed for the organization to survive and prosper. Much of this research is motivated by the "bottom line," helping managers to know how to increase productivity by involving employees in meaningful decision making.

Human resource management theory postulates that workers are happiest and most productive when they share control over their jobs. This perspective reasons that because employees know best how to perform their jobs, they should be meaningfully involved in task-related decisions intended to improve work design and job performance. Communication, according to this philosophy, flows in all directions: downward, upward, and horizontally. Employees are encouraged to offer opinions about the way tasks are performed. Managers are expected to be open and responsive to the needs of subordinates. Productivity improves, not only because employees "work smarter," but also because they are involved socioemotionally in their jobs. Supporters believe that this management philosophy encourages openness, trust, and proper distribution of control.

Comparison of these three management theories should force you to think about organizations. Your view of organizations must be encompassing enough to include a range from a family to companies with hundreds of employees. It must embrace organizations that have different missions: provide education, satisfy religious needs, deliver governmental services, serve social needs, as well as produce and sell products and services.

Toward these ends, organizations need, according to contingency theory, to be flexible in their ability to follow one managerial philosophy in preference to others. Each theory might be best in certain circumstances. For instance, while fighting a fire, one person is likely to direct the efforts of a team of fire fighters. A surgeon directs the efforts of a surgical team. But when decisions need to be made regarding the best way to perform such procedures, discussion and employee involvement has positive effect on job satisfaction, morale, efficiency, productivity, and willingness to perform the required tasks. That theme will be expanded below in the section on group decision making. The key to successful management is to decide which method is best suited to achieve the organization's goals and mission in light of its present circumstances.

This brief review of four theoretic options brings us to the necessary discussion of empowerment. Although this term has been a buzz word in research and management training for a decade, it is nevertheless a good concept to use to evaluate the effectiveness of management theories. It is sometimes thought to refer to management being expected to share "its power" with employees. That paradigm assumes falsely that management has all of the power, and employees only have power if it is granted.

Challenging that view, Albrecht (1988) approached empowerment from "a personal control framework" (p. 380). Personal control is a matter of individual perception grounded in each person's "belief that his or her actions have desirable causal effects on the environment" (p. 381). This approach to empowerment relies on an attribution paradigm, which postulates that individuals attribute causality for outcomes based on schemata that (a) emphasize either internal personal traits or external environmental traits, (b) are stable or unstable over time, and (c) are specific or global. Employees test hypotheses about power by seeing whether they have power, as they define it. Do employees believe that their individual and collective efforts lead to mutually beneficial outcomes?

These four managerial theories and the concept of empowerment force us to consider how researchers can best study how organizations become effective and what communication contributes to that outcome. Where should researchers look to determine whether organizations are healthy and employees are motivated to work wisely because of communication?

To deal with issues of that sort, the study of communication in organizations revolves around four paradigms: (a) structural functionalism, (b) psychological, (c) interpretivism, and (d) systems interaction (cf. Krone, Jablin, & Putnam, 1987; Putnam, 1982). To some extent, these paradigms overlap and support one another, but they also challenge each other. Analysis of each of these paradigms can give you different orientations for the study of organizational communication.

According to structural functionalism, organizations can be studied by examining the structure (arrangement) of people (by department or unit, for instance) who join to accomplish similar, compatible, or interlocking functions (tasks) designed to achieve shared goals. Structures are best described in terms of information flow throughout an organization, including the relationships between superiors and subordinates. Proponents of this paradigm reason that they are studying the dynamic processes of organizing (Farace, Monge, & Russell, 1977).

Drawing on a systems meta-perspective and information theory, this paradigm postulates that organizational effectiveness requires accurate and rapid transmission of clear and accurate messages to employees who need and want the information. Key concepts include barriers and communication breakdowns. A secretary, for example, might manage the information flow of others in an efficient and professional manner, eliminating barriers, and breakdowns. Departments are interlocked when their goals are complementary; for instance, the persons who work in the exploration department of a major oil company locate (goal) crude oil that the processing department makes (goal) into products such as gasoline that are sold (goal) by the marketing department. Each department has unique, but complementary goals; these support the corporate goal of making a profit, which in turn supports individual employees' goals of earning a living. Goals interlock. Individuals and groups interact with one another through communication to achieve their goals. Networks are a basic unit of analysis in this theory.

A second paradigm of organizations views them as psychological entities. Thus, a company is what employees perceive it to be. As each person enters an organization, he or she strives to be assimilated by learning its expectations for work performance (Jablin, 1980, 1984). The organization tries to mold each member to certain norms and roles. Each member must acquire "an evolving set of perceptions about what the organization is like as a communication system" (Jablin, 1982a, p. 273). You can appreciate this paradigm by recalling that you have been involved in many organizations, various schools, classes, families, clubs, cliques, and such. In each, you probably felt like a different psychological entity, a "different person." Each organizational entity has a personality, a conception of itself as an organization, the organizations around it, and its members. This view of organizations relies on measures of what individuals think about themselves, their role performance, their organization, and the other members in it.

A third paradigm, an interpretive-symbolic perspective reasons that each organization constitutes a unique social reality which its members share. Shared meaning helps employees understand the company, its employees, its product or service, and the environment where it functions, including its competitors and customers (Pacanowsky & O'Donnell-Trujillo, 1983). Communication is an interpretive process by which people coordinate their efforts by sharing meaning, often through stories, myths, rituals, and code names. Each organization exists as a "symbol" in the minds of its members and others who are affected by it (Daft & Weick, 1984).

Interpretativism relies on the principle that people create their identities and world views through symbolic interaction. For this reason, coordinated management of meaning is a major task of members of organizations; shared meanings are basic units of analysis. As members of organizations, individuals create and live a sense of social reality embedded in their unique idiom, a theme supported by linguistic relativity; each idiom provides "terministic screens" (Burke, 1966; Heath, 1986; Tompkins, 1987). To varying degrees, members take on the social reality of the organizations into which they assimilate.

For instance, a school has a unique shared reality. Some private schools require students to wear uniforms and adhere to a particular ideology. A large state-supported university may have a different social reality than does a small, private, church-supported college. The difference may be the responsibility the organization believes it has toward the moral development of students. In recent times, major state universities have opted for less moral development of students, whereas many church-supported colleges assume that as a major responsibility. Or, the social reality of one school might include being small, highly selective, and academically superior, even at the expense of athletics. Another school might emphasize athletics and other activities and accept a mediocre academic reputation.

The last of the four paradigms by which organizations can be studied is systems interaction. Viewed this way, an organization is a system, as you may recall from chapter 4. Each system has subsystems (and subsubsystems) that are hierarchically arranged. This approach to the study of organizations features concepts such as openness (in varying degrees), system interchange with other systems, balance, wholeness, hierarchy, interdependence, equifinality, and self-regulation. Organizations take in (input) what they need from their environments; this input is processed (throughput) and disseminated (output). Schools take in children and educate (throughput) them and turn out educated people. Electric utilities take in fuel, which is processed into electricity. As is discussed in chapter 4, organizations take in information that is used to make cybernetic adjustments to the environment based on feedback to ascertain how well the organization is meeting its goals by using the tactics it is employing. Newspapers are good examples of how organizations take in, process, and sell information. These principles of interaction not only describe the organization as a whole, but also its components or subsystems. Work groups, relational communication, and decision making are key units of analysis according to this perspective (Krone, Jablin, & Putnam, 1987).

Research efforts become more meaningful if directed at supporting or challenging these paradigms. For instance, structural functionalism stresses the importance of people using clear and accurate messages as they exchange information. This standard, Eisenberg (1984) contended, is dysfunctional. Ambiguity helps people deal with many situational requirements, develop and pursue multiple and even conflicting goals, and use communication that can be effective, even though ambiguous. He reasoned, "Strategic ambiguity is essential to organizing in that it: (a) promotes unified diversity, (b) facilitates organizational change, and (c) amplifies existing source attributions and preserves privileged positions" (p. 239). Organizations are organized by adhering to key metaphors, a notion compatible with the interpretive-symbolic paradigm.

This section demonstrated how managerial philosophies influence how people create, operate, and study organizations. Competing management philosophies complicate the study of organizations because each suggests a preferable way of viewing the management, performance, and interaction needed to achieve organizational goals. The problems raised by managerial philosophies are compounded when we consider competing paradigms of organizational communication. As frustrating as these competing opinions are, they demonstrate the robustness of the study of organizational communication. To appreciate the efforts of various researchers to explain and prove their perspectives requires that some avenues be explored in more detail.

SYSTEMS RATIONALE FOR ORGANIZATIONAL ANALYSIS

Since the 1940s when it emerged, systems theory or metatheory has been used to achieve insights into communication. It was especially influential for the study of organizational communication. It reasons that each organization is a system that exhibits specific dynamics. Because of the influence this view of organization has enjoyed, it deserves featured attention, although some critics believe this view treats organizations mechanistically.

A system, Fisher (1982) defined, is "the 'all' of a thing" (p. 199). It is an organic whole that not only consists of subsystems but is also part of larger systems, suprasystems that are also called environments. As discussed in chapter 4, systems theory is interested in the dynamic properties of wholes and parts, relationships, and hierarchies. Stressing its dynamism, Krippendorff (1977) reasoned that "a *system* consists of a set of states that are chained in time by a transformation. The states take account of the relations between the parts of the system, so that changes over time imply changes in the relations among the system's parts" (p. 150). As any part of a system changes or is affected, so are its other parts. A major issue in organizational communication is relationship and flow of communication between people. In this way, "parts of a system are often viewed as integrated into a whole so that they *serve a common or overriding purpose*" (p. 150). As systems, organizations constantly change (Morgan, 1982).

Cybernetics, the study of regulation and control via feedback, explains how units of a system interact to achieve their goals. Systems obtain feedback, which they use to determine whether the actions being taking are achieving the desired goal. For instance, a company may do market research to determine which product features customers like and dislike. Thus, cybernetics explains how communicative acts feed back on themselves. Through this means of control, communicators can determine whether their messages succeed and their information is useful.

A systems approach to organizational communication expands the model of sender-to-receiver to feature communication networks to explain how systems adapt to their environments. Central to this analysis is the concept of openness. A continuous variable, openness is vital to a system's successful adaptation to other systems.

The fundamental systems-interactive paradigm of organizational analysis features the continual stages of input, throughput (processing), and output, which demonstrate the concept of openness/closedness. A closed system does not interact with its environment. It does not take in information and therefore is likely to atrophy. An open system receives information, which it uses to interact dynamically with its environment. Openness increases its likelihood to survive and prosper. According to Fisher (1982), "openness is the free exchange of energy between the system and its environment. That is, to the extent that the boundaries are permeable and allow the exchange of information—what energy is to a physical system, information is to a social system—that system is said to be more nearly open than closed" (p. 199).

Open systems tend to become increasingly complex. As organizations become more complex, they develop more parts or subsystems and thereby require more networks for information exchange. To illustrate this point, compare the simplicity of a system of three people sharing information to operate a business as opposed to the complexity of information sharing in a global corporation with 30,000 employees. As a company expands, it creates new departments, each of which has specialized functions and information needs. Complexity is one of the central driving forces behind the dramatic growth in new "cyberspace" communication technologies.

Not only can a system be open to its environment and thereby take in information, but it can open itself by generating information that it shares with markets, audiences, and key publics. It uses information to define its environment and establish its boundaries (Fisher, 1982). An open system is not merely a pawn caught within the dynamics of its environment; it can shape its environment. For instance, the oil industry, as we know it today, grew because it took crude oil, a once-abundant but fundamentally worthless substance, and found marketable uses for it. This business enterprise was aided by the invention and mass production of automobiles. Together, the automobile and petrochemical industries dramatically changed society.

The dynamic quality of systems explains how each system can set goals, forecast whether they will be achieved, change how it seeks to achieve those goals, and even revise the goals based on the feedback it receives. That line of analysis can be applied in more specific terms by discussing organizational networks.

ORGANIZATIONAL NETWORKS: STRUCTURAL-FUNCTIONALISM

Information and systems theories supply conceptual underpinnings for using networks as the basic unit of analysis to define and explain the patterns of information flow within an organization. Network analysis features information flows throughout an organization by taking various pathways. Each pathway is a pattern that can be charted as a network. Since information is the life force or energy of an organization, researchers want to know how information flows and influence is exerted (Farace et al., 1977; Monge, 1987).

Such analysis justifies structural functionalism, which views organizations as structural patterns of information flow, or networks. It focuses attention on the functions individuals undertake in their work. Viewed this way, a department, such as accounting, is a network. It takes in and processes information, which is output to other departments and external organizations such as the Internal Revenue Service. The job function is accounting. The communication functions include acquiring, processing, and outputting financial information. Other departments take in different information and shape it as informative reports (communication function) and persuasive messages (communication function).

A network is the pathway or pattern by which information flows between individuals within a group and between groups in an organization. A network consists of person-to-person connections by which information is exchanged. Networks consist of people who interact. A set of pathways, such as information flow between accountants in the accounting department of a company, is a micronetwork. In this sense, a micronetwork is a system (or a subsystem). When micronetworks are put together, they form a macronetwork (a system or a suprasystem). To some extent, both types of network correspond to the organization chart, but information also flows through networks that do not correspond to formal organizational structure (Farace et al., 1977). If a macronetwork is a system, its micronetworks are subsystems. Several types of networks can be identified: line (one person contacts another, who contacts another and so on A→B→C→D), commune (open exchange, everyone interactions with everyone else), hierarchy (network as organization chart, or layers of systems), and dictator (super gatekeeper; Krippendorff, 1977).

A person in one micronetwork is a link when he or she communicates (facilitates information flow) with a person in another micronetwork. Through links, information can flow between networks. One kind of link is a bridge, which results when one person connects two networks; a manager of a department, for instance, is a bridge between his or her department and the vice president. A slightly different link is a liaison; this person connects with several people, not just one, from another network. Some people are isolates because they have little interaction with others (Farace et al., 1977). People are stars or nodes when, like the hub of a wheel, they receive information from many people and pass it to others, receptionists, for instance. Bridges, liaisons, and stars are gatekeepers who filter, pass, withhold, or distort information.

Networks are characterized by the number of persons involved and by the relationships between them. These relationships can be described in words such as "talks to," "coordinates with," or "reports to." In this way, analysis not only focuses on the number of people involved but also the strength or intensity of the relationship between them, which can be estimated by the frequency of contact and the degree of interdependence.

Networks exhibit the property of symmetry, which describes the degree to which direction or flow of information reveal balance rather than imbalance in a relationship. Relationships can be one way or two way, and they can be symmetrical (influence balanced) or asymmetrical (one party has more influence than the other). In a one-way asymmetrical relationship, for instance, one person provides information and influence for the other but does not receive much if anything in return. Two-way symmetrical relationships exhibit the most balance because influence and information flows freely between the two parties.

Another characteristic of networks is transivity, the ease by which information flows from one person to the next. Typical of a line network, Person A communicates with Person B, who communicates with C, who communicates with D. Person D depends on all of the others for information; for this reason, it may be difficult for A and D to communicate because they depend on B and C. If the information A wants to get to D flows with relative ease, the system has high transivity. If the information does not flow because one or more links are impediments, the system lacks transivity. This characteristic can easily be seen in the organizational practice of routing communication; it also refers to the ease with which communication flows across each link in the chain of authority (Monge, 1977).

Networks can be based on static and routine relationships between people. Networks can also be dynamic, in a constant state of emergence, growth, maintenance, and decline. They grow when interpersonal and group contacts become frequent and interdependent. They decline when people cease to have contact with one another. They emerge when they have not been in place before. A classic example of emerging networks is the creation of new sales contacts. Many salespeople "prospect" to make new contacts. If they succeed, a network is established, and two systems begin to interact, a process called boundary spanning.

The degree to which information flow is routine depends on demands created for the system by its environment. When a system is beginning (emerging), such as the spawning of a new department, information flow is likely not to be routine. The structures by which information flows are emerging. Over time, they become routine. For this reason, Monge and Eisenberg (1987) stressed that the degree to which each network is dynamic and changing, or routine and static, may indicate the health of an organization. According to contingency theory, the status of network development is a function of whether any network is adequate given the requirements of its circumstances (Morgan, 1986; Poole & Roth, 1989).

Structural concerns addressed by this approach to organizational communication begin with the assumption that each organization has absolute information (all of the information it possesses). Information is not concentrated in one part of an organization; rather, it exists as distributed information because it is scattered through the organization. One concern addressed by structural-functionalism is whether information is so well distributed that the people who need it can get it. This view fits comfortably with the principle that people use information to reduce uncertainty and be competent in achieving a range of personal and organizational goals.

If an individual has insufficient information, too little to do his or her job adequately, he or she suffers information (or communication) underload. When persons have so much information (or communication) to process that they are unable to extract what they need, they experience information overload. A key principle of structural-functionalism is that information must be distributed correctly if the organization is to function properly (Farace et al., 1977).

This line of analysis gives insights into many relevant issues, such as job involvement. If people have the information they want, they experience higher job involvement (identification with the organization). Increased job involvement decreases turnover and absenteeism and increases job satisfaction (Penley, 1982). Employees may become more committed to a company when they are involved in the communication networks associated with their jobs. This effect is likely to be seen in employees who have low job involvement, but it does not manifest itself in employees who are moderately or highly involved with their jobs (Eisenberg, Monge, & Miller, 1984). For instance, a receptionist may be committed to a company merely because of his or her level of involvement in the organization's communication network. But an employee who is isolated (not involved in the communication network), such as a pumping station operator for a gas pipeline company, may nevertheless feel high job involvement and high levels of commitment to the company.

In this way, systems and network analysis have produced many interesting and useful research findings. For instance, persons who are links can use information to achieve control and exert power. Links are most effective when they strive to reduce uncertainty. Because of their role and their access to information, links tend to identify closely with their jobs. Their position leads them to think in terms of teamwork and group effectiveness (Albrecht, 1984). This study demonstrates that network analysis and information flow are useful means for analyzing the health and productivity of organizations and their members.

Such conclusions seem relevant even for those dramatic and dislocating times in the history of organizations and their members: change. When dramatic change occurs in an organization, it can damage the morale and job satisfaction of employees. That can result in resistance to change. For this reason, knowing the factors that lead organizational members to support change gives valuable insights regarding how to successfully manage change. Exploring this issue, Miller, Johnson, and Grau (1994) concluded "that employees who received ample information in a timely and appropriate fashion and who had a high need for achievement were willing to participate in an organizational change" (p. 72).

Additional insights into organizational communication can be obtained by examining the effect that shared meaning has on organizational members' ability to cooperate. Interpretivism is a key for unlocking those mysteries.

ORGANIZATIONAL CLIMATE AND CULTURE: INTERPRETIVISM

The previous section demonstrated how network analysis is used to analyze organizational communication as information flow patterns between people in subsystems of an organization. However helpful this analysis is, it fails to capture all of what accounts for the effectiveness or ineffectiveness of organizations and their members' performance.

Two other concepts—climate and culture—help explain why organizational members know what is expected of them and feel motivated (or unmotivated) to support an organization's goals. These two concepts are similar enough so that some researchers treat them as synonymous. Climate and culture are viewed as being similar by researchers who use the paradigm of an organization and its members as psychological entities. According to this paradigm, climate and culture are perceptual issues that can be ferreted out by surveying employees' opinions of the company and themselves as members of it. Climate and culture are products of the perceptions collectively held by the members of the organization; they exist in their minds. An organization is "open and trusting" if they believe it is. This view reasons that most members in an organization have views of its climate and culture that enable them to coordinate their activities.

Before settling on a definition of climate, let's review several approaches. One reasons that climate consists of traits that are the product of the structure and operations of an organization, not of the people in the organization. Analyzed in this way, the climate of an organization exists even when its membership changes (Tagiuri, 1968). This is an organizational trait view of climate.

Taking a contrasting view, Falcione and Kaplan (1984) offered the perceptual measurement-individual attribute model. It treats climate as the product of the contact each individual has with each organization. Climate is based on traits of the company that are revealed by what occurs during its activities (how people act toward and react to one another) and the relationships that develop between them. Based on this interaction, they perceive the traits of a company—or any type of organization. People compare the traits they discover against those they prefer as the ideal organization. People prefer organizations that have climates that match their personalities and needs. They seek to associate with members who share their views of climate. This view of climate stresses communication variables.

For purposes of the analysis that follows, let's distinguish between climate and culture, while acknowledging that they are counterparts. Climate arises from the interactions between individuals—and the organization—and results from the quality of relationships between members of an organization, as discussed in chapter 6. One of the most important relationships occurs between superior and subordinate, and another key relationship exists between employee and organization. If management and superiors seem open, then the organization has an open climate. If they are closed and distrustful, then the climate is closed and untrusting. Culture consists of meanings that members share about an organization. We are interested in the communication variables that create and result from climate and culture. First we examine climate and then analyze culture.

Climate is easy to imagine, but difficult to conceptualize. You have experienced many organizational climates. Recall the "feeling" you had as you experienced different organizations (even different friends' homes or different teachers' classrooms). Did the climate change when a new boss was hired, new members were added, old ones left, or new tasks, goals, or rewards were implemented? One boss is friendly, open, and helpful, taking time to explain what subordinates need to know to perform their work effectively. In contrast, another boss manages by "guerrilla tactics"—explosions, sabotage, secrecy, power plays, and sneak attacks. The climate of a group changes when too much work is expected for the time available or skills and capacity of its members. Climate is different (at least perceived so) on the first days on a job when a member really likes what she or he is doing than it is later when boredom has set in and the person has learned the unpleasant aspects of the organization.

What variables should be used to study climate and its effect on individual task performance, personal satisfaction, and communication interaction? Variables typical of interpersonal relationships are often used in this regard. Redding (1979) reasoned that climate depends on (a) the extent to which an organization is supportive of its members; (b) whether members are allowed to participate in decision making, a form of interpersonal control; (c) levels of trust, confidence, and credibility—criteria by which members assess persons who are in leadership positions; (d) amount of openness and candor; and (e) effect the organization has on individual performance goals—a form of commitment. In this vein, Downs (1979) discovered that climate, the quality of feedback members receive, and supervisor communication styles are closely related. Job satisfaction and performance correlate with the quality of communication in an organization. Members' perception of communication quality depends on supervisor communication style, communication climate, and personal feedback (Pincus, 1986).

To derive a sense of climate, members of an organization assess the performance of others, especially their superiors. Supervisory and communication style differences affect how satisfied members are in an organization. For example, when asked to compare supervisory nurses who managed in "masculine" versus "feminine" styles, nurses reported experiencing higher morale and job satisfaction when their female supervisors used "feminine" rather than "masculine" management styles. Participants in this study preferred traits that promote positive relationships, lead to reception of new ideas, encourage effort, as well as show concern, attentiveness, friendliness, and approval. Supervisors who were liked least controlled the conversations in which they engaged; they were dominant and quick to challenge others (Camden & Kennedy, 1986).

Jablin (1982b) found that where members are located within the hierarchy of organizations leads them to perceive different amounts of openness in superior–subordinate relationships. The lower people are in an organization, the less they believe relationships are open. Employees in large organizations believe less openness exists than do their counterparts in small organizations.

These research findings on communication and supervisory style should help you realize that climate arises from relationships and events that occur outside each individual. Climate arises when each individual interprets these relationships and events. How these relationships affect each member depends on his or her idiosyncratic perceptions. For instance, some people like a disciplined, authoritarian climate, whereas others hate that climate. People in an organization have similar relational experiences. These perceptions become more similar for many employees because they talk about and interpret them through formal and informal communication.

Climate and organizational structure interrelate. One view of structure is that it is the organizational chart of the company. Most researchers believe that structure is something different from what is specified by that chart. Structure is enacted as people adjust to one another. Viewed this way, structure is a product of relationships between members. Structure is not mechanistic, it is not static— not the result of a rigid organization chart. It is ever changing, a product of members' values, needs, and interactions. Called *structuration,* this model postulates that "organizational climates are continually being structured through organizational practices" (Poole, 1985, p. 97).

People's sense of an organization's structure results from their perceptions of the practices or procedures, interpersonal behavior, and superior–subordinate relationships. In this way, climate is closely related to structure. Who employees communicate with and what they say and do not say goes a long way toward defining structure. The structure of each organization exists in the minds of its members. It is the product of the values they enact through communication and compliance. If an organization is autocratic, such is the case only because members verify autocracy by yielding to executives' authority. For instance, you have undoubtedly been in a classroom where a teacher tries to exert direct control over students' behavior; if the students do not yield to this control, the teacher fails to achieve control. Likewise, if the structure of an organization is democratic but the members do not accept the responsibilities of democracy, that structure will fail.

Members of each organization create its climate by their actions, which, in turn, reflect their values and perceptions. The relationship between climate and structure is dialectical; each shapes the other. The structuration of climates is affected by "(1) structural properties of the organization, (2) apparatuses that directly produce and reproduce climates, and (3) members' knowledge and skills" (Poole, 1985, p. 102).

Principles of social exchange theory support the concept of structuration. Each individual attempts to become assimilated into the organization and specific work groups by negotiating which of the organization's task and role expectations are acceptable given the reward/cost ratio. Each member negotiates, to the extent possible, a workable relationship with others (superiors, peers, and subordinates), task groups, and the total organization. Members expect an organization to be personally rewarding. They expect tangible outcomes, such as money, as well as intangible ones, such as esteem. If the relationship is rewarding, the member fosters it; if not, the member seeks to change it, reluctantly accommodates to it, or decides to leave. If the person cannot leave, the climate is likely to have negative effects on his or her performance (communication and task) as well as esteem. In turn, the person may have a negative influence on the organization.

Individual perception, values, and actions in an organization reflect each member's view of climate. This process involves attribution and uncertainty reduction. Members of an organization seek to know (assign meaning) what the climate and structure are, how they should perform to achieve reward, and what relational communication variables are typical of, and important to, the organization. They want to know whether their efforts are successful, whether how they manage, work, and communicate leads to positive or negative outcomes. They check to see whether others' views of their competence match their own views (a coorientation model). Because of these perceptions, as well as the attitudes, values, and beliefs associated with them, members develop views of the organization, work, role, and competence.

The individual is not the only unit of analysis. How a member obtains and maintains views of an organization's climate is influenced by interpersonal relationships, policies, group memberships, and actions by people at various levels in the organization, especially those in management. Through talk and other forms of communication, individual perspectives on climate become generalized as members share or oppose various views on the organization's climate.

Because experiences of members differ throughout an organization, it will have many climates. Falcione, Sussman, and Herden (1987) argued that the climate in each task group is not identical to that of the total organization. Nor is the climate in each interpersonal relationship the same as that in either the organization or the groups in which its members operate. The climate of the total organization is a product of interactions at each level of analysis: organization, group, and dyad.

Your experience can help you appreciate this point. In some organizations, such as a class, you cooperate because you like the teacher. In another class, you may try to undermine that teacher's authority. Or, you may sabotage efforts of students who are trying to ingratiate themselves with a teacher to get undeserved rewards. The climates of these relationships will reflect and produce your view of the climate of the entire organization. But your view of climate and that of others (inside and outside) is not identical, even though it may be similar.

Communication with other members, groups, and the organization gives individuals an opportunity to form attributions and match them against those held by other members. Differences occur; some members of an organization think it is open and fair and that members participate in decisions; other members of the same organization may think the climate is closed and unfair. You probably have evidence of this situation by having talked with others in an organization, each of whom has a different opinion of whether it is open or closed, supportive or not.

The creation, negotiation, and use of climate is a product of each individual's efforts to exercise autonomy, seek structure, and obtain rewards, as well as receive consideration, warmth, and support. How these climate variables operate is the result of rules and resources. Individual schemata define what the climate is and ought to be, as well as how interaction and task efforts result in structuration (ongoing efforts to create an operable system to achieve goals). As Falcione et al. (1987) concluded, "Structuration then serves as the basis of psychological climate, the individual's unique and idiosyncratic perceptions of what is happening in the organization and to him or her" (p. 220). People act in an organization and thereby create its structure in ways that fit their impressions of what the structure is and should be and what performance in that structure is likely to cost versus the rewards it offers.

What role does organizational culture play in the creation of climate? Or is the relationship the opposite—does climate shape culture? Individual experiences of climate become shared through communication. Once individual impressions of the organization's climate become translated into members' comments, especially the stories they tell, climate has become embedded in the organization's culture. By the same token, culture is likely to affect individual members' interpretations of the relationships they encounter.

One view is that the climate in each organization is instrumental to its culture. Schein (1985) concluded that culture is

a pattern of basic assumptions—invented, discovered, or developed by a given group as it learns to cope with its problems of external adaptation and internal integration—that has worked well enough to be considered valid and, therefore, to be taught to new members as the correct way to perceive, think, and feel in relation to those problems. (p. 9)

Thus, Schein (1992) reasoned, culture could be viewed as operating at different levels. Level 1 can be seen in the artifacts of an organization, such as its building or the uniforms employees wear. Level 2 consists of beliefs and values. Level 3 consists of underlying assumptions that influence the actions and decisions of organization members.

Culture provides employees with useful assumptions, Morgan (1986) reasoned, because it is "shared meaning, shared understanding, and shared sense making" (p. 128). Culture consists of "significant symbols and modes of legitimated social action that enables selective responses" by organizational members to the requirements of daily activities (Pilotta, Widman, & Jasko, 1988, p. 317). According to this view of culture, employees enact the culture of each company (what they think is expected of them) as actors perform the script of a play (Morgan, 1986).

Culture of each organization is contained in its artifacts. It is conveyed in stories (such as how the company was founded or the "characters" who have worked in a department), legends, and myths, as well as physical attributes of an organization, such as its architecture, furnishings, properties, and accomplishments. Schools, for instance, have a culture that consists of their athletic and academic traditions as well as student life. Culture allows members of an organization to describe and share views of reality, including the unique character of the organization, its members, and its environment (Smircich & Calas, 1987). Stories portray versions of reality and thereby convey a sense of what behavior is appropriate or inappropriate. Those definitions are vital to the politics and power that operate in an organization (Mumby, 1987).

Archetypes are means by which climate and culture are shared between members. For instance, managerial styles are expressed as archetypal characters in the stories members tell. Some managers, Mitroff (1983) observed, are "Sherman Tanks," whereas others are "complainers," "wet blankets," or "innovators." Similarly, companies can be characterized as "fly-by-night," "We'll get back to you," or "The check is in the mail." On the positive side, the culture of an organization might be "Service first" or "Customers know best" (Heath, 1988).

According to this analysis, organizations change when their members change the key metaphors by which they think about themselves and the organization. For instance, the structure, functions, and climate of a company will change if the "military metaphor" (highly structured, top-down, autocratic) in its culture is abandoned in favor of a "family metaphor" (open, supportive, shared power). To create a climate conducive to organizational rapport with its community, a company might abandon a culture based on a metaphor of privileged self-interest and adopt a metaphor of responsiveness.

This use of ambiguity, Eisenberg (1984) reasoned,

> is not a kind of fudging, but rather a rational method used by communicators to orient toward multiple goals. It is easy to imagine the ethical problems that might result from the misuse of ambiguity. In the final analysis, however, both the effectiveness and the ethics of any particular communicative strategy are relative to the goals and values of the communicators in the situation. (p. 239)

Organizations state ambiguous goals that are implemented with ambiguity. Total ambiguity would lead to organizational chaos. However, when employees share guidelines regarding which level of performance is expected, those principles constitute unobtrusive control over their choices and actions (Tompkins & Cheney, 1985). Persons can achieve the same corporate goals by employing different individual means, but they need to share common themes so that they can coordinate their activities.

Culture can foster or hinder employees' sense of empowerment. Chiles and Zorn (1995) discovered that in contrast to several other variables, including employees' sense of self-efficacy, their sense of culture plays a dominant role in whether they feel empowered. Thus, employees can feel empowered or hindered by their organization's culture. Their sense of empowerment was largely based on the quality of communication with and from management.

One vehicle for creating an organization's culture is its mission statement. Through this device, executive management states the organization's core values and chief objectives. Executives create mission statements and share them with employees and external audiences through many communication vehicles, such as placards, business cards, Web sites, marketing slogans, and employee newsletters. Mission statements have more impact if employees believe management is seriously committed to them, an issue of credibility. Impact increases if employees see the statements as being personally relevant. How people interpret and manage the meaning of their organization's mission statement is influenced by commitment to their managerial role, information about the future, and trust in supervisor and executive management. When people manage the meaning of an organizational mission, they personalize it and communicate enthusiasm for it; they see it as being central to their activities, to the organization, to the work unit, and to performance standards. Employees are more likely to communicate in this way when they receive information on critical topics and feel commitment to the organization. Even so, those employees are cautious to monitor executives to see whether they maintain commitment to the mission statement of the organization (Fairhurst, Jordan, & Neuwirth, 1997).

Mission statements can help employees identify with the organization, even in times of significant transition. Identification is stronger if employees receive consistent communication over time, which leads them to share a vision of the company and their roles in it (Ferraris, Carveth, & Parrish-Sprowl, 1993).

In these ways, climate and culture affect the lives of an organization's members. An organization's climate may even encourage or discourage romantic relationships between employees. Such relationships are more likely when climate is less formal, less likely in small or large organizations, and more likely to occur in medium-sized organizations (curvilinear relationship). Women who become romantically involved with coworkers are likely to be young, have less tenure in the company, and work in lower ranks (Dillard & Witteman, 1985).

Climate and culture assist each individual's ability to make self-attributions, as well as to attribute traits and motives to others in the organization. These factors assist members' efforts to reduce personal uncertainty and to learn what is expected of them to be productive. But impressions of climate are not universal throughout an organization. Management tends to believe that the climate of the organization is more positive than subordinates do. Management feels more involved in the organization and believes communication is more open than do subordinates. Subordinates do not believe managers are as effective as they think they are (Glaser, Zamanou, & Hacker, 1987).

Culture is shared and learned as a means by which organization members, employees for instance, come to know each other's views on important matters and share a social reality. We can recall the general themes from chapter 5, where we discussed social influence as a means by which people transmit and acquire attitudes and behaviors that result in positive outcomes.

If people are going to have useful sharing of culture, it should conform to coorientation principles of agreement, accuracy, and congruence (satisfaction). Using this logic, Suzuki (1997) explored the forces by which culture is transmitted through interpersonal contacts, or networks. Through their networks, individual members of organizations come to share beliefs and values. Such transmission occurs through routine interactions in the performance of general tasks associated with the roles and activities of the individuals.

Treated as a global construct, culture includes everything about a company, such as its image, size, values, place in its industry, managerial style, operating philosophies, personnel, and reputation. Culture consists of an organization's values, norms, beliefs, and structures. Whereas culture exists over longer periods of time, climate is to some extent a moment-by-moment matter that results from members' contact with the organization and others in it. According to this view, "*climate* would become an indicator of the goodness of fit between an organization's *culture* and its people" (Falcione & Kaplan, 1984, p. 301). Whereas climate, according to Krone et al. (1987), is a psychological variable, culture is a focal point for interpreting the meaning of the actions and symbols used by organizational members (Pacanowsky & O'Donnell-Trujillo, 1983).

The desire to gain insights into the creation and impact of culture spawned an analytical approach called interpretivism. As Putnam (1983) observed,

"Interpretivists adopt a meaning-centered view of organizational communication. Social reality is constituted through the words, symbols, and actions that members invoke." For this reason, messages can be treated "as the symptoms of and means for developing social meanings" (p. 40). Interpretivism sheds light onto the dynamics of organizations by revealing the meaning individual members use to share a culture.

Interpretivism views organizations as dramatic, narrative, and symbolic entities. As members create and share meaning, it guides their organizational actions. To diagnose the organization requires that prevailing symbols and their structure be revealed (Goodall, 1989, 1990; Pacanowsky & O'Donnell-Trujillo, 1983). To conduct this analysis, two lines of interpretivism have developed. One, critical theory, discovers aspects of culture that stifle human growth through the experience of being a constructive part of effective organizations. The second stream, analytical interpretivist, discloses meaning structures of organizational culture in order to reveal the forces that guide and impinge on individual and collective efforts on behalf of the organization.

Critical theory reasons that organizations should not be dehumanizing. The study of organizations, especially organizational communication, should liberate employees by revealing the power structures that work against individual preferences and needs. These power structures are created by management to control the efforts, even the lives, of employees. Critical interpretivism works to remove the privilege of management, which is called a managerial bias. This analytic perspective works to disclose the aspects of culture that marginalize employees.

Managers can influence and even dominate workers' performance by how communication occurs and what is communicated. The essence of this communication is themes, premises, metaphors, and narratives, as well as nonverbal symbols that create a meaning that privileges the views of management in preference of those of employees (S. A. Deetz, 1988; Pfeffer, 1981; Smircich, 1983a; R. C. Smith & Eisenberg, 1987). Critical interpretivists explore these issues to uncover "communication distortion and to free individuals from exploitation, alienation, and arbitrary forms of authority" (Putnam, 1983, p. 48). Critical interpretivism seeks "to remove blockages and contradictions that prevent individuals from developing their own potential and from constructing their own activities" (p. 48).

Power, its creation and use, is a focal point in such discussions. As Eisenberg (1986) argued, "power inheres in language-in-use—in the metaphors, myths, stories, and rituals through which members of dominant coalitions control the issues that those with less power feel they may address" (p. 93). Executives work to exert power through well-crafted premises and assumptions that employees are expected to adopt and use as performance guidelines. Because interpretations of reality lead to actions consonant with those views, S. A. Deetz (1982) concluded, "Meaning structures are filled with privileged interests" (p. 139). Management works to privilege its views and power.

Power meaning structures often are binary, specifying that employees should do one thing and not do another. "Power can be said to be greater if it can exert influence in the face of attractive alternatives, and it increases proportionately as there is an increase in freedom for the power receiver" (Pilotta, Widman, & Jasko, 1988, p. 329).

In contrast to its ideological counterpart, analytical interpretivism wants to explain the culture of an organization to understand why it operates as it does. In keeping with linguistic relativity, this analytical approach believes that the idioms organizations use specify how operations are conducted, employees are treated, and rewards are provided.

Based on their study of the culture of Disneyland, R. C. Smith and Eisenberg (1987) concluded, "The park or 'show' is the enactment of Walt Disney's utopian vision; it is 'the happiest place on earth'" (p. 372). Employees who worked for the theme park adopted the culture of family. This metaphor created cohesiveness among workers and gave them a positive image, which appealed to customers. When downsizing occurred, employees resisted it because they opposed breaking up the family. Thus, the metaphor that created cohesiveness also fostered resistance to change.

Climate and culture are two dominant themes in organizational analysis. They are used as key variables to discover the health of an organization and to understand why management and employees (or any members of an organization) act as they do. As linguistic relativists would argue, the idiom of any group is the view of the world that they enact as though it were true. That theme is basic to enactment theory.

ENACTMENT THEORY

With this understanding of structure, climate, and culture in mind, we can turn attention to enactment theory. It was developed to explain how people think and act as members of organizations. Organizational actions and the terms used to define them are fraught with ambiguity. To solve this problem of ambiguity, people create and impose meaningful interpretations on themselves, their organization, its environment, and all relevant activities. They enact these meanings as though they were clear and free of ambiguity.

They do this, Weick (1979b) reasoned, because they cannot separate themselves either as individuals or as members of an organization from how they think about the meaning they impose on themselves, other actors, and the environment. As people in an industry, governmental agency, or nonprofit organization view the world, for instance, it reflects their products, services, and activities. "The external environment literally bends around the enactments of people, and much of the activity of sense-making involves an effort to separate the externality from the action" (pp. 130–131).

The automobile industry offers an excellent example of enactment. Executives and employees in a car manufacturing company see the possession and use of automobiles as a dominant theme in their discussion of their industry, plant operations, identities, and society. That view dominates their planning, operations, and marketing. They see themselves, their customers, and society through the perspective of manufacturing, selling, repairing, financing, and owning automobiles. For years, as an example, anyone who worked for a domestic automobile company was likely to have his or her car vandalized by fellow employees if the car was an import. Owning a domestic automobile was an act of being a LOYAL AMERICAN!

Reflecting on Weick's theory, Bantz (1989) agreed that organizing results when employees enact change in an environment that is ambiguous, equivocal. People select an interpretation that they believe reduces the equivocality. They enact that view as though it were clear and free from ambiguity. In this way, Weick (1979b) argued that a company is not an organization, but is engaged in the process of organizing. It undergoes constant change. People enact structure by forming, maintaining, and dissolving relationships. Thus, Weick conceptualized organizations as being in a continual state of falling apart and rebuilding.

In Weick's (1979b) view, enactment transpires in stages: act, interact, and double interact. One person as an individual or representative of a company does something (act) that is meaningful to another person. The second person reacts; this is an interact, an act followed by a reaction. Reaction to the interact is a double interact. Persons involved in these relationships read each other's behavior and make attributions to comprehend what the actions mean in the given situation. Each act is defined by reactions (symbolic action) persons make to it, to themselves, and to the persons who commit it.

Weick's (1987) analysis requires an understanding of the processes people employ as they attempt collectively to interpret their environment: Enactment, selection, and retention. Enactment is "a bracketing activity" that consists of actions that define each situation by being relevant to that situation (p. 153). For instance, a sales call brackets the enactment that occurs between customer and sales representative. Selection refers to traits and themes on which people focus as they observe themselves and their environment. Retention entails remembering events, concepts, and scripts, as individuals and as groups in a company. Through interaction, people form collective interpretations that they use to lessen the equivocality about themselves, one another, and their environment.

People engage each other, their organization, and the environment. They focus on some elements and ignore others. Recurring selections transform into predictable ways of perceiving and thinking, or schema. Information derived from this process becomes retained in individual and collective memories. Each schema, Weick (1979b) reasoned, is "an abridged, generalized, corrigible orientation of experience that serves as an initial frame of reference for action and perception. A schema is the belief in the phrase, 'I'll see it when I believe it.' Schemata constrain seeing and, therefore, serve to bracket portions of experience" (p. 154).

People perceive reality selectively through perceptual filters. Weick (1979b) reasoned that they see what their orientations and assumptions—even biases—allow them to see or prevent them from seeing. Such is the case because each "person's idea is extended outward, implanted, and then discovered as knowledge. The discovery, however, originated in a prior invention by this discoverer" (p. 159). Individuals are part of the environment they perceive, and they cannot see it independent of their interest and presence in it.

Enactment is a self-fulfilling prophecy. People see what they expect to find. For this reason, Weick concluded, enactment is not merely perception. "Enactment emphasizes that mangers construct, rearrange, single out, and demolish many 'objective' features of their surroundings. When they unrandomize variables, they insert vestiges of orderliness, and literally create their own constraints" (p. 164). People can share views of reality by having common experiences and assigning similar interpretations to them. Enactment occurs when "people, often alone, actively *put* things out there that they then perceive and negotiate about perceiving. It is that initial implanting of reality that is perceived by the word *enactment*" (p. 165).

What enables individuals to achieve collective effort? Weick's (1987) answer featured two concepts, thought and interaction given form through the idiom unique to each industry, company, and work discipline. Scripted in business idiom, "measures of profitability, debt to earnings ratios, reports of capital investments and the like are vital information about any enterprise" (Mangham & Overington, 1987, p. 3). Interpretations of these "facts" arise from perspectives employees and mangers share, or should share. The "language trappings of organizations such as strategic plans are important components in the process of creating order. They hold events together long enough and tightly enough in people's heads so that they act in the belief that their actions will be influential and make sense" (Weick, 1987, p. 98). Through language, especially idioms unique to their organization, individuals make public the assumptions, expectations, justifications, and commitments they use to "span the breaks in a loosely coupled system and encourage confident actions that tighten systems and create order. The conditions for order in organizations exist as much in the mind as they do in the rationalized procedures. That is why culture, which affects the mind through meaning, is often more important than structure" (p. 98). By living the implications of these idioms, they enact the organization.

Through the shared sense that is culture, individual members learn shared expectations needed to act collectively. Through scripts that they help create, executives and employees enact the drama that is the structure of their organization.

With structural functionalism and interpretive views, including enactment, as a foundation, we can now explore these issues in contexts. Of relevance are interpersonal, groups, and organization as organization levels of analysis.

INTERPERSONAL LEVEL OF ANALYSIS

This section focuses on individuals' efforts to be efficacious in an organization, to serve its goals, and to obtain rewards in exchange. As explained by structural-functionalism, network members are connected by interpersonal and organizational bonds. From the perspective of interpretivism, each person's performance depends on his or her perception and understanding of the organizational culture, climate, structure, and the other members. Through interpersonal contacts, members develop organizational self-concepts, make reward/cost estimates, as well as understand and transmit the organization's culture. Personal contact occurs with superiors, subordinates, and coworkers, as well as the organization itself through internal mediated communication. Such interaction is not the same for all interactions, according to leader–member exchange theory, because communication styles affect the social exchange between superior and subordinate as well as with coworkers (Sias & Jablin, 1995).

In the process of assimilation and many other activities that occur to bring an organization to life, interpersonal interaction is a vital set of activities. Whenever you think of the flow of information and influence exerted within an organization, you should keep in mind that these transpire, in many cases, between two people, a dyad. For this reason, as Weick (1987) observed, "Interpersonal communication is the essence of organization because it creates structures that then affect what else gets said and done and by whom" (p. 97). You would be incorrect if you think of organizations only as units or groups, such as departments or divisions. A moment's reflection should remind you of the dyads (two people talking or exchanging memos or e-mails) that occur each day in an organization. Many activities occur interpersonally: telephone conversations, interviews, supervisors assigning and checking on the work someone is doing, negotiations, conversations at water fountains, and sales presentations, to mention only a few.

To what extent are people who compose an organization thoughtful, cognitively aware of themselves and the organization? Weick (1979a, 1979b) and Jablin (1982a, 1984) argued that organizations consist of thinking people. Jablin (1982a) challenged researchers to operationalize this assumption to explain *"how* social cognition affects and is affected by organizational communication" (p. 255). A crucial factor in social cognition is organizational assimilation.

Assimilation

One reality of organizational life is that each person must assimilate into (become a member of) many organizations. Assimilation occurs not only as a new member enters an organization but also as she or he joins departments or groups within an organization. According to Jablin (1982a), "Organizational assimilation refers to the process by which organizational members become a part of, or are absorbed into, the culture of an organization" (p. 256).

Communication is vital to the assimilation process. Jablin (1985) believed that each member's efforts to become assimilated are influenced by his or her perceptions of life and work, role expectations, and self-assessments, as well as many external forces such as whether membership is voluntary (such as a fraternity or sorority) or mandatory (such as attending grammar school).

Individuals acquire role definitions and expectations from those with whom they have close contact. Families and educational institutions are not only "organizations" into which people are assimilated, but they also shape how individuals become assimilated into subsequent organizations, such as schools or businesses. In addition to their families and schools, individuals' socialization is influenced by media, peers, and direct experiences with part-time jobs. In this way, each person, in various ways and to different degrees, prepares for the transition into an organization; this critical moment begins with employment interviews (Jablin & McComb, 1984).

During assimilation, people learn what is expected of them and what efforts and attitudes will be required for them to be accepted as meaningful participants who can predictably obtain the rewards of membership. This process, Jablin (1982a) contended, has two interlocking sets of activities and goals: (a) an organization's efforts to integrate the individual into its corporate culture by teaching appropriate attitudes, values, and behaviors; and (b) personal efforts to become part of that culture while maintaining individuality.

To explain this process, D. Katz and Kahn (1966) contended that membership in a company is a role-taking process. People take on (or are expected to take on) specific roles unique to the goals and culture of each organization to which they belong. The price of membership is the ability and willingness to comply with and follow the roles the organization prescribes.

Interpreting this role-taking process differently, Jablin (1982a) reasoned that D. Katz and Kahn failed to acknowledge that each member, including new recruits, negotiates the nature of the expected role. By taking an assimilation approach, Jablin is able to study efforts individuals make to understand and negotiate the roles organizations expect them to take. This phenomenon can be observed by looking at the communication processes organizations use to help members understand and accept their roles. This process is dynamic, not static. Members either confirm or disconfirm an organization by adopting the roles it prescribes.

Assimilation, Jablin (1984, 1985) contended, is a developmental process that consists of three stages: anticipatory socialization, encounter, and metamorphosis. The first phase, anticipatory socialization, occurs prior to a recruit's entry into an organization or when entering a different group in an organization. Prior to entry, the individual makes role choices by selecting an occupation or position and deciding to adopt relevant role expectations. This phase has two distinct aspects: vocational and organizational socialization. The first set of cognitions relates to the ability to perform the job, whereas the second set of cognitions focuses on how the individual sees himself or herself fitting into and influencing the company.

During the second phase, encounter, members seek to "break into" the organization after being hired. Each new member develops an impression of the new work environment. During this phase, she or he relies on scripts and schemata that were acquired before coming to the organization. The individual must also learn new scripts that fit his or her view of the particular organization. The encounter is easiest when the social reality of the individual fits that of the organization. What the new member thinks about this organization will be shaded by his or her personality, values, job experience, and information provided by superiors, peers, and the organization through its many forms of communication, including orientation sessions and company publications, such as newsletters and annual reports.

What happens during the encounter phase, Jablin (1985) reasoned, will affect members' metamorphosis. During this stage, the individual becomes aware of discrepancies and agreements between his or her attitudes or values and those prevailing in the organization. Metamorphosis occurs if the individual adapts to the organization. Communication plays a major role in the individual's effort to learn appropriate attitudes, values, and behaviors. Information is received from documents. It is obtained through superior–subordinate relationships and from fellow members. Part of what the member learns is how the organization communicates, what is communicated and to whom, and how decisions are made. The organization, brought to life by people who are responsible for and needful of the person making the metamorphosis, expects new members to adopt appropriate patterns of thinking and behaving. As part of successful metamorphosis, the member acquires a sense of the company's reward system and from that derives an understanding of how satisfying the job is. All of this can affect work motivation.

After new members have entered an organization, they use interpersonal contacts to learn the organization's climate and culture. They seek information about their job tasks. Whether workers think a task is "enriched" depends on variables such as feedback, skill variety, autonomy, and task identity. Investigating this situation, Blau (1985) found that participants who received information about enriched task situations exhibited significantly higher ratings of perceived job scope than did those who received information about unenriched tasks. Employees are favorably affected when they receive positive social cues from competent (credible) coworkers, and if they believe they have some control rather than being controlled by others.

Interpersonal communication in organizations is influenced by attribution processes, relationship development, discrepancy arousal, speech accommodation, and uncertainty reduction. To reduce uncertainty, employees seek information via interpersonal contacts and respond best when they encounter superiors who are credible and open, but not dominant. How they seek this information, which persons they seek it from, and how the information is interpreted by the person providing it and the one receiving it are factors that influence the ways persons become assimilated into organizations (Jablin & Krone, 1987).

As well as using communication tactics to enter an organization, people also seek and give information when they are transferring from one department to another. This process entails three phases: loosening, transition, and tightening. Loosening involves comments about leaving, including helping those who are staying behind. Transition occurs when the physical move leads the individual to develop new links while maintaining old ones. The tightening phase is similar to assimilation, whereby the person becomes part of a new unit (Kramer, 1989).

People reduce uncertainty about their jobs during a job transfer if they enjoy high quality conversation with work peers. Applying uncertainty-reduction theory, Kramer (1996) noted, however, that when transferees encounter peer conversation that is high in impersonal information about job tasks, they experience less comfort than when they receive personal information as well. Of related interest is the concern for differences between uniplex and multiplex relationships on transferee feelings of acceptance. Multiplex relationships exist when people have access to many people and many topics. This research project did not find that multiplex relationships were more effective in reducing uncertainty than were uniplex relationships.

Assimilation, Jablin and Krone (1987) reasoned, occurs as the new member communicates with superiors, peers, and the organization. For this reason, the assimilation process gives an excellent way to compare the new member's perceptions, sense of expectations, and values against those of others, especially persons who are in authority. Each member's social reality is pitted against the collective reality of all the members of the organization. Roles are building blocks of an organization, and how a person assimilates reflects his or her willingness and ability to take a role.

Personal constructions of social reality about role expectations of participating in organizations begin early in life. Children play "school" and "work." They observe those around them (parents, siblings, and acquaintances) who engage in various roles. The media portray role expectations that viewers use to create insights into the cultures and activities of organizations that they might join. Role definition and expectation may lead to specific activities such as obtaining education, training, or apprenticeships. It entails internalizing expectations, values, communication behaviors, and reward/cost matrices.

As individuals undertake to enter a role, they may experience problems with their self-perception, role expectation, or role reality. They test their skills in the performance of the role and their ability to process a lot of new information. During the encounter phase, the new member may experience difficulties of fitting in. The cognitive processes involved in this effort can be explained by social learning theory (Bandura, 1986), information integration-expectancy value theory (Ajzen & Fishbein, 1980), and involvement theory (Petty & Cacioppo, 1986a). Cognitive processes such as these interact with personality factors such as locus of control, independence, and dogmatism as well as relationships with peers, superiors, and subordinates (Jablin & Krone, 1987).

Organizational Relationships: Superior–Subordinate Dyads

Communication that occurs during superior–subordinate interaction is essential to the success of an organization. This point of contact is the source of substantial amounts of climate and culture. Leader–member exchange theory seeks to explain how communication affects superior, subordinate, and coworker ability to achieve mutually beneficial relationships. This theory features the Pelz effect, which "suggests that subordinate satisfaction with supervision is a by-product not only of an open, supportive relationship between the two parties but also of the supervisor's ability to satisfy his or her subordinates' needs by possessing influence with those higher in the organizational hierarchy" (Jablin & Krone, 1994, p. 633).

Relationships are affected by the communication styles of superiors and subordinates. Classical management style, for example, reasons that influence and instructions on how to perform jobs flow downward. By this rationale, the quality of a manager depends on the ability to give clear, accurate, and firm instruction. A more vital, albeit more complicated, model assumes that superiors and subordinates use communication to codefine and negotiate their relationship and the way work will be performed. Rather than exclusively flowing from superiors, many job instructions come from coworkers.

Relationship quality is a variable that helps researchers and managers understand superior–subordinate interaction. Fairhurst, Rogers, and Sarr (1987) studied the effect manager dominance has on subordinate performance. Dominance occurs when managers prescribe rather than negotiate role and work expectations. When subordinates perform poorly, managers are likely to exert dominance. This strategic choice can hamper the quality of their exchanges with subordinates. Subordinates whose superiors dominate begin to feel uninvolved in decisions on how to correct performance problems. Managers who are dominant believe that their subordinates desire little involvement in decisions and therefore tend to give their subordinates lower performance ratings. Managers who are dominant are more likely to misunderstand the relationship they have with subordinates than less dominant managers.

For these reasons, superiors must be skillful when they attempt to change the performance of their subordinates. Subordinates tend to view such efforts by superiors negatively. This in turn leads subordinates to become dissatisfied (Richmond, Davis, Saylor, & McCroskey, 1984).

Efforts to influence subordinate performance may involve compliance-gaining tactics. What happens if these tactics are countered by noncompliance? In that event, the superior is likely to resort to compliance-gaining tactics that feature reward and punishment; these could include bribes and threats. Women are more prone to select this strategy than are men (deTurck, 1985). As predicted by social-exchange theory, people use rewards and constraints to define and negotiate their relationships.

Managers' communication styles influence employee productivity. If managers use positive approval when dealing with subordinates, employee performance increases; the amount of positive approval correlates positively with the increase in performance. When supervisors give their subordinates autonomy to correct mistakes in ways the subordinates see fit, the length of time before the problem recurs is lengthened (Fairhurst, Green, & Snavely, 1984).

Superiors do not treat all subordinates equally well. Some subordinates receive differential treatment. Such treatment is noticed by coworkers who may discuss it with the person receiving the favors. If the special treatment is believed to be deserved because the favored employee is competent, it is considered to be fair. Coworkers discuss this treatment to make sense of it and to express their emotional reactions. Such discussion is intended to reduce uncertainty and as a form of bolstering. Persons who have low-quality relationships are prone to report more differential treatment with their supervisor than actually occurs. The quality of relationship with the boss (superior) affects the subordinate's sense of the boss and interaction with other employees (Sias & Jablin, 1995).

Supervisors' credibility affects the way subordinates respond to comments made about their performance. If employees trust their superiors' judgment and believe they posses expertise, levels of satisfaction or motivation (or both) will increase. Cusella (1982) found that post-performance feedback from high expertise sources has more impact whether it is positive or negative. Motivation is greatest when individuals receive positive feedback from sources whom they believe have expertise.

Along with credibility, other traits are important for supervisors' effectiveness: (a) perceptions of openness (willingness to listen and ability to understand), (b) shared attitudes, (c) oral communication apprehension, and (d) self-esteem. These traits lead subordinates to be more satisfied with their supervisors, but not necessarily with their jobs (Falcione, McCroskey, & Daly, 1977).

An open superior–subordinate relationship can foster flow of information and influence within an organization. Openness refers to the extent to which members are willing to send and receive information as well as make what could be perceived as negative comments. Openness will affect the content of the message (what can and will be said) and what messages are appropriate (Jablin, 1979). If a boss "blows up" at bad news, subordinates learn what constitutes bad news and avoid those statements, even to withholding information the boss needs.

Openness can include willingness and ability to express opinions. Bosses are supposed to have opinions regarding how tasks are performed, but employees like to have some autonomy in performing those tasks. Subordinates like to believe their supervisors can be effective in making a case to their superiors. Supervisory communication style is crucial in this regard. Subordinates are more satisfied with superiors who are argumentative but not verbally aggressive. This kind of boss is perceived to be an effective upward communicator. A boss who is argumentative but not verbally abusive is likely to increase his or her subordinates' career satisfaction and belief that their rights are protected (Infante & Gorden, 1985).

As is the case for all interpersonal communication, people know one another only by their perceptions and attributions of what they see and hear one another do, a central theme of social cognition. Therefore, people assign motives to one another in organizational settings. In this process, supervisors use personal and situational factors when attributing reasons while appraising subordinates' performance. If performance is below expectations, many supervisors attribute the causes to factors internal to subordinates; when positive performance occurs, external factors are used as the basis of the attributions (Green & Mitchell, 1979). These findings are typical of those reported in chapter 7. They should also remind you that even though people are not good at making accurate attributions, they think they are.

Of concern is whether superiors and subordinates accurately understand each other. Coorientation assumes that if people communicate accurately, they will have the same understanding of an object, task, or behavior, for instance Person A viewing his or her performance compared to Person B's view of Person A's performance. When supervisors are accurate in their appraisal of subordinate's performance (essentially agree with the subordinate's view), the superior is rated higher by the subordinate. When supervisors were seen by subordinates as agreeing with them on rules, subordinates evaluated the supervisors higher. Accuracy of agreement is not as important as perceived agreement (Eisenberg, Monge, & Farace, 1984).

Interpersonal relationships are a vital link in the process by which individuals assimilate into organizations. This process begins during employment interviews and carries into the orientation phase. Early in their contact with an organization, individuals begin to learn the role expectations others have of them and compare those against their own role expectations. But the parties in these situations may not have congruent or accurate impressions of one another or of what transpires, including the quality of the relationship (Jablin & Krone, 1987).

Employment interviews are an important form of interpersonal interaction. They are vital to assimilation. Examining the kinds of questions asked during employment interviews, Babbitt and Jablin (1985) discovered that nearly half of the questions asked by applicants seek job-related information. Candidates ask more questions to seek new information (especially on job and organization topics) than to clarify or elicit opinions. Applicants tend to ask questions that are closed (versus open), singular (versus multiple), and phrased in the second rather than first person. Candidates who are eventually hired by the interviewer tend to ask fewer questions that seek new information on miscellaneous (irrelevant) topics or about the interview procedures. Successful applicants make fewer self-references and ask relevant rather than miscellaneous questions and demonstrate competence by not asking as many job-related questions, thereby implying that they have done their homework on the interviewer's company.

The mechanics of the interview and communication tactics employed by persons involved have a great deal to do with whether they accomplish their objectives. The person being interviewed attempts to appraise his or her relationship with the interviewer by looking to see if the person is trustworthy, competent, composed, and organized. Both parties attribute favorable characteristics to one another if they display high rather than low levels of nonverbal immediacy, high vocal activity, and employ "response–response" rather than "question–response" conversation. During an interview, a substantial part of the exchange involves topics related to the organizational climate. Of particular interest are job duties and responsibilities, advancement potential, pay/benefits, supervision, and coworker relations. Interviewees come away from interviews with high expectations of the interpersonal communication climates in the organization (Jablin, 1985).

The kinds of information people seek and the persons they ask for information often are a function of the communication skills of the person and the rewards–cost ratios of seeking the information. For instance, people may not ask questions directly if they believe that tactic would make them to appear "dumb." Indirect communication tactics are employed, especially if risks of direct tactics appear high (Miller & Jablin, 1991).

Recruiters are more favorably impressed by job applicants who are active and dynamic communicators. But prospective employers are also scrutinized by the applicants. Applicants prefer working for bosses (recruiters) whom they perceive to be credible and who encourage applicants to express themselves (Jablin & Krone, 1994).

Research findings reported in this section indicate that superiors are wise to maintain positive relationships with their personnel. Relationships become strained as a normal part of the activities required for people to work together. One study, for instance, found that a large (50%) percentage of maintenance efforts are devoted to repair deteriorating relationships, but that many efforts are also devoted to keeping them on a positive trajectory. Several strategies are used in such relationships: avoidance, supportiveness, demonstration of positive regard, restrained expression of feelings and other reactions, and small talk. Supervisors tend to use the same communication tactics regardless of the kind of maintenance problem they are addressing. Subordinates were more likely to try several communication strategies to maintain relationships (Lee & Jablin, 1995).

Despite generalizations such as these regarding interpersonal effectiveness, organizational communication researchers have not discovered why some individuals succeed by using communication tactics that fail for others. Differences in this regard relate to a host of variables including gender, situations, and the skills of the persons using the tactics. Jablin (1985), for one, doubted "that supervisors or managers possess an 'average' communication style" (p. 630). No standard exists that people can apply to always be effective.

By examining research findings, this section has demonstrated how interpersonal relationships affect the climate and culture of an organization as well as provide focal points by which information and influence flow throughout an organization. Another of the vital contexts in an organization is the meeting, small-group task-oriented discussions and decision making.

GROUP-LEVEL ANALYSIS

Each day across corporate America, thousands of meetings transpire. In them, personnel share information and make decisions. Meetings cost millions of dollars in personnel time. Are those dollars well spent? Because of the cost and the belief that meetings are useful, researchers study small group processes to learn how groups perform their tasks effectively and how satisfied members are by their involvement in groups. In addition to making decisions, groups are also used to implement and manage complex projects and resolve conflicts (Putnam, 1989). As people stay in organizations, such as where they work, they are not only in many small groups at a given time, but they are likely to be members of many groups over the course of the years. Not only do they enter and leave groups, but they also are members of groups that other people enter and leave. For this reason, groups are a vital part of people's life spans (Jablin & Krone, 1994).

Several competing theories are used to explain why and how groups operate and to distinguish effective from ineffective groups. Although the usefulness of groups is debated, researchers suggest that they result in superior decisions in comparison to decisions made only by individuals. When employees have a chance to participate in group decision making, they believe the decisions are superior, and for that reason they are prone to help implement them.

Groups are subsystems, parts of larger systems. For this reason, they are typically approached by implementing a systems perspective. This orientation leads theorists and researchers to feature input, process, and output. Groups acquire information (input). They process it and output decisions.

Another model features communication task and socioemotional functions as independent variables that affect the success of the group. These functions include the following: Gives opinion, shares information, creates solidarity, draws attention, and makes procedural suggestions. Groups that follow the input–process–output model generate decisions that their members believe are superior. However, groups that experience more processing (have more time to converse and comment, engage in more communication) are more satisfied with group procedures. When the emphasis is on task, the quality of outcome seems higher, and when it is on process, climate or socioemotional feelings are higher (Jarboe, 1988).

This study addresses one of the controversies regarding small group (meeting management) processes. Do groups produce better decisions, and are members more pleased by what they accomplish if they have extensive communication? One assumption is that small group members voice opinions and scrutinize ideas; the opposite view is that too many comments bore members because a few people dominate the group, thereby lessening the likelihood that group decisions are superior to individual decisions. One study found that open discussion and exchange of information and ideas produces better and more satisfying decisions than do group interactions that limit the amount of communication (Burleson, Levine, & Samter, 1984).

Members of groups may have to negotiate the conclusions and decisions they achieve. During negotiation, they may use integrative (seeking to maximize wins for everyone in the group) tactics instead of distributive strategies (have some persons lose so others can win). If they use integrative strategies, they believe that they make better decisions than if they use distributive tactics (Jablin & Krone, 1994).

Does all communication help groups, or are some types of communication more useful than others? As proposed by the functional view of group processes, the answer seems to be that certain types are valuable, whereas others do not meet group needs to make sound decisions. Hirokawa (1985, 1988) found that a group must exhibit decision skills for weighing alternative decisions. Communication is best when it helps members understand the problem, develop and share requirements for an acceptable choice, and assess positive and negative qualities of alternative choices. In their efforts, groups demonstrate a rational ability to adapt their decision processes to the contingencies of the decision (Poole & Roth, 1989).

Such analysis has taken on new meaning with the invention of computer-assisted decision systems. As new communication technologies become more widely utilized, especially by global companies, they offer many new ways for people to hold meetings. Even when people meet face to face, they may employ computer programs to guide their decision making. However, such aids do not necessarily increase the precision or quality of the decision process. When the group believes that it is being orderly and logical in its decision making, it enjoys a higher level of satisfaction with its decision (Poole & Holmes, 1995).

Videoconferences are another technological innovation. Employees can see each other on television screens during a meeting. Such technology does not result in qualitatively different decisions. When individuals only experience their coworkers via videoconferences, they form a less positive impression of them. They base those impressions on features that are emphasized by television, such as facial characteristics and the ability of videoconference members to engage in appropriate turn taking—not dominate the conversation (Storck & Sproull, 1995).

Part of the impact communication has on the quality of group decisions results from the usefulness of feedback members receive in response to their comments. Feedback in task groups has more impact when it is clear, trustworthy, and presented dynamically, as well as when it fits the mood of the group. Feedback has the most effect when it is expressed in dynamic, assertive language (Ogilvie & Haslett, 1985). Even then, group members may not accurately understand one another's views, even when they think they do (Steeves, 1984).

Although evidence supports the claim that group decisions produce an assembly effect, which leads collective decisions to be superior to individual ones, not everyone believes such is the case. One critic of group processes is Janis (1972), who asserted that decisions often suffer from what he called *groupthink*. Groupthink is used to explain why decisions, especially those made in an attempt to avoid losses, can lead to fiascoes. Under this condition, groups can become so cohesive that their members avoid dissenting opinions.

Groupthink is thought to occur for several reasons:

1. Group members limit rather than increase the number of alternatives they consider.
2. If a position is initially favored by many group members, it is likely to prevail with little or no challenge.
3. If the majority of a group does not favor alternatives early in the decision-making process, those alternatives are unlikely to receive consideration in later deliberations.
4. Rarely do highly cohesive groups seek outside opinions, unless the members believe their ideas will be confirmed.

5. If the group comes to like the opinions that have emerged, it is unlikely to seek ways to disconfirm them.
6. The group can believe that it is invulnerable (Janis, 1972).

Reexamining groupthink, Whyte (1989) argued that these group dynamics are mediating variables, not independent variables. They reinforce faulty decision processes rather than prompt them. According to Whyte, groupthink results because of conformity pressures. Group members employ decision-making schemata to assess the magnitude of losses posed by a decision they must make. In such circumstances, polarization leads group members to attempt to avoid losses even if their decision entails selecting high risk alternatives that are unlikely to be successful.

Another challenge to the proposition that groups suffer from groupthink resulted from a body of studies originally called risky shift, but later referred to as choice shift. The findings of this series of studies focused on a simple, important question: Is the final decision of the group merely an average of the opinions the members held before discussion began, or can the outcome differ from this average by being either more risky or conservative? The answer: The choice can differ from the average of the members' opinions prior to discussion.

Let's think through the situation this way. Imagine that you could calculate what each member of a group thought about some issue that was going to be discussed. (Researchers do this by having respondents mark a scale; the responses are summed and averaged.) Is it not reasonable to predict that group decisions will be the average of all opinions, a kind of predetermined consensus? Despite this hypothesis, research indicates that the final decision tends to be either more risky or more conservative for many reasons.

1. Members' opinions change because of group leaders' efforts (Boulanger & Fischer, 1971).
2. Social comparison in the face of risk taking (people like to be thought of as risk takers; Blascovich & Ginsburg, 1974; Vinokur & Burnstein, 1974).
3. Diffusion of responsibility ("If this decision goes bad, don't blame me; I only went along with the group."; Yinon, Jaffe, & Feshback, 1975).
4. Subjective expected utilities (i.e., through discussion, group members get a better view of the reward–cost ratio. Discussion helps them understand better what needs to be done to maximize rewards and minimize losses; Kahan, 1975; Vinokur, Trope, & Burnstein, 1975).

Choice shift research challenged the assumption that group decisions are necessarily more cautious, the lowest common denominator of risk that group members will tolerate. Indeed, groups are capable of examining a range of alternatives, whether conservative or risky. Kellermann and Jarboe (1987) reasoned that groups help individuals check decisions by generating new arguments that they had not thought of by themselves. In this process, members become persuaded to shift their choice. The best indicator that a shift is occurring is repetition of argument and voiced agreements with arguments. In this way, the group builds consensus.

Because groups continue to demonstrate their usefulness, a small-group technique called quality circles was developed to add another option to foster employee participation in decision making. A quality circle is created when management selects a group of employees and empowers them to suggest ways for improving work design or climate.

Quality circles, Stohl (1987) discovered, are likely to serve an organization best if they are integrated into the organization and are flexible. Circles that span departmental boundaries by drawing members from throughout an organization are likely to have their recommendations accepted. Quality circle members are more likely to believe their efforts are effective if the group is cohesive. This factor does more to foster a sense of involvement and participation than does the circle's location in the organization. Managers are most likely to favor recommendations by circles that are well integrated into the decision network and consist of members with more tenure. Stohl (1986) found that being a member of a quality circle prompts employees to like the climate and feel more integrated into the organization. Circles encourage communication and innovation.

Although quality circles offer many advantages, they cannot correct deeply embedded organizational problems. They improve members' communication and decision-making skills and offer opportunities for advancement, but they do not guarantee increased employee satisfaction (Marks, 1986). They work best when they grow out of an otherwise effective organization, one that has proper structure, supportive management, established decision-making processes, adaptability to change, open communication, and good labor relations (Smeltzer & Kedia, 1985).

Groups do more than make decisions. They help new members assimilate into an organization by teaching its scripts and schemata (Jablin, 1982a). Groups help their members understand the social reality unique to the organization. As a subsystem, they obtain and process information that their members use to understand the corporate culture (Jablin, 1985), including the organization's reward/punishment system and the means by which rewards are obtained and punishment avoided (Hackman, 1976). For this reason and others previously noted, small groups are useful to organizations.

This section addressed research and theory that focuses primarily on group processes. Researchers continue to search to unlock the mysteries of group behavior, especially decision making. In closing, we turn to the sound advice of Jablin and Krone (1994) who pointed to the evidence of a contingency theory of decision development. Under certain conditions, a group's decision paths conform to a traditional, unitary sequence of activities (e.g., an orientation phase, followed by an evaluation phase, followed by a control phase). However, under other conditions, more complex (unitary and nonunitary cycles) or solution-orientation decision sequences are observed. (pp. 643–644)

Such observations conform to the principle of equifinality, that systems characteristic that predicts that different systems can achieve successful outcomes by employing different means. This research also conforms to the standard findings that people form objectives and create plans (with varying degrees of clarity and sophistication) and then set out to implement them in the company of others. Adaptation and interpersonal interaction, then, become key dynamics that do not always work in exactly the same ways.

Groups do work. They achieve beneficial outcomes. They serve as useful focal points for helping us to understand the organizational level analysis.

INTERNAL ORGANIZATIONAL COMMUNICATION: MACRONETWORKS

To this point, our discussion has emphasized subsystems of the organization. Now we address the organization communicating as an organization. This discussion postulates that each organization should enact itself through coherent and cohesive actions and statements that become a harmonious presentation—its voice. If the organization (e.g., a business) does not present itself in this manner, its discordant voices (internal and external) risk destroying itself (Heath, 1994).

Organizational analysis looks at macronetworks and company-wide climate and culture. Organizational analysis is interested in downward, upward, and horizontal communication between members of the organization. Analysis can address strategic efforts, including mediated messages, that each organization uses to communicate with its members. Executives and staff members, such as public relations and human resource personnel, communicate on behalf of the organization through many kinds of vehicles, for instance employee newsletters and policy manuals.

Organizational-level communication can affect the assimilation process. As Jablin and Krone (1987) observed, "From an organizational assimilation perspective the study of communication at the network or organizational level of analysis focuses on how formal and informal organizational communication structures affect and are affected by the organizational socialization and employee individualization processes" (p. 726). Network analysis considers how the size and kind of network affects communication outcomes.

From a network perspective, research might work to understand how kinds and sizes of networks affect the work socialization and assimilation efforts of members. This focus could address factors that influence each worker's efforts and her or his views of the organization, the efforts required for assimilation, along with their costs and rewards. This perspective, Jablin and Krone reasoned, can emphasize the structure so much that researchers lose sight of the fact that it is less of a factor than is the individual's perception of it. For this reason, researchers can consider how communication affects the assimilation process from two viewpoints: "(1) as a process that may vary as a result of formal organizational structure, and (2) as an emergent structuring process that may promote variation in assimilation outcomes (including formal structures)" (p. 727).

How effectively individuals become assimilated into networks is likely to affect whether they assume roles as "linkers" in the network or as "nonlinkers" (Jablin, 1985). Linkers tie networks together; nonlinkers do not. Where individuals are located in organizational hierarchies can affect their perceptions of factors such as openness. Employees at the lower levels of organizations are likely to believe superior–subordinate relationships are less open than do employees at higher levels of the organization (Jablin 1982b).

Throughout networks, information is shared, and influence is exerted in many directions: upward, downward, and horizontally. Distortion occurs during information transmission. Serial transmission effects occur when information is altered at each point of exchange. Each person who receives and sends a message may alter or distort it, by adding or removing detail or by making it more positive or negative. Employees may withhold some or all of the information they have.

Superior–subordinate relationships are focal points for studying the distortion of information that occurs during transmission. Several variables predict whether distortion is likely to occur as people pass information upward or downward. These include supervisor's power, amount of upward influence the supervisor has, subordinate's aspiration for upward mobility, and whether the subordinate trusts the supervisor. The relationship between superior and subordinate as well as the supervisor's communication style are factors. Supervisors who suffer from role conflict (cannot resolve the conflicts in their job) are likely to withhold information from subordinates. If the superior communicates frequently and openly, so does the subordinate. Supportive superiors promote open and undistorted information, as is the case when they are friendly, approachable, and considerate of subordinates' needs (Fulk & Sirish, 1986).

To explain network efforts, Monge (1987) featured several elements: number of people who constitute it, strength of relationships between those people, symmetry (whether the flow of information and exertion of influence is symmetrical or asymmetrical), and transitivity (flow patterns such as how A communicates with B; B communicates with C; in this way, A communicates with C.). Other factors are reciprocity and multiplexity. Reciprocity is high if organizational members experience a balance between giving and taking in their relationships (a positive social exchange ratio). Multiplexity is revealed by examining the interconnectedness and reachability of relationships between people.

Each organization is a complex macronetwork that must effectively distribute information among its members. It is a complex of interconnected inputs, processing, and outputs. Its climate and culture shape the identity and identification of its members who strive for a coherent and unified enactment of the organization. These forces transpire inside the organization. They also give insights into its connections with external individuals, groups, and organizations.

EXTERNAL ORGANIZATIONAL/MEDIATED COMMUNICATION

Research focuses on how communication transpires between a system and individuals, groups, and organizations outside of it. Information and influence flow from organizations as well as come to them from outside stakeholders. Chapter 4 features the effort required as organizations obtain information from outside, from their environment. This environment consists of individuals and other organizations who have information that each system needs to guide and regulate itself. Sometimes the information environment is turbulent; there is so much information and so many changes occurring that organization members have difficulty making sense of what is going on. Turbulent situations require people and systems who have a high information-processing capacity (Huber & Daft, 1987).

An organization's ability to achieve its goals depends on the ability of key personnel to obtain information from outside. This information must be processed and used to correct its plans. Strategic adaptations may include changing goals or selecting new means for achieving them. Without information regarding what is going on outside of itself, an organization might have a false sense of certainty. As the environment becomes more turbulent, more effort is likely to be exerted to reduce uncertainty (Dutton & Duncan, 1987; Dutton & Ottensmeyer, 1987).

Most organizations communicate outwardly, to solicit business, raise funds, notify members of a community, and resolve conflicts. As organizations communicate outwardly, they provide information and influence aimed at shaping judgments and behaviors of people who are not their members. Informational and persuasive campaigns often involve the use of mass-mediated communication, such as print or electronic ads regarding products or services.

The extent to which the organization is in harmony with key stakeholders in its environment can affect its operations. For instance, at one time, air pollution was virtually uncontrolled; then scientists recognized the health hazards associated with it. Activist groups and governmental efforts led to clean air standards. Thus, issue managers may need to observe early in a public policy debate that activist and governmental efforts are being made to change the way the organization is allowed to function (Crable & Vibbert, 1985).

To avert unreasonable regulation of their activities, organizations may respond in ways that can help shape the social reality by which people outside the organization view it and the standards by which it can operate. To do so, they need to engage in several interrelated activities: Plan strategically by being sensitive to public policy issues, monitor issue positions that are important to key publics, know and accomplish the necessary standards of corporate responsibility, and communicate with key stakeholders to achieve mutually agreeable resolution of differences (Heath, 1997). For instance, debates waged over air quality bring together companies, activist groups, governmental agencies, and media reporters and editorialists. From this dynamic interaction emerge the standards by which companies are allowed to operate.

Organizations' efforts to interact with individuals and other organizations may be best served if they employ two-way symmetrical communication (J. E. Grunig, 1992; J. E. Grunig & Hunt, 1984). Communication flows from companies to inform and influence others, but companies also take in information and yield to the influence of others. By using two-way symmetrical communication, an organization can increase trust that it is acting in the interests of others and thereby foster their willingness to act in its interest. Whether the leadership of an organization adopts two-way symmetrical communication depends on its ideology. When public relations practitioners are part of the dominant coalition of an organization, it seems most able to accomplish two-way symmetrical communication (J. E. Grunig & Grunig, 1989).

As organizations communicate with external publics, several factors influence their ability to do so. Persons are likely to become activists (whether for or against a company's interests) when they recognize problems that need to be solved, experience high levels of involvement regarding the issue, and believe that rewards of activism outweigh its costs (J. E. Grunig, 1989). High levels of involvement lead individuals to be more willing to communicate (talk, read, and teleview) about the topic. Persons who are highly involved tend to have more messages about those topics. This is true whether the persons favor or disfavor the issue affecting a company's interests (Heath & Douglas, 1990).

The communication style of organizational members (such as grocery store cashiers) can affect the attitudes of persons outside of the organization. If the effect is positive, those persons become more willing to tell others about the service, such as recommending a grocery store. Even though the service is courteous, however, customers are not significantly more likely to do other favors, such as purchase more products (Ford, 1995).

In conceptualizing organizational communication at this level, you may want to remember that organizations attempt to assimilate into the values, institutions, and expectations of society at large. Organizations attempt to get people who are not its members to support its goals, whether to buy products, donate funds, support public education, or whatever. Organizations are not likely to last long if they attempt to stand alone and are ignorant of or unresponsive to their environment.

CONCLUSION

At first thought, organizational communication would seem to consist of a set of communication activities that organizations have. As Jablin and Krone (1987) observed, however,

> the study of communication phenomena at the network or organizational level is inherently a multilevel form of analysis. In other words, since communication networks are composed of individual communicators (nodes) interpersonally linked to other communicators, it is essentially impossible to examine organizational structures without also considering intrapersonal and interpersonal level communication factors. (p. 739)

For this reason, effort is made to describe the variables and points of analysis that define communication at all levels of analysis in organizations. Through communication, members of organizations, as well as external persons whom organizations affect, form meaning regarding the organization and the quality of their relationship with it. The meaning that is derived will affect behavior of people in regard to and in behalf of the organization. To alter reactions to each organization requires changing what it means for the people it affects.

9

Mass-Mediated Communication

In chapter 2, you were asked to jot down your definition of communication and then reexamine that definition after reading the chapter. No doubt your perception of the term was somewhat altered after being exposed to the various concepts, models, and theories that are involved in the communication process. You quickly realized that no one definition of communication can be agreed on, nor can one process be applied to all types of interaction. The same can be said when trying to conceptualize the term *mass communication*. DeFleur (1970) reminded us that "in the past, the content of the field of mass communication and the directions of its inquiry have been defined by whatever happened to be currently capturing the attention of its more prominent students" (p. xiii). However, we attempt to provide a working definition of mass communication or at least provide you with characteristics that are generally recognized as unique in the process of mass communication. It may be easier to understand by contrasting mass communication with something you are already familiar with: interpersonal communication. You will also notice that many of the theories and paradigms found in chapters 1 and 2 relate directly to our understanding of the mass communication process.

In chapters 6 and 7 we examined how people use communication to shape interpersonal relationships and emphasized the interactional nature of interpersonal communication. Recall that *interpersonal communication* was defined as dyadic interaction, in which people engage to negotiate relationships by using direct and indirect communication that becomes personally meaningful as they attempt to reduce uncertainty about themselves, their partners, and their relationships. From the perspective of linear models, interpersonal communication usually involves a single source (the encoder), a single receiver (the decoder), and feedback (verbal and nonverbal) that occurs between both parties immediately. Interaction occurs. The roles of source and receiver alternate between parties; what one person says can influence future messages. In addition, there is a level of homogeneity between the source and receiver, a common bond or need to communicate.

In its most basic form, the term *mass communication* commonly refers to the process of communicating through a medium to an audience. When you think of mass communication, what immediately comes to mind? Do you think about television, radio, motion pictures, newspapers, magazines, and books? Wright (1986) reminded us that, whereas these are often essential in the process of mass communication, they represent the technological instruments or media used to convey messages and do not constitute the processes involved. Any device that is capable of carrying messages between people can be considered a medium. This would include the telephone, a personal letter, an electronic bulletin board, the Internet, and so on. Mass communication involves distinctive characteristics concerning each element within the communication process, not just the presence or absence of media technologies. You will learn that, for example, a telecast of the popular show "60 Minutes" or the latest issue of *Time Magazine* is an instance of mass communication; a closed-circuit security camera in a retail store or an interoffice memo is not.

Recall that interpersonal communication involves very individualized message "sources"; the source in mass communication usually involves a complex and highly organized media entity such as a national television network like ABC, NBC, CBS, FOX, UPN, or WB, or large publishing concerns such as Gannett or Knight-Ridder. Public access to these media is often restricted (getting to the offices of a network executive is like running a gauntlet, even if you have an appointment), and messages (television programs, for instance) are usually very expensive to produce and distribute, requiring the sale of either air time or space to keep the organization financially viable.

The audience for mass-mediated messages is also special. Typically, it is large, involving too many people for the communicator to interact with personally. Unlike interpersonal communication, there is little or no interaction or feedback from the audience back to the communicator (producers of controversial programs often get few if any complaints from audience members, unless they provide an e-mail address). Audience members are heterogeneous in that the receivers of messages are demographically diverse and are usually anonymous or unknown to the communicator.

The mass communication experience can further be defined with the following terms: public: messages are not addressed to particular individuals; rapid: messages are delivered simultaneously or in minimal time; and transient: messages are usually consumed immediately but can be stored (e.g., in video tape, libraries, or newspaper "morgues").

In discussing the functions that the mass media serve, many theorists rely on a set of four propositions stated by Lasswell (1948) and expanded by Wright (1960, 1986). They postulated that media serve the following functions:

1. Surveillance: surveying the environment and providing newsworthy information.
2. Correlation: interpreting information about the environment and editorializing or prescribing how people should react to those events.

3. Transmission of culture: binding time across generations by educating people about information, values, and social norms.
4. Entertainment: amusing people without necessarily offering any other functional values.

Wright (1986) added that these four functions can also be seen to have negative effects or dysfunctions for both the individual and society. For example, "mass communicated news about impending danger, broadcast to the general public without local mediation and interpretation by someone, may lead to widespread panic (surveillance)" (p. 18). Hearing numerous alternative political or commercial messages may either bring about sophistication or become confusing and lessen the individual's ability to think independently (correlation). "The presentation on a more or less standardized view of culture through mass communication could result in a loss of regional, ethnic, and other subcultural variety and could discourage cultural diversity and creativity (transmission of culture)" (p. 21). And finally, spending too much time on nonproductive entertaining diversions can distract people from useful social participation and interactions and result in their becoming dependent on a medium for all entertainment needs (entertainment). Over the years, narrowcasting has reversed some of these trends.

As we begin our discussion of mass communication theory, remember that these theories are complex and involve many volumes of studies conducted over several decades by diverse researchers. Every theory has its proponents and critics. This chapter is selective in that it focuses on the basic characteristics of the most prevalent theories and processes of mass communication.

PREMATURE PERSPECTIVES ON MASS COMMUNICATION THEORY

Prior to the 1930s, most mass communication theorists assumed that mass media messages were immensely powerful and capable of directly and substantially influencing the values, opinions, and emotions of people within the audience. They embraced the concept of mass society that emerged from the study of the fundamental social changes that had taken place over the last two centuries. Lowery and DeFleur (1983) explained that *mass* in this context refers not to numbers but to a distinctive process or pattern of social organization that occurs when industrialization, urbanization, and modernization increasingly modify the social order. It was thought that, as the populace of the 19th century and early 20th century moved from a rural, agricultural-based society to an urban-industrial society, open communication as a basis of social solidarity between members became more difficult. Psychological alienation and the erosion of traditional social groups resulted in an independent and culturally isolated mass of people. Early theorists assumed that, if individuals were not influenced by social variables but shared the same psychological and emotional makeup, then mediated messages would presumably have a powerful, predictable, and uniform effect on all the members. Tan (1985) added that the audience was best thought to be classified by demographic characteristics such as age, sex, socioeconomic status, and education rather than as members of a social group.

This argument of uniform and powerful direct media effects has, in retrospect, been labeled the bullet theory or hypodermic needle theory, and even later was known as the stimulus–response theory or the theory of uniform influences. Studies conducted after World War I indicated that propaganda and advertising campaigns in newspapers were highly effective in shaping the attitudes, beliefs, and consumer behavior of their audiences. Messages had only to be loaded, directed to the target, and fired; if they hit their target, then the expected response would be forthcoming. Audiences were assumed to act on impulse, emotion, instinct, and basic human nature rather than on reason. In retrospect, the results of many of these studies may have been tainted by the lack of rigorous methodology and the absence of accumulated empirical evidence; or, the results may have come about because of the naivete of the mass audience, whose members were unaccustomed to mediated messages. Regardless, proponents of the bullet theory are with us even today. Critics of the mass media continue to claim that the highly institutionalized and omnipotent mass media exercise a powerful influence over a passive, trusting, and vulnerable consumer, despite decades of research evidence that indicates that the relationships between mass media messages and audiences are seldom simple and direct.

Television is perhaps the favorite target of such critics today, although the Internet seems to be gaining ground in the race for the medium that attracts the most criticism. Television has been accused of inciting riots, promoting crime and violence, encouraging illicit sex, promoting alcohol and drug abuse, reducing the populace to a nation of mindless "couch potatoes," creating a nation of obese and passive illiterates, and breaking up the nuclear family. Granted, television may have some influence on some people some of the time, but television and other mass media obviously do not affect all people in the same manner all of the time.

It is, in fact, this realization that prompted many psychologists and social psychologists in the 1930s and 1940s to focus their research attention on the widely divergent reactions of individuals to the same media content. It was soon discovered that audience members were not passive receivers of information, but rather they were active, and various intervening variables affected their reactions to messages. Researchers began to emphasize the individual differences in audience needs, attitudes, values, motivations, and moods, as well as the psychologically oriented personality variables of audience members. It was found that these differences, as well as environmental factors, greatly influenced individuals' perceptions of the world and caused them to react in distinctly individual ways (DeFleur, 1970). Although mediated messages were believed to influence the individual, the effects were not as powerful, indiscriminate, and predictable in this model. Human nature was not uniform; rather it was comprised of diverse, complex, and highly integrated psychological characteristics. The question before researchers was not only what were the effects of mass-mediated messages, but how and why were particular media selected, and what factors influenced the selection of one medium or message over another?

Much of the early theory building at this time came from the then rapidly growing field of psychology. Experiments in behaviorism, motivation, persuasion, and conditioning led researchers to examine the processes of habit formation and learning. Differences among individual personality traits and psychological organization were found to be affected by the social environment in which people were raised. Moreover, studies in human perception showed that an individual's values, needs, beliefs, and attitudes were instrumental in determining how stimuli are selected from the environment and the way meaning is attributed to those stimuli within an individual's frame of reference (DeFleur, 1970).

From these findings, the concept of selective attention or exposure, selective perception, and selective retention were formulated to explain how individuals contend with the multiplicity of mediated messages that are available. DeFleur (1970) concluded that selective attention and perception are intervening psychological mechanisms that modify the stimulus–response model of mass communication. Individual audience members were found to selectively attend to messages, "particularly if they were related to his interests, consistent with his attitudes, congruent with his beliefs, and supportive of his values" (p. 122). Similarly, it was found that individuals tended to avoid communication that was contrary to their interests, attitudes, beliefs, and values. For example, if you were an avid sports fan and were given the opportunity to watch either the Super Bowl or a PBS documentary on the migration of the snow goose, you would probably be inclined to watch the football game. Message selection was not found to be random; in addition, much media selection was quite purposeful and deliberate.

Selectivity continues after the individual chooses which messages will be selected. Selective perception is the tendency for people to adapt mediated messages to fit their own preferences. Perception has been defined as a "complex process by which people select, organize, and interpret sensory stimulation into a meaningful and coherent picture of the world" (Berelson & Steiner, 1964, p. 88). Perception can be influenced by a myriad of psychological factors, including predispositions based on past experience, cultural expectations, motivations, moods, and attitudes. These factors can cause individuals to misperceive and misinterpret messages, so the communicator cannot assume that all receivers will extract the same meaning from the same message.

The process of selective retention or recall reveals that people tend to remember messages they consciously perceive and accept rather than those they consciously reject. Factors that influence this phenomenon include the following: whether the messages are consistent with prior attitudes and experience, the importance of the message for later use, the intensity of the message, and the medium used to receive the message. As with selective perception, selective retention also involves the distortion of the intended message. The audience may adapt the message and retain it in a form that best suits individual member needs.

Concurrent with the studies of selectivity and perception of individuals in the field of psychology, another group of social scientists, primarily sociologists, began to look at the various characteristics in common with people within social groups. Called the *social-categories perspective,* it assumed that people in various positions of the social structure shared the same demographic characteristics and would have similar reactions to mediated messages. Variables such as age, sex, income, education, religious affiliation, and ethnic background seemed to have a powerful influence on the type of communication content selected from the various media options available. For example, most prosperous urban males may prefer reading *The New York Times,* whereas most adolescent girls may prefer reading magazines like *Seventeen* (Black, Bryant, & Thompson, 1998). Also, people from different demographic categories might use the same medium or content for different reasons

AN EARLY INTERPERSONAL TWIST IN MASS COMMUNICATION RESEARCH

However, sociologists continued to assume that members of any given social group were isolated from each other and that interaction occurred only indirectly via the media. Public opinion or mass behavior was considered the summation of individual decisions of persons within each social group. Although they produced a substantial number of studies categorizing the usage patterns and knowledge acquisition of various social groups, researchers did not consider other variables that were affecting the communication process.

This was to change with a 1940 voting study conducted by Lazarsfeld, Berelson, and Gaudet in Elmira, New York, published under the title *The People's Choice* (1948). Originally the researchers had set out to compare the effectiveness of radio to that of newspapers and magazines in influencing public opinion during the 1940 presidential campaign. After several months of conducting personal interviews, it became apparent that, whereas newspapers and radio had some influence on public opinion, it was through interpersonal contacts that most people received most of their influence.

This accidental finding was significant in that it indicates that interpersonal communication about mass media messages was taking place and was modifying media effects. Recall that, in the original stimulus–response model, mediated messages were communicated from the source to an independent receiver in what was perceived as a single, linear process. Now it appeared that, not only were people talking about the election, but certain individuals began to surface as "opinion leaders." These opinion leaders were heavy users of the available media who would pass information along to their peers who had lesser or no media exposure or less expertise on the topic in question. These opinion leaders, in retransmitting the media messages to their associates, often included, gratis, their own interpretation of the information they had received. Thus was born the concept of the two-step flow of mass communication.

Prominence in the community was not a requisite qualification for opinion leaders; they were found at all levels of the social structure. Friends' and acquaintances' perceptions of one's expertise on a subject and the confidence of peers were key characteristics of opinion leaders. Subsequently, the role of opinion leader could change with any given topic. Lowery and DeFleur (1983) added that

> personal influence from opinion leaders was more likely to reach the undecided and the uninterested voter, both of whom were all but impervious to the political campaign presented via the media. . . . Opinion leaders were also likely to be trusted as a nonpurposive source of information and interpretation. (p. 109)

In addition, because the exchange of information was likely to take place in a social situation, the opinion leader was able to respond to questions and make counterarguments throughout the discussion; something that the mass media were unable to do.

The concept of two-step flow and other findings contained in *The People's Choice* were instrumental in guiding future research into the limited-effects model of mass communication and the role of interpersonal processes in communication. However, the recognition of several shortcomings would later expand the two-step flow into a multistep flow. One limitation is that the study was conducted over a relatively short period of time and dealt exclusively with a highly political matter. Also, access to the mass media was limited, and the introduction of television, our most prevalent mass medium today, was still years away.

Later studies concluded that the influence of opinion leaders was not always "downward," as in the interpretation of news events for a less informed audience. Opinion leaders were found to communicate "upward" to the media gatekeepers (i.e., newspaper editors and radio programmers), as well as share information "sideways" with other opinion leaders. Further studies of interpersonal communication showed that an individual's personal identification with an organization, religion, or other social group has a strong influence on the type of media content selected (recall selective attention, perception, and retention). Group norms apparently provide a type of "social reality" check built on similar and shared beliefs, attitudes, opinions, and concerns that tend to form barriers against mediated messages contrary to the group's point of view. Likewise, mediated messages in agreement with the group or provided by the group are usually attended to and utilized to reinforce the status quo.

In addition, research conducted by Merton in the late 1940s sought to determine the characteristics of "community influentials" or opinion leaders in a small eastern community. Merton identified two types of opinion leaders: the local influential and the cosmopolitan influential (Wright, 1986). The local influential was usually found to be born in or near the community, interested in local activities, concerned with knowing a wide variety of townspeople, have membership in voluntary associations, and take an interest in local newspapers and radio broadcasts. In contrast, the cosmopolitan influential was usually a newcomer to the town, was interested in national and international affairs, had a restrictive circle of friends on the same status level, belonged to specialized or professional associations, and sought media messages that reduced feelings of cultural isolation and helped maintain expertise on nonlocal matters.

Merton found that local influentials are most likely to have influence over a wide variety of people in various topics, whereas cosmopolitan influentials are restricted to a specific field in which they are considered expert.

SOCIAL COGNITIVE THEORY AND SOCIAL LEARNING THEORY

One theory in particular reappears time and again in media effects literature. It serves as the theoretical basis for many other media effects theories, including those in the critical and highly scrutinized area of media violence. For this reason, an acquaintance with this important theory, called social cognitive theory, is essential for a basic comprehension of media effects.

Social cognitive theory identifies the mental processes at work whenever learning takes place. It provides a framework that allows us to analyze the human cognitions (or mental functions) that produce certain behaviors. The theory emphasizes a process of triadic reciprocal causation that determines thought and actions (Bandura, 1994). The interaction and variable influence of three factors are involved: (a) behavior; (b) personal characteristics such as cognitive and biological qualities (e.g., IQ, sex, height, or race); and (c) environmental factors or events.

Social cognitive theory is a more comprehensive extension of social learning theory, which Bandura (e.g., Bandura & Walters, 1963) advanced in the 1960s.

Social learning theory emphasizes the interaction of cognitive, behavioral, and environmental factors in determining behavior. These two theories, social cognitive and social learning, have served as the theoretical bases for much research in the various areas of media effects study, including media violence, prosocial effects, entertainment effects, and persuasion.

Social learning theory (also referred to as observational learning or modeling theory) remains one of the most widely used theories of mass communication today. (See chap. 5, this volume, for an extensive discussion of this theory.) Tan (1985) stated that social learning theory explains how we learn from direct experience as well as by observing and modeling individuals and events we see in the mass media; behavior is the result of both environmental and cognitive factors. Bandura's original studies found that, under certain circumstances, children can learn aggressive behavior on television. If aggressive behavior is attended to, cognitively retained, and perceived as beneficial, it increases the probability that the children may model this behavior at a future time. Although commonly used to study how children learn aggressive behavior from watching television, learned prosocial behavior has also been observed.

There are several components to the social learning process (e.g., Bandura & Walters, 1963; Tan, 1985). An individual must first be exposed to and attend to an event or the behavior of an individual, either directly or symbolically via television or other media. Events or behavior that are simple, distinctive, elicit positive feelings, and are observed repeatedly are most likely to be modeled. Several characteristics of the observer may also influence attention (see Fig. 9.1). These are the capacity to mentally process information, usually related to age and intelligence; perceptual set as determined by needs, moods, values, and previous experiences; past reinforcement, both positive and negative, from attending to the same or similar events; and often the arousal level of the individual.

Next, an individual must be capable of mentally retaining the observed behavior or event. This is accomplished by visual imagery or the storing of mental pictures of observations, and by representing symbolically events using verbal codes or a common language. In addition, because most behaviors that are learned are not immediately performed, an individual must be able to cognitively rehearse the experience before actively repeating it.

The third step is behavioral enactment. An individual must possess the cognitive and motor skills necessary to initiate the learned behavior. Repetition, self-observation, and feedback from others are helpful in refining an accurate reproduction of the desired behavior.

Finally, the individual must be motivated to perform the learned behavior (see Fig. 9.2). Bandura stated that reinforcement is the key to motivation and will increase the probability that a behavior will be modeled. External reinforcements are the actual rewards or the expectation of rewards such as praise, social approval, and prestige. Vicarious reinforcement or observing others being

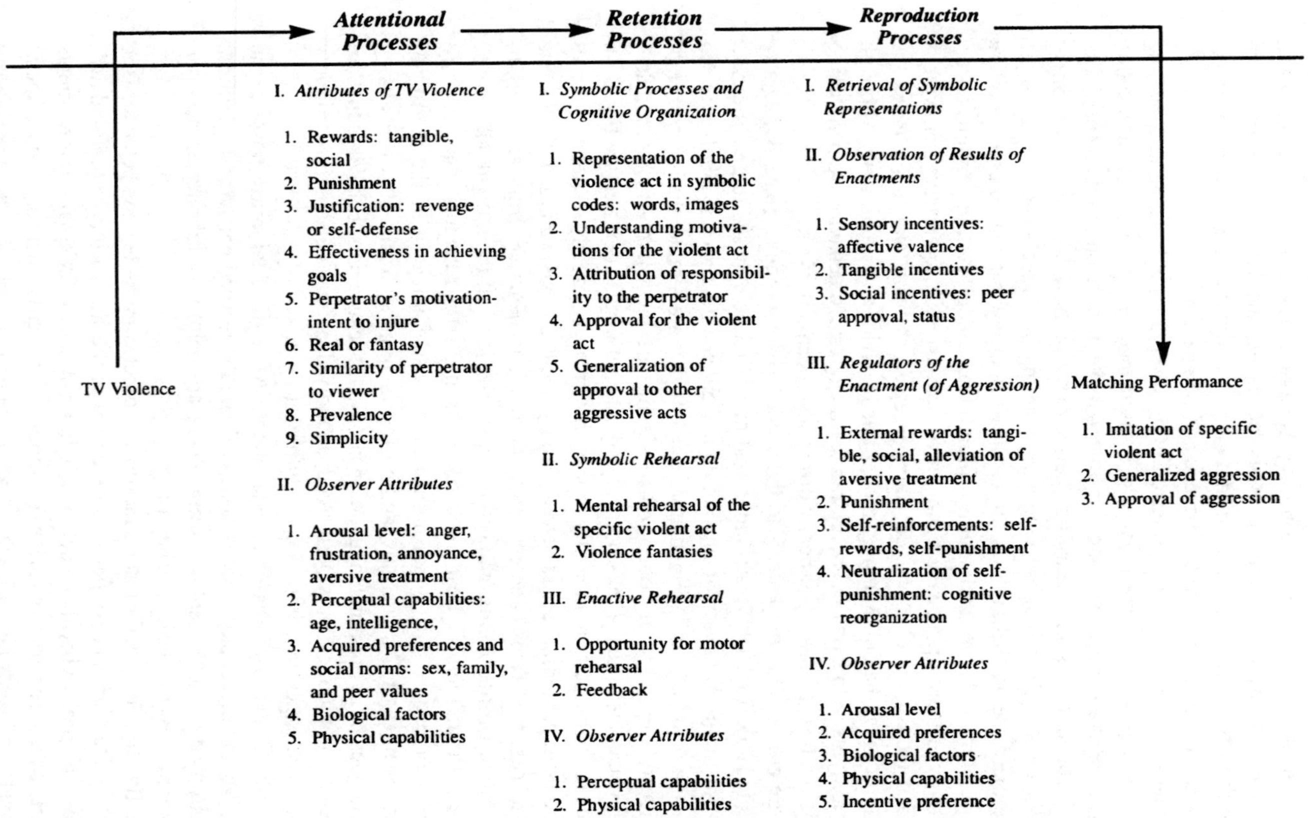

Attentional Processes	*Retention Processes*	*Reproduction Processes*	Matching Performance
I. Attributes of TV Violence	I. *Symbolic Processes and Cognitive Organization*	I. *Retrieval of Symbolic Representations*	1. Imitation of specific violent act
1. Rewards: tangible, social	1. Representation of the violence act in symbolic codes: words, images	II. *Observation of Results of Enactments*	2. Generalized aggression
2. Punishment	2. Understanding motivations for the violent act	1. Sensory incentives: affective valence	3. Approval of aggression
3. Justification: revenge or self-defense	3. Attribution of responsibility to the perpetrator	2. Tangible incentives	
4. Effectiveness in achieving goals	4. Approval for the violent act	3. Social incentives: peer approval, status	
5. Perpetrator's motivation-intent to injure	5. Generalization of approval to other aggressive acts	III. *Regulators of the Enactment (of Aggression)*	
6. Real or fantasy	II. *Symbolic Rehearsal*	1. External rewards: tangible, social, alleviation of aversive treatment	
7. Similarity of perpetrator to viewer	1. Mental rehearsal of the specific violent act	2. Punishment	
8. Prevalence	2. Violence fantasies	3. Self-reinforcements: self-rewards, self-punishment	
9. Simplicity	III. *Enactive Rehearsal*	4. Neutralization of self-punishment: cognitive reorganization	
II. Observer Attributes	1. Opportunity for motor rehearsal	IV. *Observer Attributes*	
1. Arousal level: anger, frustration, annoyance, aversive treatment	2. Feedback	1. Arousal level	
2. Perceptual capabilities: age, intelligence,	IV. *Observer Attributes*	2. Acquired preferences	
3. Acquired preferences and social norms: sex, family, and peer values	1. Perceptual capabilities	3. Biological factors	
4. Biological factors	2. Physical capabilities	4. Physical capabilities	
5. Physical capabilities		5. Incentive preference	

TV Violence

FIG 9.1. A model of social learning of aggression from television. From Tan (1986). Reprinted by permission.

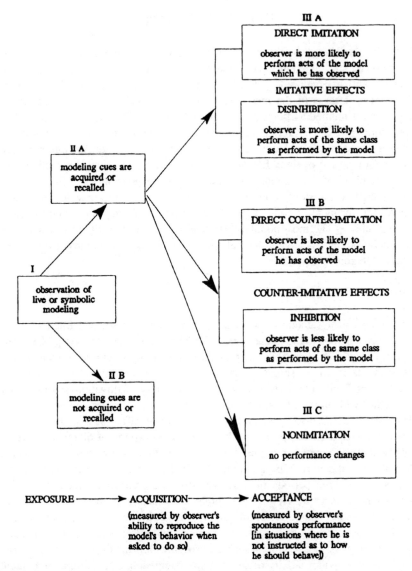

FIG 9.2. Schematic of the steps involved in social learning. From Liebert, Neale, and Davidson (1973). Reprinted by permission.

reinforced for certain behavior can also motivate similar behavior. Lastly, self-reinforcement can occur by internal rewards such as self-satisfaction.

Lowery and DeFleur (1983) pointed out an important distinction between the acquisition of new behavior and the acceptance of new behavior. Acquisition is the ability to reproduce a previously unfamiliar response, whereas acceptance is the actual performance of the same or similar response.

STALAGMITE THEORIES

With the decline of hypodermic needle theories and the inclusion of more interpersonal and social group considerations into mass communication theories, social scientists began to look to more complicated theoretical models to explain the effects of mass media messages on their audiences. One of the dominant perspectives on media effects during the 1970s and 1980s was that the impact of consuming media messages is very real and, potentially, of critical psychological and social consequence, but the effects are cumulative and transpire unnoticeably over a long period of time. Black et al. (1998) referred to such perspectives via the metaphor of stalagmite theories, suggesting that media effects occur analogously to the slow buildup of formations on cave floors, which take their interesting forms after eons of the steady dripping of limewater from the cave ceilings above. The most popular "name brand" theory that fits this perspective is cultivation theory. Several formulations of socialization theories also seem to fit this category.

Cultivation Theory

The prototypical stalagmite perspective concerning the societal impact of the mass media can be found in the work of Gerbner and his associates (e.g., Gerbner, Gross, Morgan, & Signorielli, 1986). Cultivation theory, or cultivation analysis in its most basic form, suggests that television is responsible for shaping, or "cultivating," viewers' conceptions of social reality. Cultivation theory is not concerned with any one type of media content or with a specific immediate effect. The theory states that concentrating on individual differences and immediate change misses the main point of television: the absorption of divergent currents into a stable and common mainstream (p. 20). Rather, "the pattern that counts is that of the total pattern of programming to which entire communities are regularly exposed over long periods of time" (p. 19). The combined effect of massive television exposure by viewers over time subtly shapes the perception of social reality for individuals and, ultimately, for our culture as a whole. The highly stylized, stereotyped, and repetitive messages and images portrayed by television have become our most common source of socialization and everyday information. "Television provides a daily ritual of highly compelling and informative content that forms a strong cultural link between elites and the rest of the population" (p. 18). Gerbner called this effect *mainstreaming,* or the homogenization of our perceptions of social reality, and argued that it results in significant personal and social consequences. In the words of Gerbner et al. (1986), "Mainstreaming means that television viewing may absorb or override differences in perspectives and behavior that stem from other social, cultural, and demographic influences. It represents a homogenization of divergent views and a convergence of disparate viewers" (p. 31).

Through content analysis of prime-time television, Gerbner and his associates found that the television world does not necessarily mirror the real world. Discrepancies included the following: three times more male characters than female; few minority characters, usually portrayed in minor roles; misrepresentation of various social groups such as the elderly; and a preponderance of violent media content. Gerbner argued that repeated viewing of such portrayals contributes to the development of particular beliefs about the world and reinforces those beliefs once they are established. One such belief was termed the "mean world syndrome," or the belief, acquired by massive exposure to violent media fare, that the world is a mean and dangerous place, which can instill in people a fear of violent crime (Gerbner et al., 1986, p. 28).

Cultivation analysis recognizes the "cultivation differential" between light viewers and heavy viewers. Heavy viewers are more likely to be influenced by television viewing than are light viewers. In addition, Gerbner and his colleagues (Gerbner et al., 1986) "observed a complex relationship between the cultivation of general orientations or assumptions about facts of life and more specific personal expectations . . . . Television may cultivate exaggerated notions of the prevalence of violence and risk out in the world, but the cultivation of expectations of personal victimization depends on the neighborhood of the viewer" (p. 29). Likewise, social interaction and prior knowledge of the subject matter can also influence the acceptance of television reality.

In spite of its prominence, cultivation theory has not been without its critics. Some researchers have attempted to replicate cultivation studies and failed to support their findings; others have questioned the dominant methodologies of cultivation research. For example, Hirsch (1979) questioned the differences found between heavy and light viewers when controls for demographic and social characteristics are used. Hughes (1980), another critic, also tried and failed to replicate Gerbner's findings when strict statistical controls for extraneous variables were in place. Gerbner and his associates, of course, disagreed with these criticisms.

Regardless of the debate, cultivation theory has made a valuable contribution by emphasizing the totality of the television viewing experience. Rather than focusing on the impact of a single mass-mediated message, concentration is placed on the effect of the cumulative exposure pattern and the homogeneity of media fare.

Socialization Theories. Numerous other scholars have conducted research that has shared, either explicitly or implicitly, many of the perspectives of what we are calling *stalagmite theories.* Some of this research might be identified generically as socialization theories.

One important and expansive body of literature that tends to fit under this rubric looks at the effects of advertising on young children. A descriptive title from one volume in this tradition is *How Children Learn to Buy* (Ward,

Wackman, & Wartella, 1977). For obvious reasons, most of the research in this tradition has focused on television.

A glance at several of the assumptions that distinguish this literature indicate why it fits under the category of stalagmite theories. First, children have been considered to be a special audience, particularly vulnerable to media effects (Adler, 1980), primarily because they have been assumed not to have the cognitive capacity to recognize, as well as to resist, various effects derived from repeated exposure to television advertisements. Secondly, it has been alleged that much of the content of advertising directed to children is for unhealthy or otherwise undesirable products and is, at least, somewhat misleading in the way it is presented (Barcus, 1980). And, finally, it has been first presumed and then substantially demonstrated that children's repeated exposure to the vast number of advertising messages they watch has subtle but powerful effects over their requests for products, on their rate of consumption of products, on their emotional state, and even on the way they interact with their parents (Atkin, 1980). By and large, once children reach the level of cognitive and emotional maturity whereby they can consciously determine the validity of advertising claims and recognize their intent, social and policy concerns, as well as research interest, have greatly diminished. Given the findings in other stalagmite theory domains, it may be invalid to assume that the effects of long-term exposure to advertising will be inconsequential once an individual reaches cognitive maturity.

Many similar perspectives undergird the area of mass communication theory known as political socialization. This category of socialization theory has examined the role of the mass media in creating political awareness and political values among children and adolescents. Because political ideas and values begin rather early in childhood, communication scholars and political scientists have examined the relationships between the content of media message systems used by children and the political norms, values, attitudes, and beliefs to which they adhere (Van Evra, 1998). It has been found that the mass media provide a great deal of the political information children and adolescents receive; moreover, children frequently cite the media as their most important sources of political information and opinion (e.g., Nimmo, 1978). Most of the studies are necessarily of long-term nature, for only a reckless scientist would claim a direct cause–effect relationship between a particular media message and a specific subsequent political behavior. Nevertheless, evidence is accumulating that the media are an important, though subtle, influence in children's definitions of political reality and subsequent political behavior.

Following an extensive review of the media socialization literature, Van Evra (1998) posited a developmental model of media socialization effects. Her model, which can be seen in Fig. 9.3, predicts a range of effects dependent on the use youngsters make of media content, their perceptions of the reality of the content they consume, their amount of media consumption, and the number of information alternatives available in the child's environment. Van Evra predicted maximal stalagmite effects, which she refers to as "drip" effects, when children (a) view for diversion, (b) perceive the media content to be realistic, (c) are heavy viewers, and (d) have few information alternatives available. Empirical tests of complex socialization models, such as Van Evra's, are sorely needed.

A provocative but untested socialization hypothesis has been advanced by Meyrowitz (1985). This author presumed that, for some time now, mass media has been a major force of socialization for children. Two suppositions form the basis for his argument: (a) "book [print] information is still thick and strong, but television now provides children with a large keyhole through which to view the adult world" (p. 151); and (b) "now, children of every age are presented with 'all age' social information through electronic media" (p. 151). He sees the results as an "homogenization of socialization stages" (p. 152). These arguments are closely related to Postman's (1982) thesis that modern mass-mediated reality has led to *The Disappearance of Childhood*. Although such claims by Postman and Meyrowitz are for potent media effects, they too seem to presume a cumulative, gradual buildup of media impact rather than a "big bang" effect from single exposures to media messages. In this way, they too are stalagmite theorists, although it might be argued that, in their views, the monuments of Mammoth Cave were created more rapidly than many of their contemporary spelunkers might imagine, and some might argue that Postman and Meyrowitz see these fascinating stalagmites as more central to the keystone of our "caverns' structures" than do most of us.

AGENDA SETTING

Another influential mass communication theory that deals with media and political behavior, broadly defined, that also rests its case on relatively subtle media effects, is that of agenda setting. McCombs and Gilbert (1986) defined the agenda-setting function of mass communication as the "ability of the mass media to structure audience cognitions and to effect change among existing cognitions" (p. 4). More simply put, agenda setting is the creation of public awareness and concern of salient issues by the news media. The agenda-setting role of the news media has frequently been traced back to the publication of Walter Lippmann's *Public Opinion* (1922) and his argument that the public responds, not to actual events in the environment, but to a pseudo-environment or, as Lippmann described it, "the pictures in our heads" (p. 271). However, it was not until after the 1968 presidential election that this concept was empirically tested by McCombs and Shaw (1972).

Many commentators on agenda setting have stated that the process occurs because the press must be selective in reporting the news. The media employ

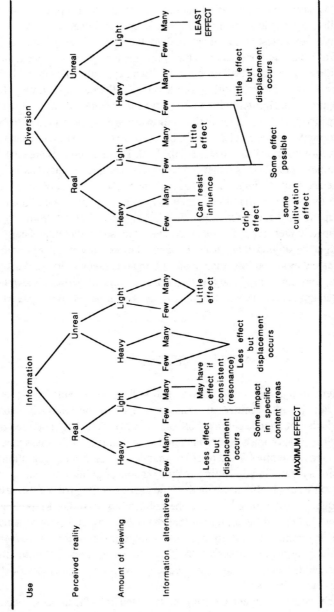

FIG 9.3. A developmental model of media socialization effects. Interactions among use and amount of viewing with perceived reality and information alternatives. Developmental level, socioeconomic level, race, gender, and other factors determine use made of television, reality perceived, amount viewed, and information alternatives. From Van Evra (1998). Reprinted by permission.

professional "gatekeepers" who daily make informal choices about what to report and how to report it. In addition, the media "cue" the public as to which news items are deemed most important. Such cues include the frequency with which the item is repeated, the prominence with which items are displayed (front page or lead story), the length or time allotted for the item, and the framing (in what context and on what occasion the media give attention to an item).

McCombs and Gilbert (1986) stated that "one of the most critical aspects in the concept of an agenda-setting role of mass communication is the time frame for this phenomenon" (p. 8). Determinants of the time frame include: (a) the overall time frame, which is the total period of time under consideration; (b) the time lag, which is the elapsed time between the appearance of an item on the media agenda and its appearance on the public agenda; (c) the duration of the media agenda; (d) the duration of the public agenda measure; and (e) the optimal effect span, which is the peak association between media emphasis and public emphasis of an issue (p. 8).

In addition, there is evidence that, over time, different media have different agenda-setting potential. Shaw and McCombs (1977) found that, in a 1972 political campaign, newspapers were initially more effective in agenda setting than in influencing public opinion. However, television supplanted newspapers as election day grew closer. McCombs concluded that "technological and stylistic differences between the media accounted for the different functions during distinct phases over time. . . . Television news is more like the front page of a newspaper, so that readers have a longer period of experience with an issue than do viewers. But once an issue is on television, the treatment tends to be more intensive and its salience is more apparent" (McCombs & Gilbert, 1986, p. 9).

Lowery and DeFleur (1983) stated that another issue associated with the agenda-setting function of the media is "the degree to which the meanings attached to issues by the public (e.g., perceived importance) play a part in formulating public policy. . . . If the press emphasizes a given topic to a point where the public comes to believe that it is truly important, do political leaders then take action to 'do something' about the issue?" (p. 381). It appears that this may be true, although empirical evidence regarding this complex effect is only beginning to be marshalled in a useful way.

Invariably, when discussing the concept of agenda-setting, one is reminded of Cohen's (1963) statement to the effect that the press may not be successful much of the time in telling people what to think, but it is stunningly successful in telling its readers what to think about.

FRAMING

The concept of framing is related to the agenda-setting tradition but expands the research by focusing on the essence of the issues at hand rather than on a particular topic. A frame refers to the way media and media gatekeepers organize and present the events and issues they cover, and the way audiences interpret what they are provided.

Gitlin (1980) defined frames as "persistent patterns of cognition, interpretation, and presentation, of selection, emphasis, and exclusion, by which symbol-handlers routinely organize discourse" (p. 7). In other words, frames are abstract notions that serve to organize or structure social meanings. Examples of much-used frames include the "war on drugs," or a person's "battle with cancer," or the "cold war," phrases that elicit widely shared images and meanings.

USES AND ENTERTAINMENT

Uses and Gratifications

A number of classic and recent media theories have focused, not on what media messages do to audiences, but on what media users do with media. The most prominent of those is uses and gratifications. Uses and gratifications research assumes that individuals take an active role in the communication process and are goal directed in their media behavior (from which we derive the term *uses*). This approach also assumes that alternate choices are available to gratify the needs or motives of the individual (gratifications or rewards; Rubin & Windahl, 1986).

In a historical perspective, uses and gratifications research began under other rubrics in the 1940s in the few social scientific areas concerned with mass communication (McQuail, 1984). Throughout that decade, empirical mass communication research centered on studying the "effects" of media content, rather than differences in individual gratifications. "Researchers were investigating 'why' people engaged in various kinds of mass communications behavior, such as listening to radio quiz programs and daytime serials, reading comic books, and reading the newspaper" (Tan, 1985, p. 233). Early descriptive research was hindered by both conceptual and methodological limitations. One serious limitation was an inability to determine whether the gratifications sought and the gratifications received were one and the same. Researchers were able to tell who the heavy users were but often were unable to determine what precise gratifications they were receiving from their communication experience. However, these surveys, case studies, and other forms of audience analysis did provide an empirical base from which to build (Black et al., 1998).

In the late 1950s and early 1960s, researchers became disappointed with results of measuring the short-term effects from exposure to mass media campaigns. "It reflected a desire to understand audience involvement in mass communications in terms more faithful to the individual user's own experience and perspective than the effects tradition could attain" (Blumler, 1979, p. 10).

Katz (1959) summarized when he stated the following:

> Less attention should be paid to what media do to people and more to what people do with the media. Such an approach assumes that even the most potent of mass media content cannot ordinarily influence an individual who has no "use" for it in the social and psychological context in which he lives. The "uses" approach assumes that people's values, their interests, their associations, their social roles, are pre-potent and that people selectively "fashion" what they see and hear to these interests. (p. 2)

It is important to note that, during this time, television was fast becoming the dominant mass medium that it is today. Naturally, as with any developing mass media, much skepticism and conjecture concerning television's potential for "good" or "evil" spawned a flurry of scholastic attention.

Throughout the 1970s, many assumptions of the uses and gratifications approach were revised as researchers began to work toward theoretical integration. There are several widely accepted approaches to identifying and measuring audience needs and the functions mass media serve, but most of them adhere to a set of basic assumptions found in Blumler and Katz's (1974) volume, *The Uses of Mass Communication: Current Perspectives on Gratifications Research*. This book was extremely instrumental in conceptualizing the focus of uses and gratifications research. The authors proposed that the uses and gratifications approach concerns the following:

1. the social and psychological origins of
2. needs, which generate
3. expectations of
4. the mass media or other sources, which lead to
5. differential patterns of media exposure (or engagement in other activities), resulting in
6. needs gratification and
7. other consequences, perhaps mostly unintended ones. (p. 20)

Palmgreen, Wenner, and Rosengren (1985) provided a more contemporary view of uses and gratifications research. They mentioned eight important assumptions:

1. the audience is active, thus
2. much media use can be conceived as goal directed and
3. competing with other sources of need satisfaction, so that when
4. substantial audience initiative links needs to media choice,
5. media consumption can fulfill a wide range of gratifications, although
6. media content alone cannot be used to predict patterns of gratifications accurately because
7. media characteristics structure the degree to which needs may be gratified at different times, and further, because

8. gratifications obtained can have their origins in media content, exposure in and of itself, and/or the social situation in which exposure takes place (p. 14).

Although audience activity is a central theme throughout uses and gratifications research, researchers no longer regard audience members as universally active. Rubin (1994) analyzed the work of several researchers and suggested several influences:

> Activity depends, to a large extent, on the social context and potential for interaction. Elements such as mobility and loneliness are important. Reduced mobility and greater loneliness, for example, result in ritualized media orientations and greater reliance on the media. Attitudinal dispositions such as affinity and perceived realism are also important. Attitudes filter media and message selection and use . . . .These attitudes, which result from past experiences with a medium and produce expectations for future gratification-seeking behavior, affect meaning. (p. 427)

In the study of uses and gratifications, the seeking of gratifications is seen as a significant determinant of an individual's exposure to mass communication. Early uses and gratifications research indicated that newspapers, radio, and television seemed to connect individuals to society, whereas books and cinema appeared to cater to more "selfish" needs such as those dealing with self-fulfillment and self-gratification. Further research, however, led to the argument that the same set of media materials was capable of serving a multiplicity of audience needs. The contemporary view is that the relationship between the content of specific media and the needs of audience is rather complex. Experiences with the media are probably highly individualized, and the utility of particular media content is unique to the consumer (Black et al., 1998).

Tan (1985) stated that "the uses and gratifications model begins by attempting to classify human needs into distinct and theoretically meaningful categories" (p. 235). Rather than focus on a lengthy list of specific needs, he cited a typology of media-related needs that groups specific needs into five categories.

1. *Cognitive needs:* needs related to strengthening of information, knowledge, and understanding of our environment. They also satisfy our curiosity and exploratory drives.
2. *Affective needs:* needs related to strengthening aesthetic, pleasurable, and emotional experiences. The pursuit of pleasure and entertainment is a common motivation that can be satisfied by the media.
3. *Personal integrative needs:* needs related to strengthening credibility, confidence, stability, and status of the individual. They are derived from the individual's desire for self-esteem.
4. *Social integrative needs:* needs related to strengthening contact with family, friends, and the world. These are based on an individual's desire for affiliation.

5. *Escapist needs:* needs related to escape, tension release, and desire for diversion (pp. 235–236).

One approach that has advanced the understanding of why people use mass media the way they do integrates expectancy-value theories within the uses and gratifications framework. (Recall that this theory is discussed in chap. 5, this volume; there it is applied to a broad array of decisions, whereas here it is used to explain media selection.) In regard to media selection, Rayburn and Palmgreen (1984) stated the following:

> The concept of audience expectations concerning the characteristics of the media and potential gratifications to be obtained is essential to the uses and gratifications assumption of an active audience. If audience members are to select from among various media and nonmedia alternatives according to their needs, they must have some perception of the alternatives most likely to meet those needs. (p. 538)

Expectancy-value theory suggests that "people orient themselves to the world according to their expectations (beliefs) and evaluations" (Littlejohn, 1989, p. 275). Utilizing this approach, behavior, behavioral intentions, or attitudes are seen as a function of "(1) expectancy (or belief)—the perceived probability that an object possesses a particular attribute or that a behavior will have a particular consequence; and (2) evaluation—the degree of affect, positive or negative, toward an attribute or behavioral outcome" (Palmgreen, 1984, p. 36).

From an expectancy-value perspective, Palmgreen has constructed a process model of gratifications sought and gratifications obtained that states that

> the products of beliefs (expectations) and evaluations influence the seeking of gratifications, which, in turn, influence media consumption. Such consumption results in the perception of certain gratifications obtained, which then feed back to reinforce or alter an individual's perceptions of the gratification-related attributes of a particular newspaper, program, program genre, or whatever. (pp. 36–37)

Palmgreen's formula for this generalized orientation to seek various gratifications parallels that of the general expectancy-value formula and is stated:

$$\sum_{i=1}^{n} GS_i = \sum_{i=1}^{n} b_i e_i$$

In other words, if an individual evaluates information about football and believes (expects) that the Entertainment Sports Programming Network (ESPN) would best supply that information, he or she will be motivated to seek such information from ESPN, as is explained in Fig. 9.4. If the individual obtains the expected information about football (gratifications obtained), it should feed back in a cyclical process to reinforce previous beliefs about ESPN being a good source of information. In addition, if the individual obtains football information at a higher or lower level than expected, it should produce a subsequent change in beliefs about ESPN as well as affect the motivation to seek football information from that source. Thus, the combination of beliefs and evaluations developed via this process about a program, a program genre, the content, or a specific medium could be either positive or negative. If positive, it is likely that the individual would continue to use that media choice; if negative, then one would avoid it.

However, although expectancy-value theory can be used to explain central concepts in uses and gratifications research, there are other factors that influence the process. Palmgreen (1984) devised a schematic model that

> integrates what is known about media consumption on the basis of uses and gratifications research and research in other social science disciplines. . . . The integrative model, while taking into account the feedback from gratifications obtained to those sought, also considers (among other things) the social and psychological origins of needs, values, and beliefs, which give rise to motives for behavior, which may be guided by beliefs, values, and social circumstances into seeking various gratifications through media consumption and other nonmedia behaviors. (p. 46)

No single element or concept dominates the model, but, as is indicated in Fig. 9.5, it shows that gratifications sought cannot be viewed in isolation, connected as they are in both antecedent and consequent fashion to a host of media, perceptual, social, and psychological variables. In addition to the expectancy-value approach, several other categories of uses and gratifications research are currently being pursued. Rubin (1994) listed six active research directions:

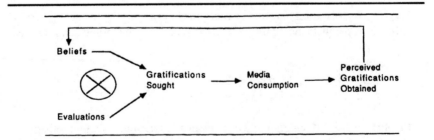

FIG 9.4. Schematic model of expectancy-value theory. From Palmgreen (1984). Reprinted by permission.

1. Links among media-use motives and their associations with media attitudes and behaviors.
2. Comparing motives across media or content.
3. Examining social and psychological circumstances of media use.
4. Links between gratifications sought and obtained when using media or their content.
5. Assessing how variations in background variables, motives, and exposure affect outcomes such as the effects of exposure or motivation on relational perceptions, cultivation, involvement, parasocial interaction, satisfaction, and political knowledge.
6. Methods for measuring and analyzing motivation including reliability and validity.

Although the study of uses and gratifications has been an extremely active media research tradition, especially during the 1970s and 1980s, it has been criticized from its beginning by a host of mass communication scholars. One recurring complaint, voiced by McQuail (1984), is that "no common model, set of procedures or purposes informs the tradition . . . it is essentially lacking in theory and such theory it has is inadequate and confused" (pp. 181–182). That critique seems dated in light of current theory development in this area. Another criticism focuses on social and political objections from the perspective of critical theory, which has depicted uses and gratifications research as "Pollyanaish," in that it tends to view media consumption almost exclusively in positive terms. By focusing on the fact that media meet people's needs, the criticism tends to ignore the overall negative effects of media on the culture.

A final common criticism of uses and gratifications research is that it offers a more rational view of media users than is realistic. This criticism notes that people frequently use media without thinking about their needs and gratifications, operating "mindlessly" or ritualistically. Then when asked to complete a questionnaire, they "rationalize" their viewing in ways that may not accurately reflect their true motives. Rubin (1986, 1994) addressed these criticisms rather convincingly.

Play Theory and Entertainment Theories

Closely related to uses and gratifications research is play theory and entertainment theory. As previously stated, many mass communication theories have originated in other social scientific disciplines. For example, psychological theories, such as learning theories, have been extended and generalized to include media socialization. Freud's pleasure principle, an early theory of psychological gratifications, has been applied to the consumption and enjoyment

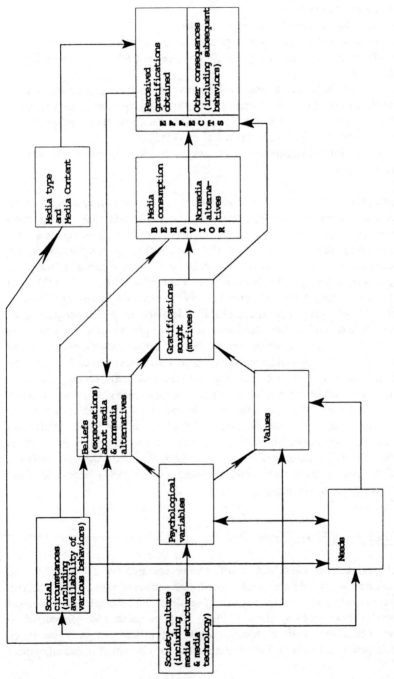

FIG 9.5. Integrative model of uses and gratifications research. From Palmgreen (1984). Reprinted by permission.

of media messages. Freud stated that all activities, psychological and social, are the product of a fundamental need to reduce emotional tension. People are motivated to alleviate disagreeable states that they experience consciously and painfully. Pleasure is a means of tension reduction, and humans seek pleasure from both internal and external sources. The mass media are one source of pleasure readily available in our everyday environment. These pleasure-gratifying situations become learned and recognized, which increases the likelihood of repeating the pleasurable situation. You may recognize that this principle has been incorporated in some of the theories described thus far.

Drawing on Freud's principles, Stephenson (1967) proposed and empirically supported a mass communication theory based on such concepts of pain and pleasure, work and play. Stephenson's play theory maintains that audiences, whenever they are given the chance, will manipulate their media to serve their own needs. In addition, he stated that when pursuing media in their daily lives, audiences are engaged in pleasurable, ritualistic, and self-serving activities that are essentially playlike in nature. Enjoyment and contentment are inherent in activities that allow freedom of choice rather than social control. Play theory and the psychological principles on which it is based posit that individuality is preferable to being forced to work and to conform to the expectations of someone else. In a similar vein, Mendelsohn (1966) added that "when most people are confronted with a choice between deriving pleasure from serious nonentertainment fare or from nonserious entertainment fare, they will choose the latter in much greater proportions than the former" (p. 143).

However, not all communication is characterized by play and pleasure. Purposeful activities expected to elicit a specific reaction from us, according to Stephenson, incorporate elements of work, pain, and social control. The distinction between play and pain rests, not in the communication per se nor in the motivations of the communicators and gatekeepers, but rather in the minds and behaviors of the audiences. For example, a medical student may derive much pleasure from viewing a television drama that includes a scene with a particularly complex operation. In contrast, a humanities student may find the experience distasteful and psychologically painful. Thus, it is the psychological orientation of the consumer that is critical in determining the extent to which that consumer is able to enjoy media content.

An emerging area that shares some concepts with play theory has been labeled entertainment theory (e.g., Zillmann & Bryant, 1986). The research focuses on message and audience variables in attempting to build more cohesive theories of mass entertainment. Such studies have examined the elements within media messages and the psychological and personality factors that, for example, cause viewers to ultimately enjoy a movie after the strain of watching 90 minutes of agonizing suspense sequences capped off with a mere 5-minute "happy ending" (or suspense resolution). A combination of physiological factors (such as varying levels of excitation experienced), and cognitive factors (such as how well the viewers like the resolution of the suspense), help determine the moviegoers' ultimate level of enjoyment of the presentation. Other related entertainment theories have been applied to understanding and predicting enjoyment from televised sporting events, horror movies, music videos, humor and comedy, and various other genres of media fare. Over 30 years ago, Mendelsohn (1966) stated the following:

> What is essential in the psychological study of mass entertainment is the precise discernment of those psychological needs that impel individuals to seek mass entertainment rather than other available sources of satisfaction. Nor will a mere cataloguing of such needs—either a priori or post hoc—suffice. What is called for here is a series of studies that first ascertain specific psychological needs via testing and clinical observation; second, trace the specific pathways, including the mass media, through which these explicitly stated needs are satisfied both temporarily and over relatively long time periods; third, weigh the relative importance of mass entertainment vis-a-vis other "outlets" in satisfying these specific needs; and fourth, determine the over-all consequence of these experiences to the totality of the individual's psyche. (pp. 172–173)

This is a rather tall order that should keep mass communication scholars busy for some time. Nonetheless, entertainment theory seems to be taking some important first steps in this direction.

SEMIOTICS AND MEANING THEORIES IN MASS COMMUNICATION

Throughout our discussion of the various concepts and theories of mass communication, two assumptions have been made. We have assumed that the audience is an active participant in the mass communication process (e.g., selective attention, perception, and retention; uses and gratifications research) and that mediated messages do have some "effect" on the audience (e.g., cultivation analysis, cultural and critical studies, social learning theory, or entertainment effects). Hall (1980) stated that contemporary research in mass communication concentrates on behavior manifestations of communication. It is assumed that meaning is constituted behaviorally or that behavior is meaning made manifest. Hall argued that "before a message can have an 'effect,' satisfy a 'need,' or be put to a 'use,' it must first be appropriate as a meaningful discourse and be meaningfully decoded" (p. 130). He called for increased research into the processes through which mediated messages become meaningful to audiences. Similarly, other researchers have questioned how identical mediated messages may be interpreted differently or in unintended ways by individuals. Such research postulates are not new but are being examined with fresh approaches utilizing both centuries-old and new methods.

Semiotics, or the analysis of signs and symbols, especially in language, has been used extensively in advertising and public relations research. One branch of semiotics attempts to decipher hidden messages and the system of codes through which people communicate both verbally and nonverbally, consciously and unconsciously. Charles Sanders Peirce is recognized as one of the great figures in the history of semiotics and as the founder of the modern theory of signs. Combining the work of Peirce at the turn of the century with more contemporary research by Umberto Eco, Fry, and Fry (1986) attempted to reconceptualize the process of mass communication by utilizing the principles of semiotics. They merge Peirce's concepts of sign and interpretant with Eco's theory of semiotics "in which the process of signification is explained in terms of codes and the production of new signs" (Fry & Fry, 1986, p. 444). Fry and Fry's synthesis and extension of this research attempts to "account for both the media text and the audience's interpretation without reducing the importance of either" (p. 444). Fry and Fry stated that

> it is necessary to adopt an orientation that places total power neither in the media text (as has been implicit in some semiotic textual analyses) nor in the interpretive capacities of the audience member (a position that has been often implicit in the uses and gratifications approach). Thus, a semiotic model must address the question of the relative power of both the text and audience in determining the meaning of media texts. (p. 444)

The following postulate is essential to Fry and Fry's (1986) developing semiotic model: "Mass media messages are textual resources capable of engendering multiple levels of potential meanings. Because signs convey numerous intertwined meanings, that which is normally called a mass media message is, more appropriately, a text capable of producing multiple levels of meaning" (p. 445). Such applications of semiotic theory would seem to hold substantial promise if they retain their focus on the interplay of audiences and the meaning of media messages.

OTHER MODERN MASS COMMUNICATION THEORIES

Recently, mass communication theory has taken many interesting turns. It is beyond the potential of this chapter to represent all the perspectives and theories that currently comprise the body of knowledge of contemporary mass communication theory. Instead, we have selected and present three emerging formulations that we think characterize fruitful lines of representative theory development in mass communication today.

Integrated Theories

One potentially significant development in mass communication theory construction features attempts to consolidate various research perspectives and traditions into more integrated theories. Perhaps the outstanding exemplar in this tradition is DeFleur and Ball-Rokeach's (1989) media system dependency theory of mass communication. This theory is integrative in many ways: First, it combines perspectives from psychology with ingredients from social categories theory. Second, it integrates systems perspectives with elements from more causal approaches. Third, it combines elements of uses and gratifications research with those of media effects traditions, although its primary focus is less on effects per se than on rationales for why media effects typically are limited. Representative of this perspective are statements such as, "The surrounding sociocultural context provides controls and constraints not only on the nature of media messages but also on the nature of their effects on audiences" (p. 234). And, finally, a contextualist philosophy is incorporated into the theory, which also features traditional concerns with the content of media messages and their effects on audiences.

To date, research generated by this model has tended to be more descriptive than explanatory or predictive. Nonetheless, although "the jury is still out" on the place of dependency theory in the annals of mass communication theory, it continues to serve a useful role in casting researchers' gazes upon some of the more molar sociocultural issues that surround concerns with media effects.

Cognitive Theories

A second interesting turn in mass communication theory construction has been an increased emphasis on cognitive dimensions of mass communication. The 1980s and 1990s bore witness to extensive and seemingly productive inquiry into the "black box" of human cognition. Cognitive psychologists and sociologists joined forces with specialists in computer modeling and artificial intelligence to explore more carefully what might be going on in the minds of viewers, readers, and listeners of mass media messages. With this cognitive emphasis came a shift from an examination of effects to a focus on processes, a regular feature of our first mass communication formulations that seems to have been lost during the period of radical behaviorism during which much early mass communication theory developed. With this new focus on cognition came a shift in the nature of researchers' perceptions of communicators. Specifically, that portion of our theories that had referred to passive audiences during the period of the "magic bullet" gradually began to reconceptualize them as active users of media fare, users who have sometimes emerged as the "sovereign consumers" of media messages in today's rich media environments.

One common concern of the cognitive media theorists has been to identify and examine the place of purposeful or goal-directed media use. For example, one cognitive psychologist (Bargh, 1988) concluded that the nature of the media users' cognitive goals are critical in determining more than just what information they receive from media messages: "The type of information one attends to, how much attention one pays to it, how one encodes and interprets it, and consequently how one remembers it all are greatly influenced by one's processing goals while encountering the information" (p. 18). Furthermore, cognitive scientists have posited mental analogs, such as schemas, to explain why we process different types of media fare differently. For example, it has been claimed that well-developed cognitive schemes allow us to process highly repetitive media fare with minimal effort, so-called "top-down" processing; whereas exposure to novel or highly complex mediated information or entertainment requires a qualitatively different sort of process if such fare is to be mastered. Compare, for example, the simplicity of the schema required to follow your 100th episode of "The Beverly Hillbillies" with that required for fully comprehending "Mystery" on public television.

Like Van Evra's (1998) model of developmental socialization and DeFleur and Ball-Rokeach's (1989) dependency theory, many cognitive models of mass communication processes have exhibited considerable complexity and elegance. For example, as expressed in Fig. 9.6, Thorson (1989) presented a model for the cognitive processing of television commercials that includes consideration of goal specification, memory mechanisms, language structure, emotional state, and distraction. Although complexity for complexity's sake certainly is not desirable, what we have learned in recent years about the cognitive processing of mass communication suggests that our models must be complex if they are to fairly and accurately represent the processes undergirding the complex behaviors involved in selecting and using media messages.

Another recent perspective that some consider to be a cognitive-based theory is that of third-person effects on perception. This perspective predicts that people perceive that others, rather than themselves, are more vulnerable to influence from media messages. Studies have revealed that people who perceive themselves as more knowledgable than others on particular subjects are more likely to experience this third-person effect (Lasorsa, 1989). Third-person effects have been found in a number of studies, including those that examined pornography (Gunther, 1995), advertising (Price, Tewksbury, & Huang, 1998), body image (David & Johnson, 1998), message arguments of various strengths (White, 1997), and media orientations (Price, Huang, & Tewksbury, 1997). Such effects have been found to be influenced by the message content itself and by preexisting beliefs regarding particular media messages (Driscoll & Salwen, 1997).

Others have examined the third-person effect in an attempt to understand its theoretical underpinnings. Atwood (1994) found that third-person effects are

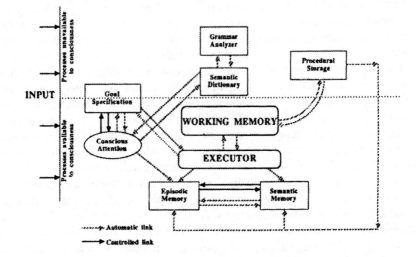

FIG. 9.6. A cognitive model of information processing of television commercials. From Thorson (1989). Reprinted by permission.

based on two theoretical perspectives: social comparisons and cognitive adaption theory. These effects "result from downward social comparisons following from differences in belief in the message, accuracy of information . . . and perception of the beliefs of others about the message" (p. 269). Gunther and Mundy (1993) found that the psychological mechanism of "optimistic bias" accounted for third-person effects. Brosius and Engel (1996) expanded on this finding by identifying two mechanisms in addition to unrealistic optimism: impersonal impact and generalized negative attitudes towards media effects. They wrote the following:

> The concept of unrealistic optimism would predict that media effects described in a negative way will produce large third-person effects because individuals want to preserve a positive self. The same can be expected when subjects are described as passively suffering media effects. Empirically this means that the third-person effect will be smaller if media influences are described as a benefit, or the recipient suggested to be actively controlling the effects. The concept of impersonal impact suggests that the extent of the third-person effect varies with the psychological distance between the first and the third person. If third persons are described as psychologically close, the third-person effect will be smaller. The third concept of generalized negative attitudes towards media effects suggests that, regardless of the description, a third-person effect will always occur because negative predispositions to media influence are so strong that they cannot be overriden by variations in question wording . . . . Depending on the kind of media effects, all three concepts can account for some of the results. (p. 142)

Cultural Studies and Critical Theory

Another set of approaches to mass communication theory that have received considerable scholarly attention of late are cultural studies and critical theory. These approaches to mass communication theory were spawned by European researchers in the 1950s, but it has only been during the past decade that they have captured much of the interest of American communication scholars. Many of these theoretical perspectives have their roots in the Marxist critical tradition, which typically has been seen as having two main areas of focus: the "politics of textuality" and the "problematic of cultural studies." Grossberg (1983) made this statement:

> The politics of textuality concerns the ways in which media producers encode messages, the ways in which audiences decode those messages, and the power domination apparent in these processes. . . . The problematic of cultural studies examines more closely the relation among media, other institutions in society, and the ideology of culture. (p. 52)

These traditions frequently are concerned with the evils and injustices of a ruling elite and a social class system, as well as how the social structure is formed and reinforced via the actions of individuals, groups, and institutions. It is important to note that although proponents of these traditions view the mass media as important and powerful institutions, the media are perceived to be but one influence in a complex social structure that attempts to dominate the ideology of a people. Other influences include education, government, and religion.

One of the prevalent traditions to emerge in this domain is that of British Cultural Studies. Many scholars adhering to this approach have sought to change or reform western society via their scholarship. This change is said to occur by identifying contradictions in society and suggesting resolutions that will lead to positive change.

Many American critical theorists have also seen themselves as agents of social change. For example, via detailed scholarship, they have first identified and publicized how the agents of control—media, for example—have sustained the dominant ideology of capitalism. Such revelations are intended to help people realize how media are instruments of a power struggle controlled by an elite group. Another step that has been taken quite frequently has been to point out to the populace what can be done to shift power back to them. Becker (1984) articulated this role clearly: "These communication scholars want to keep jarring both the audience and the workers in the media back from becoming too accepting of their illusions or existing practices so they will question them and their conditions" (p. 67).

The usefulness of the cultural studies tradition to American mass media studies is evidenced by its growth in prominence. As we have suggested, it is substantially different from the other theories we have discussed. A primary reason for this is that most of its roots are in the humanities, whereas those of the other theories we have reviewed are in the social and behavioral sciences. To some people, this makes cultural studies incompatible with mass communication theory construction. We do not see it that way. We find these diverse positions complementary and ideally reflective of the complexity of the contemporary mass communication milieu. As Grossberg (1983) indicated, cultural studies, "as a theory of communication . . . opens new possibilities for the discipline by interrogating the place of communication within the production of the real, a place that we recently have begun to take for granted" (p. 70).

NEW DIRECTIONS IN MASS COMMUNICATION THEORY AND RESEARCH

Bryant and Thompson (in press) examined the "standard" history of media effects (i.e., bullet theory to limited-effects model to more powerful effects model), reexamined the classic works on media effects, and located some relatively unrecognized but important works that provided a clearer understanding of the actual history of media effects inquiry (e.g., Fenton, 1910, 1911; Klapper, 1960; Stouffer, 1942; Waples, 1942). They identified several points of contention with the standard history and several theoretical and empirical issues that have been obscured by the repetitive recounting of the standard version and the passage of time.

First of all, labels of "powerful," "limited," or "moderate" effects have been the qualitative judgments of individual researchers through the years. Bryant and Thompson (in press) stressed the need for standardized, empirical lines of demarcation based upon statistical effect sizes, percentages of people found to be effected, or some other criterion, that would separate the various levels of effects. They also noted the conspicuous lack of a "no effects" model. Secondly, they determined that findings of "powerful" and "limited" effects can be identified in any period of the history of media effects inquiry; thus the actual history of media effects emphasizes "a body of research that has, from the beginning, found overwhelming evidence for significant effects from mass media communications on audiences, based for the most part upon scientific methods and traditional statistical models" (Bryant & Thompson, in press).

Also, they noted that the generalizations of Klapper (1960) have generally been reduced to supporting a "limited effects" model, yet several of his generalizations clearly state that direct effects from mass media are possible. He repeatedly warned about the danger of blindly minimalizing the potential effects of media communication. Moreover, Klapper seems to be the only media effects scholar who has even attempted to make generalizations toward an overall, blanketing theory on media effects.

Forty years after Klapper insisted that generalizations needed to be made, the challenge remains unmet. . . . The generalizations should sufficiently explain circumstances and conditions necessary for either powerful, limited, direct, indirect, short-term, long-term, cumulative, cognitive, affective, and behavioral effects from mass media communications, and if possible, the factors present in a "no-effects" scenario. (Bryant & Thompson, in press)

A FINAL WORD

Mass communication is a rather young field of inquiry, but, as this chapter has shown, scholars have been prolific in both theory construction and research throughout the previous century. The field has gained academic respectability and public support in recent years, due in large measure to the practical value of much of the research being conducted.

The study of mass communication has developed at a rapid pace, and it will continue to do so. In this, the information age, researchers will be challenged to keep up with the ever-changing media environment and how it may affect individuals or our society as a whole. With a basic knowledge of the theoretical developments thus far, students will be better prepared to understand the opportunities and limitations of mass communication study in today's changing world.

10

New Communication Technologies

T raditional mass communication media such as television and radio are so much a part of our lives that we sometimes fail to notice technological innovations that are changing the nature of media as we know them. Oftentimes, the "early adopters" among us are the only ones aware of these "new media," these new communication technologies. The rest of us simply live life without considering the implications of these innovations. We think that we have all we need in order to be informed and productive, until we are either forced to use the new methods of communicating or until we see direct and personal advantages to making use of them. Once confronted with them directly, we wonder at how suddenly our lives have been altered by a new or modified technology (and also how we ever got along without it in the past). We also tend to take innovation for granted without stopping to give serious consideration to its impact on our lives.

New technologies are also changing the very nature of mass communication processes. In the past few decades, traditional forms of mediated communication with large, heterogeneous, and anonymous audiences (e.g., television and radio broadcasts) have gradually given way to other forms of mediated communication in which audience members have far more potential for feedback and much more "user power." In other words, one-way (primarily), mass communication has been slowly evolving into a more interactive or transactive process. Many of the new communication technologies allow and even foster interpersonal communication as well as mass communication among users. Moreover, the interactive components of certain new communication technologies make it difficult to distinguish between the classic "sender" and "receiver" that for so long were seen to be basic components of the mass communication model.

The characteristics of the new technologies force us to take a step beyond the realm of mass communication. We label this new domain *transactional mediated communication*. Transactional implies a give and take situation—an interpersonal communication relationship in which parties alternate in their roles as sender, receiver, and information processor and thereby exchange information. Mediated signifies that media—technologies—are still involved. In most media systems that support transactional communication, mass communication is also possible. In other words, communication transactions may occur between many users. Any one individual or institutional entity has the opportunity to address numerous other users.

In today's information age, change has become the constant. As we shall see in the next section, the marriage of the computer to contemporary media is causing these sweeping changes to occur before our eyes. Accordingly, scholars are having to change their traditional views of media audiences. We are also having to confront ethical issues and concerns that have not troubled us in the past. Such change ultimately forces us, whether practitioners or as academicians, to revise existing communication theories and models and to develop new ones as the old constructs lose their viridicality. As we enter the new millennium, the continual challenge for communication scholars will be to not only keep abreast of new media technologies as they become available, but also to reconsider prevailing theories and models with a fresh eye and to explicate new and different processes of communication as they emerge.

THE DIGITAL FRONTIER

Among the marvelous accomplishments of human study and genius, nothing, all facts considered, can well be regarded as more important than man's triumph over space and time in the matter of the intercommunication of widely separated individuals and nations.

—(Greeley et al., 1872, p. 1111)

This quote only sounds like something from the 1990s used in a discussion of the wonders of electronic communication. Believe it or not, it is actually a product of the 1870s! The quote opens a chapter called "The American Magnetic Telegraph" in a book by Horace Greeley and others, *The Great Industries of the United States: Being an Historical Summary of the Origin, Growth, and Perfection of the Chief Industrial Arts of this Country.* (Greeley et al., 1872) The quote serves to remind us that "new" communication technologies have been around for some time, and, through the years, people have filled many pages discussing the impact these new technologies have made, are making, or will make on everyday lives.

This leads us to an important question: When we say "new communication technologies" or "new media technologies" at the cusp of the 21st century, what exactly do we mean? Basically, we are referring to communication technologies on the cutting edge; therefore, our definition of new technologies continues to change, or perhaps evolve, as time goes on and new technologies emerge. This makes a discussion of new media difficult at best, when you consider that by the time this book sees publication the new media discussed in it will more than likely be well worn or, in some cases, even obsolete. Media technologies are the consummate illustration of the validity of the claim that in the information age, the rate of change of change is constantly increasing.

If we were pressed to list some of the new communication technologies of today we might start with a list compiled by Rogers "way back when" in the 1980s, which included microcomputers, teletext, videotext, interactive cable television, communication satellites, and teleconferencing (E. M. Rogers, 1986). (Teleconferencing is considered by some to be an application of new media technology rather than a new media technology in itself.) We would add to his list the technologies of high-definition television (HDTV) and other forms of digital television. HDTV provides 1,920 vertical lines of detail and 1,080 horizontal scan lines and offers pictures and sound as sharp and crisp as a movie theater experience. Digital TV, often called interactive television, is the result of the convergence of the television and the computer. This medium allows viewers to click on icons during television shows to get more information, for instance, sports statistics on certain players, or biographical information on stars, and so forth. About 1 million homes in the United States have interactive TV capabilities; by 2005, the number of interactive TV subscribers is expected to skyrocket to 24.5 million (Haring, 1999).

In a recent biblioessay, Marien (1996) surveyed the literature and offered a comprehensive list of new technologies already in place or projected for the future. His list included the likes of voice-access computers, language translators, and 500-channel cable television, among many others. Yet he noted that compiling such lists and discussing their implications proves difficult for several reasons:

> No one has a good, up-to-date grasp of the emerging technologies. The enthusiastic advocates have no communication with the critics and the empiricists. Communications scholars are notably unhelpful, with the vast majority losing themselves in behaviorist trivia and minutia. There are remarkably few journals in this area, and no yearbooks to survey the "knowledge industry" in its broadest dimensions (in contrast, the travel industry has several yearbooks). Futurists and their publications have made many contributions (often on the upbeat/enthusiast side), but still largely focus on single topics rather than broad patterns and frameworks. (Marien, 1996, p. 382)

One of the ways in which communication scholars have attempted to define the new technologies is by describing their essential nature. Dizard (1986) argued that new communication technologies cannot be accurately termed *mass media* by the conventional definition of that phrase. The specialized nature, decentralized products, and interactive format of these new media make them very different from traditional mass media.

Mass media historically has meant centrally produced standardized information and entertainment products, distributed to large audiences through separate channels. The new electronic challengers modify all of these conditions. Their products often do not come from a central source. Moreover, the new media usually provide specialized services for large numbers of relatively small audiences. Their most significant innovation, however, is the distribution of voice, video, and print products on a common electronic channel, often in two-way interactive formats that give consumers more control over what services they want, when they get them, and in what form. (Dizard, 1994, p. 2)

E. M. Rogers (1986) made many of the same points, and some additional ones, using a different vocabulary. He listed several ways in which human communication had changed since the advent of new technologies:

1. All of the new communication systems have at least a certain degree of *interactivity,* something like a two-person, face-to-face conversation....
2. The new media are also *de-massified,* to the degree that a special message can be exchanged with each individual in a large audience....
3. The new communication technologies are also asynchronous, meaning they have the capability for sending or receiving a message at a time convenient for an individual. (pp. 4–8)

Perhaps the best way to come to grips with all the new technologies and facilitate a broad-based understanding of them is to identify the common bond that they all seem to share: their need for broader bandwidths to support digital technology rather than the old analog variety. The conversion from analog to digital has been described as being as significant as the fundamental change that occurred when transistors replaced vacuum tubes (Grant, 1997). Another commentator referred to the changes in broadcast production and transmission as "revolutionary," even though the conversion has been occurring for decades and continues to this day.

The conversion to digital transmission represents the first fundamental change in television broadcasting since color was added to the NTSC standard more than 40 years ago. It is a transition with multibillion dollar consequences for broadcasters who are the first adopters of these technologies, and consumers who will eventually need to replace their analog radio/TV receivers, VCRs, camcorders, and other related peripherals. (Seel, 1997, p. 8)

The key to understanding the nature of digital technology can be found in three *c* words: compression, conversion, and convergence. More information—much more information—can be transmitted and stored using digital technology than the old analog form. In addition, digitalization makes possible the integration or conversion of this compressed information into computer systems and applications. As a result of digitalization, broadcast communications, wireless communications, and telecommunications are converging due to their sudden ability to share information with one another.

The new digital formats require larger bandwidths, or network pathways. Construction of these new networks is already underway throughout the world. Once fully developed, telecommunications will be very different from that to which we are now accustomed. Hodge (1995) described this transformation and its consequences in this way:

> Highly evolved telecommunications networks, interconnected and delivering telecommunications and data services around the country and the world, will enable the delivery of virtually unlimited numbers of channels of video, telephony, switched data, wide area networking, business data links, etc. These networks will carry services (sometimes called video dial tone) including broadcast video, time-shifted TV, Pay-per-view TV, multimedia services, premium channels, video on demand, home shopping, tele-education, interactive games, etc. This interconnected high-performance network is often referred to as the Information Superhighway, or the National Information Infrastructure (NII). (p. xv)

The technological, operational, and functional shifts that are taking place in the communication infrastructure of modern society soon can be felt by virtually every citizen. Already, more than half a million homes in the United States are wired for broadband services, and by 2002, that number is expected to increase anywhere from 7 million to 16 million, depending on the research firm doing the forecasting (Berman & Bunzel, 1999; Bowles, 1998). In the transition period, the conversion box business is booming. About 10 million digital set-top boxes were sold throughout the world in 1998 for digital direct broadcast systems, and about 14 million satellite, cable, and digital television product sales with revenues of $4.7 billion forecasted for 1999 (Brown, 1999). Digital set-top boxes allow people to use existing wiring in their homes to pick up digital signals.

In the future we will have an intelligent network, an advanced information system supported by a spinal column comprised of a fiber-optic-based backbone. In all likelihood, although fiber optic cable will comprise the backbone, the vein-like extensions of the network will also include coaxial cable, telephone lines, and wireless, microwave, and satellite communications. This high bandwidth capacity network will have the potential to deliver diverse, customized functions and incredibly specialized media messages. When media messages are encoded into a digital format, video, audio, and textual messages can be combined in an almost unlimited way. As Brand (1988) wrote quite poetically in *The Media Lab: Inventing the Future at MIT*:

> With digitalization all of the media become translatable into each other—computer bits migrate merrily—and escape from their traditional means of transmission. A movie, phone call, letter, or magazine article may be sent digitally via phone line,

coaxial cable, fiber optic cable, microwave, satellite, the broadcast air, or a physical
storage medium such as tape or disk. If that's not revolution enough, with
digitalization the content becomes totally plastic—any message, sound, or image
may be edited from anything into anything else. (p. 19)

This network of networks currently under construction extends around the
globe. Countries in Europe and Asia are rushing to construct fiberoptic lines so
that they maintain parity with, if not supremacy over, the United States. A report
to the European Union in 1994 emphasized the importance of being among the
first countries to construct information infrastructures (Commission of the
European Communities, 1994). In Japan, one corporation recently announced
plans to wire all schools, homes, and offices in the country with fiberoptic cable
by the year 2010. This initiative should cost somewhere between $150 billion
and $230 billion, according to the country's Ministry of Posts and
Telecommunications. In Singapore, a similar project is well underway by the
island government. Ironically, that same government holds very tight controls on
information access for its citizens (Hudson, 1998).

As some hurry to lay cable, others experiment with radiowave technology,
which avoids the use of wires altogether for broadband network access. In recent
years, a number of wireless products and services has appeared on the market.
Some believe that wireless may lead the way in broadband networking in the
future. One electronics expert wrote recently, "There's every indication that
wireless will begin to take a leading role in the broadband multimedia future"
(Mathias, 1999, p. 6).

The Personal Communications Industry Association's (PCIA) 1998 Wireless
Market Portfolio clearly issued a clarion call for head-to-head competition with
wireline services. After detailing many breakthroughs in wireless during 1998,
PCIA President Jay Kitchen noted, "Taken as a whole, these developments
demonstrate the wireless industry's commitment to challenge entrenched wireline
service providers for every customer in every segment of the telecommunications
industry to bring the benefits of wireless connectivity and true competition to the
world" (PCIA's 1998 Wireless Market Portfolio, 1999, p. ii).

In early 1999, *The New York Times* reported that Motorola, a corporation that
makes wireless products, and Cisco Systems Inc., a major provider of Internet
equipment, were undertaking a joint venture that would result in a wireless
Internet system (Barboza, 1999). The Motorola-Cisco alliance was the latest in a
series of giant mergers that had occurred during the previous year. The article
reported that a number of leading Internet equipment providers and leading
makers of telecommunications equipment were racing to offer greater wireless
Internet access for customers.

A cover story for *PC World* noted that cell phones, beepers, and personal digital assistants are merging, and that powerful handheld devices will soon take advantage of a wireless technology called Bluetooth.

> Set your Bluetooth-capable palmtop device next to a similarly equipped PC, and they'll transfer e-mail and update contact lists at about 1 megabit per second. American Airlines and other airlines are talking about installing Bluetooth stations in airport lounges, so fliers can place their notebooks next to a transmitter and check their e-mail. (Desmond, 1999, p. 116)

Another recent article in *The Chronicle of Higher Education* explored the subject of wireless networks on college campuses throughout the country. Thus far, experimental wireless systems have received mixed reviews among administrators, but some future campus communication infrastructures will include a mixture of wired and wireless technology (Young, 1999). Many colleges and universities are now experimenting with wireless Internet connections that operate via radio-equipped laptops. Students do not have to "plug in" for network access and therefore have more flexibility; they can do their work in a comfortable chair or on a soft patch of grass in the sunshine. The downside of these networks thus far has been the cost (about $400 per student to lease wireless network adaptors) and their connection speed (slower than attachments to network cables).

NEW ENVIRONMENTS

The move to digital communication has resulted in new media "environments" such as virtual reality and cyberspace. As these environments have emerged, scholars have set themselves to the tasks of naming and explaining them and describing their implications for practical use. Virtual reality is a form of communication that takes place between a computer and a person. Biocca and Levy (1995) offered the following illuminating definition:

> Part computer simulation, part 'consensual hallucination', virtual reality offers us the opportunity to surf through information-rich cyberspace; to 'be' in worlds that exist only in our imaginations, more so than we have with other media, and to manipulate (for better or worse) virtual environments, ranging from the smallest chemical compound to the entire surface of a distant planet. Communication becomes simulation. (p. vii)

Many definitions of virtual reality concentrate on the technological hardware, but Steuer (1995) emphasized that the concepts of presence and telepresence should be the key to defining and understanding virtual reality.

Presence is defined as the sense of being in an environment. . . . Telepresence is defined as the experience of presence in an environment by means of a communication medium. . . . In other words, presence refers to the natural perception of an environment, and telepresence refers to the mediated perception of an environment. This environment can be either a temporally or spatially distant "real" environment (for instance, a distant space viewed through a video camera), or an animated but nonexistent virtual world synthesized by a computer (e.g., the animated "world" created in a video game). (pp. 35–36)

Cyberspace is another term that some use to describe a new media technology. Others, however, view virtual reality as the technology and cyberspace as a computer-driven environment. "Some equate cyberspace with virtual reality, others with the electronic storage and transmission of information, or with computer-mediated communication, or with communication over computer networks. Some see cyberspace as an individual conceptual space, others as a product of social interaction" (Strate, Jacobson, & Gibson, 1996, p. 4).

As these new environments become more common among masses of users and their practical value becomes more evident, our definitions of them are likely to solidify. Our conceptual understanding of the communication processes inherent in them or available through their use should become clearer as well.

NEW CONCEPTIONS OF AUDIENCES

The new media technologies are also forcing us to reexamine our traditional conceptions of media audiences and with that a refined view of the mediated communication process. In the previous chapter, we discussed the concept that mass media assumes a dominant to powerful sender and a subordinate to completely passive receiver. New media empower users to become more active in the communication process and to be more selective with regard to the messages they receive. This power makes them active agents rather than passive receivers of information.

The decade of the 1990s has yielded a generation of addressable users of micromultimedia. By addressable we mean that media messages are no longer being sent "to whom it may concern." Indeed, media messages may be selected and downloaded by parties whose names, addresses, identification numbers, and demographic and marketing profiles are a part of the message distributor's data base. The degree of efficiency and profitability such communication systems will provide surely will make them commonplace as the new century dawns, despite the increased expenses of initial installation and start-up.

What we formerly referred to as an *audience* must now be termed *users*. How can we call *an audience* an active aggregate of media users who can and will, by programming a scanner, actively select from thousands of informational, educational, and entertainment options? We cannot. Some have called him or her "the sovereign consumer of the information age." We prefer the less pretentious label of "media user."

Finally, what do we mean by micromedia or micromultimedia? The changes that support this seemingly innocent term are revolutionary. They are also multidimensional. At the core are essential alterations to the communications skeleton of our nation (and, indeed, our world!), a backbone of which many of us are not even aware. This plastic translation of messaging from computers to microprocessors in practically everything electronic is the latest computer revolution destined to affect us all. It's "computers in everything. Everything connected to the Net" (Levy, 1999, p. 58). The fact that the form can readily be shaped to suit the desires of an individual user is signaled by the term *micromedia*.

> The infrastructure has yet to be created—a process that might take nearly a decade— but the vision is well drawn. A mix of broad-band information "pipes" and wireless high-speed data transfer will toss a blanket over our homes, offices and motorways. Your home, for instance, will probably have one or more items hot-wired to the Internet. . . . These would be the jumping off points for a tiny radio-frequency net that broadcasts throughout the house. That way, the Internet would be, literally, in the air. (p. 58)

Certainly the prototypical scenario for typical media use under these new media environments is miles removed from what our intellectual ancestors meant by mass communication.

New Models for New Media

Traditionally, communication scholars have debated the notions of an active versus a passive audience; that is, audience members as a passive mass of people exposed to a mass medium and influenced in some way by its messages versus audience members as active individuals who make purposive selections based on individual choices. As a result of new media technologies, new theoretical models of the audience are moving away from this traditional passive versus active dichotomy. They recognize the different nature of different media audiences.

Webster (1998) made a compelling argument against viewing media audiences as either all passive or all active in orientation and, at the same time, provided an interesting framework for conceiving the audience in today's world of interactive media and transactive mediated communications. He offered three models to describe media audiences, and termed them audience-as-mass, audience-as-outcome, and audience-as-agent. The audience-as-mass model defines audience members as those who have common exposure to a mass medium. With this model, the mass or "the body of the audience" assumes utmost importance (p. 192). Attempts to measure audience numbers have fallen under this category. The audience-as-outcome model focuses more broadly on media effects. Propaganda studies, media violence and pornography studies, attitude change studies, and other media effects studies have fallen within this category. The audience-as-agent model differs considerably from the other audience models. It recognizes the power that new media technologies offer today's audience members. It shows an audience member as an individual who enjoys more personal options and choices whenever consuming media fare. This audience member is more active, more involved in the communication process than ever before.

This brief discussion should help you rethink some of the issues that were raised about the definitions of the components of the communication process in chapter 2. For its time, the S–M–C–R model was fine, but it has to be refined and updated to reflect changes in how people communicate and how we think about the way they communicate.

The beauty of Webster's (1998) conception of audience models is its capacity to classify combinations of the various perspectives of media audiences. He ingeniously uses a Venn diagram to denote the different areas of communication research that conceive of the audience as either mass, outcome, agent, or some combination of the three (see Fig. 10.1).

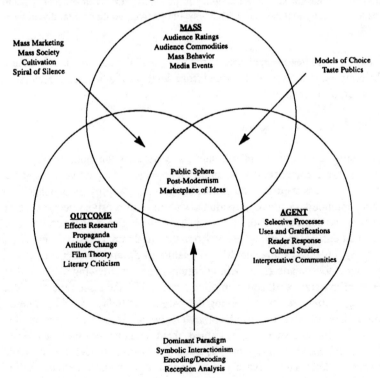

FIG. 10.1. Various traditions of audience studies. From Webster (1998). Reprinted by permission.

The areas of intersection on the diagram may be used to describe the various conceptions of the audience from all the various areas of communication research and theoretical approaches, including critical theory, cultivation, symbolic interactionism, and even postmodernism, in addition to the more conventional areas of effects research, propaganda studies, uses and gratifications, and cultural studies.

ETHICAL CONSIDERATIONS AND POLICY CONSIDERATIONS

In today's techno-hungry world, as new communication technologies are developed and adopted, they present us with a number of public policy and ethical considerations. Some of these issues have been around for some time, whereas others are new concerns created by the advent of brand new media technologies.

Cooper (1998) provided a useful and thoughtful inventory of 40 leading ethical concerns that are the result of the use of new communication technologies.

> Understanding effects and ethical issues accompanying new technologies includes studying a myriad of overt and submerged social, cultural, and institutional factors within corporations and countries. To have dominion over such new technologies and to predict at least some of their effects, it is important to recognize, systematize, analyze, and tentatively evaluate not only technologies but their relations to corporations, individuals, and societies. (pp. 86–87)

Included in his list were the diverse ethical issues associated with fairness or equality, an information underclass, obscenity and pornography, plagiarism, and bootlegging, or the copying of other people's data for resale purposes. On the issue of fairness or equality, Cooper (1998) wrote the following:

> One of the most ancient ethical issues is magnified when discussing resources (technology rich and technology poor countries, regions, and peoples), access, and even air space. Questions about how the air spectrum should be allocated, about whether foreign owned satellites may orbit over domestic military sites, about who should be charged and how much for transmission and transponder time magnify questions of global equality, inequality, and fairness. Similarly, questions of intellectual property, ownership, royalties, and so forth raise questions of distributive justice. Who, if anyone, should profit from the distribution of information? (p. 76)

A good example of the bootlegging issue is the controversy of late associated with MP3, a compression technology that results in computer files with sound quality that rivals compact disks. MP3 music available on the World Wide Web has been called "the biggest thing to happen in the business in about 40 years," by a senior vice president for a major recording label (Jensen, 1999, p. 34). Music fans can "call up" tunes via their computer and illegally download or copy them for future play or for resale. The difference between this type of bootlegging and the old variety (simply taping a song from an album or from the radio) is in the quality of the sound.

The MP3 bootlegging problem attracted the notice of the recording industry when a new device called the Diamond Rio came onto the market. The recording industry objected to its introduction because PC peripherals such as the Diamond Rio are not required by law to pay royalties, even though the device allows digital audio recording and permits online music to become portable. The industry responded by filing suit against Diamond Rio. The Recording Industry Association of America and five major recording labels created a task force called the Secure Digital Music Initiative. The Initiative will study the MP3 problem and come up with new standards that will protect music distributed in digital formats.

In addition to ethical concerns, the new technologies are also associated with a number of public policy considerations. In 1998, the FCC complied with the Telecommunications Act of 1996 by forming an Advanced Networks Inquiry and Rulemaking initiative. This initiative is attempting to define a new regulatory framework to provide guidance as the country's public switched, voice-based telecommunications network is transformed into a high-speed and broadband network. Another goal is to stimulate the growth of alternative networks such as hybrid wireless, wireline, CATV, and satellite networks (A. Pearce, 1998).

The policy associated with high-definition television serves as another good example. The FCC has set several requirements that will facilitate the transition from analog to digital television in the near future. An April 1997 order required (a) that network affiliate stations in the top-10 television markets construct digital television facilities by May 1, 1999; (b) that network affiliates in the top 30 markets construct their facilities by November 1, 1999; (c) that all other commercial stations construct their facilities by May 1, 2002; (d) that all noncommercial stations construct by May 1, 2003; and (e) that all analog services cease by 2006 (Dupagne, 1998; Federal Communications Commission, FCC, 1997).

Since that order, however, FCC Chairman Bill Kennard has come under fire for not offering enough regulatory guidance to broadcasters during this period of conversion from analog to digital. In the winter newsletter of the Communication and Technology Policy division of the Association for Education in Journalism and Mass Communication, Dupagne criticized Kennard's apparent decision to curtail FCC involvement in HDTV policy.

Such a call for disengagement is both premature and inconsistent with prior FCC policymaking. It is unreasonable to expect broadcasters to meet aggressive build-out deadlines without contributing appropriate policies enabling them to achieve these objectives. As HDTV enters American homes, it is imperative that the commission continue to provide a nurturing, albeit flexible, regulatory environment, to ensure an orderly and expeditious transition to HDTV broadcasting. (Dupagne, 1998, p. 3)

Whether the government offers too many regulations or not enough is a matter of opinion, but it serves to illustrate the one constant in telecommunications policy of today: controversy. With so many players vying for a piece of the broadband network pie (broadcasters, cable companies, telephone companies, computer companies, satellite companies, etc.) finding a common regulatory ground that will satisfy all seems next to impossible. Additionally, policymakers are still searching for the balance between regulation versus deregulation of the major players and assurance that various publics—including the disadvantaged—will be served.

One of the key issues of late has been the question of digital must-carry on the part of cable companies. The National Association of Broadcasters has urged the FCC to adopt a ruling that will force cable companies to carry digital signals in the future, so that cable customers will have access to digital television. Cable operators, on the other hand, are resisting being forced to carry digital signals of broadcast stations in a particular market. They would prefer to offer more cable channels on the extra channel capacity.

Perhaps the key to solving policy dilemmas lies in the conceptualization of the new technologies themselves, their uses, their users, and the stakeholders. In her award-winning dissertation, Holman (1998) offered a regulatory framework for emerging communication media based on First Amendment principles. This framework, which she called *information commons,* takes into consideration the interactive and convergent nature of new communication technologies and provides policymakers with an appropriate metaphor to describe new, digital-based communication environments.

Commons can be conceptualized as any set of social acts characterized by voluntary participation, common purpose, shared resources, mutuality, and fairness. This concept of the commons, or koinonia, which dates back to the ancient Greeks, has five principles: 1) participation must be free and uncoerced; 2) participants must share a common purpose; 3) participants must have something in common that they share, such as jointly held resources, a collection of precious objects, or a repertory of shared actions; 4) participation involves a sense of mutuality or friendship; and 5) social relations must be characterized by fairness and justice. A commons describes any self-defining collective of individuals who voluntarily associate to create communities and to reproduce social worlds—a setting very akin to the groups and communities that comprise the new information environment. (Holman, 1998, pp. 248–249)

Another framework for understanding current telecommunications policy involves a communication theory perspective, but also emphasizes an integration or common ground approach. Lenert (1998) used the concepts of liberalization and democratization to characterize two recurring themes in telecommunications policy discourse, and he associated those concepts with two models of communication advanced earlier by Carey (1989), the transmission model and the community-cultural-ritual (CCR) model. According to Lenert, liberalization (also known as deregulation) can be associated with the transmission model of communication that emphasizes the transporting of messages, or "the movement of messages in space" (p. 6). Lenert defined democratization as "a focus on a political system characterized by popular participation in decision making in the context of liberal guarantees of equality and individual rights" (p. 4). He associated democratization with the CCR model, which views communication as "the representation of shared beliefs, rather than the imparting of information . . . directed toward the maintenance of society in time as well as the extension of messages in space" (p. 7). In his essay, Lenert called for an integration of the transmission and CCR models "to provide the basis for a more fully democratized telecommunications policy in the context of a liberalized global economy" (Lenert, 1998, p. 5).

RESEARCH ON NEW MEDIA TECHNOLOGIES

"As new information technologies become available, a whole new program of research is required to learn techniques for their effective utilization." This was the farsighted opinion of Parker (1973, p. 596), one of the few communication scholars of the 1970s who felt that technology variables should be given greater attention in communication research.

Since the 1970s, the study of new communication technologies has followed a trend set by past precedents. As each new communication technology has appeared, researchers have studied it using research methods that were used to study technologies immediately previous to the new one. Using early television studies as an example, one finds similar methods of research on the effects of message content as those used for earlier film and radio studies (Williams, Rice, & Rogers, 1988)

Most recent research has followed tradition by making use of existing communication theories as a guide in exploring the uses and consequences of new media technologies. Williams, Strover, and Grant (1994) reviewed the literature and found a number of studies related to new media technologies, from the areas of uses and gratifications and diffusion of innovation research.

Researchers have studied the motives of cable television subscribers to learn what gratifications they obtained from cable (Becker, Dunwoody, & Rafaell,

1983; Ducey, Krugman, & Eckrich, 1983; Jeffres, 1978; McDermott & Medhurst, 1984; Metzger, 1983). Others have investigated the relationship between viewer motives and actual program choices to find that different people watch certain programs for different reasons at different times. Zillmann and Bryant (1985) found that people experiencing emotional distress preferred to watch soothing programs. Rubin (1984) distinguished two different styles of watching television: instrumental, in which viewers selected a program carefully and with a definite purpose in mind; and ritualized, in which viewers watched television habitually in an effort to pass time or to forget their loneliness. Heeter and Baldwin (1988) studied cable viewers and found that the variety of programming offered by cable provided opportunities for both instrumental and ritualized viewing. These and other uses and gratifications studies revealed that new media technologies offered audiences more content choices, opportunities to alter messages, time-shift alternatives, and opportunities for interaction with other users (Williams, Strover, & Grant, 1994).

Other researchers have studied new media technologies in relation to the rapidity of their diffusion among users. Some have examined the phenomenon of critical mass, or that explosive point when the greatest number of people suddenly adopt the new technology. Markus (1987) pointed out that the success of certain technologies such as e-mail or the telephone was entirely dependent upon achieving the critical mass due to the reciprocal nature of these technologies. For example, if only a few people had adopted the telephone, those users would have had very few people to call. Without achieving the critical mass, telephone usage would have declined and probably vanished entirely. E-mail and the fax machine are other technologies for which mass adoption was critical to their success.

Another arm of research into new technologies has involved their effects upon children and adolescents. Van Evra (1998) provided a survey of research on children and their use of new communication technologies such as the VCR, video games, virtual reality, and the Internet. New technologies are causing changes in program content for children and making much more diverse content choices accessible to them. Sometimes this programming is educational and positive in nature, sometimes it is not.

The availability of additional channels via cable and VCRs has meant that children may be exposed to inappropriate content such as violence, graphic sex, or programs with adult themes. This, along with the interactive component built into many of the new technologies, has had important developmental and behavioral implications for today's children. Oftentimes children do not have the developmental maturity and experience to understand completely the adult information they are being exposed to. The borders that separate reality from fantasy may become confusing for them.

Children who are watching material intended for adults may still be having considerable difficulty sorting out real information from fantasy material; they may not be cognizant of some of the formal features of television and hence they may find flashbacks, dream sequences, and other dramatic techniques confusing and incomprehensible. They may still be unable to grasp subtle messages or "morals to the story" and hence they may overreact to salient, but irrelevant or inappropriate, aspects of a program. (Van Evra, 1990, p. 199)

On the positive side, new technologies such as the V-chip and electronic locks on televisions are allowing parents greater powers to screen out programs they do not wish for their children to see. On the down side, there has also been concern that the new technologies and their greater diversity of content are more readily available to gifted children or those with affluent or well-educated parents (Cantor, 1980; Sprafkin, Gadow, & Abelman, 1992; Webster, 1989).

PRACTICAL ADVANTAGES OF THE NEW TECHNOLOGIES

New media technologies are already proving to be exceptionally valuable tools, especially for educational purposes, in many different areas. The computer has become a central part of modern day schooling (Marien, 1996; Papert, 1993). The ease and availability of electronic communication has made it possible for students in remote corners of the globe to access information previously available to a select few.

A recent survey showed that the use of new communication media in college instruction is on the rise (Deloughrey, 1996; Panici, 1998). More and more college instructors are making use of e-mail, the World Wide Web, and multimedia materials in their courses.

The introduction of new technologies has brought many changes in traditional modes of education for communication professors and students. In mass communication, especially, mastery of new technologies has become an essential part of undergraduate and graduate education. Instructors teaching skills courses in journalism, public relations, advertising, and broadcasting must keep abreast of new technologies in order to prepare their students for modern work environments. In communication and other fields, distance education has become more and more prevalent in recent years and has allowed and sometimes forced faculty members to embrace new technologies.

Journalism and mass communication are not the only subject areas undergoing profound changes due to new media technologies. In the area of personal and public health, for instance, new media are viewed as tools for both health care systems and individuals concerned about their health (Harris, 1995). These new media are allowing more public access to health information, and they are "making expertise portable" (p. 14). Interactivity and simulation are combining to make medical knowledge available to audiences who would not normally have access to such information (McGinnis, Deering, & Patrick, 1995). Multimedia programs are now being used in medical schools, allowing doctors in training to encounter simulated experiences that they may face when in actual medical practice (Henderson, 1995). New media technologies are also being viewed as a means for reducing health care costs. These new technologies allow patients to have more health information and take more responsibility for their own health and their needs. Armed with such information, people may recognize when unnecessary services are about to be rendered (Vickery, 1995).

NEW THEORY AND NEW MODELS

Attempts to build comprehensive communication theory that would account for transactional mediated communication and explain both the interpersonal and multimedia aspects of new technologies have occurred at two different levels. Macro-analytical models have been offered to guide our understanding of the relationships between communications infrastructure, technologies, communication policies, and society. Micro-analytical models (rare at this time) provide us with a clearer picture of the specific components of transactional communication among users via the new technologies.

Williams et al. (1994) suggested that two recent theories, media system dependency theory and social information processing theory, may prove useful in explaining in macro-analytical terms the complex nature of communication processes via new media technologies. Media system dependency theory (Ball-Rokeach, 1985, 1988) provides a framework for understanding relationships of dependency among mass media, various audiences, and societal groups or systems. For example, individual audience members may develop a dependency on a medium such as television to satisfy certain needs such as entertainment or instruction. The media system itself is dependent on advertisers for financial support, and this relationship is dependent on the individual viewers in order to provide audiences for the advertised products.

Social information processing theory (Fulk, Steinfield, Schmitz, & Power, 1987) holds that when evaluating new media and making selections for use, media users are as much or more influenced by the information and evaluations they hear from others rather than by personal appraisals of media performance. The theory has been used to predict adoption and use of an electronic mail system (Rice, Grant, Schmitz, & Torobin, 1990) and electronic message evaluation (Schmitz & Fulk, 1991).

One of the best examples of the macro-analytical type of model is the "Interactive Model of Communication and Society," provided by the Office of Technology Assessment (U.S. Congress, 1990, p. 35) of the U.S. Congress. This model was contained in an extremely comprehensive and useful report called

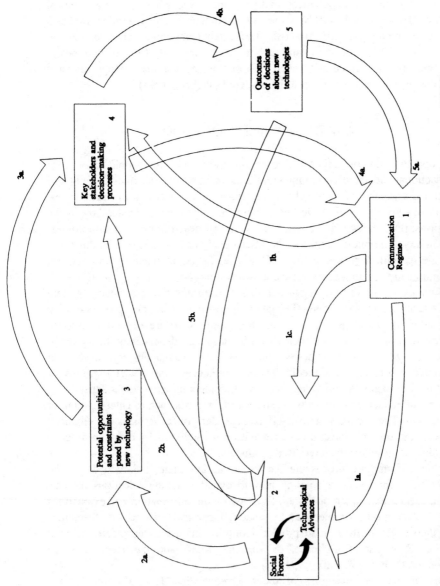

FIG 10.2. An interactive model of media and society. From Office of Technology Assessment (1990).

Critical Connections: Communication for the Future. In Fig. 10.2, la. represents the effect of all social, economic, political, and cultural activities engendered by the activities of the "communication regime" represented as 1; lb. plots the effects of the communication regime on the values and positions of key decision makers; and 1c. indicates how activities within the communication regime will also affect the level and direction of technological development. All of the "operations" associated with 2 refer to the interaction of social forces and technological advances. 2a. indicates that their interaction will create new ways of carrying out economic, political, cultural, and social activities, as well as new opportunities and constraints. That these same interactions also create new communication needs and desires and change the key parties' perceptions of their interests is indicated in 2b. The potential opportunities and constraints posed by new technology is presented as 3. 3a. shows that these opportunities and constraints may alter the position and status of the key participants (e.g., opinion leaders) in the process—the so-called stakeholders, represented in 4. 4a. is the pathway for stakeholders to influence the communication regime via their decisions; 4b. represents how the stakeholders' decision-making processes affect the outcomes of decisions about new technologies in society (5). Finally, 5a. plots the pathway by which outcomes of decisions about new technologies affect the communication regime.

This molar model is useful if it accurately describes the overarching "players" and essential relationships in the realm of communication and society, and if it guides research that explains and predicts how technology changes society and vice versa. Nonetheless, it is presented at a much more macroanalytic level than most of the models and theories we have considered in previous chapters. Those models that have focused on the human and message elements of the new multimedia environment have also tended to depart rather radically from orthodoxy—for example, the Shannon-Weaver paradigm. (Recall the discussion in chaps. 2 and 3, this volume.) If they are to be accurate representations of the new media environment and the communication processes of the users of new media, they must depart radically from orthodoxy. Rogers (1986) indicated the following:

> The new media are having a powerful influence on the nature of communication research, unfreezing this field from many of its past assumptions, prior paradigms and methods. As we have stated previously, the predominant linear models of one-way communication effects must give way to convergence models of communication as a two-way process of information exchange, due to the interactivity of new media. (p. 213)

The Office of Technology Assessment (U.S. Congress, 1990) report offered a slightly different slant but reflected similar concerns:

> The sender/receiver model is also much too orderly to describe many of today's mediated communication processes. It assumes that communication takes place as a

consistent, linear sequence of events—an assumption that is not supportable in today's technology-mediated information environment. With a computerized bulletin board, for example, how does one identify and distinguish between who is the sender and who is the receiver? And, similarly, who is considered the sender when the receiver can now access information on demand? (pp. 31–32)

As for microanalytical models, the Office of Technology Assessment (U.S. Congress, 1990, p. 33) offered the following simple model (Fig. 10.3) to indicate the transactional nature that veridical communication theories must assume in the multimedia environment. Their model "highlights interrelationships and interdependencies and institutions" (p. 32) and brings a multidimensional approach to communication, which is defined in the context of this model as "the process by which messages are formulated, exchanged, and interpreted" (p. 31).

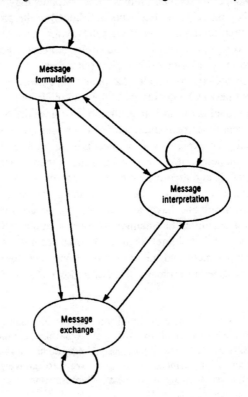

FIG. 10.3. A transactional model suitable for both interperson communication and interactive mediated communication. From Office of Technology Assessment (1990).

The dearth of theoretical models to illustrate the transactional nature of modern mediated communication underscores the rapid development and deployment of the new communication technologies. Simply put, theory has not been able to keep up with technology. New communication theories that would explain the uses of new technologies are sorely needed. As the new century begins, the continual challenge for communication theorists will be to catch up and keep up.

References

Adler, R. P. (1980). Children's television advertising: History of the issue. In E. L. Palmer & A. Dorr (Eds.), *Children and the faces of television: Teaching, violence, selling* (pp. 237–249). New York: Academic.

Ajzen, I., & Fishbein, M. (1980). *Understanding attitudes and predicting social behavior.* Englewood Cliffs, NJ: Prentice-Hall.

Alberts, J. K. (1988). An analysis of couples' conversational complaints. *Communication Monographs, 55,* 184–197.

Albrecht, T. L. (1984). Managerial communication and work perception. In R. N. Bostrom & B. H. Westley (Eds.), *Communication yearbook 8* (pp. 538–557). Newbury Park, CA: Sage.

Albrecht, T. L. (1988). Communication and personal control in empowering organizations. In J. A. Anderson (Ed.), *Communication yearbook 11* (pp. 380–390). Newbury Park, CA: Sage.

Albrecht, T. L., Burleson, B. R., & Goldsmith, D. (1994). Supportive communication. In M. L. Knapp & G. R. Miller (Eds.), *Handbook of interpersonal communication* (2nd ed., pp. 419–449). Thousand Oaks, CA: Sage.

Allen, M., Hale, J., Mongeau, P., Berkowitz-Stafford, S., Stafford, S., Shanahan, W., Agee, P., Dillon, K., Jackson, R., & Ray, C. (1990). Testing a model of message sidedness: Three replications. *Communication Monographs, 57,* 275–291.

Allport, G. E. (1935). Attitudes. In C. Murchison (Ed.), *Handbook of social psychology* (Vol. 2, pp. 798–844). Worcester, MA: Clark University Press.

Alper, S. W., & Leidy, T. R. (1969). The impact of information transmission through television. *Public Opinion Quarterly, 33,* 556–562.

Altman, I., & Taylor, D. A. (1973). *Social penetration: The development of interpersonal relationships.* New York: Holt, Rinehart & Winston.

Altman, I., Vinsel, A., & Brown, B. B. (1981). Dialectic conceptions in social psychology: An application to social penetration and privacy regulation. In L. Berkowitz (Ed.), *Advances in experimental social psychology* (Vol. 14, pp. 107–160). New York: Academic.

Andersen, P. A. (1985). Nonverbal immediacy in interpersonal communication. In A. W. Siegman & S. Feldstein (Eds.), *Multichannel integrations of nonverbal behavior* (pp. 1–36). Hillsdale, NJ: Lawrence Erlbaum Associates.

Andrews, P. H. (1987). Gender differences in persuasive communication and attribution of success and failure. *Human Communication Research, 13,* 372–385.

Aristotle (1954). *Rhetoric* (W. R. Robert, Trans.). New York: Modern Library.

Ashby, W. R. (1963). *An introduction to cybernetics.* New York: Science Editions.

Atkin, C. K. (1980). Effects of television advertising on children. In E. L. Palmer & A. Dorr (Eds.), *Children and the faces of television: Teaching, violence, selling* (pp. 287–304). New York: Academic.

Atwood, L. E. (1994). Illusions of media power: The third-person effect. *Journalism Quarterly, 71*, 269–281.

Aune, K. S., Buller, D. B., & Aune, R. K. (1996). Display rule development in romantic relationships: Emotion management and perceived appropriateness of emotions across relationship stages. *Human Communication Research, 23*, 115–145.

Austin, J. L. (1962). *How to do things with words.* Cambridge: Harvard University Press.

Austin, J. L. (1964). *Philosophy of language.* Englewood Cliffs, NJ: Prentice-Hall.

Babbitt, L. V., & Jablin, F. M. (1985). Characteristics of applicants' questions and employment screening interview outcomes. *Human Communication Research, 11*, 507–535.

Babrow, A. S., & Swanson, D. L. (1988). Disentangling antecedents of audience exposure levels: Extending expectancy-value analysis of gratifications sought from television news. *Communication Monographs, 55*, 1–21.

Baglan, T., Lalumia, J., & Bayless, O. L. (1986). Utilization of compliance-gaining strategies: A research note. *Communication Monographs, 53*, 289–293.

Ball-Rokeach, S. J. (1985). The origins of individual media-system dependency: A sociological framework. *Communication research, 12*, 485–510.

Ball-Rokeach, S. J. (1988). Media system dependency theory. In M. L. DeFleur & S. J. Ball-Rokeach (Eds.), *Theories of mass communication* (pp. 297–327). New York: Longman.

Bandura, A. (1977). *Social learning theory.* Englewood Cliffs, NJ: Prentice-Hall.

Bandura, A. (1994). Social cognitive theory of mass communication. In J. Bryant & D. Zillmann (Eds.), *Media effects: Advances in theory and research* (pp. 61–90). Hillsdale, NJ: Lawrence Erlbaum Associates.

Bandura, A. (1986). *Social foundations of thought and action: A social cognitive theory.* Englewood Cliffs, NJ: Prentice-Hall.

Bandura, A., & Walters, R. (1963). *Social learning and personality development.* New York: Holt, Rinehart & Winston.

Bantz, C. R. (1989). Organizing and The Social Psychology of Organizing. *Communication Studies, 40*, 231–240.

Barcus, F. E. (1980). The nature of television advertising to children. In E. L. Palmer & A. Dorr (Eds.), *Children and the faces of television: Teaching, violence, selling* (pp. 283–285). New York: Academic.

Barboza, D. (1999, February 8). Joint venture aims to help the Internet go wireless. *The New York Times*, C1.

Bargh, J. A. (1988). Automatic information processing: Implications for communication and affect. In L. Donohew, H. E. Sypher, & E. T. Higgins (Eds.), *Communication, social cognition, and affect* (pp. 9–32). Hillsdale, NJ: Lawrence Erlbaum Associates.

Bateson, G. (1978). *Mind and nature: A necessary unity.* New York: E. P. Dutton.

Bauchner, J. E., Brandt, D. R., & Miller, G. R. (1977). The truth/deception attribution: Effects of varying levels of information availability. In B. D. Ruben (Ed.), *Communication yearbook 1* (pp. 229–243). New Brunswick, NJ: Transaction Books.

Bavelas, J. B., & Coates, L. (1992). How do we account for the mindfulness of face-to-face dialogue? *Communication Monographs, 59*, 301–305.

Baxter, L. A. (1982). Strategies for ending relationships: Two studies. *Western Journal of Speech Communication, 46*, 223–241.

Baxter, L. A. (1990). Dialectical contradictions in relationship development. *Journal of Social and Personal Relationships, 7*, 69–88.

Baxter, L. A., & Bullis, C. (1986). Turning points in developing romantic relationships. *Human Communication Research, 12*, 469–493.

Baxter, L. A., & Wilmot, W. W. (1984). "Secret tests": Social strategies for acquiring information about the state of the relationship. *Human Communication Research, 11,* 171–201.

Becker, L., Dunwoody, S., & Rafaell, S. (1983). Cable's impact on use of other news media. *Journal of Broadcasting, 27,* 127–142.

Becker, S. L. (1984). Marxist approaches to media studies: The British experience. *Critical Studies in Mass Communication, 1,* 66–80.

Bell, R. A., & Daly, J. A. (1984). The affinity-seeking function of communication. *Communication Monographs, 51,* 91–115.

Bell, R. A., Buerkel-Rothfuss, N. L., & Core, K. E. (1987). "Did you bring the yarmulke for the Cabbage Patch Kid?" The idiomatic communication of young lovers. *Human Communication Research, 14,* 47–67.

Bem, D. J. (1965). An experimental analysis of self-persuasion. *Journal of Experimental Social Psychology, 1,* 199–218.

Bem, D. J. (1968). Attitudes as self-descriptions: Another look at the attitude–behavior link. In A. G. Greenwald, T. C. Brock, & T. M. Ostrom (Eds.), *Psychological foundations of attitudes* (pp. 197–215). New York: Academic.

Bem, D. J. (1970). *Beliefs, attitudes, and human affairs.* Belmont, CA: Brooks/Cole.

Bem, D. J. (1972). Self-perception theory. In L. Berkowitz (Ed.), *Advances in experimental social psychology* (Vol. 6, pp. 2–63). New York: Academic.

Berelson, B. (1959). The state of communication research. *Public Opinion Quarterly, 23,* 1–6.

Berelson, B., & Steiner, G. A. (1964). *Human behavior: An inventory of scientific findings.* New York: Harcourt, Brace & World.

Berger, C. R. (1975). Proactive and retroactive attribution processes in interpersonal communications. *Human Communication Research, 2,* 33–50.

Berger, C. R. (1977a). The covering law perspective as a theoretical basis for the study of human communication. *Communication Quarterly, 25,* 7–18.

Berger, C. R. (1977b). Interpersonal communication theory and research: An overview. In B. D. Ruben (Ed.), *Communication yearbook 1* (pp. 217–228). New Brunswick, NJ: Transaction Books.

Berger, C. R. (1985). Social power and interpersonal communication. In M. L. Knapp & G. R. Miller (Eds.), *Handbook of interpersonal communication* (pp. 439–499). Newbury Park, CA: Sage.

Berger, C. R. (1987). Communicating under uncertainty. In M. E. Roloff & G. R. Miller (Eds.), *Interpersonal processes: New directions in communication research* (pp. 39–62). Newbury Park, CA: Sage.

Berger, C. R. (1988). Planning, affect, and social action generation. In L. Donohew, H. E. Sypher, & E. T. Higgins (Eds.), *Communication, social cognition, and affect* (pp. 93–116). Hillsdale, NJ: Lawrence Erlbaum Associates.

Berger, C. R. (1994). Power, dominance, and social interaction. In M. L. Knapp & G. R. Miller (Eds.), *Handbook of interpersonal communication* (2nd ed., pp. 450–507). Thousand Oaks, CA: Sage.

Berger, C. R., & Bell, R. A. (1988). Plans and the initiation of social relationships. *Human Communication Research, 15,* 217–235.

Berger, C. R., & Bradac, J. J. (1982). *Language and social knowledge: Uncertainty in interpersonal relations.* London: Edward Arnold.

Berger, C. R., & Calabrese, R. J. (1975). Some explorations in initial interaction and beyond: Toward a developmental theory of interpersonal communication. *Human Communication Research, 1,* 99–112.

Berger, C. R., & DiBattista, P. (1992). Information seeking and plan elaboration: What do you need to know to know what to do? *Communication Monographs, 59,* 368–387.

Berger, C. R., & Douglas, W. (1982). Thought and talk: "Excuse me, but have I been talking to myself?" In F. E. X. Dance (Ed.), *Human communication theory: Comparative essays* (pp. 42–60). New York: Harper & Row.

Berger, C. R., Karol, S. H., & Jordan, J. M. (1989). When a lot of knowledge is a dangerous thing: The debilitating effects of plan complexity in verbal fluency. *Human Communication Research, 16,* 91–119.

Berger, C. R., Weber, M. D., Munley, M. E., & Dixon, J. T. (1977). Interpersonal relationship levels and interpersonal attraction. In B. D. Ruben (Ed.), *Communication yearbook 1* (pp. 245-261). New Brunswick, NJ: Transaction Books.

Berger, P., & Luckmann, T. (1966). *The social construction of reality.* Garden City, NY: Doubleday.

Berlo, D. K. (1960). *Communication: An introduction to theory and practice.* New York: Holt, Rinehart & Winston.

Berlo, D. K. (1977). Communication as process: Review and commentary. In B. D. Ruben (Ed.), *Communication yearbook 1* (pp. 11-27). New Brunswick, NJ: Transaction Books.

Berlo, D. K., Lemert, J. B., & Mertz, R. J. (1969). Dimensions for evaluating the acceptability of message sources. *Public Opinion Quarterly, 33,* 563–576.

Berman, S. J., & Bunzel, M. (1999, March 1). The rapid bandwidth explosion. *Electronic Media, 20.*

Bertalanffy, L. (1968). *General system theory: Foundations, development, applications.* New York: Braziller.

Bineham, J. L. (1988). A historical account of the hypodermic model of mass communication. *Communication Monographs, 55,* 230–246.

Biocca, F., & Levy, M. R. (Eds.). (1995). *Communication in the age of virtual reality.* Hillsdale, NJ: Lawrence Erlbaum Associates.

Black, J., & Bryant, J. (1998). *Introduction to mass communication* (5th ed.). Dubuque, IA: Wm. C. Brown.

Black, J., Bryant, J., & Thompson, S. (1998). *Introduction to media communication* (5th ed.). New York: McGraw Hill.

Blankenship, J. (1974). The influence of mode, sub-mode, and speaker predilection on style. *Speech Monographs, 41,* 85–118.

Blascovich, J., & Ginsburg, G. P. (1974). Emergent norms and choice shifts involving risk. *Sociometry, 37,* 205–218.

Blau, G. J. (1985). Source-related determinants of perceived job scope. *Human Communication Research, 11,* 536–553.

Blumler, J. G. (1979). The role of theory in uses and gratifications studies. *Communication Research, 6,* 9–36.

Blumler, J. G., & Katz, E. (Eds.). (1974). *The uses of mass communications: Current perspectives on gratifications research.* Newbury Park, CA: Sage.

Bochner, A. P. (1994). Perspectives on inquiry II: Theories and stories. In M. L. Knapp & G. R. Miller (Eds.), *Handbook of interpersonal communication* (2nd ed., pp. 21–41). Thousand Oaks, CA: Sage.

Booth-Butterfield, S. (1987). Action assembly theory and communication apprehension: A psychophysiological study. *Human Communication Research, 13,* 386–398.

Bormann, E. C. (1983). Symbolic convergence: Organizational communication and culture. In L. L. Putnam & M. E. Pacanowsky (Eds.), *Communication and organizations: An interpretive approach* (pp. 99–122). Newbury Park: Sage.

Boster, F. J., & Mongeau, P. (1984). Fear-arousing persuasive messages. In R. N. Bostrom (Ed.), *Communication yearbook 8* (pp. 330–375). Newbury Park, CA: Sage.

Boster, F. J., & Stiff, J. B. (1984). Compliance-gaining message selection behavior. *Human Communication Research, 10,* 539–556.

Boulanger, F., & Fischer, D. G. (1971). Leadership and the group-shift phenomenon. *Perceptual and Motor Skills, 33,* 1251–1258.

Bowers, J. W. (1963). Language intensity, social introversion, and attitude change. *Speech Monographs, 30,* 345–352.

Bowers, J. W., & Bradac, J. J. (1982). Issues in communication theory: A metatheoretic analysis. In M. Burgoon (Ed.), *Communication yearbook 5* (pp. 1–27). New Brunswick, NJ: Transaction Books.

Bowles, J. (1998, November 16). The future Internet: Faster, smarter, mobile, scarier. *Newsweek,* 12.

Boyanowsky, E. O. (1977). Film preferences under conditions of threat. *Communication Research, 4,* 133–144.

Bradac, J. J., Bowers, J. W., & Courtright, J. A. (1979). Three language variables in communication research: Intensity, immediacy, and diversity. *Human Communication Research, 5,* 257–269.

Bradac, J. J., & Mulac, A. (1984). A molecular view of powerful and powerless speech styles: Attributional consequences and specific language features and communicator intentions. *Communication Monographs, 51,* 307–319.

Brand, S. (1988). *The media lab: Inventing the future at MIT.* New York: Penguin.

Brenders, D. A. (1987). Fallacies in the coordinated management of meaning: A philosophy of language critique of the hierarchical organization of coherent conversation and related theory. *Quarterly Journal of Speech, 73,* 329–348.

Broadhurst, A. R., & Darnell, D. K. (1965). An introduction to cybernetics and information theory. *Quarterly Journal of Speech, 51,* 442–453.

Brosius, H-B., & Engel, D. (1996). The causes of third-person effects: Unrealistic optimism, impersonal impact, or generalized negative attitudes towards media influence? *International Journal of Public Opinion Research, 8,* 142–162.

Brown, P. (1999). Set-top box market frenzy: Industry trend or event? *Electronic News, 45,* 50.

Bryant, J. (1990). *Television and the American family.* Hillsdale, NJ: Lawrence Erlbaum Associates.

Bryant, J., & Street, R. L., Jr. (1988). From reactivity to activity and action: Evolution of a concept and a Weltanschauung in mass and interpersonal communication. In R. P. Hawkins, S. Pingree, & J. M. Wiemann, (Eds.), *Advancing communication science: Merging mass and interpersonal processes* (Vol. 16, pp. 162–190). Newbury Park, CA: Sage.

Bryant, J., & Thompson, S. (in press). *Fundamentals of media effects.* Manuscript submitted for publication.

Buber, M. (1965). *Between man and man.* (R. G. Smith, Trans.). New York: MacMillan.

Buller, D. B., & Aune, R. K. (1988). The effects of vocalics and nonverbal sensitivity on compliance: A speech accommodation theory explanation. *Human Communication Research, 14,* 301–332.

Buller, D. B., & Burgoon, J. K. (1986). The effects of vocalics and nonverbal sensitivity on compliance: A replication and extension. *Human Communication Research, 13,* 126–144.

Buller, D. B., Strzyzewski, K. D., & Comstock, J. (1991). Interpersonal deception: I. Deceivers' reactions to receivers' suspicions and probing. *Communication Monographs, 58,* 1–24.

Burggraf, C. S., & Sillars, A. L. (1987). A critical examination of sex differences in marital communication. *Communication Monographs, 54,* 276–294.

Burgoon, J. K. (1975). Conflicting information, attitude, message variables as predictors of learning and persuasion. *Human Communication Research, 1,* 133–144.

Burgoon, J. K. (1994). Nonverbal signals. In M. L. Knapp & G. R. Miller (Eds.), *Handbook of interpersonal communication* (2nd ed., pp. 229–285). Thousand Oaks, CA: Sage.

Burgoon, J. K., & Aho, L. (1982). Three field experiments on the effects of violations on conversational distance. *Communication Monographs, 49,* 71–88.

Burgoon, J. K., Birk, T., & Pfau, M. (1990). Nonverbal behaviors, persuasion, and credibility. *Human Communication Research, 17,* 140–169.

Burgoon, J. K., Buller, D. B., Dillman, L., & Walther, J. B. (1995). Interpersonal deception IV. Effects of suspicion on perceived communication and nonverbal behavior dynamics. *Human Communication Research, 22,* 163–196.

Burgoon, J. K., Buller, D. B., Hale, J. L., & deTurck, M. A. (1984). Relational messages associated with nonverbal behaviors. *Human Communication Research, 10,* 351–378.

Burgoon, J. K., Coker, D. A., & Coker, R. A. (1986). Communicative effects of gaze behavior: A test of two contrasting explanations. *Human Communication Research, 12,* 469–493.

Burgoon, J. K., & Hale, J. L. (1984). The fundamental topoi of relational communication. *Communication Monographs, 51,*193–214.

Burgoon, J. K., & Hale, J. L. (1987). Validation and measurement of the fundamental themes of relational communication. *Communication Monographs, 54,* 19–41.

Burgoon, J. K., & Hale, J. L. (1988). Nonverbal expectancy violations: Model elaboration and application to immediacy behaviors. *Communication Monographs, 55,* 58–79.

Burgoon, J. K., & Koper, R. J. (1984). Nonverbal and relational communication associated with reticence. *Human Communication Research, 10,* 601–626.

Burgoon, J. K., Pfau, M., Parrott, R., Birk, T., Coker, R., & Burgoon, M. (1987). Relational communication, satisfaction, compliance-gaining strategies, and compliance in communication between physicians and patients. *Communication Monographs, 54,* 307–324.

Burke, K. (1934, May 2). The meaning of C. K. Ogden. *New Republic, 78,* 328–331.

Burke, K. (1952). "Ethan Brand": A preparatory investigation. *Hopkins Review, 5,* 45–65.

Burke, K. (1958). The poetic motive. *Hudson Review, 40,* 54–63.

Burke, K. (1961). *Attitudes toward history.* Boston: Beacon Press. (Original work published 1937)

Burke, K. (1964). On form. *Hudson Review, 17,* 103–109.

Burke, K. (1965). *Permanence and change.* Indianapolis: Bobbs-Merrill. (Original work published 1935)

Burke, K. (1966). *Language as symbolic action.* Berkeley, CA: University of California Press.

Burke, K. (1969a). *A grammar of motives.* Berkeley, CA: University of California Press. (Original work published 1945)

Burke, K. (1969b). *A rhetoric of motives.* Berkeley, CA: University of California Press. (Original work published 1950)

Burleson, B. R., & Denton, W. H. (1992). A new look at similarity and attraction in marriage: Similarities in social-cognitive and communication skills as predictors of attraction and satisfaction. *Communication Monographs, 59,* 268–287.

Burleson, B. R., Levine, B. J., & Samter, W. (1984). Decision making procedure and decision quality. *Human Communication Research, 10,* 557–574.

Burleson, B. R., Wilson, S. R., Waltman, M. S., Goering, E. M., Ely, T. K., & Whaley, B. B. (1988). Item desirability effects in compliance-gaining research: Seven studies documenting artifacts in the strategy selection procedure. *Human Communication Research, 14*, 429–486.

Buzzanell, P. M., & Burrell, N. A. (1997). Family and workplace conflict: Examining metaphorical conflict schemas and expressions across context and sex. *Human Communication Research, 24*, 109–146.

Cacioppo, J. T., Harkins, S. G., & Petty, R. E. (1981). The nature of attitudes and cognitive responses and their relationships to behavior. In R. Petty, T. Ostrom, & T. Brock (Eds.), *Cognitive responses in persuasion* (pp. 31–54). Hillsdale, NJ: Lawrence Erlbaum Associates.

Cacioppo, J. T., & Petty, R. E. (1979). Effects of message repetition and position on cognitive responses, recall, and persuasion. *Journal of Personality and Social Psychology, 37*, 97–109.

Camden, C. T., & Kennedy, C. W. (1986). Manager communicative style and nurse morale. *Human Communication Research, 12*, 551–563.

Canary, D. J., & Stafford, L. (1992). Relational maintenance strategies and equity in marriage. *Communication Monographs, 59*, 243–267.

Cantor, M. G. (1980). *Prime-time television: Content and control.* Beverly Hills, CA: Sage.

Cappella, J. N. (1977). Research methodology in communication: Review and commentary. In B. D. Ruben (Ed.), *Communication yearbook 1* (pp. 37–53). New Brunswick, NJ: Transaction Books.

Cappella, J. N. (1985). The management of conversations. In M. L. Knapp & G. R. Miller (Eds.), *Handbook of interpersonal communication* (pp. 393–443). Newbury Park, CA: Sage.

Cappella, J. N. (1987). Interpersonal communication: Definitions and fundamental questions. In C. R. Berger & S. H. Chaffee (Eds.), *Handbook of communication science* (pp. 184–238). Newbury Park, CA: Sage.

Cappella, J. N. (1994). The management of conversational interaction in adults and infants. In M. L. Knapp & G. R. Miller (Eds.), *Handbook of interpersonal communication* (2nd ed., pp. 380–418). Thousand Oaks, CA: Sage.

Cappella, J. N., & Greene, J. O. (1982). A discrepancy-arousal explanation of mutual influence in expressive behavior for adult–adult and infant–adult interaction. *Communication Monographs, 49*, 89–114.

Carey, J. W. (1989). *Communication as culture.* Boston: Unwin Hyman.

Cassirer, E. (1946). *Language and myth* (S. K. Langer, Trans.). New York: Harper & Brothers.

Cassirer, E. (1953). *The philosophy of symbolic forms. Vol. 1. Language* (R. Manheim, Trans.) New Haven: Yale University Press.

Chaffee, S. H. (1988). Differentiating the hypodermic model from empirical research: A comment on Bineham's commentaries. *Communication Monographs, 55*, 247–249.

Chaffee, S. H., & Roser, C. (1986). Involvement and the consistency of knowledge, attitudes, and behaviors. *Communication Research, 13*, 373–399.

Chaffee, S. H., & Wilson D. G. (1977). Media rich, media poor: Two studies of diversity in agenda-holding. *Journalism Quarterly, 54*, 466–476.

Chaudhuri, A., & Buck, R. (1995). Affect, reason, and persuasion: Advertising strategies that predict affective and analytic-cognitive responses. *Human Communication Research, 21*, 422–441.

Cheney, G. (1991). *Rhetoric in an organizational society: Managing multiple identities.* Columbia, SC: University of South Carolina Press.

Cherry, C. (1978). *On human communication* (3rd ed.). Cambridge, MA: MIT Press.

Chiles, A. M., & Zorn, T. E. (1995). Empower in organizations: Employees' perception of the influence of empowerment. *Journal of Applied Communication Research, 23,* 1–25.

Cialdini, R. B., Petty, R. E., & Cacioppo, J. T. (1981). Attitude and attitude change. *Annual Review of Psychology, 32,* 357–404.

Cody, M. J., & McLaughlin, M. L. (1980). Perceptions of compliance-gaining situations: A dimensional analysis. *Communication Monographs, 47,* 132–148.

Cody, M. J., & McLaughlin, M. L. (1985). The situation as a construct in interpersonal communication research. In M. L. Knapp & G. R. Miller (Eds.), *Handbook of interpersonal communication* (pp. 263–312). Newbury Park, CA: Sage.

Cohen, B. (1963). *The press and foreign policy.* Princeton, NJ: Princeton University Press.

Coker, D. A., & Burgoon, J. K. (1987). The nature of conversational involvement and nonverbal encoding patterns. *Human Communication Research, 13,* 463–494.

Commission of the European Communities. (1994). *Europe and the global information society.* Brussels: European Commission.

Conant, R. C. (1979). A vector theory of information. In D. Nimmo (Ed.), *Communication yearbook 3* (pp. 177–194). New Brunswick, NJ: Transaction Books.

Cooper, T. W. (1998). New technology effects inventory: Forty leading ethical issues. *Journal of Mass Media Ethics, 13,* 71–92.

Crable, R. E., & Vibbert, S. L. (1985). Managing issues and influencing public policy. *Public Relations Review, 11*(2), 3–16.

Craig, R. T. (1979). Information systems theory and research: An overview of individual information processing. In D. Nimmo (Ed.), *Communication yearbook 3* (pp. 99–121). New Brunswick, NJ: Transaction Books.

Craig, R. T (1993). Why are there so many communication theories? *Journal of Communication, 43*(3), 26–33.

Cronen, V. E., & Davis, L. K. (1978). Problems in the laws-rules-systems trichotomy. *Human Communication Research, 4,* 120–128.

Cronen, V. E., Pearce, W. B., & Harris, L. M. (1982). The coordinated management of meaning: A theory of communication. In F. E. X. Dance (Ed.), *Human communication theory: Comparative essays* (pp. 61–89). New York: Harper & Row.

Cronkhite, G., & Liska, J. R. (1980). The judgment of communicant acceptability. In M. E. Roloff & G. R. Miller (Eds.), *Persuasion: New directions in theory and research* (pp. 100–139). Newbury Park, CA: Sage.

Cusella, L. P. (1982). The effects of source expertise and feedback valence on intrinsic motivation. *Human Communication Research, 9,* 17–32.

Daft, R. L., & Weick, K. E. (1984). Toward a model of organizations as interpretive systems. *Academy of Management Review, 9,* 284–295.

Daly, J. A., Vangelisti, A. I., & Daughton, S. M. (1987). The nature and correlates of conversational sensitivity. *Human Communication Research, 14,* 167–202.

Dance, F. E. X. (1967). Toward a theory of human communication. In F. E. X. Dance (Ed.), *Human communication theory* (pp. 288–309). New York: Holt, Rinehart & Winston.

Dance, F. E. X. (1970). The "concept" of communication. *Journal of Communication, 20,* 201–210.

Dance, F. E. X. (1978). Human communication theory: A highly selective review and two commentaries. In B. D. Ruben (Ed.), *Communication yearbook 2* (pp. 7–22). New Brunswick, NJ: Transaction Books.

Dance, F. E. X. (1985). The functions of human communication. In B. D.Ruben (Ed.), *Information and behavior* (Vol. 1, pp. 62–75). New Brunswick, NJ: Transaction Books.

Danes, J. E. (1978). Communication models of the message-belief change process. In B. D. Ruben (Ed.), *Communication yearbook 2* (pp. 109–124). New Brunswick, NJ: Transaction Books.

Daniels, T. D., & Spiker, B. K. (1987). *Perspectives on organizational communication.* Dubuque, IA: Wm. C. Brown.

Darnell, D. (1971). Toward a reconceptualization of communication. *Journal of Communication, 21*(1), 5–16.

David, P., & Johnson, M. A. (1998). The role of self in third-person effects about body image. *Journal of Communication, 48*, 37–58.

Deetz, S. (1973). Words without things: Toward a social phenomenology of language. *Quarterly Journal of Speech, 59*, 40–51.

Deetz, S., & Mumby, D. (1985). Metaphors, information, and power. In B. D. Ruben (Ed.), *Information and behavior* (Vol. 1, pp. 369–386). New Brunswick, NJ: Transaction Books.

Deetz, S. A. (1982). Critical interpretive research in organizational communication. *Western Journal of Speech Communication, 46*, 131–149.

Deetz, S. A. (1988). Cultural studies: Studying meaning and action in organizations. In J. A. Anderson (Ed.), *Communication yearbook 11* (pp. 335–355). Newbury Park, CA: Sage.

DeFleur, M. L. (1970). *Theories of mass communication* (2nd ed.). New York: David McKay.

DeFleur, M. L., & Ball-Rokeach, S. (1989). *Theories of mass communication* (5th ed.). New York: Longman.

Delia, J. G. (1977). Constructivism and the study of human communication. *Quarterly Journal of Speech, 63*, 66–83.

Delia, J. G., O'Keefe, B. J., & O'Keefe, D. J. (1982). The constructivist approach to communication. In F. E. X. Dance (Ed.), *Human communication theory: Comparative essays* (pp. 147–191). New York: Harper & Row.

Deloughrey, T. J. (1996, November 22). Campus computer use is increasing but not as fast as in previous years. *The Chronicle of Higher Education, 43*, A21–22.

Denzin, N. (1992). *Symbolic interactionism and cultural studies: The politics of interpretation.* Oxford: Basil Blackwell.

Desmond, M. (1999). The incredible shrinking computer, subnotes emerge, cell phones and handhelds converge. *PC World, 17*, 116.

Derlega, V. J., Winstead, B. A., Wong, P. T. P., & Greenspan, M. (1987). Self-disclosure and relationship development: An attributional analysis. In M. E. Roloff & G. R. Miller (Eds.), *Interpersonal processes: New directions in communication research* (pp. 172–187). Newbury Park, CA: Sage.

Desmond, R. J., Singer, J. L., Singer, D. G., Calam, R., & Colimore, K. (1985). Family mediation patterns and television viewing: Young children's use and grasp of the medium. *Human Communication Research, 11*, 461–480.

deTurck, M. A. (1985). A transactional analysis of compliance-gaining behavior: Effects of noncompliance, relational contexts, and actors' gender. *Human Communication Research, 12*, 54–78.

deTurck, M. A. (1987). When communication fails: Physical aggression as a compliance-gaining strategy. *Communication Monographs, 54*, 106–112.

deTurck, M. A., & Miller, G. R. (1985). Deception and arousal: Isolating behavioral correlations of deception. *Human Communication Research, 12*, 181–201.

Devito, J. A. (1986). *The communication handbook: A dictionary.* New York: Harper & Row.

Dillard, J. P., & Burgoon, M. (1985). Situational influences on the selection of compliance-gaining messages: Two tests of the predictive utility of the Cody-McLaughlin typology. *Communication Monographs, 52,* 289–304.

Dillard, J. P., Hunter, J. E., & Burgoon, M. (1984). Sequential-request persuasive strategies: Meta-analysis of foot-in-the-door and door-in-the-face. *Human Communication Research, 10,* 461–488.

Dillard, J. P., Palmer, M. T., & Kinney, T. A. (1995). Relational judgments in an influence context. *Human Communicaton Research, 21,* 331–353.

Dillard, J. P., & Witteman, H. (1985). Romantic relationships at work: Organizational and personal influences. *Human Communication Research, 12,* 99–116.

Dindia, K. (1987). The effect of sex of subject and sex of partner on interruptions. *Human Communication Research, 13,* 345–371.

Dizard, W. P., Jr. (1982). *The coming information age: An overview of technology, economics, and politics.* New York: Longman.

Dizard, W. P., Jr., (1994). *Old media new media: Mass communications in the information age.* New York: Longman.

Doelger, J. A., Hewes, D. E., & Graham, M. L. (1986). Knowing when to "second-guess": The mindful analysis of messages. *Human Communication Research, 12,* 301–338.

Donohue, W. A., & Diez, M. E. (1985). Directive use of negotiation interaction. *Communication Monographs, 52,* 305–318.

Donohue, W. A., Weider-Hatfield, D., Hamilton, M., & Diez, M. E. (1985). Relational distance in managing conflict. *Human Communication Research, 11,* 387–406.

Douglas, D. F., Westley, B. N., & Chaffee, S. H. (1970). An information campaign that changed community attitudes. *Journalism Quarterly, 47,* 479–487, 492.

Douglas, W. (1984). Initial interaction scripts: When knowing is behaving. *Human Communication Research, 11,* 203–219.

Douglas, W. (1987). Question-asking in same- and opposite-sex initial interactions: The effects of anticipated future interaction. *Human Communication Research, 14,* 230–245.

Douglas, W. (1991). Expectations about initial interaction: An examination of the effects of global uncertainty. *Human Communication Research, 17,* 355–384.

Downs, C. (1979). The relationship between communication and job satisfaction. In R. Huseman, C. Logue, & D. Freshley (Eds.), *Readings in interpersonal and organizational communication* (pp. 363–376). Boston: Allyn & Bacon.

Driscoll, P. D., & Salwen, M. B. (1997). Self-perceived knowledge of the O. J. Simpson trial: Third-person perception and perceptions of guilt. *Journalism & Mass Communication Quarterly, 74,* 541–556.

Ducey, R., Krugman, D., & Eckrich, D. (1983). Predicting market segments in the cable industry: The basic and pay subscribers. *Journal of Broadcasting, 27,* 155–161.

Duck, S. (1982). A topography of relationship disengagement and dissolution. In S. Duck (Ed.), *Personal relationships 4: Dissolving personal relationships* (pp. 1–30). London: Academic.

Duck, S. (1985). How to lose friends without influencing people. In M. E. Roloff & G. R. Miller (Eds.), *Interpersonal processes: New directions in communication research* (pp. 278–298). Newbury Park, CA: Sage.

Duck, S. (1990). Relationships as unfinished business: Out of the frying pan and into the 1990s. *Journal of Social and Personal Relationships, 7,* 5–28.

Duck, S., & Miell, D. E. (1986). Charting the development of personal relationships. In R. Gilmour & S. Duck (Eds.), *The emerging field of personal relationships* (pp. 133–143). Hillsdale, NJ: Lawrence Erlbaum Associates.

Duck, S., & Pittman, G. (1994). Social and personal relationships. In M. L. Knapp & G. R. Miller (Eds.), *Handbook of interpersonal communication* (2nd ed., pp. 676–695). Thousand Oaks, CA: Sage.

Dupagne, M. (Winter, 1998). The two faces of HDTV policymaking: United States enters new era of TV broadcasting. *Communication & Technology Policy Newsletter, 3.*

Dutton, J. E., & Duncan, R. B. (1987). The creation of momentum for change through the process of strategic issue diagnosis. *Strategic Management Journal, 8,* 279–295.

Dutton, J. E., & Ottensmeyer, E. (1987). Strategic issue management systems: Forms, functions, and contexts. *Academy of Management Review, 12*(2), 355–365.

Eisenberg, E. M. (1984). Ambiguity as strategy in organizational communication. *Communication Monographs, 51,* 227–242.

Eisenberg, E. M. (1986). Meaning and interpretation in organizations. *Quarterly Journal of Speech, 72,* 88–97.

Eisenberg, E. M., Monge, P. R., & Farace, R. V. (1984). Coorientation on communication rules in managerial dyads. *Human Communication Research, 11,* 261–271.

Eisenberg, E. M., Monge, P. R., & Miller, K. I. (1984). Involvement in communication networks as a predictor of organizational commitment. *Human Communication Research, 10,* 179–201.

Ekman, P., & Friesen, W. V. (1974). Detecting deception from the body or face. *Journal of Personality and Social Psychology, 29,* 288–298.

Fairhurst, G. T., Green, S. G., & Snavely, B. K. (1984). Face support in controlling poor performance. *Human Communication Research, 11,* 273–295.

Fairhurst, G. T., Jordan, J. M., & Neuwirth, K. (1997). What are we here? Managing the meaning of an organizational mission statement. *Journal of Applied Communication Research, 25,* 243–263.

Fairhurst, G. T., Rogers, L. E., & Sarr, R. A. (1987). Manager-subordinate control patterns and judgments about the relationship. In M. L. McLaughlin (Ed.), *Communication yearbook 10* (pp. 395–415). Newbury Park: Sage.

Falcione, R. L., & Kaplan, E. A. (1984). Organizational climate, communication, and culture. In R. N. Bostrom & B. H. Westley (Eds.), *Communication yearbook 8* (pp. 285–309). Newbury Park, CA: Sage.

Falcione, R. L., McCroskey, J. C., & Daly, J. A. (1977). Job satisfaction as a function of employees' communication apprehension, self-esteem, and perceptions of their immediate supervisors. In B. D. Ruben (Ed.), *Communication yearbook 1* (pp. 363–375). New Brunswick, NJ: Transaction Books.

Falcione, R. L., Sussman, L., & Herden, R. P. (1987). Communication climate in organizations. In F. M. Jablin, L. L. Putnam, K. H. Roberts, & L. W. Porter (Eds.), *Handbook of organizational communication* (pp. 195–227). Newbury Park, CA: Sage.

Farace, R. V., Monge, P. R., & Russell, H. (1977). *Communicating and organizing.* Reading: Addison-Wesley.

Farace, R. V., Stewart, J. P., & Taylor, J. A. (1978). Criteria for evaluation of organizational communication effectiveness: Review and synthesis. In B. Ruben (Ed.), *Communication yearbook 2* (pp. 271–292). New Brunswick, NJ: Transaction Books.

Federal Communications Commission (1997). *Advanced television systems and their impact upon the existing television broadcast service (Fifth Report and Order),* 12 FCC Rcd. 12809.

Fenton, F. (1910). The influence of newspaper presentations upon the growth of crime and other anti-social activity. *The American Journal of Sociology, XVI,* 342–371.

410   References

Fenton, F. (1911). The influence of newspaper presentations upon the growth of crime and other anti-social activity. *The American Journal of Sociology, XVI,* 538–564.

Ferraris, C., Carveth, R., & Parrish-Sprowl, J. (1993). Interface precision benchmarks: A case study in organizational identification. *Journal of Applied Communication Research, 21,* 343–357.

Festinger, L. (1957). *A theory of cognitive dissonance.* Stanford, CA: Stanford University Press.

Festinger, L., & Carlsmith, J. M. (1959). Cognitive consequences of forced compliance. *Journal of Abnormal and Social Psychology, 58,* 203–210.

Finn, S., & Roberts, D. (1984). Source, destination, and entropy: Reassessing the role of information theory in communication research. *Communication Research, 11,* 453–476.

Fischhoff, B. (1985). Managing risk perceptions. *Issues in Science and Technology, 2,* 83–96.

Fishbein, M., & Ajzen, I. (1975). *Belief, attitude, intention, and behavior: An introduction to theory and research.* Reading: Addison-Wesley.

Fishbein, M., & Ajzen, I. (1981). Acceptance, yielding and impact: Cognitive processes in persuasion. In R. E. Petty, T. M. Ostrom, & T. C. Brock (Eds.), *Cognitive responses in persuasion* (pp. 339–359). Hillsdale, NJ: Lawrence Erlbaum Associates.

Fisher, B. A. (1978). Information systems theory and research: An overview. In B. D. Ruben (Ed.), *Communication yearbook 2* (pp. 81–108). New Brunswick, NJ: Transaction Books.

Fisher, B. A. (1982). The pragmatic perspective of human communication: A view from system theory. In F. E. X. Dance (Ed.), *Human communication theory: Comparative essays* (pp. 192–219). New York: Harper & Row.

Fitzpatrick, M. A. (1977). A typological approach to communication in relationships. In B. D. Ruben (Ed.), *Communication yearbook 1* (pp. 263–275). New Brunswick, NJ: Transaction Books.

Folger, J. P., & Poole, M. S. (1982). Relational coding schemes: The question of validity. In M. Burgoon (Ed.), *Communication yearbook 5* (pp. 235–247). New Brunswick, NJ: Transaction Books.

Ford, W. S. Z. (1995). Evaluation of the indirect influence of courteous service on customer discretionary behavior. *Human Communication Research, 22,* 65–89.

Foss, S. J., & Griffin, C. L. (1995). Beyond persuasion: A proposal for an invitational rhetoric. *Communication Monographs, 62,* 1995.

Fry, D. L., & Fry, V. H. (1986). A semiotic model for the study of mass communication. In M. L. McLaughlin (Ed.), *Communication yearbook 9* (pp. 443–462). Newbury Park, CA: Sage.

Fulk, J., & Sirish, M. (1986). Distortion of communication in hierarchical relationships. In M. L. McLaughlin (Ed.), *Communication yearbook 9* (pp. 483–510). Newbury Park, CA: Sage.

Fulk, J., Steinfield, C. W., Schmitz, J., & Power, J. G. (1987). A social information processing model of media use in organizations. *Communication Research, 14,* 529–552.

Gerbner, G. (1967). An institutional approach to mass communications research. In L. Thayer (Ed.), *Communication: Theory and research* (pp. 429–445). Springfield, IL: Charles C. Thomas.

Gerbner, G., Gross, L., Morgan, M., & Signorielli, N. (1986). Living with television: The dynamics of the cultivation process. In J. Bryant & D. Zillmann (Eds.), *Perspectives on media effects* (pp. 17–40). Hillsdale, NJ: Lawrence Erlbaum Associates.

Gergen, K. J., & Gergen, M. M. (1988). Narrative and the self as relationship. In L. Berkowitz (Ed.), *Advances in experimental social psychology* (Vol. 21, pp. 17–56). New York: Academic.

Giles, H., Mulac, A., Bradac, J. J., & Johnson, P. (1987). Speech accommodation theory: The first decade and beyond. In M. L. McLaughlin (Ed.), *Communication yearbook 10* (pp. 13–48). Newbury Park, CA: Sage.

Giles, H., & Powesland, P. F. (1975). *Speech style and social evaluation*. London: Academic.

Giles, H., & Street, R. L., Jr. (1985). Communicator characteristics and behavior. In M. L. Knapp & G. R. Miller (Eds.), *Handbook of interpersonal communication* (pp. 205–261). Newbury Park, CA: Sage.

Giles, H., & Street, R. L., Jr. (1994). Communicator characteristics and behavior. In M. L. Knapp & G. R. Miller (Eds.), *Handbook of interpersonal communication* (2nd ed., pp. 103–161). Thousand Oaks, CA: Sage.

Giles, H., & Wiemann, J. M. (1987). Language, social comparison, and power. In C. R. Berger & S. H. Chaffee (Eds.), *Handbook of communication science* (pp. 350–384). Newbury Park, CA: Sage.

Gitlin, T. (1980). *The whole world is watching*. Berkeley: University of California Press.

Glaser, S. R., Zamanou, S., & Hacker, K. (1987). Measuring and interpreting organizational culture. *Management Communication Quarterly, 1*, 173–198.

Golden, L. L., & Alpert, M. I. (1987). Comparative analysis of the relative effectiveness of one- and two-sided communication for contrasting products. *Journal of Advertising, 16*(1), 18–25.

Goldsmith, D. J., & Baxter, L. A. (1996). Constituting relationships in talk: A taxonomy of speech events in social and personal relationships. *Human Communication Research, 23*, 87–114.

Goldsmith, D. J., & Fitch, K. (1997). The normative context of advice as social support. Human *Communication Research, 23*, 454–476.

Goodall, H. L., Jr. (1989). *Casing a promised land*. Carbondale, IL: Southern Illinois University Press.

Goodall, H. L., Jr. (1990). A theater of motives and the "meaningful orders of persons and things." In J. A. Anderson (Ed.), *Communication yearbook 13* (pp. 69–94). Newbury Park, CA: Sage.

Graber, D. A. (1989). An information processing approach to public opinion analysis. In B. Dervin, L. Grossberg, B. J. O'Keefe, & E. Wartella (Eds), *Rethinking communication: Particular exemplars* (Vol. 2, pp. 103–116). Newbury Park, CA: Sage.

Grant, A. E. (1997). Introduction. In P. B. Seel & A. E. Grant (Eds.), *Broadcast technology update, production and transmission*. Boston: Focal Press.

Greeley, H., Case, L., Howland, E., Gough, J. B., Ripley, P., Perkins, F. B., Lyman, J. B., Brisbane, A., Hall, Rev. E. E., et al. (1872). *The great industries of the United States: Being an historical summary of the origin, growth, and perfection of the chief industrial arts of this country*. Hartford: J. B. Burr & Hyde.

Green, S. G., & Mitchell, T. R. (1979). Attributional processes of leaders in leader–member interactions. *Organizational Behavior and Human Performance, 23*, 429–458.

Greenberg, B. S., & Salwen, M. B. (1996). Mass communication theory and research: Concepts and models. In M. B. Salwen & D. W. Stacks (Eds.), *An integrated approach to communication theory and research* (pp. 63–78). Mahwah, NJ: Lawrence Erlbaum Associates.

Greene, J. O. (1984). A cognitive approach to human communication: An action assembly theory. *Communication Monographs, 51,* 289–306.

Greene, J. O. (1995). Production of messages in pursuit of multiple social goals: Action assembly theory contributions to the study of cognitive encoding processes. In B. R. Burleson (Ed.), *Communication yearbook 18* (pp. 26–53). Thousand Oaks, CA: Sage.

Greene, J. O., O'Hair, H. D., Cody, M. J., & Yen, C. (1985). Planning and control of behavior during deception. *Human Communication Research, 11,* 335–364.

Grimes, T., & Meadowcroft, J. (1995). Attention to television and some methods for its measurement. *Communication yearbook 18* (pp. 133–161). Newbury Park, CA: Sage.

Grossberg, L. (1982). Does communication theory need intersubjectivity? Toward an immanent philosophy of interpersonal relations. In M. Burgoon (Ed.), *Communication yearbook 6* (pp. 171–205). Beverly Hills, CA: Sage.

Grossberg, L. (1983). Cultural studies revisted and revised. In M. S. Mander (Ed.), *Communications in transition* (pp. 39–70). New York: Praeger.

Grunig, J. E. (1989). Sierra Club study shows who become activists. *Public Relations Review, 15,* 3–24.

Grunig, J. E. (Ed.). (1992). *Excellence in public relations and communication management.* Hillsdale, NJ: Lawrence Erlbaum Associates.

Grunig, J. E., & Grunig, L. A. (1989). Toward a theory of the public relations behavior of organizations: Review of a program of research. In J. E. Grunig & L. A. Grunig (Eds.), *Public relations research annual* (Vol. 1, pp. 27–63). Hillsdale, NJ: Lawrence Erlbaum Associates.

Grunig, J. E., & Hunt, T. (1984). *Managing public relations.* New York: Holt, Rinehart & Winston.

Grunig, J. E. (Ed.). (1992). *Excellence in public relations and communication management.* Hillsdale, NJ: Lawrence Erlbaum Associates.

Gudykunst, W. B., & Hammer, M. R. (1988). The influence of social identity and intimacy of interethnic relationships on uncertainty reduction processes. *Human Communication Research, 14,* 569–601.

Gudykunst, W. B., Yang, S., & Nishida, T. A. (1985). Cross-cultural test of uncertainty reduction theory. *Human Communication Research, 11,* 407–455.

Gunson, D., & Collins, C. (1997). From the *I* to *We*: Discourse ethics, identity, and the pragmatics of partnership in the west of Scotland. *Communication Theory, 7,* 277–300.

Gunther, A. C. (1995). Overrating the X-rating: The third-person perception and support for censorship of pornography. *Journal of Communication, 45,* 27–38.

Gunther, A. C., & Mundy, P. (1993). Biased optimism and the third-person effect. *Journalism Quarterly, 70,* 58-67.

Habermas, J. (1984). *The theory of communicative action* (Vol. 1, T. McCarthy, Trans.). Boston: Beacon Press.

Hackman, J. R. (1976). Group influences on individuals. In M. D. Dunnette (Ed.), *Handbook of industrial and organizational psychology* (pp. 1455–1525). Chicago: Rand McNally.

Hall, S. (1980). Encoding/decoding. In S. Hall, D. Hobson, A. Lowe, & P. Wilis (Eds.), *Culture, media, language: Working papers in cultural studies, 1972–1979* (pp. 128–138). London: Hutchinson.

Hample, D., & Dallinger, J. M. (1988). Individual differences in cognitive editing standards. *Human Communication Research, 14,* 123–144.

Haring, B. (1999, January 20). Linking the clicker and the cursor: Interactive TV is finally real, but services are jumbled. *USA Today*, 4D.

Harris, L. M. (1995). Differences that make a difference. In L. M. Harris (Ed.), *Health and the new media: Technologies transforming personal and public health* (pp. 3–18). Mahwah, NJ: Lawrence Erlbaum Associates.

Hawes, L. C. (1973). Elements of a model for communication processes. *Quarterly Journal of Speech, 59,* 11–21.

Hawes, L. C. (1975). *Pragmatics of analoguing: Theory and model construction in communication.* Reading, MA: Addison-Wesley.

Heath, R. L. (1976). Variability in value system priorities as decision-making adaptation to situational differences. *Communication Monographs, 43,* 325–333.

Heath, R. L. (1986). *Realism and relativism: A perspective on Kenneth Burke.* Macon, GA: Mercer University Press.

Heath, R. L. (1988). The rhetoric of issue advertising: A rationale, a case study, a critical perspective—and more. *Central States Speech Journal, 39,* 99–109.

Heath, R. L. (1994). *Management of corporate communication: From interpersonal contacts to external affairs.* Hillsdale, NJ: Lawrence Erlbaum Publishers.

Heath, R. L. (1997). *Strategic issues management: Organizations and public policy challenges.* Thousand Oaks, CA: Sage.

Heath, R. L., & Douglas, W. (1990). Involvement: A key variable in people's reaction to public policy issues. In L. A. Grunig & J. E. Grunig (Eds.), *Public relations research annual* (Vol. 2, pp. 193–204). Hillsdale, NJ: Lawrence Erlbaum Associates.

Heeter, C., & Baldwin, T. (1988). Channel types and viewing styles. In C. Heeter & B. Greenberg (Eds.), *Cableviewing* (pp. 167–176). Norwood, NJ: Ablex.

Heider, F. (1958). *The psychology of interpersonal relations.* New York: Wiley.

Heikkinen, K. J., & Reese, S. D. (1986). Newspaper readers and a new information medium: Information need and channel orientation as predictors of videotext adoption. *Communication Research, 13,* 19–36.

Henderson, J. V. (1995). Meditation on the new media and professional education. In L. M. Harris (Ed.), *Health and the new media: Technologies transforming personal and public health* (pp. 185-205). Mahwah, NJ: Lawrence Erlbaum Associates.

Hewes, D. E., Graham, M. L., Doelger, J. A., & Pavitt, C. (1985). "Second-guessing": Message interpretation in social networks. *Human Communication Research, 11,* 299–334.

Hewes, D. E., Graham, M. L., Monsour, M., & Doelger, J. A. (1989). Cognition and social information-gathering strategies: Reinterpretation assessment in second-guessing. *Human Communication Research, 16,* 297–321.

Hewes, D. E., & Planalp, S. (1982). There is nothing as useful as a good theory: The influence of social knowledge on interpersonal communication. In M. E. Roloff & C. R. Berger (Eds.), *Social cognition and communication* (pp. 107–150). Newbury Park, CA: Sage.

Hewes, D. E., & Planalp, S. (1987). The individual's place in communication science. In C. R. Berger & S. H. Chaffee (Eds.), *Handbook of communication science* (pp. 146–183). Newbury Park, CA: Sage.

Hirokawa, R. Y. (1985). Discussion procedures and decision-making performance: A test of a functional perspective. *Human Communication Research, 12,* 203–224.

Hirokawa, R. Y. (1988). Group communication and decision-making performance: A continued test of the functional perspective. *Human Communication Research, 14,* 487–515.

Hirsch, P. (1979). The role of television and popular culture in contemporary society. In H. Newcomb (Ed.), *Television: The critical view* (2nd ed., pp. 249–279). New York: Oxford University Press.

Hocking, J., Bauchner, J., Kaminski, E., & Miller, G. (1979). Detecting deceptive communication from verbal, visual, and paralinguistic cues. *Human Communication Research, 6,* 33–46.

Hodge, W. W. (1995). *Interactive television, A comprehensive guide for multimedia technologists.* New York: McGraw-Hill.

Hoffman, E., & Roman, P. M. (1984). Information diffusion in the implementation of innovation process. *Communication Research, 11,* 117–140.

Holman, J. M. (1998). *An information commons: Protection for free expression in the new information environment.* Unpublished doctoral dissertation, Indiana University, Bloomington.

Honeycutt, J. M., Cantrill, J. M., & Greene, R. W. (1989). Memory structures for relational escalation. *Human Communication Research, 16,* 62–90.

Hovland, C. I., Janis, I. L., & Kelley, H. H. (1953). *Communication and persuasion.* New Haven: Yale University Press.

Huber, G. P., & Daft, R. L. (1987). The information environments of organizations. In F. M. Jablin, L. L. Putnam, K. H. Roberts, & L. W. Porter (Eds.), *Handbook of organizational communication* (pp.130–164). Newbury Park, CA: Sage.

Hudson, H. E. (April, 1998). Global information infrastructure: Eliminating the distance barrier. *Business Economics, 33,* 25.

Hughes, M. (1980). The fruits of cultivation analysis: A re-examination of television in fear of victimization, alienation and approval of violence. *Public Opinion Quarterly, 44,* 287–302.

Hunter, J. E., & Boster, F. J. (1987). A model of compliance-gaining message selection. *Communication Monographs, 54,* 63–84.

Huspek, M. (1997). Toward normative theories of communication with reference to the Frankfurt School: An introduction. *Communication Theory, 7,* 265–276.

Infante, D. A., & Gorden, W. I. (1985). Superiors' argumentativeness and verbal aggressiveness as predictors of subordinates' satisfaction. *Human Communication Research, 12,* 117–125.

Infante, D. A., Rancer, A. S., & Jordan, F. F. (1996). Affirming and nonaffirming style, dyad sex, and the perception of argumentation and verbal aggression in an interpersonal dispute. *Human Communication Research, 22,* 315–334.

Innis, H. (1951). *The bias of communication.* Toronto: University of Toronto Press.

Jablin, F. M. (1979). Superior–subordinate communication: The state of the art. *Psychological Bulletin, 86,* 1201–1222.

Jablin, F. M. (1980). Organizational communication theory and research: An overview of communication climate and network research. In D. Nimmo (Ed.), *Communication yearbook 4* (pp. 327–347). New Brunswick, NJ: Transaction Books.

Jablin, F. M. (1982a). Formal structural characteristics of organizations and superior–subordinate communication. *Human Communication Research, 8,* 338–347.

Jablin, F. M. (1982b). Organizational communication: An assimilation theory. In M. E. Roloff & C. R. Berger (Eds.), *Social cognition and communication* (pp. 255–286). Newbury Park, CA: Sage.

Jablin, F. M. (1984). Assimilating new members into organizations. In R. N. Bostrom & B. H. Westley (Eds.), *Communication yearbook 8* (pp. 594–626). Newbury Park, CA: Sage.

Jablin, F. M. (1985). Task/work relationships. A life-span perspective. In M. L. Knapp & G. R. Miller (Eds.), *Handbook of interpersonal communication* (pp. 615-654). Newbury Park, CA: Sage.

Jablin, F. M., & Krone, K. J. (1987). Organizational assimilation. In C. R. Berger & S. H. Chaffee (Eds.), *Handbook of communication science* (pp. 711–746). Newbury Park, CA: Sage.

Jablin, F. M., & Krone, K. J. (1994). Task/work relationships: A life-span perspective. In M. L. Knapp & G. R. Miller (Eds.), *Handbook of interpersonal communication* (2nd ed., pp. 621–675). Thousand Oaks, CA: Sage.

Jablin, F. M., & McComb, K. B. (1984). The employment screening interview: An organizational assimilation and communication perspective. In R. N. Bostrom & B. H. Westley (Eds.), *Communication yearbook 8* (pp. 137–163). Newbury Park, CA: Sage.

Jacobs, S. (1985). Language. In M. L. Knapp & G. R. Miller (Eds.), *Handbook of interpersonal communication* (pp. 313–343). Newbury Park, CA: Sage.

Jacobs, S. (1994). Language and interpersonal communication. In M. L. Knapp & G. R. Miller (Eds.), *Handbook of interpersonal communication* (2nd ed., pp. 199–228). Thousand Oaks, CA: Sage.

Janis, I. L. (1972). *Victims of groupthink: A psychological study of foreign policy decisions and fiascos.* Boston: Houghton Mifflin.

Janis, I. L., Hovland, C. I., Field, P. B., Linton, H., Graham, E., Cohen, A. R., Refe, D., Abelson, R. P., Lesser, G. S., & King, B. T. (1959). *Personality and persuasibility.* New Haven: Yale University Press.

Jarboe, S. (1988). A comparison of input–output, process–output, and input–process–output models of small group problem-solving effectiveness. *Communication Monographs, 55,* 121–142.

Jeffres, L. (1978). Cable TV and viewer selectivity. *Journal of Broadcasting, 22,* 176–177.

Jensen, J. (March 12, 1999). Everything you wanted to know about MP3 but were afraid to ask. *Entertainment Weekly,* 33–37.

Johnson, W. (1946). *People in quandaries.* New York: Harper & Brothers.

Kahan, J. P. (1975). Subjective probability interpretation of the risky shift. *Journal of Personality and Social Psychology, 31,* 977–982.

Kaplan, A. (1964). *The conduct of inquiry.* San Francisco, CA: Chandler.

Katz, D., & Kahn, R. L. (1966). *The social psychology of organizations.* New York: Wiley.

Katz, E. (1959). Mass communication research and the study of culture. *Studies in Public Communication, 2,* 1–16.

Katz, E., Blumler, J. G., & Gurevitch, M. (1974). Utilization of mass communication by the individual. In J. G. Blumler & E. Katz (Eds.), *The uses of mass communications: Current perspectives on gratifications research* (pp. 19–32). Newbury Park, CA: Sage.

Kazoleas, D. (1993). The impact of argumentativeness on resistant to persuasion. *Human Communication Research, 20,* 118–137.

Kellermann, K. (1987). Information exchange in social interaction. In M. E. Roloff & G. R. Miller (Eds.), *Interpersonal processes: New directions in communication research* (pp. 188–217). Newbury Park, CA: Sage.

Kellermann, K. (1992). Communication: Inherently strategic and primarily automatic. *Communication Monographs, 59,* 288–300.

Kellerman, K., & Jarboe, S. (1987). Conservatism in judgement: Is the risky shift-ee really risky, really? In M. L. McLaughlin (Ed.), *Communication yearbook 10* (pp. 259–282). Newbury Park, CA: Sage.

Kelley, G. (1955). *The psychology of personal constructs.* New York: Norton.

Kelley, H. H. (1972). Attribution in social interaction. In E. E. Jones, H. H. Kanouse, H. H. Kelley, R. E. Nisbett, S. Valins, & B. Weiner (Eds), *Attribution: Perceiving the causes of behavior* (pp. 1–26). Morristown, NJ: General Learning Press.

Kelley, H. H. (1973). The processes of causal attribution. *American Psychologist, 28,* 107–128.

Kennamer, J. D., & Chaffee, S. H. (1982). Communication of political information during early presidential primaries: Cognition, affect, and uncertainty. In M. Burgoon (Ed.), *Communication yearbook 5* (pp. 627–650). New Brunswick, NJ: Transaction Books.

Kerlinger, F. N. (1973). *Foundations of behavioral research* (2nd ed.). New York: Holt, Rinehart & Winston.

Kippax, S., & Murray, J. P. (1980). Using the mass media: Need gratification and perceived utility. *Communication Research, 7,* 335–360.

Klapper, J. T. (1960). *The effects of mass communication.* New York: Free Press.

Knapp, M. L. (1978). *Social intercourse: From greeting to goodbye.* Boston: Allyn & Bacon.

Knapp, M. L., Ellis, D. G., & Williams, B. A. (1980). Perceptions of communication behavior associated with relationship terms. *Communication Monographs, 47,* 262–278.

Knapp, M. L., Miller, G. R., & Fudge, K. (1994). Background and current trends in the study of interpersonal communication. In M. L. Knapp & G. R. Miller (Eds.), *Handbook of interpersonal communication* (2nd ed., pp. 3–20). Thousand Oaks, CA: Sage.

Knowlton, S. W., & Berger, C. R. (1997). Message planning, communication failure, and cognitive load: Further explorations of the hierarchy principle. *Human Communication Research, 24,* 4–30.

Koolstra, C. M., & Van Der Voort, T. H. A. (1996). Longitudinal effects of television on children's leisure-time reading: A test of three explanatory models. *Human Communication Research, 23,* 4–35.

Korzybski, A. (1948). *Science and sanity: An introduction to non-Aristotelian systems and general semantics* (3rd ed.). Lakeville, CT: International Neo-Aristotelian Library.

Kramer, M. W. (1989). Communication during intraorganizational job transfers. *Management Communication Quarterly, 3,* 219–248.

Kramer, M. W. (1996). A longitudinal study of peer communication during job transfers: The impact of frequency, quality, and network multiplexity on adjustment. *Human Communication Research, 23,* 59–86.

Krippendorff, K. (1975). Information theory. In G. J. Hanneman & W. J. McEwen (Eds.), *Communication and behavior* (pp. 351–389). Reading, MA: Addison-Wesley.

Krippendorff, K. (1977). Information systems theory and research: An overview. In B. D. Ruben (Ed.), *Communication yearbook 1* (pp. 149–171). New Brunswick, NJ: Transaction Books.

Krone, K. J., Jablin, F. M., & Putnam, L. L. (1987). Communication theory and organizational communication: Multiple perspectives. In F. M. Jablin, L. L. Putnam, K. H. Roberts, & L. W. Porter (Eds.), *Handbook of organizational communication* (pp. 18–40). Newbury Park, CA: Sage.

Krull, R., Watt, J. H., & Lichty, L. W. (1977). Entropy and structure: Two measures of complexity in television programs. *Communication Research, 4,* 61–86.

Kuhn, T. S. (1970). *The structure of scientific revolutions.* Chicago: University of Chicago Press.

Langer, S. K. (1951) *Philosophy in a new key* (2nd ed.). New York: New American Library.

LaPiere, R. T. (1934). Attitudes vs. action. *Social Forces, 13*, 230–237.

Lasorsa, D. L. (1989). Real and perceived effects of "Amerika." *Journalism Quarterly, 66*, 373–378, 529.

Lasswell, H. D. (1927). *Propaganda technique in the World War.* New York: Knopf.

Lasswell, H. D. (1948). The structure and function of communication in society. In L. Bryson (Ed.), *The communication of ideas* (pp. 37–51). New York: Harper.

Lazarsfeld, P. F., Berelson, B., & Gaudet, H. (1948). *The people's choice.* New York: Columbia University Press.

Lee, I. J. (1941). *Language habits in human affairs: An introduction to general semantics.* New York: Harper.

Lee, I. J. (1952). *How to talk with people.* New York: Harper.

Lee, J., & Jablin, F. M. (1995). Maintenance communication in superior–subordinate work relationships. *Human Communication Research, 22*, 220–257.

Lenert, E. M. (1998). A communication theory perspective on telecommunications policy. *Journal of Communication, 48*, 3–23.

Levy, S. (1999, May 31). The new digital galaxy. *Newsweek,* 57-62.

Lewin, K. (1951). *Field theory in social science.* Westport, CT: Greenwood.

Liebert, R. M., Neale, J. M., & Davidson, E. S. (1973). *The early window: Effects of television on children and youth.* New York: Pergamon.

Lippmann, W. (1922). *Public opinion.* New York: Harcourt Brace.

Littlejohn, S. W. (1989). *Theories of human communication* (3rd ed.). Belmont, CA: Wadsworth.

Lometi, G. E., Reeves, B., & Bybee, C. R. (1977). Investigating the assumptions of uses and gratifications research. *Communication Research, 4*, 321–338.

Lowery, S., & DeFleur, M. L. (1983). *Milestones in mass communication theories and research: Media effects.* New York: Longman.

Mangham, I. L., & Overington, M.A. (1987). *Organizations as theatre: A social psychology of dramatic appearances.* New York: Wiley.

Mares, M. (1996). The role of source confusions in television's cultivation of social reality judgments. *Human Communication Research, 23*, 278–297.

Marien, M. (1996). New communications technology, a survey of impacts and issues. *Telecommunications Policy, 20*, 375–387.

Marks, M. L. (1986). The question of quality circles. *Psychology Today, 20*(3), 36–46.

Markus, M. L. (1987). Toward a "critical mass" theory of interactive media: Universal access, interdependence and diffusion. *Communication Research, 14*, 491–511.

Marwell, G., & Schmitt, D. R. (1967). Dimensions of compliance-gaining behavior: An empirical analysis. *Sociometry, 30*, 350–364.

Mathias, C. J. (1999). An expert opinion: Wireless—still chasing wire, but catching up. *Electronic Design, 47*, 6.

McCombs, M. E., & Gilbert, S. (1986). News influence on our pictures of the world. In J. Bryant & D. Zillmann (Eds.), *Perspectives on media effects* (pp. 1–15). Hillsdale, NJ: Lawrence Erlbaum Associates.

McCombs, M. E., & Shaw, D. L. (1972). The agenda-setting function of the mass media. *Public Opinion Quarterly, 36*, 176–187.

McCornack, S. A., & Levine, T. R. (1990). When lovers become leery: The relationship between suspicion and accuracy in detecting deception. *Communication Monographs, 57*, 219–230.

McDermott, S., & Medhurst, M. (1984, May). *Reasons for subscribing to cable television.* Paper presented to the International Communication Association conference, San Francisco.

McGinnis, J. M., Deering, M. J., & Patrick, K. (1995). Public health information and the new media: a view from the public health service. In L. M. Harris (Ed.), *Health and the new media: Technologies transforming personal and public health* (pp. 127–141). Mahwah, NJ: Lawrence Erlbaum Associates.

McGuire, W. J. (1864). Inducing resistance to persuasion: Some contemporary approaches. *Advances in Experimental Social Psychology, 1,* 192–229.

McGuire, W. J. (1968a). Personality and attitude change: An information-processing theory. In A. G. Greenwald, T. C. Brock, & T. M. Ostrom (Eds.), *Psychological foundations of attitudes* (pp. 171–196). New York: Academic.

McGuire, W. J. (1968b). Personality and susceptibility to social influence. In E. F. Borgatta & W. W. Lambert (Eds.), *Handbook of personality theory and research* (pp. 1130–1187). Chicago: Rand McNally.

McGuire, W. J. (1981). Theoretical foundations of campaigns: In R. E. Rice & W. J. Paisley (Eds.), *Public communication campaigns* (pp. 41–70). Newbury Park, CA: Sage.

McLaughlin, M. L. (1984). *Conversation: How talk is organized.* Newbury Park, CA: Sage.

McLeod, J. M., Becker, L. B., & Byrnes, J. E. (1974). Another look at the agenda setting function of the press. *Communication Research, 1,* 131–166

McLeod, J. M., & Chaffee, S. H. (1973). Interpersonal approaches to communication research. *American Behavioral Scientist, 16,* 469–499.

McLuhan, M. (1964). *Understanding media: The extensions of man.* New York: New American Library.

McQuail, D. (1984). With the benefit of hindsight: Reflections on uses and gratifications research. *Critical Studies in Mass Communication, 1,* 177–193.

McQuail, D. (1987). Functions of communication: A nonfunctionalist overview. In C. R. Berger & S. H. Chaffee (Eds.), *Handbook of communication science* (pp. 327–349). Newbury Park, CA: Sage.

Mead, G. H. (1934). *Mind, self, and society.* Chicago: University of Chicago Press.

Mehrabian, A. (1981). *Silent messages: Implicit communication of emotions and attitudes* (2nd ed.). Belmont, CA: Wadsworth.

Mendelsohn, H. (1966). *Mass entertainment.* New Haven, CT: College and University Press.

Mendelsohn, H. (1973). Some reasons why information campaigns can succeed. *Public Opinion Quarterly, 37,* 50–61.

Meringoff, L. K., Vibbert, M. M., Char, C. A., Fernie, D. E., Bunker, G. S., & Gardner, H. (1983). How is children's learning from television distinctive? Exploiting the medium methodologically. In J. Bryant & D. R. Anderson (Eds.), *Children's understanding of television: Research on attention and comprehension* (pp. 151–179). New York: Academic.

Metts, S., & Cupach, W. R. (1990). The influence of relationship beliefs and problem-solving responses on satisfaction in romantic relationships. *Human Communication Research, 17,* 170–185.

Metzger, G. D. (1983). Cable television audiences: Learning from the past and the present. *Journal of Advertising Research, 23,* 41-47.

Meyer, T. P., Trandt, P. J., & Anderson, J. A. (1980). Nontraditional mass communication research methods: An overview of observational case studies of media use in natural settings. In D. Nimmo (Ed.), *Communication yearbook 4* (pp. 261–275). New Brunswick, NJ: Transaction Books.

Meyrowitz, J. (1985). *No sense of place: The impact of electronic media on social behavior.* New York: Oxford University Press.

Millar, F. E., & Rogers, L. E. (1976). A relational approach. In G. Miller (Ed.), *Explorations in interpersonal communication* (pp. 87–103). Newbury Park, CA: Sage.

Millar, F. E., & Rogers, L. E. (1987). Relational dimensions of interpersonal dynamics. In M. E. Roloff & G. R. Miller (Eds.), *Interpersonal processes: New directions in communication research* (pp. 117–139). Newbury Park, CA: Sage.

Miller, G. R. (1980). On being persuaded: Some basic distinctions. In M. E. Roloff & G. R. Miller (Eds.), *Persuasion: New directions in theory and research* (pp. 11–28). Newbury Park, CA: Sage.

Miller, G. R. (1987). Persuasion. In C. R. Berger & S. H. Chaffee (Eds.), *Handbook of communication science* (pp. 446–483). Newbury Park, CA: Sage.

Miller, G. R., Boster, F. J., Roloff, M. E., & Seibold, D. R. (1987). MBRS rekindled: Some thoughts on compliance gaining in interpersonal settings. In M. E. Roloff & G. R. Miller (Eds.), *Interpersonal processes: New directions in communication research* (pp. 89–116). Newbury Park, CA: Sage.

Miller, G. R., & Burgoon, M. (1978). Persuasion research: Review and commentary. In B. D. Ruben (Ed.), *Communication Yearbook 8* (pp. 29–47). New Brunswick, NJ: Transaction Books.

Miller, G. R., & Steinberg, M. (1975). *Between people: A new analysis of interpersonal communication.* Chicago: Science Research Associates.

Miller, V. D., & Jablin, F. M. (1991). Information seeking during organizational entry: Influences, tactics, and a model of the process. *Academy of Management Review, 16,* 92–120.

Miller, V. D., Johnson, J. R., & Grau, J. (1994). Antecedents to willingness to participate in a planned organizational change. *Journal of Applied Communication Research, 22,* 59–80.

Mitroff, I. I. (1983). *Stakeholders of the organizational mind: Toward a new view of organizational policy making.* San Francisco, CA: Jossey-Bass.

Monge, P. R. (1977). The systems perspective as a theoretical basis for the study of human communication. *Communication Quarterly, 25,* 19–29.

Monge, P. R. (1987). The network level of analysis. In C. R. Berger & S. H. Chaffee (Eds.), *Handbook of communication science* (pp. 239–270). Newbury Park, CA: Sage.

Monge, P. R., & Eisenberg, E. M. (1987). Emergent communication networks. In F. M. Jablin, L. L. Putnam, K. H. Roberts, & L. W. Porter (Eds.), *Handbook of organizational communication* (pp. 304–342). Newbury Park, CA: Sage.

Morgan, G. (1982). Cybernetics and organization theory: Epistemology or technique? *Human Relations, 35,* 521–537.

Morgan, G. (1986). *Images of organization.* Newbury Park, CA: Sage.

Morley, D. D., & Walker, K. B. (1987). The role of importance, novelty, and plausibility in producing belief change. *Communication Monographs, 54,* 436–442.

Morton, T. L., Alexander, J. F., & Altman, I. (1976). Communication and relationship definition. In G. R. Miller (Ed.), *Explorations in interpersonal communication* (pp. 105–125). Newbury Park: Sage.

Moschis, G. P. (1980). Consumer information use: Individual versus social predictors. *Communication Research, 7,* 139–160.

Motley, M. T. (1992). Mindfulness in solving communicators' dilemmas. *Communication Monographs, 59,* 306–314.

Muehling, D. D. (1987). An investigation of factors underlying attitude-toward-advertising-in-general. *Journal of Advertising, 16*(1), 32–40.

Mumby, D. K. (1987). The political function of narrative in organizations. *Communication Monographs, 54,* 113–127.

Mumby, D. K. (1988). *Communication and power in organizations: Discourse, ideology, and domination.* Norwood, NJ: Ablex.

Nelson, C., Treichler, P. A., & Grossberg, L. (1992). Cultural studies: An introduction. In L. Grossberg, C. Nelson, & P. A. Treichler (Eds.), *Cultural studies* (pp. 10–22). New York: Routledge.

Newcomb, T. M. (1953). An approach to the study of communicative acts. *Psychological Review, 60,* 393–404.

Nimmo, D. (1978). *Political communication and public opinion in America.* Santa Monica, CA: Goodyear Publishing.

Office of Technology Assessment (1990). *Critical connections: Communications for the future.* Washington, DC: U.S. Government Printing Office.

Ogden, C. K., & Richards, I. A. (1923). *The meaning of meaning.* New York: Harcourt, Brace Jovanovich.

Ogilvie, J. H., & Haslett, B. (1985). Communicating peer feedback in a task group. *Human Communication Research, 12,* 79–98.

O'Keefe, B. J. (1988). The logic of message design: Individual differences in reasoning about communication. *Communication Monographs, 55,* 80–103.

O'Keefe, B. J., & Delia, J. G. (1982). Impression formation and message production. In M. E. Roloff & C. R. Berger (Eds.), *Social cognition and communication* (pp. 33–72). Newbury Park, CA: Sage.

O'Keefe, B. J., & Lambert, B. L. (1995). Managing the flow of ideas: A local management approach to message design. In B. R. Burleson (Ed.), *Communication yearbook 18* (pp. 54–82). Thousand Oaks, CA: Sage.

O'Keefe, B. J., & McCornack, S. A. (1987). Message design logic and message goal structures. *Human Communication Research, 14,* 68–92.

O'Keefe, B. J., & Shepherd, G. J. (1987). The pursuit of multiple objectives in face-to-face persuasive interaction: Effects of construct differentiation on message organization. *Communication Monographs, 54,* 396–419.

O'Keefe, D. J. (1987). The persuasive effects of delaying identification on high- and low-credibility communicators: A meta-analytic review. *Central States Speech Journal, 38,* 63–72.

O'Keefe, D. J. (1990). *Persuasion: Theory and research.* Newbury Park, CA: Sage.

O'Keefe, D. J., & Figge, M. (1997). A guilt-based explanation of the door-in-the-face influence strategy. *Human Communication Research, 24,* 64–81.

Oliver, R. L. (1981). Measurement and evaluation of satisfaction processes in retail settings. *Journal of Retailing, 51,* 25–48.

Osgood, C. E. (1953). *Method and theory in experimental psychology.* New York: Oxford University Press.

Osgood, C. E. (1963). On understanding and creating sentences. *American Psychologist, 18,* 735–751.

Osgood, C. E., Suci, G. J., & Tannenbaum, P. H. (1957). *The measurement of meaning.* Urbana, IL: University of Illinois Press.

Pacanowsky, M. E., & O'Donnell-Trujillo, N. (1983). Organizational communication as cultural performance. *Communication Monographs, 50,* 126–147.

Palmgreen, P. (1984). Uses and gratifications: A theoretical perspective. In R. N. Bostrom & B. H. Westley (Eds.), *Communication yearbook 8* (pp. 20–55). Newbury Park, CA: Sage.

Palmgreen, P., & Rayburn, J. D., II (1982). Gratifications sought and media exposure: An expectancy value model. *Communication Research, 9,* 561–580.

Palmgreen, P., & Rayburn, J. D., II (1985a). A comparison of gratification models of media satisfaction. *Communication Monographs, 52,* 334–346.

Palmgreen, P., & Rayburn, J. D., II. (1985b). An expectancy-value approach to media gratifications. In K. Rosengren, L. Wenner, & P. Palmgreen (Eds.), *Media gratifications research: Current perspectives* (pp. 61–72). Newbury Park, CA: Sage.

Palmgreen, P., Wenner, L. A., & Rayburn, J. D., II. (1981). Gratification discrepancies and news program choice. *Communication Research, 8,* 451–478.

Palmgreen, P., Wenner, L. A., & Rosengren, K. E. (1985). Uses and gratifications research: The past ten years. In K. E. Rosengren, L. A.Wenner, & P. Palmgreen (Eds.), *Media gratifications research: Current perspectives* (pp. 11–37). Newbury Park, CA: Sage.

Panici, D. A. (1998, Spring). New media and the introductory mass communication course. *Journalism & Mass Communication Educator, 53,* 52-63.

Papert, S. (1993). *The children's machine: Rethinking school in the age of the computer.* New York: Basic Books.

Parker, E. B. (1973). Implications of new information technology. *Public Opinion Quarterly, 37,* 590-600.

Parks, M. R. (1994). Communicative competence and interpersonal control. In M. L. Knapp & G. R. Miller (Eds.), *Handbook of interpersonal communication* (2nd ed., pp. 589–618). Newbury Park, CA: Sage.

Parks, M. R., & Adelman, M. B. (1983). Communication networks and the development of romantic relationships: An expansion of uncertainty reduction theory. *Human Communication Research, 10,* 55–80.

Patterson, M. L. (1982). A sequential functional model of nonverbal exchange. *Psychological Review, 89,* 231–249.

Patterson, M. L. (1983). *Nonverbal behavior: A functional perspective.* New York: Springer-Verlag.

Patterson, M. L., Churchill, M. E., Burger, G. K., & Powell, J. L. (1992). Verbal and nonverbal modality effects on impressions of political candidates: Analysis from the 1984 presidential debates. *Communication Monographs, 59,* 231–242.

Pavitt, C., & Cappella, J. N. (1979). Coorientation, accuracy in interpersonal and small group discussions: A literature review, model, and simulation. In D. Nimmo (Ed.), *Communication yearbook 3* (pp. 123–156). New Brunswick, NJ: Transaction Books.

PCIA's 1998 Wireless Market Portfolio. (1999). Washington, DC: PCIA Wireless Information Resource Center.

Pearce, A. (1998). Exciting times in Washington; FCC rulemakings gives us respite from sex, lies and videotape. *America's Network, 102,* 74.

Pearce, W. B., & Cronen, V. E. (1980). *Communication, action, and meaning.* New York: Praeger.

Penley, L. E. (1982). An investigation of the information processing framework of organizational communication. *Human Communication Research, 8,* 348–365.

Penman, R. (1992). Good theory and good practice: An argument in progress. *Communication Theory, 2,* 235–250.

Perry, D. K. (1996). *Theory and research in mass communication: Contexts and consequences.* Mahwah, NJ: Lawrence Erlbaum Associates.

Petronio, S., Martin, J., & Littlefield, R. (1984). Prerequisite conditions for self-disclosing: A gender issue. *Communication Monographs, 51,* 268–273.

Petty, R. E., & Cacioppo, J. T. (1979). Issue-involvement can increase or decrease persuasion by enhancing message-relevant cognitive responses. *Journal of Personality and Social Psychology, 37,* 1915-1926.

Petty, R. E., & Cacioppo, J. T. (1981). *Attitudes and persuasion: Classic and contemporary approaches.* Dubuque, IA: Brown.

Petty, R. E., & Cacioppo, J. T. (1986a). *Communication and persuasion: Central and peripheral routes to attitude change.* New York: Springer-Verlag.

Petty, R. E., & Cacioppo, J. T. (1986b). The elaboration likelihood model of persuasion. In L. Berkowitz (Ed.), *Advances in experimental social psychology* (Vol. 19, pp. 123–205). New York: Academic.

Petty, R. E., Cacioppo, J. T., & Goldman, R. (1981). Personal involvement as a determinant of argument based persuasion. *Journal of Personality and Social Psychology, 41,* 847–855.

Petty, R. E., Cacioppo, J. T., & Schumann, D. (1983). Central and peripheral routes to advertising effectiveness: The moderating role of involvement. *Journal of Consumer Research, 10,* 135–146.

Petty, R. E., Kasmer, J. A., Haugtvedt, C. P. & Cacioppo, J. T. (1987). Source and message factors in persuasion: A reply to Stiff's critique of the elaboration likelihood model. *Communication Monographs, 54,* 233–249.

Pfau, M., Tusing, K. J., Koerner, A. F., Lee, W., Godbold, L. C., Penaloza, L. J., Yang, V. S., & Hong., Y. (1997). Enriching the inoculation construct: The role of critical components in the process of resistance. *Human Communication Research, 24,* 187–215.

Pfau, M., Van Bockern, S., & Kang, J. G. (1992). Use of inoculation to promote resistance to smoking initiation among adolescents. *Communication Monographs, 59,* 213–230.

Pfeffer, J. (1981). Management as symbolic action: The creation and maintenance of organizational paradigms. In B. M. Staw & L. L. Cummings (Eds.), *Research in organizational behavior* (Vol. 3, pp. 1–53). Greenwich, CT: JAI.

Pilotta, J. J., Widman, T., & Jasko, S. A. (1988). Meaning and action in the organizational setting: An interpretive approach. In J. A. Andersen (Eds.), *Communication yearbook 11* (pp. 310–324). Newbury Park, CA: Sage.

Pincus, J. D. (1986). Communication satisfaction, job satisfaction, and job performance. *Human Communication Research, 12,* 395–419.

Planalp, S. (1985). Relational schemata: A test of alternative forms of relational knowledge as guides to communication. *Human Communication Research, 12,* 3–29.

Planalp, S. (1989). Relational communication and cognition. In B. Dervin, L. Grossberg, B. J. O'Keefe, & E. Wartella (Eds). *Rethinking communication: Particular exemplars* (Vol. 2; pp. 269–279). Newbury Park, CA: Sage.

Planalp, S., Graham, M., & Paulson, L. (1987). Cohesive devices in conversations. *Communication Monographs, 54,* 325–343.

Planalp, S., Rutherford, D. K., & Honeycutt, J. M. (1988). Events that increase uncertainty in personal relationships II: Replication and extension. *Human Communication Research, 14,* 516–547.

Poole, M. S. (1985). Communication and organizational climates: Review, critique, and a new perspective. In R. D. McPhee & P. K. Tompkins (Eds.), *Organizational communication: Traditional themes and new directions* (pp. 79–108). Newbury Park, CA: Sage.

Poole, M. S., & Holmes, M. E. (1995). Decision development in computer-assisted group decision making. *Human Communication Research, 22,* 90–127.

Poole, M. S., & Roth, J. (1989). Decision development in small groups V: Test of a contingency model. *Human Communication Research, 15,* 549–589.

Porat, M. U. (1977). *The information economy.* Washington, DC: U.S. Department of Commerce.

Postman, N. (1982). *The disappearance of childhood.* New York: Delacorte.

Potter, W. J. (1987). Does television viewing hinder academic achievement among adolescents? *Human Communication Research, 14,* 27–46.

Price, V., Huang, L-N., & Tewksbury, D. (1997). Third-person effects of news coverage: Orientations toward media. *Journalism & Mass Communication Quarterly, 74,* 525–540.

Price, V., Tewksbury, D., & Huang, L-N. (1998). Third-person effects on publication of a Holocaust-denial advertisement. *Journal of Communication, 46,* 3–26.

Putnam, L. L. (1982). Paradigms for organizational communication research: An overview and synthesis. *Western Journal of Speech Communication, 46,* 192–206.

Putnam, L. L. (1983). The interpretive perspective: An alternative to functionalism. In L. L. Putnam & M. E. Pacanowsky (Eds.), *Communication and organizations: An interpretive approach* (pp. 31–54). Newbury Park, CA: Sage.

Putnam, L. L. (1989). Perspectives for research on group embeddedness in organizations. In S. S. King (Ed.), *Human communication as a field of study* (pp. 163–181). New York: SUNY Press.

Ragsdale, J. D. (1996). Gender, satisfaction level, and the use of relational maintenance strategies in marriage. *Communication Monographs, 63,* 354–369.

Rayburn, J. D., & Palmgreen, P. (1984). Merging uses and gratifications and expectancy-value theory. *Communication Research, 11,* 537–562.

Reardon, K. K. (1981). *Persuasion: Theory and context.* Newbury Park, CA: Sage.

Reardon, K. K., & Rogers, E. M. (1988). Interpersonal versus mass media communication: A false dichotomy. *Human Communication Research, 15,* 284–303.

Redding, W. C. (1979). *Communication within the organization: An interpretive review of theory and research.* New York: Industrial Communication Council

Redding, W. C. (1985). Stumbling toward identity: The emergence of organizational communication as a field of study. In P. K. Tompkins & R. D. McPhee (Eds.), *Organizational communication: Traditional themes and new directions* (pp. 15–54). Newbury Park, CA: Sage.

Reeves, B., Chaffee, S. H., & Tims, A. (1982). Social cognition and mass communication research. In M. E. Roloff & C. R. Berger (Eds.), *Social cognition and communication* (pp. 287–326). Newbury Park, CA: Sage.

Reinard, J. C. (1988). The empirical study of the persuasive effects of evidence: The status after fifty years of research. *Human Communication Research, 15,* 3–59.

Reinsch, N. L., Jr. (1974). Figurative language and source credibility: A preliminary investigation and reconceptualization. *Human Communication Research, 1,* 75–80.

Rice, R. E., Grant, A. E., Schmitz, J., & Torobin, J. (1990). Individual and network influences on the adoption and perceived outcomes of electronic messaging. *Social Networks, 12,* 27–55.

Richards, I. A. (1925). *Principles of literary criticism.* New York: Harcourt, Brace Jovanovich.

Richards, I. A. (1936). *The philosophy of rhetoric.* New York: Oxford University Press.

Richmond, V. P., Davis, L. M., Saylor, K., & McCroskey, J. C. (1984). Power strategies in organizations: Communication techniques and messages. *Human Communication Research, 11,* 85–108.

Ritchie, L. D. (1986). Shannon and Weaver: Unravelling the paradox of information. *Communication Research, 13,* 278–298.

Ritchie, L. D. (1991). Another turn of the information revolution: Relevance, technology, and the information society. *Communication Research, 18,* 412–427.

Rogers, E. M. (1962). *Diffusion of innovations.* New York: Free Press.

Rogers, E. M. (1986). *Communication technology: The new media in society.* New York: Free Press.

424 References

Rogers, E. M., & Kincaid, D. L. (1981). *Communication networks: Toward a new paradigm for research.* New York: Free Press.

Rogers, R. W. (1975). A protection motivation theory of fear appeals and attitude change. *Journal of Psychology, 91,* 93–114.

Roloff, M. E. (1981). *Interpersonal communication: The social exchange approach.* Newbury Park, CA: Sage.

Roloff, M. E. (1987). Communication and reciprocity within intimate relationships. In M. E. Roloff & G. R. Miller (Eds.), *Interpersonal processes: New directions in communication research* (pp. 11–38). Newbury Park, CA: Sage.

Roloff, M. E., & Berger, C. R. (1982). Social cognition and communication: An introduction. In M. E. Roloff & C. R. Berger (Eds.), *Social cognition and communication* (pp. 9–32). Newbury Park, CA: Sage.

Roloff, M. E., & Campion, D. E. (1987). On alleviating the debilitating effects of accountability on bargaining: Authority and self-monitoring. *Communication Monographs, 54,* 145–164.

Roloff, M. E., & Janiszewski, C. A. (1989). Overcoming obstacles to interpersonal compliance: A principle of message construction. *Human Communication Research, 16,* 33–61.

Roloff, M. E., Janiszewski, C. A., McGrath, M. A., Burns, C. S., & Lalita, A. M. (1988). Acquiring resources from intimates: When obligation substitutes for persuasion. *Human Communication Research, 14,* 364–396.

Roskos-Ewoldsen, D. R. (1997). Implicit theories of persuasion. *Human Communication Research, 24,* 31–63.

Ruben, B. D. (1985). The coming of the information age: Information, technology, and the study of behavior. In B. D. Ruben (Ed.), *Information and behavior* (Vol.1, pp.3–26). New Brunswick, NJ: Transaction Books.

Rubin, A. (1984). Ritualized and instrumental uses of television. *Journal of Communication, 34,* 67-77.

Rubin, A. M. (1986). Uses, gratifications, and media effects research. In J. Bryant & D. Zillmann (Eds.), *Perspectives on media effects* (pp. 281–301). Hillsdale, NJ: Lawrence Erlbaum Associates.

Rubin, A. M. (1994). Media uses and effects: A uses-and-gratifications perspective. In J. Bryant & D. Zillmann (Eds.), *Media effects, advances in theory and research* (pp. 417–436). Hillsdale, NJ: Lawrence Erlbaum Associates.

Rubin, A. M., & Windahl, S. (1986). The uses and dependency model of mass communication. *Critical Studies in Mass Communication, 3,* 184–199.

Salmon, C. T. (1986). Message discrimination and the information environment. *Communication Research, 13,* 363–372.

Saltiel, J., & Woelfel, J. (1975). Inertia in cognitive processes: The role of accumulated information in attitude change. *Human Communication Research, 1,* 333–344.

Samter, W., & Burleson, B. R. (1984). Cognitive and motivational influences on spontaneous comforting behavior. *Human Communication Research, 11,* 231–260.

Schein, E. H. (1985). *Organizational cultures and leadership.* San Francisco, CA: Jossey-Bass.

Schein, E. H. (1992). *Organizational culture and leadership* (2nd ed.). San Francisco, CA: Jossey-Bass.

Schiller, H. I. (1983). The privatization of information. In E. Wartella, D. C. Whitney, & S. Windahl (Eds.), *Mass communication review yearbook* (Vol. 4, pp. 537–568). Newbury Park, CA: Sage.

Schmitz, J., & Fulk, J. (1991). The role of organizational colleagues in media selection. *Communication Research, 18,* 487-523.

Schramm, W. (1954). How communication works. In W. Schramm (Ed.), *The process and effects of mass communication* (pp. 3–26). Urbana, IL: University of Illinois Press.

Schramm, W. (1955). Information theory and mass communication. *Journalism Quarterly, 32,* 131–146.

Schramm, W. (1973). *Men, messages, and media.* New York: Harper & Row.

Searle, J. R. (1969). *Speech acts: An essay in the philosophy of language.* Cambridge: Cambridge University Press.

Searle, J. R. (1976). A classification of illocutionary acts. *Language in Society,* 5, 1–23.

Seel, P. B. (1997). The transition from analog to digital broadcasting. In P. B. Seel & A. E. Grant, (Eds.), *Broadcast technology update, production and transmission* (pp. 7–20). Boston: Focal Press.

Seibold, D. R., Cantrill, J. G., & Meyers, R. A. (1994). Communication and interpersonal influence. In M. L. Knapp & G. R. Miller (Eds.), *Handbook of interpersonal communication* (2nd ed., pp. 542–588). Thousand Oaks, CA: Sage.

Seibold, D. R., & Spitzberg, B. H. (1982). Attribution theory and research: Review and implications for communication. In B. Dervin & M. J. Voigt (Eds.), *Progress in the communication sciences* (Vol. 3, pp. 85–125). Norwood, NJ: Ablex.

Shannon, C. E., & Weaver, W. (1949). *The mathematical theory of communication.* Urbana, IL: University of Illinois Press.

Shapere, D. (1974). Scientific theories and their domains. In F. Suppe (Ed.), *The structure of scientific theories* (pp. 518–589). Urbana, IL: University of Illinois Press.

Shaw, C. M. (1997). Personal narrative: Revealing self and reflecting other. *Human Communication Research, 24,* 302–319.

Shaw, D. L., & McCombs, M. E. (1977). *The emergence of American political issues: The agenda-setting function of the press.* St. Paul, MN: West.

Shepherd, G. J. (1987). Individual differences in the relationship between attitudinal and normative determinants of behavioral intent. *Communication Monographs, 54,* 221–231.

Sherif, C. W., Sherif, M., & Nebergall, R. E. (1965). *Attitude and attitude change: The social judgment-involvement approach.* Philadelphia, PA: Saunders.

Sherif, M., & Cantril, H. (1947). *The psychology of ego-involvement.* New York: Wiley.

Sherif, M., & Hovland, C. I. (1961). *Social judgment: Assimilation and contrast effects in communication and attitude change.* New Haven: Yale University Press.

Sherif, M., & Sherif, C. W. (1967). Attitude as the individual's own categories: The social judgment-involvement approach to attitude and attitude change. In C. W. Sherif & M. Sherif (Eds.), *Attitude, ego-involvement, and change* (pp.105–139). New York: Wiley.

Shimanoff, S. B. (1987). Types of emotional disclosures and request compliance between spouses. *Communication Monographs, 54,* 85–100.

Shrum, L. J. (1996). Psychological processes underlying cultivation effects: Further tests of construct accessibility. *Human Communication Research, 22,* 482–509.

Sias, P. M., & Jablin, F. M. (1995). Differential superior–subordinate relations, perceptions of fairness, and coworker communication. *Human Communication Research, 22,* 5–38.

Sillars, A. L. (1980). Attribution and communication in roommate conflict. *Communication Monographs, 47,* 180–200.

Sillars, A. L. (1982). Attribution and communication: Are people "naive scientists" or just naive? In M. E. Roloff & C. R. Berger (Eds.), *Social cognition and communication* (pp. 73–106). Newbury Park, CA: Sage.

Sillars, A. L., Pike, G. R., Jones, T. S., & Murphy, M. A. (1984). Communication and understanding in marriage. *Human Communication Research, 10,* 317–350.

Sillars, A. L., & Weisberg, J. (1987). Conflict as a social skill. In M. E. Roloff & G. R. Miller (Eds.), *Interpersonal processes: New directions in communication research* (pp. 140–171). Newbury Park, CA: Sage.

Sillars, A. L., Weisberg, J. Burggraf, C. S., & Wilson, E. A. (1987). Content themes in marital conversations. *Human Communication Research, 13,* 495–528.

Singelis, T. M., & Brown, W. J. (1995). Culture, self, and collectivist communication: Linking culture to individual behavior. *Human Communication Research, 21,* 354–389.

Slovic, P., Fischhoff, B., & Lichenstein, S. (1987). Behavioral decision theory perspectives on protective behavior. In N. D. Weinstein (Ed.), *Taking care: Understanding and encouraging self-protected behavior.* (pp. 14–41). Cambridge: Cambridge University Press.

Smeltzer, L. R., & Kedia, B. L. (1985). Knowing the ropes: Organizational requirements for quality circles. *Business Horizons, 28*(4), 30–34.

Smircich, L. (1983a). Implications for management theory. In L. L. Putnam & M. E. Pacanowsky (Eds.), *Communication and organizations: An interpretive approach* (pp. 221–241). Newbury Park, CA: Sage.

Smircich, L. (1983b). Organizations as shared meanings. In L. R. Pondy, P. J. Frost, G. Morgan, & T. C. Dandridge (Eds.), *Organizational symbolism* (pp. 55–65). Greenwich, CT: JAI Press.

Smircich, L., & Calas, M. R. (1987). Organizational culture: A critical assessment. In F. M. Jablin, L. L. Putnarn, K. H. Roberts, & L. W. Porter (Eds.), *Handbook of organizational communication* (pp. 228–263). Newbury Park, CA: Sage.

Smith, D. H. (1972). Communication research as the idea of process. *Speech Monographs, 39,* 174–182.

Smith, D. R. (1970). The fallacy of the "communication breakdown." *Quarterly Journal of Speech, 56,* 343–346.

Smith, M. J. (1984). Contingency rules theory, context, and compliance behaviors. *Human Communication Research, 10,* 489–512.

Smith, R. C., & Eisenberg, E. M. (1987). Conflict at Disneyland: A root metaphor analysis. *Communication Monographs, 54,* 367–379.

Snider, J., & Osgood, C. (1969). *The semantic differential technique.* Chicago: Aldine.

Sorrentino, R. M., Bobocel, D. R., Gitta, M. Z., Olson, J. M., & Hewitt, E. C. (1988). Uncertainty orientation and persuasion: Individual differences in the effects of personal relevance on social judgments. *Journal of Personality and Social Psychology, 55,* 357–371.

Spitzberg, B. H., & Hecht, M. L. (1984). A component model of relational competence. *Human Communication Research, 10,* 575–599.

Sprafkin, J., Gadow, K. D., & Abelman, R. (1992). *Television and the exceptional child: A forgotten audience.* Hillsdale, NJ: Lawrence Erlbaum Associates.

Stafford, L., & Daly, J. A. (1984). Conversational memory: The effects of recall mode and memory experiences on remembrances of natural conversations. *Human Communication Research, 10,* 379–402.

Steeves, H. L. (1984). Developing coorientation measures for small groups. *Communication Monographs, 51,* 185–192.

Stephenson, W. (1967). *Play theory of mass communication.* Chicago. University of Chicago Press.

Steuer, J. (1995). Defining virtual reality: Dimensions determining telepresence. In Biocca, F., & Levy, M. R. (Eds.), *Communication in the age of virtual reality.* Hillsdale, NJ: Lawrence Erlbaum Associates.

Stewart, J. (1972). Concepts of language and meaning: A comparative study. *Quarterly Journal of Speech, 58,* 123–133.

Stiff, J. B. (1986). Cognitive processing of persuasive message cues: A meta-analytic review of the efforts of supporting information on attitudes. *Communication Monographs, 53,* 75–89.

Stohl, C. (1986). Quality circles and changing patterns of communication. In M. L. McLaughlin (Ed.), *Communication yearbook 9* (pp. 511–531). Newbury Park, CA: Sage.

Stohl, C. (1987). Bridging the parallel organization: A study of quality circle effectiveness. In M. L. McLaughlin (Ed.), *Communication yearbook 10* (pp. 416–430). Newbury Park, CA: Sage.

Storck, J., & Sproull, L. (1995). Through a glass darkly: What do people learn in videoconferences? *Human Communication Research, 22,* 197–219.

Stouffer, S. A. (1942, August). A sociologist looks at communications research. In D. Waples (Ed.), *Print, radio, and film in a democracy: Ten papers on the administration of mass communications in the public interest.* Paper presented to the Sixth Annual Institute of the Graduate Library School (pp. 133–146). Chicago: The University of Chicago Press.

Strate, L., Jacobson, R., & Gibson, S. B. (1996). Surveying the electronic landscape: An introduction to communication and cyberspace. In L. Strate, R. Jacobson, & S. B. Gibson (Eds.), *Communication and cyberspace, social interaction in an electronic environment* (pp. 1–22). Cresskill, NJ: Hampton Press, Inc.

Street, R. L., Jr. (1984). Speech convergence and speech evaluation in fact-finding interviews. *Human Communication Research, 11,* 139–169.

Street, R. L., Jr., & Buller, D. B. (1988). Patients' characteristics affecting physician–patient nonverbal communication. *Human Communication Research, 15,* 60–90.

Street, R. L., Jr., & Giles, H. (1982). Speech accommodation theory: A social cognitive approach to language and speech behavior. In M. E. Roloff & C. R. Berger (Eds.), *Social cognition and communication* (pp. 193–226). Newbury Park, CA: Sage.

Sunnafrank, M. (1990). Predicted outcome value and uncertainty reduction theories: A test of competing perspectives. *Human Communication Research, 17,* 76–103.

Suzuki, S. (1997). Cultural transmission in international organizations: Impact of interpersonal communication patterns in intergroup contexts. *Human Communication Research, 24,* 147–180.

Sypher, B. D., & Zorn, T. E., Jr. (1986). Communication-related abilities and upward mobility: A longitudinal investigation. *Human Communication Research, 12,* 420–431.

Sypher, H. E., & Applegate, J. L. (1984). Organizing communication behavior: The role of schemas and constructs. In R. N. Bostrom & B. H. Westley (Eds.), *Communication yearbook 8* (pp. 310–329). Newbury Park, CA: Sage.

Tagiuri, R. (1968). The concepts of organizational climate. In R. Tagiuri & G. H. Litwin (Eds.), *Organizational climate: Exploration of a concept* (pp. 11–32). Boston: Harvard University Press.

Tan, A. S. (1985). *Mass communication theories and research* (2nd ed.). New York: Wiley.

Tan, A. S. (1986). Social learning of aggression from television. In J. Bryant & D. Zillmann (Eds.). *Perspectives on media effects* (pp. 41–55). Hillsdale, NJ: Lawrence Erlbaum Associates.

Taylor, D. A., & Altman, I. (1987). Communication in interpersonal relationships: Social penetration processes. In M. E. Roloff & G. R. Miller (Eds.), *Interpersonal processes: New directions in communication research* (pp. 257–277). Newbury Park, CA: Sage.

Thorson, E. (1989). Processing television commercials. In B. Dervin, L. Grossberg, B. J. O'Keefe, & E. Wartella (Eds.), *Rethinking communication: Paradigm exemplars* (Vol. 2, pp. 397–410). Newbury Park, CA: Sage.

Tompkins, P. K. (1987). Translating organizational theory: Symbolism over substance. In F. M. Jablin, L. L. Putnam, K. H. Roberts, & L. W. Porter (Eds.), *Handbook of organizational communication* (pp. 70–96). Newbury Park, CA: Sage.

Tompkins, P. K., & Cheney, G. (1985). Communication and unobtrusive control in contemporary organizations. In R. D. McPhee & P. K. Tompkins (Eds.), *Organizational communication: Traditional themes and new directions* (pp. 179–210). Newbury Park, CA: Sage.

Tracy, K. (1984). The effect of multiple goals on conversational relevance and topic shift. *Communication Monographs, 51,* 274–287.

Tversky, A., & Kahneman, D. (1986). Judgment under uncertainty: Heuristics and biases. In H. R. Arkes, & K. R. Hammond (Eds.), *Judgment and decision making* (pp. 38–55). Cambridge: Cambridge University Press.

Valente, T. W., Paredes, P., & Poppe, P. R. (1998). Matching the message to the process: The relative ordering of knowledge, attitudes, and practices in behavior change research. *Human Communication Research, 24,* 366–385.

Van Evra, J. (1998). *Television and child development* (2nd ed.). Mahwah, NJ: Lawrence Erlbaum Associates.

Van Lear, C. A., Jr. (1987). The formation of social relationships: A longitudinal study of social penetration. *Human Communication Research, 13,* 299–322.

Van Rheenen, D. D., & Sherlbom, J. (1984). Spoken language indices of uncertainty. *Human Communication Research, 11,* 221–230.

Vickery, D. M. (1995). Demand management, self-care, and the new media. In L. M. Harris (Ed.), *Health and the new media: Technologies transforming personal and public health* (pp. 45-63). Mahwah, NJ: Lawrence Erlbaum Associates.

Villaume, W. A., & Cegala, D. J. (1988). Interaction involvement and discourse strategies: The patterned use of cohesive devices in conversation. *Communication Monographs, 55,* 22–40.

Vinokur, A., & Burnstein, E. (1974). Effects of partially shared persuasive arguments on group-induced shifts: A group-problem-solving approach. *Journal of Personality and Social Psychology. 29,* 305–315.

Vinokur, A., Trope, Y., & Burnstein, E. (1975). Decision-making analysis of persuasive argumentation and the choice shift effect. *Journal of Experimental Social Psychology, 11,* 127–148.

Walton, R. E. (1982). Social choice in the development of advanced information technology. *Human Relations, 35,* 1073–1084.

Waples, D. (Ed.). (1942, August). *Print, radio, and film in a democracy: Ten papers on the administration of mass communications in the public interest.* Paper presented at the Sixth Annual Institute of the Graduate Library School (pp. 133–146). Chicago: The University of Chicago Press.

Ward, S., Wackman, D., & Wartella, E. (1977). *How children learn to buy: The development of consumer information processing skills.* Newbury Park, CA. Sage.

Warfel, K. A. (1984). Gender schemas and perceptions of speech style. *Communication Monographs, 51,* 253–267.

Watzlawick, P., Beavin, J. H., & Jackson, D. D. (1967). *The pragmatics of human communication.* New York: Norton.

Webster, J. G. (1989). Assessing exposure to the new media. In J. L. Salvaggio & J. Bryant (Eds.), *Media use in the information age: Emerging patterns of adoption and consumer use* (pp. 3–19). Hillsdale, NJ: Lawrence Erlbaum Associates.

Webster, J. G. (1998). The audience. *Journal of Broadcasting & Electronic Media, 42,* 190-207.

Weick, K. E. (1979a). Cognitive processes in organization. In B. M. Staw (Ed.), *Research in organizational behavior* (Vol. 1, pp. 41–74). Greenwich, CT: JAI Press.

Weick, K. E. (1979b). *The social psychology of organizing* (2nd ed.). Reading, MA: Addison-Wesley.

Weick, K. E. (1987). Theorizing about organizational communication. In F. M. Jablin, L. L. Putnam, K. H. Roberts, & L. W. Porter (Eds.), *Handbook of organizational communication* (pp. 97–122). Newbury Park, CA: Sage.

Weiner, M., & Mehrabian, A. (1968). *Language within language: Immediacy, a channel in verbal communication.* New York: Appleton-Century-Crofts.

Weiner, N. (1948). *Cybernetics or control and communication in the animal and the machine.* Cambridge, MA: MIT Press.

Weiner, N. (1950). *The human use of human beings: Cybernetics and society* (Rev. ed.). Garden City, NY: Doubleday Anchor.

Werner, C. M., & Baxter, L. A. (1994). Temporal qualities of relationships: Organismic, transactional, and dialectical views. In M. L. Knapp & G. R. Miller (Eds.), *Handbook of interpersonal communication* (2nd ed., pp. 323–379). Thousand Oaks, CA: Sage.

Westley, B. H., & MacLean, M. S., Jr. (1957). A conceptual model for communication research. *Journalism Quarterly, 34,* 31–38.

Wheeless, L. R., & Cook, J. A. (1985). Information exposure, attention, and reception. In B. D. Ruben (Ed.), *Information and behavior* (Vol. 1, pp. 251–286). New Brunswick, NJ: Transaction Books.

White, H. A. (1997). Considering interacting factors in the third-person effect: Argument strength and social distance. *Journalism & Mass Communication Quarterly, 74,* 557–564.

Whorf, B. L. (1956). *Language, thought, and reality.* Cambridge, MA: MIT Press.

Whyte, G. (1989). Groupthink reconsidered. *Academy of Management Review, 14,* 40–56.

Wiemann, J. M., Hawkins, R. P., & Pingree, S (1988). Fragmentation in the field—and the movement toward integration in communication science. *Human Communication Research, 15,* 304–310.

Wiio, O. A., Goldhaber, G. M., & Yates, M. P. (1980). Organizational communication research: Time for reflection? In D. Nimmo (Ed.), *Communication yearbook 4* (pp. 83–97). New Brunswick, NJ: Transaction Books.

Williams, A., & Giles, H. (1996). Intergenerational conversations: Young adults' retrospective accounts. *Human Communication Research, 23,* 220–250.

Williams, F., Rice, R., Rogers, E. M. (1988). *Research methods and the new media.* New York: The Free Press.

Williams, F., Strover, S., & Grant, A. E. (1994). Social aspects of new media technologies. In J. Bryant & D. Zillmann (Eds.), *Media effects: Advances in theory and research* (pp. 463–482). Hillsdale, NJ: Lawrence Erlbaum Associates.

Wilmot, W. W., Carbaugh, D. A., & Baxter, L. A. (1985). Communicative strategies used to terminate romantic relationships. *Western Journal of Speech Communication, 49,* 204–216.

Wilson, S. R. (1995). Elaborating the cognitive rules model of interaction goals: The problem of accounting for individual differences in goal formation. In B. R. Burleson (Ed.), *Communication yearbook 18* (pp. 3–25). Thousand Oaks, CA: Sage.

Wilson, S. R., Cruz, M. G., & Kang, K. H. (1992). Is it always a matter of perspective? Construct differentiation and variability in attributions about compliance gaining. *Communication Monographs, 59,* 350–367.

Winett, R. A. (1986). *Information and behavior: Systems of influence.* Hillsdale, NJ: Lawrence Erlbaum Associates.

Witte, K. (1992). Putting the fear back into fear appeals: The extended parallel process model. *Communication Monographs, 59,* 329–349.

Witteman, H., & Fitzpatrick, M. A. (1986). Compliance-gaining in marital interaction: Power bases, processes, and outcomes. *Communication Monographs, 53,* 130–143.

Woelfel, J. C. (1977). Changes in interpersonal communication patterns as a consequence of need for information. *Communication Research, 4,* 235–256.

Wood, W., Kalgren, C., & Priesler, R. (1985). Access to attitude relevant information in memory as a determinant of persuasion: The role of message attributes. *Journal of Experimental Social Psychology, 21,* 73–85.

Wright, C. R. (1960). Functional analysis and mass communication. *Public Opinion Quarterly, 24,* 605–620.

Wright, C. R. (1986). *Mass communication: A sociological perspective* (3rd ed.). New York: Random House.

Wright, P. L. (1973). The cognitive processes mediating acceptance of advertising. *Journal of Marketing Research, 10,* 53–62.

Wright, P. L. (1974). Analyzing media effects on advertising responses. *Public opinion Quarterly, 38,* 192–205.

Wright, P. L. (1981). Cognitive responses to mass media advocacy. In R. E. Petty, T. M. Ostrom, & T. C. Brock (Eds.), *Cognitive responses in persuasion* (pp. 263–282). Hillsdale, NJ: Lawrence Erlbaum Associates.

Yinon, Y., Jaffe, Y., & Feshback, S. (1975). Risky aggression in individuals and groups. *Journal of Personality and Social Psychology, 31,* 808–815.

Young, J. R. (1999, February 5). Are wireless networks the wave of the future? *The Chronicle of Higher Education,* A25.

Zillmann, D., & Bryant, J. (1985). Pornography, sexual callousness and the trivilization of rape. *Journal of Communication, 34*(4), 10–21.

Zillmann, D., & Bryant, J. (1986). Exploring the entertainment experience. In J. Bryant & D. Zillmann (Eds.), *Perspectives on media effects* (pp. 303–324). Hillsdale, NJ: Lawrence Erlbaum Associates.

Zuckerman, M., DePaulo, B. M., & Rosenthal, R. (1981). Verbal and nonverbal communication of deception. In L. Berkowitz (Ed.), *Advances in experimental social psychology* (Vol. 14, pp. 1–59). New York: Academic.

Author Index

431

Subject Index